THE RELIGION
OF AN
INDIAN TRIBE

THE RELIGION
OF AN
INDIAN TRIBE

VERRIER ELWIN

GYAN

Published by

Gyan Publishing House
5, Ansari Road
Daryaganj, New Delhi-110002
Phone: 011-47034999, 9811692060
E-mail: books@gyanbooks.com

Distribution Network
gyanbooks.com
India, USA, Canada, UK, Australia

ISBN: 978-93-6280-524-9 (PB)
First Published, 1955

2nd Impression 2024

Printed at: Gyan Press, Delhi.

THE RELIGION OF AN INDIAN TRIBE
Author: VERRIER ELWIN

THE RELIGION OF AN INDIAN TRIBE

ALSO BY VERRIER ELWIN

MONOGRAPHS

The Baiga (1939, Murray), out of print
The Agaria (1942, O.U.P.), out of print
Maria Murder and Suicide (1943, O.U.P., second edition, 1950)
Folk-Tales of Mahakoshal (1944, O.U.P.), out of print
Folk-Songs of Chhattisgarh (1946, O.U.P.)
Myths of Middle India (1949, O.U.P.)
The Muria and their Ghotul (1947, O.U.P.), out of print
Bondo Highlander (1950, O.U.P.)
The Tribal Art of Middle India (1951, O.U.P.)
Tribal Myths of Orissa (1954, O.U.P.)

GENERAL

Leaves from the Jungle (1936, Murray), out of print
The Aboriginals (1943, O.U.P., second edition, 1944), out of print
Motley (1954, Orient Longmans)

NOVELS

Phulmat of the Hills (1937, Murray), out of print
A Cloud that's Dragonish (1938, Murray), out of print

WITH SHAMRAO HIVALE

Songs of the Forest (1935, Allen & Unwin)
Folk-Songs of the Maikal Hills (1944, O.U.P.), out of print.

THE RELIGION OF AN INDIAN TRIBE

VERRIER ELWIN

GEOFFREY CUMBERLEGE
OXFORD UNIVERSITY PRESS

To

B. S. GUHA

CONTENTS

ILLUSTRATIONS

PLATES

FIGURES

COLOUR PLATE

MAPS

PREFACE

JUST about a hundred years ago, in the first week of January 1852, John Campbell, the brave and sympathetic officer who persuaded the Konds to abandon human sacrifice, pitched his camp at Godairy, a large village on the banks of the 'Bangsadara' (Vamsadhara) River. 'At this place', he says, 'I first came in contact with the Sourah race. They are of a fairer complexion, and their features, resembling the Gentoos of the plains, have a better expression than those of the Konds. They speak a different dialect, are less dissipated in their habits, and consequently more athletic in their persons, which they adorn with beads and bangles; this custom, however, is more common with the women than with the men. Their arms are the battle-axe, bow and arrow, though a few have matchlocks. They are professed thieves and plunderers, and are the terror of the inhabitants of the plains.' They readily promised, however, to have nothing to do with the Meriah rite of their Kond neighbours, agreeing to refrain from it 'even as spectators'.[1]

Anthropology is the poorer for the fact that Campbell did not make his way up into the Saora hills, for he was an accurate observer and his notes on the condition of the tribe at that time would have been invaluable. Another officer, S. C. Macpherson, in a report which he wrote on the Konds in 1841, says that he proposed 'on a future occasion to submit the results of his enquiries respecting the "Sourah" race, the only other Hill people of Orissa with respect to which he possessed any information'.[2] In view of Macpherson's account of Kond theology, which has misled historians of religion for over a century, anthropologists may perhaps be thankful that this writer did not carry out his ambition.

Perhaps the earliest European to come into close contact with the Saoras was G. E. Russell, a member of the Madras Board of Revenue. In 1832, the disturbances in the Vizagapatam District and the Parlakimidi Taluk of Ganjam District were so serious that Russell was appointed Special Commissioner with very wide powers to establish law and order in the area. It was he who in 1836 discovered the

[1] J. Campbell, *A Personal Narrative of Thirteen Years Service amongst the Wild Tribes of Khondistan* (London, 1864), p. 203.

[2] S. C. Macpherson, *Report on the Konds* (1841, reprinted Madras, 1863).

practice of human sacrifice among the Konds. He had to deal with the Hill Saoras in rebellion, and at one time had no fewer than two hundred in custody. His notes upon them, though tantalizingly few, are of great interest.

In 1862, the Rev. William Taylor published a *Catalogue Raisonné* of the manuscripts in the Government Library at Madras. Among these were some Telugu documents, bound in 'a small quarto, of medium thickness, much damaged', which gave an account of the Konds, and the Maliya Savaralu and Conda Savaralu; they are undated, but some must go back at least to 1838, when Taylor started his researches. The Maliya Savaralu, who are described as being in the 'proximate neighbourhood' of Vizagapatam, Kimedi and Ganjam, and as being less 'civilized' than the Conda Savaralu, are undoubtedly our Hill Saoras. The document describes them as 'a people with small eyes, noses, ears, and very large faces. Their hair is thickly matted together. They bind either a cord, or a narrow bit of cloth around their head; and in it stick the feather of a stork, or of a peacock, and also wild flowers, found in the forests. They go about in the high winds, and hot sunshine, without inconvenience. They sleep on beds formed of mountain-stones. Their skin is as hard as the skin of the large guana-lizard. They build houses over mountain-torrents, previously throwing trees across the chasms; and these houses are in the midst of forests of fifty, or more, miles in extent.' They are regarded as essentially independent, and more than ready to attack when provoked. The Conda Savaralu are equally warlike, and they 'do not regard the wound of a musket ball, as they have a remedy for it; they are afraid only of a cannon ball; for which, of course, they have no remedy'.

In the autumn of 1870, the geologist Ball accompanied a Calcutta surgeon, Dr Palmer, in search of a sanatorium which the unique natural advantages of the Mahendra Hill seemed likely to supply. It was here, in the last week of September, that the party first encountered Saoras, known previously as 'a wild intractable race' but by that date 'perfectly docile'. In appearance Ball found the Saoras small but wiry, often very dark in colour, sometimes quite black. 'Their hair is generally tied in a top-knot, and sometimes it is cut short over the forehead, two long locks being permitted to hang over the ears. A few individuals have frizzled shocks, with which no such arrangement is attempted. Most of the men have small square beards.' They made little display of their weapons and had few personal ornaments.

Unhappily, although another member of the party, a Captain Murray, took photographs of groups of Saoras, they were not reproduced by Ball in his book *Jungle Life in India* (London, 1880), from which the above account is taken.

In 1881-2, Major-General Cunningham, then Director-General of the Archeological Survey, made a long tour of the Central Provinces and in the course of his report (which forms Vol. XVII of the Archeological Survey reports) devotes twenty-six pages to a discussion of the history and dispersion of the Saoras. He himself was personally acquainted only with the western Saoras, but he has a few notes on our Hill Saoras, and refers to a visit paid by Mr J. D. Beglar to Ganjam in 1875.

Another early writer, whose elegant and romantic pen was well fitted to describe this splendid people and their lovely hills, was Colonel E. T. Dalton. But he has only scattered references to the Saoras in his great *Descriptive Ethnology of Bengal* (1872), and the Saoras he met were either Bendkars or the near-Bhuiya Saoras of Keonjhar. His travels never led him as far as the Ganjam and Koraput hills.

It is to Mr Fred Fawcett, Superintendent of Police, that we owe our first detailed account of the Saoras of Ganjam District (which was then in the Madras Presidency) to which he was posted in the course of his duties in 1887. Fawcett was a careful and accurate observer (even if in the fashion of his time he was rather too apt to describe prayers and incantations which he could not understand as 'gibberish'), and he has also given us valuable notes on the Muppans, the Kondyamkottai Maravars and the Nayars of Malabar. He presented his Saora material in the form of a lecture to the Anthropological Society of Bombay in 1888. It is interesting to note that at the date of Fawcett's lecture this Society had no fewer than 300 ordinary members and 16 honorary and corresponding members. The President was R. C. Temple, whose *Legends of the Punjab* was in course of publication. J. M. Campbell and H. H. Risley were among the Vice-Presidents, and members of Council included K. R. Cama, the Rev. D. Mackichan, K. T. Telang, Sir W. Wedderburn and J. J. Modi. Among the subjects then engaging the attention of anthropologists in India were A Report on the Hairy Man of Burma, Indian Necromancy, Embalming in Ancient India, the Night Demon, Demonolatry in Southern India (by an Anglican Bishop), the Evil Eye among the Modern Persians, and Personal Vows with Respect to Sexual Abstinence. Malinowski was then a child of three.

Fawcett's paper was printed in the Journal of the Society (Vol. I, No. 4, 1888) and since it is the work of a man who mixed freely with the people and knew many individuals as personal friends, it is of exceptional value. Much of the material was used by Thurston, sometimes slightly misquoted, in his section on the 'Savaras' in his *Castes and Tribes of Southern India* (Madras, 1909). Risley, in his *Tribes and Castes of Bengal* (Calcutta, 1891), has a few pages on the 'Savars', but only a line or two on the branch of the tribe which lived 'near Mahendragiri in Ganjam'. The Saoras of his account are, quite properly, those of what was then called Bengal. So too, Russell and Hira Lal, in their *Tribes and Castes of the Central Provinces of India* which is dated 1916 but contains material collected many years previously, describe an entirely different branch of the tribe with which the Hill Saoras of this book have nothing in common.

'Our' Saoras, as perhaps we may call them, are the 'Savaras' of Thurston who, although he does not seem to have had any first-hand acquaintance with the tribe, managed to compile a valuable account from the reports of Fawcett, the Gazetteers and one Mr G. V. Ramamurti Pantalu.

Thurston does not tell us anything about this author, and in his own books Ramamurti describes himself modestly as 'a retired teacher of Parlakimidi'. He was in fact a man of some scholarship, a great capacity for controversy—he fought Government on the merits of a phonetic script for schools and assailed the Maharaja of Parlakimidi over the amalgamation of his zamindari with Orissa—and above all a devoted affection for the Saoras of Ganjam. He gave over thirty years of his life to studying the tribe and its language, and published a *Manual of the So:ra (or Savara) Language* (Madras, 1931) and a *Sora-English Dictionary* (Madras, 1938). I must here acknowledge my very great debt to Ramamurti's linguistic studies.

From 1938 onwards, Ramamurti's son, G. V. Sitapati Pantalu, published a series of articles on 'The Soras and their Country' in the *Journal of the Andhra Historical Research Society*. Sitapati's researches were conducted mainly in the area round Serango—both he and his father were close friends of the Canadian missionaries there and Sitapati helped one of them, Miss A. C. M. Munro, to translate the Gospels into Saora. Sitapati also published an article on Saora Musical Instruments in the *Bulletin d'Ethnographie du Trocadero*, No. 5 (Paris, 1933), a rather charming paper on 'Sora Songs and Poetry', and collaborated with Miss Munro in some notes for the Census Report of 1931. Although I cannot always follow Sitapati in his conclusions and I suspect that he relied a little too much on information given him by schoolmasters and other semi-educated informants, I found his account of the Saoras stimulating and its enthusiasm for the people he described infectious.

Other work on the Saoras has been of an incidental character. Miss Munro wrote an article on 'S'Ora (Savara) Folk-Lore' in *Man in India*, Vol. X (1930). Baron E. von Eikstedt visited the Gumma and Serango Muttas for about three weeks in 1927, and wrote two short papers on the tribe.[1] Dr J. H. Hutton and Mr M. W. M. Yeatts contributed very short notes to the Census Reports of 1931.

When I began my investigations among the Saoras in 1944 I had, therefore, certain guide-posts to put me on my way. During the succeeding seven years I visited all the chief Hill Saora villages, even those far to the north where their country merges into that of the Konds. I have had the good fortune to witness nearly all the ceremonies described in this book; of the rest I obtained trustworthy accounts which were checked by several informants. And at many ceremonies, particularly the funerary rites and sacrifices designed to heal the sick, I assisted over and over again.

Where this was possible, I was able on the first occasion to give my attention to observing and recording what the shamans were doing; on subsequent occasions to overhear and to record what they were saying. I took down the incantations, prayers and trance-dialogues directly, usually squatting on the floor as near as possible to the officiating shaman, who invariably ignored my presence. The constant repetitions made this task easier, even if more tedious, than it sounds, and I would like to emphasize that these transcriptions are an exact and literal translation of what I heard—with this exception, that I have not included all the proper names and the repetitions.

Another fruitful source of information was the recording of the life-histories of shamans and other religious functionaries. Many of these are keen theologians and like nothing better than to describe their experiences and discuss the points of doctrine that arise from them. The study of myths, ikons and the material apparatus of ritual

[1] See E. von Eikstedt, 'Die Soras', *Anthrop. Anz.*, IV (1927), pp. 208–19 and 'Die Soras', *Ethnol. Anz.*, I (1928), pp. 376–82.

provided a mass of material which it was possible to check against the information gained in conversation.

My introduction to the Saoras was facilitated by the late Mr J. W. Nicholson, C.I.E., I.F.S., then Conservator of Forests, and members of his staff, in particular Mr M. Riazuddin who, with Mrs Riazuddin, was my generous host in Parlakimidi and whose guidance was invaluable to a stranger making his way through unknown forests for the first time.

On some of my tours I had the company of Mr Shamrao Hivale, whose genial presence created an atmosphere of friendliness which revealed many secrets, and on others that of Mr D. V. Sassoon, the most delightful of field-companions. On one occasion I was accompanied by Mr Asutosh Bhattacharyya, on another by Mr Sachin Roy, both of the Department of Anthropology: to the first I owe a deeper knowledge of the Hindu background to tribal life in India, to the second I am indebted for many acts of kindness.

My friend Mr Saurindranath Roy, of the National Archives of India, placed his scholarship and time unreservedly at my disposal. I am especially grateful to him, as well as to Mr B. S. Kesavan of the National Library and to Mr Mukherjea of the Library of the Department of Anthropology for providing me with books and verifying references for me when I was in the field. My personal staff was laborious and faithful as ever. I cannot overpraise the work of my chief assistant, Mr Sundarlal Narmada Prasad. He quickly obtained a mastery of the Oriya language and a considerable knowledge of Saora. He managed the camp, arranged supplies, nursed me when I was ill, made friends with everyone, and recorded a great deal of information. He was ubiquitous and indispensable. His tact, his affection and his knowledge made a great appeal to the Saoras, and it was widely believed that he was a Saora boy whom I had adopted many years ago and who had now returned to visit his old tribe. Sunderlal's remarkable versatility may be gathered from the fact that similar legends have made him in turn a Muria, a Gadaba and a Bondo.

'I confess', says Ramamurti, author of the Saora Dictionary, 'that I found it extremely difficult to learn Saora, and I have spent more than thirty years to understand some of the main features of the language.' Although I was able to conduct simple conversations and knew enough to check the work of translation, I could not dispense with interpreters, but I was fortunate in being able to engage the services of three men who were quite first-rate, each in his own way, and after careful training became expert. The first of these was Somra, an elderly Saora, husband of a famous shamanin, who had long served the Forest Department and had retired. Intelligent, tactful, informative, he was an ideal interpreter.

Equally good was Gandorbo, a Dom from Serango, who had lived his entire life in contact with the Saoras. He was a friendly and charming person, good-natured to a fault, and a careful and assiduous worker. Saoripani, another Dom but from Pottasingi, was also a first-rate translator.

I must not forget the little group of hard-worked and often forgotten camp-assistants. In the early days I had as cook a Goan named Fero, who had once provided banquets for the Palace at Jagdalpur and had fallen on evil days; he proved a master of the *haute cuisine* in the remotest villages, and I have never eaten so well since. Later I had Bhajan, a Pardhan of Patangarh, who was always cheerful and witty, and at various other times Haricharan, Phaggu, Jailal and Chakropani. They all behaved admirably in camp and helped to make what was always an arduous life comparatively easy and comfortable.

A grant from Merton College materially assisted the field-work for this book in its early stages. Later the generosity of the Sir D. J. Tata Trust, the J. R. D. Tata Trust and my friend Mr J. P. Patel helped to make the work possible. For part of the time I was engaged as Anthropologist to the Government of Orissa, part as Deputy Director of the Department of Anthropology in the Government of India; but most of my tours were in my private capacity.

Part of Chapter X appeared as an article 'The Saora Pictographs' in *Marg*, Vol. II, No. 3. Chapter V is a revised version of an article, 'The Saora Priestess', which has appeared in the *Bulletin* of the Department of Anthropology. Some of the drawings and photographs in my *The Tribal Art of Middle India* will serve to illustrate the themes of this book. The full text of the myths will be found in my *Myths of Middle India* and *Tribal Myths of Orissa.*

V.E.

1 *January* 1952

NOTE

THE name Saora has been spelt in almost as many different ways as the name Shakespeare. I have noted the following: Sabar, Sabara, Sahara, Sahra, Saonr, Saor, Saora, Saoura, Sar, Saur, Saura, Saurah, Savar, Savara, Savaralu, Savra, Sawara, Sayar, Sobor, Soeri, Soiri, Sora, Sor'a, So:ra, Soura, Sourah, Sowra, Sowrah, Suir, Swiri.[1] The most common spelling among the older European writers was Savara; this was the use of Thurston and Penzer. Russell and Risley, however, give the name as Savar. Ramamurti spells it So:ra in his *Manual*, Sora in his *Dictionary*; Sitapati and von Eikstedt also spell Sora.

In the Census of 1931, Yeatts adopted the spelling Saora, which had been used long before by Fawcett. His reasons are worth quoting. 'The common spelling of this name,' he says, 'is "Savara". This "v" is a Telugu intrusion. One of the marked characteristics of that language is to dislike the juxtaposition of two vowels. If it were written . . . "Sawara", a closer approximation to the real pronunciation would be obtained and the form thereby made less objectionable. Rao Sahib Ramamurti considers the true rendering to be "Sora". This, though possibly technically accurate, departs rather from the ordinary sound of the word. The form now given, "Saora", is probably as close as ordinary transliteration can get to the name which the tribe give to themselves and to their language.'[2] I have adopted the spelling Saora as a compromise which is not too distant from the traditional usage, and at the same time represents the pronunciation as nearly as is possible without the use of phonetic symbols.

Throughout this book certain Saora words recur continually, and for the convenience of English readers I have translated these wherever possible. This is a legitimate literary, and scientific, device, provided that the Saora words are invariably represented by the same English equivalents. In the following list, therefore, the English words, when

[1] 'As a curious specimen of the disintegration of a word,' said Hunter in 1872, 'the name is still spelt Savara in the police reports of Ganjam district; Sourah in the collectorate records; and Saur, Sur, or Sar, in the official documents of the adjoining district of Puri.'—W. W. Hunter, *Orissa* (London & Calcutta, 1872), vol. i, p. 175.

[2] M. W. M. Yeatts, in *Census of India*, 1931, vol. xiv, pt. i, p. 286. Yeatts also protests against the spellings Khond and Kondh: for the intrusion of the 'h' at the beginning of the first 'there is no warrant whatever'; for the 'h' hanging in the air at the end of the second, there is no meaning. He adopts the spelling 'Kond' and I have followed him in this book.

used in a Saora context, always have the same meaning and translate the same expressions.

Ancestor. I use this word to describe all those who have been admitted to the company of the ancestral dead, in the Under World or elsewhere, as a result of the Guar ceremony. The most common Saora word for these spirits is *idaisum*, which implies 'deified dead'; they are also called *jojonji* or *yoyonji*, grandfathers or grandmothers. I also, when the literary form of a passage demands it, use the word 'ghost' as a synonym for 'ancestor'.

Chief. This translates the Saora Gamangan, usually shortened to Gamang, the head of a village. It seems to me that the word 'Chief', which I have adopted from its use throughout Africa, is a more suitable title for these responsible and often well-to-do tribesmen than the usual 'headman'.

Custom. Saora *ukkan*, a word adapted from the Oriya, has the general meaning of custom, rule, practice, tradition.

Dead. Whenever I use the expression 'the dead' it should be understood that I refer to *all* the dead, *kulbānji* or shades, and *idaisumji* or ancestors, as well as to those ghosts who have been transformed into tutelaries or gods.

Deity. I sometimes use this as a synonym for 'god'.

Family. This always means the extended family, the *birindān*, of all persons descended from a single male ancestor, which is the only exogamous unit among the Saoras.

Ghost. I use this as a synonym for 'ancestor', since it is often necessary to refer to 'the ghost of such and such a person'. It never translates *kulbān*, shade.

God. I have adopted this word, after much consideration, as a translation of the Saora *sonuman* or *sonumbojan* (goddess), which occur in compounds shortened to *-sum* or *-sumboi*. The Saoras distinguish four types of spirit in the unseen world, the *sonumanji* proper, the tutelaries, the ancestors and the shades. But although popular theology gives the title of *sonuman* to the first three of these, the tutelaries and ancestors are distinguished in practice from the ordinary gods. I use the word 'god', therefore, for those spirits to whose names are attached the suffix *-sum* or *-sumboi*, and to certain others whose names are not so distinguished but are commonly classified with them, but who are not tutelaries, ancestors or shades.

Household. I use this for the individual family, the single economic unit, consisting of parents and children with dependent relatives, which is part of the larger *birindān* family.

Ikon. The Saoras make ceremonial paintings on the walls of their houses which are called *ittalan, jodartalan* or *jotalan.* The root *id-* means to scratch, write or make pictures; *tal* is a contraction of *kintalan,* a wall. Previously I described the *ittalan* as 'pictographs', but the word seemed rather pretentious and since these paintings are sacred and the objects of worship, the translation 'ikon' seemed to me sufficiently appropriate.

Liquor. I use 'liquor' for the spirit distilled from the corollas of the *Bassia latifolia* tree, and 'wine' for the spirit distilled from the fermented sap of the palm *Caryota urens.*

Measure. I use this to denote the Indian *seer,* which is approximately equivalent to 2 lb. avoirdupois.

Medicine. The Saora word *regaman* refers to a vegetable substance used in magical and sacrificial rites to avert certain dangers and diseases.

Medicine-man. A literal translation of the Saora Regamaran, a shaman who has the knowledge and power to administer magic medicines.

Priest. The Buyyan, who in the villages of Ganjam, and very rarely in Koraput, holds an official position below the Chief. Every member of the priest's family is called Buyyan, but the word as I use it only applies to the head of the family. The priest may also be a shaman, but he often is not, and then his chief religious duties consist in officiating at the Harvest Festivals.

Sacrifice. This always translates the Saora *purpuran,* usually contracted to *-pur* in suffixes, as in Doripur, Ajorapur.

Shade. After death the soul becomes a *kulbān,* which is sharply distinguished from the ancestors into whose company it is only admitted by the buffalo-sacrifice and menhir of the Guar rite. In this book *kulbān* is always translated 'shade', never 'ghost', but the *kulbānji* are included in the collective expressions 'the dead' and 'the spirits'.

Shaman, Shamanin. These are the very important Kuranmaran (usually called Kuran) and Kuranbojan (usually Kuranboi). There are several types of shaman, distinguished by different Saora words. Whenever it is necessary, I use the technical Saora words; but normally shaman or shamanin covers all the different types.

As there is no word in English for a female Shaman, I have ventured to coin the word Shamanin which, whenever it is used, means some kind of Kuranboi.

Shrine. The Saora *sadrun*, the little temple or shrine for a god or ancestor in the street or just outside a village.

Sorcerer. Saora *tonaimaran*; a witch is *tonaibojan* or *tonaiboi*. The sorcerer is always evil, and sorcery is dangerous, hostile magic directed against the community.

Soul. The Saoras distinguish two *purādanji*, or souls; one is the *rup-rup purādan*, the little soul, which gives life to the body and terminates at death; the other is the *suda purādan*, the big soul, which can leave the body in dreams and after death becomes a shade and then an ancestor. In this book whenever I use the word 'soul', I refer to the 'big soul'.

Spirit. It is often necessary to refer collectively to all the inhabitants of the unseen world, gods, tutelaries, ancestors, shades, and for this purpose I speak of 'the spirits'. This does not translate any particular Saora word.

Taboo. A fairly close translation of the Saora *ersin*.

Tutelary. The lords of the Under World, male or female, who 'marry' human beings and thus make them shamans or shamanins, are known by a number of different words—Ildasum, Ildabatan, Sedasum, Mannesum and Raudasum—according to the locality. But all the different names refer to the same thing, and the word tutelary translates any of them.

Under World. The Saora Under World is called Kingoraidesan or Kinnorai, the country of the ancestors, ruled over by the tutelaries and certain gods.

Wine. This always means the fermented sap of the palm *Caryota urens*.

I have generally referred to the form of cultivation known variously in India as *jhum*, *podu* or *bewar*, as 'axe-cultivation', and for the clearings on the hillsides made for this purpose I have adopted Izikowitz's word 'swidden'. This author points out that there is no single word in ordinary English which covers the meaning, since this method of cultivation no longer exists in England, and he continues: 'In contrast to English, the Swedish language has a single word, *svedja*, a burnt clearing (n.), and to burn a clearing (v.), in ordinary use today, because the method has been continued up until modern times. In searching for an English word I have taken the helpful suggestion of Professor Eilert Ekwall (of the University of Lund), a dialect word, *swidden.*'[1] To me the word seems admirable; it has a rustic air; and it fills an awkward gap in our vocabulary.

It is not easy to achieve a standard transliteration of Saora words, for the language itself is not uniform. 'It varies from Mutta to Mutta and from village to village. Even in the same village variations of pronunciation are noticed. It varies sometimes with sex and age.'[2] In his *Dictionary*, Ramamurti sometimes spells the same word differently on different pages; in his articles, Sitapati spells the same word differently on the same page. I have, in the main, followed Ramamurti's *Dictionary* and *Manual*, which give the dialect of the Gumma Mutta, though I have had to depart from it occasionally.

Another point on which it is difficult to be consistent is in the use of contracted forms and in the insertion of the noun suffix *–n* or *–an*. Technically, every Saora noun (with certain exceptions occurring in compounds) should end in *–n* or *–an*. But in ordinary speech this termination is often dropped. If a Saora is asked to give his name, he will give it formally with the full suffix. But when someone talks to him, he will usually omit it. Similarly, the everyday practice is to use contracted forms of many words—Kuran instead of Kuranmaran or even Kuranmar.

I have been frankly inconsistent over this. I follow all previous writers, including the linguists Ramamurti and Sitapati, in speaking of the Guar and Karja instead of Guaran and Karjan, because that is the way I have always heard the words spoken. I have used *–maran* in full, but *–boi* in the contracted form, because I think that in their transliterated guise they are the more attractive words. I omit the suffix in all proper names. But in words used only occasionally, I have usually added the suffix to the nouns.

[1] K. G. Izikowitz, *Lamet: Hill Peasants in French Indochina* (Goteborg, 1951), p. 7.

[2] G. V. Ramamurti, *A Manual of the So:ra (or Savara) Language* (Madras, 1931), p. xii.

Chapter One

INTRODUCTION

I. *The Hill Saoras*

THE Saoras described in this book are a fragment of a great tribe to which there are many, if confused, references in the ancient literature of India, and which today is widely distributed in groups of different traditions and manners.

It is possible that the word Saora (Sabara, Savara), or something like it, was used in ancient times much as people in India today use the words 'aboriginal', 'Bhumijan' or 'Adibasi', for it seems to have been synonymous with such names as Matanga, Kirata, Janangana, Pulinda and Bhilla, and can hardly have been employed in any ethnographic sense. 'My conclusion is,' says Cunningham, 'that in early times, where the name of the Savara is used, it probably covers all the different divisions of the Kols, as they are now called, including Kurkus and Bhils in the west, with Santals and Bhuiyas, Mundas and Hos, Bhumij and Juangs in the east. In later times, when Somadeva wrote the *Katha Sarit Sagara,* the name of Savara is used as synonymous with Pulinda and Bhilla, and, therefore, means only a man of an aboriginal tribe, of whom the writer knew nothing except by hearsay.'[1]

But the persistence with which the name recurs suggests that the Saoras were an important and widely scattered tribe; perhaps the confusion about the name is due to the fact that from the earliest period the Saoras were broken up into different sections; certainly today many of them have lost their language and have been assimilated in culture and religion to their neighbours.

Cunningham continues, 'There seems good reason to believe that the Savaras were formerly the dominant branch of the great Kolarian family, and that their power lasted down to a comparatively late period, when they were pushed aside by other Kolarian tribes in the

[1] A. Cunningham, 'Report of a Tour in the Central Provinces and Lower Gangetic Doab in 1881-82', *Archeological Survey of India,* vol. XVII (Calcutta, 1884), p. 139.

north and east, and by the Gonds in the south'.[1] B. C. Mazumdar is of the same opinion: 'All the Kolarians are but branches of the Sabara people.'[2] S. C. Roy agrees and refers to the fact that the Kolarian Santals are called Savaras by the Male Paharias.[3] The Parna-Savaras mentioned by Varaha Mihira (about A.D. 550) are supposed to be the leaf-clad Juangs, another tribe of the same group, though they may equally well be the leaf-clad Saoras. The Bendkars living between Singhbhum and Keonjhar described themselves as Saoras in the Census of 1872, and Risley includes them in his section on 'Savars'.[4] The Males of the Rajmahal Hills call, or used to call, themselves Savar Paharia or Sauria, and they resemble the Hill Saoras of this book in one remarkable particular: they too have no exogamous septs.[5]

The Hill Kharias of Dhalbhum trace their ancestry back to Sabbar-Burha and Sabbar-Burhi. 'This would appear to indicate,' says Roy, 'that the Kharias originally formed a branch of the great Savara people. The tradition of the Mayurbhanj Kharias that they are descendants of Basu Savara lends further support to this conjecture.'[6] Cunningham advances evidence to suggest a link, which had already been traced by Dalton, between the Saoras and the Bhuiyas.[7] The Purans, who are probably also to be classed with the Bhuiyas, claim racial affinity with the Saoras as well as with the Kharias.[8] And Crooke, following Nesfield, shows how the Musahars are connected with both Cheros and Saoras.[9] 'There can be little doubt,' says Hutton, 'but that the Sawars of the Orissa Maliahs and of Chhattisgarh, the Saoras of Saugor, Damoh and Bundelkhand, and the Saharia caste of Malwa and Gwalior all belong to the same original stock.'[10]

Cunningham divides the Saoras proper, that is to say tribesmen specifically calling themselves by this name, into two great divisions,

[1] Cunningham, p. 139. Modern scholars, of course, no longer classify the peoples of India by what are essentially linguistic terms—Dravidian and Kolarian. Eikstedt classifies the Saoras as Kolid.

[2] B. C. Mazumdar, *The Aborigines of the Highlands of Central India* (Calcutta, 1927), p. 13. Mazumdar is not perhaps a very reliable authority, but he devoted considerable attention to this subject, and some of his suggestions are of value.

[3] S. C. Roy, *The Mundas and their Country* (Calcutta, 1912), pp. 52f.

[4] H. H. Risley, *The Tribes and Castes of Bengal* (Calcutta, 1891), vol. II, p. 243.

[5] ibid., vol. II, p. 56.

[6] S. C. Roy and R. C. Roy, *The Kharias* (Ranchi, 1937), vol. I, p. 30.

[7] Cunningham, p. 134.

[8] S. C. Roy, *The Hill Bhuiyas of Orissa* (Ranchi, 1935), p. 24.

[9] W. Crooke, *The Tribes and Castes of the North-Western Provinces and Oudh* (Calcutta, 1896), vol. IV, pp. 16f. See also, infra, p. 31.

[10] J. H. Hutton, in *Modern India and the West*, edited by L. S. S. O'Malley (London, 1941), p. 436.

the western and the eastern. On his 1881 tour he travelled from Allahabad to the south-west and 'on turning to the westward', he says, 'I first came across some Saoras in the District of Damoh, and from thence westward to Sagar and Bhilsa I found them almost every day'. He traced them further in the hilly tracts to the south of Lalitpur and as far as Gwalior, in the vicinity of which they were called Sabarias and were known as wood-cutters and charcoal-burners. He estimated that at that date, there were not less than 120,000 of the western Saoras.[1]

He found some Saoras mixed with Bhils, and those towards Hoshangabad and Nimar touched the Korkus, 'a cognate race'. The western Saoras all spoke the same Hindi dialect. They were short, and their features were 'generally of the Tartar type', with broad flat noses, slightly oblique eyes and dark skins. They could endure great fatigue and were 'active and vigorous foresters'.

Cunningham also notices small numbers of Saoras living in the hills to the south of Shahabad and Bihar, where they were known by the name of Suir. There were also a few, called Suirai, in the Allahabad District, and they appeared again in the Ghazipur district to the north of the Ganges, and another small body 'of apparently the same clan' lived in eastern Oudh under the name of Sarhia.[2] Russell and Hira Lal notice the large numbers of Saoras in the Bundelkhand districts; they numbered about 100,000 in 1911.[3] The Suirs or Swiris of Ghazibad were studied by Garrick, but he had the greatest difficulty in meeting any of them, and estimated their total population as only 47.[4]

The eastern Saoras, as Cunningham points out, are separated from their brethren by a broad tract of country extending from Allahabad to Jabalpur in one direction, and from the Betwa river to the Mahanadi in the other. From the Mahanadi they extend in scattered groups across Chhattisgarh, through Sambalpur, and down to Ganjam and Koraput.[5] Russell and Hira Lal say that the eastern

[1] Cunningham, p. 116. Many years later Grigson found the Saoras of Saugor District landless and depressed.—W. V. Grigson, *The Aboriginal Problem in the Central Provinces and Berar* (Nagpur, 1944), p. 18.

[2] Cunningham, pp. 117f.

[3] R. V. Russell and Hira Lal, *The Tribes and Castes of the Central Provinces of India* (London, 1916), vol. IV, p. 500.

[4] H. B. W. Garrick, 'Report of a Tour through Behar, Central India, Peshawar and Yusufzai', *Reports of the Archeological Survey of India*, vol. XIX (1885), pp. 36ff. Crooke (*Tribes and Castes*, vol. IV, pp. 320ff.) gives some account of the 'Soeri, Soiri or Suiri' of Allahabad and Benares.

[5] Cunningham, p. 119.

Saoras have two main divisions called Laria and Uriya, or those belonging to Chhattisgarh and Sambalpur respectively.[1]

Kitts's *Compendium*[2] gives the distribution of Saoras in 1881 as follows:

Bengal	82,952
Central Provinces	130,719
Madras	131,981
North-West Provinces	2,099
Hyderabad	8

This makes a total of 347,759 individuals for the whole of India. But this figure is doubtless only approximate, for the Census of 1881, on which Kitts's work was based, had neither staff nor equipment to survey the remoter areas adequately.

By 1941 there had been considerable redrawing of the maps. At this Census there were no Saoras returned from the United Provinces, Central India, Bengal or Gwalior. They were concentrated mainly in Orissa, the Central Provinces (now Madhya Pradesh), Madras and Bihar. In Orissa the names of 326,236 persons were recorded, and the main centres of the Saora population were these:

Athgarh	6,584	Keonjhar ..	5,414
Balasore	1,993	Koraput	52,518
Cuttack	36,435	Mayurbhanj ..	3,583
Dhenkanal ..	27,270	Pal Lahara ..	1,239
Ganjam (Agency) ..	95,479	Patna	2,207
Ganjam (Plains) ..	29,521	Puri	26,385
Kalahandi	20,014	Sambalpur ..	7,602

These figures show some remarkable decreases from those recorded in 1931; the Saoras in Sambalpur District went down by no fewer than 71,504, in the Ganjam Plains by 33,505, in Patna State by 24,743. Census returns for individual tribes reveal the most erratic variations, due sometimes to redistribution of territory, sometimes to the fact that the tribesmen often change the official name of their community in the hope of gaining social advancement, sometimes to the inefficiency of semi-literate enumerators.

[1] Russell and Hira Lal, vol. IV, p. 504. See also A. E. Nelson, *Bilaspur District Gazetteer* (Allahabad, 1910), p. 92.

[2] E. J. Kitts, *Compendium of the Castes and Tribes found in India* (Bombay, 1885), p. 17.

In the Central Provinces also the Saora population decreased by 24,106. In 1941 it was distributed as follows :

Bilaspur	9,197
Chhattisgarh States	349
Raigarh	10,037
Raipur	22,039
Saugor	11,712

This gives a total for the whole area of what is now called Madhya Pradesh of 53,334 individuals. Mazumdar suggests that the Saoras formerly occupied the areas watered by the Savari River, and thus once dominated the eastern part of Bastar.[1] But there are very few Saoras now in Bastar. In 1941 I visited some Saora villages in Sarangarh; they are an attractive people there, and Grigson speaks of the 'magnificent specimens of baskets in brightly coloured patterns' made by Saoras and other tribesmen for sale in the bazaar in Sarangarh town.[2]

Bihar returned a Saora population of 2,754 in 1941, of which the majority (1,752) were in Manbhum District.

Most of the Saoras of Madras were transferred to Orissa with the adjustment of the boundaries in 1936, but there remained in 1941 a total of 14,696, of whom 12,842 were in the Vizagapatam Agency. An account of these, taken almost entirely from Sitapati's description of the Hill Saoras of Ganjam, is given in A. Aiyappan's *Report on the Socio-Economic Conditions of the Aboriginal Tribes of the Province of Madras* (Madras, 1948), pp. 77-81. The Report includes a photograph of Saoras with head-dresses of bison-horns and peacock feathers, which seem to be peculiar to this area.

When we compare the above Census figures with the earliest reports it appears that the western Saoras have almost entirely disappeared as a separate community; even in the days of Cunningham and Garrick they had adopted a great many Hindu ways; and they have now been so fully assimilated by their neighbours that they have even lost their distinctive name.

But the Saoras of all the other parts of India, except perhaps those of the Vizagapatam Agency, show few signs of affinity with

[1] Mazumdar, *Aborigines of Central India*, p. 8. And the Halbas, an important caste of Raipur and Bastar, include 'Sawara' among their family or section names. —A. E. Nelson, *Raipur District Gazetteer* (Bombay, 1909), p. 103.

[2] Grigson, *The Aboriginal Problem in the Central Provinces and Berar* (Nagpur, 1944), p. 284.

the Hill Saoras of Ganjam and Koraput. In most cases they have assimilated themselves to the local population, adopting its language, its dress, its manners and its gods. The Saoras described by Russell and Hira Lal have customs that are not only different but are in sharp contrast to those of the Hill Saoras. They have totemistic exogamous divisions;[1] they worship such deities as Bhavani and Dulha Deo; their women 'abstain from wearing nose-rings'; they are famous for their sorceries. The Saoras discussed by Risley are different again. The Bankura Saoras had exogamous and totemistic septs; Brahmins served them as priests; they forbade widow-remarriage. The Orissa Saoras (and it must be remembered that in Risley's day, Orissa did not include Ganjam and Koraput) worship Thanpati and Bansuri or Thakurani. The Bendkar Saoras described by Tickell in 1842 spoke Ho or Uriya; they worshipped Kali; were particular about food-taboos; did not collect ashes from a pyre; danced in Bhuiya fashion. In fact Dalton, who describes the Bendkars as a 'somewhat isolated fragment of Savaras' regards them as members of 'the great Bhuiya family'. Unhappily, Dalton 'never fell in with' any large community of true Saoras, though he notes that those who occupy 'the country between the Kandh Maliahs or hill tracts and the Godavery' retain a primitive form of speech.[2]

Where a name covers such diverse populations that it has come to mean little more than 'aboriginal' it is necessary to make very clear to whom exactly I refer when I use the word 'Saora' in this book. I mean the Hill Saoras of the Agency Tracts of the Ganjam and Koraput Districts of the modern State of Orissa, and I shall normally call them simply Saoras for convenience. They may be further defined by territory and by culture. A Saora, for purposes of this book, is someone calling himself by this name and living within a rough rectangle above the Vamsadhara River; one side of the rectangle stretches north from the Agency boundary near Parlakimidi for about forty miles; another runs east from Gunupur for twenty. The most typical of these Saoras live in the Gumma and Serango Muttas (sub-divisions) of the Ganjam District, and in the villages within ten miles of Pottasingi in Koraput. To the north through

[1] It is very odd for anyone who has spent a long time among the proud and independent Hill Saoras to find Frazer classifying the Saoras, 'an aboriginal tribe of cultivators and menials' as a 'totemic people'.—J. G. Frazer, *Totemism and Exogamy* (London, 1910), vol. II, p. 229.

[2] E. T. Dalton, *Descriptive Ethnology of Bengal* (Calcutta, 1872), p. 149.

Peddakimidi and Chinnakimidi are other Saora villages which gradually change their character as they approach the country of the Konds.

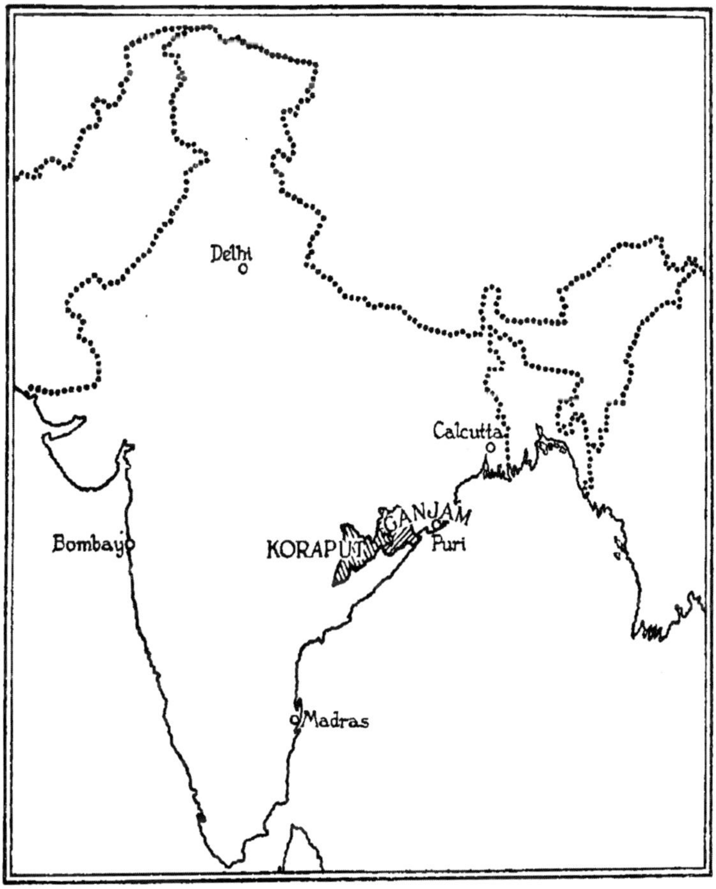

The Ganjam and Koraput Districts of Orissa

Not all the Saoras living in this area are Hill Saoras, though most of them are. The Hill Saoras, therefore, may be further distinguished by certain cultural traits: they live in long streets, in which they build little shrines; they erect menhirs and sacrifice buffaloes for their dead; their religious needs are served by male and female shamans; they engage in both terraced and shifting cultivation; their men put on a long brightly-coloured loin-cloth and their women wear a hand-woven brown-bordered skirt and do not usually wear anything else; the women also greatly enlarge the lobes of their ears and have a characteristic tattoo mark down the middle of the forehead. Most important of all, the Hill Saoras retain their own language and very few of them speak any other.

Sitapati rightly says that the country of the Hill Saoras must formerly have extended southwards to include the three talukas of Palakonda, Parlakimidi and Tekkali, but the Telugus, a stronger and more cunning people, drove them back and those who did not leave (and 'there are still hundreds of Saora villages in these talukas') they assimilated, teaching them their language and many of their social and religious customs.[1]

Those Saoras who have been assimilated into the surrounding populations are known by a number of different names. Those who talk Telugu are called Kampu Saoras—Kampu meaning Telugu: the word actually is the name of a Telugu Sudra caste. Other 'civilized' Saoras are the Sudda and Sarda or 'reformed' Saoras, who dress and look like untouchables; the Based Saoras, who live towards the coastal areas (*based* means 'sạlt'); the Bimma Saoras in the direction of Jirango; and a number of other small groups. Some of these retain their language, but most of them have lost or are losing it. They have begun to worship Hindu gods, to adopt Hindu food-taboos, and to wear different clothes and ornaments from their brethren in the hills.

The Hill Saoras are called Lombo Lanjhia Saoras by their Oriya neighbours in reference to the long-tailed loin-cloth which they wear. Ramamurti considers that this nickname is contemptuous and that the Saoras resent it.[2] I have not found this so myself; some Saoras are rather proud of being called Lanjhia, which they take to be synonymous with 'hillman'. Indeed people who can call themselves Arsis, monkeys, can hardly complain if outsiders call them long-tailed.

Lombo Lanjhia is the only single term which covers all the Hill Saoras as distinct from the plains Saoras of the Kampu or Sudda type. The Hill Saoras themselves use a variety of names for the different sections of their tribe. One branch, and perhaps the most important branch, calls itself Jati. Jati is not, of course, a Saora word, but an Oriya one which these Saoras have borrowed to show that they are the real thing, the true caste (*jāt*), pure in blood, custom and

[1] G. V. Sitapati, 'The Soras and their Country', *Journal of the Andhra Historical Research Society*, vol. XII, pp. 57f.

[2] G. V. Ramamurti, *A Manual of the So:ra (or Savara) Language* (Madras, 1931), p. v.

religion. The only characteristic, however, that distinguishes them from other Hill Saoras is that officially they do not eat beef. Another group is called Arsi. Arsi means monkey, but the name has no totemic reference and the only reason for it seems to be the curious affinity which many Saoras have for monkeys, and perhaps the long-tailed cloth. The Arsi Saoras eat monkeys, but so do most of the others. Some of the Arsis weave cloth and are the only Hill Saoras who do so.

The Jadu[1] Saoras live on the tops of hills and in the wilder tracts north of Serango. There is little difference between them and the Jati Saoras, for they too claim that they do not eat beef. But Jati Saoras insist that this is untrue, and that—whatever their pretensions may be—both the Jadu and Arsi Saoras have no real reverence for the cow and are therefore inferior breeds.

Beside these main divisions there are a few occupational groups, whose members live with the other Saoras and resemble them in every particular except in the special craft they have adopted.

The Kindal and Takala Saoras are basket-makers. They also do general bamboo work, weaving mats and winnowing-fans and making brooms. At Karja ceremonies the Kindals ceremonially exchange mats and baskets for a share in the rice and meat of the feast.

The Kumbit Saoras are potters. The Gontaras work in bell-metal and brass. The Luaras are blacksmiths: they do not smelt iron, and their little forges can only handle the roughest work. None of these are numerous.

The different groups are vaguely endogamous. But nobody thinks very much of it if a Jati Saora marries an Arsi or a Jadu. The barriers between the cultivating and occupational groups are a little stronger, yet an elopement between a Kumbit and a Jadu is not taken very seriously and is forgiven after the payment of a small fine. It is said, however, that members of priests' families have to be more careful: a Jati Buyya cannot marry an Arsi Buyya or Jadu Buyya, still less—for example—a Kumbit Poroja.

Yet members of all these groups look, dress, and behave alike. Even the blacksmiths and potters have their fields and cattle, and when they are cultivating there is nothing whatever to distinguish them from the others. They often live together in the same street;

[1] *Jadu* has no reference to magic; it is a genuine Saora word meaning wild, as in *jadu-medan*, a wild goat. The *a* is short.

at Boramsingi, there were Jatis, Takalas and Luaras living next door to one another. Sometimes, however, the members of different groups tend to associate in separate quarters of a village. Kumbit potters had their own street in Alangda. Arsis had a special quarter in Tumulu, Takalas occupied most of Karanjaju. A blacksmith's forge is often, from fear of fire, built outside a village, and the blacksmith may make his house near by. But there are no rules about this. In time the divisions will probably increase in importance; one group will decide not to eat pork, another will change its style of dress, a third will not let its women wear glass bangles; but at the moment the divisions do not matter very much to anyone.

The Saora hills are remarkably homogeneous. The only other inhabitants are the Doms and, in Ganjam District, the Paiks who work for the Bissoyi and Patro overlords. These Doms and Paiks, with a very few exceptions, live in their own villages, at Pottasingi, Nuagada, Gumma, Serango.

In 1941, there were 326,236 Saoras in Orissa, of whom 95,479 were in the Ganjam Agency, and 52,518 in Koraput. Approximately, two-thirds of these are Hill Saoras, whose number may thus be estimated at about 100,000.

II. *The Saoras in Literature and History*

THE early history of the Saoras is shrouded in the mists of legend and can only be glimpsed through tantalizing hints and obscure references but, as we have seen, what evidence there is suggests that they composed at one time a powerful tribe, including under their name all the different branches of Kols as we know them today; indeed they were so important that they are among the few tribesmen who are mentioned by early western geographers. There can be little doubt that they are the Suari of Pliny and the Sabarai of Ptolemy.

'In the interior', says Pliny, 'behind these (the Palibothri) are the Monedes and the Suari, among whom is Mount Maleus.'[1] And in another place he speaks of the Mandei and the Malli as being in the neighbourhood of the same mountain. Cunningham thought that the Monedes were the Mundas, living in the interior to the south of Patna or Palibothra; the Malli were perhaps the people of the

[1] J. Bostock and H. T. Riley, *The Natural History of Pliny* (London, 1855-6), vol. II, p. 46. Pliny's words are: *Ab iis in interiore situ Monedes et Suari, quorum Mons Maleus.* Another reading gives the name of the mountain as Mallus.

Rajmahal Hills who are called Maler—Malli in fact might, it was suggested, be equivalent to the Hindi *pahari*, or hillman. Cunningham tentatively identified Mount Maleus with the celebrated Mount Mandar, to the south of Bhagalpur, which is fabled as having been used by the gods and demons at the churning of the ocean.[1] Ganguly, however, considered that Mount Maleus was the beautiful Malyagiri in Pal Lahara, in whose vicinity I certainly found Saoras in 1942. Mahendragiri has also been suggested, but Ganguly rightly holds that the weight of the evidence is against this identification.[2] It is quite possible, however, that Beverley's suggestion is correct. Maleus or Mallus, he thought, was simply the Indian vernacular for the Latin *mons*. 'If a native were asked the name of a hill in the present day, he would reply, as Pliny's informant probably replied years ago, that it was a "hill"; and if asked the name of the people who lived there, he would probably say they were hillmen.'[3]

Ptolemy says that 'towards the Ganges River are the Sabarai, in whose country the diamond is found in great abundance; their towns are Tasopion and Karikardama'.[4] There has been much, not always very fruitful, speculation about the meaning of this passage: Cunningham observes that it places the Saoras to the south-west of the Gangetic delta and at a short distance from the sea-coast;[5] Yule considers that the Saoras must have been further north in Dosarene, towards the territory of Sambalpur 'which produced the finest diamonds in the world'.[6] Lassen thought that Karikardama was probably somewhere in Singbhum. But there is no certainty about this and the 'towns' have never been properly identified.

Interesting as these references are, yet as Cunningham says, 'the native notices of the Saoras ascend to a much earlier period'. Although the hymns of the *Rigveda* do not mention them explicitly, they have a great deal to say about the Dasyus who are identified by S. C. Roy with the great Kol race. 'For a time,' he says, 'the Mundas and other allied tribes appear to have waged wars on equal terms with

[1] Cunningham, p. 125. See also *Cunningham's Ancient Geography of India*, edited by S. M. Sastri (Calcutta 1924), p. 583.

[2] M. M. Ganguly, *Orissa and her Remains* (Calcutta, 1912), p. 13.

[3] H. Beverley, *Report of the Census of Bengal*, 1872, p. 184.

[4] *McCrindle's Ancient India as Described by Ptolemy*, edited by S. M. Sastri (Calcutta, 1927), p. 172; bk. VII, i, 80. Oldham suggests that in the first centuries of the Christian era, the Saoras occupied the inland hill and jungle country to the south and south-east of what is now the Ranchi District.—C. E. A. W. Oldham, 'Diamonds in Bihar & Orissa', *J.B.O.R.S.*, vol. XIII (1927), p. 198.

[5] Cunningham, p. 125. [6] Sastri, p. 173.

their Aryan opponents', and he suggests that they had not yet sunk to the condition of savagery and anarchy which later classical writers describe.[1] The Dasyu leader Sambara had a hundred cities,[2] Vangrira a hundred more,[3] Pipru had ninety-nine.[4] We read of castles—which were not all, perhaps, castles in the air—and 'firm forts built by men'.[5] Sambara had strongholds stored with wealth within his mountain. There are hints of social organization, of wives and families[6] and commonwealths of cities. 'The arts of war and peace were not unknown. Stone and flint weapons were used in warfare and implements of the same materials appear to have been utilized for household purposes.'[7] But in the end the Aryans conquered the older inhabitants of the land, 'the sun of Kol prosperity sank below the horizon' and in the first explicit reference to the Saoras, in the *Aitareya Brahmana*,[8] we find them classed with such Dasyu tribes as the Andhras, Pulindas, Pundras and Mutibas, and living as outcastes on the fringe of the Aryan settlements. This places the Saoras in trans-Vindhyan India about 800 B.C.

The *Aitareya Brahmana* describes the Saoras as the descendants of the elder sons of Visvamitra, who were cursed by their father for an act of disobedience, and this epitomizes the general attitude of the Hindu classical writers towards the 'aboriginals'. 'The Saoras', says Hunter, 'appear in very early Sanskrit writings and are spoken of by them with even more than usual detestation. As the Sudras or aboriginal tribes, who had been subdued into the servile caste of the Aryan Commonwealth, sprung from the feet of Brahma, so the Savara and other forest races, who successfully withstood the invaders, proceeded from the sweat of a cow. They were goblins, they were devils, they were raw-eaters, they were man-eaters, and the *Vishnu Purana* has concentrated the national antipathy towards them in its picture of a dwarfish race, with flat noses and a skin the colour of a charred stake. Another sacred text assures us that they were as black as crows, with tawny hair, red eyes, a chin jutting out, short arms and legs, and the typical flat nose. A third Sanskrit sage adds a protuberant belly, drooping ears and an ogre mouth. They seem

[1] S. C. Roy, *The Mundas*, p. 55.
[2] *Rigveda*, II. 14, 6. [3] ibid., 1, 53, 9. [4] ibid., I, 174, 8. [5] ibid., VI, 45, 9.
[6] ibid., XXIV, 2. [7] Roy, op. cit., p. 59.
[8] *Aitareya Brahmana*, VII, 18, 2. See N. K. Dutt, *The Aryanisation of India* (Calcutta, 1925), p. 68 and H. Raychaudhuri, *Political History of Ancient India* (Calcutta, 1932), p. 64.

to have made their individuality very strongly felt in ancient India. The beginning of their territory long marked the last point of the Aryan advance. They are often spoken of as border tribes, who resisted the Sanskrit invaders, scattered their armies, and earned for themselves the name of the "terrible Saoras".'[1]

Some of the Saora references in the *Mahabharata*[2] reflect this attitude. The origin of the Saoras is traced to the cow of Vasishtha Nandini, which was desired by Viswamitra, King of Kanyakubja (Kanauj). He offered the owner an *arbuda*, or ten crores of his own kine, or even his kingdom itself, in exchange, but in vain. He then tried to take the cow by force. 'To prevent this the cow attacked Visvamitra's troops; from her tail she brought forth Pahlavas, from her udders Dravidas and Sakas, from her vagina Yavanas, from her dung Sabaras, from her urine Kanchis, from the froth of her mouth Paundras, Yavanas, Simhalas, Barbaras, Vasas, Chivukas, Pulindas, Chinas, Hunas, Keralas and other Mlechchas.'[3] This is the reading of the Calcutta text, and it suggests a link between the Saoras and the Kanchis, people of Conjeevaram in the south, the one originating from dung, the other from urine. But in the text published by the Bhandarkar Oriental Research Institute the Sabaras are associated with the Sakas, a northern people. The attitude of the ruling race, however, is clear: the Saoras can be used as mercenaries, but they are not fit, in view of their birth from dung, to be admitted into Aryan society.

Other passages are equally derogatory in tone. 'He (Siva) assumes the form also of men and women, *pretas* and *pisachas*, Kiratas and Sabaras and of all aquatic animals'[4]—Saoras are placed between goblins and fishes. Janamejaya, son of Parikshit, is reported as saying that wretches like himself had forfeited all claim to the respect of the world and after death would have to dwell in hell like Pulindas and Sabaras.[5]

But in other, probably later, passages there is a change of attitude. For example, when Mandhatri asks what duties should be performed by a number of peoples, of whom the Saoras are one, who have

[1] W. W. Hunter, *Orissa* (London & Calcutta, 1872), vol. I, pp. 176f.

[2] My friend Mr Saurindranath Roy, of the National Archives of India, translated the passages from the *Mahabharata*, generally following the Calcutta text, with some help from P. C. Roy's version. This shows some divergence from the text published by the Bhandarkar Oriental Research Institute, particularly in references to ethnic names: where such differences are relevant they are noticed.

[3] *Mahabharata*, I, 174. [4] ibid., XIII, 14. [5] ibid., XII, 151.

sprung from the four main castes who reside in the domain of the Aryan kings, Indra replies: 'All the robber tribes should serve their parents, their preceptors and other seniors and recluses living in the woods. All the robber tribes should also serve their kings. The duties inculcated in the Vedas should also be followed by them. They should perform sacrifice in honour of the Pitris [manes], dig wells, give water to thirsty travellers, give away beds and make other seasonable presents to Brahmins.' In this passage there appears to be recognition of the Saoras as of the same blood as the ruling race, for they are derived from one of the four castes, even though they are degraded because they have become a robber tribe. It is the King's duty to reclaim them by teaching them the laws of the land and the ideals of piety.[1]

This change of attitude, suggests Mr Saurindranath Roy, may have been due to the influence of Buddhism or to a missionary zeal on the part of the rulers to Hinduize the tribal peoples as well as the foreign settlers in the country, refusing to make any distinction between them.

Another passage which refers to the Saoras in friendly terms is that which places a Sabaralaya, a residence of Saoras, in the northern region inhabited by Mlechchas. A Brahmin named Gautama belonging to the middle country went to this region and reached a village which was peopled by Dasyus. He was kindly received by one of them who was wealthy, truthful and munificent. The house of this Dasyu is described in the text as a Sabaralaya, and we gather that the village was a colony of Saoras who lived by hunting birds, their chief weapons being bows and arrows. They were sufficiently well-to-do to present Gautama with new clothes and on his arrival he was offered and accepted the hand of a widowed girl, whose husband had recently died.[2]

There is some evidence that the Saoras were not only a robber tribe, but well organized to arms. There is a reference to the 'terrible Saoras' created by Vasishtha's cow who caused great carnage among the troops of Visvamitra.[3] Cunningham considered that the Saoras were among the seven tribes of Dasyus inhabiting the mountains, the Utsavansanketas, who were conquered by the Pandavas. Among those vanquished by Saineya, Krishna's charioteer, were the Kambojas, Sakas, Sabaras, Kiratas and Varvaras; on this occasion 'the

[1] ibid., XII, 65. [2] ibid., XII, 168, 171, 173. [3] ibid., IX, 40.

earth was covered with the helmets and shaven and bearded heads of the Dasyus'.[1]

It is not easy to draw any conclusion from the references in the *Mahabharata* about the location of the Saoras in early times. Sometimes the name Sabara occurs in association with northern, sometimes with southern tribes. In one passage they are definitely described as a southern people.

> I shall now, O son of Kunti, speak to you about the sinful creatures of the earth. Listen to me. These men, O King, are born in the southern region and are called Andhrakas, Guhas, Pulindas, Sabaras, Chuchukas, Madrakas. Those that are born in the northern region I shall also mention. They are Yavanas, Kambojas, Gandharas, Kiratas and Barbaras. All of them, O sire, are sinful and move on the earth characterized by practices similar to that of Chandalas, ravens and vultures. In the Krita [Golden] Age they were nowhere on the earth.[2]

Two other references to the origin of the Saoras may be given. In the first we read:

> The Mekalas, the Dravidas, the Lathas, the Paundras, the Konwasiras, the Saundikas [wine-sellers], the Darvas, the Chauras, the Sabaràs, the Kiratas, the Yavanas, and numerous other tribes of Kshattriyas have become degraded to the status of Sudras through the wrath of the Brahmanas.[3]

This idea of the degradation of the Saoras from a high to a low caste appears to be comparatively modern; it is repeated in the second passage.

> Then some of the Kshattriyas afflicted with the terror of Jamadagni's son, entered mountain fastnesses, like deer afflicted by the lion. Of them that were unable, through fear of Rama [that is, Rama of the axe, Jamadagni's son] to discharge the duties ordained for their order, the progeny became Vrishalas [Sudras] owing to their inability to find Brahmanas. In this way the Dravidas and Abhiras and Pundras together with the Sabaras became Vrishalas, though these men had Kshattriya duties assigned to them.[4]

During the first thousand years of the modern era, we have only a few scattered references to the Saoras. The Puranas describe them

[1] Cunningham, p. 126.
[2] *Mahabharata*, XII, 107. Mr S. Roy points out that the mention of the Madrakas (who belong to the western Punjab) as a southern people hardly encourages us to regard the author as an authority on geography.
[3] ibid., XIII, 35. [4] ibid., XIV, 29.

as *Dakshina-patha-vasinah* and *Vindhyamaulika*,[1] which places them towards the south. In the period A.D. 500 to 600, Amara Sinha classes the Saoras with such barbarians as Kiratas and Pulindas. Varaha Mihara speaks of the 'naked Sabaras and the Parna Sabaras' as living with the Purikas and Dasamas in the south-east, and of the Sauris and Kirnas as living in the south.[2] Cunningham quotes Kern as holding that the Parna Sabaras were 'manifestly the Phyllitae of Ptolemy': he explained the name as 'feeding upon leaves'. But Cunningham suggests that since the Juangs, a 'cognate race', still wear leaves, it is more probable that the term means 'leaf-clad'[3] —as late as 1886 the Saoras of Ganjam were reported as wearing leaves. Varaha Mihira also speaks of the 'Sabara savages' and the 'savage Sabaras and Pulindas'.[4]

The *Natya-Sutra*, attributed to Bharata Muni of the sixth century A.D., refers to the Saoras as charcoal-burners, and lays down the rule that when they or other barbarians such as the Odras are represented on the stage, they should be made to talk *vibhasa*, which probably means that they were to use a rough dialect flavoured with tribal words.[5]

The poet Bana tells the story of how Harsha Vardhana, immediately after his accession in A.D. 607, went to search for his sister Rajya Sri in the wild forests of the Vindhyan Mountains. As he travelled across the hills, he met a Chief named Vyaghraketu, son of Sarabhaketu, and Nirghata, commander-in-chief of the Bhukampa Sabaras. 'The King made enquiries of the Sabara Chief regarding Rajya Sri; he replied that no woman answering to the description given by the King was known to have been seen in his jungles, but promised to make vigorous efforts for her discovery.' He suggested that she might have taken refuge in a hermitage and guided the King thither.[6] Although the names seem to be fictitious—the Bhukampa Sabaras means the 'earthquake' Sabaras—the story suggests that at this time the Saoras were still powerful in the Vindhyan Hills.

It is, however, in his *Kadambari* that Bana elaborates his account of the Sabaras. Bana is a very luxuriant writer; every paragraph

[1] *Matsya Purana*, 114, 46-48; *Vayu Purana*, 45, 126.

[2] *Brihad Samhita*, vol. XIV, 10-22.

[3] Cunningham, p. 128.

[4] *Brihad Samhita*, vol. IX, 15, 29; XXXII, 15.

[5] See chap. XVII, slokas 44, 47. Grierson has discussed the possible meaning of *vibhasa* in *J.R.A.S.*, 1918, pp. 489-517.

[6] Bhau Daji, 'Discovery of complete Manuscript Copies of Bana's *Harsha Charita*', *J.B.B.R.A.S.*, vol. x (1871-4), pp. 39-41.

flowers with a score of similes; every sentence is garlanded with jasmine and champak buds. His descriptions, therefore, cannot be taken too seriously, yet they are interesting, in their curious combination of severity and almost reluctant admiration, as a picture of the attitude towards the tribal people of the day, and some of the details may well be based on fact.

Bana opens his account of the Sabara army with a procession of fifteen unflattering similes. The Sabaras were like 'all the nights of the dark fortnight rolled into one', 'a crowd of evil deeds come together', 'a caravan of curses of the many hermits dwelling in the Dandaka Forest'. Their leader's name was Matanga. 'He was as the child of the Vindhya Mountains, the partial avatar of death; the born brother of wickedness, the essence of the Iron Age.' Like the trident of Durga, 'he was wet with the blood of buffaloes'—as most of his descendants still are. 'Like a summer day, he always showed a thirst for deer.' Yet Bana cannot altogether withhold his admiration. 'Horrible as he was, he yet inspired awe by reason of his natural greatness and his form could not be surpassed.' He was hard as iron.

And he was certainly good to look at. He filled the woods with beauty that streamed from him sombre as dark lotuses, like the waters of Yamuna; he had thick locks curled at the ends and hanging on his shoulders. To ward off the heat he had a swarm of bees which flew above him like a peacock-feather parasol. Yet he bore the marks of his profession; his shoulders were rough with scars from keen weapons often used to make blood-offerings to Kali; his chest was scarred 'by constant and ceaseless fatigue'. He was surrounded by hounds whose throats were covered with strings of cowries.

Matanga's warriors were equally remarkable. 'Some had seized elephants' tusks and the long hair of yaks; some had vessels for honey made of leaves closely bound; some like lions had hands filled with many a pearl from the frontal bones of elephants; some, like demons, had pieces of raw flesh; some, like goblins, were carrying the skins of lions; some, like Jain ascetics, held peacocks' tails; some, like children, wore crows' feathers.'

We need not, perhaps, take this description very seriously; what is of greater interest is the narrator's reflections upon it. 'Ah,' he says, 'the life of these men is full of folly, and their career is blamed by the good. For their one religion is offering human flesh to Durga; their meat, mead and so forth, is a meal loathed by the good; their exercise is the chase; their *shastra* is the cry of the jackal; their teachers of good and evil are owls; their knowledge is skill in birds; their bosom friends are dogs; their kingdom is in deserted woods; their feast is a drinking bout; their friends are the bows that work cruel deeds; and arrows, with their heads smeared, like snakes, with poison, are their helpers; their song is what draws on bewildered deer; their wives are the wives of others taken captive; their dwelling is with savage tigers; their worship of the gods is with the blood of beasts, their sacrifice with flesh, their livelihood by theft; the snake's hood is their ornament; their cosmetic, elephants' ichor; and the very wood wherein they dwell is utterly destroyed root and branch.'[1]

The love of spirituous liquor, animal-sacrifice, marriage by capture, the love of dogs, axe-cultivation that destroys the forest—the same complaints are still made against the tribesmen by the orthodox Hindu. But how far the Saoras ever practised human sacrifice is doubtful, and will be discussed later.

Another poet, Kavi Vakpati, who flourished during the last half of the seventh century A.D., describes a shrine at Vindhyachal, near the present Mirzapur, which had a Sabara goddess to whom Sabaras clad in leaves offered human sacrifice.[2]

Epigraphic records are few and the information they give us is so disconnected that it is of little value. A Korni copperplate grant of Anantavarma Choda Ganga tells us that Karmavarna, the founder of the Kalinga Ganga dynasty, defeated and killed the previous ruler Sabaraditiya somewhere to the east of Mount Mahendra, about A.D. 720.[3] In the Udayendiram plates of the twenty-first year of the reign of the Pallava King Nandivarman Pallavamalla, he is said to have defeated the Saora King Udayana and captured his mirror banner made of peacock feathers. This was about A.D. 736.[4]

Another Saora Chief is mentioned in the Sanskrit and Kanarese *prasasti* of the Western Ganga Chief Marasimha II, who was a subordinate of the Rashtrakuta King Krishna III and placed Indra IV on the throne. This inscription is at Sravana Belgola in Mysore and

[1] *The Kadambari of Bana*, translated by C. M. Ridding (London, 1896), pp. 27ff.
[2] Mazumdar, *Aborigines of Central India*, p. 10.
[3] Sitapati, 'The Soras', *J.A.H.R.S.*, vol. I, pp. 107f.; G. Ramadas, 'Tri-Kalinga Country', *J.B.O.R.S.*, vol. XV (1929), p. 635.
[4] *South Indian Inscriptions*, vol. I, p. 365; *Indian Antiquary*, vol. VIII (1879), pp. 275-6; R. D. Banerji, *History of Orissa* (Calcutta, 1930), vol. I, p. 20. Hultzsch considers that the 'Sabara' of the plate cannot be identified with the Saoras, but Foulks and Mazumdar hold that he can.

states that Marasimha II (963–74) defeated a Saora Chief named Naraga.[1] The Naihati grant of Vellasena dated about 1100 declares that the children of the Kings who were Vellasena's enemies were reduced to living in the houses of Saoras; this gives us Saoras in the Burdwan District of Bengal.[2] A rock inscription of the time of Bhojavarman (A.D. 1300) in the Ajayagarh Fort records that Ananda the Governor subdued the wild tribes of Bhillas, Sabaras and Pulindas.[3] A Khadavada inscription dating from Gyasahi of Mandu, A.D. 1484, declares that one of Mandu's military officers put down a Saora rebellion at Khidavada on the Chamanvati.[4]

The only inscription, however, from the area now populated by the Hill Saoras occurs in the Kurmesvara temple at Sri-Kurmam in the Vizagapatam District; this records that the famous Vaisnava scholar Narahari-tirtha had protected the people of Kalinga and defended the temple against an attack by the wild Saoras. This was some time in the latter part of the thirteenth century.[5]

We have already seen how unfavourable was the attitude of the early Aryans towards the Saoras and Dasyus generally. But in the *Katha Sarit Sagara*, that great anthology of tales current in India in the eleventh century, we find a kindlier and almost romantic approach. It is true, as Bühler says, that the names of tribes are 'used very vaguely in the Sanskrit story-books'[6] and that here the words Savara, Bhilla[7] and Pulinda are almost interchangeable; possibly they were used, as Cunningham suggests, according to the demands of the metre. Yet since the Saoras were, even at this date, still predominant among the tribes, we may assume that Somadeva's references are not without some significance for our inquiry.

On one side, indeed, the picture is still unfavourable. The Saoras are brigands and cattle-lifters;[8] they practise human sacrifice;[9] they maintain prisons characterized by appalling barbarity;[10] they attack

[1] *Epigraphica Indica*, vol. v, p. 176; Banerji, op. cit., vol. I, p. 20.
[2] ibid., vol. XIV, p. 18, No. 10. [3] ibid., vol. I, pp. 330-8.
[4] Sitapati, 'The Soras', *J.A.H.R.S.*, vol. XII, p. 61.
[5] *South Indian Inscriptions*, vol. v, No. 1312; *Epigraphica Indica*, vol. VI, pp. 266-8; Banerji, op. cit., vol. I, p. 271.
[6] N. M. Penzer, *The Ocean of Story* (London, 1924-8), vol. I, p. 100.
[7] Hira Lal considers that the frequent confusion of the names Savara and Bhilla suggests that they were 'two branches of the same tribe descended from a common ancestor'.—Hira Lal, 'The Aborigines of Central India', *Man in India*, vol. II (1922), p. 35. Saletore, following the lexicographers Amara and Dandin, considers that the Kiratas and Sabaras are identical.—B. A. Saletore, *The Wild Tribes in Indian History* (Lahore, 1935), p. 38. [8] Penzer, op. cit., vol. I, p. 152.
[9] ibid., vol. I, p. 115; II, p. 141. [10] ibid., vol. VII, p. 154.

and kill King Dharma;[1] there is a story of a Saora girl who is a wanton and a murderess.[2]

Yet though many of the Saoras are wild and savage enough, they are not altogether unattractive in their simplicity. A Saora messenger appears, 'bow in hand, with his hair tied up in a knot behind with a creeper, black, and wearing a loin-cincture of *bhilwan* leaves'.[3] Other Saoras are 'adorned with peacock's feathers and elephant's teeth, clothed in tiger's skins and living on the flesh of deer'.[4] The palace of the Saora Chief Ekakikesarin is 'crowded with Saoras, having its high walls covered with the tusks of elephants, adorned with tiger-skins; in which the women had for garments the tails of peacocks, for necklaces strings of *gunja* fruit and for perfume the ichor that flows from the forehead of elephants'.[5] Saora women dance 'delighted' at a great feast.[6]

Even the wildest Saoras appear to have some social sense. When Mrigankadatta sees them, he exclaims, 'See! These men live a wild forest life like animals, and yet, strange to say, they recognize Durgapisacha as their King. There is no race in the world without a King.'[7]

The ruling Saoras are wealthy and are accepted on equal terms by other Kings. The Saora King, Mayavatu, is able to entertain a visiting host, 'giving them all splendid baths, unguents, food, arms and beds'.[8] King Amaradatta and his son camp in his palace at Kanchanapura and spend an agreeable day there, with 'song, music and dancing'.[9]

The Saora King in Jimutavahana's story is merciful and intelligent; he goes to find pearls on the heads of elephants and on the way meets an exquisite maiden 'like the digit of the moon resting in the lap of an autumn cloud'; she is riding on a lion. He at once thinks of his friend, Vasudatta, goes to fetch him, takes him to the Himalayas, and arranges his marriage. Here we have an important Hindu of good family, son of a rich merchant, cherishing the friendship of a tribal Chief. Indeed he considers that he has attained all that the heart could wish 'in having Manovati for a wife and the Saora prince for

[1] Penzer, op. cit., vol. VII, p. 117. [2] ibid., vol. III, p. 94. [3] ibid., vol. VII, p. 158. [4] ibid., vol. VII, p. 167. [5] ibid., vol. IX, p. 46. [6] ibid., vol. VII, p. 158. Saletore quotes from a seventeenth-century Kannada poet, Braham-kavi, a description of Saora women: 'With black bodies, wearing the sprouts of the asoka plant and the [beautiful scarlet and black] seeds of the wild liquorice, and the black pearls obtained from the bamboos in their braids, the Sabara women shone like *sandhya-Lakshmi* [goddess of twilight].'—Saletore, op. cit., p. 47. [7] ibid., vol. VII, p. 167. [8] ibid., vol. VII, p. 171. [9] ibid., vol. VII, p. 184.

a friend'. It is interesting to note the effect of this friendship on the Saora; he spent most of his time with Vasudatta, 'finding that he took less pleasure in dwelling in his own country than he formerly did'[1]—a not uncommon result of acculturation.

The King of Vatsa also owed much to a Saora who came from the mountain of the sunrise and guided him to find his wife.[2]

Vishnudatta describes the husband of the wanton Saora girl, in whose house he stayed, as performing an act of 'surprising courage, characteristic of men of mighty minds'.[3]

And finally, Mrigankadatta says to the Saora King Mayavatu, 'When the Creator made you here, he infused into your composition qualities borrowed from your surroundings, the firmness of the Vindhya hills, the courage of the tigers, and the warm attachment to friends of the forest lotuses'.[4]

The important thing about these references is that they show that, in Somadeva's time, the tribal peoples were regarded with respect and even affection; there is indeed a certain sentimentalizing of them, a Rousseau-like attitude that there may be something to be said for the noble savage and his free life of skins and leaves and feathers.

I have deferred discussion of the *Ramayana* because of its influence on contemporary traditions, to which we must shortly turn. But probably the most famous of the historical references to the Saoras is that connected with Ramachandra. These all ultimately derive from Valmiki's *Ramayana* where, in Book III, Canto 74, we read how Rama and Lakshman, in the course of their search for Sita, came to the banks of a lake or river, Pampa, lying to the west of 'Rishyamukha's wood-crowned height', where an aged ascetic Savari had made her home. Before her time the hermitage had been occupied by Matanga and other rishis, and Matanga had given his name to the neighbouring forest. Knowing that her visitors were on the way, Savari collected the fruits for which the place was famous and offered them to Rama for his comfort. She showed Rama the hermitage saying, 'See the charming great forest abounding in flowers and fruit, resembling a bank of clouds, filled with all sorts of deer and birds; this is famed on earth as Matanga's forest'. Rama then gave her

[1] Penzer, op. cit., vol. II, pp. 141ff.
[2] ibid., vol. III, p. 94.
[3] ibid., vol. III, p. 67.
[4] ibid., vol. VII, p. 167.

permission to depart from this world. In the presence of the two brothers, Savari[1] went into a fire and ascended into the heavens while all the sky was lighted by her glory.

It has been suggested that Valmiki introduced the character of Savari for no other reason than to give us a clue as to what tribes were then inhabiting the Forest of Dandaka, for she has no real bearing on the story and the incident does not advance the plot in any way. Ramadas in fact believes—rather optimistically—that it is from the Saora language that we may discover the real meaning of some of the names in the *Ramayana*. Thus, he derives the name of Rawan's capital, Lanka, from the Saora *lankan*, meaning tall, high or above, for the most striking characteristic of the city of Lanka was its lofty and inaccessible position on the Trikuta. Similarly, he suggests that the low-lying Janasthana is derived from Saora *jaitan*, below. The Forest of Dandaka itself, which was famous for its 'lucid pools, floods and lakes, rills leaping from their parent hills' does not mean the Forest of King Danda, but 'full of water', from the Saora word for water *dān* or *dāk*, repeated twice for emphasis.[2] But these, and some other derivations which appear very far-fetched, have been controverted by Ambika Prasad, who points out, for example, that Lanka really means 'white' and that the name refers to the shining white buildings of the city.[3]

Ramadas has also made an ingenious attempt to identify the Vanars of the *Ramayana* with our Hill Saoras. Both Vanars and Saoras are afraid of strangers; both delight in revelry; both love alcoholic refreshment; both enjoin a younger brother to marry an elder brother's widow; both drink from leaf-cups. More convincing is the point that while the Vanar men had tails, the women apparently did not have 'this appendage'. This suggests that the 'monkey-hosts' of Sugriva were none other than the Arsi (monkey) Saoras with their long-tailed loin-cloth. 'Since the Vanars of the *Ramayana* resemble in dress, customs and manners the Saoras of today, and many of the names of persons, places and objects existing between the Ganges

[1] Savari is known as the Sramana Savari: Sramana suggests a 'woman of low caste' as well as a female mendicant. There can be no doubt that the author intends her to be regarded as a Saora. See F. E. Pargiter, 'The Geography of Rama's Exile', *J.R.A.S.* (1894), pp. 252ff.

[2] G. Ramadas, 'Aboriginal Names in the Ramayana', *J.B.O.R.S.*, vol. XI (1925), pp. 41ff.

[3] Ambika Prasad, 'Some Names in the Ramayana', *J.B.O.R.S.*, vol. XII (1926), pp. 290ff.

and Lanka are of Saora origin, it is clear that Sugriva and his men were Saoras or of tribes allied to them.'[1]

To this we may add the very high place which 'Ramma' has in Saora mythology, though obviously Ramadas's identifications can be no more than conjectural.

The story of Savari is told today in many different forms. The Kols of Middle India regard her as their mother; children are born in answer to her prayers; by her merit they are clothed and fed. The Kol tradition differs in many particulars from the story in the *Ramayana*. Rama, Lakshman and Sita were together in exile in the forest and one day when they were very hungry they met 'Shivari' who fed them with wild plums. After this she used to gather the fruits daily for her divine visitors, but one day she forgot what she was doing and as she picked them she took a bite from each before dropping it into her basket. When she returned home, Rama asked her for the plums, but when she realized what she had done, she was ashamed to offer them to him. But he pressed her to do so, and in spite of the fact that they were half eaten, Sita and he enjoyed them. But Lakshman refused to touch them—for to do so was to eat the 'leavings' of an aboriginal[2]—and as a result he was struck down by an arrow and only recovered when he changed his mind. Rama was so pleased with the woman's devotion that when he left her home, he gave her the boon that she should have many descendants and that they should never lack for food and clothing.[3]

Other Kol stories say that Shivari or Sheori was a devotee of Bhagavan, who is sometimes called Siva and sometimes Krishna. She used to follow her lord wherever he went, gathered wild plums for him, and spread large leaves for his couch in the forest. According to the Kols, Shivari's hermitage was near the modern Seori-Narayan, not far from Raipur.[4]

Russell and Hira Lal also refer to the story of Savari, which they attribute to 'local tradition'. Their version traces the origin of the Saoras 'to the celebrated Seori of the *Ramayana*, who is supposed to have lived somewhere near the present Seori-Narayan in

[1] G. Ramadas, 'The Aboriginal Tribes in the Ramayana', *Man in India*, vol. v (1925), pp. 28ff.

[2] For the great importance of this in the Indian mind, see below p. 488.

[3] W. G. Griffiths, *The Kol Tribe of Central India* (Calcutta, 1946), p. 207.

[4] ibid., p. 8. Sheori is sometimes called Kolni, and sometimes Bhilni; this branch of the tribe is thus linked with both Saoras and Bhils.

the Bilaspur District and to have given her name to this place. Ramachandra in his wanderings met her, ate the plums which she had gathered for him after tasting each one herself, and out of regard for her devotion permitted her name to precede his own of Narayan in that given to the locality.'[1] It will be noted that in this version of the story the Saora woman tastes the plums as an act of devotion, presumably to see if they are sufficiently ripe, not from forgetfulness. The Saoras living in this area still call themselves Seori-Narayan Saoras.

The claim of Seori-Narayan to be the scene of this incident is not undisputed. The people of Sirpur, to the north-east of Rajim and forty miles lower down the right bank of the Mahanadi, claim that the original name of their village was Savaripura, since it was here that the anchoret Savari offered her plums to Rama. The *Ramayana* itself describes the Pampa lake or river, on whose banks Savari lived, as being to the west of 'Rishyamukha's wood-crowned height'. But if Sirpur was the site of Savari's hermitage, then the Mahanadi must be identified with the Pampa, and the hills to the east with the Rishyamukha Mountain, and this is improbable.[2] Pargiter places Pampa as far west as Sholapur,[3] and S. N. Roy declares that Matanga's hermitage was in the neighbourhood of Nasik.[4] The matter can hardly be concluded with certainty, but the general modern tradition is that Savari lived somewhere in what is now Chhattisgarh and it is probable that the Panchapsaras lake, where Rama spent ten years of his exile, was in this region.[5] It is of much significance, says Mazumdar, that 'so late as the eighth century A.D. Pallavamalla of South India in recording his military expedition against Udayana —the ruler of this tract—has called this country the land of the Sabaras'.[6]

[1] Russell and Hira Lal, vol. IV, p. 502. But the Gazetteer says that Seori-Narayan gets its name from the hermit Sawar who worshipped Jagannath there.—Nelson, *Bilaspur Gazetteer* (Allahabad, 1910), pp. 92 and 294.

[2] Cunningham, p. 24.

[3] Pargiter, 'The Geography of Rama's Exile', *J.R.A.S.* (1894), p. 246.

[4] S. N. Roy, 'The Savaras of Orissa', *Man in India*, vol. VII (1927), p. 281.

[5] Mazumdar, *Aborigines of Central India*, p. 8; Pargiter, op. cit., p. 246.

[6] Mazumdar, p. 8. But Cunningham refers to a Sanskrit inscription at Sirpur which speaks of 'King Udayana of the Savara tribe'. 'He was a tributary of Siva Gupta, the Pandava King of Mahakosala, who reigned in the last quarter of the fourth century A.D. I think it probable that Udayana may have been the Raja of Suarmar and Khalari to the eastward of Sirpur, where the Saoras are still found in considerable numbers.'—p. 138. Hira Lal, however, says that the attribution of Saora lineage to Udayana is due to a misreading of the inscription: the King actually belonged to the family of Sasadhara, of the lunar race.—See Hira Lal, *Inscriptions in the Central Provinces and Berar* (Nagpur, 1932), p. 98.

We must now turn from the literature to comparatively modern oral traditions. Garrick was the first to emphasize the fact that the dominion of the Swiris or Saoras once extended as far as the present districts of Azimgarh and Ghazipur; near the modern town of Ghazipur indeed there still exist ruins which are supposed to mark the site of an ancient Swiri town, and in and around Vaidyanath Garrick discovered many remains to which he attributed a Swirani origin.[1]

Garrick was not very successful in his attempts to contact living members of the Swiri or Saora race, but he met a few and from them and the local Hindus he collected what he could of their traditions. They were, he records, of the Solar Race and their progenitor was Savaran. Their ancient capital, long before the time of Rama, was Ayodhya, but in the reign of the fourth Swiri King Sainjith it was removed to Vrithavr, near Kasiji, in which was the royal palace. In this King's reign and in that of his successors 'many fortresses and castles were built, and the races who inhabited them were called Swiris by all'. When King Purmedh, whose family is fabled to have belonged to the Silver Age, ascended the throne, great were the rejoicings of the Cow and the Brahmin; old and young, rich and poor, were contented and happy.

In the meantime other powerful tribes became envious, and the three races of Bhrighu, Raghu and Nag entered that kingdom very humbly and became the Swiris' servants. It is related that some time after the advent of these three tribes into Swirani territory, a tributary king died, on which there was a large gathering of people, and these *vansas* slew the Swiris by a stratagem which their menial capacity greatly facilitated, namely, when their masters (the Swiris) called for sherbet, these foreigners mixed a herbaceous poison, *yhr*, in the beverage, on drinking which large numbers of the Swiri-vansa died instantly. Then the Swiris, being considerably weakened, and thus affording an easy chance of conquest, an attack was made by the Bhrighu-vansa, Raghu-vansa and Nag-vansa conjointly, in which the three races were victorious, and in this manner the kingdom passed from the race of Swiri, and the descendants of Bhrighu (contrary to custom) began to reign in their stead. The few Swiris who escaped from this great war fled to the woods and lived in concealment, some taking refuge in mountain-caves, others going on

[1] Garrick, 'Report of a Tour through Behar, Central India, Peshawar and Yusufzai', *Reports of the Archeological Survey of India*, vol. XIX, pp. 40ff. In a rather patronizing Preface to Garrick's report, Cunningham, who was then Director-General of the Archeological Survey, points out that this was Garrick's first complete tour as an Assistant of the Survey, and that 'some of his deductions and derivations are perhaps too strongly and positively stated'.

durjatra, or distant sacred places of pilgrimage unknown to the three tribes, who entered their kingdom as cupbearers and usurped their throne.[1]

Garrick considers that this event may 'with comparative security' be assigned to some time in the first 225 years of the present era; this means that the people who were 'once the rulers of the vast tract of country before named, of which they are the aborigines, have been homeless wanderers for nearly 2000 years'.

Another tradition, however, makes the Saoras conquerors; this ascribes to them the conquest of the Cheros, and their expulsion from the plateau of Shahabad, about A.D. 500. 'A number of ancient monuments in the Shahabad District,' says Risley, 'are still put down to the Savars or Suirs, who are supposed to have been driven south by the inroad of Rajputs under the Bhojpur chief, which made an end of their rule.'[2]

But S. C. Roy doubts the likelihood of this. 'Not a single remnant of the supposed Saora conquerors of the Cheros is to be found in Shahabad at present, the name of Saora as that of a particular tribe being unknown in the district... On the other hand, a number of Cheros still live in the Shahabad District and point to a later Chero predominance. According to another tradition, it was a tribe of the name of Hurihobans, and not the Saoras, who expelled the great body of the Cheros from Shahabad.'[3]

We must now turn south. Cunningham says that according to the universal belief of the people of Raipur, the whole of the plain country of Chhattisgarh formerly belonged to the Haihaya princes, while the hilly districts of Balaghat and Bhandara were occupied by the Gonds. 'The jungly districts to the north and east of the Mahanadi river would appear to have been occupied by the Baigas and Sabaras. Then the Haihayas, following the course of the Narbada, first displaced the Sabaras in Mandla (where the Baigas still remain) and the Gonds in Balaghat, and extended their sway over the plains of Chhattisgarh . . . But the Sabaras and Gonds must still have held all the more jungly tracts to the south-east and south-west as

[1] Garrick, op. cit., p. 42. Garrick also gives the names of the traditional Swiri Kings—Savaran and Soviroth who lived in the Satyuga; Reponjea, Baharith and Sainjith who ruled in later fabulous ages; and Purmedh, who was dethroned by the alien forces. It may be remarked that, according to a tradition formerly current in Saugor, the Gonds conquered the Saoras of this District by treacherously making them drunk.

[2] Risley, vol. II, p. 242.

[3] S. C. Roy, *The Mundas*, p. 53.

tributaries of the Haihayas', until in the lapse of time the Gonds conquered Mandla from the degenerate Haihayas and greatly extended their kingdom. Cunningham considers that the dominion of the Haihayas on the Narbada cannot lay claim to a greater antiquity than the middle of the third century A.D.[1]

When we come to Orissa, we find, as we might expect, many more and more precise traditions about the Saoras. For the ordinary citizen of the State the most important is that which connects them with the famous temple of Jagannath at Puri. The legend describing how the image was originally in the charge of Vasu or Basu Saora and how it came to Puri exists in a number of variants; it is recorded in the *Madala Panji*, or palm-leaf chronicles of Jagannath; it is described in a poem *Deul-tola* by a sixteenth-century Oriya poet, Krishnadas;[2] Hunter based his account on oral tradition.[3] For some reason it was not known to Stirling (1825) who gives an entirely different story. L. S. S. O'Malley combines the versions of Hunter and the *Madala Panji*, but regards the latter as the more authoritative.[4] I myself recorded a Saora version at Maneba. The story briefly is as follows:

In the Golden Age, Indradyumna, King of Malwa, sent out Brahmins to search for Vishnu, and one of them, named Vidyapati, travelled through the jungle until he came to the country of the Saoras. There he dwelt in the house of a fowler named Viswabasu, who was a servant of the god Jagannath and used to go daily to offer him fruit and flowers in secret. The Brahmin won the confidence of the Saora and the latter, in proof of his friendship, showed him his god in the form of a blue stone image at the foot of a fig-tree. But the god did not come to partake of Viswabasu's offerings. Only a voice was heard saying, 'O faithful servant, I am wearied of thy jungle flowers and fruits, and crave for cooked rice and sweetmeats. No longer shalt thou see me in the form of thy blue god. Hereafter I shall be known as Jagannath, the Lord of the World.'

The Brahmin returned to tell the King of his discovery, but when the King reached the holy spot he found the image had disappeared. But a voice from heaven declared that if he offered a thousand *asvamedha* sacrifices, he would be blessed by the sight of Vishnu, not indeed in the shape of the blue image but as a log with certain marks

[1] Cunningham, p. 81.
[2] S. N. Roy, 'The Savaras of Orissa', *Man in India*, vol. VII, p. 287.
[3] Hunter, *Orissa*, vol. I, p. 89.
[4] L. S. S. O'Malley, *Puri District Gazetteer* (Calcutta, 1908), pp. 89f.; L. S. S. O'Malley, *Census of India*, 1911, vol. V, pt. I, p. 505. See also *Asiatic Researches*, vol. XV, p. 317; Brij Kishore Ghose, *History of Puri* (Cuttack, 1848), p. 65; W. Ward, *A View of the History, Literature and Religion of the Hindoos* (Serampore, 1815) vol. II, p. 163.

upon it. Indradyumna performed the sacrifices demanded and the god appeared in the form of a log floating in the sea.

The King then summoned all the carpenters in his kingdom and ordered them to fashion the log into the image of Jagannath. But when they put their chisels on the wood, the iron lost its edge; and when they struck them with their mallets, the mallets missed and crushed their hands. At last Vishnu himself came down in the form of an aged carpenter and promised to make the image if he was shut up alone for fifteen days. At the end of this period, Indradyumna found that the carpenter had disappeared and had left three images (of Jagannath, his brother Balabhadra and his sister Subhadra) fashioned from the waist upwards, Jagannath and his brother having only stumps for arms, while his sister had none at all.

FIG. 1 Traditional image of Jagannath

'In this legend,' says Hunter, 'at least two distinct stories are mixed up. Its latter part probably refers to the exile of Jagannath during the Yavana occupation of Orissa, A.D. 318 to 473. The pious founder of the Lion dynasty, who expelled the intruders, is still called the second Indradyumna; and the rebuilder of the temple in A.D. 1198 also enjoys this title. The first part of the legend shadows forth the original importation of Vishnu-worship by an Aryan king from the north-west, and its amalgamation with the aboriginal rites existing in Orissa.' In most of such legends, 'the aboriginal race turns up again and again, long after the first Aryan settlement among them. Nor do the primitive tribes appear invariably as serfs or as hewers of wood, but sometimes as warlike allies, or, as in the case of Basu the fowler, in mysterious connection with the introduction of the present Hindu faith.' In the legend of the Divine Log, we find the aboriginal people —the Saoras—worshipping a blue stone in the depths of the forest. But 'the deity has grown tired of the jungle offerings of the primitive people, and longs for the cooked food of the more civilized Aryan race. When the Aryan element at length comes on the scene the rude blue stone disappears, and gives place to a carved image.'

The name of the Saora fowler, Vasu or Vishwabasu, is said to mean 'the dweller'. It was possibly given to him by the Sanskrit writer of the legend 'by a reflex process from the name of his god Vasudeva, or because he is the typical aboriginal dweller in the land throughout the story. The word is also used as a name for Vishnu, and the writer of the legend may mean that the aboriginal fowler was himself Vishnu in an earlier form.'[1]

There has been much discussion about the possible Buddhist origin of the worship of Jagannath and in particular it has been noticed that there is similarity between the form of the image and the Buddhist symbols of an open *trisula* on a wheel. But O'Malley rightly points out that 'the anthropoid development of the *trisula* is sufficient to account for the modern triple image, though it is also possible that they are imitations of crude images originally set up by the aboriginal Saoras'.[2] Certainly the Jagannath images, in their curiously stunted form, look as if they might have come down from the Ganjam Hills, and there is a curious parallel in the image of the maimed Kittung to which I refer in chapter XVII.

In view of the traditional origin of the image, it is not surprising to find that some of the temple attendants at Puri are credited with descent from Vishwabasu. The Suars who cook the celebrated *mahaprasad* are probably Saoras, though Hindu orthodoxy derives their name from the Sanskrit *supakar* or cook. The Daitas, who have the privilege of touching the image on certain occasions are also Saoras in origin, and their name is probably the same as Daitya, a word which was applied to non-Aryans in classical times. The Kalapitha, or 'black-backed' Saoras pull the car of Jagannath at the great festival.

Russell and Hira Lal record other legends connecting the Saoras with the temple of Jagannath. They were specially created to carry stones for its construction and to drag the car. They are descended

[1] Hunter, op. cit., vol. I, pp. 93ff.

[2] O'Malley, *Census*, p. 94.

from an old Bhil hermit called Sawar, who lived in Karod, two miles from Seori-Narayan.

The god Jagannath had at this time appeared in Seori-narayan and the old Sawar used to worship him. The King of Orissa had built the great temple at Puri and wished to instal Jagannath in it, and he sent a Brahmin to fetch him from Seori-narayan, but nobody knew where he was except the old hermit, Sawar. The Brahmin besought him in vain to be allowed to see the god and even went so far as to marry his daughter, and finally the old man consented to take him blindfold to the place. The Brahmin, however, tied some mustard seeds on a corner of his cloth and made a hole in it so that they dropped out one by one on the way. After some time they grew up and served to guide him to the spot. The Brahmin then went to Seori-narayan alone and begged the god to go to Puri. Jagannath consented and assuming the form of a log of wood, floated down the Mahanadi to Puri, where he was taken out and placed in the temple. As a consolation to the old man, the god ordained that the place should bear the hermit's name before his own as Seori-narayan.[1]

Similar traditions connect the Saoras with other famous temples in Orissa. The Barus, who serve as cooks and priests in the temples at Bhubaneswar, are probably of Saora descent. A devotee happened to laugh at Parvati, not realizing who she was, and she cursed him, thereby transforming him into a black snake. In this form he was eaten by a peacock. A Saora killed the peacock and left its body near his wife, who was fast asleep. The snake left the dead body of the peacock and entered the Saora woman through the nostrils and she conceived. When the child was born he was brought up as a Saora, but when he grew up he discovered his identity and went to worship Lingaraja at Ekambraban. Siva was pleased with him and gave him the boon that in the Kaliyuga his descendants would have the right of worshipping him in the temples at Bhubaneswar.[2]

At Mukhalingam in the Ganjam District there is a large temple of Siva, called Mukkalingeswar, to which is ascribed a connexion with the Saoras similar to that given in the legend about Jagannath.[3]

An interesting link between the Saoras and the god Jagannath is found in a Kharia tradition. Out of the primeval egg, from which came the ancestors of the Bhanja Kings, the first Purans and the first Brahmana Kharias, came also the ancestor of Jara Saora. The present

[1] Russell and Hira Lal, vol. IV, p. 503; Nelson, *Bilaspur Gazetteer* (Allahabad, 1910), pp. 92, 294.

[2] S. N. Roy, op. cit., p. 293.

[3] O'Malley, *Puri District Gazetteer*, p. 94.

descendants of Jara Saora are the Brahmana Kharias, who have the privilege of placing a silken cloth over the sacred car of Jagannath at the Rath-jatra festival at the capital of Mayurbhanj, just as the descendants of Vishwabasu Saora do at Puri.[1] Jara is the name of an old hunter in the *Mahabharata*, who shot Krishna in the forest.[2] Russell and Hira Lal say that this Jara was himself a Saora, the first ancestor of the tribe, and that it was in the form of a deer that he shot Krishna.[3]

The word Jara resembles Jadu, or jungly, which is the name of one of the divisions of the Hill Saoras, and in fact Maltby gives it with this spelling in his early *Manual* of the Ganjam District.[4] Risley says that the Saoras of the Orissa Tributary States were divided into four branches—Bendkar, Parira, Jharua and Palli, and it may be that Jharua is another variant of the same name.[5] Roy suggests that 'it will not be unreasonable to infer that the Hill Kharias who claim to have been intimately associated or connected with the Jara-Saoras may have found their way from their original home in some part of the central hill belt of India by the same route as the Saoras of the Ganjam District, and thus reached the Mayurbhanj hills which became the centre of their subsequent dispersion'.[6]

Another tribe whose traditions appear to connect them with the Saoras is the Musahar, which also has associations with the Bhuiyas and Cheros.[7] Nesfield recorded the following legend:

Arjuna had retired to the forest to meditate on the 108 names of Siva, and to test him the god caused a wild boar to run before him. But Arjuna first finished his devotions and then seized his bow and arrow and gave chase to the animal which led him to a hermit's hut. Here Siva and Parvati had assumed the disguise of a Saora and his wife. Arjuna and the Saora both commenced pursuing the boar and when the animal had been hunted down and killed, a contention arose as to who had the right claim to it. It was agreed that the matter should be decided next day by a wrestling match. Arjuna wrestled with the disguised god all the day till sundown, when he pleaded that he must go and repeat his evening devotions, to which his antagonist

[1] S. C. and R. C. Roy, *The Kharias* (Ranchi, 1937), vol. I, p. 29.
[2] *Mahabharata*, XVI.
[3] Russell and Hira Lal, vol. IV, p. 502.
[4] T. J. Maltby, *The Ganjam District Manual* (Madras, 1882), p. 70.
[5] Risley, vol. II, p. 243.
[6] S. C. and R. C. Roy, op. cit., vol. I, p. 33.
[7] J. C. Nesfield, 'The Musheras of Central and Upper India', *The Calcutta Review*, vol. LXXXVI (1888); Risley, vol. II, pp. 113ff; Crooke, *Tribes and Castes*, vol. IV, pp. 12ff.

consented. In the course of these Arjuna realized who the Saora really was and, returning to the hut, threw himself at the feet of his divine antagonist and received his blessing. Now in this hermitage there was a maiden of unknown parentage whom the hermit cherished as a daughter. She had just completed her period and after bathing returned to the hut where she found Siva and Parvati in their Saora disguise. The eye of the god fell on her. From the glance of that eye she became pregnant, and gave birth in due course to twins, one a male and the other a female, who bore an exact resemblance to the Saora and his wife whom she had seen in the hermitage. The hermit, judging from the uncouth features and dark complexion of the babes that she had been guilty of unchastity with some wild man of the woods, sent her out of his hermitage. From the two children whom she had borne sprang the Musahar tribe.[1]

The small principalities of Dhenkanal (where over 20,000 Saoras are still living) and Pal Lahara are both traditionally associated with the Saoras. Dhenkanal is said to derive its name from a Saora named Dhenka, who owned a strip of land on which the present residence of the Raja stands. In the middle of the seventeenth century the country was conquered by Singh Bidyadhar, and Dhenka Saora was captured. Before he was put to death, he prayed that his head should always be worshipped, and there still exists near the Raja's palace a stone which is named Dhenka Savar Munda, to which sacrifice is offered once or twice a year.[2] The Chintapatris who cook the offerings which are made at the Kapilas temple near Dhenkanal are supposed to be of Saora origin, and high-class Brahmins will not accept the cooked rice-offerings of the god for this reason.[3]

The first Rajput Raja of Pal Lahara, Santoshpal, went to Puri with a body of his followers and, as he was returning home, he was chosen by Saoras, Konds, Malhars and Thoras to rule over them. He was given the name Pal because he was hidden by the Saoras under a heap of straw (*pala*) during a battle.[4]

The Borasambar Zamindari of Sambalpur also has a link with the Saoras. The ruling family is an aristocratic representative of the tribal Binjhals, who resemble the Saoras in having no exogamous clans and determining marriage simply by relationship.[5] One of the

[1] Nesfield, op. cit., pp. 15f.

[2] This account seems to have been given first by L. E. B. Cobden-Ramsay, *Feudatory States of Orissa* (Calcutta, 1910), p. 164. It is repeated by L. S. S. O'Malley, *Census of India*, 1911, vol. v, pt. I, pp. 504ff.

[3] S. N. Roy, op. cit., p. 294.

[4] Cobden-Ramsay, op. cit., p. 276.

[5] Russell and Hira Lal, vol. II, p. 332.

1. Scenery outside Kerubai village

2. Shrine and stuffed monkey, to avert disease from village, outside Arangulu

recent zamindars edited an old book named *Nrisimha Mahatmya*, in which he claimed a Kshattriya origin, describing how four heroic youths, filled with magic power, married Saora girls and became the ancestors of the Binjhals. 'This fact', says B. C. Mazumdar, 'shows that Binjha was once the name of a section of the Saoras who came to Orissa by migrating from the Vindhyan region.'[1] Suarmar Zamindari, in the Raipur District, is believed by some to have taken its name from the Saoras. It has been held by a Gond family for many generations, and 'according to family tradition the name Suarmar was given to the zamindari on account of an enormous boar which devastated the country and which was slain by Puranrai, the first zamindar, but antiquarians say that the present name is a corruption of *Sawar mal*, the land of the Sawar tribe, who are said to have originally occupied the tract'.[2]

From these traditions we cannot obtain more than the vaguest picture of the ancient Saoras. But they do enable us to assert that at one time they were distributed right across middle and eastern India, and that at least during the period 800 B.C. to A.D. 1200 they were the dominant race of aboriginals. 'In none of the authorities which I have quoted,' says Cunningham, 'either native or classical, is there any mention of Gonds, or Kols, or Bhils, but only of Andhras, Pulindas, Savaras, Kiratas, Pundras, Mutibas and Barbaras. In the middle ages we find repeated notices of Saora chiefs and generals, who may be supposed to have held much the same position in the Vindhyan district, which the Gonds afterwards held in the provinces on both banks of the Narbada.' The Saoras were clearly organized and living under their own Chiefs down to a fairly recent date, and it is probable that they were characterized by those qualities of bravery in war and independence in social and political affairs that their descendants have revealed in modern times.

III. *The Saora Hills*

THE whole of the area considered in this book lies within what are known as the 'Agency' tracts of the Ganjam and Koraput Districts of Orissa. It is only, of course, in comparatively recent times that

[1] B. C. Mazumdar, *Orissa in the Making* (Calcutta, 1925), p. 89.
[2] A. E. Nelson, *Raipur Gazetteer* (Bombay, 1909), p. 348.

these districts have been included in Orissa—indeed Orissa itself was only constituted a separate province (or State, as it is now called) in 1936. Formerly the districts were part of the Madras Presidency, and this explains why, in the older literature, such tribes as the Saoras, Konds and Gadabas were included among the tribes and castes of Madras.

Under Act XXIV of 1839, the Districts of Vizagapatam (out of which Koraput was ultimately formed) and Ganjam were each divided into two sharply contrasted portions, the plains and the Agencies, which presented different problems and were administered under different sets of rules and orders.[1] This was one of the earliest attempts made in India to make special administrative arrangements for a tribal population. It was found difficult in practice, and in 1920 an Agency Commission was set up, by which the Agency areas of Vizagapatam, Ganjam and East Godaveri were all put in charge of a Commissioner who had his headquarters in Waltair. The present Koraput District was divided into four subdivisions, called the Kond, Saora, Oriya and Ghats divisions, and each was in charge of a special Assistant Commissioner. This was an excellent plan, for through it there was established a great tract of country largely populated by tribesmen, to whose problems its officials were able to devote themselves without being distracted by the many preoccupations of the plains. But the practical difficulties of communications, accommodation and expense led to the abandonment of the scheme after only three years, and the districts were reconstituted as before.

On the foundation of the separate Province of Orissa in 1936, Koraput District was created, and for the first seven months of its life it included the Parlakimidi Taluk. The restoration of this taluk to Ganjam had the unfortunate result of splitting the Hill Saora area into two political divisions which had the support of history, but no basis in geography, ethnography or administrative convenience. It would have been greatly to the advantage of the Hill Saoras had they been united in a single district.

In the Koraput District, which is more or less coterminous with the old Jeypore Zamindari under the nominal headship of its Maharaja, there are no overlords or landlords in the Saora area and the people pay their taxes direct to the state. But the Saora part of the

[1] R. C. S. Bell, *Koraput District Gazetteer* (Cuttack, 1945), p. 143.

Ganjam District is not only divided into a number of zamindaris and maliahs, but these are further divided into what are called Muttas, tracts of territory which in the early years of the nineteenth century were put in the charge of feudal overlords called Patros or Bissoyis. For the purpose of this book the important Muttas are those of Serango, Gumma and Ajayagad in the Parlakimidi Maliahs, the Chandragiri Mutta of Chinnakimidi, and the Ramagiri Udayagiri, Khajaripada, Nuagada and Keradang Muttas of Peddakimidi.

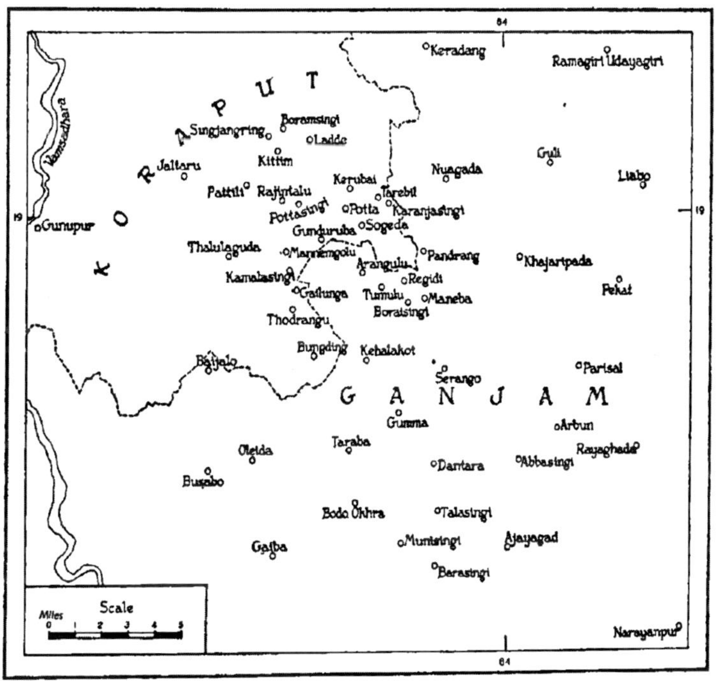

Saora villages in the Ganjam and Koraput Districts

The Bissoyis and Patros have been described as 'wardens of the marches anciently established in a species of feudal tenure' and their forts were placed in the hills or immediately below them to command the passes leading down to the plains. At that time there was good reason for their existence, for the Saoras and Konds made frequent raids on the towns and villages of the low country, and the Bissoyis and Patros with their small armies of 'home guards' called Paiks and Pessaniyas undoubtedly contributed to the establishment of law and order in what was then a very wild region. There is no reason whatever why these arrangements should have continued to modern times.

The Gumma Mutta as it is today represents an amalgamation of the Gumma and Gaiba Muttas, Gaiba having been handed over to the Bissoyi of Gumma as a reward for surrendering his own brother to execution after an abortive rebellion, thus 'gaining his fief', in MacCartie's words, 'as the price of blood'. It is 120 square miles in extent and Taylor's *Manual* gives the number of Saora villages as 71.[1] The villages are large, and there is considerable pressure on the land. The Serango Mutta, divided from Gumma by a high range of hills to the north-east, is much smaller, consisting of only 23 villages in its 20 square miles. Ajayagad is even smaller: some of its 10 Saora villages lie on the eastern slopes of the Deogiri Mountain.

Although in his day Fawcett was probably right in saying that it was around Kehalakot that 'the purest customs exist',[2] at the present time the classic Saora area is in Koraput. Round Serango the missionary labours of thirty years have had some effect, even on the refractory people of Kehalakot itself, and in the Gumma valley the Saoras have been exposed to a certain degree of external influence. But the great valleys round Pottasingi remain the home of customs and ideas which are very old. It is remarkable that this area, only twelve miles from a railway, only five from the thriving Hindu centre of Jaltaru, should have remained much more untouched than villages in the heart of the forest fifty miles from any town. The reason is the exceptionally wealthy, independent and aggressive character of the Saoras here and the influence of three great Chiefs—of Sogeda, Pattili and Rajintalu—and of a number of lesser yet still important Chiefs—of Kerubai, Potta, Boramsingi and Gunduruba. The villages in the hills are even more isolated; a village like Ladde, for example, is so notorious for its sorceries that even other Saoras are afraid to visit it.

[1] C. F. MacCartie's *Report*, printed in W. D. Taylor, *Memoir on the Ganjam Maliahs*, p. 46. This *Memoir*, which is an official document, was based on C. H. Mounsey's *Manual*, which was revised by F. A. Coleridge.

[2] F. Fawcett, 'On the Saoras (or Savaras), an aboriginal Hill People of the Eastern Ghats of the Madras Presidency', *Journal of the Anthropological Society of Bombay*, vol. I (1888), p. 213.

Here are no Saora schools, no missions, no roads.[1] The police come, reluctantly, to make an occasional arrest for murder; other officials keep away as much as they can. Even money-lenders ply their trade with discretion.

It is a lovely part of the world. Hills rise from two to three thousand feet, and valleys radiate out in every direction from Pottasingi. A prosperous and fertile valley runs due east to Sogeda and its fine terraced fields, broadens out to Borai, Kerubai and Potta and loses itself in the hills round Tarebil. Another valley goes south to Gunduruba, a third west through the substantial villages of Rajintalu and Pattili to the commercial centre, Jaltaru. From Rajintalu there is a path through hills and woods down into the picturesque glades of Boramsingi and Singjangring, which are overlooked by the splendid but sinister heights of Ladde.

From Pattili is another route due south to Regaisingi, but this is soon caught by the hills, on the far side of which is the Thalulaguda valley which leads to the Bangthala Jodi, a stream that flows fairly direct south-east through hills and forest to the group of villages round Bungding. High up in the hills is Gailunga below an impressive peak of rock and, on the brow of a great cliff, Thodrangu. A little below Gailunga are Kamalasingi and Mannemgolu, each in cups of the hills.

A description of the Gumma and Serango Muttas is difficult, in view of the extraordinary complexity of the hills and the large number of villages. But perhaps the most striking feature of this area is the great range of hills from Serango running south to the noble 4532-feet high Deogiri. This range overlooks the spacious valley of Gumma to the west and the villages of the Ajayagad Mutta to the east, and on it are situated some of the most charming villages—Barasingi, Dantara, Talasingi—in the whole of the Saora country. Rice gives a good description of the general appearance of this area. 'Far away,' he says, 'lies the sea, more than twenty miles as the crow flies. Underneath the hills—great rugged mountains looked at from below—stretch out on either hand, tumbled and in disorder, like some giant children resting after their game of play, while from above, the parent Mahendra looks down and watches over them. In the distance, paddy fields and pastures are unrolled to the sea-shore, while here and there shining strips show where the tanks are dotted over the face of the

[1] This was written in 1950. There may have been changes since.

country. Immediately below, trees lie in the lap of a lower spur—bright green, red, yellow and olive, all mingled together.'[1]

IV. *The Saoras at Home*

A SAORA village is a matter of streets; long rows of houses, each built on to its neighbour with a common veranda running right along, are arranged in every conceivable relation to each other. Often the rows are face to face with a broad street between; sometimes one row turns its back on the other and opens onto a separate street; sometimes the houses stand round a square. Or the streets may be built one above another up a hillside, and the houses all face the same way towards the view. This is a development of the terracing principle, and indeed some villages are built on old terraces, for in fact the Saoras love to be on a slope. Where the ground is very irregular, the arrangement in streets breaks down, and the houses are simply huddled together wherever it is possible to build them.

G. M. Young has said of English villagers that 'we may be quite sure that they planted their houses exactly at the most advantageous point for people who had to economise every ounce of muscular effort for themselves and their oxen'. It was a 'ploughman's eye that the early settler measured by and the muscles of a ploughman's back'.[2] I doubt if this could be said of many Saora villages, which are built in the most difficult and inaccessible sites that can be imagined, far away from water or grazing-grounds. The reason probably goes back to the days when the country was unsettled and every man's hand was against his neighbour; the first Saora villages were forts—they were less convenient for the purposes of agriculture.

All round the villages are little gardens where tobacco, maize, and sometimes ginger are grown. Not too far away are the burning-grounds and groups of menhirs. In the streets and down the paths leading to the village boundary are shrines for gods or ancestors. A well or spring may be carefully built up with large stones. Everywhere are sago and date palms, and many villages are well shaded by great trees.

[1] The charming, if slightly florid, pages of S. P. Rice's *Occasional Essays on Native South Indian Life* (London, 1901) give a quaint, yet attractive, picture of the Hill Saoras. Rice gives the *feel* of the country, but he is inaccurate in detail. He found the Saoras pleasant but mediocre: 'In a life of such simplicity,' he says, 'it is hard to discover manners and customs which are worth our notice.'

[2] G. M. Young, *Last Essays* (London, 1950), p. 164.

There is nothing of the nomad about these substantial villages, with their strongly built houses, the endless stone walls piercing the forest on every side, the wonderfully constructed terraces, the menhirs whose number often suggests considerable antiquity. Occasionally a village may be deserted; sometimes the interference of Paik tax-gatherer or Dom money-lender becomes unbearable; sometimes a pestilence convinces the elders that the local gods are too hostile to be endured. But even Bungding, with its rows of widows' houses and deserted streets, did not shift when it fell under the heavy hand of the goddess of smallpox. Saora villages in fact resemble established Gond or Santal settlements rather than the rough and ready camps of Baigas and Konds, for whom shifting cultivation means shifting homes. But shifting cultivation means that some Saora villages are very small, with only three or four houses, high in the hills, lonely and remote, but convenient for the swiddens.

The Saora has an eye for beauty. It would be hard to find a more excitingly lovely place than Thodrangu, clinging to the hillside with a superb view of the lower hills and plains. Talasingi too is built on the brow of a hill and from its cliffs you can look across to the splendid heights of Jumtangbaru. Bodo Okhra is another beautiful village in a cup of the hills; great rocks overlook it. Sogeda is in a valley surrounded by steep hills and terraced fields: the eye is enchanted by the quiet beauty of the scene. Tumulu must be one of the loveliest places in India, where you look across green-carpeted terraces and waving palms to range upon range of near and distant hills.

Unfortunately these villages, so beautifully situated, so picturesquely arranged, are sometimes filthy beyond words, though curiously enough once you step off the street you find the interior of the buildings kept spotlessly clean.

As you travel north towards the Kond country, the character of the Saora village alters. Kond influence is seen in wider streets approximating to the Kond rectangles, verandas are not raised so high above the ground, wooden pillars take the place of stone memorials, there may be a bamboo fence embracing the whole village. The *sadru*-shrine, which is so important a feature of Saora villages elsewhere, tends to disappear, and its place is taken by little stone 'boxes' for the gods.

The Saora idea of the evolution of their villages and homes is interestingly suggested in a myth from Kamalasingi.

At first men lived under trees: they were small then, only about two feet high. In the rains they found it very troublesome and they dug holes in the ground and lived like hares. But in the rains the roofs fell in and buried many of them alive. In this way the population rapidly decreased. Then one Jangu Saora decided to build a house. First he used the leaves of the toddy palm and made something like an umbrella, as we make shrines today. In such houses men lived for many years. Later, they made similar houses out of wood, and these buildings were dry and pleasant. At last, in order to be near each other, they built their houses in rows.

The Saora house is a dark rectangular box, raised well above the ground, and divided inside into two sections, with a veranda in front and often, when there is a second door, at the back also. The buildings are solidly constructed; the walls are built up of stone or rubble or of upright pieces of wood and covered with a thick plaster of mud; there may be substantial doors with padlocks; there are often double roofs, the lower of poles laid close together and plastered with mud, the upper of ordinary thatch. The verandas, which are rather narrow, are usually at least three, and may be as much as six feet above the ground, and are reached by a flight of stone steps. Built into the veranda there is often a pigstye though this may be located on the back veranda instead.[1]

Every Saora house is in a sense a temple, for nearly every sacrifice begins indoors, the ancestors use it as a hostelry on their visits to earth, and there are half a dozen resident deities. Dakosungboi presides over the welfare of the building; Kudasum is god of the hearth; Ganonroialsum lives in the eaves, Madaboi in the loft, Garnadasum on the threshold; perched like flies on the wall, other spirits are attracted by the ikons.

Every house is built on the same general plan. The door opens onto a small room, which may have another door immediately opposite. In the middle of this is a wooden mortar let into the floor, and the children sleep here, the boys on one side of the mortar, the girls on the other. The rest of the building is filled with a loft, a platform about four feet high which supports the grain-bins and other possessions. Under this platform the women have to crawl for the important task of cooking, for the hearth is always placed in the far corner

[1] Ball says that the Saoras living on Mahendragiri in 1870 had houses of wattled bamboos.—*Jungle Life in India* (London, 1880), p. 267. But Fawcett found Saora houses substantial enough.—op. cit., p. 228.

below it. The head of the house and his wife sleep here, near the hearth. From the roof hangs a great variety of objects, baskets, gourds, bundles of cloth, umbrellas, spears, bows and arrows, pots. The walls may be decorated with ikons in honour of the gods or ancestors; in front of them are hung dedicated gourds and pots, and sometimes baskets in which the special cloths of the dead or tutelaries are carefully preserved. Outside on the veranda there may be a small wooden pillar for a god: as the menhirs stand on guard outside the village, so pillars and pots keep watch before the home.

In the northern area, where Kond influence is strong, a pillar is placed in the centre of the house, at the point where the platform ends, in front of the mortar. On this pillar, about two feet from the ground, is a small ledge on which offerings may be placed, and below it is carved a pair of female breasts. The purpose of these is rather obscure: one Saora said, 'they were for beauty'; another declared that 'when we feel lonely because we have no one to sleep with, we can console ourselves with these'. When people bring an arrow and a bangle to betroth a girl, they drive the arrow into the ground between the wooden breasts.[1]

Under Kond influence, the level of the houses sinks down almost to the ground; the common veranda often disappears, being either walled in or at least divided all along the line; and some attempt at decoration of doors and pillars may be observed.

The houses of the great Chiefs are very large, with several lofty buildings built round an inner courtyard, and are furnished with beds and chairs.

When building a new house, the Saoras put rice and wine in the hole dug for the first pillar to be erected: this is for Labosum, the Earth-god, to prevent white ants damaging the wood. After the pillar has been set up, they tie to it a little bundle of rice wrapped in a mango leaf: this is for Uyungsum, the Sun-god, to prevent the house catching fire. When the building is complete, the shaman is called to offer wine to the ancestors, who are likely to be all too frequent visitors, and there is a house-warming party, to which the Chief and members of the family are invited.

It is fortunate that the Saoras spend most of their lives in the open air, for their houses are dark and stuffy, for ever filled with wood-

[1] They are illustrated at p. 115 of my *The Tribal Art of Middle India* (Bombay, 1951), henceforth referred to as *TAMI*.

smoke that forces tears from the eyes and a cough in the throat, and except in the small space round the mortar it is impossible to stand upright. In fact, the Saoras still live, as their traditions say they lived at first, like hares in burrows.

The real clothing of the Saoras is 'the eternally dressed nakedness of the brown skin', which adorns them with beauty and dignity. There is a rule, founded in the mythology, that they should not wear too much: there is a common tradition that they originally dressed in leaves.[1] The traditional cloth for both sexes is woven for them by Doms, from yarn hand-spun by the Saoras themselves; it is generally woven very well, and artistically is most attractive. The women wear a simple skirt with a brown border top and bottom; it is wound round the waist and tucked in at the front. In the chill of the early morning, they cover themselves with miscellaneous wraps—many of them the cast-off cloths of ancestors or tutelaries—but later in the day they discard these and work in nothing but the skirt.

The traditional dress of men is the loin-cloth, which may be a plain white strip or it may be gay with coloured patterns and tassels of red cotton. It is passed between the legs, covers the genitals in a sort of bag, and hangs down in a flap before and behind; the rear flap is very long, like a tail.[2]

Men do not normally wear anything else. If they have been to Assam, the dubious inspiration of civilization may inspire them to put on a dirty khaki shirt or a tattered waistcoat, sometimes even an old sola topi. Headmen have special coloured turbans. But a Saora usually only wears a turban when he is dancing or going somewhere. Then he brings out a length of coloured cloth—sometimes it is silk and very old—winds it round his head, puts in a tuft of feathers and looks very smart indeed.

The Saoras are not good at ornaments. They tend to attach to their bodies or hang from them anything they can get hold of, indifferent to whether it looks well or not.

[1] This is how they are described in the *Katha Sarit Sagara*. *The Manual of the Administration of the Madras Presidency*, published in 1886, describes the Saoras of Ganjam as dressing in leaves (p. 59).

[2] G. E. Russell, writing in 1837, says that the Hill Saoras of Ganjam, 'when equipped for war, cover their breast with leather or bear skin, and decorate their heads with cock's feathers; some of them wear also a slip of bear-skin under the chin'.—'Report on the Disturbances in Purla Kimedy, Vizagapatam and Goomsoor in 1832–36', *Selections from the Records of the Madras Government*, No. XXIV, (Madras, 1856), vol. II, p. 13.

Examples of cloth worn by Saora men and women. The yarn is spun by the Saoras themselves and is then woven by Doms under Saora direction

For a woman the most important ornamental zone, a zone where she must endure a painful operation and discomfort lasting a decade,

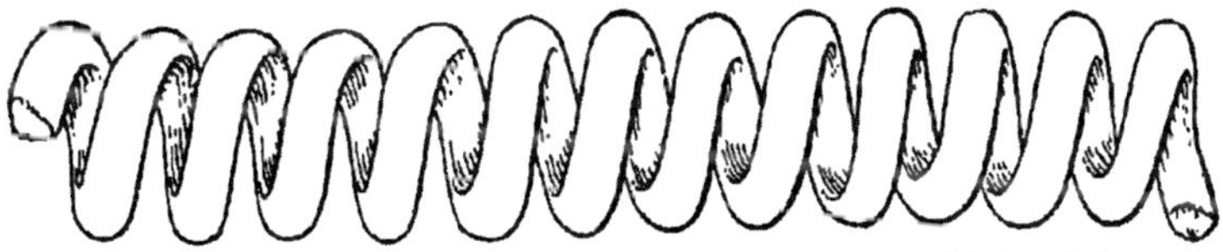

FIG. 2 Spiral of bell-metal worn by women in the distended lobe of the ear
Actual size ; sometimes rather smaller

is the ear. While she is still a little girl, holes are made in the lobes, and these are gradually enlarged, first by the insertion of bits of straw and reed, and then by wooden plugs of tamarind or the spadix of the sago palm.[1] This plug gets larger and larger until it reaches a diameter of as much as three inches and the skin stretched round it looks like a strip of brown leather. There is often asymmetry in the development of the holes and there may be different decorations in the two ears. For when the plugs are removed, their place is taken by the most incongruous of ornaments, ordinary brass spiral springs from the bazaar (Fig. 2). Into the fossa of the anti-helix many little holes are also made and small rings are inserted.

After the ear, attention is given to the hair and throat. A woman combs her hair carefully, collects it into a bun and tucks it underneath so that it makes a ball slightly to the left, and fixes it in place with a brass hairpin. The front locks are brushed back towards the crown and are often held in place by a band of fibre or black cloth inlaid with tiny bits of glass. In the northern villages many young girls bob their hair and look very pretty as a result. Women also wear little brass chains, sometimes brass flowers, but the most characteristic ornament is the brass pin with its large spike (Fig. 3). It is common to see women with the pin projecting to the left and a leaf pipe projecting to the right like a pair of little horns. This pin is said to be comparatively

FIG. 3 Saora woman's brass hair-pin
6″ to 8″

[1] Kadir women wear similar disks of wood coated on one side with brass. For the dilation of the lobe, see E. Thurston, *Castes and Tribes of Southern India* (Madras, 1909), vol. II, p. 63.

modern: the women illustrated by Fawcett and Thurston are not wearing it; and Somra's wife told me that she formerly wore an ornament 'broad as the sun and moon' in her hair, but later turned to the fashion of the present day.

A Saora woman decorates her beautiful throat with a number of necklaces which add little to its grace, though she uses fewer than is customary among people who expose the breasts. The Bondos put on a mass of bead and brasswork which almost serves the purpose of a blouse. The Marias cover their bosoms with heavy decorations. But the Saoras wear none of the chains and bands loved by the Bondos and Marias, and they do not seem to have acquired the art and patience to thread their beads into patterns; they simply sling a number of strings of beads, just as they are sold in the bazaar, round their necks and think that is enough.

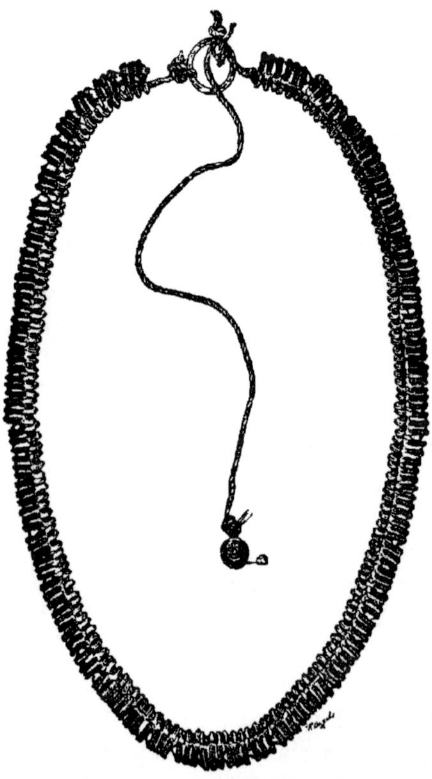

FIG. 4 Saora woman's necklace
3½' long

In the nose a woman wears three little rings; those in the alae are flat and round, the one in the septum is thicker and often shaped like a heart. She puts cheap aluminium or brass bracelets on her wrists and covers her fingers with rings—there may be as many as twenty on each hand.

Many of the tribal women of Orissa pay a lot of attention to the girdle. The Juangs used to make an elaborate affair of baked earthenware cubes; the Kuttia Konds tie round their waists a thick belt consisting of a large number of ordinary bits of string; the Gadabas take pride in their bustles and the girdles that go with them; the Bondos support their scanty skirts with a special girdle that used to be made of bark fibre. Saora women too wear a girdle composed of many strings of dark blue beads that hang down a little over the buttocks; others put on a belt of one or more strands of brass cubes made by the Gontaras. This girdle seems to be entirely for ornament; it does not hide anything and it does not hold anything up.

On the legs women wear bronze or aluminium anklets and rings on the toes; in some places the Chief's wife wears a particularly large and tawdry anklet.

Saora men are not very distinguished to the eye. They put cheap bazaar ornaments in the ears and nose and round their wrists. They sometimes hang a floppy necklace of beads round the neck, but do not tie it tightly in Kond or Muria fashion; as a result they look untidy and careless. A young man often sticks a feather or a few flowers in his hair. Girls do the same, and they specially love marigolds, which were created specially to please the gods.

From Fawcett's descriptions and from the talk of the older men, I should judge that there has been little change in fashion in the past half-century. But Maltby refers to a 'curious ornament' which I have never seen; it was 'a piece of brass, half an inch wide and about a foot and a half long, beaten out until it is quite thin and pliant. This being polished up and shining and quivering with every movement of a man's head has a very curious effect'.[1] Fawcett also speaks of a head ornament which seems to have gone out of fashion: it was 'a piece of wood, about eight or nine inches in length and three quarters of an inch in diameter, with a flat button on the top, all covered with hair or coloured thread'.[2]

The distinctive thing about the Saora tattoo is the line down the middle of the forehead. Most women have this and a few men. Women also have dots on either side of the line, on their cheeks and on the point of the chin. But that is all. Since the Saoras do their own tattooing and are not very good at it, they do not attempt elaborate patterns, and they leave the breasts, arms and legs alone. The usual reason for the tattoo marks is either that 'we do it because it looks nice' or that 'our parents had these marks on their foreheads, and unless we had the same they would not recognize us when we went to the Under World'.

Clothes and ornaments are important in a study of Saora religion, because in every house there is a store of the old clothes and ornaments belonging to the dead, which have to be brought out and shown

[1] Maltby, *Ganjam Manual*, p. 88. [2] Fawcett, p. 213.

to the shaman, whenever the ancestors come upon him and insist on seeing their property. And then too a shaman has to keep a set of women's clothes and ornaments, and a shamanin has to keep a man's cloth for the tutelaries. From time to time a tutelary demands new things and then permits the old ones to be used by members of the household. The ancestors do gradually give their clothes away, but sometimes insist on their being replaced. It may well happen that in a home that has lost something of a former prosperity, the dead are better dressed than the living, and that while children shiver with cold, the store holds plenty of cloth which it is taboo to use.

Food, of course, is another very important subject for Saora religion. Nearly every sacrifice, festival and ceremony ends in a corporate feast which is shared by the living and the dead, the human and the divine. Although religion is undoubtedly a severe strain on the Saora economy, it is the means by which the poorest people get the only really good meals they have a chance to enjoy. On the whole, however, the Saoras do themselves fairly well. The majority are comparatively prosperous, far more so than most tribesmen of Middle India, and they believe in enjoying life while they can.

In the early morning and at sunset, the men go out to the palm trees for their wine, a nourishing as well as a stimulating drink, and they usually bring some home for the women and children. They often take a little gruel at the same time, and they prepare tasty snacks, tit-bits of crab and chilli, special scraps of meat which are set aside and dried for the purpose after certain sacrifices, and chutneys of various kinds. Bones may often be observed hanging from a veranda; they are taken out to the palms, and the marrow is extracted and cooked in the wine.

At midday the Saoras have a substantial meal; they have another just before it gets dark; and at night, before going to bed, they have a bit of supper.

The basis of their food is rice, millet and pulse. They do not use wheat. The most common dish is a gruel made by boiling rice or millet together with pulses and vegetables. This is not flavoured with salt or chillies, but a sort of chutney is made separately and tasted from time to time.

The Saoras seem to have no idea of frying; everything is roasted or boiled. They never use ghee and very rarely (unless they have picked up the habit in Assam) cook in oil. Another characteristic of their cookery is to boil everything together: rice or millet along with the pulses, unhusked and in their skins, and meat and vegetables as well.

Although they do not use wheat, they make a flour from rice, the pith of the sago palm and the bones of animals; with this they prepare flat cakes which they roast between leaves in the embers of a fire.

They make a sort of pudding out of the corollas of the *Bassia latifolia* flowers and tamarind, which they boil together in a little water all night. They also roast the corollas with *amaru* seeds in a dry pot and make it into balls which are very popular with children. They do not, however, seem very fond of sweets; they do not buy *gur*, and if they collect any honey, they sell it.

Their great love is meat. This they usually boil with rice or millet, though they sometimes prepare it separately, cooking it with salt, chillies and occasionally turmeric. Turmeric is useful if the meat is beginning to go bad. They make a nourishing soup with blood and rice boiled together.

Crabs are boiled or roasted between leaves. Fish are boiled. Roots are boiled separately, and kept for use when required. Bamboo shoots are very popular. Field-rats are roasted on a skewer. Red ants are tied up with mushrooms in a leaf-bundle which is put in the embers to roast.

And of course the Saoras, like everyone else in tribal India, collect every sort of wild herb, and edible leaves, berries, wild plums, mangoes, jackfruit, and a score of other simple things that lie ready to their hand. They are fond of cucumbers, gourds, pumpkins and wild melons which they often grow with other crops in their clearings.

Every meal is in a sense a communion, for a good Saora should always place a few grains on a leaf for the ancestors and gods who will come and share the meal.

At sacrifices, although there are a few attended only by men, the cooking is usually done by women, and from an early age every child learns its way about the kitchen.[1]

[1] Stirling gives an early (1825) account of Saora food. 'They will eat', he says, 'almost any kind of food, whether animal or vegetable. A great part of their subsistence is derived from the roots and produce of the jungles. The flowers of the Madhuka (*Bassia latifolia*) and the Keora (*Pandanus odoratissimus*) yield them an intoxicating liquor; in lieu of rice they consume the seed of the bamboo, a very heating and indigestible food; the wild yams, arums, and other roots furnishing a nutritious, and not unwholesome substitute for bread; and for a dessert they have the wild mango, the fruit of the Bela everywhere abundant, and the seeds of the *Bauhinia racemosa*, served up on the large ribbed leaf of the *Ravya* (apparently a species of *Dillenia*), which answers the purposes of a dish.'—A. Stirling, 'An Account, Geographical, Statistical and Historical of Orissa Proper, or Cuttack,' *Asiatic Researches*, vol. xv (1825), p. 43.

V. *The Saora Language*

ALTHOUGH the great majority of Saoras in their dispersion across India have lost their own language and now speak that of their neighbours, the Hill Saoras have preserved their ancient tongue, and very few of them speak any other. Saora is an Austro-asiatic language of the Munda family; it seems to be most closely allied to Gutob and Pareng, but it has some affinities also with Kharia and Juang.

Grierson considered that Saora had been 'largely influenced by Telugu, and was now no longer an unmixed form of speech',[1] but his opinion seems to have been based on linguistic specimens obtained from the plains Saoras. The language of the hills is remarkably pure, and contains only a few Telugu and Oriya words.

Among the main characteristics of the language may be mentioned the frequent use of prefixes, infixes and suffixes, the dual case in addition to singular and plural, the existence of semi-consonants which are imperfectly articulated and indistinct,[2] the common contractions of words when incorporated with the verb in clauses or other nouns in compounds, reflexive and impersonal forms in place of the English passive.[3]

Emeneau, in a study of 'echo-words', remarks that Saora 'seems to be particularly rich in formations of this kind',[4] and Ramamurti lists no fewer than 158 examples, which are formed in a number of ways: the additional word may be a synonym (current or archaic, obsolete or dialectal), or a coinage, or the suffix *ite*—the tag, or echo, is always of the same grammatical form and rhymes or at least balances the first word.[5] Examples are *jelu-melu*, flesh; *jojonji-yoyonji*, ancestors; *kokede-kakode*, crooked; *tangli-mangli*, cattle; *regam-surtam*, medicine; *panurpuran-janujunan*, sacrifice. The frequent use of such words is characteristic of a people who love repetition, and are accustomed to utter or hear long lists of names and words which have very little meaning. The shamans use echo-words constantly in their incantations, padding them out to give sonority and impressiveness.

Another characteristic of Saora is its gift for onomatopeia, which suggests that the people have a love of sound and music, an instinct

[1] G. A. Grierson, *The Linguistic Survey of India*, vol. IV (1906).
[2] Bell, p. 58. [3] Ramamurti, *Manual*, p. xiv.
[4] M. B. Emeneau, 'Echo-Words in Toda', *New Indian Antiquary*, vol. I (1938-9), p. 109.
[5] Ramamurti, *Manual*, p. 150.

for mimicry and keen powers of observation. Among the many examples listed by Ramamurti are the following: *andelai-sundelai*, the bubbling of water; *budu-budu*, to express rapid movement in dancing; *bung-bung*, the humming of bees; *dading-dading*, the tinkle of coins; *gutur-gutur-gutur*, the cry of a falcon; *kadik-kadung kadik-kadung*, the cry of wild fowl; *kekkerjub kekkere-keb kokkorjub kekkor jum kekkere keb*, the crowing of a cock; *lujur-lajur*, the growl of a tiger on noticing a tigress; *sob-sob*, the padding of a cat walking softly on dry leaves; *taku-kai-taku-kai-bud*, the chattering of a monkey.

The Saoras, who give the impression of being rather matter-of-fact and prosaic, are surprisingly picturesque and metaphorical in their speech. I have not studied their poetry, but Sitapati has published a charming account of Saora songs, which unfortunately he has translated into English rhymed verse. Even so it is possible to trace the veil of romantic imagination which the Saoras, like other tribesmen, throw over common things.

In ordinary speech too they constantly use highly condensed metaphors. Thus we have such descriptions of ugliness as a *santui-tam-maran*, a mouse-mouth-man; a *kuddadaji-maran*, a hoe-tooth-man; a *paidi-bob-maran*, a coconut-head-man. A beautiful girl is *kulpad-me-boi*, a bael-fruit-breast-girl, having breasts shaped like the fruit of *Aegle marmelos*. Her body is tender as fresh leaves; the bun of her hair is like a bulbul's nest; she is like the palm tree. *Dangadi-boi aduban titi langten*, 'the young maiden gives us milk'—the palm gives us its sap.

Clouds may be described as 'striped like a tiger' and as the veil of the sun: *uyungan taruban jungkum-n-eten*, the sun put on a veil of cloud.

A man may be active as a rat, nimble as a squirrel; when astonished, his face grows large as a basket; he may be fat as a liquor-pot; his drinking-tube tapers like a cow's tail.[1]

The Saoras play at riddles, some of which are vivid and clever. Tamarind fruit is described as 'curved knives hanging from the sky'. A sickle is the 'sharp little son of a dwarf'. A hearth is a woman with three breasts. A broom licks up its food with its tail; thunder sounds when the palm-leaf umbrella of the sky cries *dueng-dueng*; a bow is sated in the forest, but starved at home. Indian corn is a man whose whole body is covered with hair; the leech is a little man with no

[1] Most of these examples are from Ramamurti's *Manual*.

bones; a muzzle-loader is a man who drinks with his mouth and spits with his mouth.[1]

The usual discreet similes are used when a party goes to betroth a girl. They have a black he-goat in their house, and want a black mate for it. 'A flower has blossomed in your garden and the scent has come to our nostrils.' The boy has burnt his hand and wants a spoon to eat with.

The Saora language is flexible, always ready to coin new words, vigorous and full of colour, well adapted to the demands made upon it. It is not rich in abstract or theological terms, but since Saora religion is largely a matter of personal relationships, it is a ready instrument in the cause of prayer and praise.

VI. *Marriage and the Family*

The most remarkable thing about the organization of Saora society is its lack of organization. Its endogamous divisions are vague and often disregarded and, in sharp contrast to all the neighbouring tribes, it has no exogamous totemic clans, no phratries, no moieties. The one essential unit is the extended family descended from a common male ancestor, but there are also divisions into aristocracy and proletariat and by villages.

Saora aristocracy consists of the families of the Chiefs and, where they exist, of the Buyya priests. The Chiefs are known by various names, the most common being Gamang—the word also means 'rich' and 'important'. But they may also be called Naiko, Janni, Karji, Dora; a Mandal may be the head of a village, or merely a Gamang's assistant. The Dhol-behera has an important, though somewhat subordinate, position.

The Gamangs and Buyyas are not only the most wealthy, but they are recognized by Government, and in the old days used to receive an official turban which was greatly prized. The Gamang, the Chief, is of great importance, for he is the intermediary between Government and the people; it is by his orders that the villagers go to work for officials or the Bissoyis; his presence is essential at all village functions; in Koraput he is the arbiter in matrimonial disputes; and in practice everywhere he has the final say in the allocation of land. Where the Buyya priest, in his secular capacity, is head of a

[1] I owe some of these riddles to G. V. Sitapati.

separate quarter in a village, he may be of almost equal importance to the Chief himself.

Most Saora villages are divided into a number of groups of houses called *sahis*, hamlets or quarters, each named after its most important resident. Thus the quarter where the Gamang and his family resides is called the Chief's quarter; the Buyya-sahi is the priest's quarter; there may also be a Karji-sahi or a Dhol-behera-sahi. Often, however, the quarters are not named after families, but by some geographical or occupational word. In Rajintalu, for example, there were three quarters named respectively after the Gamang (the Chief), Gamangsing (the old Chief), the Dhol-behera (the Chief's assistant), and two quarters called simply the Jata (lower) and Lanka (upper). In Kerubai the quarters were the Jata (lower), Tarangdi (central) and Lanka (upper); one family group lived in the first, three in the second and two in the third. In Tumulu there were five families settled in five quarters—the Chief's family in the Jata quarter, the priest's in the Akurup, the Karji's in the Bongri, the Jadu Poroja's in the Tarangdi and the Arsi Poroja's in the Lanka.

In Boramsingi, nine families were distributed in four quarters; two of these groups were occupational, Arsis and Kindals; four were official, the Chief's, two groups of priests, and the Dhol-Behera's; and three were different groups of Poroja.

These *sahi*-quarters may be simply different streets in a single settlement, or they may be widely separated hamlets as at Boramsingi and Barasingi.

Naturally members of the Chief's family live in the Chief's quarter, and every member of the group may attach the word Gamang to his own name as a sort of surname. But there may be members of other families living in the Chief's hamlet and these do not call themselves Gamang.

Similarly, if there is a Mandal quarter, it will be mainly populated by members of the Mandal's family, each of whom can call himself Mandal, but it will not be exclusively populated by them, though it may be. And the Dhol-beheras will live in the Dhol-behera quarter, the Buyyas in the Buyya quarter, the Karjis in the Karji quarter and so on.

Members of these large families form the Saora aristocracy. Below them are members of a large number of families who are called by the general term Poroja or Ryat, which simply means peasant. The heads of these families have no official standing, no representative capacity and are generally poor. But the shamans and funerary officiants may be drawn from these or from any groups whatever their social or economic standing.

Marriage between the aristocratic and proletarian families is admitted only in a typically aristocratic way. The Chiefs will accept girls from the proletarian families, but will not give girls to them. Generally, however, the Chiefs prefer their sons to marry girls from the families of other Chiefs; Buyyas like to marry Buyyas, Mandals like to marry Mandals. But there is no objection to a Gamang marrying a Buyya, or a Mandal or a Naiko, if they are sufficiently well-to-do.

While the village is the more important unit (people pay their taxes and celebrate most of their festivals as a village), the quarter —especially if it is something more than a row of houses in a street —also has its significance. Many ceremonies take place within it for its own members who owe a special loyalty to their particular leader.

Neither the village nor the quarter is an exogamous unit. There is no real territorial exogamy among the Saoras; there may once have been, but Fawcett, writing in 1888, says that 'a Saora may marry a woman of his own village or of any other village'. But since most of the inhabitants of a quarter are generally of one family, it is natural for its men to seek wives elsewhere. But it is the family, not the quarter or village, which makes this necessary.

The family is called *birinda*, and it is this which is the one fundamental division of Saora society. It consists of all the descendants of a common male ancestor, 'men and women of the same blood'. This family group has no name and no totem. It is distinct from the hamlet, though only rarely from the village. Thus members of two families may live together in one hamlet, or members of one family may be divided between two hamlets. But nearly every family is to be found contained within the boundaries of a single village.

The *birinda*-group controls first of all the marriage arrangements of the tribe. 'We go by the blood,' as a Saora once said to me. That is the only real rule, breach of which is regarded as incest, as the ultimate taboo. A youth can, if he tries, marry a girl of a different tribal type; he can elope with a girl outside his social class; he can marry within his own village or quarter; but he cannot under any circumstances whatever marry a girl of his own *birinda*. And since the family boundaries are widely drawn, this means that he cannot marry his mother's brother's daughter or his father's sister's daughter, for both have his blood. Here is another remarkable difference between the Saoras and other Indian tribesmen: cross-cousin marriage, so popular elsewhere, is not allowed.

A very important fact is that a woman does not change her *birinda* by marriage; she does not join her husband's family but continues in the group of her birth till death. Theoretically, therefore, a man should be able to marry his maternal grandmother, his mother's sister, a widowed daughter-in-law, his wife's brother's wife, his wife's elder sister, his mother-in-law, his younger brother's wife and his father's elder brother's wife. But in practice this is not allowed.

There is some disagreement as to whether a man may marry his stepmother. But some Saoras consider it is not improper for the son of a polygamous father to marry after his father's death one of the younger widows, a younger co-wife of his own mother. I know a Saora who married a woman who had left her first husband by whom she had a daughter. The woman then died and the man married the daughter. 'There is no harm in it,' I was told, 'she was of different blood.' A Saora is expected to marry his elder brother's widow and even his father's elder brother's widow.

The *birinda*-family also controls the funerary arrangements. There are separate burning-grounds and separate groups of menhirs for each family. Separate Idaimarans and Idaibois, who officiate at funerals, are appointed for each group and cannot normally function for others. Since a woman does not enter her husband's *birinda*, it means that she must be taken home if the funerary arrangements are to be properly made. From this arise all the complications of the Guar, the bringing home of the bones and the soul, the double expense, which I describe in chapter IX.

It is rare for a son or brother to migrate from his own to another village. If he does so, he retains the membership of his own family and when he dies his bones, or if possible his actual corpse, should be brought to his original home for disposal. Sometimes, if there is bad feeling between, say, two brothers and one of them leaves his home and goes elsewhere, he may make a separate burning-ground and erect his own menhirs, but he has to abide by the marriage rules.

The *birinda* also controls certain sacrifices, and in particular the ceremonial eating of food. The Doripur and Ajorapur ceremonies, for example, are performed only for and by members of a particular family. At the great funerary rites of the Guar, Karja and Lajap, members of the family concerned eat their food in their own homes and get more; members of other groups eat out in the fields and get less. The family food is cooked in a new pot, other food in an old one, and the two lots of food must not touch and cannot be shared. At a funeral only members of the deceased's family attend.

The Saora marriage ritual has been studied in detail by Fawcett,[1] Ramamurti[2] and Sitapati.[3] It is unusually secular in character, a business contract rather than a religious union. Its function is the stabilizing of society round the institution of the family and the canalization of sex into the fruitful field of child-production. Saora marriage, which takes place rather early, at sixteen or seventeen for the boy, fifteen or sixteen for the girl, does not initiate its partners into sexual experience, either generally or with one another.[4] As in most tribes at this level of development, pre-marital life is fairly (though not exceptionally) free, but great value is placed on the integrity of the marriage-bond.

The marriage ceremony and its preliminaries are simple and economic. It is curious that a tribe which never loses an opportunity for ceremonial display should surround this critical event with so little. The betrothal is effected by a series of visits (which may extend over many months) from the bridegroom's family to the girl's house; on the first visit the suitors take an arrow and a bangle and put them in the roof or, where the central pillar of the house has breasts carved on it, in the ground between them. Gifts of palm wine are made and the bride-price is paid. The betrothal is important and should it not end in marriage, compensation must be paid by the family of the girl—if she is at fault—proportionate to the gifts that have been received.

The actual ceremony is marked by a feast and a dance. The bride visits all the houses of her own village to bid farewell, and is then escorted by a party of relations and friends, with drums and trumpets, to her new home. There she is welcomed and taken into her husband's house. A priest or shaman makes offerings to the ancestors. There is plenty of eating and drinking, and a lot of noise. But there are

[1] Fawcett, pp. 230ff. [2] Quoted by Thurston, vol. VI, pp. 319ff.
[3] Sitapati, 'The Soras', *J.A.H.R.S.*, vol. XII, pp. 189ff.
[4] But if a man has become a shaman before marriage, he is expected to refrain from anticipating his marital privileges.

none of the usual marriage rites observed by other tribes: no wedding furniture of turmeric or vermilion, no booth, no circumambulation of a pole, or tying the pair together. And there is no bedding of the married pair as among Bondos, Marias and Murias.

About a week after the marriage the young husband and wife go to the girl's house with presents for the parents. The father returns the betrothal arrow to the youth saying, 'I have given you my daughter; see, I also give you back this arrow'. After a marriage a man builds his own house and sets up a separate establishment as soon as he can.

There is very little religion in all this. At the time of paying the bride-price, a shaman makes offerings to the gods and ancestors. When the bride is brought to her husband's house her father says to the boy's father, 'From today we give you our own life. Now our life has become yours. If the gods or ancestors trouble her, that is your affair. If she elopes with someone else, if she dies, that is your affair, not ours. You be happy; we will be happy.' When the bride cleans the house and cooks for the first time, her mother-in-law says, 'From today this will be your home. The pots and pestles are yours; the gods and the dead are yours. The seeds of rice and millet, pulse and beans are yours. We are old and ignorant; feed and take care of us.'

The nearest thing to a ceremony I have recorded occurs when the bride arrives at her husband's house. Bride and bridegroom stand before the door, and a priest or shaman puts *Bauhinia vahlii* leaves in their hands. He makes a libation of palm wine, puts a little rice into each leaf and says, 'O Kittung Mahaprabhu, you are Darammasum, you are Uyungsum. You made the world. You know the fate of men. Today we have joined these two as man and wife. You are above; Labosum is below.' He makes a mark with rice on the foreheads of the boy and girl, and they salute Darammasum. Then they go into the house, carrying the rice in their hands. There they tie the rice up in the leaves and hang them in one bundle from the roof.

The Saoras, like other tribesmen, have the custom of engaging a suitable youth to serve for a period of years for a girl. This is usually done when there is no son in a household, or when the parents are particularly attached to a daughter and do not want her to leave them for another home.

Marriage by capture seems to have been fairly common at one time; in fact Fawcett was told that 'formerly every one took his wife by force'.[1] But even in his day this practice had become greatly modified, and now only occurs sporadically.

A widow is expected to marry her husband's younger brother or one of an elder brother's sons, if there are no younger brothers. If she marries someone else, compensation must be paid to the husband's brothers.

Divorce is simple, though emphatically disapproved. There is no ceremony; it is effected by the payment of compensation, for no woman leaves her husband except for another man. The dispossessed husband has the right to follow his wife to her new home and kill and eat any goat or pig he can find there, whether it is the property of the new husband or not. 'A woman', says Fawcett, 'may leave her husband whenever she pleases . . . Formerly, it is said, if he did not pay up, the man she left would kill the man to whom she went.'[2] Divorce usually comes from the woman's side, but a man may turn out a wife if she does not work properly, if she gives away his property to her own relations or a lover, or if he catches her in the act of adultery. Even then, if anyone marries her, the new husband must pay compensation.

Polygamy is fairly common. In Dokripanga I found every married man had at least two wives. Fawcett has some interesting remarks about the situation in his day. Men usually married their wives' sisters, as this was less expensive. 'In some places all a man's wives are said to live together peaceably. It is not the custom in the Kehalakot villages. Knowing the wives would fight if together, domestic felicity is maintained by keeping up different establishments. A man's wives will visit one another in the day time, but one wife will never spend the night in the house of another. An exception to this is that the first wife may invite one of the other wives to sleep in her house with the husband: unless so invited the other wife will not go to the house. As each wife has her separate house, so has she her separate piece of ground on the hillside to cultivate. The wives will not co-operate in working each other's cultivation, but they will work together, with the husband, in the paddy fields. Each wife keeps the produce of the ground she cultivates in her own house. Produce of the paddy fields is divided into equal shares among the wives.'[3]

I found much the same arrangement persisting to the present time. At Parisal, for example, there was an old priest with five wives—his

[1] Fawcett, p. 235. [2] ibid., p. 230. [3] ibid., p. 231.

father had had nine—and each had her own house, and her individual pigs, fowls and swidden. The eldest wife arranged how the husband was to sleep; he usually had each wife four days at a time. When he was sleeping with a wife, he would take his food and spend his time in her house. If he spent a day or two too long with one wife, the others would abuse her saying, 'What god has carried him off? Was it Mardisum? Was it Labosum?' After a husband's death, each of the widows retains her own house, swidden and domestic animals, but the fields are divided among the sons.

The Saora household is generally—so far as it is possible to generalize on such a point—a happy one. Both men and women are devoted to their children and are very good to them. I have rarely seen people so fond of babies. There is exceptionally little crying in a Saora village. Children have to work hard, especially in looking after still younger children and in tending the cattle and other animals. But so long as they work well, their parents allow them a great deal of freedom, and from a very early age they begin to share the life of their elders. They attend all the rituals, and even funerals and trance-sessions, and their most popular games are those in which they imitate religious ceremonies. At Sogeda I watched little boys solemnly bring in a menhir stone; four of them tied it to poles in the correct fashion, and marched up and down a terrace with it. At Ladde a group of boys did a capital imitation of a buffalo sacrifice; one of them was the buffalo, and the others cut him up in the approved way, pulled out his entrails in the form of a strip of cloth, pretended to cut off his penis, shared out the meat, while a 'shaman' fell into trance near by. Hunting-games too include the religious motif. The boys shoot one of their number, tie him by arms and legs to a pole and carry him in, then cut him up and eat him. The 'shaman' sacrifices appropriate portions of the kill.

Smaller children play at winnowing, cleaning grain, cooking, rice-husking, beating pulse; they make mud pies and little toys with sticks and leaves. But above all they like to play at shamans.

The general impression of a Saora village, despite the acrid disputes that occasionally disfigure it and the stress and anxiety involved in some of the religious practice, is that it is a very happy place. The people sing at their work, and there is always laughter in the fields.

VII. *Poverty and Wealth*

THE Saoras are in many respects better off than the people of the plains. They sit in the lap of Nature and she spoils them with a thousand simple gifts. Axe-cultivation, however much and rightly it may be deplored by the forest official, gives splendid harvests. The terraces so laboriously constructed give a rich return for the toil they demand. Free from tiresome and enervating food-taboos, the Saora has before him an abundant spread of all wild things, fruit, herbs, roots, leaves and every kind of living creature.

As a result of this, and of their own exceptional industry, the Saoras are the most prosperous tribesmen I have seen anywhere in India; they might be the most secure and happy if they were given adequate economic protection. They have always been lightly administered; in modern times at least, Government has been content to drive them with a light rein and gentle whip and they have responded with increased mettle and a finer gloss. They waste little of their substance on liquor, for the palm trees at their door give them almost all they need. Their commercial dealings are very restricted.

The Saoras go, but not in large numbers, to the few local bazaars, to Jaltaru, Rayaghada, Serango and Gumma, occasionally to Parlakimidi and Gunupur. But much of their business is done at home, where they are visited by itinerant Dom merchants who bring salt, tobacco, yarn and pots.

The Saoras sell rice, *Eleusine corocana*, pulses, dates, chillies, tamarind, the products of the *Bassia latifolia*; the larger families press and sell oil from various seeds. Often they take goods instead of money in exchange—from the Doms, salt and tobacco; from the Kumbits, pots; from the Kindals, bamboo baskets and fans; from the Luaras, iron tools. They sometimes sell, illegally, the spirit they distil at home. Even in Stirling's time (1825), they 'gained a subsistence' by clearing the jungles and providing fuel. 'They likewise collect the produce of the woods, and dispose of large quantities to the druggists and fruit-sellers in the neighbouring bazaars.'[1] This enterprise is now restricted, but they can still make something at it.

The Saoras do not use a great deal of money, but they use some; they need it for taxes; for cloth—not the tribal cloth,

[1] Stirling, 'Account of Orissa', *Asiatic Researches*, vol. xv, p. 42.

which is woven for them by the Doms and paid for in kind, but for shawls, shirts and blankets; for ornaments, beads and combs; for brass pots; for salt, garlic and onions, sometimes for turmeric; for tobacco and matches; for gunpowder, which they are allowed to buy without licence from the Doms who make it; for dried fish.

But the chief need for cash is to purchase the animals which are in constant demand for religious ceremonial. This is the chief cause of Saora indebtedness; it is said that a Saora never gets into debt for food or clothing, but only for religion.

As I show in greater detail in a later chapter, were it not for the economic claims of their religion, the Saoras would be well-to-do; were it not for the exploitation of the Bissoyis and their servants, they would be actually wealthy. They spend little money on clothes for themselves, but they are always having to buy cloth for their tutelaries and the dead. They are careful to a fault over their own food; they waste meat and rice in the most prodigal manner when it comes to feeding the spirits. Their countryside is beautiful but malarious, and malaria not only saps the Saora blood of its strength, but drains the Saora purse of its wealth. For an attack of fever is not to be prevented by a few pills of paludrine (which can be bought for an anna or two at a dispensary); it may demand a fowl on the first day, when the ague is acute, a pig when the fever becomes remittant, perhaps a buffalo if it persists. And the custom of treating disease by the therapeutics of animal sacrifice means that the Saora always goes to his shopping in a hurry. If a man must have a buffalo to save his daughter's life, he will not think too closely about the cost. The gods are angry and impatient; every hour is of importance; he pays whatever price is demanded or binds himself to a debt that will cripple him for years.

In the neighbourhood of the Saoras lives a caste (held in social detestation by the Hindus and often classified as criminal by authority) to which I have already had occasion to refer, the Doms.[1] Throughout Ganjam and Koraput the Doms (who are also known as Panos, Gandas and Pankas) have established themselves in close contact with the Saoras, living side by side with them, though usually in separate hamlets. Nearly all these Doms have become Christians, but their conversion to the religion of brotherly love and fair dealing

[1] The Saora attitude to Doms is illustrated by their myth of the origin of the caste. The first Dom had a head of the abominated horse.

has done little more than to sharpen their wits by a little education and encourage their aggressiveness. Their original task in the Agency was to provide the Saoras with cloth, and no praise can be too high for the artistic and durable material they turn out from their primitive looms. Unfortunately many of them have now abandoned the tedious pursuit of weaving, finding that finance is much more profitable. Their superior cunning and intelligence have now established them as the agents, usurers and advisers of the aboriginals throughout Orissa.

It is the Christian Dom who provides the Saora distracted by illness or disaster with the sacrificial animal for his 'heathen' ceremonies. This would have made Augustine stare and gasp, but after all in the modern world it is money that talks, and it is money that the Dom gets from his agitated tribal neighbour. He sets a high price on the animal and usually arranges that it should be paid in grain at rates that bear no relation to the likely price at the next harvest, plus an appropriate interest of fifty per cent a year. When harvest time comes round, the Doms spend their days standing on the Saoras' threshing-floors scooping in their dues, filling their baskets with whatever they consider to be their rights. The Saora's threshing-floor in Ganjam is indeed one of the saddest places in India. This symbol of a lifetime's toil, this shrine into which Mother Earth pours her choicest gifts, is the scene of persistent and wholesale economic trickery and exploitation.

One day I walked from Gumma to Bungding, a distance of about five miles. As I went there passed me an almost unbroken procession of Saoras, staggering along under great baskets of the grain their toil had gathered, bringing it in for the Bissoyi overlord, his Paik bodyguard and for the Dom money-lenders. The labour, devotion, the enthusiasm was being carried away; it was a funeral procession I saw, for they were carrying out the life and substance of the ancient people of the land.

In a later chapter, I give some account of the violent reactions against this spoliation which from time to time sweep across the Saora hills.

The Saoras of Koraput are in a happier position. They have no overlords, no army of agents to rob and terrorize them, they deal direct with Government. It is an extraordinary contrast to go from one district to the other. In Ganjam, there is perpetual brooding discontent; in Koraput, there is comparative prosperity, freedom and confidence. In Ganjam, the Saoras are serfs; in Koraput they are lords of field and forest. For a hundred years the evil arrangements of the Ganjam Agency, despite a score of protests from administrators, have persisted, but I hope that happier, more equitable days are now ahead.

VIII. *The Outside World*

THE Saoras know much more about the other world than this. In a sense they feel more at home 'below' than abroad. They have few contacts outside their own circle and have proved remarkably resistant to the few influences that have been brought to bear upon them.

The most powerful instrument of change is Assam, whither the Saoras go in fairly large numbers to the Tea Gardens; during the war many young men worked in a Labour Corps and enjoyed the experience. Indeed the Tea Gardens are generally popular with the younger people; one can go there and earn enough money for a marriage—or a divorce; one can escape from an embarrassing domestic or economic situation at home; here is an arena for adventure, a way of seeing the world. To go to Assam rather than to attend a cheap and nasty little school in his own village is the Saora's idea of a liberal education.

The journey to Assam and residence there for several years is of course a very drastic form of contact with the outside world, yet its effect is largely in externals. One reason for this is probably the fact that most of the young explorers can speak no language other than their own; they can therefore copy things they see, but there is no way by which ideas can penetrate their minds. When they come home, therefore, they continue to live exactly as before and observe their religious duties without any alteration. But they dress up a little. The women put on singlets and blouses, which soon become filthy beyond description, but curiously they do not make any change in their ornaments. Men attempt to enhance their personal prestige by wearing jerseys, singlets, coats, shirts, shorts, trousers; they soon become tattered and filthy but the boys wear them to the last rags, as a traveller might keep old hotel labels on his suitcase. It is rather pathetic to see a Saora boy, who in his natural finery is a prince, dressing himself like a chaprasi with the mistaken notion that it will give him a social lift.

Psychologically, the travellers often become lawless and arrogant, and for this reason the older men are strongly opposed to visits to Assam. The Chief of Kerubai said to me, 'Our women become whores, our boys grow proud and violent, they care nothing for the elders, they obey no one. And while they are away, the neglected gods and ancestors bother the rest of us.' This is true; the moral effect of a year or two in the Tea Gardens is generally deplorable.

The moral loss is seldom compensated by economic gain. The meagre earnings of tea-picking are soon exhausted. There are often expensive sacrifices to be made on return to neglected and indignant spirits. There is sometimes a vague attempt at a different way of living; a man may make a chair and put it on his veranda, but no one uses it unless a police or forest official visits the village. Of all the useful and valuable things that the Saoras might bring home, I have never seen one. They bring nothing that is not useless or even harmful; it is not their fault—there is no one to advise them how to spend their money.

Assam has had no effect on religious or social custom; some important shamans have been there, but I noticed little effect on them, except that in trance they could weave Oriya and Bengali words into their prophecies; that they occasionally talked about 'the god of Calcutta'; and that they showed an unusual artistry in the construction of altars, which they decorated with tridents, plates, little mirrors and boxes of matches. There were sola topis on a shrine at Bhubani, and near Maneba I saw a tin plate nailed on the spire of a shrine to Tangorbasum.

My assistant Gandorbo, who has lived all his life (he is now about fifty) among the Saoras, tells me that he has noticed no change at all since he was a boy, and discussions with the older men confirmed this. An intelligent man like Somra, after thirty years of close association with British officials in the Forest Department, still lived in the usual pitch-dark, smoke-filled little box that is a typical Saora house.

But what of contacts and influences nearer home? The Saoras are, up to a point, free of one of the chief vices of tribal India—intolerance. They have no caste feeling, and they do not excommunicate one of their number if he changes his religion. Most of them have no idea of untouchability and accept food even from Doms.

It is the Doms, of course, with whom the Saoras are most closely in touch. But the Doms do not influence them very much because everyone regards them as an inferior people, because the great majority have become Christians and because the Saoras' relations with them are usually financial and unpleasant. One is not likely to be spiritually inspired by someone who is charging you fifty per cent interest on a loan.

The Saoras regard Hindus with respect, for the tutelaries are Hindus and the great Saora shamans become Hindus after death. In any case, I have been told, 'the Hindu religion is good, for its gods help ours'. I never found a Saora who knew what a Mussalman was.

A greater problem for the Saoras is Christianity. There are missions at Parlakimidi and Serango, and groups of Christian Doms —Lutherans, Baptists and Roman Catholics—scattered throughout the Agency areas. By far the most important mission, led by the spiritual genius of Miss A. C. M. Munro, is at Serango. At least up to 1948, this mission conducted its work with the wise and intelligent policy of non-interference with the life of the people. Their few converts continued to dress and live like ordinary Saoras; even polygamy was winked at, provided a second wife was not taken after baptism; Christian and non-Christian Saoras were permitted to marry. In practice most Christian Saoras continued all the old ceremonies in secret; they attended Church on Sunday and sacrificed to Uyungsum on Monday.

More recently I have noticed an increased evangelistic zeal which has led to violent anti-Christian reactions in some Saora villages and an intensified antagonism to the Christian Doms. Indeed to many Saoras, Christianity is the Dom religion, and for a Saora to become a Christian is to become a Dom. But that, it is sometimes said, 'is all to the good, for he need not make so many sacrifices'.

At Gunduruba, I was told that 'the Christian religion is no good. It is not a religion at all. It has no ancestors, no sacrifices, no gods. Unless the gods help us, how can we get good crops?'

The most reasoned criticism of Christianity I have heard came from the celebrated Chief of Pattili.

My grandfather went to a woman. My father went to a woman. I go to a woman.

My grandfather ploughed and sowed his fields. My father ploughed and sowed his fields. I plough and sow my fields.

My grandfather sacrificed buffaloes and planted stones. My father sacrificed buffaloes and planted stones. I sacrifice buffaloes and plant stones.

Ramma-Bimma taught us these things. We know they are good.

But who is this new Bhagavan Christ and where does he come from?

The Christians go to church every week and they do no work on Sundays. Who grazes the cattle, who watches the fields on Sundays? This is why the Christians are so poor.

It is true they do not spend so much on their religion. But as a result they do not have their sacrifices and feasts, the gods are not pleased, and they end up poorer than we are.

What is their religion when the Christians come to beg sacrificial meat from us at our festivals?

3. Women ploughing at Sogeda

4. Threshing-floor at Pattili

5. A Saora girl reaps millet on the hillside near Guli

6. Women transplanting rice on a terraced field at Maneba

7. Boys and girls threshing beans at Barasingi

8. Typical Dom agents who live in small groups among the Saoras

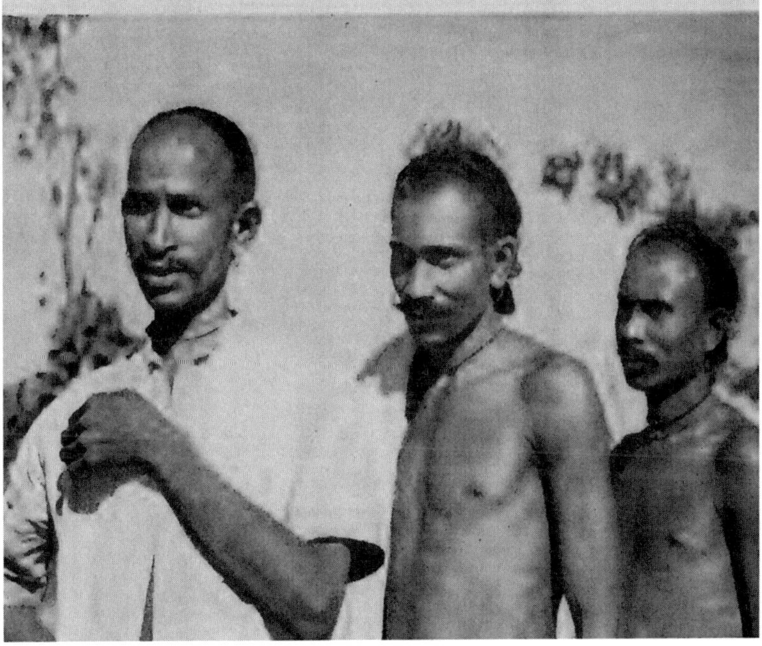

Chapter Two

THE SOUL AND ITS DESTINY

I. *The Two Souls*

SAORA eschatology is confused and its doctrines vary from place to place, but it is possible to define certain broad principles that are generally accepted. Man has two 'souls'—the *suda purādan* or big soul and the *sanna purādan* or little soul, which is also called the *baleng-purādan* or *rup-rup-purādan*. *Balengan* is the roof of a house, and the use of the word here seems to suggest that the 'little soul' is as essential to the life of the body as a roof is to the existence of a house. *Purādan*, used by itself, means 'life' or 'heart', and the 'little soul' is in fact the animating principle, the life of the body, which has its seat in the *rup-rup* beating heart. The 'little soul' does not outlast the destruction of its physical integument; its departure means death; the body cannot exist without it.

But the body can get along very well without the *suda purādan*, which I will henceforth translate simply as 'soul'. This can exist independently of the body both in life and after death. During life, it can leave the body in sleep and wander about the world; it can meet and converse with gods and tutelaries; from time to time it may even descend to the Under World and return enriched by panoramic visions. These experiences are, of course, what we call dreams, but to the Saoras they are something more; they are actual and real events.

When a shaman goes into trance and a spirit comes upon him, the soul is temporarily expelled and the spirit takes its place in the heart or the Adam's apple. The shaman's own soul 'goes away somewhere'. This is why a shaman has his eyes shut during trance; it is because he has no soul; he can remember nothing; and afterwards he cannot say whether the liquor he drank or food he ate had any taste. It is sometimes said, however, that when an ancestor comes upon a shaman, he sits in the throat and does not drive out the soul, which remains in the body 'but below: it cannot say anything'.

II. *The Soul after Death*

WHEN it leaves the body at death, the soul first becomes a shade and then an ancestor. About its immediate fate Saora opinion is confused and contradictory, but there is general agreement that it is unpleasant. Immediately after death the soul makes a brief visit to the Under World, but it is not allowed to stay there and as soon as the funeral is over, it is sent back to wander on earth until it can be admitted into the full fellowship of the ancestral dead. A shaman at Potta described this.

A man's shade wears the clothes he had when he died. He goes to the Under World, but the ancestors there drive him away. He returns to earth and lives near his pyre until the Guar rites are performed. After that he becomes an ancestor and gets better clothes to wear. But if a man dies of epilepsy or smallpox, he has to dress in leaves and fly in the wind.

I recorded a more detailed account in the remote hill-village Thodrang.

When a soul leaves the body in life and goes down to the Under World, it finds a great wooden fence and at the door chaprasis armed with guns and swords marching up and down. One of them goes in to tell the tutelaries that a visitor has come and they hurry to the gate to greet him. If the visitor is a shaman the spirits treat him with honour; they wash his feet and make him sit down and take a drink of wine. But when a soul leaves the body in death, the ancestors catch it and bind it hand and foot. They carry it to the gate of the Under World and the chaprasis let them in. There they make the soul stand —they do not let it sit for a moment—until the corpse is burnt and the bones removed, whereupon they send it back to earth. The soul searches for its body, but naturally it cannot find it, and so it lives hungry and wretched above the pit where its bones are buried. It is when the mourners see the discoloration of the charred bones that they know that the soul has returned.

The first incident, therefore, in the shade's adventures after death is a brief visit to the Under World, which lasts only so long as the period between death and cremation. The next stage is a period of waiting, which may be from a few months to several years, until the elaborate and expensive Guar ceremony with its buffalo sacrifice and erection of a menhir can be performed. This is the period during which the dead are supposed to work their greatest mischief. For it is the time of their greatest misery. The clothes they had at death soon wear out; the little soul-house built above the pyre falls down;

relatives soon forget to provide them with food and liquor; they flit uneasily from place to place, shivering under rocks, nesting in trees, or desolate upon a mountain-side. Above all they are companionless, outcasted by the stain of death. Small wonder then that they are so assiduous in infecting their heirs with their own pains and agues in the hope of hastening the blessed release of the Guar.

For the Guar is the great turning-point in the life of the dead. Its effect may sometimes have to be driven home, as it were, by the Karja ceremonies, but for all practical purposes, in the majority of villages, the Guar changes the shade into an ancestor and admits him to the Under World.

We now approach an obscure and difficult aspect of Saora eschatology. Although the Saoras speak in general terms of the ancestral dead as living in the Under World and as one community, the more speculatively inclined among them insist that it is not quite so simple as this. Everything depends on the cause of death. Those who have been taken out of this world by their own relations, who are themselves known as Idaisum, become Idaisum too and live with them. But if a man dies of smallpox or cholera or is killed by a tiger, that is to say (as a Saora would put it) if he has been taken away by Rugaboi or Mardisum or Kinnasum, he does not become an ordinary Idaisum; he becomes Rugaboi or Mardisum or Kinnasum, as the case may be.

It is not clear what exactly happens. Some Saoras speak of such ghosts as being themselves Rugaboi or Mardisum, as if they were merged in the gods who carried them away; others, however, say that they become their chaprasis and preserve their individuality. But a man who has died of cholera can certainly come in the form of Mardisum to a village and infect his heirs with cholera, and a man killed by a tiger can be very dangerous to the living as a Kinnasum who incites tigers to attack them. And when a shaman wishes to summon a ghost who died as the result of an attack by Ratusum, he has to call on him by the name of Ratusum. To take another example, Dorisum is not only a congeries of all the deities who preside over cattle-graziers but the word covers everybody who has ever died from an attack by one of them: it is a collective noun covering an entire community of spirits.

Shamans and shamanins are often taken away by their tutelaries, and when this happens they may become tutelaries themselves. In this case they retain their individuality and are invoked by their own names, often assuming the character of local gods. Here we have, in fact, the business of god-making visibly at work.

Some of the gods, such as Uyungsum or Kittungsum, are regarded as living in the sky, and the ghosts whom they summon to them do not live in the Under World, but go above to a vaguely imagined heaven.

In the other world, therefore, there are several different classes of spirits. At the head of all are the tutelaries, the beings known variously as Ildasum, Sedasum, Mannesum or Raudasum. Then there are the ordinary dead, the Idaisum. And then, living apart from the rest, are the dead attached to or merged in various deities—Dorisum, Mardisum, Labosum and a host of others. Most of these are regarded as living in the Under World, in their separate quarters, but those who die of the sky-gods go to live with them in the sky.

III. *The Under World*

ALL these beings, tutelaries and ancestral dead alike, are called *sonumanji* or 'gods'. But the tutelaries are of definitely higher rank and possess greater powers. They are dressed better, they have more appetising food, they live in bigger houses, they have greater freedom of movement, they are more respectable. They are regarded as Hindus and observe some of the rules and taboos of caste: they may, for example, eat goats and fowls but no other meat; their women observe menstruation restrictions. Their relations with the ancestors are not unlike those between the Hindus of the plains and the Saoras of the hills.

The tutelaries do not only govern the Under World and the company of the dead; they maintain vitally important relations with the living. As we shall see in another chapter, it is the marriage of a tutelary to a human being that makes him a shaman, and no ceremony of divination can succeed without a tutelary's presence and support. Although they usually contract their marriages with human beings, it is not impossible for tutelaries to marry between themselves, though this is rare. When they do, they are very troublesome to mankind, for they are always searching for food to give their children. If a male tutelary marries in this way, he cannot take a human wife. But a female tutelary can have husbands both on the earth and below it.

The widespread confusion over the use of the word 'Ildasum' is probably due to the fact that there are young tutelaries and old tutelaries. When an Ildasum is young, he is a handsome and obliging spirit, fit mate for a human shamanin. But when he grows old, 'his hair gets long and has to be tied in tresses, his teeth are big as a pestle and his nails are sharp as the teeth of a bear'. In this form he appears as an ogre or hill-god to be feared and placated. It is not quite clear whether the tutelaries can die, but they can certainly grow old. It is said that, if a young tutelary is rejected by a shamanin whom he has chosen, he calls an old Ildasum to frighten her into acquiescence.

Such are the rulers; what of the ghostly country they control? The Under World is known as Kinorai or Jaitanadesa, and the Saoras devote a good deal of imagination to its description and portrayal. The shamans frequently visit it in dreams and the ancestors often come at the time of trance and describe their condition there. The ikons give many vivid representations of its houses and furniture, its dances, marriages, animals and natural scenery. The country is believed to lie to the south, 'for the east and the west are the paths of the Sun and Moon, and the north is the path of the rain'. Here is a typical description from Sogeda.

> The Under World is like this world; there are hills, rivers, rocks and trees, but it is always moonlight there. There is no brighter light than that, there is no sun and the clouds are very low. You cannot recognize people at a distance, the light is so dim. The tutelaries are the officials and the ancestors are the peasants of the land. Since there is so little light the ancestors cannot get about very much. But when they do find a path, they come to this world and cause a lot of trouble.

Another description comes from Kamalasingi; it also stresses the bad light and unhappy condition of the country.

> It is more mountainous than this world and the valleys are deeper. But there is little jungle. It is always moonlight. It is hard to get sufficient food, though the ordinary dead plough their fields. But the rulers, the tutelaries, who dress and behave like Hindus, are rich and prosperous; they sleep on beds; sahibs and forest officers come to their marriages; they keep many servants and soldiers; they ride on elephants and horses and have lizards, snakes and tigers as pets. As men keep dogs, they keep tigers in their houses. But the ancestors, who are the peasants of that country, look just as they did at the time of death, thin, weary, deformed and sad. They cannot get proper clothes to wear and it is always cold under the infernal moon. The wind too blows so hard that it carries their thin bodies up into the air. When they can find the way, they come to their old homes on earth

and give their relatives fever and ague; that is why we shiver when we get fever, because the dead who give it are themselves shivering with cold; they do not let us be until we give them clothes.

I recorded another account with some fresh detail at Boramsingi.

The tutelaries' houses there are like the offices in Parlakimidi. But the houses of the dead are very small and are thatched with porcupine quills. The doors are so small that you have to climb in and out. There are many little hills, bare of trees but covered with rocks. Among the houses stand tall sago palms. It is very hard to climb these trees, but their sap flows as freely as a stream does on earth. But it is so bitter that there is no pleasure in drinking it. The day there is like the night here. The whole country is always full of sound, like the noise of a great bazaar. The bear and the porcupine perform priestly duties for the dead. The bear divines with rice in the fan and the porcupine knows many charms and medicines. When the tutelaries want to visit the earth, they ride on the horses of the wind; when important ancestors come, they travel on elephants.

The way down to the Under World is described in a manner that recalls folk-lore motifs throughout the world.[1] There is a thread from this world to that; there is a great ladder, very perilous; there is a steep and winding path, set with great rocks, but with steps cut here and there where one can sit and rest. Many shamans have described to me their sensations of terror as they slid in dream down the slender thread or climbed the swaying ladder. But, as we have just seen, when the tutelaries come up to earth, they fly on 'wind-horses' and there are also 'wind-elephants' on which important people travel, and these are often represented in the ikons.

According to one tradition the tutelaries employ an enormous hairy caterpillar, the Kurobudjadan, as a sort of watchman on the way. Its function is entirely benevolent: when spirits try to go up to earth to trouble mankind it stops them whenever possible. It also keeps a watch on unauthorized shades (whose Guar ceremonies have not been performed) from coming down. This creature is also called Bungbungbudan and is described as an insect covered with black hair but with a bald head.

In many of the ikons, drawings of bears and porcupines may be seen. One tradition declares the bear (or sometimes the mountain-rat) to be the priest and the porcupine to be the shaman of the Under

[1] See the motifs listed under F80-109 in Stith Thompson, *Motif-Index of Folk-Literature* (Helsinki, 1932-6), henceforth referred to as *Motif-Index*.

World, and these animals are sometimes shown exercising their sacred duties.[1] In another tradition, however, the porcupine is simply the tutelaries' watchman. Its business is to look after the guns and stores and drive away any mischievous god or ghost who tries to tamper with them. When a shaman is divining, if any spirit refuses to obey his summons, he calls him in the name of the porcupine which frightens him into obedience with its quills. This is why ikons dedicated to tutelaries usually include a porcupine.

The bear too may have a purely secular function as the tutelaries' dog. 'As dogs behave here, so do bears behave there.' When the tutelaries go hunting, they take a bear with them. When visitors come to the gate of the Under World, bears run to bite them, and that is why the ancestors hasten to welcome them and escort them in.

IV. *The Ancestors in the Under World*

THE life of the ancestors in the Under World is not unlike that of the living, but it is dwarfed and frustrated. Tikari, a shamanin of Thalulaguda, described how shocked she had been at a dream during which she had seen her dead ancestors. 'My mother,' she said, 'had a wound in her foot; my father was blind; my brother lame in both feet; my father's brother was a hunchback; my paternal grandfather had a great swollen belly; my grandmother was crawling about on her hands and knees. The house in which they lived was so small that they could not stand up in it.'

The ancestors are heavy drinkers, even though their palm wine is bitter, and the reason why shamans normally do not like to perform their divinations after midday is that the ancestors are generally sleeping off their potations at this hour and object to being roused. If it is absolutely necessary to wake them, a special offering should be made in compensation.

The ancestors wear the clothes that they are given at the Guar ceremony, but these soon wear out, and they suffer an additional irritation at seeing the tutelaries always well and 'brightly' dressed in shining garments.

The dead have one physical abnormality which is specially noticeable. Their eyes are in the back of the neck. For when the funeral pyre is fired, the eyes of the corpse swivel round behind. This is why

[1] See *Motif-Index* B154: Oracular animal. Animal acts as soothsayer; and B191: Animal as magician.

the dead make so many mistakes in their attacks on the living; they cannot recognize people properly and frequently trouble the wrong relations.

In the old days the ancestors had conches, which they used to carry with them when they visited the earth. But when they sounded them, the sick recovered and no one died. Kittung thought that if this continued, he would have no inhabitants for the Under World, so he took the conches away and gave them to the gods instead.

The ancestors quarrel, murder, commit suicide just as if they were alive. They are great litigants and the courts are always crowded. This sometimes complicates the work of the shaman, for he may call on a particular ancestor and be told, 'Don't send for him; we're not on speaking terms; there's a case on in so-and-so's court'.

What of the relations of husband and wife after death? It often happens that, when both grow old together and then one dies, the ghost, lonely and neglected in the Under World, comes to call the survivor. In this case, the couple will live together as before and they can even have children, though these children do not have the power of visiting the earth. As always, everything depends on the cause of death. If, for example, a husband is killed by Labosum and a wife by Kinnasum, they will be for ever separate. But if both are taken by Mardisum in a cholera epidemic, or if both are carried away by their own ancestors, they will be together and will be able to resume their marital relations.

When a shaman dies, the position is complicated by the fact that he already has a spirit-wife in the Under World. Let us suppose that a shaman is 'taken away' by his tutelary, leaving a widow on earth. He will then live with his tutelary wife in the Under World. Suppose then that when his widow dies it is as a result of an attack by Ratusum. She will see her husband in the Under World, but there will be a social as well as a domestic barrier between them. Her husband, having joined the tutelaries, on the way perhaps to becoming a tutelary himself, has had a social rise; he has become a Hindu. His wife, having joined a Saora god, remains a Saora. He has a jealous and possessive tutelary-wife watching all he does. If the human wife tries to speak to her former husband, the tutelary-wife falls into a rage, drives her away and loses no opportunity of making life unpleasant for her. She must live alone, unless she can find an unmarried male ghost among

Ratusum's chaprasis. She can marry him, but only if he pays compensation to her former husband's ghost.

Take another case. Suppose a young married shamanin dies, being taken away by her tutelary. She will live with him as her husband in the Under World. Then suppose her husband also dies as a result of a visit from a tutelary. Husband and wife will both be in the same group, the tutelaries' group, and they can meet and talk to one another. But the shamanin cannot live with her human husband; she must be with her tutelary, and if she herself at last becomes a tutelary she will go to find yet another husband among the living.

V. *Transmigration*

THE Saoras' attitude to reincarnation is obscure. Many children are named after an ancestor or at the request of a tutelary. If, after receiving its ordinary name (generally derived from the day of the week on which it was born), a child refuses its milk or cries a great deal, the shaman may declare that one of the ancestors wishes it to bear his name, and an elaborate ceremony is performed. When this happens there is some talk of the ancestor being reborn in the child; indeed I have heard the theory that the ancestors themselves have two souls, just like human beings, and that it is the *sanna purādan* or little soul that is reborn, while the big soul continues to live in the Under World. This is an ingenious way of explaining how it is that even after an ancestor's name has been given to a child and he is vaguely imagined as reborn in it, he continues to be invoked in the Under World.

Tutelaries also give their names to children. This generally happens to a child who is related to a shaman; he gives the name of his own tutelary or that of one of her relations. Such a child is expected to become a shaman. It is also possible for the spirit-child of the union of a human shaman and a tutelary to be born as an ordinary child in this world. In this case the child is given the name it had in the Under World. For example, Aganti, a shamanin of Boramsingi, had a child called Saitino from her tutelary in the spirit world, and later this child took birth in her womb here and was given the same name.

The Saoras, however, insist that there is no real reincarnation; there is not a rebirth of the person, but only of the name. But the name itself has a kind of real existence, and the ancestor or tutelary who gives a name to a human child does in some way live in it, even though he continues another life in the Under World.

On the other hand, it must be admitted that the language used at a Name-giving ceremony at Singjangring in 1950 was undoubtedly suggestive of a belief in a real rebirth. On this occasion a baby was named after his paternal grandfather Saitino. Saitino had been a well-known shaman and after his death he became a tutelary and was called Ribano. When his little grandson was born he insisted that he should be given both his names—Saitino and Ribano. The ceremony is described at p. 390 and here Saitino-Ribano is certainly imagined as continuing to live in the Under World, though the following address to him by the celebrant equally suggests that he has come back to live in this.

> You are great; you are Brahmins; you are Hindus; yet you have come here to us . . . Now that you are born here, you must eat the flesh and blood of the excreta-eating pig. Did you get permission to come from your relatives in the Under World? How were you able to leave the dead there, thick as leaves on the tamarind? But however you did it, you are born here now. Now you will have to use the plough, you will have to clear the forest, you must eat what others eat, and live just like the rest of us . . . You had great happiness in the Under World; how is it that you have come to taste sorrow here?

It is noteworthy that throughout this ceremony the shamanins addressed the tutelary in the plural, as if he were two persons, because he had two names, Saitino and Ribano.

Some light is thrown on Saora ideas of reincarnation by incidents in the mythology. There are a dozen stories of the transformation of a dead person into something else. In one type of tale, the soul goes to Kittung and is sent back to earth in another form. A woman, beaten and abused by her husband, dies in sorrow. Her soul goes to Kittung and he places a handful of paddy chaff on her head; it turns into a swarm of bugs. 'Go and live in your husband's cot,' says Kittung, 'and all night you can bite him and drink his blood.'[1] A girl who dies old and a virgin asks Kittung that 'as I wept for men, let me be the cause whereby men may weep for me'. Kittung sends her back to earth as a scorpion.[2] Another frustrated girl asks that she who was ignored by all men may return as something which all men desire. A tobacco plant grows from her bones.[3] A drowned girl is allowed to live in a stream as a leech and drink the blood of those who killed her.[4]

[1] For the full text, see p. 240 of my *Tribal Myths of Orissa* (Bombay, 1954), henceforth referred to as *TMO*. [2] See my *Myths of Middle India* (Bombay, 1949), p. 160, henceforth referred to as *MMI*. [3] *MMI*, p. 329. [4] *TMO*, p. 216.

In another type of tale, trees grow out of a human body, an ebony tree from a girl who dies of snake-bite, a bamboo from a three-months' foetus. From a Saora's bones, duly buried in the ash-pit, come two frogs. A girl eaten by a tiger turns into a bird.

Yet at the same time the ghosts have a separate and independent existence. The girl from whose body grew the ebony tree comes to her parents in a dream and tells them what has happened. The man whose bones turned into frogs comes to his wife and says, 'I have been born again on earth and I desire to see you'.

These folk-tale motifs may be borrowed,[1] as indeed the whole conception of reincarnation may have come to the Saoras from outside and is still hesitating uneasily on the fringe of their thought, waiting to be assimilated. On the whole, I doubt whether any belief in reincarnation, at least of the classical type, is native to Saora theology.

VI. *The Immortality of the Soul*

Do the Saoras believe the soul to be immortal? 'The primitive belief in a future life,' says Pringle-Pattison, 'is not, of course, a belief in immortality in the strict or philosophical sense of an endless life. Such a conception of endlessness we may well consider to be beyond the grasp of primitive man: it is too abstract.'[2] Munro and Sitapati, on the other hand, assert that the immortality of the soul is inferred by the Saoras from their experience in dreams, and further that they believe 'in the immortality of the body, which prevailed in by-gone ages when men could slough off the worn out elements and rejuvenate. The power was later lost, but the idea is still present. *Labana-mar*, which literally means "sloughman" indicates the idea of an immortal person. The benediction, "May you live long" or "Live for ever" is expressed by *jadan-a-laba-labanaba* which literally means "Snake's slough, slough you".'[3]

[1] Some of these motifs are listed in the Stith Thompson *Motif-Index*: A2611·2: Tobacco from grave of bad woman. E613: Reincarnation as bird. E615·1. Reincarnation as frog. E631: Reincarnation in plant (tree) growing from grave. See also *TMO*, pp. 666f.

[2] A. S. Pringle-Pattison, *The Idea of Immortality* (Oxford, 1922), p. 12. The author goes on to illustrate the 'ebbing of the soul's vitality with the lapse of time' from Mexican eschatology and recalls how souls pass from one division to another of the Maori Hades, losing a little of their vitality each time, until at last they die outright.

[3] A. C. M. Munro and G. V. Sitapati, 'The Soras of the Parlakimidi Agency', *Census of India*, 1931, vol. I, pt. iiiB, p. 202.

These authors have confused the idea of immortality with that of survival, a very different thing. The benediction 'Snake's slough, slough you', which incidentally is used by only a very small group of Saoras in the neighbourhood of Serango, does not suggest an immortality of the body, but merely that it can be rejuvenated and go on a little longer. Nor can the immortality of the soul be deduced from meetings with the dead in dreams; all that can be inferred is its continuance. In fact, the Saoras believe in a second death. An ancestor in the Under World can fall ill and die. When this happens the other ghosts carry the body to a great flat rock and burn it with castor wood. Guriya, a Saora of Sogeda, told me that he once saw this in a dream. 'There were many ancestors sitting on a hillside. One of them had died, and the others were burning the body on a pyre of castor wood, but the corpse would not burn. When I saw this I crawled back to the world on my hands and knees.'

After such a death and the due performance of the proper rites, one of three things may happen. The ancestor may simply disappear; his second death is the end of him. Or he may turn into an owl; he is then kept as a pet by Mardisum (god of cholera) or Yuyuboi (small-pox) and may be sent by them to warn villagers of their approach. Thirdly, if the ancestor had been a shaman during his lifetime, and at his death had been taken away by his tutelary, he himself may turn into a tutelary.

It is only in this last case that the soul achieves some kind of immortality through apotheosis. In ordinary cases, I have noticed that the Saoras rarely recall the names of very old ghosts. After two or three generations their weary spirits find an ultimate release in a second and final death.

Chapter Three

THE SAORA PANTHEON

I

For a proper understanding of the drama of Saora religion, it is necessary to have clearly in mind the names of the chief actors, and I make no apology for describing them thus early in the book.

It is not easy to list the Saora gods, for there is a bewildering variety of them;[1] each area, sometimes each village, has its special cult; the same god may be known by different names; and a god who is of great importance in one area may be almost unknown in another. The important deity Jaliyasum is hardly known today in the Gumma Mutta; Karnosum, who is sometimes regarded as the Supreme Being in Ganjam, is not recognized even by name in Sogeda and its neighbourhood.

The Saora word for 'god' is *sonuman*, of which *suman* is the contracted form; in compounds this is still further shortened to *-sum*. This is a masculine suffix, which is added to the name of any god irrespective of sex. The word *-bojan* or *-boi*, which is a feminine suffix often added to a woman's name, is also indifferently attached to the names of gods, sometimes even when, as in the case of Uyungan the Sun, they are certainly male. Sitapati suggests that the *-boi* thus added

[1] J. C. Molony, who gives some account of the Saora gods in his 1911 Census report, says that, 'of the Saoras of Ramagiri, and those of Parlakimidi, I have received detailed information from Messrs Dinabandha Pandu and G. H. Welchman. The complete disagreement of their accounts, which in each case are founded on undoubted knowledge of the people described, indicates the difficulty of any general statement as to religious belief.'—*Census of India*, 1911, vol. xii, pt. i, p. 64. The gods listed, with the exception of 'Jhallia', 'Korono' and 'Kitum', are Hindu. An anonymous writer in the *Manual of the Administration of the Madras Presidency* (Madras, 1886), vol. i, p. 109, tells us explicitly of the Saoras that 'they have no gods. Their goddesses are three in number; Joolva, to whom they sacrifice goats, Gangy, to whom they sacrifice a pig, and Jommo, to whom they sacrifice a fowl.' And Stirling observes that the Saoras 'are said to worship certain rude forms of Devi and Mahadeo or rather the Hindus so interpret the adoration paid by them to a few natural objects, as stumps of trees, masses of stone, or clefts in rocks, in which an impure imagination may discern some resemblance to the human organs of generation'.—Stirling, 'Account of Orissa', *Asiatic Researches*, vol. xv, p. 43.

is not really the feminine suffix at all, but 'is probably a variant of *bong*, contraction of *bongan* (cf. *bonga*, deity, in almost all the languages of the Kol-Munda group)'.[1] But, although the Saoras have a vague notion of a deity called Sing-bonga, they do not really use the word *bonga*, and I have always been assured by them that the suffix *-boi* is intended to be feminine, the apparent contradiction being explained by the fact that many gods have wives; when, for example, Uyungan the Sun is called Uyungboi, a reference is intended to the Sun's wife who is regarded as part of himself.

Sitapati, apparently following his father Ramamurti,[2] divides the Saora gods into no fewer than twenty-one 'Orders or Classes of Deities and Spirits'. Although his knowledge of this subject is considerable, I am unable to follow him here, for I found it impossible to verify this classification, or anything like it, among the Saoras themselves, and indeed of half a dozen of his 'Orders' Sitapati himself admits that no definite information was to be had beyond the names. The Saoras certainly distinguish the *sonumanji*, the Kittungs, the tutelaries, the shades and the ancestors, but Sitapati's other divisions seem to me to represent a schematization which is characteristic of Hindu rather than of Saora thought.

We have then first the *sonumanji*, whom I rather reluctantly call 'gods', each of whom has his own name and attributes. Some of these are comparatively aloof sky-gods, others are local deities of limited cult, others are malevolent authors of human tragedy and pain. Many deserve to be called 'demons' or 'furies' rather than 'gods', but since the Saoras themselves describe both the benevolent and the most vicious spirits by the same name, I have not thought it proper to distinguish between them.

The Kittunganji, whom I call for convenience the Kittungs, are also 'gods', though they are not usually described with the suffix *-sum*, and most of them are not worshipped. But there is a sort of collective deity called Kittungsum, who is the object of a widespread and important cult. The Kittungs are imagined in greater detail and in more human terms than the other gods, and a being who is generally called simply Kittung is the hero of the majority of the myths, where he appears as the creator of the world and the author of human institutions.

[1] Sitapati, 'The Soras', *J.A.H.R.S.*, vol. XIII, p. 117.
[2] Ramamurti, *Manual*, p. 92; Sitapati, loc. cit.

Next in importance are the tutelaries. They are dignified with the dominical suffix and may thus be classified as 'gods'. They receive special attention from the shamans who give them individual names and genealogies.

Then come the dead. The *kulbanji*, shades, are human souls who have not yet been admitted to the company of the ancestors and, though they receive considerable attention, are not the object of worship. They are not to be included among the gods. But after the Guar ceremony, the dead are regarded as in some way deified; they are known as Idaisum, and are invoked as *jojonji* and *yoyonji*, grandfathers and grandmothers: they are, in fact, the ancestors, the word I use for them throughout this book.

Sitapati's other 'Orders' are extremely vague. The Jnonadanji are properly to be included among the other gods; there is nothing, apart from the form of the name, to distinguish them. The same may be said of the Daiyunji, who are of very limited cult, the Kuaranji, the Adanganji, Mallanji, Bullunji, Jalbanji, Bulkanji, Rudobanji and Rajanji. Where there is anything to be said for them at all, I see no reason to classify them separately. Most of their names appear to have been taken from the invocations of the shamans. The shamans, as we shall see, are accustomed to indulge in interminable lists of names in the course of which they refer to everyone they have ever heard of, in order to be on the safe side. But many of these words are meaningless and certainly cannot be taken to denote orders or classes of spirits.

Only a few of the gods receive anything like regular worship. Even fewer have shrines erected or ikons made in their honour. Some are not worshipped at all. Many are only remembered at times of crisis. But this great company of spirits surrounds and often invades Saora existence, and neither the social, domestic nor economic life of the tribe can be understood without a knowledge of who and what they are.

II. *The Home of the Gods*

THE gods are great tourists, and one of the things that makes a shaman's business so complicated is that he never knows where a particular god is to be found at any given moment. Most of the gods, however, do seem to have permanent homes, some in the sky, some on earth and some in the Under World.

The great Sun-gods—Uyungsum, Darammasum and Lankasum—are naturally located in the sky. The Kittungs too, after their long sojourn on the earth which they have done so much to improve, are vaguely pictured as living 'above'.

In the sky are the Kittungs. They cook in the sky. The fire of their hearth is the light of the sun. They warm themselves with it when it is cold. When they sleep and the fire dies down, there comes the night.

In the sky also is the Moon, the wife of the Sun, who is deified as Angaiboi, and her children the stars and planets. The god of the wind, Ringesum, finds his natural home there, and so does Ganurboi, the goddess of rain, and Ilingbongsum the rainbow.

Many gods are believed to live on earth. Local gods are attached to hills and streams. Tokens of their presence may still be seen: in one place a long stone rather like a sword reminds the people that a god once placed his sword on the ground there and forgot it when he went away. A hollow rock is said to be the mortar where the gods once pounded human bones. A yellow-coloured stone shows by its colour that the gods once prepared turmeric paste upon it. Near Sarsang village is a stone shaped like a drum; this is the Kittungs' drum.

The hill-gods are specially dangerous to mankind, for they are jealous of their property, and attack anyone who picks herbs or cuts trees without acknowledging their authority. Although such gods are usually named after the hills on which they live, there is some idea that they are all Labosum, the god of earth. Labosum himself is generally imagined as living beneath the soil: there is a story that he pushed the first broom up through the ground into a girl's hand;[1] he also pushes up seedlings and trees.

Other gods seem to live in the Under World, where they each have their own quarters, where they live with their servants and the ghosts of their own dead. Here too, of course, live the tutelaries and the ancestors.

But all the gods come to visit earth and they, with the earth-dwelling deities, are to be found in every conceivable place. A shamanin at Boramsingi, in the course of her invocations at the Rogonadur ceremony, addressed the gods:

You who live in clearings now overgrown with trees, you who live in pits, you who live above, you who live in water, you who live in

[1] *TMO*, p. 594.

water where there are fishes, you who live in the fish, you who live in bones, you who live in the bones of men, you who live in the stone walls between fields, you who live in the trees of the forest.

I do not think that this is a belief in divine immanence. When a Saora says a god is living in a tree he does not mean that he pervades the tree with an unseen power; what he means is that the god is perched on the tree as if he was a bird. Samiya, the shaman of Sogeda, described how he saw in a dream the gods of the Under World. 'The gods fly about like birds; they are small as little birds.' And when an ikon is made for a god, he is said to live in it 'like a fly sitting on the wall'.

The gods are always travelling. Groups of them go to and fro, summoned by importunate shamans; others travel far in quest of food or to avenge an injury. On the way they halt beneath banyan trees and drink their gruel; they sit down by the roadside for a smoke; occasionally a human traveller treads on them or trips over their cooking-pots.

Probably the Saoras' last word on the home of the gods would be a phrase of a shaman's prayer: 'O Great Ones, though we cannot see you, you live on every side.'

III. *Apotheosis*

It has been suggested that the mighty anthropomorphic figures of the gods have resulted from the synthesis of an ideal human being with a tribal god or demon. The demon gives the hero his supernatural qualities; the hero gives the demon his human features. We can see something of this sort happening when we compare the Saora myths with the prayers; in these the all too human heroes of legend become powerful, though anthropomorphically imagined, demons or gods.

Among the Saoras the process of god-making never ceases. As we have seen, every ancestor, on entering the Under World after the proper performance of the Guar, becomes an Idaisum, one of the *sonumanji* or deities. If the dead person was a shaman (or shamanin), he may under certain conditions become a tutelary himself and thus attain a higher rank in the scale of deification. He will be invoked and honoured by name, and in time may become established as a local god.

We have also seen how those who die as the result of being attacked by a god join that god after death and in some way not clearly defined become part of him and are called by his name. At a Doripur ceremony at Potta (described in full at pp. 267ff.), the shaman addressed his invocations to 'Dorisum wandering in the forest, Dorisum in the stones, Dorisum in the trees, Dorisum on the mountains, Dorisum in the moon, Dorisum in the sun, Dorisum in the Under World, Dorisum in the sky, Dorisum on this earth'. That this was not an affirmation of belief in the universal pervading of the universe by Dorisum was indicated by the shaman's prayer, 'Come all of you,' and by his identification of some of the Dorisum by name. The invocation implies that the collection of spirits who have become Dorisum may be scattered anywhere on their daily duties or expeditions and must now be collected to accept the sacrifice which is offered to the god in his collective form: it is most important that not one of the Dorisums should be left out.

I do not know how far we can assume that the Kittungs are deified human beings, or that their fantastic adventures have any place in history. Probably not at all. The Kittungs are the heroes of tribal legend, and were not at first objects of worship, though under the name of Kittungsum their cult is gradually increasing in importance. The human origin of Gadalsum, however, is expressly stated. He was, according to one tradition, a priest who cut grass before the proper time. The local hill-god was annoyed and sent a tiger to devour him. The priest ran to a cave and managed to get his head, but not his legs, inside. The tiger ate him to the waist and what was left turned into Gadalsum, the god of grass-cutters. According to another tradition, Gadalsum was born from the blood of an old man who was killed by a tiger while cutting grass.

The Rajanji may, as Sitapati suggests,[1] be a class of deified kings. He names a number of them—Daramma Raja, Gulusu Raja, Gurbada Raja, Indura Raja, Pattika Raja, Sindima Raja and Sodanga Raja. But the word 'Rajan' can be applied in flattery to any god, and Sitapati admits that he was unable to get any information about these kings, though he suggests that Sodanga may be Chodanga Deo, a king of Kalinga-desa, that Indura Raja may be Indra or the Raja of Indora and that Daramma Raja may be Yama's son and the eldest of the Pandus. It is just possible that these names may recall very old memories of Saora migrations in ancient times.

[1] Sitapati, 'The Soras', *J.A.H.R.S.*, vol. xiii, p. 125.

Sitapati also refers to a class of spirits called Pataranji and suggests that some Patros 'might have been deified on account of their importance or special merit'. But since the Patros and Bissoyis are cordially hated for their exactions, and no one has ever been able to think of a Patro or Bissoyi who was either important or of special merit, this seems unlikely.

Moreover, so far as I can see, the path to godhead is by a certain type of death, but this applies only to Saoras. The most wealthy and famous chief who is carried off by his father's ghost will not become a god; but the most insignificant cripple who is killed by Ratusum will, and will be all the more powerful and malignant on account of his deformity.

It is evident, however, that the Saoras have recruited their pantheon widely from among the human population. The process is still going on, and as old local gods lose their influence and are forgotten, new ones are found to take their place.

IV. *A Supreme Being*

Do THE Saoras believe in a Supreme Being? The answer to this question must depend, of course, on the definition of our terms. If we simply mean, Do the Saoras believe in a high god who towers above the rest? the answer is simple. It is equally simple if our question refers to what Söderblom calls a 'Producer' (*Urheber*),[1] a being who is postulated to answer the universal human need for an explanation, whose existence tells us how and why all things were made. But let us give the expression 'Supreme Being' its fullest and most difficult meaning, descriptive (in the words of Andrew Lang) of 'a primal, eternal Being, author of all things, the father and the friend of man, the invisible omniscient guardian of morality'.[2] We shall also assume that such a being is not a mere *deus otiosus* who has lost interest, but one who continues to have a vital concern for the world he made. Have the Saoras any idea of a being who could be described in some such terms as these?

Fawcett, writing nearly seventy years ago, is emphatic in his reply. 'There is no idea,' he says, 'of a supreme and beneficent Creator of all things.' In villages 'where the Saoras have been free from Hindu

[1] N. Söderblom, *Gudstrons uppkomst* (Stockholm, 1912), p. 175. Quoted by R. Karsten, *The Origins of Religion* (London, 1935), pp. 185, 198.

[2] A. Lang, *The Making of Religion* (London, 1900), p. 173.

influence nothing is known of a beneficent deity. They have no notion of any deity of whom they will ask anything in expectation of their request being granted through love.'[1] Sitapati, who studied the subject many years later and in villages where there had been a good deal of missionary preaching and influence, is of the opinion that there is a Supreme Deity, but that he is not yet clearly defined in the Saora mind. He considers that this deity is the Sun, Uyungsum, who is also known as Darammasum, Lankasum and sometimes Gadelsum or Gadejangboi, and he points out that in recent years the Saoras have learnt to use the words Maprun (Sanskrit, Mahaprabhu) and Paramesaran (Sanskrit, Paramesvar) from the Hindus and the Christian missionaries. 'The use of these foreign names,' he says, 'is very significant.' It shows that the Saoras felt that there was no word in their own language (which incidentally is a flexible one, well able to create words which will serve as the vehicle of new ideas) to express the idea of a benevolent and moralized Creator. And Sitapati concludes that even though the Saoras have borrowed these words (and I myself must add that very few have borrowed them), 'they have not yet acquired the idea of an all-merciful and benevolent Supreme Being'.[2]

In their social and political life the Saoras attach great importance to precedence. In the Pottasingi valley there is continual strife between the great Chiefs as to who is the greatest. I myself have often been asked just how important I was; was I, for example, 'bigger' than the Deputy Commissioner or the Forest Officer? Once, to my mortification, I was asked whether I was greater than the Sub-Inspector of Police. The Saoras, in fact, like to arrange people in order, and the idea of settling the question of precedence among the gods is thus in no way alien to them. The difficulty is that they do not seem able to make up their minds. Not only is there great difference of opinion in different areas, but even the same informant will attribute supreme qualities today to one god and tomorrow to another.

There is no doubt that the Sun has a very high place in the pantheon. As Uyungsum he causes children to be conceived; as Gadejangboi he forms the bones in the womb; as Darammasum he is the witness who watches the doings of men. He has some control over lesser spirits and sometimes sacrifices are offered to other gods on

[1] Fawcett, p. 248.
[2] Sitapati, 'The Soras', *J.A.H.R.S.*, vol. XIII, p. 133.

the understanding that they will be passed on to him. It is he 'who gives and takes away' and he is on the whole benevolent, though he is believed to punish 'sinners' with leprosy or epilepsy.

But not all Saoras give the Sun-god this pre-eminent position. At Ladde they were emphatic that Galbesum was the greatest of the gods and they emphasized their opinion by building him a splendid shrine. In some villages, again, Karnosum is the Supreme Being, in others Patha Munda, in one the earthworm Labosum who creates earth, in many Kuraitu Kittung, the 'god of the gourd', who made the world and all that it contains. In the large number of myths which I have collected from all parts of the Saora country, the active agent who not only creates the world at the beginning, but also makes all sorts of things for men and teaches them how to live, is called Kittung. Occasionally Uyungsum appears as a consultant; sometimes Labosum, Jammasum and the ancestors have a creative function; but in the great majority of instances it is Kittung and Kittung only who creates.

This raises a further problem. As we see later in this chapter, there are a number of different Kittungs and the Saoras are entirely uncertain as to which of them is the Creator. The myths contain obscure references to a Kittung Mahaprabhu who is greater than the Kittung who is known to men. In the days before the sun and moon were made, men complained to *their* Kittung about the inconvenience of living in perpetual darkness, and he went to *his* Kittung, Kittung Mahaprabhu, to ask him what to do. Mahaprabhu made the sun, but it was so hot that 'rocks split open, trees were withered, and men died of heat'. It was Kittung who then dealt with the matter, cursing the sun so that one of its eyes burst open and its heat was lessened. In the confused Creation stories,[1] the original couple who survived the primal flood are sometimes said to be Kittung and his sister; in one tale this Kittung makes the new world, in another 'the great Kittung in the sky' does so. But in yet other stories, the first couple are ordinary human beings, and it is Kittung who creates and guards them.

Probably the inconsistency arises from the fact that the Saoras have never been able to make up their minds whether Kittung is a supra-mundane deity or a simple cult-hero. This is why, according to some myths, he made, and, according to others he was, the first man. Sometimes he is pictured as very definitely a sky-god, far above

[1] See *MMI*, pp. 43ff. and *TMO*, pp. 9ff.

the world; at others he is a homely person, a shaman of extraordinary powers, walking the ways of earth and teaching the Saoras the details of cultivation.

Our difficulty is that the Saora myths are confused and even contradictory. There is no such thing as a corpus of Saora myth, known throughout the tribe and universally accepted as an explanation or a motive-force for modern ritual behaviour. The stories occur sporadically and are often known only in limited areas. There is no class of story-tellers; there are no famous raconteurs; and, except for those recited at the Jammolpur and Ajorapur, there is no virtue in the myths and no set time when they should be told.

Yet the myths, which are printed in full in my books *Myths of Middle India* and *Tribal Myths of Orissa*, are of the first importance, for they are the only way by which the rather inarticulate Saora can tell us what he is thinking about the great problems of the origin and meaning of life. Myth, as Tylor said, 'is the history of its authors, not of its subjects',[1] and from this point of view Saora mythology is of great value for the light it throws on the Saora mind. That mind is not a philosophizing or abstract mind; it always seeks the concrete, and one can see the relief with which the Saora theologian escapes from abstract ideas when he clothes them in concrete form. This view of myth has been admirably stated by a recent American writer. 'Whereas fairy tales', says David Bidney, 'are held to be the expression of wishful thinking and personal gratification, myth, at its best, is to be regarded as a recognition of the drama of human existence. Its ultimate aim is not the wishful distortion of the world, but rather serious comprehension and envisagement of its fundamental nature. Myth is regarded as representing metaphorically a world-picture and insight into life generally and may, therefore, be considered as primitive philosophy or metaphysical thought.'[2]

The Saora world-picture, thus metaphorically displayed, presents us with Kittung (whoever he may be) as the Creator of this earth and of mankind, and the originator of many human institutions. There was a former world, which sank down below the primeval waters. All living creatures were destroyed, except for a male and a female

[1] E. B. Tylor, *Primitive Culture* (London, 1929: the first edition was in 1871), vol. I, p. 416.

[2] David Bidney, 'The Concept of Myth and the Problem of Psychocultural Evolution', *American Anthropologist*, vol. LII (1950), p. 17. Bidney is summarizing the views of S. K. Langer expressed in *Philosophy in a New Key* (New York, 1948).

(who are often described as Kittungs), who took refuge in a gourd which floated on the surface of the great sea. The new world was made in a variety of ways, according to different local traditions. Ramma-Bimma's hen laid an egg in the sky; it fell into the sea and broke; the white spread over the water and hardened into the new world. The gourd floating on the sea broke open and the pieces turned into the earth. Kittung's rat burrowed below the ocean and brought up earth, which Kittung spread over the waters. The seven suns rained down heat and dried up the sea and the dry land appeared.

The man and woman emerged from the gourd and settled on the earth. Soon the woman conceived—some say it was by Kittung's rat, some say by her brother. Her children were the first human beings, the Saoras. Other stories say that Kittung made the first men directly, by vitalizing little clay images or paintings on the wall of his house.

There is no consistency in these myths, which from their resemblance to similar stories known to other tribes, and indeed to the whole sub-Puranic tradition, appear to be importations from outside. The position of Kittung is obscure. Sometimes he appears as the Creator, making a kite from the dirt of his body and sending it out to discover whether there have been any survivors of the flood. Sometimes he appears as the first man and it is from his sister that the rest of mankind comes. The general opinion, however, is that it was Kittung who made the new world. As in parallel tales of other tribes, the world as we know it is made of pre-existent matter and indeed everything seems to have come from something else—grass from hair, salt from a dead man's bones, the cock from a marking-nut, fish from bits of wood, frogs from ashes in a grave. We watch Kittung actually at work creating things. Some he makes with dirt from his own body: he turns dirt from his tongue into the poison for a snake's fangs, he makes a crab with his dirt and puts little sticks for legs. Sometimes he has things transformed; he cuts off his beard and buries it and it becomes a sago palm; a buried necklace is transformed into grubs, chaff into mosquitoes. His curse turns a girl into a dog, a boy into a fowl. His blessing sends an angry woman back to earth as a scorpion, a neglected girl back as a tobacco plant, a girl unkindly drowned as a leech, a hungry shade as the jackal which never wants for food.

To provide men with nails, Kittung buys a potsherd, breaks it into little bits, spits on them and sticks them on the fingers and toes.

To give a dog a tail, he finds a gourd, breaks off the long handle and fixes it to the animal's backside.

Examples could be multiplied and they all point the same moral: that everything is made out of something else. Kittung must have his materials; he is not able simply to wave his hand and say 'Let there be fish'. He has to cut some wood up into little bits, put the bits into a new pot, strip his wife naked, send her with the pot down to a pond, and make her throw it into the water.

Koppers considers that this belief is ultimately Hindu; the idea of *creatio ex nihilo sui et subjecti* (which he claims to have discovered among the Bhils) is 'one which runs counter to almost every system evolved by Hindu mentality',[1] and he quotes Monier Williams as saying that all Hindu sects 'believe in some material cause (*upādana*) —some eternal substance out of which the universe is evolved'.[2] Held also points out that 'when there is talk of creation, we must beware of considering that idea in the light of western philosophy, thereby laying undue stress upon the act of creation as generation out of nothing instead of on the arranging, the ordering of primordial matter. . .There never was a time when nothing existed'.[3]

But I doubt whether we need trace anything so portentous as Hindu influence here; the Saora has certainly never considered this as a problem; his picture of Kittung at work is natural enough to someone who thinks of the gods as acting very much like men, and men—often enough—as acting very much like gods: it was a man, in Saora myth, who made the clouds, a man who started the moon and stars shining. If we want to make something, we first have to get our materials: Kittung has to do the same.

Kittung, in a tale from Mannemgolu, is called 'the one who made the earth and all mankind', but it is in his activities after the creation of the earth as a whole, after the birth of the first men, that we get the clearest picture of his character.

The world at the beginning was a strange mixture of fairyland and nightmare. Human beings were only two feet high, and they lived in burrows like hares, eating leaves and grass, until the roofs caved in and smothered them. As they grew larger they developed strange physical characters; they had three eyes, their noses were

[1] W. Koppers, 'Bhagwan, the supreme deity of the Bhils', *Anthropos*, Tome XXXV-VI (1940-41), p. 275.

[2] Monier-Williams, *Brahmanism and Hinduism* (London, 1891), p. 119.

[3] G. J. Held, *The Mahabharata* (London and Amsterdam, 1935), p. 118.

so long that they hung across their shoulders, their umbilical stumps drooped over their bellies, the male organ was so large that it was kept wound about the waist. Women's genitals used to detach themselves from the body and wander about the streets at night. Men had horns, and these could be very inconvenient when one was making love. They had tails which they used to sweep the floor. They were completely covered with hair, except for the head which was quite bald. Under the circumstances it was perhaps just as well that they had no tongues and could only converse by signs.

For a long time, human beings had no blood in their bodies, and they suffered greatly from the heat. Neither had they nails and, since they had to do everything with their hands—with which they husked rice and often swept the ground—they found it very tiresome.

At death, at first they simply threw corpses away. Later when they learnt to bury them, they left the heads sticking out of the ground. When they learnt to cook, they broke the skulls and used them as hearths.

The animal world was very close to the human at this time. Animals could speak before men could, for they got their tongues first. They were all very friendly. Monkeys and tigers lived in the same huts. When Ramma-Bimma ruled the world, people rode on deer, tigers and peacocks. Elephants flew about on great wings, and in fact became rather a nuisance, for when they perched on a roof it would collapse under their weight. There was no enmity between house animals and wild animals. When the latter visited a village the house animals received them hospitably and made them rest on the veranda and have a bite to eat.

The gradual amendment of all this, and the furnishing of the world with the amenities of food and drink, clothing and houses, the reduction of the fantastic to the ordinary, we owe to Kittung.

In all he did to reform the world, Kittung is seen as generally benevolent. He teaches men the operations of agriculture and provides them with seed and plough-cattle. He shows them how to build houses, how to grow cotton and wear clothes, how to cook, how to extract wine from the palms. He is quickly moved by the sight of suffering: he takes pity on an abandoned bastard child; when he sees people sleeping on the damp ground, bitten by scorpions, their ears tortured by insects, 'he feels very sorry'. He decides that people must have cots, 'for if they have trouble like this,' he says, 'they will die. Men must be happy.' At a time of drought, he 'feels sad for the misery of men'.

Kittung is always ready to promote domestic happiness. He teaches a neglected wife to tickle her husband and excite him. He creates mosquitoes for no other purpose than to force a frigid wife into her husband's bed. He puts blood in the human body to prevent it drying up and make it capable of bearing children. He takes pity on the soul of an unmarried girl and sends her back as a tobacco plant, to be desired by all men.

Kittung does all he can to brighten the dull existence of mankind. He teaches boys and girls to dance. He persuades people to do their hair properly and look nice. He invents musical instruments to cheer the company at weddings and funerals. He makes frogs to clean the water of tanks and wells so that people will enjoy their baths.

He makes the first shaman to save men from the exactions of the spirits. He forces a witch to cure one of her victims.

Kittung is fond of animals. He gives dogs their tails and teaches them to recognize each other by their smell. He shows them how to avoid dangerous animals which would kill them. He makes horns for the buffalo so that the yoke will rest comfortably in place. He makes the cock a comb with a scarlet thread from his own loin-cloth. Although he teaches men to eat meat, he realizes what this will mean for the animals and warns them not to be too familiar with human beings but to keep them a little afraid.

A lover of trees, Kittung sits down and weeps when he sees the devastation caused by the Saoras' axes, and goes to a great deal of trouble to find the seeds of new trees to grow instead.

Kittung was always very good fun.[1] The first men seem to have regarded him with a sort of amused affection. When, in order to force

[1] 'In a certain sense these mythologies are a safeguard of reverence in that they provide a theme for humour and profanity and rough handling, which is thus expended, not on the sacred realities themselves, but on their shadows and images. Among certain savages, God's personal name is too holy to be breathed but in mysteries; yet His mythological substitute is represented to be as grotesque, freakish, and immoral as the Zeus of the populace. We can hardly enter into such a frame of mind, though possibly the irreverence and buffooneries of some of the miracle-plays of the middle ages are similarly to be explained as the rebound from the strain incident to a continual sense of the nearness of the supernatural . . . If we possessed a minutely elaborated history of the Good Shepherd and His adventures, or of the Prodigal's father, or of the Good Samaritan, interspersed with all manner of ludicrous and profane incidents, and losing sight of the original purport of the figure, we should have something like a mythology.'—G. Tyrrell, *The Faith of the Millions* (London, 1901), p. 268.

them to do their hair, he scattered on their heads a powder which would turn into lice, they thought it was just one of his little jokes and took no notice. Everyone was very amused at the discovery of Kittung's mermaid daughter, for they said he must have slept with a fish. He was always ready to join in the rough and tumble of boys and girls and once when the girls were throwing their hairs at the boys and screaming with merriment, he pranced about in the crowd sticking little bits of reed on the boys until they too had their bushes. It was also a tremendous joke, the day Kittung trod on one of the female organs which at that time used to go wandering about the streets on their own; it cried '*Cher-cher*' in fright and he turned it into a tortoise. But the best of the stories is the one about Kittung's tail.

In the days when men had tails, they used them to sweep the floor. But as the population increased, the tails got in the way, and at weddings and funerals people used to tread on each other's tails and trip over, and this caused a lot of amusement.

One day Kittung went to the Under World bazaar and found it crowded as usual. As he went round the stalls searching for some good tobacco, someone trod on his tail and he went sprawling on the ground. Unfortunately he fell against a stone and knocked out two of his front teeth. The whole bazaar roared with laughter and Kittung lost his temper. He picked up his own tail, pulled it out and threw it away. When the other tails saw this, they were frightened and they all of their own accord detached themselves and ran away. Kittung's own tail became the sago palm and the rest turned into the grass which is now used for making brooms.

Kittung is, of course, lacking in many of the attributes which the more highly developed religions have given to the Supreme Being. He is far from being omnipotent: he has to go to his Mahaprabhu to get light; he has to force a witch to cure her victim, but is not able to perform the cure himself; he makes bees, but he cannot control them. During a great epidemic, when corpses are littering the villages, he cannot stop the disease; all he can do is to provide a vulture as scavenger. He is not omniscient, for he does not know where grain is and has to send someone to look for it; he has to send a kite to see if there are any survivors of the great flood; he has to undertake a long and rather humiliating journey in search of goats; he makes tongues for men, but only after several mistakes; he is forgetful—he makes trees, but forgets the all-important *Bassia latifolia*. He is not omnipresent, for he is always shown as definitely located in some particular place, and people have to make long journeys to see him.

In many ways Kittung appears as a cult-hero of the type of Nanga Baiga or the Muria Lingo. He is a simple and thoroughly human person. He has his farm and his tobacco patch. He is greatly attached to his pig; he builds it a fine clean house and gives it a bed to sleep on. He is a true peasant, expert on the quality of seed and the best way to plough and thresh and winnow. He is a good cook, and not only does he teach mankind the art, but when his wife is in her period he himself does the cooking while she guards the crops. We see him with his wife going to their little hut on a mountain-side and sitting by the fire roasting cobs of maize.

Kittung's domestic life is hardly one which we would normally associate with a Supreme Being. We are not told the name of his wife or sisters, but we hear of a son Maru, a daughter Maderari, and the unfortunate child 'with the head of a girl and the body of a fish' who causes so much scandal that Kittung quietly puts her out of the way. Maderari makes an unfortunate marriage with a man who eats nothing but beef; the family cooks in a cow's skull, husks grain with a cow's leg, uses a cow's ear for a fan and a hoof as a bin; and Kittung refuses to have anything to do with her. Maru is murdered and his widow's tears fall to the ground as rain. Kittung's sister disgraces herself by becoming pregnant as a result of an affair with a rat.

Kittung's wife is obviously a very useful and knowledgeable woman, just the sort of wife that a not altogether omniscient Creator needs. After the creation of bees, which in Kittung's hands was rather a fiasco, his wife comes to the rescue and promises them food on condition that they do not bite her husband. She finds that Kittung has made the crab without any claws, so she makes them herself with her own pubic hairs. In the days when there was no such thing as menstruation or childbirth, she puts a lotus on a girl's head; it turns into a placenta and since then women have menstruated regularly. She makes the first necklaces, stringing marking-nuts on a cord of wild bean-vine, threading bits of goat's meat and scraps of roast liver on the entrails—transforming the unpleasant things into shiny red and black beads. She works very hard, even when she is pregnant, distributing grain to mankind. She gives away her own comb so that men will be able to do their hair.

Unfortunately the peace of the home is marred, not only by the discreditable conduct of his relatives, but by Kittung's own almost pathological jealousy. One day, when his wife brings water from a stream, a little red earth from the bottom of the pot sticks to her hair. Kittung decides that some young man has been throwing mud at her—this being a common tribal method of initiating an intrigue. Another day he quarrels with her so violently that she leaves the house, and it takes him a week to find her.

Significantly, it is Uyungsum who finally breaks up the home. Kittung's wife falls for this splendid god, with the flower of light 'strong and beautiful' in his hair, and whenever her husband goes to work in his swidden she flirts with him. But Kittung's little daughter watches and protests with tears, and one day the older woman loses her temper and kills the child. She tells Kittung that a snake has bitten her, but somehow he discovers the truth and drives his wife from the house. He has never, we are told, remarried.

The Saoras cannot create a perfect god. Uyungsum, the noble Sun-god who stands for truth and justice, pesters babies with fever and the aged with leprosy. Darammasum, whose very name means 'righteousness', gives leprosy and epilepsy to mankind. And Kittung's character, in some ways so admirable, is a *complexio oppositorum* and has a darker side.

At the very beginning, when he emerged from the gourd with his sister, he made grubs to devour trees, put insects in water and created disease. Later, finding that fowls had somehow escaped, he made special diseases for them with dirt scraped from his tongue. He cursed his favourite pig for eating excrement. He created the tiger to prevent human beings having too much happiness and freedom. He allowed his adopted daughter Rugaboi to take revenge on mankind by spreading smallpox. Although he first made snakes and scorpions without venom he changed his mind later and put dirt from his tongue on their fangs so that with the poison they became venomous, proud and haughty. He made weeds to prevent men growing rich and fearless.

These are not the actions of a wholly benevolent deity, though it might be argued on Kittung's behalf that his ultimate design was a moral one: to save men from falling into the evil of pride. Without disease, or tigers, snakes and scorpions, without weeds, human beings were becoming altogether too prosperous and were in danger of making themselves equal with the gods. Kittung was forced to put them in their place, however drastic and distasteful the means.

This may be so, but Kittung's own character too is not above reproach. He is hot-tempered and hasty. When the bastard child on whom he had taken pity as a baby grew up and sought a wife, he fell into a rage and turned him into a cock. He transformed another boy who offended him into a monkey. He raped the daughter of Ramma-Bimma, and when she refused to marry him he turned her into a dog. He refused to do anything for his daughter, so unhappily married to an eater of beef, and fearing defilement and 'thinking only of himself', deserted her. In a fit of temper he made the animals 'dumb as madmen'.

But on the whole, compared with other tribal heroes and even more with other tribal gods, Kittung is a kindly and even a noble figure. The benefits he confers on mankind far outweigh the evils, and even the evils may in the long run have been for good. If he created disease, at least he also made the shaman to fight it. If he made weeds, at least he taught men how to pull them up.

Kittung, then, is for many Saoras, and perhaps for all Saoras in certain moods, at least an approximation to a Supreme Being. But other gods, and in particular the Sun-god under his different names, are also given positions of pre-eminence. The situation is not unlike that in early Rigvedic times, when we see the seers and poets struggling to escape from a primitive polytheism to a fuller philosophy of life. 'The plurality of gods,' says a Hindu writer in the authoritative history, *The Vedic Age*, 'could not satisfy the intellect of the Rigvedic seers. One god was therefore identified with another, or gods were invoked in pairs or conjointly in groups of three or more. Systematization took the form of the classification of the gods into different categories or of the amalgamation of them all into one comprehensive group of the "All-gods". This systematization was but a step forward towards the more logical monotheism. There cannot be more than one supreme and unlimited being. The appearance of what Max Müller calls henotheism is due to this unconscious urge towards monotheism imperfectly moulding polytheistic tendencies and thus presenting an inconsistent picture. When "individual gods are alternately regarded as highest", a large number of attributes, personal characteristics, and functions become common to all the gods, the merging of all these qualities into one divine figure becomes easy, and thus polytheistic anthropomorphism evolves into a kind of spiritual monotheism.'[1]

I have quoted this passage at length, for it throws some light, I think, on the Saora situation. Although the Saoras are obviously very far away indeed from any kind of spiritual monotheism, there is already apparent the effect of the unconscious urge towards it, moulding, however imperfectly, their polytheistic tendencies. Individual gods are alternately regarded as highest and many of their attributes are already interchangeable. The very confusion of the present time is a sign that the Saoras are on the way to some sort of conception of a Supreme Being, even though they have a long way to go before their incipient henotheism turns into monotheism.

V. *The Saora Pantheon*

I NOW give a list, or catalogue, of Saora gods. In order to avoid any sort of classification not accepted by the Saoras themselves, I have arranged the names in alphabetical order. I have not included what I may call 'nonce-gods' of very restricted local cult, and I do not pretend to any kind of completeness. But the reader will find here all the chief *dramatis personae* in the theological histories—and tragedies—which I am to narrate later.

ABUSUM

Abun means a red ant, and this god is somehow connected with red ants. Abusum makes his home in a village, but never with more than one family, which thenceforth observes a taboo on eating red ants and has the duty of propitiating the god on behalf of the whole community. When Abusum is angry he makes the eyes of his victims red and painful as if they had been stung by ants, and he may also damage the ripening crops.

ADANGSUM

This is the kite-god—*adangan* in Saora is a kite. He is very dangerous; if he flies over a baby it may fall ill and 'cry like a kite'. When this happens, the parents place an old pot on the roof of their house; they make a bamboo model of a kite and sacrifice a brown cock before it, crying like kites as they do so.

ADUNUNKISUM

A form of Uyungsum, the Sun.

[1] V. M. Apte, 'Religion and Philosophy' in *The Vedic Age*, edited by R. C. Majumdar and A. D. Pusalker (London, 1951), p. 378.

AJADANG KITTUNG

According to one account, the mother of Ramma-Bimma. As Ajadangsum, she gives people headaches, but can be appeased with a fowl.

AJORASUM

A snake-god who lives in streams. Elaborate stories are told about him (see pp. 272ff.) and he has his own priests. He troubles pregnant women and babies, causing miscarriage and death. He has to be appeased by an elaborate ceremony which includes the sacrifice of a buffalo, for he himself, it is said, has the horns of a buffalo. His first priest, who had the body of a man but the pelt of a bear, was named Kurutameru-Arangtameru.

ALAMBASUM

Gives children fever and rickets. The cure is to pass the sick child under the belly of a cow and make appropriate offerings.

ALLARMANNESUM

A tutelary (Mannesum) who lives on the hill Allar, near Dantara. Local cult only.

ANGAJAN, ANGAIBOI

The Saora name for the Moon, who is regarded as the wife of the Sun. But when worshipped she is often addressed as Sandraboi, from the Sanskrit *chandra*.

ARENGSUM

Arengan is the menhir erected at the Guar ceremony. The Saoras sacrifice to Arengsum just before this stone is erected, but not at other times.

ARGATTA KITTUNG

Sometimes called the first of the Kittungs, and brother-in-law of the others. Hinduized Saoras identify him with Krishna.

ARSIBASUM

Arsin is a monkey, and Arsibasum is one of several monkey-gods. It is curious in view of their interest in monkeys that the Saoras have not adopted Hanuman into their pantheon, though they have accepted Rama and Sita.

ATTUNGSUM

A gourd of seed is preserved in every forest clearing. This god lives in the gourd and prevents insects spoiling the crops.

9. Girl spinning at Olleida

10. Saora woman ginning cotton at Liabo

11. Saora girl carrying plough

12. Ceremonial on threshing-floor at Sogeda

Photo: D. V. Sassoon

13. Saora youths at Tumulu

BABUSUM

One of the village deities; an Oriya-speaking Saora once described him to me as a '*grām-devata*'. At Sogeda he was said to be the husband of Karnosum, and the couple were identified with Ramma and Bimma, in spite of the fact that all four deities are male. Babusum is said to ride round a village at night, and if anyone hears the sound of his horse's hoofs he falls ill. He is worshipped with plantains, gourds and country sugar, and anything cooked for him must be in an aluminium, not an earthen, pot. In the ikons he is always shown riding on his horse.

BALUSUM

Ordinarily a hill-god, but in some places, owing to the likeness of the name to the common Oriya word for bear, he is regarded as the bear-god. Once, when the people of Liabo went to hunt, a bear mauled and killed one of them. The man's soul turned into Balusum who now seeks revenge; when he attacks someone his victim feels as if he was being mauled by a bear.

BANUMBASUM, BANUMSUM

Banumban or *banuman* is Saora for ant-hill. Tigers are everywhere associated with ant-hills; for example, when a man is killed by a tiger, the ghost is located in an ant-hill, and the mourners sacrifice a cock before it. It is said that when Banumbasum attacks a man, he feels sometimes 'as if he was being chewed by a tiger', sometimes as if he was being eaten by white ants, 'as if they had filled the body and were devouring it'. Banumbasum gives coughs, colds and sore throats; if sacrifice is made before an ant-hill, the 'ants' leave the body.

I recorded the following story at Burda. 'Long ago, Kittung's wife gave birth to a baby and her organs were greatly enlarged. When Kittung saw this he was frightened, and went to get some clay to make them smaller. He found an ant-hill and broke off a piece of the clay. He took it home and smeared it over his wife's parts. But the following day it dried and fell off. Kittung went back to the ant-hill to get some more, and found that the ants had already repaired the hole he had made. As he stood staring in astonishment at this, he put his hand in to break off another piece, but the ants bit him and Banumbasum caught his hand so that he could not withdraw it. Then Banumbasum said to him, "You are a fool; you know nothing. Just as our hole mended of its own accord, so if you wait three months, your wife's parts will mend of themselves." With this, Banumbasum let go of Kittung's hand, and Kittung said, "From today I shall honour you as a god, and I shall see that men do so also".'

BARABOI

A spirit who haunts pathways.

BARONGSUM

The word *barongan* is an archaic word meaning a high hill or mountain; it occurs in this sense in old songs. Barongsum is thus a hill-god, specially associated with the forest-clearings, whence he may send snakes or tigers if he is offended. He should be pacified with a white hen.

In some villages, however, Barongsum is better known for his attentions to young big-breasted girls. 'When he sees a breast round and lovely as a bael fruit, he is very happy.' When such a girl is troubled by him, the shaman should offer a silver ornament and five silver rupees, on a plantain leaf placed in a winnowing-fan, to the god on a path leading out of the village.

BARUSUM

A god of the hills and clearings, who is worshipped whenever a new clearing is made. Like other hill-gods he resents the invasion of his territory by cultivators and is easily offended.

BAYISUM

This is the god of madness, the name being derived from Oriya. He is blind, deaf, dumb and never eats. He is both male and female. If he attacks a man in his female form or a woman in his male form, there is no hope for the victim. But if he attacks someone of the same sex, there is a chance of recovery. Bayisum is sometimes called the messenger of Uyungsum.

BENASUM

A god of local cult living on a hill near Arangulu.

BIMMA

One of the Kittungs. He is probably identical with the Hindu Bhima or Bhimsen, honoured by tribes throughout Middle India as a rain-god. But the Saoras hardly ever mention Bimma except in the combination Ramma-Bimma, or at least in close association with Ramma, under whose name a full account will be found.

BIRADISUM

From the Telugu word *bidaru*, caravan. This god originally used to accompany caravans making their way into the Saora country from the plains; nowadays he may go with any group of travellers.

BODBODIYASUM

A local god who lives under a rock on a hill near Kankaraguda.

BOMERSUM

A bazaar-god who lives with the bullocks tethered at a market-place. When Saoras buy anything from a merchant, this god may follow them home and make them ill. As a precaution, a brown cock should be offered to him on the road leading from the bazaar.

BUBUJISUM

A god who makes the face swell and ache.

BUTTAMBOI

The spirit which is known elsewhere in India as Churel. The ghost of a girl who dies young and beautiful at the time of the menarche, she comes to men in dreams and saps their manhood.

DAIYU

Sitapati gives a list of Daiyus, whom he describes as 'superhuman beings'. He mentions Adongan-daiyu, the Daiyu with a body; Ajadang-daiyu, the Daiyu who is mature; Kandedeng-daiyu, the noisy Daiyu; Pattika-daiyu, a Daiyu who lives in a tree; Rana-daiyu, the golden Daiyu; Saron-daiyu, the corn Daiyu; Sudangar-daiyu, the Daiyu of the big stone. I myself have been unable to get confirmation of any of these and Sitapati himself admits that 'no definite information could be had about any of them or about the class in general'. The word *daiyu* may be connected with the Telugu *dayyam*, which is used in the classical literature for 'god', but now means 'ghost'.

DAKOSUNGBOI

A *dakosungboi* is a pregnant woman, hence someone who stays at home. Dakosungboi is thus a house-god, generally benevolent, who watches over a house. If someone steals, the god is said to come to the householder in a dream and report who it was.

DANGARASUM

A god who troubles women during delivery and may interfere with subsequent lactation unless he is pleased by sacrifice, in which case he can be very helpful.

DANUNKISUM

Also called Dakusum, Danudakisum and Dakosumboi. He is specially concerned with childbirth and the life of babies. If neglected or offended, he may cause a miscarriage, stop a mother's flow of milk or give a baby diarrhoea. There are various methods of cure, but the most popular is to tie an amulet of date-palm root or the bark of *Trewia nudiflora* round the child's throat.

DARAMMASUM, DARAMMABOI

One of several names for the Sun-god. The word is probably derived from the Sanskrit *dharma*, righteousness, and is used in ordinary speech to mean goodness, pity or kindness; to some extent Darammaboi is endowed with these qualities. The Sun-god is the witness of 'goodness, fate and sin'; he punishes 'sinners' with leprosy or epilepsy. Although he gives people headaches when he is hungry, 'he does not generally give very much trouble; he is merciful'. The curious confusion about the sex of the Sun, who in the myths is definitely male, the father of the stars, is resolved by some Saoras by the theory that the god should be addressed as Darammasum at the time of sacrifice, and as Darammaboi when taking an oath. To swear on Darammaboi is regarded as very binding, and in a quarrel the Saoras sometimes call on Darammaboi as a witness saying, 'Let the one at fault suffer!'

DARISUM

Dāri means a prostitute. Darisum is another name for Labosum, the Earth-god. If anyone falls ill while ploughing or hoeing, offerings are made to Labosum in the name of Darisum. For when the plough enters the earth it is as though one was copulating with her, and since the whole world does this, the earth is regarded as a prostitute who gives her favours to everyone. If a youth is betrothed and his girl dies, and he goes to betroth someone else, his girl's ghost follows him in the form of Darisum, and must be appeased, for since he is going to a second girl he has made the first a whore.

DINGARASUM

Offerings are made to this god when a party goes to another village to fetch home the bones of someone who has died abroad. But he is not honoured at other times.

DOBASUM

A rather mischievous god who stops the flow of sap from a palm, steals grain from a threshing-floor and sends snakes, bears and tigers to attack people on the way to their clearings. Crabs and eggs are offered to him, and the grain on the threshing-floor is protected against his attacks by winnowing-fans and ash-patterns.

DORISUM

A god of cattle-graziers. He gives fever and makes people very thin. An elaborate buffalo-sacrifice is made in his honour, and in some places he has a special shaman.

DRUGASUM

The Hindu goddess Durga. In some villages a shrine is built for her outside the boundary, and offerings are made there to check the attacks of dysentery which she is believed to cause.

DUBBASUM

Dubbasum is the ghost of a girl who has died during her menstrual period. Her touch spoils the products of the *Bassia latifolia* tree, making them smell unpleasantly.

DUMASUM

This is the Oriya version of Idaisum, the deified dead.

EDANGSUM

Edang is to cut fuel, and Edangsum is the god of wood cut for fuel. He is also the god of the funeral pyre. When angry, he attacks little children and makes their bodies burning hot and their faces 'white as a burnt corpse'.

ERDANASUM

A god who causes wounds.

ETTANG–JAMBUSUM

Ettang is a dialect form of *atangliyan*, a cow, and Jambu (Jamma) is the god of the dead. Ettang-Jambusum is thus the god of the dead to whom cows are sacrificed. 'When this god catches hold of a man's soul, he beats it and gives great pain to the body, but when a cow is offered the pain is eased.'

GABALDATUNGBOI

Jaliyasum's wife. She is represented by two bits of wood with peacock's feathers on the veranda of a house. She makes babies cry.

GADALSUM

Gadalsum is the god of thatching grass; it is taboo to cut this before the annual sacrifice at the Festival of Red Gram. When offended Gadalsum gives toothache, but this can be cured if one makes a little grass doll and offers it to him with a pig outside the village.

There are two stories about the origin of Gadalsum. The first comes from Dantara. 'In the old days there was no special sacrifice connected with cutting grass. The people just went to get it after they had finished the Red Gram Festival. But one year the priest of Dantara found that he did not get very good grass then, so he went before the Festival instead. Barusum was annoyed at this, and sent a tiger to attack him. The priest ran to a cave, and managed to get his head inside, but his legs stuck out. The tiger ate him up to the waist. What was left turned into Gadalsum.'

The other story is from Tumulu. 'One day, long ago, when the peasants went to cut grass, a very old man went with them. After cutting it, they tied the grass in bundles and went on their way, but the old man lagged behind and was lost in the forest. A tiger found him and he was running for his life when he cut his foot on the sharp grass. Gadalsum was born from the blood and frightened the tiger away. The old man went home. The people went again for grass, but now when they tried to lift up their bundles they found themselves stuck to the grass, stuck just as they were, bending down.[1] The old man went to find his son, who was one of the grass-cutters, and found everybody stuck to his bundle. He was a shaman and he divined the cause—that Gadalsum demanded food-sacrifice. He offered a pig, whereupon the people at once stood up and took their bundles home.'

GADELSUM, GADEJANGBOI

These are names for the Sun-god, and stress his creative power. Sitapati has an interesting note on the meaning of the words.[2] *Gadel* means 'to come about', 'to evolve', and in its causative form is often used in the sense of 'to create'. *Jangan* is an old Kol-Munda word found not only in Saora, but also in Santali, Mundari and Birhori. 'It is used in many senses, including seed, kernel, stone of fruit, bone, wood, fibres, stalk, etc. *Jangadan* is an old Saora word used in

[1] In a Muria story, Lingo Pen indicates his wishes by making a bundle of grass stick to a girl's head.—Verrier Elwin, *The Muria and their Ghotul* (Bombay, 1947), p. 248.

[2] Sitapati, 'The Soras', *J.A.H.R.S.*, vol. XIII, p. 131.

incantations to mean "life". The word *jang* in the compound Gadejang may, therefore, be understood to mean life-giving seed or essence.'

Whether Sitapati is justified in inferring from this that Gadelsum is the Supreme Creator may be doubted, for she does not appear in this sense in any of the myths, and in actual practice Gadejangboi appears as a god who wanders about troubling little children. She is associated with various rocks where she is supposed to rest on her travels, and ikons are made on them to please her. On the other hand, she is worshipped to avert barrenness, and is said to make the bones of a child in the womb. At an Ajorapur ceremony, the shaman addressed her, saying, 'You brought us into being'. We may, therefore, accept the fact that Gadejangboi has a creative function without implying that she is the creator of the world.

GADESUM

A lame god, very bad-tempered, who cannot be influenced by sacrifice. He attacks babies, making them lame even while they are in the womb.

GAJJISUM

Gajjin is itch. The actual giver of itch is Uyungsum, but offerings to cure it are made to Gajjisum, who passes them on to the higher deity.

GALBESUM

In most places, but not in all, Galbesum is associated with Jaliyasum and with Jaliyasum's emblem, the peacock. If a man is attacked by Galbesum, he dreams of peacocks and 'his soul flies up like a peacock into a tree'. After a death from this cause, the shade demands peacock feathers at the funeral, and a peacock hunt is a feature of the Limma ceremony. Wherever a pot is dedicated to Galbesum or Jaliyasum, peacock feathers are tied to it. If neglected, Galbesum may give the cattle foot and mouth disease.

GANGAMALLA

Malla in Sanskrit is a wrestler. Gangamalla and Surmalla are said to be the messengers of the god of death. Gangamalla, who lives in the sky, takes away the souls of those who die by hanging, accident or murder. Surmalla, who lives 'below', takes to the Under World the souls of those who die of other causes.

GANONROYALSUM

This god is associated with the eaves (*ganonroyalan*) of a house. Sometimes a child reaches three or four years without being able to walk. Then the sacrifice of a fowl and rice offered on a *kurlu* leaf below the eaves to Ganonroyalsum may mend matters.

GANURSUM, GANURBOI

The god, or goddess, of rain. The Saoras sacrifice to her both to increase and to lessen the rainfall. At Barasingi the people described how in time of drought they make a special pilgrimage to the Madiabur Hill where Madia Kittung lives and sacrifice a buffalo to Ganurboi. They believe that as they eat the sacrificial feast, the rain will begin to fall.

GARANNASUM, GARNADASUM

The god of the threshold (*garannan*) who prevents hostile gods or ghosts from entering a house; if a sorcerer tries to enter a place under his protection he will be sure to bang his head against the door. At Dantara, Garannasum was regarded as the 'Inspector' of the gods, who went round to check the supply of rice in the dedicated pots.

GARSADA KITTUNG

One of the original Kittung brothers.

GAYARA–BULLU

A goddess who, unless properly appeased, interferes with a woman's delivery.

GIREJANGSUM

A house-god who gives children rickets.

GORUSUM

The god of the Gour graziers and hence, like Dorisum, of all graziers. He is represented by a small pot suspended in the cowshed by a cord woven from the hair of a cow's tail. If offended he attacks both cattle and their owner.

GUNGUSUM

A hill-god who lives in a cave on Gungu Hill, above Keradang. He is lord of all the animals of his forest; he also controls the rain. From time to time, when food is scarce or the rains fail, the men of twelve villages unite under the leadership of the Chief of Sogeda for a special hunt on Gungu Hill. They do not call this a hunt but a *dandān*, a fee or levy, which implies that they are begging for a gift from the gods. In each village, the shamans shout, 'Tomorrow we go for *dandān*; before we start let no woman fetch water, let no one clean the streets'. The next day, fasting and abstinent, the leading shaman of Sogeda offers rice and wine to Gungusum and blows his horn 'to attract the animals'. Then they go for the hunt. It is said that if an arrow so much as grazes an animal on this day it will fall. When this happens, the shaman runs to it, cuts off the tail, chops it up and roasts it over a little fire. He offers it to Gungusum, sitting by the animal's head. Only then do the people take the carcass home. If they fail to make the offering of the tail, the animal, they say, will get up and escape. A successful hunt is expected to bring rain that very day.

GUSADAJNOD

This is one of the three Jnonadanji, supernatural beings of whom little is known, but who are regularly invoked by the shamans and appear to be on the whole benevolent. The others are Panosijnod and Kusalijnod.

IDAISUM

The deified dead, the ancestors.

ILDASUM

A common name for a tutelary. In some villages, however, Ildasum is a malignant and dangerous demon. At Dariambo, for example, I was told that the Ildasum there was a cannibal who came in the form of a great crab to devour men.

ILINBONGSUM

The rainbow-god. If he appears during an epidemic, it is generally believed that he has come to indicate that the worst is over.

INDARAIKA KITTUNG

A Kittung, probably named after the Hindu sky-god Indra.

INTANGSUM

A god who causes swelling of the hands and feet. He should be offered a cow, but since he is not of great importance, 'an old one will do'.

JAGANTHA KITTUNG

Sometimes described as a grandson of Ramma-Bimma.

JAGDUMBASUM

A cannibal god. He has a great head, long hair, small hands and feet, but nails like a tiger's claws. He lives in dried-up streams and in caves. If he catches a man, he at once eats the flesh raw. He sometimes comes in dreams and makes people ill. He is offered a toy gun made of date-palm wood.

JAKERSUM

This is a Kond god worshipped in the Saora villages which border on the Kond country to the north. In Kui, *jakeri* means a patriarch, or founder of a village. He is said to have been born under a stone in a river and is the same as Darni Pinnu, Mother Earth. At Ladde he was the object of a special cult: there was a circular stone shrine for him inside the village, and the priest sacrificed three times a year, at the main Harvest Festivals.

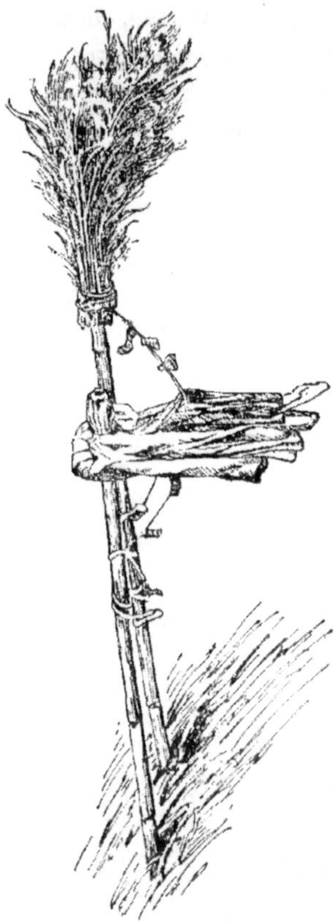

FIG. 5 Symbol of Jaliyasum on the roof of a shaman's house

JALIYASUM

This god seems to have lost something of his former importance, for Fawcett—writing of 1887—describes him as 'the most widely known, very malevolent, always going about from one Saora village to another causing illness or death; in some places said to eat people. Feared and receives most attention. Almost every illness that ends in death in three or four days is attributed to Jaliya's malevolence.'[1] Fawcett describes sacrifices made to Jaliya at the Mango Festival and says that in 1887 shrines were built to him inside villages for the first time. He concludes, 'There are a few villages in or near which there are no Jaliya erections; the people saying that Jaliya does not trouble them, or that they don't know him. In one village where there was none, the Saoras said there had been one, but they got tired of Jaliya, and made a large sacrifice with numerous goats and fowls, burnt his temple and drove him out. Jaliya, like any other

[1] Fawcett, p. 242.

Saora, is fond of tobacco. Near one village is an upright stone in front of a little Jaliya temple, by a path-side, for passers-by to leave the ends of their cheroots for Jaliya.'

Francis, writing in 1907, also says that 'the hill Saoras chiefly fear the deity Jaliya, who in many villages is provided with a small habitation with a circular thatched roof in which are placed wooden images of household implements and requisites and figures of men, animals and birds'.[1]

It seems likely that in the past fifty years many villages have 'got tired of Jaliya', for today his cult has dwindled and he is known simply as one of many malicious deities who disturb the Saora home. I have seen a few ikons, but only one shrine, in his honour; at Luangpadar, there was a large bunch of peacock feathers tied with bits of cloth and leaves to a pole which was stuck in the roof of the priest's house. In this village I was told that Jaliyasum was the chaprasi of Jammasum, the god of death. Jammasum does not himself come to fetch souls away; he sends his chaprasis who, like all chaprasis, cause far more trouble than their master. At the Harvest Festivals Jaliyasum's pole is brought out and carried round in the dance. It is washed with turmeric water and offered fish and rice. At Jamudia village, I found a wooden snake in Jaliyasum's shrine; the shaman dances with this on ceremonial occasions.

JAMBUMDASUM

Also called Assumdasum. A sky-god who gives people sore eyes.

JAMMASUM

This god, whose name is derived from the Sanskrit Yama, god of death, is probably a recent importation, for little is known of him, and in fact the Saora theory of death does not require a special god; there are already many other agents of mortality. There is a story which associates him with the origin of sorcery, and he is worshipped to make a barren woman fertile, presumably with the idea that he who takes away life should also give it. But Jammasum and his chaprasis do not fit properly into the Saora picture of the Under World; the idea has not yet been assimilated.

JAMMOLSUM

The god of seed (*jammolan*). Before removing his seed from the store for sowing, a householder must perform the appropriate ceremonies described at pp. 315ff.

[1] W. Francis, *Vizagapatam District Gazetteer* (Madras, 1907), p. 26.

JANANGLOSUM

A village god worshipped at Dariambo, where a sort of stone box was made for him.

JARASUM

A hill-god. There is a story that Jarasum used to keep a male buffalo. It grew very strong and fat, and one day it strayed away into a village at the foot of the hills. The people thought it would be a good thing to mate such a fine animal with their own cattle, but they found that every she-buffalo it covered died. They decided to kill it, and cooked and ate the flesh. This greatly angered the god and ever since he has been a menace to young children.

JATTARASUM

Yatra in Sanskrit means 'pilgrimage' and Jattarasum is a god vaguely associated with the rare pilgrims who enter the Saora hills.

JAYODENSUM

A snake-god, distinguished by the red crest on its head, who lives on the banks of streams. He is specially dangerous to young children and must be appeased by a special and expensive ceremony, the Jayodenpur. For a full account see pp. 275ff.

JEMRA KITTUNG

A long story about Jemra Kittung and his wife Sidibiradi is recited at the Jammolpur ceremony (see pp. 316ff.).

JORABASUM

A river-god who takes the form of a snake. He attacks babies, and it is said that the fontanelle is due to Jorabasum who knocks a bit of bone down into the skull.

JUMTANGBUR KITTUNG

This is a Kittung who lives on the hill Jumtangbur in the Gumma Mutta. He is a beef-eater, and in the old days, whenever cattle went to graze on the hill, he used to steal them. When the people realized what was happening, they began cow-sacrifices for the safety of their herds and the fertility of their crops, and the Kittung was satisfied with one cow a year instead of two or three a week.

KACHHINOSUM

This god lurks by the roadside, and whenever he sees a mother taking her children with her as she goes to the forest for roots or firewood, he attacks them with fever.

KADUSUM

A blind god who lives in hills where there is a lot of thatching-grass. Since he is blind (*kadun*) he does not often manage to catch people, but when he does he makes them blind too.

KAMBUTUNG (KITTUNG)

The very dangerous bear-god. Anyone killed by a bear turns into Kambutung, and then attacks the living; he comes first in the form of a bear, and then turns into a whirlwind which sweeps round the victim and so kills him. He is supposed to lurk in bushes near some path which leads from a village to the forest; when he attacks a man, blood flows from the nose, mouth and ears. Sacrifice must be offered immediately on the path or the man will die. Many people, however, believe that there is no hope for anyone attacked by this Kittung.

At Sogeda I was told that Kambutung's special function was to guard the road to the Under World, and to prevent the shades of the newly dead from descending thither.

KANCHEDSUM

There is a tradition that in the old days the Saoras offered human sacrifice to this god.

KANENGSUM

He gives sores and boils, very bad ones, for it is said that nothing can be done about them.

KANNISUM

A very dangerous god who causes epilepsy. He is said to have 'come down from the sky'. According to Fawcett, he lives in big trees, and such trees are never cut in groves which he is supposed to haunt.[1]

KANTIARSUM

This god gives people rheumatism. He is commonly represented by an old ploughshare which is erected on the veranda of the sufferer's house.

KARNOSUM

In some villages this god is believed to be female and is then called Karnoboi and said to be the wife of Patha Munda. At Busabo, the Saoras said that Karnoboi was 'of good caste', a Hindu, though her

[1] Fawcett, p. 244.

husband was a Saora. As a Hindu she refused to enter the village because there were pigs in it and the people sacrificed cows and buffaloes. She had therefore a little shrine outside where she received offerings from the passers-by. She used to stop and interrogate any strange god wishing to enter the village.

But in many villages Karnosum is regarded as male, the son of Gadelsum, and is sometimes regarded as a Kittung. I have even heard him described as the greatest of the gods, but this belief is not widely held.

KARSADA KITTUNG

The Kittung of the east, as Muara Kittung is the Kittung of the west. From time to time, some Saoras offer eggs to them to ensure their assistance at sunrise and sunset.

KARUDSUM

This god, it is said, was born in a black-plum tree among monkeys, and he himself looks like a little monkey. When he attacks anyone, he makes him look wizened as a monkey.

KETTARAJI–KETTARGUMI

According to one, but only one, tradition, the father of the Kittungs and creator of the world.

KIMENGSUM

A god of seed and the growing seedlings. Probably the same as Jammolsum.

KINCHESUM

This is a Kond god: it is said that *kinche* means Kond. I found his cult in such villages as Dariambo, Sundruba and Sinkulipadar, where Saoras have migrated into Kond territory. The special priest of Kinchesum is called, in Kond fashion, the Janni. Custom varies; in some places a black goat is sacrificed to him every third year; in others Kinchesum is worshipped twice every year, once before sowing and again at one of the harvest festivals.

At Sundruba Kinchesum was associated with the *Bassia latifolia* tree. If anyone eats the fruit of this tree before the annual sacrifice has been made to the god, Kinchesum may give him white watery swellings that look like the corollae of the tree. On the other hand, if the god is pleased, he makes the trees give abundant crops of flowers and fruit.

KINNADASUM

The tiger (*kinnan*) of the water (*dān*) god, in other words the crab.[1] He lives in streams and attacks people while they are bathing. Crabs are sacrificed to him.

KINNALOSUM

Kinnalosum lives in a stream between two rocks. If anyone drinks water there, he slips into the belly with the water and makes it ache. Anyone, it is said, can recognize the symptoms; there is no need to go to a shaman. The cure is a sacrifice of crabs.

KINNASUM

The tiger-god. When a man is killed by a tiger, after his menhir has been erected with special Guar rites, his ghost turns into Kinnasum and goes to live with Banumbasum in an ant-hill. Kinnasum's attacks are very virulent. 'You feel as if you were being torn by a tiger's claws,' said one informant; 'it is as though you were being pierced by thorns, and your body aches as from a good flogging,' said another. When Kinnasum enters a house, the first thing he does is to put his paw on the pot of gruel simmering on the hearth; at once it begins to stink, and must be thrown away. If there is no pot on the fire, he touches one of the store-bins, and the grain is spoilt.

FIG. 6 Image of Kittung in a shrine at Karanjaju 18″ *high*

KITTUNG

In Saora the word *kittung* means 'god': so does the Gutob *kituon* and the Remo and Pareng *kittung*. There is no point in Saora theology about which there is more confusion. Although it is generally agreed that there are a number of divine beings called the Kittungs, in ordinary talk—and particularly in the myths—the word is used in the singular, as if there was only one. No one can agree on how many Kittungs there are, who they are, or which of them is the most important. Sitapati gives the names of eleven Kittungs—

Argatta	Jodebulla or Jodepulu	Ramma
Bimma	Mutta	Rungrung
Garsada	Peda or Pedramadtung	Tete
Jagantha		Tumanna

To these he adds the names of their sisters, Sidibiradi and Sitaboi.[2]

[1] See *TMO*, pp. 235ff. [2] Sitapati, 'The Soras', *J.A.H.R.S.*, vol. XIII, p. 122.

I have recorded a number of lists which show considerable variation. At Kankaraguda I was given a catalogue of no fewer than twenty-one Kittungs, completely different from Sitapati's, but I found that the Saoras of this village called their hill-gods Kittung and that their list was simply one of all the hills in the neighbourhood. At Dantara, in the Gumma area, the Saoras knew of seven Kittungs:

Garsada	Ranadiu
Indaraika	Sunaraika
Kuraitu	Udurkuara
Maddia	

These, I was told, were the chief Kittungs, the original seven brothers. They had seven sons:

Jagantha	Rungrung
Jodebulla	Tumanna
Mutta	Yete-tete
Pedramadtung	

At Pattili, in the Pottasingi valley, the Saoras knew of these:

Argatta	Jodebulla
Bimma	Labosum
Garsada	Peda
Jagantha	Ramma
Kuraitu	Sitaboi

In Sogeda I was told that Uyungsum and Darammasum were Kittungs and elsewhere I have heard Jammasum called a Kittung.

Finally at Taburda a shaman gave me a descriptive list of sixteen Kittungs:

Alangtung, who made the grass
Alotung, who makes the streams flow (*alon*)
Anebtung, who made the trees (*aneban*)
Arengtung, who made the rocks (*arengan*)
Arumotung, who swallows men (*mo-*)
Barutung, who made the mountains and hills (*barun*)
Ganurtung, who gives rain (*ganuran*)
Jammatung, who causes death
Kinorai Kittung, who made the Under World
Kuraitung, the greatest, who gave birth to all
Labo Kittung, the earth

Ramma-Bimma, who made all living creatures
Ringetung, who makes the winds (*ringen*) blow
Ruangtung, the sky (*ruāngan*)
Talobatung, who made the great rocks (*tālān* is a stone)
Uyungan Kittung, the Sun.

Kuraitu, as in the above list, is often said to be the greatest of the Kittungs: the name refers to the hollow gourd in which a boy and girl survived the Deluge; there are stories of how he created the world and all mankind. But at Sogeda I was told that the greatest Kittung was the earthworm, who is the symbol of Labosum, for earth comes from it, and it made the world and all things. Others again say that Ramma-Bimma, often mentioned as a single individual, is the greatest, and there are stories of a Kittung Mahaprabhu who is worshipped by the other Kittungs. Finally there is a god called Kittungsum, who seems to be a sort of collective deity, in whom all the other Kittungs are included. Shrines are made for him, and he is worshipped at the greater festivals. Oaths are taken on his name, and he behaves very much like any other of the Saora gods.

The Kittungs are much more human in character than the other gods, and for this reason they appear—either under their individual names or called simply 'Kittung'—as the heroes of many stories. Indeed, Sitapati considers that they are 'deified heroes or demigods in human form', and he records a tradition that they came originally from 'Orissa-Maindura', which is probably the Mahendra Hill near Mandasa in the Ganjam District. The Kittungs lived in the Saora country for a long time and then went away to the Basengdesa, the salt-country or the sea-coast. I have not been able to verify this, and the Saoras I have consulted deny that the Kittungs have left their country except in the sense that their real home is 'above', somewhere in the sky.

KONDASUM

A Kond god worshipped by Saoras living on the borders of the Kond territory. He is a drinker of human blood, but this the Saoras refuse to give, offering him pig's blood instead.

KUDASUM

This is the god of the hearth (*kudan*); he is also known as Togisum—*togin* is Saora for fire. If he is neglected, he may set fire to a house and inflame the eyes.

KUKKUSUMBOI

Kukkun is Saora for a cough. Kukkusumboi, therefore, is the goddess who gives people coughs and, in severe cases, pneumonia. Sacrifices are made to Uyungsum to effect a cure.

KUKUDANSUM

A god whose cult seems to be confined to the neighbourhood of Sundruba village. He first manifested himself by killing five children in one family.

KUMBIRSUM

A forest-god who gives leprosy and yaws.

KURAITUNG

This, sometimes called the greatest of the Kittungs, is said to have made the sun, moon and world. There is a curious idea that the high position given to the sun in Saora theology is due to a mistake. 'When men were first created, they could not see Kuraitu Kittung on account of the glare of the Sun, and so they supposed that the Sun was the greatest god and honoured him instead.' Kuraitu taught men that it was taboo for them to drink milk and gave them palm wine instead.

KURASUM

A god of fire. He makes men vomit and causes their hands and feet to swell.

KURTISUM

A hill-god who lives on Deogiri.

KUSALIJNOD

Kusali is the vegetable *Luffa aegyptica*, and the bodies of those attacked by the god are supposed to take its shape. Kusalijnod also causes anaemia, jaundice and great septic wounds.

LABOSUM

The Earth-god, sometimes regarded as male, sometimes as female. He is worshipped at most agricultural ceremonies for the fertility of the soil. For a fuller account, see pp. 298f.

LAMBUSUM

A god of the forest clearings. If he is offended, he is like 'an insect which eats paddy' and quickly destroys a crop. A rite which involves the impaling of a pig, called Lambapur, is performed for him.

LANKASUM

Lankan is the Saora word meaning 'above', the sky. Lankasum, who is often identified with the sun, is thus god of the sky and has a creative function. 'In his hands are bones, flesh and blood. He is the giver of children.' But he is also a menace to children, and to pregnant women, and if one meets him on the way to get wood or water, he may attack one's eyes.

LURNISUM, LURNIBOI

A deity of indeterminate sex, sometimes called Lurniboi, who shares with Rugaboi and Yuyuboi the odium of giving smallpox to the world. He is usually worshipped in small stone shrines. For a detailed account, see pp. 286ff.

MADASUM

A god of the loft (*mādān*) which in Saora houses is built to accommodate the grain-bins.

MADUSUM

A god who gives leprosy. He is also called Muttasum—the word *mutta* is used of anything that is mutilated.

MAKRISUM

Makrin is the Saora word for a small red-faced monkey. When this god attacks a baby, it grows thin and develops red spots on its face and cries like a baby monkey. Known only in the north, round Dariambo.

MAMMOSUM

A god who causes sores.

MANDUASUM

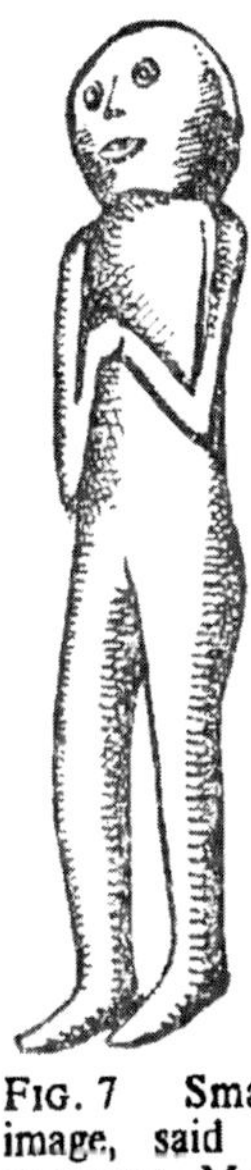

FIG. 7 Small image, said to represent Manduasum, in a shrine at Karanjaju
16″ high

God of the *sadru*-shrine, which is also known as *mandua* (from Sanskrit *mandapa*). He is called Manduasum when he settles inside a village, and Tangorbasum when he has his shrine outside. The distinguishing characteristic of his cult is that he has a 'merry-go-round' type of shrine. A single pole supports an umbrella-like roof, and this pole is in two pieces, a peg at the bottom of the upper shaft fitting into a slot in the lower, so that the roof can be whirled round. At festivals, the shamans seize the roof and, while dancers and drummers move about them, they revolve it as rapidly as they can, thus affording (so they say) the god much pleasure.

At Mandidi an ancestor told the villagers: 'Manduasum is the great friend of the dead. We want to entertain him. Build a shrine that will go round and round.'

At Ladiguda, the Saoras said that Manduasum was a newcomer to their village, for he had come from the Serango hills. 'Formerly', they said, 'we did not know of him. Then one day he came from Serango with many other gods and a great noise of drums and trumpets. The gods went round and round, dancing round the village. Only the shaman could see them and he said that they looked like little dolls about an arm's length in height. The next day we all fell ill. The shaman sent the other gods away by sacrificing on the roadside, but he said that we must make a shrine for Manduasum inside the village and that the roof must go round and round in memory of the way the gods danced round the village.'

MANGDARASUM

The Tuesday god. But in most villages he is the god of only one Tuesday in the year, the Tuesday of the week in which seed is brought out for sowing before the rains. If he is offended, he gives a man itch.

MANNESUM

In Saora *mānne* means to be docile and obedient. Thus the Mannesum, of whom there are many, are spirits who are helpful to mankind. The word is sometimes used as synonymous with Sedasum or Ildasum, when it means a tutelary. These gods are invoked at the beginning of nearly all communications between a shaman and the unseen world.

In villages round Abbasingi and Angda there is a special cult of Mannesum. He lives, I was told, in the sky; he is like a Bissoyi and has papers on which the names of all men are written. His clerk is Dobasum, his chaprasis are the Ildasums. The shamans chosen by him are the most powerful of all.

MAPRUSUM

From the Sanskrit Mahaprabhu, title of the great Jagannath of Puri. The cult of this god, so popular throughout Orissa, is slowly penetrating the hill country. At Olleida, I found Maprusum located by the side of a path, and anyone bringing food into the village had to offer him a share on pain of falling ill.

MARDISUM

The name is derived from the Telugu word for cholera. Mardisum, I was told at Tumulu, 'eats human flesh. He enters into a man's body and eats it away from the inside; you can tell what is happening from the blood in his excreta'. Sorcerers can send Mardisum to trouble a village and rob its palm trees. He may also attack fowls, causing them to moult.

MERIAHSUM

Meriahsum is the god of human sacrifice, *meriah* being the word both for the victim and the rite. The Saoras probably never practised human sacrifice (for a fuller discussion of this, see pp. 494ff.) but they evidently regarded it as a solemn and important matter, one which placed the Konds very definitely in a superior position in relation to the supernatural. And whether or no anyone now pays him his proper tribute, the Meriah god remains supreme ruler of the hills to the north of the Saora country. When therefore Saoras wish to migrate to the north, they have to be very careful, for—as I was told at Dokripanga —'it is the Kond land, not ours. So when we want to settle anywhere, we must first get permission from the Konds and their gods, and only afterwards from Government. It is the Konds, not the forest guards, who give us permission to make clearings in the jungle. So to please the Konds, we sacrifice a cow and a pig every year for Meriahsum and the Kond ancestors, so that they will not torment us, and we all share the feast.'

At Ladiguda, I was told that ten years previously there had been a Kond hamlet near the site of the present Saora village. The Konds moved on somewhere and the Saoras took their place. 'Then Meriahsum began to trouble us. We called the Konds to help and they told us to put up a wooden pillar in the place where the old Kond pillar used to be, and to sacrifice a buffalo there every third year.' In Karanjaju, the Saoras described how when they first settled there Meriahsum ruined their crops. He came upon the shaman and said, 'This is the Kond country. You have no business here. But if you worship me I will see that all goes well with you.'

MIDDIASUM

Middiaburan, or Madiaburan, is the Saora name for Deogiri (about 4,600 feet), the sacred mountain to the north of Parlakimidi, sometimes described as the roof of the world. Middiasum or Madia Kittung is one of the many deities who live there. Indeed the Kittungs were born on this mountain and spread thence throughout the Saora hills.

Of the first seven Kittung brothers, the youngest was Middia or Madia (also called Mutta). He got this name because he was conceited, idle and a leper. As he grew up, the other brothers used to grumble saying, 'We do all the work and he just sits and eats'. And one day they said to him, 'Go and work in the clearings. If you won't work, we won't give you food.'

But when they reached the clearing, the brothers thought, 'How can this diseased fellow do any work? We'd better let him cook for us instead.' So when they came to a stream, they sat him down under a mango tree and said, 'You cook our food and we'll go to work. When we've finished, we'll come back for our dinner.'

Off they went and Middia began to cook. He prepared the gruel and herbs, but there was no salt—for salt had not yet been discovered. He wondered how he could make the food tasty, and he took some pus from his wounds and put it in. When the six brothers came for their dinner they thought it delicious. 'Our mother never cooked like this.'

This went on for some days. Then one morning the eldest brother hid behind a tree to discover the secret of Middia's cooking. When he saw him put the pus into the food, he was very angry. He called the others and they killed the boy. They threw his body away in the Basengdes, the salt country. His soul turned into Middiasum, and his pus and bones became salt, and the people of that land grew rich through trading in it.

Middiasum or Madiasum is thus the giver of leprosy. He is still proud and conceited. He stops the rain from falling and the Saoras living below Deogiri have to sacrifice to him if they would have good crops. He lives between three great rocks, and from time to time these fall over or go crooked as a sign that he is angry. To straighten them, the Saoras offer milk and wine.

MOKROSUM

A god who attacks the throat, making it dry and swollen.

MUTTATUNG

Another name for the leprous Kittung, Middiasum—*muttan* is a leper.

ORISSA–MANJORASUM

The god of Puri. He is represented in ikons as two men with a woman between them, an obvious reflection of the images of Jagannath.

ORUBSUM

God of the evening (*oruban*). If anyone gets fever regularly in the evening, it is supposed that Orubsum is causing it. But he is not a vindictive or greedy god, and a little rice and wine is generally sufficient to satisfy him.

OSARASUM

This god lives in the *osara* tree, and gives people bad headaches.

OSMAIDARULI

Kittung's wife, who gives magic 'medicines' to be used in sorcery.

OYJNODSUM

When peasants go to their fields, they honour Oyjnodsum to avoid backache. His emblem is a small pot placed upside down on the handle of an old plough fixed on a veranda floor.

PANDAI

According to one tradition, Pandai was the daughter of Ramma-Bimma and sister of the first seven Kittungs. She married the horned snake Sarapunda-Tikapunda (who is the same as Ajorasum). He was murdered by his brothers-in-law, but Pandai restored him to life.

PANGUNASUM

This god, whose name is derived from the Oriya word for sorcery, lives on Panguna Hill near Kankaraguda. He is the helper and guide of practitioners of black magic. He appears to the sorcerer in dreams, first in the form of a tiny green chilli, then as a pig. See also pp. 234f.

PANOSIJNOD

He is worshipped at Harvest Festivals with Gusadajnod. But whereas Gusadajnod receives sacrifice publicly from the priest, Panosijnod is honoured by individual householders in the privacy of their own homes.

PATHA MUNDA

A god of lofty but rather restricted reputation. In 1943, at Bodo Okhra I found many small wooden figures; they were said to represent Patha Munda and Galbesum, who had created the world. They were worshipped at the Harvest Festivals and before the forest was cleared for cultivation.

PIDAJNOD–KARNOSUM

A god who looks 'grand as a Raja'. He is highly esteemed at Dantara.

PINDASUM

God of the veranda (*pindan*).

PUDOISUM

The god of the *pudoi* (Hindi, *gui*) tree. Should a man's first children die, then if his wife conceives again, the shaman dedicates a pot to Pudoisum. If this child survives, the shaman takes him when he is about four years old to the *pudoi* tree and makes him salute it.

PUNGPUNGDASUM

Dān is the Saora for water; *pung-pung* is to be bloated. Pungpungdasum is thus the god who makes a man bloated with water; in other words, he gives people dropsy.

RADAJTUMMADSUM

A spirit whose eyes burn like live coals.

RAMMA

Traditionally Rama and Sita visited the country of the Saoras during their exile; they were hospitably received by Sabari and Rama treated her with honour. It is doubtful, however, how far the Ramma of the Saora pantheon is to be identified with the hero of the *Ramayana*. Knowledge of the great epic was spread in Orissa by Ramats who came on pilgrimage to Puri, but they were few in number and the cult of Rama, which had to compete with the powerful influence of Chaitanya and his disciples, and the far more popular worship of Radha-Krishna, has not been of major importance in this part of India.[1] The Saora Ramma is a Kittung; he is nearly always coupled with Bimma, in the expression Ramma-Bimma, of whom he is alternately the brother, sister or wife. Sitaboi is also a Kittung, but is described as Ramma's sister, not his wife.

But Ramma-Bimma are of great importance. It was from them that the Saora tribe was born, indeed some say that from them came all mankind. Ramma is but another name for Labosum: he is the earth, while Bimma is the sky. Ramma-Bimma established Saora custom and taught the people how to live well. They invented tobacco; they taught men and women how to love; they discovered fire; at one time they ruled the world. It is possible that where the word 'Kittung' is used in the myths without further qualification, it refers

[1] Cf. M. M. Chakravati, 'Notes on the Language and Literature of Orissa', *Journal of the Asiatic Society of Bengal*, vol. LXVII (1898), p. 351.

to Ramma-Bimma; if this is so, Ramma-Bimma are the chief of all the personalities of Saora legend.

RANKALASUM

A god of waste land.

RATUSUM

A singularly malignant deity, a cannibal, the god of night. If he attacks anyone, there is no hope; the victim dies within a few hours. When I was camping at Sogeda in December 1945, the whole place was shocked by a tragedy which occurred in the neighbouring village of Potta. A girl went to cut branches along a path which led out of the village; as she came home in the twilight, she lagged behind the friends who were with her, and Ratusum caught her. Terrified, she ran home, developed high fever, and was dead by morning.

Ratusum is also known as the giver of night-blindness; he causes people to fall into fires at night. His sacrifices should be performed at night, and only black animals should be offered.

RAUDASUM

The Saora verb *raud-* means to faint, to lose one's senses, to be under the influence of a spirit. Raudasum, therefore, is a god who possesses people—in this sense he is regarded as a tutelary—or causes them to lose their senses, to faint or fall into trance. He lives in the Under World.

RINGESUM, RINGEBOI

The god of the wind (*ringan*). He manifests himself in various ways. He may come as a storm of wind, blowing grass from the roof and flattening the crops: he should then be offered a pig. He is sometimes said to be the god of aeroplanes. He makes people constipated, yet at the same time he has a sinister association with Mardisum, the cholera-god; when Mardisum is angry, the wind blows hot and people die of cholera. He also causes umbilical hernia. 'Ringesum fills the stump with wind and puffs it out.' A girl with this is called Pudin and a boy Puda (*pudin* is Saora for navel). Finally Ringesum may attack cattle with every kind of disease.

RONASUM

Gives pneumonia, but may be appeased by a she-goat.

RUGABOI

One of the names of the smallpox goddess. She is the elder sister of the sun; under this name she is associated with *rogon*, the red gram, which the pustules are supposed to resemble. See also pp. 286ff.

RULENGSUM

A god who causes cattle-pox.

RUNGRUNGBOI

Rung-rung means to be sick, and Rungrungboi seems to be a Kittung who causes sickness.

SAHIBOSUM

The 'sahib-god', described in detail at pp. 180ff., whose images are erected outside Saora villages to keep away alien gods who may be brought in by touring 'sahibs': the word 'sahib' nowadays is applied to any educated or well-to-do person.

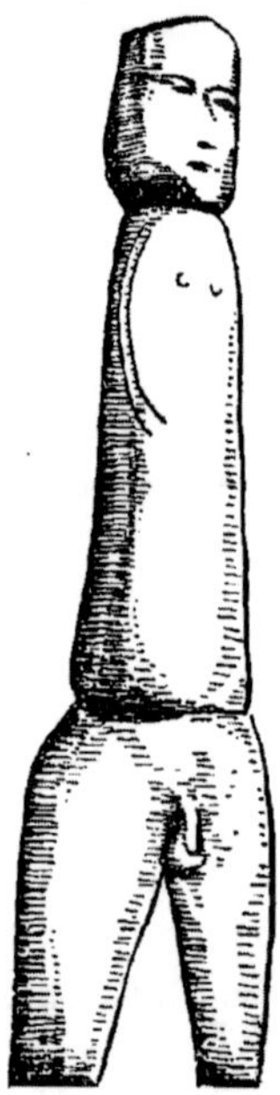

FIG. 8 Image of Sahibosum
5′ high

SAILUNGDASUM

A daughter of Labosum. She makes springs and streams, boring holes in the rock to allow water to flow out.

SAKURASUM

A god who gives goats sores in their mouths.

SALENGDASUM

Salengan is a pot, *dān* is water. Salengdasum is thus the god of water-pots. When he is angry, he gives babies vomit and motions. When this happens, the mother should take two new pots, putting one above the other on her head, and go for water early in the morning. On her return to the house, the shaman should make certain patterns on the pots, hang them up, sacrifice a fowl, and the child should recover.

SAPTUNGTONGSUM

Tong- is to dance. Saptungtongsum is the god of dancing. At the Guar and other ceremonies, people put ploughs, hoes and baskets on their heads and dance in his honour; when they have done, they offer him rice and wine.

SARDASUM

God of the Sarda or reformed Saoras of the plains. From time to time he comes up into the hills, makes people ill, obtains his food-sacrifice and goes away.

SATTIRASUM

A god who presides over the growing crops.

SEDASUM

The name for a tutelary in some villages. The Saora verb *seda-* means to choose or select, and the name probably has reference to the way a tutelary chooses a human husband or wife.

SENAISUM

A god who attacks cattle.

SIDIBIRADI

The wife of Jemra Kittung; her story will be found on pp. 316ff. She is a goddess of wealth.

SING-BONGA

Sing-bonga, regarded in Kol-Munda tradition as the Sun, is occasionally worshipped by the Saoras in the same sense. 'He lives above, above all, and he sees all.' But the use of the name is rare.

SITABOI

A sister of Ramma-Bimma; she and her sister Manneboi are the givers of wealth and prosperity. There is a story that she was compelled to marry a tiger and had seven cubs from it. The Kittungs, her brothers, were angry at this and killed all but one of the cubs, the lame tiger Kuntikinna. There is little beyond the name to connect Sitaboi with the beautiful and heroic Sita of Hindu tradition.

SIYURASUM

Siyur- means to be out of one's senses as a result of love-fever or intoxication. Siyurasum is thus a god who drives men crazy.

SURMALLA

Sura in Sanskrit is a hero and *malla* is an athlete or wrestler. See under Gangamalla, his fellow messenger of the god of death.

SUTARKADSUM

A god who affects the lungs, causing tuberculosis.

SUTORDUBSUM

Another name for the god who gives backache and is represented by an old ploughshare on a veranda.

TABARDASUM

The god of the banyan tree. Anyone afflicted with bloody motions should go to the banyan and sacrifice to Tabardasum.

TADENGDASUM

Tadeng- is to carry, *dān* is water. Tadengdasum is therefore the god who helps women to balance two or more pots on their heads. If he is neglected, he knocks them over.

TADIDANGSUM

A god whose symbol is a small pot, in shape something like a cup (*tadin*).

TAMBASUM

The god of midday. When the midday fever attacks a man, the people say it is due to Tambasum, and they sacrifice when the sun is directly overhead.

TANGOLBOBSUM

A god who chooses as his seat a bundle of leaves brought in from the forest and stored in a corner of the house. He gives headaches and pains in the nose.

TANGORBASUM

The god of the path (*tangoran*). He gives people high fever, and must be satisfied with sacrifices made on the path leading to a village.

TANGSIRBASUM

The god of the *tangsir* tree. He causes headache.

THAKURANI

The Hindu goddess of smallpox who is gradually ousting the old Saora gods, Lurnisum and Rugaboi, from public attention.

TILJANGSUM

This god makes holes (*til-* is to bury) in paths down to the Under World; he also digs up paths in this world. Witches send him to make pit-traps to catch gods who might come to help the victims of their magic. Another way in which sorcerers can cause a lot of annoyance is this. Suppose a party of gods or ancestors have come to drink wine from the palms of a village. That is not too serious. But the sorcerer sends Tiljangsum to dig pits in the path that is to take them home; they fall into them and return and stay on the palms, and drink all the wine there is. Tiljangsum also attacks babies, making them cry and putting blood in their motions. Sacrifice must then be offered on a path, and afterwards all the leaves used should be put in a pot and buried in the middle of the path.

TONAISUM

This god, whose name is derived from the Oriya, serves the function of a familiar to Saora sorcerers. They send him to attack their enemies with internal pains and dysentery. He visits men in dreams and drinks their blood. He must be kept away by the sacrifice of a pig on the threshold of one's house.

TUNDRUBLUTSUM

A very touchy god, who will allow no one to watch his ceremonies or share his liquor. When angry he makes the fields 'barren as a childless woman'.

TUTIYUNGSUM

The god of a mother's nipples. He has the power to stop the flow of milk.

TUTTUMSUM

The bloodsucker god—*tuttuman* is a bloodsucker. He makes babies thin and weak.

URALBASUM

Chiefly notorious for his attacks on little children. 'He gives them fever and makes them pant.' The origin of this god, or rather goddess —for in spite of the form of the name, Uralbasum is probably female —is this: when a woman loses child after child and not one survives, and she at last dies of sorrow, she turns into Uralbasum and attacks other people's children out of jealousy. *Ural* is evil; an *uralmaran* is a cruel, dangerous man, with a face of foreboding.

URALJUNGSUM

A local god of Sogeda village. He is deformed, with a hare-lip and only half a penis.

URNASUM

A god presiding over childbirth. In some places the first cutting of a child's hair is done in his name.

UYUNGSUM, UYUNGBOI

Uyungan is the Sun in Saora, and the most popular names for the Sun-god are Uyungsum and Uyungboi, for although in the myths the Sun is definitely male and the father of the stars, the male or female suffix is used indifferently. Some Saoras explain this by saying that when they speak of Uyungboi, they are referring to the Sun's wife Abdrungdari, who is invisible to us, but part of him and equally powerful.

The Sun-god has several other names—Darammaboi, Lankasum, Gadelsum, Gadejangboi and Marandakumsum. It is sometimes said that the Sun should be called Uyungsum in the morning and Darammaboi in the afternoon, and there is a general rule that Uyungsum should be worshipped in the morning, the shaman being careful that the rays do not go into his eyes: to ensure this he shades his face with a plantain leaf. Darammaboi, however, should always be worshipped in the afternoon. It is more probable, however, that the different names are intended to emphasize different qualities: the name Darammaboi emphasizes the 'righteous' character of the Sun; Gadejangboi stresses his creative power; and Lankasum refers to his abode 'above' (*lanka*) in the sky.

Uyungsum is often regarded as the greatest of the gods, though it is not clear whether he is superior to Kuraitung, the chief of the Kittungs. It is he 'who gives and takes away'; birth and death are in his hands. He is specially worshipped to promote human fertility, and a year after marriage a goat may be given him and a pot dedicated for this purpose. He is, up to a point, benevolent. 'As a mother gives milk to her child, so Uyungboi draws milk from her breasts and gives it to men in the form of rain.' On the other hand, when he is displeased, he gives fever and headaches, sometimes great sores, and often leprosy.

There are many, often contradictory, stories about the Sun-god. A shaman at Tumulu described how Uyungsum 'has a flower, strong and beautiful, in his hair. When he wears it, and goes to see the Moon, the world gets very hot, for it means the Sun is on heat. When he couples with the Moon, sweat falls from his body. He fans himself, the wind blows and the world grows cold again.' In another story, from Liabo, we find the Sun delighted with marigolds. He came to a Saora in a dream and said, 'Offer me marigolds as a sacrifice'. The Saora did so and the Sun was pleased. 'Since then marigolds have spread throughout the world, and the Saoras offer them to every god.' Uyungsum caused the first mango tree to grow from an egg, declaring that 'the fruit will be like an egg. When it is unripe you must remove the skin; when ripe it will be yellow inside; it will be sweet as an egg to the taste.' We find the Sun-god, in fact, associated with beautiful things, with the mango, and marigolds, and the strong and beautiful flower in his hair.

Uyungsum is sometimes called a Kittung, and there are stories which show him behaving in the human fashion usually associated with the Kittungs—for example, he seduces Kittung's wife and breaks up his home. But in Burda I was told: 'Uyungsum is not a Kittung; he is the eye of Kittung. We sacrifice to the Sun because Kittung cannot see without him. His eye is strong and hot as it is, because so long as he is hungry he glares across the world looking for food. At midday he is famishing, and so he glares all the more hotly, but when he has eaten he gradually cools down.'

The eminence of Uyungsum is suggested by the fact that he has a number of gods subservient to him, and they have to pass on to him any sacrifice they may receive. Gajjisum is one of these; Adununkisum is another. It is said that when sacrifice to all other deities has failed, the Saoras approach the Sun-god for redress.

Chapter Four

PRIESTS AND SHAMANS

I. *The Buyya*

THE placation of the vast other-world of invisible and often hostile beings occupies the energy of a small army of dedicated men and women who, armed with the fragile weapons of bow and fan, earthen pot and bamboo fiddle, and devoting themselves to supplication and sacrifice, fight bravely to protect mankind.

The Saoras recognize four different kinds of male religious functionary, each with his special duties and rewards. The Buyya is a village official who performs the office of priest in most of the Ganjam villages. The Kuranmaran is the shaman—diviner, medicine-man and celebrant at every kind of sacrifice. The Idaimaran is an acolyte who assists the shaman and performs menial duties at the funerary ceremonies. The Siggamaran[1] has the duty of cremating the corpse and performing other duties at a funeral.

The word Buyya, unlike Kuranmaran which only applies to individuals, describes both an official and a whole class of people. The official Buyya, who is often called the Sadi Buyya (the priest who has been given a turban, *sādi*, by Government), is generally the head of one of the quarters of a village, and in the Ganjam (but not the Koraput) villages acts as second in command to the Gamang chief. But the word Buyya is also given to every member of the quarter of which the official Buyya is the head, and in many villages therefore there are many people who call themselves Buyya. From among these it sometimes happens that a Purpur Buyya—*purpuran* means sacrifice—is appointed to perform priestly functions, leaving the Sadi Buyya to attend to social and governmental duties. More often, however, these functions are united in the same person.

The Gamang chief and the Buyya priest are of great social and political importance in the Ganjam villages. The priest officiates at the Harvest Festivals, and has his part to play at marriages, funerary

[1] The name is probably associated with the Saora verb *siggod,* which means to 'offer rice-grain to the gods'. The word *siyan* describes a corpse placed on a funeral pyre.

14. Saora brings sheaves of rice from the fields at Sogeda

15. Man and wife at Taraba

16. Women at Sogeda removing grain

rites and other sacrifices. Ramamurti points out that 'sales and mortgages of land and liquor-yielding trees, partition and other dispositions of property, and divorces are effected in the council of village elders, presided over by the Gamang and Buyya, by means of long and tedious proceedings, involving various religious ceremonies'.[1] In the old days the village Chief and priest had quasi-magisterial functions, and the authority to settle a number of criminal and civil cases and to impose fines.

But apart from attending to the general affairs of his own hamlet, the Buyya is essentially a priest. He can offer sacrifice for the whole of his village (not only for his own quarter), but he is not usually invited—as the shamans are invited—to visit other villages for this purpose. The reason probably is that his special function is to maintain the cult of the *sadru*-shrines and to guard the village lands from the interference of hostile spirits and sorcerers.

Although a Buyya is distinct from a shaman, he may become one, and his activities and influence are then greatly enlarged. Lakhia, the priest of Barasingi, became a shaman when he was a boy and was 'married' to no fewer than three tutelaries at once. This meant that he was able to add to his priestly and official duties the ability to divine and interpret the will of the gods.

In most of the Koraput villages, there are no Buyyas,[2] and the Saoras there say that one reason why the Ganjam Saoras are so much poorer and their crops are so often ruined is that they depend on priests instead of shamans to conduct their ceremonies. For the Buyya as such is not married to a tutelary, and from the point of view of the great orthodox shamans his work seems uninspired.

The priest's position is hereditary, and this is natural in view of his official functions. When a new priest is to be appointed, a shaman is called and he, falling into trance, asks the gods and ancestors whether the proposed candidate is acceptable to them. If they agree, the shaman summons the ghost of the last priest to hold office in the village. If he too approves, the shaman (possessed by and representing the dead priest) puts his hands on the head of the new priest and tells him to do his work well. The villagers subscribe sufficient money to buy a goat, which is sacrificed in the new priest's house. After fasting for

[1] Quoted by Thurston, vol. VI, p. 343.

[2] Ladde is one of the few Koraput villages where there is a Buyya, but there he has special functions, for he is mainly attached to the cult of the god Jakersum.

twenty-four hours, he cooks a meal entirely by himself. Then, still keeping away from everyone, he sacrifices to Kittung in a new pot which he afterwards hangs from the roof of his house.

The story of Mangu, the priest of Vangarada, is significant; it shows how the tradition of succession works in practice and illustrates the custom of dedication.

> My father was a priest, and on his death my younger brother succeeded him. But soon afterwards, at the Jammolpur feast, my elder brother murdered him and was sent to jail for three years. Then the shade of my younger brother came to me and said, 'Now I have been killed and my son is too young to do the work of a priest. You must do it instead.' He also told me that I must arrange his Guar ceremony. I could not afford it, so he began to plague me with fever. I escaped to the Tea Gardens and after two years I returned with a hundred rupees, and paid for the Guar. The people then insisted that I should be their priest. My younger brother, now an ancestor, came upon the shaman and told him to dedicate me, and the shaman put his hands on my head and made me a priest. My father's ghost also came and said, 'You must do the work of a priest.'

Lakhia's father, who was a priest, had three wives. The son of his eldest wife became priest after his death. But he died also, and Lakhia who was son of the third wife became priest, since the elder man's son was too young for the post. The ghosts of his father and half-brother appeared in dreams and insisted on this.

The Buyya priests have to observe a number of taboos. Someone once said to me, 'A Buyya is like a Brahmin'. At ceremonies he must always cook his own food apart from the rest. He must fetch his own water for cooking. If he is a Jati, he must not eat from the hands of Arsi, Luara or Kindal Saoras. As a result of this the priests sometimes develop a rather superior attitude towards their fellows.

II. *The Kuranmaran*

FOR practical purposes the Kuranmaran, the shaman, is the most important religious figure in a Saora village. He has the power not only to diagnose the source of trouble or disease, but to cure it. He is doctor as well as priest, psychologist as well as magician, the repository of tradition, the source of sacred knowledge. His primary duty is that of divination; in case of sickness he seeks the cause in trance or dream. Every shaman has a tutelary-wife in the Under World, and she comes to assist him in any perplexity and often guides him in his duties. He may inherit his powers, and is generally trained by his father or some other relative, but he is chosen by the direct intervention of a tutelary, and his marriage with her effects his dedication. Once that is done he is continually in touch with the gods and ancestors of the other world, and if he is adept he may develop a wide practice, for he is not confined to his own village, but may go wherever he is summoned. He is regarded with respect and often with affection, as a man given to the public service, a true friend in time of affliction.

The first shaman, according to a story recorded at Ladde, was appointed by Kittung himself.

In the days before the gods and the dead troubled mankind, there were no shamans. But in time the gods were born and in their search for food-sacrifice they began to make men ill.

A Saora called Baori lived alone on Jungor Hill; he had no wife or child. When Kittung saw how men were troubled by the gods, he came to find someone whom he could make a shaman to help them. No one was ready to do it, but after a long time Kittung found Baori and said to him, 'I will make you a shaman to protect and heal men'. Baora said, 'But how can I do such a thing? I am a poor man and ignorant.' Kittung put rice in a new fan and liquor in a new pot, and gave Baori goats, fowls and pigs, and sent him to Anglur village, where there were many sick. Baori sacrificed to the gods there, and they were pleased and left men alone for a time.

Five different types of shaman may be distinguished. The first, and probably the most important, are the Raudakumbmarans. They are shamans who are married to tutelaries, and learn their duties in dreams and trance. They are qualified to perform the great rituals—Doripur, Uyungpur, Ratupur, Jammolpur—and can deal with all the small routine matters that constantly arise. But they do not assist in funerary rites or in such ceremonies as the Ajorapur, except in special cases. There are, however, in some areas, shamans of this type who can take part in every rite of the Saora tradition.

Secondly, there are the Guarkumbmarans. They too are married to tutelaries, but they have to be trained for their duties by another shaman: they cannot learn them from dreams. Their work is largely confined to the funerary rites—the Guar, Karja, Lajap—and to divination and ceremonies which have mainly to do with the dead. They can, for example, perform a Name-giving ceremony if the name to be given is that of an ancestor.

Thirdly, there are the specialist shamans who can conduct the Ajorapur and similar rites, but no others. They are not usually capable of trance, and their main duty is to be familiar with the ritual, preside at the buffalo-sacrifice, administer 'medicine' and recite the relevant myths.

Fourthly, there are the shamans who are not supported by the presence of tutelaries. Some of these are simply omen-takers. They can divine by various mechanical means, such as the fan or the bow, but no spirit comes upon them, they are not capable of possession. Their special field of activity is the Tonaipur, where a long series of names of villages and persons is mechanically tested to discover the source of hostile magic.

Finally, there is the very important shaman known as the Regamaran, the medicine-man, who supplies supernatural 'medicines' against sorcery, the infection of suicide and the menace of man-eating tigers.[1]

The shamans differ from one another in the extent to which they are capable of communicating with the spirit world and in the ceremonies which they are qualified to conduct. But they are all competent to offer some sort of sacrifice, except that no shaman should ever kill an animal with his own hands. Where there is no Buyya priest, the Raudakumbmaran performs most of his functions, offering sacrifice before cutting a forest-clearing, at the time of taking out seed, to Labosum in the fields, on the threshing-floor, at the shrines during the Harvest Festivals.

A shaman is attached to a village, and often to one quarter and family within it, though there is sometimes a feeling that a shaman should not treat members of his own household. But he is not confined to his village. Famous shamans are indeed constantly being invited to other places, sometimes at a considerable distance. There is a rule that when a shaman goes to officiate at certain rites in another village, he should not eat there, but should bring home the food he is given. On his return he puts the food on the mortar in the central room of his house, and offers his ancestors a little of it. Then he and his family can eat it. 'But the ancestors must always have their share first.'

[1] In Barasingi, the Saoras also recognized a Sarkakumbmaran whose work was confined to protective rites against tigers, and a Kujarikumbmaran, who only officiated for the deities of smallpox. I describe the activities of the Regamaran in chapter VII, pp. 257ff.

The office of shaman is not hereditary, but in practice it often runs in families. Daipano of Amrasingi was the son of a shaman and his father used to make him sit beside him and study his technique. Dume's father and grandfather were both shamans; Tarendu's father was a shaman; Samiya's mother was a shamanin. Pingo was initiated by his mother's brother. On the other hand, Kintaru's parents were lay people, and so were Lango's.

The impetus to become a shaman seems often, but by no means always, to arise from dreams about a father's tutelary. Thus, when Dume's father died, his tutelary came to Dume with her daughter and arranged for the boy to marry her. The same thing happened to Daipano. Samiya was visited by his mother's tutelaries, who brought him two girls to marry.

The young man, subject to these visitations, often reacts strongly against the suggestion that he should become a shaman. The profession is no sinecure; it is exacting and sometimes dangerous; there are tiresome taboos to be observed; the income hardly compensates for the long hours of labour. Nearly every 'marriage' with a tutelary is preceded by a period of struggle.

Dume was one of those who refused to marry his tutelary at first, and the inner conflict made him so ill that he felt 'as if ants were biting him all over and his whole body was being pricked by thorns'. Until he gave in and accepted his 'call' he behaved like a madman, weeping, laughing and sometimes falling to the ground unconscious. Kintara was 'driven' by his tutelary and robbed of his memory for a whole year before he consented to marry her and thus accepted the duties of a shaman. Tarendu's father was attacked by his tutelary in the form of a wild boar, after which he decided that he had better give up the struggle. Tarendu himself gives (p. 139) in symbolic form a description of what was evidently a period of sharp conflict during which he lost his appetite and was tortured by dreams of falling from a height. For several months he wandered crazily in the forest.

But in every case, once the surrender is made, and the dedication to the new life accepted, the young shaman recovers his health and poise and settles down happily to his duties.

The shamans, like the shamanins, are expected to observe a rather stricter way of life than ordinary people. They are carefully watched by their tutelaries, who take special note of their relations with women. One shaman told me how, after his dedication, he went to several girls, but that whenever he did so, his tutelary visited his wife in a dream and told her about it. 'Then in the middle of the night, fresh from her dream, my wife would wake up and quarrel with me. After this had gone on for some time, my tutelary came to me and said that if I continued to go with other women, she would leave me for ever. "You have a woman in your house," she said. "Why do you want to go to others?" After that I left the girls alone.' Kintara's tutelary rebuked him for approaching his future wife before marriage.

The reason for this control is not that the tutelary wife is jealous, but that since she is a Hindu she is expected to have a higher standard of conduct in such matters.

Other taboos are not really burdensome. Before any major sacrifice the shaman must fast and abstain from sexual intercourse, and this is probably very good for him. Breach of the rule leads to immediate disaster. Samiya described how he got drunk one year on the evening before the Red Gram Festival and in a fuddled way approached his wife. Next morning he realized what he had done, but decided to go ahead and officiated as usual at the shrine. Almost at once he went down with high fever. Dume also got drunk before a Name-giving ceremony, so drunk that he could not remember whether he had eaten anything or no. But he evidently had, for when he took his place before the altar he began to tremble all over and felt very ill. He forced himself to finish the sacrifice, but added a fowl to appease the indignant spirits.

The fasting rules are not, however, a very great burden, and shamans and shamanins often appear well nourished, as they should do, for they are continually fed on meat. Although they drink largely on ceremonial occasions, I have noticed that they rarely get drunk at other times. Indeed, a shaman develops the habit of walking warily, for he is beset by many pitfalls. He avoids excess, and undoubtedly makes some effort to keep himself in spiritual condition.

This is all the more necessary since it is believed that a shaman makes many spiritual enemies and is far from popular in the other world. And naturally, for if there were no shamans the gods and ancestors could exercise unrestricted dominion over the world; they could trick the simple laity into giving them extravagant food-offerings; they could rob the sago palms without interference; they could revenge themselves on the living or carry them away in death just as they felt inclined. The shaman stands between mankind and the greed of the unseen empire of the dead. He bargains with the gods and reduces their demands to more reasonable figures. The shaman Ipan told me:

> I have cured many sick people, though many too have died. The gods were angry with me for saving so many people from them. One day, many of the dead assembled—I saw them in a dream—and standing far off said to me, 'You are always saving these people by bribing us with fowls and wine. We can't have you here any longer. We are going to take you away.' They came towards me in a great crowd, but my tutelary flew to my rescue and drove them away.

Another shaman named Passino was curing his brother of fever, which was attributed to the shade of his father who had recently died. The shade attacked the shaman saying, 'Why are you helping this worthless son of mine? He refuses to do the Guar for me, and keeps me wandering about hungry and thirsty with no place to live. I won't have it, and I am going to take him away and you as well.' Passino had to fight with this shade for a whole week, until his tutelary came and rescued him.

III. *Reminiscences*

WHEN their confidence is won, the shamans show themselves as ready to indulge in autobiographical detail as any other clerics, and the stories they tell are to my mind of great interest, for here they are not answering questions, but allowing themselves to wander at will down the path of memory.

The life-story of Kintara, an elderly Saora of Hatibadi on the borders of the hill-country to the north, illustrates the strange twilight life of the shaman, whose experiences and relationships in the other world are almost as real to him as those here.

> I was born in Jaltal, an ailing child with a great head that caused my mother much pain. While I was still in the womb, my father mistook a snake for a bit of wood and struck it with his axe. This snake was really the god Ajorasum, and when I was born he made me very ill. But my father called a shaman, who sacrificed a fowl to the angry god and dedicated a pot with many promises and I recovered. Later, when I was old enough to play with other children and take the cattle out to graze, my father sacrificed a buffalo to Ajorasum on the bank of a stream.
>
> When I was about twelve years old, a tutelary girl called Jangmai came to me in a dream and said, 'I am pleased with you; I love you; I love you so much that you must marry me.' But I refused, and for a whole year she used to come making love to me and trying to win

me. But I always rejected her until at last she got angry and sent her dog [a tiger] to bite me. That frightened me and I agreed to marry her. But almost at once another tutelary came and begged me to marry her instead. When the first girl heard about it she said, 'I was the first to love you, and I look on you as my husband. Now your heart is on another woman, but I'll not allow it.' So I said 'No' to the second girl. But the first in her rage and jealousy made me mad and drove me out into the jungle and robbed me of my memory. For a whole year she drove me.

Then my parents called a shaman from another village and in his trance my tutelary came upon him and spoke through his mouth. She said to my parents, 'Don't be afraid. I am going to marry him. There is nothing in all this; don't worry, I will help the boy in all his troubles.' My father was pleased and bought a she-goat, and two cloths, bangles, a ring and a comb and arranged the wedding. The shaman sat down in the house, put the gifts and a new pot in front of him, tethered the goat near by and, singing, singing, fell into a trance. My tutelary's mother, father and sisters brought her to me, and I fell to the ground unconscious. Jangmai asked for her cloth and the shaman dressed me in it. Then she demanded the other things, gift by gift, and they put the ring on my finger and gave me the bangles and necklace, and did my hair with the comb. They gave the second bit of cloth to my tutelary's elder sister. They killed the goat for Jangmai's father, mother and brother. Then the others went away and only Jangmai remained. She said to the shaman, 'Tie up a pot in my name and put rice for me in a cooking-pot. I have married this boy in order to protect him and care for him.' The shaman then made me sit with rice in a winnowing-fan and my hand moved over it of its own accord, and I danced for a long time. Then I put some rice in a new pot for my tutelary and tied up all the things we had bought for her in a bundle and hung it from the roof.

Jangmai's possessions are always there, hanging from the roof, and when she asks for them I take them down and show them to her. Often at the Harvest Festivals she comes for her coloured cloth; I put it on and dance in her name. Whenever I go on a journey I put a little palm wine by her pot and say, 'Now I am going on a journey. If a god meets me on the way he may catch hold of me, but I am going to wear your cloth so that the spirits will recognize me and leave me alone.' Then I put the coloured cloth over my shoulder or tie it round my head as a turban, and when gods see me they say to themselves, 'This is a tutelary's husband; we had better leave him alone.'

Four years after I became a shaman I married a [human] wife, Dasuni. Before we were married, my wife and I lived in the same village and I tried to seduce her. The first time I tried I failed, and my tutelary said, 'If you do this sin, your eyes will burst open,' so I left the girl alone till we were married. After the wedding, Jangmai came upon me and spoke through my mouth to my wife Dasuni saying, 'Now you are going to live with my husband. You will fetch his water, husk his rice, cook his food: you will do everything, I can do nothing. I must live below. All I can do is to help when trouble comes. Tell me, will you honour me or no, or are you going to quarrel with me?' Dasuni answered, 'Why should I quarrel with you? You are a god-wife and I will give you everything you need.' Jangmai was pleased at that and said, 'That is well. You and I will live together as sisters.' Then she said to me, 'Look! Keep this woman as you have kept me. Do not beat her. Do not abuse her.' So saying, she went away.

Every year, when I give Dasuni a new cloth, I also get one for Jangmai. When her clothes get old I ask her permission to let Dasuni or her children wear them. For now I have a son and three daughters from Dasuni; the boy is twenty-four years old. And from Jangmai I have a son and two daughters in the Under World. The boy is now about twenty and his name is Darsana. One of the girls—Sundri—is fifteen, and the youngest—Sugmi—is ten. When Darsana was born his mother brought him to me and told me his name; she put him in my lap and asked me to make arrangements for his food. When I said I would, she took him down again to the Under World. I sacrificed a goat for the child and dedicated a pot. But I did not dedicate pots when the girls were born, for a boy stays at home but a girl goes to a stranger's house. At the Harvest Festivals these children bother me a lot, for they come crying, 'O father, give us rice and a fowl, give us some liquor, for we're awfully hungry.' This is a nuisance, for it means I have to make sacrifices for them as well as for their mother.

When my tutelary is in her period she does not visit me, and I cannot do the work of divination at that time. When she washes her head she tells Dasuni, 'Now I am clean; wash the clothes and clean the house.' So Dasuni washes all our clothes and cleans the house. My tutelary's periods last three days.

In the year I became a shaman, my mother died in child-birth. A year later my father planted a stone for her. We didn't get enough to eat, so we moved to Lugurmundi and it was there I married Dasuni. I have never been to any woman except my wife. A year after my marriage, my father died, for my mother's ghost came to him and said, 'You are an old man now, and you don't get enough to eat. Come and join me.' When he heard this, my father died peacefully the following day. At one time I often used to see him in dreams, but a few years ago he died a second time in the Under World, and they burnt his body with castor wood. Now I see him no more.

In Lugurmundi I was always sick and hungry, and my tutelary said, 'You will never be happy in this village. Don't stay here. Go and build a house in Hatibadi.' That was twelve years ago. At first when I asked Kittung for a place to live in, he would not give it to me. But I sacrificed a pig to him, and he relented; he gave me a site for a house, and now we live there happily.

Shortly before he died at the age of about fifty-five in 1949, Samiya, the shaman of Sogeda, gave me a brief account of his professional experiences.

My mother was a shamanin. When she fell ill for the last time, she said to me, 'Now I am going to die. My tutelary will come to you; whatever he tells you, follow it exactly.' The old lady died and as she had foretold, her tutelaries—she had two of them, one named Lausa, the other Sarker—came to me in a dream. They said to me, 'Son, your mother is dead; now who will serve us? You must look after us; if you do, we will arrange your marriage.' So I began by serving my mother's tutelaries and at every festival I used to give them rice and wine.

Then one night they came to me with two young girls. One was a Paik, the other a Dom by caste. They both wanted to marry me, but I didn't want a Dom girl and refused to have her. My mother's tutelaries were very angry and beat me with thorn bushes until I agreed to do what they wanted. At the wedding I sacrificed a goat and three fowls, and I dedicated four pots, for my mother's two tutelaries and my own two, and I drew a separate ikon for each of them.

From my Dom tutelary I have had one daughter, Ilianti, who is now ten years old. Every now and then all four tutelaries come and take me to the Under World. Since I fly with them I get there very quickly. The ancestors there are miserable enough, some lame, some blind, some with only one side to the face, many with great wounds. But the gods fly about like birds; they are small as little birds. They have large and splendid houses and keep every kind of animal as pet.

As a shaman I cure so many people that the gods and the dead dislike me. They say, 'When we come to fetch the sick, you stop us and drive us away with your goats and cocks.' Once the ancestors were so annoyed that they sent Dorisum to attack me and I fell very ill with pneumonia and nearly died. I consulted two other shamans, but they could not do anything, and in the end I had to cure myself.

One of my most difficult patients was a man named Antanu. He was driven mad by the shade of his dead brother, whose widow Antanu had beaten and driven from his house. 'Look at this good-for-nothing creature,' said the shade to me. 'He shares none of his things with his unhappy brother. He refuses to arrange the Guar for me, and just sits about in my house drinking and enjoying himself, while I have to wander in the woods, cold and hungry and thirsty. Well, now I am going to make him wander with me.' So he drove Antanu out of his wits and made him roam about in the jungle, sleeping at night under trees, without proper food. At last he came home, haggard and raving, and we thought he was going to die. I stayed five days by him; I ate my food where I was, I never left his side. All those days the shade took no notice of me whatever, then at last he said, 'I will only let him alone when he does the Guar for me.' Antanu promised to do it at once, but directly he got better, he forgot all about it, and the shade was so annoyed that this time he attacked me for deceiving him, as he put it, and I had to sacrifice a buffalo at my own expense.

Tarendu, a shaman at Pattili, a man of about fifty when I recorded his life-history, was himself the son of a shaman.

My father at first refused to marry his tutelary, so she took the form of a wild boar and attacked him. I too had a lot of trouble before I was married, for several tutelary girls were after me. First a potter woman came to my house. I hid inside and she put a pot on the veranda and went away. When she had gone I came out and smashed the pot. Then a Pano girl came with skins and again I hid inside. She put the skins on the veranda. When she was gone, I came out and threw the skins away. Then came two Saora tutelaries, sisters, the elder was cross-eyed, the younger lame and fat. When they arrived I was up a sago palm. They called to me, 'Give us some wine too: we are both going to marry you.' I looked at them and said, 'O no you aren't.' At last came a Paik girl, a lovely girl in fine clothes; she smiled at me from a distance. She said, 'I am a Paik girl, and you are only a Saora, but I am going to marry you.' I said no, but she caught hold of me and took me to the Under World, where she shut me up in a stone house and gave me nothing to eat. I grew thin as a tamarind leaf, and then she took me to the top of a high date palm and shook it until I was so terrified of falling that I promised to marry her after all. Her name was Sirpanti.

But I forgot all about it, and the result was that I went crazy and wandered about the fields like a lunatic until after several months I suddenly remembered what I had promised. At once I arranged for the wedding, sacrificed a goat, dedicated a pot, drew her an ikon, and in no time I was quite well again and began my work as a shaman.

Sirpanti always says to me, 'If you do any sin, you will die.' Every year I give her a new cloth and a bangle. One day she gave her cloth to my human wife, for Sirpanti likes her and looks after her.

One year Labosum was angry because I had not sacrificed to him for three seasons. I am always forgetting things like that. He wanted to carry off my wife, but Sirpanti quarrelled with him and drove him away. Another time Galbesum came from Boramsingi and told me in a dream, 'You are a great shaman. I like you. Keep me in your house and I will help you in every way.' Of course I forgot all about this too, and Galbesum sent a tiger which killed two of my cows. Then I sacrificed a pig, and made a pot and an ikon for her, and now Galbesum too lives in my house.

The story of Lango, a shaman of the neighbouring village of Tollana, contains some interesting circumstances.

When I was born my mother fell very ill, and for a month she could not feed me. My father sent for a shaman and he had a fowl killed over my mother's breasts, so that the blood poured over them. After that the milk came and I drank it and stayed alive.

When I was about twenty years old I was married to a girl in this world. Soon afterwards Labosum came to me in a dream and taught me how to work as a shaman. Then from the Under World came a tutelary named Rajaboi and said, 'Marry me and keep me as your wife.' I said, 'No, I've got one wife already. What am I to do with another?' The next day I got very high fever. The shaman came and said to me, 'You must marry this tutelary girl.' I did so, and I have been happy with her. She has given me three fine boys—Lingru, Sinru and Gamdu. In this world also I have three sons and a daughter —Balsingo, Molika and Kumbub: the girl's name is Kakli.

At first I had no idea how to make love, and my wife had to teach me what to do. I had never done it before I was married. The first time I felt as if the earth and the sky had become one.

When my first son was born in the Under World, Rajaboi came and told me about it in a dream. She said, 'Put some millet flour in your winnowing-fan, and at night the child will play in it. In the morning you will see the marks of its little feet.' And so I did.

At Potta there is a shaman who has lived all his life completely naked. His name is Tikano, the son of Baria; he is about forty-five and his hair is a little grey. He has never married, but a woman once fell in love with him and came of her own accord to live in his house. It is said that he found himself impotent, 'for all his seed was in his head'. As a shaman, however, he has a wife and children in the Under World. He was married to his tutelary while he was still in the womb, and this is one reason why he cannot wear clothes.

Tikano is quite a well-to-do person, a clever and even aggressive business man; he once drove a hard bargain with me over the purchase of a goat. He has a good house in the middle of the village; it has a substantial gate and a pleasant garden. He had an elder brother, Kishi, now dead, who also lived naked. Tikano spoke freely of his experiences.

When I was a little boy of about five years, my parents tried to make me put on a scrap of cloth. But directly I tied it round me I fell down senseless and stayed like that for hours. No one could rouse me and my parents were very frightened. A shaman came, and after a long time, Labosum came upon him and said, 'Look! I live out in the fields and clearings. I have a wife and a son and daughter. We all live naked and are not ashamed of it. We love this boy and he has got to live as we do. If you put clothes on him, we won't let him live in your world, but will take him away to live with us.' When he heard this, my father pulled the cloth off me, and I at once sat up and was perfectly well again. I have never worn clothes since then, for I am very much afraid of Labosum and his wife, who live naked as I am.

The other villagers, however, told me that there had been several attempts to dress Tikano in more conventional fashion. But every time he fell down in a frenzy and bit his own body or seized an axe and attacked the bystanders. One day a visiting Congress busybody lectured him on the impropriety of his appearance; since then, when strangers are about, Tikano drapes himself in a sort of toga. But this is not 'clothing' in the Saora sense and so does not count.

IV. *The Idaimaran*

WHILE the shaman's activities are almost unrestricted, and the priest's are confined to his own village, the duties of the Idaimaran are usually only performed for his own family. As a result there are many more Idaimarans and Idaibois than there are shamans, for each group in a village must have at least one man and one woman set apart for this purpose.

The work of the Idaimaran is entirely concerned with the funerary rituals. At these he acts as an assistant or acolyte to the shaman and Siggamaran. At a divination, when the dead are summoned, he may sit with the shaman and may be possessed by the spirits and speak in their name. He has an important, if subordinate place at Name-giving rites, at funerals, and at the Guar, Karja, Sikunda and Lajap ceremonies. He may actually officiate at the Lajap rite so long as the sacrifice is only of a fowl; he cannot offer a buffalo to the dead.

A boy becomes an Idaimaran when he is still young, and always before marriage. The profession usually runs in the family and most Idaimarans are sons and grandsons of Idaimarans. They are usually appointed in dreams—though in this case there is no marriage with a tutelary—and after a period of training they take up their duties without any formal ceremony. If there is any doubt of a boy's fitness for the task, a shaman may test the omens by passing a knife through the flame of a wick or by burning leaves.

The experience of Dora, a middle-aged Idaimaran of Borai village, is instructive. At his birth his mother's pains lasted three days: 'she sat on the birth-stone all that time'. The reason was that he was, as he said, 'his own grandfather'. By this he meant that, while he was still in the womb, his paternal grandfather's ghost came to his father in a dream and said, 'I am coming in this boy. You must give him my name and sacrifice a goat for me.' But the father forgot his dream, and it was only when the mother's pains were so greatly prolonged that he remembered and hastily sacrificed a goat and gave the name of Dora, the old man's name, to the as yet unborn child.

This first Dora had been an Idaimaran, so was his son. When the time came for training a boy to carry on the family tradition, the father did not choose Dora but his eldest son. But old Dora's ghost came in a dream and said, 'I used to be an Idaimaran, and it was to your second, not your eldest, son that you gave my name. It is him whom you should teach to be an Idaimaran.' The father turned, therefore, to young Dora and taught him by example and precept what to do. The boy learnt quickly and began work on his own even while his father was alive.

Both father and grandfather of Jonia, an Idaimaran of Potta, were Idaimarans. Jonia was trained by his own father. 'He used to make me offer sacrifice in the name of the dead; he made me sit beside him and watch him until I knew exactly what I was to do. When he died, his ghost and my grandfather's ghost came to me and said, "Now you must carry on our work without mistakes. Never eat or drink before a ceremony." Then many of the ancestors came to me in a dream and said, "We like you. We will take food and liquor from your hands." Encouraged by this, I began the work of an Idaimaran, though I was still a young boy.'

The Idaimarans have their own set of rules and taboos which must be strictly observed. They must fast before any ceremony. They must never eat beef. They must not eat the entrails, lips or tongue of any animal. They must not eat the feet of pigs or fowls, though they may take the feet of other animals. They must not touch river snails.

It is dangerous to break these rules. Jonia described how, in the early days of his profession, he had made three great mistakes which nearly cost him his life. 'Once at a Guar,' he recalled, 'I ate some food before going to assist in the sacrifice. When the ancestors came upon the shaman he pushed me over and sent me sprawling. The dead cried, "Do you expect us to eat your leavings?" I was ill for some time after that and people looked down on me. But I did the very same thing at the next Guar I attended, and this time I got a nasty sore throat. On each occasion I had to sacrifice a cock to the dead whom I had offended.

'My third mistake was at a Karja ceremony, when we have to go hungry for three days, taking nothing but wine. At one point of the rite we had to carry the dead buffalo's dung out of the village, with offerings of meat and rice. When the others went back I stayed behind and I was so hungry that I secretly ate the food offered to the dead. I was drunk on all the wine I had taken, or I would not have done it. Immediately my throat swelled up, and I was in terrible pain; I could not speak, indeed I could hardly breathe. When the shaman called on the spirits to say why this was, an ancestor came and said, "This is the third and worst of his offences, for this time he has robbed us of our food. We cannot forgive him; we are going to take him away." But the shaman begged them to forgive me, and sacrificed a buffalo for me, and after a long illness I recovered. Since then I have never made a mistake, not once in twenty years.'

An Idaimaran can become a shaman, and this sometimes happens if he shows himself capable of passing into a state of dissociation and is visited by a tutelary in his dreams.

It will be convenient to consider here the work of the Idaiboi, who is the female counterpart of the Idaimaran, and has very similar duties and responsibilities. Like him she has no duties at ordinary sacrifices and festivals; her concern is with the dead. When a child dies it is her duty to carry the little body to the pyre. When a woman dies, she washes the body, anoints it with oil and turmeric, and helps to carry it out for cremation. At the pyre itself, when it is dismantled, she bathes the unburnt logs with water. She assists the Siggamaran and the Idaimaran at the Limma ceremony, both in the actual worship and in the routine cooking of sacrificial birds and animals. At the Guar rite, she has to clean and husk the rice, fetch dedicated water wrapped in a sacred cloth, cook rice on a special hearth, clear and clean the ground before a menhir and anoint it with turmeric. She has the task of carrying home the bones of any woman who has died in a strange village.

At the Karja ceremony her duties are unending. She has to sit hour after hour before the sacred bamboo pole, exhibiting their clothes and ornaments to the exacting dead, offering them wine a hundred times a day. And at all such celebrations she has many small duties of hospitality and organization which are not readily classified, but are none the less important.

An Idaiboi can only work for her own family, and it is important to note that she cannot function for her husband's group, but only for the one into which she was born. This is why an Idaiboi should always take up her duties before marriage, and why most Idaibois are young girls of twelve to sixteen years of age. Since a girl usually goes to another village on marriage, her profession is automatically terminated; she cannot act for her husband's family, and her own family is elsewhere.

Chapter Five

THE SAORA WOMAN AS SHAMAN

I. *Four Kinds of Kuranboi*

IN EVERY Saora village, in addition to the professional male priests and shamans, there is an equal—and sometimes even larger—number of women devoted to the same religious interests. There is no such thing as a female Buyya or a female Siggamaran, but the other male offices all have their feminine counterparts.

I have already given an account of the Idaibois, the girls who assist at funerary ceremonies. They correspond to the Idaimarans. Similarly there is a class of Kuranbois[1] who correspond to the Kuranmarans. They too, like the men, are of different kinds, with varying powers and duties.

The Raudakumbois are shamanins whose essential quality is the capacity to fall into trance: the Saora verb *raud-* means to faint, to be in trance, to be under the power of a spirit. They can officiate at a wide variety of ceremonies, at the Doripur, the Uyungpur, all ordinary sacrifices, and in the Boramsingi area at least at the Harvest Festivals. But only men can perform the Ajorapur and the rites after such ill-omened deaths as suicide, murder or accident.

The Guarkumbois, who are sometimes also known as Gobgobkumbois—the women who sit, from the great length of some of the funerary ceremonies—resemble the Idaibois in being concerned primarily with the rites for the dead. But they differ from the Idaibois in having tutelaries, in being capable of trance, and in the fact that they take a leading part in ceremonial, while the Idaibois are mere assistants.

The theory and practice of the shamanins has been very fully worked out by the Koraput Saoras. Here at least a number of distinctions in addition to the difference in function are made between the Raudakumbois and the Guarkumbois. The Raudakumboi's tutelary is either a real tutelary or the apotheosized ghost of a

[1] *Kuranboi* is the contracted form, used in ordinary speech, of the word *kuranbojan*.

Raudakumbmaran. The Guarkumboi's tutelary is one who on earth was a Guarkumbmaran.

A Guarkumboi ought not to marry and have children; a Raudakumboi may. A Guarkumboi is usually trained and initiated by a father's sister; a Raudakumboi may be initiated by anyone (including the father's sister) or by her tutelary in dreams. A Guarkumboi must receive the gift of a sacred lamp from an older woman who initiates her; the Raudakumboi finds this an advantage, but it is not essential.

A third type of shamanin is one who has no tutelary and cannot be possessed by the spirits in trance. She may be like Arari of Boramsingi, who was disqualified, as it were, because she broke the rules by marrying (although she was a Guarkumboi) before she received the gift of a lamp.[1] She may be just inefficient, like several of the older women who are content to work as omen-takers. She may have been appointed by Labosum, as Bejonto of Sogeda was, and be in a position to perform simple sacrifices in the home and assist at the Harvest Festivals, but not to do anything complicated that would require the assistance of a tutelary.

There are also Regambois, the feminine counterparts of the Regamarans, who are chiefly concerned in providing 'medicine' against sorcerers, but I have never come across one.

Every shamanin is called to her sacred duties at about the time of puberty as a result of a remarkable dream-experience (which is paralleled in the experience of the shamans) which results in her 'marriage' to a tutelary from the Under World. This spiritual marriage is not generally a bar to marriage on earth (though it may be in the case of the Guarkumbois), for the Saoras have no special belief in the magical efficacy of chastity, and the girl usually marries a human husband after a few years. But her dream-lord seems to be equally real to her; to hear a shamanin talking, it is not always easy to say which of her two husbands means more to her.

This experience may follow or precede some formal training in divination. Sometimes a girl whose family has had no previous association may be called to it in a dream and the dream-husband himself may teach her the art. More commonly a girl belongs to a family

[1] A shamanin who has done the wrong things is regarded rather as a nun who has broken her vows. Arari, a very pretty girl, had a secure place in Saora secular life, but the other shamanins had very little use for her.

where the shamanin tradition already exists; the mother or, as so often, the father's sister is a shamanin and begins to prepare the little girl from an early age for her future life. The dream experiences, therefore, are not unexpected (though the convention is to regard them as a great surprise) and this is why they follow a regular pattern, conditioned by the mythology and the social tradition.

The dream which forces a girl into her profession and seals it with supernatural approval takes the form of visits of a suitor from the Under World who proposes marriage with all its ecstatic and numinous consequences. This 'husband' is a Hindu, well-dressed and handsome, wealthy, and observant of many customs to which the Saoras are strangers. He comes, according to tradition, in the depth of night; when he enters the room the whole household is laid under a spell and sleeps like the dead.

In nearly every case, the girl at first refuses, for the profession of shamanin is both arduous and beset with dangers. The result is that she begins to be plagued with nightmares: her divine lover carries her to the Under World or threatens her with a fall from a great height. She generally falls ill; she may even be out of her wits for a time, and wanders pathetically dishevelled in the fields and woods. The family then takes a hand. Since in most cases the girl has been having training for some time, everyone knows what she is in for, and even if she herself does not tell her parents what is happening they usually have a shrewd idea. But the proper thing is for the girl herself to confess to her parents that she has been 'called', that she has refused, and that she is now in danger. This immediately relieves her own mind of its burden of guilt and sets the parents free to act. They at once arrange the girl's marriage with her tutelary.

For of course the mysterious suitor from below is none other than one of the tutelaries whom I have already described in chapter II. An ikon must be painted for him; sacrifice must be prepared; and on the appointed day there is an elaborate ceremony, much more elaborate than an ordinary marriage between human beings, at which the girl is both 'married' to her tutelary and dedicated as a shamanin. Either now or a little later, when she has proved herself, her dedication is confirmed by a gift of a sacred lamp from the older woman who has trained her.

After the marriage, the shamanin's spirit-husband visits her regularly and lies with her till dawn. He may even take her away into the jungle for days at a time, feeding her there on palm wine. In due course a child is born and the ghostly father brings it every night to be nursed by the girl. But the relationship is not primarily a sexual one; the important thing is that the tutelary husband should inspire and instruct his young wife in her dreams, and when she goes to perform her sacred duties he sits by her and tells her what to do.

At first a girl sits with other shamanins until she is thoroughly adept and experienced, for this is a profession where mistakes may lead to tragic consequences. When she is completely ready the young shamanin starts her own practice and she will soon be in as great a demand as any of the others. Her duties are many and exacting. If she is a Guarkumboi, she must attend every funeral within the area she serves; she must officiate or assist at the Guar, Karja, Sikunda and Limma ceremonies; she must take part in the lengthy Name-giving rituals. A Raudakumboi may not only have to attend to the funerary rites (though in the Boramsingi area she is excluded from these), but in addition she has the enormous burden of treating the sick, and of assisting at the Harvest Festivals. Most shamanins have at least three ceremonies a week to attend, and some are engaged every day.

It is in the treatment of the sick that a shamanin finds her greatest scope and fulfilment. Her methods of diagnosis and cure are varied and ingenious; she uses the fan and the lamp, the bow and the sword, handfuls of rice and pots of wine. Now she dances in ecstasy, now lies lost to the world in trance. When she has found the cause of disease or tragedy, she is at infinite pains to heal the wounds; she sucks infection from her patient's body, burns it with flashes of gun-powder, bites and kisses it, massages it to expel the evil, orders the sacrifice of goat or buffalo, directs the village artist in the composition of sacred pictures flattering to the spirits, dedicates pots, speaks healing and consoling words. She works ceaselessly, for she is inspired not only by pride in her profession, but also by her love for the tribal community she serves.

II. *The Spiritual Marriage and its Sequel*

LET us listen to the accounts which some of these shamanins themselves give of their supernatural experiences. In the village of Bung-ding, on the boundary between Ganjam and Koraput, there was living in 1944 a beautiful and accomplished shamanin named Sondan. This is how she described her initiation and subsequent experiences.

When I was a little girl of about ten years, some tutelaries came from below to betroth me with pots of wine. One of them took me by force at night, and gave me a lot to drink. They were very pleased with me. When I told my parents they knew that the gods would be pleased with us and would help us. As I grew older, I used occasionally to lose consciousness, but generally only for a few minutes at a time. My father called a shaman and he said, 'A tutelary wants to marry her. That is why he gave her wine to drink. Now give her a winnowing-fan.'

I had no one to teach me, no guide or instructor. But I took the fan and poured rice into it. Soon a tutelary came. My father asked him, 'Why do you keep on troubling this girl? She may die if you don't leave her alone.' But the tutelary said, 'No, I am pleased with your daughter. I have given her a lot of wine to drink and I am going to marry her. Then if anyone falls ill and she sends for me, I will tell her what is the matter, and help her to cure her patient. I insist on marrying her. Give me a she-goat and I will come into the house.' At that my father killed a she-goat, filled a pot with rice and hung it to the roof and the tutelary came into the house.

So now I was married and five years ago I had a child from my tutelary. I knew it was born, for my tutelary used to bring him at night for my milk. He came when everyone was asleep and cried and drank my milk. People in the village heard him, but my own family slept as if they were dead. Later I married a man in this world, but because I have had a child in the other world I don't think I will ever have one here.

Sondan was mistaken in this, for she soon had a fine boy. Her own fate is shrouded in mystery. Her husband was the son of a man who had been murdered, and when I visited Bungding in 1951 I found that Sondan herself was dead and no one would say why.

Sondan was a Raudakumboi, permitted to live a full life in this world as well as in the next. Amiya of Singjangring was older, about 35 when I recorded her story in 1948, a Guarkumboi and still a virgin.

My tutelary's name is Narsingo; he dresses like a Government official and lives in a big white house. My father's sister Sintam was a shamanin; her tutelary's name was Daiyo; she had a son Kartino and a daughter Sarjanni from him. Narsingo is Daiyo's father's sister's son. So long as Sintam was alive she taught me everything she knew. At my first menses, a tutelary named Vittam came to me in a dream and said, 'I want to marry you. For your sake I have left my brother and my family and I have come to you.' I made no reply, and he mounted his horse and rode away.

But a few days later another tutelary came: he was riding on an elephant and had two servants armed with guns. This was my Narsingo. He sat down beside me and said, 'I've come for you; don't listen to anyone else; I want to marry you.' I still kept silent, and he mounted his elephant and rode away.

Then back came Vittam on his horse saying, 'Will you marry me or not?' This time I summoned up my courage and said No. He was very upset; he dragged me out of my house, put me on his horse and flew away with me; his horse flew like a kite. As I looked down at the great spaces below me I fainted with fear. But he held me tightly in his arms and when I came to, I found myself in his house in the Under World. The house had four doors and it was fenced all round with thorns. He locked me up and went away.

Then my father's sister's tutelary Daiyo, and Narsingo, and four other tutelaries got an aeroplane and came to look for me. When they saw Vittam's house with all the doors shut and the fence of thorns, Daiyo said, 'There can't be anyone there.' But just as they were about to go away Narsingo heard a little noise, it was the sound of my tears, and he said, 'There she is.' He drew his sword and cut a way through the fence, took a great stone and broke down the door, and came in. There was a grain bin on the loft and I crept into it and hid, for I was not sure what would happen. Narsingo lit a torch and searched for me. Suddenly he saw my hair and he caught hold of it and pulled me out of the grain-bin. We all got into the aeroplane and flew back to earth and I returned to my own house.

After this experience I told my aunt that I did not want to be a shamanin; it was altogether too exciting. I have never been one for the men, and there were too many tutelaries after me. But Sintam said, 'No, marry Narsingo, and all will be well.' Soon after that she died. At her Guar ceremony, the shamanin Jigri said, 'I can't sit for this by myself; you must sit with me.' I could not disobey her, no one could, so I sat down beside her and presently Sintam's ghost came on Jigri and Narsingo came on me. Narsingo said, 'I have taken a great deal of trouble to win this girl; that aeroplane alone cost me a fortune; I love her very much; she has got to marry me.' I said to Jigri, 'Very well, when the Guar is finished, I will marry him.'

So next day I had an ikon made for Narsingo and for his brother Iganu and I sacrificed a goat. But I said to Narsingo, 'I will not sleep with you for five years.' Very soon now the time will be up and I will have to sleep with him. Narsingo said, 'That's all right, but if you don't sleep with me, you are not going to sleep with anyone else.' I said, 'I have no desire to sleep with anyone; I am not that sort of girl.'

That is why I have never married and have never been to a man. Many people have come to betroth me, but I have always refused them. Many men have tried to seduce me too, but they leave me alone when I tell them about my tutelary. All the same I never sleep away from home, however important the ceremony on which I am engaged, for fear that I may be seduced. I come home alone even at midnight and I am not afraid. So long as I am not seduced I shall be all right.

Amiya received the lamp which confirmed her dedication from her aunt Jigri, whose name often appears in these pages. In 1950 I found Amiya training her own niece Rogi, to whom she would in turn hand a sacred lamp when she was ready. Jigri set the fashion of virginity in this area and the very attractive little Rogi declared that she was going to follow her example. Jigri herself began life as an Idaiboi, but when she was about fifteen she 'married' a tutelary. He gave her 'sterility-medicine' to eat so that they should not have any spirit-children, and because of this he insisted that she should be a Guarkumboi and not officiate at any but funerary rites. The reason why she did not marry, however, was not directly connected with her profession. After the tragic death of her brothers from sorcery (see p. 236), she had a dream in which her father's ghost, her tutelary, Labosum and Uyungsum visited her and told her that if she married, all her babies would die in infancy and that she should therefore remain a virgin and adopt and care for her brothers' children and look after the family property.

In the Boramsingi area, Jigri was of great influence during her life, and her ghost is almost as important now she is dead. An old leper woman called Idan suffered all her life because she refused to conform to Jigri's exacting standards. She was a Raudakumboi of Boramsingi and this is her story.

I was born in the upper hamlet of Boramsingi about two score and ten years ago. My mother and my maternal grandmother were both shamanins and both were lepers, but no other members of my family have had the disease. My mother Sachuni had a tutelary named Rasuno.

When I was about sixteen I married a man called Bujuno in the lower hamlet of my village, and a year later I had a child by him. Shortly afterwards my mother died and I had a dream in which her tutelary Rasuno came to me and said, 'I was married to your mother, but since she died I have been alone. So I am going to marry you.' I replied, 'But I have a child; how can I do the work of a shamanin?' But Rasuno took no notice of what I said and after a few days made me ill with high fever. I sent for a shamanin and Rasuno came on her and said, 'I am going to marry her; if she does not agree, she will go mad.' I sacrificed a fowl and begged him to leave me alone, but it was no use. Soon afterwards I went mad and used to wander about the village and out into the woods, dancing and singing. Then I sent for another shamanin, and this time Rasuno said, 'It is my desire. If she does not consent, I shall take her away.' My husband was frightened when he heard this and said, 'Don't take her away. I will give you anything you want, and she shall marry you. But don't take her away.' So the next day my husband sacrificed a goat, had an ikon painted and dedicated a pot for Rasuno. No one gave me a lamp, for Jigri was angry that I was becoming a shamanin after marriage and a child. But my mother's ghost and Rasuno gave me my lamp in a dream. No one taught me; I learnt everything in dreams.

Then I had a son and a daughter in the Under World, and another child in this world, and soon afterwards my husband died. I was all right then, but about five years later Uyung-Madusum came to me and ran his hands all over my body, tickling me and making me laugh. But afterwards I found sores on my body, and gradually my fingers and toes rotted away. I went to a shamanin and Uyung-Madusum came to her, and said, 'It was I who attacked Idan.' My tutelary came and quarrelled with him saying, 'She is my wife; leave her alone.' But Madusum said, 'She may be your wife, but I am going to marry her as well. I won't do anything with her, but I like to come and tickle her a bit, and we can laugh and joke together.' I tried my best to send Uyung-Madusum away; I offered a pig and then a fowl; but he refused to go, and in the end I had to have an ikon and a pot for him. He is greater than Rasuno, and when I die I shall not join my tutelary, but I shall go to Uyung-Madusum.

Ever since I became a leper I have had many dreams. Sometimes I dream that I am going to catch fish, but the fish slip through my hands, and crabs bite my toes and fingers. Sometimes I dream that I am very cold; I crouch over the fire and fall asleep. Then I fall into the fire and burn my hands and feet. Often I dream that I am cutting grass and the sickle slips and cuts my fingers. Or I am on my way to the hills to get wood and grass and I stub my toes against rocks on the path. Sometimes I dream of a young and handsome youth who tickles me and we sit and laugh together.

Since becoming a shamanin I have cured many people. I chiefly deal with Uyungsum and Madusum—perhaps six times every month. Everybody remembers how I cured a man called Mapru who was very ill, attacked by Dorisum. He went to three other shamanins before coming to me; only I was able to cure him. And there was another man with bad eyes, who went to several others, but it was I who made him well.

But in fact, although she considered herself an expert, Idan was not highly regarded in Boramsingi, where the orthodox Jigri insisted that no true shamanin should be married, at least not before dedication, and that she must be initiated by the gift of a lamp from an older woman. Idan was in less demand than other shamanins, and when she was employed for a ceremony she was paid less. Poor people, who could not afford the more expensive shamanins, used to send for her.

Although in the course of her treatment, Idan handled her patients freely, passing her hands over their bodies, blowing in their ears and sucking at their skin, I was unable to find any evidence that she had spread her disease. Her account of Uyung-Madusum, the god of leprosy who works for the Sun-god, as a handsome youth who tickled her and made her laugh, is grimly horrible.

Champa, a middle-aged shamanin of Borai, was named after her paternal grandmother, who had also been a shamanin and had insisted that her name should be given to the child.

My father's mother was a shamanin, so was his sister. After her death, my father's sister's tutelary came to me in a dream, bringing with him another tutelary called Potnadeyi. He was a Paik by caste and was dressed in smart Hindu clothes. My aunt's tutelary said, 'I have brought this man to marry you, but you must serve me as well.' I was afraid, saying to myself, 'This is a Paik; how can I marry him?' and I refused. Again and again he came to me in dreams, and I always refused. Then one night he took me up in a whirlwind and carried me away to a very high tree, where he made me sit on a fragile branch. There he began to sing and as he sang he swung me to and fro. I was terrified of falling from that great height and I hastily agreed to marry him. Then we sat for a time swinging and singing together. The following night, my tutelary came and taught me how to use the winnowing-fan. Many other gods came with him and they said, 'We are all very pleased with you; now celebrate your marriage with a feast.' When I woke and the memory came to me I was like a mad woman and I fell unconscious to the ground. For six months I did nothing and was unwell all the time.

At last my father said to the tutelary, 'If you like this girl, by all means marry her, but don't go on pestering her.' The following Friday I made offerings to my tutelary and hung up a pot. My father gave a goat, four fowls, and some parched rice. Then my tutelary came upon me and using my hands drew a picture on the wall. He said to me, 'Now we are married, do not waste your time, and if you have any trouble, call me at once.' After a year a child was born to me in the Under World, and my tutelary brought him to me to drink my milk. I was frightened, for the child screamed and screamed. In the morning the neighbours asked, 'Who was that child crying in the night?' I said, 'I have no idea.' The following night my tutelary said, 'This is your own child; why are you afraid?' After that he used to bring him to me every day. A year afterwards a daughter was born in the

Under World. The boy's name is Pasno, and he is now ten years old, and the girl is called Pasuni and is six. At festivals the two children come to me in dreams crying, 'We are dying of hunger; give us something to eat.' I feed them first and then their father. A year after Pasuni was born, I married a human husband from Gundruba.

It occasionally happens that a shamanin has to 'marry' two or even three tutelaries; this is curious, for polyandry is unknown even as a legend among the Saoras. For example, at Kittim a shamanin had a tutelary called Tikamo, who had a younger brother (also of course a tutelary) called Dahipano. Dahipano's 'wife' was a Luara Saora girl of Boramsingi. She died young, and as a result Dahipano went blind. One day he came with his elder brother to the Kittim shamanin and said, 'I am all alone, blind, childless; you must have me too.' Tikamo magnanimously said, 'By all means, let him have anything of mine that is left over.' The shamanin accordingly took him as her second tutelary husband, and made an ikon for him below his brother's. Tikai, a young shamanin of Gundurba, had a similar experience.

My paternal grandmother was a shamanin and she used to make me sit with her and she showed me what to do. Five years after her death, three tutelaries, Siggan, Ilari and Dukhi, came to me in a dream. The first two were young, but Dukhi was rather old. They sat round me and said, 'We are all going to marry you.' I replied, 'I will marry one of you; how can I marry all three?' Dukhi said, 'If you don't marry us all, we will take you away into the Under World,' and in a rage he caught me by the hair and pulled it hard. He picked me up and was going to throw me into the sky and I was so frightened that I agreed to marry all three at once. Dukhi told me to make separate ikons and dedicate separate pots for each of them.

I had heard that people who delayed obeying the orders of the tutelaries fell ill, so early next morning I told my father what had happened. He got everything ready for the wedding. I fasted and after the pictures had been made and the pots hung from the ceiling, three hens were sacrificed and the marriage was celebrated.

After this I began to work as a shamanin, but so far I have only been able to treat simple diseases, as we are too poor to give a big enough feast to satisfy my three husbands. They come to me from time to time, but they are still careless about me and stay only for a little while. They take me along the road to the Under World, but half-way there they send me back saying that they cannot take me the whole way until I give a proper marriage feast. So far I have had six patients; I have cured four, but two of them have died.

In one unusual case, a little girl was 'married' to her tutelary when she was only a year old. It came about this way. A man called Jagu at Talasingi had a paternal grandmother called Suganni who was a shamanin. When Jagu's wife had her first baby, Suganni's ghost came on the shaman at the Name-giving ceremony and said that she was coming to the child and that her name should be given. They agreed and named the baby after her. Then came Suganni's tutelary and said, 'You have given this child the name of my shamanin, so I am going to marry her.' The parents protested, 'She is but a baby; let her grow up and then you can do what you will.' But the tutelary said, 'No. In the meantime, other tutelaries will be after her. I won't do anything to her, but she must be married to me. If you refuse I will take her to the Under World and marry her there.' At that the parents agreed, and they made an ikon for the tutelary, and sacrificed, and made the baby a shamanin then and there.

Many other examples of shamanins' reminiscences might be given, but they tend to resemble each other so closely that it is not necessary. Each account stresses the importunity of the spirit-lover, the disastrous consequences of rejecting him, the happiness that the spirit-children bring. 'The only dreams I remember', says old Chhimari of Lakkikai, 'are those in which I go below and see my children. For I have no children here and my husband has been long dead.'

The realism with which this relationship is imagined is very striking. A shamanin knows the names not only of her tutelary and her children, but the names of his relatives and even of his servants. She has to feed and clothe her children and as they grow up has to get them clothes of larger size. Kumpanti of Garabhand gave birth to her daughter Indapiro in a dream. 'After she was born, her father took her with the cord and placenta dangling from her to the Under World.'

Even the quarrels of earth may be reflected in the Under World. Arari, the young shamanin of Boramsingi who went wrong, was supposed to have paid a fine of a buffalo to her family when she got married. The quarrel went on for years in the village, but in the meantime the tutelary of Jigri, Arari's aunt, fined Arari's tutelary and the latter had to sacrifice a buffalo and give a feast in the Under World.

The shamanins talk very freely about their tutelaries, and get teased about them. Boys say to a young shamanin, 'How can a great creature like so and so—naming the tutelary—enter you with his enormous organ?' And people used to say to the virginal Amiya,

'You won't sleep with us; you must be saving it all up for Narsingo (her tutelary). What a lucky fellow he is; if only we could change places' and so on. The shamanins take all this in very good part and join in the laughter against themselves. On one occasion, Narsingo accused Amiya (through the lips of a shamanin) of betraying him and demanded a buffalo in compensation. Amiya indignantly denied the charge which caused great amusement and was, I believe, entirely false. No one took the accusation seriously, for what the spirits say is not evidence.

III. *A Shamanin's Marriage*

On 20 April 1946, I assisted at Sogeda at the dedication of a young shamanin named Sarpoli, a girl of about fifteen years who had recently passed the menarche. Two years later she was forcibly married to the Chief of her village as his fourth wife. The ceremony was conducted by the talented shamanin Sinaki and was lengthy and confused, for there were many irrelevant features.

Sarpoli had contracted to marry her tutelary, who was named Naianto, some months before and she had told her friends that he was young and handsome. She had several dreams in which he came to her and said, 'I have travelled everywhere, but I have never seen anyone who attracts me so much as you do.' After some persuasion she agreed to marry him. But she then changed her mind, and this led to another dream of a less pleasant kind; now Naianto carried her down to the Under World and shut her up in his house. But she managed to make a little hole in the wall and her soul slipped through and escaped. Naianto was very angry and followed her home and made her unconscious. Through the shaman he threatened that if she did not agree to marry him, he would keep her tied up in his house—thus suggesting that she would remain out of her wits for a long time. Her family promised that the marriage would be celebrated as soon as possible and a fowl was sacrificed, after which the girl recovered.

On the day of the dedication ceremony, the first task was to paint a suitable ikon on the wall of Sarpoli's house, and the official artist, the Ittalmaran, was summoned. He painted a large picture representing the tutelary's house and his many servants and friends in the Under World. Sinaki then made an altar beneath the ikon with little mounds of rice, a lamp and cups of wine. She sat before it, and presently her own tutelary came upon her, closely followed by Naianto.

She rose to her feet and carefully examined the painting with her lamp, and Naianto said, 'It is good, but there should be drawings of my mirror and a comb.' For he had asked Sarpoli to give him these things as a wedding present. The artist completed the picture, and then Sinaki and Sarpoli's mother made the girl sit between them and washed her hands and feet with palm wine, saying, 'Today you are married; today you will become great.' Then Naianto again possessed Sinaki and said, 'I am well pleased with this girl and I will marry her and take her to the Under World, where she will see all her new relations.' Sarpoli's mother was distressed at this and cried, 'We have made you a beautiful house on the wall and have prepared the marriage feast; if you take the girl below she will die.' This annoyed the tutelary and he said, 'Don't talk to me like that; if you won't do what I want, I'll have nothing more to do with you,' and he went away. Then Sarpoli herself got frightened and ran away and hid behind a grain-bin. When she did this, the tutelary returned, very annoyed, and demanded to know where his future wife was hiding.

Members of the family quickly brought the girl back, made her sit down and her mother and the shamanin Sinaki held her by the hands and began to chant the usual incantations. A cock had been dedicated for sacrifice to the tutelary, and it was persuaded to perch on Sarpoli's head: it remained there for a considerable time. A very large company had assembled by now, and two other shamanins took swords in their hands and began to dance. Sinaki picked up two new earthen pots and tossed them in the air, throwing them up and catching them again and again. This was a test—if the pots did not break it would be a happy marriage. When she had finished and the pots were undamaged, Sinaki began to instruct the younger girl in her duties, saying, 'This is the day of your marriage; from today you will be great, and from today you are to work in such and such a way.' She told her the names of the gods, and how to divine, and how to offer sacrifice, and though none of the information can have been new to her, the instruction took over an hour.

Sarpoli seems to have been rather alarmed at the multiplicity of the duties that were falling to her, or it may have been just a natural modesty, for she again ran away to hide. The tutelary repeated his protests, and the girl's mother pleaded with him. 'Don't be angry; she is still very young and does not know how to do things properly yet. You yourself must teach her what to do, and then she will know how to behave.' They again brought Sarpoli back and made her sit down in front of the altar. Then Sinaki prepared to dedicate the two pots with which she had already tested the omens; she cleaned and husked some rice and put it with a ring and some turmeric into one; tied a thread with a brass bangle round the other, and hung them both up in front of the new ikon. Then she sat down and made the dedicated cock perch on her shoulder. She fed it with rice and wine, and gave it a little bit of mango, after which mangoes were distributed to everyone present. Somebody killed the cock and it was taken into the kitchen to be cooked. Then Sinaki took Sarpoli in her arms and called on the tutelary to visit them. He came and Sarpoli fell into a trance for the first time. The two girls lay down together, and Sinaki put one of her legs across Sarpoli's body as a symbol of the physical aspect of the marriage. Some of the people laughed at this and Sinaki rebuked them. 'We are gods; we do what we will. Do not laugh and do not interfere.' Then Sinaki addressed Naianto: 'Now you are married to this girl, don't trouble her, don't desert her, but always come willingly to help her.'

After this the whole party went round the village, and wherever there was a house of shaman or shamanin, they showed Sarpoli the ikons on the wall and the sacred implements of divination. They returned, and once again Sinaki held the young bride in her arms; she rubbed her body with turmeric and again explained her duties, taught her and nursed her as if she were a little child.

The ceremonies continued throughout the day. There was dancing and many shamanins came from neighbouring villages and fell into trance and prophesied. The proceedings concluded with a feast to which the members of Sarpoli's family group and a number of important persons were invited.

IV. *The Shamanin's 'Conversion'*

How far does this crisis in the life of a Saora girl—or youth—compare with the experience of conversion, which has been studied by many psychologists[1] and has been called 'the most striking of adolescent religious phenomena'? Pratt, who has described, among others,

[1] See J. B. Pratt, *The Religious Consciousness* (New York, 1923); W. James, *The Varieties of Religious Experience* (London, 1902—I quote from the 1922 reprint); E. D. Starbuck, *The Psychology of Religion* (New York, 1903); J. H. Leuba, 'The Psychology of Religious Phenomena—Conversion', *American Journal of Psychology*, vol. VII (1896).

the conversions of Chaitanya, Ramakrishna Paramahamsa and Devendranath Tagore, distinguishes two types of conversion, corresponding to William James's distinction between the 'healthy-minded' and the 'sick' soul. The first, which is usually characteristic of the healthy-minded optimistic extrovert, is a gradual process. 'The new ideals grow rather silently, at times break out into somewhat noisy conflict with each other and with the more primitive powers of unmodified impulse, but in the main they win their victories by the subtle modification of values, and by the end of the adolescent period the young man finds himself a fairly unified person.'[1] In this sense, conversion is a perfectly normal adolescent phenomenon, 'incidental to the passage from the child's small universe to the wider intellectual and spiritual life of maturity'.[2]

The 'sick soul', sensitive, thoughtful and introverted, has a harder struggle, but often attains its end by a short and dramatic crisis that shortens the period of adolescent stress. The feeling of guilt and imperfection, religious and theological doubt, introspective brooding over the future life throws the soul into the depths of despair, yet at the same time prepares it to rise to heights undreamt by more placid and perhaps more commonplace natures.

But in either case the end is the same; the soul grows up, the adolescent antedates his physical development and becomes spiritually mature; equilibrium takes the place of uncertainty; a sense of unity and strength transforms the old division of purpose and weakness of will. If the conversion is a religious one, to say a man is converted means that 'religious ideas, previously peripheral in his consciousness, now take a central place, and that religious aims form the habitual centre of his energy'.[3]

In this sense the experience of the Saora shamanin[4] is certainly a form of conversion. It occurs during the critical period of adolescence; it has far-reaching consequences that affect her entire life; it organizes her personality round an ideal. But two elements often prominent in religious conversion are absent. There is no idea of turning from a life of sin to a life of virtue, and there is no change from an attitude of disbelief to the discovery and acceptance of theological truth.

A sense of sin is rare in tribal, as in most oriental, religion; there was no hint in her dedication ceremony that Sarpoli had ever been

[1] Pratt, op. cit., p. 124. [2] James, op. cit., p. 199. [3] ibid., p. 196.
[4] This discussion applies, of course, equally to the youth who becomes a shaman.

a naughty girl and that she must now repent, though there was certainly some stress on her need to live virtuously hereafter. The 'spiritual marriage' of the shamanin is a highly-moralized experience, and undoubtedly plays its part in building up that high sense of marital fidelity that is characteristic of Hill Saora womanhood. For the shamanin finds a surrogate for promiscuity in the dream-fantasy —and it must be noted that this fantasy is always of a husband, not of a lover, in the other world.

And since this husband belongs to a community which the Saoras regard as morally superior to themselves, the shamanin has to observe many of the rules and taboos of the Hindu caste into which she has 'married'. She has to be strict about menstruation rules which other Saora women ignore; she must be careful about the disposal of left-over food; she must maintain her dignity with truth and honesty; she must prove her loyalty to her tutelary lord by her fidelity to her human husband; above all she must work hard both at home and before the altar, and maintain the highest standard of ritual exactitude.

But none of this involves any violent break with the past. For some time before the dramatic crisis of her 'marriage', every shamanin goes through a period of training, in the course of which she becomes acquainted with the duties that will be required of her. In this respect, therefore, we have a typical healthy-minded conversion situation. The appalling pains of conscience that afflicted Bunyan, the self-questionings of Tolstoi, the lust of the spirit against the flesh that divided the great soul of Augustine, are absent here. But the claims of conscience will henceforth be no less insistent, the demands of the moral law no less imperative. Even the youngest shamanin is a person set apart, and a girl's failure to live up to the terms of her dedication brings swift and drastic punishment.

Saora conversion does not involve a turning from irreligion to religion, from doubt to faith, for there is no such thing as an irreligious or unbelieving Saora, certainly not an irreligious or unbelieving Saora woman. But when a girl accepts the position of a shamanin, religion undoubtedly becomes more real to her. 'Youth', says Garrison, 'is confronted with the problem of making the transition from the religion of childhood to that of his elders, which is to become a personal possession, an internal experience. To the child, God is away off somewhere; to the developing adolescent, he becomes an internal presence.'[1]

[1] K. C. Garrison, *The Psychology of Adolescence* (New York, 1946), p. 112.

17. Sinaki, a well-known shamanin of Sogeda

18. A typical Idaiboi from Olleida: such girls generally cease to perform funerary functions after marriage

This language is not exactly applicable to the Saora, but we may modify it and say that to the Saora child, as to the 'unconverted' Saora woman, the whole complex of religion is external and remote, a tribal interest rather than a personal need, a thing for emergency, an antidote to danger and disaster, rather than an intimate cherished possession. But a tutelary brings religion into a girl's heart; the alien, rather forbidding theological scene becomes alive, peopled by relatives and friends; from the very beginning the young shamanin is possessed by spirits who enter into her and use her body to express themselves; the whole tedious business of cups and leaves and drops of wine becomes alive and fascinating; now the Saora faith is hers and she is its servant.

And on the purely practical plane, religion is now the shamanin's profession; it is quite literally meat and drink to her; it controls her dreams as well as the more important moments of her waking hours.

Saora conversion, though essentially of the 'healthy-minded' type, is often marked by conflict. The girl refuses her suitor from the Under World; she delays as long as possible her act of dedication. Her refusal is followed by terrifying dreams and she falls ill, sometimes for a long period. She can be cured only by acceptance and surrender.

This conflict can be traced to two causes. Conversion is one of those means by which an adolescent is freed from her conventional infantile dependence on her parents. In several of the case-histories I have recorded the young girl may be seen clinging to an aunt or mother, depending on her for everything, looking to her as teacher and guide. Marriage with a tutelary, bringing as it does a new source of instruction and inspiration, frees the girl from this dependence. But the deliverance is not won easily. The emotional ties of childhood are not readily severed. New objects of attachment are not quickly accepted. Deutsch emphasizes the fact that shortly before the new objects are found, the rising intellectual drives turn for a time to the old objects, and this creates a characteristic difficulty. 'Affective struggles take place between an intense desire to "get away" and an equally intense urge to "go back", and this backward movement, which is now endowed with sexual force, actually arises from the re-establishment of an old situation that existed before the beginning of the latency period.'[1]

[1] H. Deutsch, *The Psychology of Women* (London, 1946), p. 91.

But the conflict is not only due to a fear of being independent of the mother. The girl plays with her fantasies, yet at the same time she is desperately afraid of them; she has a very natural dread of her awe-inspiring contact with the other world and of the strange beings who haunt her dreams. In any case, it may generally be said that the adolescent girl prefers an imaginary to a real relationship and desires to postpone realization. The girl shrinks too from the taboos and discipline, the responsibility, the arduous labour and the risk which acceptance involves.

This conflict frequently leads to illness and hysteria, which may be connected with both causes. It may be partly due to the girl's identification with or dependence on the mother for, as Deutsch says, 'a number of conversion symptoms, particularly lack of appetite and similar disturbances, all kinds of phobias and paranoiac ideas (fear of poisoning) are connected with such an inability to dissolve the old attachment to the mother'.[1] The refusal to accept the tutelary also seems to lead to a sense of guilt. Normally this refusal is kept a secret—for directly it is revealed to the parents they insist on the performance of the necessary rites—and it is well known that a guilty secret often leads to nervous collapse. 'The belief that guarding a guilty secret results in sickness,' says Aldrich, 'is very prevalent among primitives; and persons who have studied modern psychology know that the savages are absolutely correct in this belief.'[2] Confession, in the sense of telling the parents what has happened, and surrender, in the sense of undergoing the dedication ceremony and making the necessary sacrifices, invariably leads to recovery. The conversion is complete, and the girl who but a few days before was prostrate and helpless is filled with vigour and enthusiasm.

An important point made by Cole is that conversions are often socially conditioned. 'The number of conversions is steadily becoming smaller. Except among a certain class of Negroes, it is no longer the fashion in America to "get religion". Conversion is undoubtedly quite as much a pattern of social behaviour as a spontaneous individual experience. In the past, situations have often been deliberately arranged so as to produce conversions; people remained in church for many successive hours, in the midst of singing, praying, shouting

[1] Deutsch, op. cit., p. 92.

[2] C. R. Aldrich, *The Primitive Mind and Modern Civilization* (London, 1931), p. 219.

and general excitement.'[1] The social conditioning of Saora conversion is obvious; it is one of the things that happens to adolescent girls; people expect it and do their best to make things easy; the general social approval and applause must be a strong factor in helping a girl to make up her mind.

Cole also stresses the place of fatigue in conversion. The first result of the long-drawn services in church is extreme physical and emotional exhaustion. A similar result is achieved by the endless ceremonies and inquiries to which a girl, sick as a result of rejecting her tutelary, is subjected. 'A person in such a condition is highly suggestible.' And the Saora girl has her doubts and hesitations still further inhibited by copious draughts of wine. The social setting, the fatigue, the excitement, the stimulus of alcohol combine to produce a condition of suggestibility in which the girl willingly turns from her former careless and childlike life to one of responsibility and toil.

The 'marriage' of the shamanin, then, is akin to conversion in that it is one of the phenomena of adolescence; it frees a girl from dependence on her mother; it makes religion central to her life and subjects her to strong moral imperatives. The experience is often marked by resistance and conflict and consequent illness which, however, disappears on confession and surrender. On the other hand, ideas about delivery from sin and the transformation of disbelief to faith are absent. The shamanin's conversion is rather an organization of psychic energy around a new interest. It marks the transition from disassociation to unity and thus from mediocrity to significance. The girls who have given themselves to this arduous and sometimes dangerous adventure are unusually self-possessed and dignified. They have an air of authority. Their actions are marked by what I can only call charity; they are interested in people, for they have the power to allay and cure their ills. And these virtues do not pass with time. The older shamanins retain much of the devotion and enthusiasm of their younger years. For them, as for others, 'youth is the time for hailing the vision and coming to love the light; the religious task of the great middle years is to live and act in the light that has been seen.'[2]

[1] L. Cole, *Psychology of Adolescence* (New York, 1943, revised edition, 1947), p. 277.
[2] Pratt, *Religious Consciousness*, p. 120.

V. *Some Special Cases*

THE Saoras regard eunuchs with some reverence. At Sogeda there was a eunuch about forty years old, Saronti by name, a very nice person, who practised as a shamanin. Although the male characters were rather more prominent (he had a rudimentary penis and no breasts), he dressed as a woman, and even had the lobes of his ears enlarged. His experiences 'throbbing between two worlds' may be of interest.

My mother was a shamanin. Formerly I lived in the Under World where I was a Saora and a woman. But while I was still in my mother's belly, Labosum and my mother's own tutelary quarrelled over me, for both wanted to marry me. As a result I was born as a man. At the time of my birth, Labosum, who was very annoyed by what had happened, did his best to kill my mother, but they gave him a pig and he went away. When I grew up a little, however, Labosum caught me and made me mad. He took me about and hid me in fields and streams. In the end my father had to go out into the jungle and sacrifice a pig and a goat and I recovered. But after this I found that I wanted to live like a woman and be with women, though I never went with boys.

Whenever my mother went away anywhere, I used to get hold of her winnowing-fan and try to work as a shamanin. One day my mother's tutelary came to me in a dream and asked me to marry him. I said nothing, and next day again found myself out of my wits. My mother took her fan and her tutelary came upon her and told her what had happened. Because he wanted to marry me, I had to dress and wear ornaments like a woman. He gave me my present name—Saronti. As soon as my mother agreed to the marriage, I recovered. After a few days my mother made me sit with a fan and taught me what to do. My tutelary came to me and said, 'Do your work carefully and many other tutelaries will come with me to help you.'

At my marriage I gave a goat for my tutelary and a buffalo for his friends. I myself painted an ikon for him and dedicated a pot. It was very expensive entertaining all his friends. After it was over I was able to do my work properly.

But when my mother next took her fan, she could no longer do anything with it, for her tutelary had left her for me. After this, therefore, she gave up doing the work of a shamanin.

My tutelary is a Paik by caste; his name is Donsi. When he was married to my mother, they had a son and daughter; now I too have a child from him and he brings her to me to drink my milk. My tutelary often says to me, 'If you try to marry a girl in this world, you will die.' So I have not married and I do not want to.

One day many tutelaries came to me and said, 'What are you doing here? You are one of us.' For of course I had been a tutelary myself when I was in the Under World before. They said, 'Come down and live with us.' The result was that I fell very ill, but my uncle sacrificed a buffalo and I recovered.

There are some unusual circumstances in this account. In the first place, Saronti believed that he was formerly a tutelary himself and that he had come to earth, possibly to escape the embarrassing attentions of those who wished to marry him there. His marriage with his own mother's tutelary is exceptional, but not unique, and it is interesting that when this happened his mother lost her powers and had to stop her work. Saronti is also unusual in apparently wanting to be a shamanin; he used to practise secretly when his mother was away; and made none of the usual resistance before his 'marriage'.

On the whole, the astonishing fantasies and strange twilight existence of the shamanins do not seem to do them any harm. Most of them are tough and healthy young women or genial hard-working ancients, who have preserved their normality with remarkable success. But fantasy is not always a good companion. 'A girl's strong bent towards fantasy and subjective experience,' says Deutsch, 'while giving birth to the positive qualities of intuition and sympathy, involves certain dangers. Excessive withdrawal from reality strengthens neurotic tendencies. The girl's intellectual development, her social adjustment, and her professional activity can naturally be disturbed by excessive fantasying.'[1]

An interesting example of this is found in the case of Sungan, a Saora girl living in Gundruba, who in 1945 must have been about twenty years old. The remarkable thing about her was that she had lived naked from birth. She was not herself a shamanin, but she was believed to be the daughter of a shaman and his ghostly bride. Her father, the shaman, was a pleasant old man, with no evident psychopathic symptoms, and he told me that his daughter had always been a little 'odd'. She was originally intended, I gathered, to be a boy, but as she was coming into the world, Labosum caught her and changed her into a girl so that she would not reveal any of the secrets of the Under World. Labosum is a god who is supposed to be female in some places, male in others; here Labosum was female, dark and long-haired, and always lived naked. Sungan had to resemble her in every way. Her father described what happened.

[1] Deutsch, *Psychology of Women*, p. 91.

We tried to dress her, but she would say, 'What am I to do with these rags? I have already got the finest clothes to wear. Can't you see that I am already dressed as a Rani?' Even now, if anyone tries to clothe her, she says, 'Can't I plough, build a house, climb a sago palm, and work as well as any man in the fields? What do you want to put rags on me for?' When she was about eight years old, I sent for the shaman and he said, 'It is the tutelaries and the ancestors who are stopping her putting on clothes. They have told her to wear their cloth, not ours. You must be very careful, for if anyone forces her to wear something, he may die.' So we let the girl be, and she lives happily, and we have got used to her. She does every kind of man's work now, even sowing seed.

And in fact, though she was one of the most aggressively feminine creatures I have ever seen, she refused to do women's work; she never carried anything on her head and would not husk grain or cook or fetch water. She avoided men and morally bore a spotless reputation. She never went to dances and slept by herself in a lonely corner of her parents' house. It was said in 1945 that she had not yet menstruated. If anyone asked her, 'Why do you live naked?' she would reply, 'I have to, for I am a goddess.'[1]

VI. *The Shamanin and her Personal Relationships*

THE public benefactor is often a private nuisance, and many a woman who supports the Church undermines the home. Does the shamanin make a good wife and mother? Or do her many duties and the sense of authority and self-importance which she inevitably develops make her careless of her domestic duties and intractable in her domestic relationships? On the whole, I think not. It is true that sometimes a hungry family will find their mother lost in trance when she ought to be cooking the dinner. On the other hand, she may be the only member of the household who produces any dinner to cook. For her perquisites from divination and sacrifice, which I study in chapter XI, are an important addition to the ordinary income of a family. An occasional irritation is more than balanced by a solid profit. The shamanin, like every other Saora woman, works hard in the kitchen and the fields, but naturally she is often called away. But she is usually paid, in cash or in kind, for her services, and I doubt if she is ever really an economic liability in a home.

[1] I describe elsewhere the experiences of a Bison-horn Maria girl which provide an interesting parallel to the Saora fantasies. See my article 'The Saora Priestess' in the *Bulletin of the Department of Anthropology*, vol. I (1952), pp. 72f.

But a shamanin is often out for meals, and generally eats a good deal better than the rest of the family. Husbands do not always like this. This is one reason for the tradition that the Guarkumbois should avoid marriage if possible. 'She may have to sit at a Karja for two whole days; the baby cries; there is no one to cook; she may break a taboo which will make everyone ill; it is better for her not to have a husband.' When the shamanin Sinaki had her first child, she asked her tutelary for 'leave', pointing out that it was impossible to nurse a baby, run a home and maintain her practice at the same time. She sacrificed a fowl, and gave up her duties for over a year.

Things go by fashions. In Boramsingi the shamanins are in control, respected, admired, authoritative; never a word is said against their virtue, but in Tumulu in 1951 I found that shamanins had almost been eliminated from the village, and their place had been taken by shamans. One husband stopped his wife working as a shamanin because, he said, it brought her too closely into touch with other men. 'Shamanins,' he said, 'drink too much; they rub their hands over men's bodies; they go out at any time of the day or night.' This man abused and beat his wife, but he died soon afterwards. Another girl was trained and dedicated as a shamanin in Sogeda; she married a man in Tumulu, went there and began to practise her profession. Her husband soon grew jealous, and since they had no child he began to attribute everything that went wrong to the fact that she was a shamanin. He used to curse her and everyone who sent for her; he would follow her and create unpleasant scenes. In the end he managed to stop her working, with the result that for a time she went out of her mind. In the end she left her husband and went alone to Assam so as to be free to follow her vocation.

Often the conflict is less drastic than this. But the shamanin's unusual position is bound to make her relations with her husband a little delicate. After all, he has a powerful rival; invisible, but all the more attractive for that; of higher social standing, greater wit, an ampler purse; few human husbands can compare with tutelaries. And the wife's position of easy familiarity with the other world, the crowd of powerful and wealthy relations she has there, her ability to pull strings in more than one spiritual hemisphere, makes her independent, self-confident and resentful of any neglect or interference. Somra of Taraba told me how he once—but only once—quarrelled with his wife who was a well-known shamanin.

One day I said to her, 'Give me some hot rice to eat.' All she did was to pour some hot water over stale cold rice and feed me on that. I was very much annoyed and I abused her. Next day I went down with fever. It lasted for two days, and when I thought I was going to die, I had to ask my wife to find out what was the matter with me. Her husband, her tutelary, came to her from the Under World and said to me, 'If you ever abuse your wife like that again, I shall take her away. I am pleased with her; that's why I married her, and I'd very much prefer to have her with me here. She may be yours, but she is also mine. I have one child from her, though you may have had a son from her too, as well as a daughter that I have not had. But from today, never abuse or beat her, or I will come at once and take her away.' Since that day I have never quarrelled with my wife. My fever stopped that very evening.

It is significant of the strength of the Saora belief in the sincerity of the shamanins, even when they are their own wives, that it never seems to have entered Somra's head that his wife had developed an ingenious technique for controlling the household; he accepted the message (which came after all from his wife's own lips) as a divine instruction which must be implicitly obeyed.

Somra went on to describe the very strong hold that his wife had over him in other ways. 'If I go to any other woman, my wife knows of it at once. When she questions me, if I deny it, she takes the sacred rice from the winnowing-fan and puts it in my hand. Then I dare not tell any lies.' His amorous adventures must have been very modest. When he was on tour with me at the beginning of 1945, Somra stayed away from home rather longer than had been expected. His wife began to pester him in dreams saying, 'You promised to return quickly; what are you doing with that man? Why have you deceived me?' And she used, so he said, to catch him by the hair and bang his head against the ground. It was impossible to keep Somra after that; I had to let him go home.

Somra felt greatly cut off from his wife's inner life. There was always something going on, she had a range of interests into which he could not enter. She had a baby from her tutelary and a lot of her heart was wrapped up in the boy whom she only saw in dreams, but who was as real to her as any human child. Once she wandered out into the jungle and stayed there three days, living entirely on palm wine. She said she had been with her tutelary and had enjoyed the experience. No wonder that some husbands regard their shamanin wives with suspicion.

But Somra and his wife were a happy couple compared to Kitri and Panchgu at Gailunga. On 14 December 1944 I camped in this village and on the following day went with a party of dancers bearing ritual gifts for a Guar ceremony at the neighbouring village of Thodrangu. That evening I returned, and at about eleven o'clock at night was awakened by appalling screams from a house not far from my camp. My whole party was aroused, and we hastened to the spot and found an old woman completely naked rolling about on the floor of her kitchen, while her husband—a most evil-looking man—sat by, laughing to himself and every now and then striking her with a heavy stick. After a great deal of discussion, we succeeded in quieting the woman, and Panchgu was taken off by a constable. He continued to laugh and made spasmodic attempts to return to his house and kill his wife and eventually had to be tied up.

When he had gone Kitri told us her story in a lively and dramatic manner. There were certainly marks of cruel beatings on her wasted body. Panchgu appeared to me to be an unbalanced neurotic who resented enormously the position that the female members of his family (for his mother too had been a successful shamanin) had attained as a result of their priestly functions. Some years previously he had decided to put his mother in her place. He put some of his own excreta in a leaf-cup and, covering it with rice and pulse, gave the mixture to her to eat. Kitri tried to interfere but he frightened her into silence. The mother sat down to her meal and after eating most of it, found the stinking mess at the bottom of the cup. 'When she saw what her own son had put there,' Kitri told us, 'she asked herself what was the use of living any longer. That night she hanged herself from the main beam of the house and her feet swung to and fro above us as we slept.'

That was in 1943. Panchgu's neurosis then took the form of a passionate jealousy and suspicion of his wife whenever she went anywhere to fulfil her duties as a shamanin. His distempered mind fixed on the elderly Chief as her paramour. Kitri was one of the ugliest old women I have ever seen, and the Chief had two wives already and was in any case, one would have thought, rather beyond that sort of thing; we heard privately in the village that there was nothing in it. But Panchgu was determined to humble his conceited wife who was on such familiar terms with the other world and did what she liked in this. One day the Chief had a cow-sacrifice at his house and naturally Kitri who, whatever her looks, was very important spiritually, went to assist. She brought home as her normal perquisite the head, a leg and a handful of chopped meat, and tied them up to the roof beside the pot dedicated to her tutelary. Panchgu, instead of being thankful to the gods for bringing him a bellyful of beef, lost his temper and shouted, 'You don't go for sacrifice, you go to stuff yourself with anything that's going.' He threw the unfortunate woman on the floor and seizing some bits of meat thrust them into her parts. All this Kitri, throwing off her tattered garments, showed us in pitiless detail.

A few weeks later there was a pig-sacrifice in the Chief's place at which Kitri again officiated. When she returned home, Panchgu beat her shouting, 'You are just pretending to be a shamanin; all you went there for was to lie with the Chief and his brother.'

The reason for the disturbance on the day we went to Thodrangu was similar. Kitri went with us, and so there was no one to cook Panchgu's food. But his wife had a heavy meal and came home slightly drunk on palm wine. All along the road, the Chief who—like so many elderly Saoras—became quite adolescent whenever a buffalo was sacrificed, danced beating a hide-gong, and Kitri very properly danced before him. When she got home, there was Panchgu chuckling to himself and saying, 'I know what you shamanins are. You've been lying with the Chief and his brother a score of times along the road. Now I am going to smash your god-pots.' He began by breaking one of them, the one dedicated to Kitri's tutelary, but she then threw herself upon him to prevent further sacrilege. He responded by beating her mercilessly, stripping her naked and dishonouring her in a singularly cruel and obscene manner. I think he would probably have killed her that night if we had not intervened.

In June 1948 I again camped at Gailunga, and Kitri and Panchgu were still there, still quarrelling, but there was more reason for it now, for Panchgu had taken a second wife, a young and pretty girl who was not a shamanin, and most of the quarrels now came from Kitri's side.

We must not be misled by the exceptions. On the whole, husbands live very happily with their shamanin wives and are often genuinely proud of the position that they win for themselves in tribal life.

VII. *Conclusion*

WOMEN have a high and honoured place in Saora society. Protected by their innocence and their fidelity, they move freely about their lovely hills; gay and happy, their laughter and their singing echoes at all hours among the palms. They have an important role alike in festivity and funeral; their voice is not unheard in tribal and village affairs; they can more than hold their own with their men. It would be hard to find women more industrious; they toil laboriously in terraced field and remote swidden, and when they return home the work of the spinning-wheel or the kitchen fills what might well be hours of leisure. But this is not mere drudgery; because they are free and self-reliant, respected and loved by their menfolk, adored by their children, their life is full, interesting and satisfying.

To this happy state of affairs the institution of the shamanin has made its contribution. For here is a body of women dedicated to the public service and fulfilling that dedication with grace and energy. Here are women, believed to be vitally in touch with supernatural affairs, on whom one can rely, women who respond to the needs of the sick and anxious with professional thoroughness and affectionate concern. For the shamanin really cares about her patients.

The shamanin is indeed an impressive and honourable figure. She lives a dedicated life on the boundary between this life and the next. A young girl like Sondan of Bungding had the absorbed look of the idealist and dreamer; she knew herself to be someone apart; she must not enter too much into the ordinary business of life or be stained by vulgar contacts; quiet, dignified, efficient, she made one think of a world of values foreign to this. The mysterious other-world 'below' was already more real to her almost maiden imagination than the coarse realities of earth. And even bustling business-like efficient little Amiya, who was a thoroughly 'this-world' type, did by her obstinate and life-long refusal to seek carnal pleasure in the world of temptation that enveloped her, establish the priority of spiritual things. The dedication, the sacrifice, the tutelary came first.

To the sick and lonely, the shamanin is the nurse and friend, the guide, the analyst. To the stranger's eye, she may be just one more dirty old village woman; but to the Saora whose life is broken by tragedy, she may well be an angel of strength and consolation.

Chapter Six

THE APPARATUS AND TECHNIQUE OF RITUAL

I

WHERE people are so inarticulate, where there is no written deposit of doctrine for our study, where many customs and traditions have come down from antiquity with their meaning forgotten, the examination of actual examples—life-histories, rites, the material objects used in worship, things that we can touch and see—becomes of unusual importance.

The technical apparatus of religion provides us with one of those clues or pointers which show the way to understanding, and in this chapter I propose to examine first the physical environment of worship—the shrine, the altar, the image; then the materials of sacrifice—wine, blood and grain; then the general impedimenta of worship—knives and fans, pots and sacred lamps, guns, leaves, ladders, swings, fire and instruments of music. In this way we shall not only get a clear and concrete picture of Saora religion, but we shall see how closely that religion is related to Saora life for, as Heiler says, 'nowhere in religious worship is the material civilization of a people or a period so clearly mirrored as in the objects offered in sacrifice, such as food and drink, holy gifts in the form of objects of use and adornment'.[1]

II. *The* Sadru *Shrine*

THE people of Orissa, in the hills as in the plains, are sociable and lazy; they love to sit about. For this amiable purpose both Hindus and tribesmen make platforms in their villages, building them up with stone and rubble, plastering them neatly with mud and cow-dung if they are Hindus, facing them with stone if they are tribesmen. The Oriyas call these platforms *sodoru* (probably from the Prakrit *chadaru*); the Bondos call them *sindibor* ; the Gadabas, Parengas and Ronas call them *sodor*. The Bondos and Gadabas have elaborated their platforms, giving them an important ceremonial purpose, while

[1] F. Heiler, *Prayer* (Oxford, 1932), p. 25.

preserving their value as centres of rest, gossip and discussion. The Saora *sadru* is a platform which does not seem ever to have had any other purpose than a ceremonial one.

The strenuous and earnest-minded Saoras, so different in temperament from the mild and casual Gadabas or the lazy Bondo men, have no time for lounging about; their one opportunity for gossip and discussion is when they go to fetch wine from the palms—and here you will occasionally find a circle of stone seats beneath the trees. But in the villages, their *sadrus* are not places for recreation; they are strictly shrines.

These shrines are of the simplest possible construction. Above a small altar built of rubble plastered with mud, some three feet high and two to three feet square, rises a pointed circular roof raised six to eight feet above the platform, thatched with grass, and topped by a wooden spire which carries a wooden peacock, the 'watchman' of the shrine. The roof is sometimes supported by four pillars, sometimes by one; in a few shrines, those dedicated to Manduasum, the central pole is in two pieces so that the umbrella-like roof can be rotated at certain ceremonies in honour of the god (Fig. 9). A stone step may facilitate approach to the altar plinth. There are no walls.

FIG. 9 Shamans propelling the roundabout shrine of Manduasum

The shrines are furnished with images and offerings. Fawcett describes 'the furniture kept for Jaliya's use and amusement'. There were 'two new cloths in a bamboo box, two brushes of feathers to be held in the hand when dancing; oil for the body; a small looking-glass; a bell and a lamp; a brush for sweeping; a wooden gun, sword and knife'. In most of the shrines, there is a small earthen pot hung from the rafters: this is 'fed' with rice at every festival. Wooden guns, swords, knives and spoons are very common, so are wooden birds. There is often a wooden altar, supported on a roughly carved upright, on which offerings may be made. In some shrines there may be found a small block of wood pierced with little holes to represent a piece of honeycomb. This is put here because 'at the beginning, when the first brother and sister were starving in the gourd that floated on the face of the ocean, they found some grass with a little honey on it, and this kept them alive'. At Bodo Okhra I was told that formerly the Saoras there made offerings of real honey. But one day the priest stole it for himself and died, since when the honeycomb has been made of wood.

FIG. 10 Image of Kittung from Bungding *2' high*

In some villages the shrines contain small wooden images of the gods. At Bodo Okhra there were male and female figures representing Patha Munda and Galbesum. At Bungding there was an image of Kittung (Fig. 10). At Karanjaju there was a male figure representing Manduasum in one of the rotating shrines (Fig. 7).

The shrines are to be found both inside the village, in front of particular houses, and outside. Generally—though the rule is by no means universal—the shrines in the village are private, erected by individuals for their own ancestors or special gods, and those outside are public, for the gods of the community.

The private shrines are usually built for an ancestor, or for the god who killed him, or rather—since the ancestor becomes the god—for both. For example, in the little village of Kittim there were in 1947 two shrines. The first was for the ghost of a man called Panchiya and stood in front of his house in the village street. The story behind it was that Galbesum attacked Panchiya and in order to appease him the shaman ordered a shrine to be built and a goat and a fowl to be sacrificed. The shrine was accordingly made in the name of Galbesum, but a year later the god came again and this time Panchiya died. After the Guar ceremonies were completed, Galbesum came in a dream to Panchiya's son and said, 'Now that your father is with me, you should sacrifice to both of us.' The shrine thus stands for both god and ancestor.

The other shrine in this village was also for Galbesum, but in this case the victim was of a different family, a man called Lingan. Lingan and Galbesum receive equal or identical honour at the Harvest Festivals.

At Pandrung I was told that the ancestors had complained to the shaman that they were cold and lonely by their menhirs. 'They said, "How can we live outside among these stones? It is always cold and raining. Make houses near yours for us."' Shrines were accordingly built for the dead in the streets opposite the houses where they used to live, and were dedicated to them and to the gods who had taken them away. The Chief of Maneba told me, 'When a man dies, his ghost may visit any of his children and say that a shrine should be built for him. He may ask a younger rather than an elder brother, a daughter rather than a son. But whoever is bidden must make the shrine, and then the whole family is free of trouble.' These instructions are often forgotten or ignored and are a frequent cause of sickness, for the ghost continues to attack his neglectful heir until he does what he is told.

The public shrines may be inside a village. Thus at Ladde there was a very large shrine in the middle of the village for Galbesum. Its plinth was six feet high and the roof rose to over twenty feet; it contained a male human figure and several wooden guns. For Galbesum was regarded here as a great hunter, and the shrine was supposed to be his chariot 'like the one they make for the Maharaja'. At this shrine a peacock is sacrificed every year at the Rice Festival. Fawcett describes how in 1887 shrines were built for Jaliyasum inside villages for the first time. 'The reason given for building *in* the villages was that Jaliya had come into the village. Usually erections are outside villages, and sacrifice is made there in order that Jaliya may be there appeased and go away. But sometimes he *will* come to a village; and if he does, it is advisable to make him comfortable.'[1]

But most of the public shrines are outside. There is often a shrine for Tangorbasum, the god of the path, who prevents hostile spirits from entering, near one of the approaches to a village. Other shrines may be for Karnosum, or for Kittungsum, or for a particular Kittung

[1] Fawcett, p. 243.

such as Garsada Kittung. In some places there is a custom for anyone going out of the village to halt at one of these shrines, and to take a pinch of rice from the pot hanging there. He ties it in his cloth and exclaims, 'I go abroad; go with me and preserve me.' When he returns, if everything has gone well, he restores the rice to the pot and says, 'In truth you have preserved me.'

At the public shrines, offerings are made by the whole village, which unites to subscribe for the purpose. For the private shrines each family is responsible. The upkeep of a private shrine passes as a duty from father to son, and in spite of the fact that failure to keep it in repair is believed to rouse the dead to inevitable and dangerous anger, families tend to treat their shrines very casually. The public shrines are repaired and cleaned at the main agricultural festivals and everyone is expected to co-operate.

It is at these festivals that the shrine is mainly used. Offerings may indeed be made at it at any time, according to the inspirations of the shamans, but the normal routine offerings are at the Harvest Festivals. The new grain or fruit is piled upon it; it is decorated with bunches of leaves and flowers; and the priest or shaman makes his offerings under its roof.

Shrines for Lurnisum, a god of smallpox, are of an entirely different pattern. They are usually made like ordinary huts, though smaller, and the walls are of upright slabs of stone. Inside are small pillars of stone for Lurnisum and his wife. In some villages, there are small stone 'hearths' for Kittungsum. These are almost like boxes—four slabs of stone enclose a square, and a fifth stone makes a roof. Inside there may be a small stone pillar to represent the god. More often the 'box' is empty, and when the cover-slab is removed it can be used as a hearth whereon sacrificial food is cooked. Occasionally little huts are built for Sahibosum and his wife, to give the images some shelter from wind and rain.

III. *The Saora Altar*

THE Saoras make four different kinds of altar—of stone, wood, grain and patterned on the ground.

Stone altars are to be found in front of anthropomorphic images of the gods and near wooden pillars erected for the dead. Images of Sahibosum usually have a stone slab in front of them on which offerings may be placed. There are altar stones in front of many forest shrines. Occasionally, there is nothing but an altar—just a stone slab by the side of a field or at the top of a pass, where offerings may be given to the spirits of the field or hill.

Wooden altars consist of small flat planks mounted on a single support. Such altars are used for offerings which have to be made before the dedicated pots, and are sometimes found in the shrines where the offerings of first fruits are placed upon them.

FIG. 11 Wooden altar of a kind sometimes erected before a house or shrine

Benches about 12″ above ground

The simplest of all the altars is that made on a piece of cow-dunged ground, where patterns are traced with rice flour and sacrifice offered upon them. These patterns are probably of an apotropaic character and aim at confusing any hostile spirit who may approach to disturb the rite. They are often made in the middle of a path with the intention of preventing a god who is being taken out of a village from returning to it.

But the most important Saora altar, and it is to this that I refer whenever I use the word without a qualifying adjective, is the temporary altar (usually of grain) made at the time of sacrifice. These altars are prepared in all sorts of places, inside a house, outside the village, by a stream, on a hillside, in the middle of a path. When it is made inside the house, an altar may be built up against the central pillar, under an ikon on the wall, or above the mortar in the middle of the main room. Sometimes the sacrificial grain is piled up in a mound on the floor; often it is kept in baskets, which are carefully arranged with pots of wine, and a winnowing-fan in front.

The Saoras have a very good eye for this sort of thing. At a Rogonadur ceremony at Taribel in 1944, I watched the priest construct a carefully symmetrical altar of rice-grains. He put a bunch of green pulse on either side of it, and then a row of little baskets of rice in front. He arranged mirrors, match-boxes, bits of ginger, sticks of tobacco and ears of maize in a pleasant pattern. In front of everything he made a row of leaf-cups filled with wine. At the Barasingi Sikunda ceremony in 1951, the shamans cowdunged a bit of ground under a great mango tree. They made a pile of grain and set a sword upright in it. Then before it they placed a winnowing-fan with a lamp, and beside it a bunch of peacock feathers.

Where, as so often happens, the second part of a ceremony takes place outside, by a stream or on a path, the shaman has to make another altar. He now places the most important object of the sacrifice as a sort of centre-piece. It may be a ploughshare, or a little bamboo shrine for the god, or a stake of ebony. Then he arranges round it his baskets of rice and grain, his pots of wine and water, and lays out leaf-plates and cups in rows. At the Guar ceremony, a small bamboo hut is built and everything is placed in or near it. When an animal is sacrificed, the head is placed on or beside the altar.

IV. *Images*

IN TRIBAL India anthropomorphic images of the gods are rare. The Baigas make no image of Nanga Baiga, though they picture him in all too human terms; the Murias do not attempt carvings of Lingo Pen, the heroic founder of their tribe. Still less are there attempts to represent the Supreme Being. I do not know of even so much as a shrine, still less an image, of Bhagavan among the Gonds and Baigas, or of a temple to Mahapurub among the Marias and Murias. In Orissa, the Gadabas, Didayis, Parengas, Jhorias and Bondos do not make images of any of their gods, certainly not of any tribal hero or Creator. But the Saoras occasionally make rude little images of their deities and set them up either in their shrines or out in the woods with a stone altar before them.

Thus at the top of the pass as you approach Bodo Okhra from the west are—or were in 1944—two wooden figures about three feet high with a stone slab in front of them.[1] They represented Patha Munda and his wife Galbesum, who in that place were identified

[1] Illustrated at p. 119 of my *TAMI*.

with the supreme Kittung. Offerings were made to them when the Saoras fired the jungle, at the Mango Festival, indeed at all the major festivals. And any visitor to the village would pause a moment and, throwing a pinch of rice or tobacco on the stone, exclaim, 'Drive back any god or ghost that may be following me.' The priest of the village explained how these images came to be erected.

Long ago Patha Munda gave a dream to the priest of Bodo Okhra and said, 'I am Patha Munda. In my name make an image of a man and woman and offer sacrifice to me before them and I will help you.' But when the priest woke up he forgot his dream and so there was a plague in the village and many people died. Then the priest recalled his dream and called the shaman to help him. They carved the figures of a man and woman and put them on the path with a stone before them, and when they had offered sacrifice the sickness ceased. This still goes on, and every priest has the dream in turn.

There were similar figures in the shrines standing within the village and they received the same honours.

At Bungding there was a small male figure in one of the shrines; this was said to represent Kittung (Fig. 10). At Karanjaju, there was another Kittung figure, very crudely fashioned, in the central shrine of the village (Fig. 6). At Ladde, in the very large and imposing central shrine, there was a male figure holding a gun: this was Galbesum, and the image was intended to persuade the god to encourage hunting. At Bongthalda there was a carved wooden head on the spire of one of the shrines: it stood for Randrasum, which was the name of a local Kittung.

Very occasionally, when a really important person, someone who is very rich or a great shaman, dies, small clay images are made for use in the Guar or Karja ceremonies. These little images may also, as in the case of the two illustrated here (Plate 56), which were made by Indamo of Alangda, represent ancestors of long standing, who have become Chiefs of the ghosts in the Under World. The Saora potter who makes them must do so fasting, and he must make a special sacrifice to assuage the possible jealousy of any lesser ghost who is not so honoured. It is regarded as a risky business, and the potter's fee is accordingly high: a cow or a buffalo should be given for the tiny figures. After the ceremony, they are put into a dedicated pot.

I have never seen a figure in a grave-hut such as the one noticed by Hutton in 1931, but it was probably of the same order as the clay images I have just described, and I am very doubtful if it was intended to serve 'to accommodate the soul until the Guar ceremony'.[1] Saora images are intended to flatter, and so to banish, not to accommodate, the spirits.

The most important, as they are the most common, of the Saora images are connected with Sahibosum and his consort. Sahibosum is the sahib-god, but not, it must be noted, the god of the sahibs. A sahib, to the Saora mind, is not a European, he is rather an official and especially a touring official. Sahibosum, therefore, goes round the country like a forest officer or a policeman, visiting village after village, and making a nuisance of himself wherever he goes. The images carved in his honour are an attempt to keep him out or at least to divert his attentions elsewhere.[2]

FIG. 12 Wooden figure of Sahibosum from Dokripanga 3′ *high*

One of Sahibosum's earliest manifestations was in a wild little village called Karanjaju, where he gave everyone cholera. At that time, no one had ever heard of him, and when the old familiar gods, interrogated in the usual way, denied responsibility for the disaster, the shamans were nonplussed. One night, however, Sahibosum appeared in a dream and declared, 'I am a new god. I live in the land of the sahibs and with my wife go touring through the world. Now I have come to see you Saoras.' The shaman replied, 'Then take what you will and go on your way.' The god answered, 'I want no sacrifices. But make images of me and of my wife, and set them on the path towards the west and sacrifice to me there.' The Saoras hurriedly obeyed and it is said that the epidemic ceased.

There was a similar tradition at Parisal in the open country near Rayaghada. Here the shaman dreamt that a man and his wife, wearing garlands and with flowers in their hair, were dancing in the village street. When he asked them what they were doing, they replied 'We are from Assam, the land of sahibs, and we have come here to dance from place to place.' The following day, many people fell ill with vomiting and fever, and that night the worried shaman had another dream, and when he saw what he must do, he had images made and so checked the trouble.

[1] J. H. Hutton, *Census of India*, 1931, vol. I, pt. iiiB, p. 4.
[2] For another account, and additional photographs, see my *TAMI*, pp. 123ff.

The images are worshipped regularly, and once the cult has started it has to be maintained. It is always dangerous to drop a god. In some places new images are made every year; in others only when the old ones decay. Old images are allowed to lie rotting on the ground; once they have fallen down, there is nothing sacred or dangerous about them.

The images are roughly carved in wood, sometimes with a certain distortion of the erogenous areas; the male is usually, though not always, taller than the female. Anyone 'who knows how' can make the images; there is no special class of dedicated craftsmen. The carpenter goes fasting to the forest in search of a suitable *Shorea robusta* tree. He carries the wood to one of the shrines, and a shaman offers it rice and liquor. Then, still fasting, the carpenter fashions the figures with axe and knife. When he has finished, the shaman again offers rice and liquor, and the people carry the images down the path out of the village, escorted by drums and a great company of children. At the chosen place, the shaman digs holes in the ground and erects the images; once he has done so, the drums must cease and not sound again. Then he offers a pig and a goat saying, 'You came to our country and our village. We have taken a lot of trouble to please you; now depart and trouble us no more.'

The images of Sahibosum range in size from three to seven feet, and impress the traveller not only by the rugged strength and sometimes fantastic caricature of their carving, but also by the wild and lonely places where they stand: I shall not easily forget the shock of surprise and awe when I saw them for the first time at the top of a desolate pass near Karanjaju.

On the whole, images are only rarely found in the Saora hills. I have never, for example, found one in the Pottasingi valley. There is a vague notion that images are Hindu rather than Saora, even that the Hindus once stole what Saora images there were, as the following story from Mancba suggests.

Formerly Kittung's shrines were always away out in the forest, among thick trees, and were built up large and noble like Hindu temples. There was an old shaman with his wife and daughter. One day a Brahmin youth came to the house and said, 'I will live with you and serve seven years for your daughter if you will give her to me.' The old man replied, 'We are Saoras; you are a Brahmin; how can such a thing be?' But the young man insisted, and at last the old man said, 'Very well, I will ask my daughter. If she agrees, you may stay.' When he asked his daughter she said, 'I will do whatever you think is best.' So the Brahmin remained and worked for the old shaman and he grew to like the boy and said to himself, 'When I die I will give him the work of ministering at the shrine.' For every day this shaman went far into the forest, where Kittung's shrine was, to offer sacrifice.

One day the Brahmin begged to be allowed to visit the shrine. The old shaman only consented on condition that he went with his eyes blindfolded. But the Brahmin secretly hid cotton seeds in his cloth and let them fall as he went along. When they reached the shrine, the shaman undid the Brahmin's eyes and he saw Kittung and Kittung's wife. He stood by while the shaman worshipped them with offerings of uncooked food. A week later the Brahmin went secretly to the shrine, following the trail of cotton seeds, and when he found Kittung he said to him, 'This Saora only gives you raw food. If you will come with me, I will give you cooked food, with ghee and milk and sugar.' Kittung agreed and the Brahmin removed the images and took them to Puri.

When the shaman came to the shrine later in the day, he found his gods gone, and when he returned home he found his son-in-law gone. Since then we have always made Kittung's shrine inside the village, but it is always empty, for the images were stolen by the Hindus.[1]

Besides the carved images of the gods, the Saoras make wall-drawings which show in elaborate detail the figures of the gods and the dead, and portray their palace, attendants, furniture and pets, and incidents of their life in the other world. These are so important and so common that I devote a special chapter to them. But they must be mentioned here, for the Saoras themselves seem to regard the ikons and the images as equal in importance and as deserving similar honour.

What is the Saora attitude towards their images and ikons? What do they really suppose them to be?

Images may, of course, be regarded in a number of different ways. There is first the simple and straightforward belief of the 'idolator' that the image before him is the actual god, a view which leads logically to such customs as putting it to bed at night and waking it in the morning, feeding it and treating it in every way as if it were

[1] Different versions of this story can be heard all over the Saora country. It is an aboriginal rehash of the old tradition that the original image of Jagannath was discovered among the Saoras and that its first priest was a Saora fowler named Basu or Viswa Basu. See L. S. S. O'Malley, *Census of India*, 1911, vol. v, pt. i, p. 505. See also pp. 27ff. of this book.

alive. Religious history is full of miracles arising out of this belief, where images move, speak, bleed and even menstruate. This is rare among Indian tribesmen, but the Marias and Murias of Bastar seem to regard their clan-gods, the Anga Pen, in this way. These are not anthropomorphically designed, but they are undoubtedly anthropomorphically imagined. In their construction the processes of birth are recapitulated; there is even an umbilical cord to be severed. The Angas are married and have children; each has a 'soul', generally a bit of iron wrapped in straw and kept somewhere in the shrine.

I doubt if any Saoras regard their images like this. There is no ceremony of installation, for example, without which no Hindu god would be regarded as really 'alive'. Old images are left lying about and are not taken, in Hindu fashion, to a river to be 'cooled'. Food-offerings are made before the images, but I have never noticed any attempt to feed the god as if he were a person.

Another attitude to images regards them as aids to worship. The image is like a picture; it is not the god, of course, that would be absurd, but it reminds the worshipper what he is like and assists him in focussing his attention. The Crucifix, for example, is generally regarded in this way. I do not think that this either is the genuine Saora attitude. Indeed at first sight it is hard to imagine anyone being reminded of any kind of god by the crude images made by the Saora handicraftsmen. Yet the evidence of the ikons suggests that the Saoras do actually think of the gods and ancestors as rather like human beings, but wearing a few more clothes. And so the queer little images with hats and coats, and the drawings of gods holding umbrellas and riding on elephants represent a genuine Saora conception. In one village a shaman saw a great crowd of gods descend from the hills; they were about eighteen inches high and looked like little human beings, only they were very smartly dressed.

A third notion is that an image is a symbol. It is not a portrait of a god, but it attempts, by representing certain symbolic values in human form, to convey their spiritual meaning to the worshipper, and so help him to concentrate his attention on the divine. This is commonly held by the more sensitive and intelligent Hindus, but I do not think the Saoras have arrived at it.

The Saora attitude is at once simpler and more primitive than any of these beliefs. The images are made, not to bring god near but to drive him away, not to remind the worshipper of him, but to help him to forget. They are man's notice-boards to warn off trespassers from eternity. Patha Munda and his wife attacked the people of Bodo Okhra with sickness until they made images of them, and then they went away. Sahibosum tormented the people of Karanjaju and Dokeripanga until they carved the images, whereupon they did not take up their abode in the images but hurried off somewhere else. It is the same everywhere; the images do not symbolize anything, they are not a focus to devotion, they do not bring the gods near: they keep the gods away. And the offerings that are made from time to time before them are to ensure the continued absence of the gods.

V. *The Materials of Sacrifice: Wine*

THE SAGO palm, *Caryota urens*, Linn., was given to mankind by Kittung himself and its wine has an important place in all Saora ceremonial, which only rarely uses *Bassia latifolia* spirit, the popular ritual offering of other tribes.

FIG. 13 Carving of a sago palm on a door at Mandidi

A number of myths stress the sacrificial importance and divine origin of the palm. It grew from Kittung's beard; it is Kittung's tail transformed; it is the hairpin of a dancing girl from the Upper World. One story describes how Kittung gave a Saora three seeds, the seeds of the sago, date and toddy palms, in a dream, and when the man awoke he found that in truth there were three seeds on his cot. He planted and tended them, but did not think of extracting the sap until his son was attacked by Jammosum who, showing himself indifferent to the goats, pigs and chickens he was offered, demanded wine to drink. Kittung gave the Saora another dream showing him how to get the wine, and when he offered this to the god, his son recovered.

Another significant story was recorded at Potta.

At first the Saoras had no gods and of course no need of shamans and shamanins. But when the gods were born among the Saoras, Jungo and his wife Kaiti became the first shaman and shamanin. They offered every kind of food-sacrifice, but at that time they knew nothing about palm wine and the gods were not satisfied.

One day Kittung gave Jungo a dream and told him what to do. 'Give wine to every god,' he said. Next morning Kittung went to a palm tree and cut a branch and hung his pot there. When it was full he called Jungo and gave him some of the wine to drink. Kittung said to Kaiti, 'You drink some too'; she did so and was pleased. Since then the shamans have always offered wine to the gods.

FIG. 14 Saora drinking-tube

Yet another story, from Boramsingi, describes how Kittung produced a palm from a blackened grain of maize which had burnt his mouth. When the tree was ready, he called Ramma and showed him how to extract the sap and drink it, telling him that if he did so he would soon be drunk and happy.

The number and diversity of these tales,[1] of which I give only a sample here, testifies to the popularity of the tree and the value of the wine it gives. The Saoras are not great drunkards, but they cannot do without their drink. Palm wine is so much part of the day's routine that a man is lost without it. Every Saora must be up early in the morning for his drink of wine, which 'settles his mind and belly for the day'. It is like the Englishman's attachment to his cup of early morning tea.

The wine is usually taken, as by the Bondos, hot. It is warmed on a simple hearth of stones immediately below the tree where it has been tapped, and it is said that this kills off insects and makes the wine more efficacious and digestible. 'If it is taken cold, it gives you a headache; when warmed it can do nothing but good.' In some places, as at Talasingi and Gunduruba, there are circles of stone seats, with a hearth in the centre, out in the forest where the palms grow most thickly.

[1] Nine of these stories are given in *TMO*, pp. 194 ff.

The men gather morning and evening in this open-air tavern; some of them fetch the wine, mixing the sap from two or more trees if possible, for this improves it; they place it in a large pot on the hearth and light a fire beneath it. They drink from a tube, a small gourd open at one side is attached to a long hollow spout or handle, see Fig. 14, which is passed round and round. The etiquette, which is strictly observed, is for each person to fill the gourd from the pot and pass it to his right-hand neighbour. He takes it in his right hand and, raising the bowl of the gourd into the air, pours the wine down the spout into his mouth. He then refills the gourd and passes it on, always to the right. Experts can pour the stream of wine into a barely open mouth from a distance of from six to ten inches. Between drinks, bits of roasted crab, dried meat and small but fiery green chillies are eaten.

Women do not go out to the trees, but a good husband usually brings something home for the family, and most houses have a small reserve of wine available for visitors.

Such is the ordinary routine drinking of the Saoras, what we may call the secular drinking. Religious drinking is made heavier by the convenient belief that the gods who gave wine to the world are as fond of it as men are. When a shaman in trance is possessed by a spirit, he becomes the spirit, and if the spirit is to drink he can only do so through the shaman's mouth. In a lengthy ceremony, in the course of which a shaman may be possessed by a score of different gods and ancestors, each clamorous for refreshment, he has to put down a considerable quantity to satisfy them all. And the assistants and onlookers too feel it their duty to drink with the divine visitants, with the result that most ceremonies conclude with everyone more than a little drunk.

In some villages, it is taboo to offer wine or spirits to Madusum or Kannisum, for these two gods are believed to be great drunkards, 'and if they once began to get wine from us, we would never be rid of them; they would always be coming to make us ill in order to force us to give them more'.

The wine is often offered to the spirits in charming little brass jugs, with spouts which facilitate the sprinkling of the wine over the altars and offerings (Fig. 15). It is said that if such an offering is unacceptable, it remains sweet and strong; but if a spirit touches it, it loses all its flavour and becomes weak as water.

Wine then is a genial and strengthening background to the whole of Saora life. To bodies enervated by a lifetime of fever, it is an essential stimulant; to minds appalled by the menace of the Under World, it gives much-needed courage. It is used at the birth of a man, when he is named and whenever he falls ill. When he would be betrothed it is one of the symbols of a proposal; it is the chief delight of a wedding and the one consolation at death. It is offered on every ceremonial occasion and at every

FIG. 15 Brass pot used by shamans for offering wine at sacrifice

place—when the shaman sits with his divining-fan, when a ghost comes home to demand his property, when the priest sacrifices in the village shrines, at each Harvest Festival, for the Guar and Karja sacrifices. Even on ordinary and familiar occasions the people do not drink it without letting fall to the ground a few drops in honour of the dead.

A pot of wine is currency in any ritual exchange of gifts. It is a necessary part of any bride-price. It is one of the ingredients in any fine inflicted by society on an offender. Without it the entire fabric of Saora social life would be dislocated.

No one has expressed more cogently the value of alcohol for the religion of simple people than William James.

The sway of alcohol over mankind is unquestionably due to its power to stimulate the mystical faculties of human nature, usually crushed to earth by the cold facts and dry criticisms of the sober hour. Sobriety diminishes, discriminates, and says no; drunkenness expands, unites and says yes. It is in fact the great exciter of the *Yes* function in man. It brings its votary from the chill periphery of things to the radiant core. It makes him for the moment one with truth. Not through mere perversity do men run after it. To the poor and the unlettered it stands in the place of symphony concerts and of literature; and it is part of the deeper mystery and tragedy of life that whiffs and gleams of something that we immediately recognize as excellent should be vouchsafed to so many of us only in the fleeting earlier phases of what in its totality is so degrading a poisoning. The drunken consciousness is one bit of the mystic consciousness, and our total opinion of it must find its place in our opinion of that larger whole.[1]

VI. *The Materials of Sacrifice: Blood*

ULTIMATELY all blood is human blood, and every sacrifice a human sacrifice. This is the sanction behind animal sacrifice, for although the Saoras were never at any time guilty of the Meriah offerings, the entire Orissa countryside is saturated in the idea that the earth cries out for blood and that blood will bring fertility and plenty.

The Saoras have, it is true, a few vegetarian deities and bloodless sacrifices, but the great majority are 'drinkers of blood'. Buffaloes, cows and bullocks, goats, pigs, fowls and peacocks are the animals used, and it is remarkable that the only non-domestic creature considered suitable is the peacock, which has a special relation with the dead and appears as 'watchman' on the roofs of most Saora shrines.

The blood of the sacrificed animals is used in various ways. It may be sprinkled from the body of the still living creature round an object—such as a shrine or a stack of grain—which it is to preserve or dedicate. It may be mixed with palm wine and drunk, as when a particularly dangerous ghost is to be kept away. It may be scattered over an altar or mixed with seed to make it fertile. Sometimes it is caught in a pot or leaf-cup and placed as an offering before an image or a stone. I have seen a woman dip her fingers in the still warm blood of a dead buffalo and make a mark with it on her baby's forehead.

[1] James, *Varieties*, p. 387.

At a sacrifice of a buffalo to Yuyuboi to avert smallpox, the goddess 'came upon' several of the participants who buried their heads in the bleeding carcass, tore off bits of the raw flesh, and danced with them hanging from their lips as they waved their blood-stained hands in the air.

In the sacrifice of animals, certain traditions may be noted. There are no rigid rules about the colour of an animal; it is not true, for example, that a white fowl should always be offered to the Sun-god. It is a common practice, but the rule is not absolute. Nor are there any rules about the markings on an animal's body, or the shape of its horns, nor is it necessary that it should be unblemished or even free of disease.

A shaman must never do the actual killing of an animal, and no woman, still less a shamanin, should do so. Otherwise, there is no rule; anyone 'who knows how' may strike the blow, there are no kinship regulations here.

Before it is killed, an animal must eat a little consecrated rice and drink a little consecrated wine. If it cannot be persuaded to do this, it is taken as a sign that the spirit to whom it is to be offered has rejected it.

Often a little hair is plucked from the neck of a pig or goat, or some feathers from the neck of a fowl, and waved over a patient's head. The tail of a buffalo may be burnt, or wicks may be attached to its horns and set alight. Sometimes animals are dressed in the cloth and garlands offered to the spirits.

After sacrifice, the animal's head is usually placed on the altar and the rest of the body is cut up and cooked.

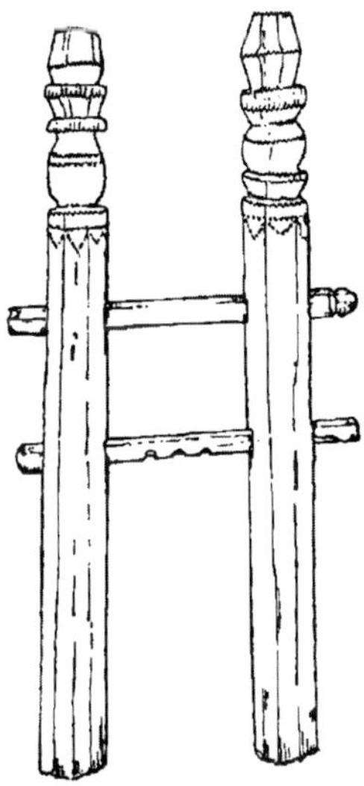

FIG. 16 Lunette sometimes used at the sacrifice of buffaloes

The great sacrificial animal is the buffalo. There must always be one or more buffaloes sacrificed at the Guar, and the ceremonial exchange of buffaloes is an important feature of this rite. At the Karja many buffaloes are offered.[1] These are the classic offerings for the dead, but buffalo-sacrifice is also necessary at the Doripur to appease Dorisum and at the Ajorapur. Well-to-do Saoras may also sacrifice a buffalo on any occasion that seems to demand it; often,

[1] In Hindu tradition the buffalo is the *vahana* or vehicle of Yama, god of death.

in a case of severe illness, a shaman asks first for a fowl, then for a goat, and then if these fail, for the costly buffalo.

In former times I think it is possible that the Saoras killed their buffaloes in Kond fashion: one man struck the animal to the ground with a blow from the sharp edge of his axe, and then the entire company fell upon it and cut it to pieces with their knives. This is still done occasionally by the Saoras, notably in the case of a buffalo which is dedicated to Uyungsum and sacrificed three years afterwards,[1] but the modern practice is to kill the animal with a blow on the back of the neck with the blunt side of the axe.

Occasionally, a special kind of lunette (Fig. 16) is made; two poles are set upright, and a horizontal pole is fixed rather low down across them. The buffalo's head is inserted, and a second horizontal pole is placed over it so that it cannot escape.[2] But in this case too the blunt edge of the axe is used.

The reason for this is not religious, but economic. The Doms, from whom the Saoras now purchase all their cattle, insist on the return of the skins in perfect condition; it is said that they levy a fine of one rupee for every hole or tear. I have seen Saoras fall upon the carcass and cut it about after the skin was removed, but never before. The price of a buffalo is always settled on the understanding that the skin will be returned intact.

Koppers has suggested that certain Indian tribes distinguish between gods and ancestors in their method of killing sacrificial animals. An animal offered to a god is decapitated and blood is shed; an animal offered to the dead is killed by a blow on the back of the neck and its death is 'unbloody'. 'In this matter of the unbloody killing of animals destined as a sacrifice for ancestors,' he says 'there is complete agreement between Gonds, Mundas and Santals' and he refers to Bodding who says that 'sacrifices to *bongas* (gods) are performed by beheading the sacrificial animal, whilst to the forefathers it is always done by a stroke of an axe-head on the neck'. The Mundas also kill horned cattle for the dead in this way, and so do the Marias when a menhir is erected.[3]

[1] The reason is that such a buffalo is the villagers' property, and the skin does not have to be returned to anyone.

[2] The form of this suggested to Hutton 'the incisions on the stones at Kasomari'. —*Census of India*, 1931, vol. I, pt. iiiB, p. 4.

[3] W. Koppers, 'Monuments to the Dead of the Bhils', *Annali Lateranensi* (1942), vol. VI, p. 193; P. O. Bodding, *Studies in Santal Medicine*, Calcutta, 1925, pt. i, p. 17; J. Hoffmann and A. van Emelen, *Encyclopedia Mundarica* (Patna, 1930), vol. VII, p. 2001; W. V. Grigson, *The Maria Gonds of Bastar* (Oxford, 1938), p. 278.

But among the Saoras, there is no such distinction. Sacrifices to gods and ancestors are made in the same way, and in so far as they are unbloody the reason is, as we have seen, a purely economic one, to save the skin, which may be worth as much as twenty rupees, no small sum for a poor Saora.[1] The killing of goats and pigs, for ancestors as for gods, is usually 'bloody'.

The sacrifice of cows and bullocks is now very rare. In a great emergency a cow may be offered to Rugaboi; it is then killed in the same way as a buffalo. At Boramsingi in 1947, when an old man died, his shade asked that his favourite cow should die with him, and this unusual *sati* was offered by his pyre. But cow-sacrifice, under Hindu pressure, is rapidly disappearing. As a routine measure it has gone; it now only occurs occasionally under the express instructions of a shaman.

Goats may be offered at all ordinary sacrifices, and according to the legend of their origin they were created specially for this purpose. A story recorded at Mannemgolu describes how a shaman who wanted to reap the harvest in his clearing on a certain hill was unable to do so because the god of the hill kept him away with tigers, bears and snakes.

So the shaman went to Kittung and told him his trouble. Kittung said, 'Give the god a she-goat to eat.' The shaman had never seen a goat and had no idea what it was, and though he searched everywhere he could not find one. Then Kittung himself went out in search of one; he had to go a long way, all the way to the star Sukua. On this star was a she-goat which had given birth to two little goats. Kittung fell at the star's feet and said, 'Let me take your children home for fifteen days, and then I will return them.' The star gave its consent and Kittung took the she-goat and its kids away and sent them to the Saora's house. The Saora went to the god of the hill and said, 'These goats are very small at the moment; let them grow and you'll get a much better meal next year. Don't have them killed now, they are far too small.' The god agreed and let him reap his crop. At the end of the year, the Saora hid the mother-goat and sacrificed the kids, and from the mother came the whole race of goats.

When a goat is offered to Babusum, Rugaboi or Galbesum, it is decapitated with a single blow of an axe. On one occasion when a goat was sacrificed for an ancestor who in his lifetime had possessed

[1] If a buffalo is sacrificed in the course of the ceremonies for an ill-omened death, although it is strictly taboo to bring anything from the spot, the rule is relaxed to permit the skin to be returned to the Dom vendor.

a fine sword, it was decapitated with this weapon. At other times, if it is small, it is lifted by the hind legs and stunned by being smashed on the ground, or if it is large it is hit on the head with a bit of wood or a heavy stone. Then someone makes two holes in the throat with a knife and lets the blood flow into a pot. He cuts through the body just in front of the forelegs, and then cuts this piece again in half, removing the head and placing it on the altar. Then he slits the skin down the body on the under side, and after removing the skin chops up the rest into pieces for the cooking-pot.

Pigs are sacrificed on a large number of occasions. When a pig is offered to Ratusum, Uyungsum or Labosum, it is hit on the head with a stone and the throat is cut in order to let out the blood. For Kinnasum, it is trampled to death. For the Lambapur, a small pig may be impaled on a sharpened pole of ebony. Often, if the animal is not too big, it is stunned by being dashed on the ground; then the throat is cut and the blood allowed to drip on the altar and into a special pot; the head is then carved off and placed on the altar, and the blood is cooked as a sort of soup.

Traditionally, the first fowls were made by a famous shaman specifically for use in sacrifice, as the following story from Pandrung shows.

Meheru was the shaman of twelve villages. He had five sons and five daughters and, since he was a great shaman, he had no trouble about getting them married. But when the youngest girl was married, Labosum made her ill. Meheru himself sought to divine the reason. Labosum came upon him and said, 'Sacrifice a black cock and a black hen, and I'll leave your daughter alone.'

But the shaman did not know what this 'cock' and 'hen' was; he had never heard of such things and was much disturbed in mind. But next day his wife went to the forest and brought home a marking-nut. She said to her husband, 'By your power put life into this and it will be a cock.' The shaman got up at midnight, made himself naked, and at dawn put life into the nut. It became a cock and crowed. From this one nut came seven cocks and seven hens. The shaman gave a black cock and a black hen to Labosum and the girl recovered. In this way the tribe of fowls entered the world.

I do not know why fowls should be associated with the marking-nut tree, but the story is interesting as showing once again the Saora tendency to relate everything, even the most homely and domestic thing, to his religion. Fowls were not made for men to eat, but to offer to the gods.

19. Sondan, the shamanin, divines with her winnowing-fan

20. Typical terraced cultivation in the Koraput hills

21. At Sogeda, the shaman Samiya treats a sick child, afflicted by Tut-tumsum, with the help of a blood-sucker lizard

22. Shamanin at Muniguda

At the Guar ceremony, fowls are killed by being smashed on the ground or against the carcass of an already sacrificed buffalo. At other times they are killed and dissected in a peculiar fashion which I have not seen elsewhere. The person engaged in killing the fowl begins by making a small incision in the right ear and letting a few drops of blood fall on whatever object it is proposed to protect or fertilize; then he makes a similar incision in the left ear and lets the blood fall on the altar. He slits the throat and allows more blood to fall into a leaf-cup. Then he removes the head by cutting the neck as low down as he can go. He removes the bones of the throat and places these and the head separately on the altar. Then gradually he cuts up the fowl, but he does not pluck it. He first removes the wings, then the legs and finally cuts the body into pieces.

When a fowl is sacrificed for Rugaboi (goddess of smallpox) its neck should be wrung, but the throat should not be cut while it is alive.

The Saoras do not seem to sacrifice ducks, which in any case are rare in their country, but after firing a new forest-clearing, they may offer a pigeon to any god living in the trees or rocks.

VII. *The Materials of Sacrifice: Fish and Crabs*

Fish and crabs are not plentiful and they do not grow large in the mountain streams of the Saora country. But, roasted, they provide a popular relish to be taken with palm wine. They are used also in a number of sacrifices.

If the flow of sap from a palm tree ceases, the Saoras cook fish, crabs and rice with a little turmeric and offer it to the dead. For it is believed that one reason for the failure of the sap is that the dead are robbing the tree, and this little meal diverts them, 'for it is sweet and pleasant'. If fish and crabs are offered at the foot of a tree, this prevents Tonaisum and Kinnasum from robbing it.

At the Guarsal ceremony, described at pp. 308ff. when a menhir is erected, a fish is substituted for the buffalo which should be sacrificed. The fish is dragged about, killed with a blow from an axe, slung on a pole and carried to the hearth for cooking just as if it were a real buffalo.

When the threshing and winnowing of a crop is done, women go for fish and crabs and cook them with rice and turmeric on the threshing-floor. They put portions of the meal on leaves and place them at the corners of the last mound of grain to be taken home. This will prevent any foreign ghosts or gods from stealing. Afterwards the labourers sit down and share the feast.

At the Ajorapur ceremony, when a buffalo is sacrificed in the bed of a stream, after buffalo-flesh and rice has been offered to the god on behalf of a child, the child's mother herself catches a few fish and crabs and cooks them with a little rice. Then she and her husband offer them to Ajorasum, and they—but no others—eat them. It is said that this makes it certain that Ajorasum will never trouble them again.

At the Lambapur for the success of a growing crop, after the sacrifice of a pig, the Saoras offer fish and crabs; the pods of pulses are expected to become strong and luscious as the legs of a crab.

So too if a rice harvest shows signs of failing, crabs may be sacrificed to Kinnasum. The shaman makes a hole in the carapace of the crab, attaches a cord to it, climbs on the roof of the house of the owner of the affected field, pushes the crab through the thatch and lets it hang down inside. Then he prepares rice in a new pot and sacrifices a hen before the crab.

Fish and crabs are regarded as specially valuable as prophylactics against sorcery. On 24 November 1950 I attended a ceremony at Sogeda intended to relieve one Manji of acute pains in his stomach. A shamanin had declared that a witch in a neighbouring village had taken a marking-nut in her hand and had thought of Manji's name: this had caused him great pain. A shaman was invited to deal with this and he had some fish and crabs cooked between leaves and offered to Tonaisum; he also made Manji eat some of it, and as a result his pain was much relieved.

VIII. *The Materials of Sacrifice: Bloodless Offerings*

ALTHOUGH nearly all the gods and ancestors are, as the Saoras put it, 'blood-drinkers', there are a few vegetarian gods and even to the blood-drinkers a number of bloodless sacrifices are acceptable.

One of the vegetarian gods is Manduasum, and I remember how at the Boramsingi Karja the fear was expressed that he might be offended by 'all the throwing about of blood'.

Nearly all the products of the fields are, at some time or other, offered in sacrifice. At each of the Harvest Festivals, the appropriate crop is offered and the shrines are hung, now with mangoes, now with bunches of pulse, now with cucumbers or sweet potatoes. But for routine use all the year round, the most common of such offerings is husked or unhusked rice. The greater millets are also used but rice is more popular.

Rice-grain is offered at every sacrifice; it is often used to make the altar; it forms the basis of the sacrificial feast; it is given to the gods in little cups, it is thrown to them outside the threshold and to the four points of the compass, it is fed to sacrificial animals, it is pressed on the forehead of a patient or waved round his head; it is as essential and ubiquitous to Saora religion as it is in the Saora kitchen.

Rice-grain is also commonly used in divination: it is poured into the winnowing-fan and helps the shaman to pass into a state of trance; grains are placed on a knife which is heated in the flame of a lamp and are counted or measured as a means of testing omens.

Another very popular offering is tobacco.[1] It is said that while gods and ghosts like the smell of tobacco, the tutelaries love it. Whenever they attend a sacrifice they demand it, and if they are given cheroots, 'they laugh with pleasure and promise to do no harm'. A stick of tobacco or a cheroot is therefore usually added to the other gifts on an altar, and leaf-pipes are often tied to the dedicated pots that are hung in front of ikons.

It is considered a wise thing to keep a pipe or cheroot constantly in one's mouth, for if a hostile spirit approaches the smell may so please him that he may depart without doing any harm. And in fact, the Saoras, both men and women, are perpetually shrouded in a sort of haze of tobacco smoke: I have seen girls keep their pipes going even when they were bathing in a stream.

Ginger is another gift acceptable to all spirits. Shamans use it at the time of trance to clean their teeth, for it is supposed to help them to talk sweetly to the gods. When a shamanin goes abroad, she may carry a bit of ginger with her. She puts a little bit in a corner of her mouth and when she returns home she chews it up, spits it out onto her hands, and rubs her face, arms and thighs with it. By

[1] G. S. Forbes, who was Collector of Ganjam 1858-67, in his *Wild Life in Canara and Ganjam* (London, 1885), remarks that the Saoras in his day preferred to use their tobacco in the form of snuff. 'Every man of them carries somewhere about him a tiny snuff-box, shaped like a humming-top, and made from the rind of the wood-apple; it contains pale, high-dried snuff, made from the baked stalk of the leaf, and is very strong.'—p. 174.

this means any hostile spirit who has followed her will be frightened away.[1]

Turmeric is slowly invading Saora life from the outside world. But it is not yet an important element in Saora cookery; it is not used at marriages; and only very rarely do girls rub themselves with the yellow paste on some special occasion when they want to look unusually attractive. A rhizome may be offered at any sacrifice, and is sometimes used in cooking a sacrificial feast. Turmeric and oil may be rubbed on the menhirs at a Guar ceremony.

The cheap and handy egg is constantly in demand. It is used on the threshing-floor where it is placed on a mound of grain in a little basket to keep away thievish spirits. At the burial of the ashes after a cremation, an egg, rice and dupi grass is put into the pit. An egg may be added to any other sacrificial gifts if the spirit demands it.

IX. *The Minor Impedimenta of Sacrifice*

Bows and Arrows. The Saoras use a rather small simple bamboo bow with a bamboo string.[2] There is little hunting nowadays, for the forests have been long since stripped of game. A shaman uses a bow and arrows ceremonially on a number of occasions; he dances shooting at the head of a decapitated goat when it is sacrificed to the dead for the good of the crops (see p. 306). He drives an arrow into the trunk of a tree to close a village boundary against tigers. He uses a special bow and arrow to shoot at a patient during the Doripur and similar rites. There is a special ritual of divination or taking the omens with a bow. When anyone goes to betroth a girl, an arrow is one of the symbolic gifts presented to the future parents-in-law.

Feathers. Peacock's feathers are specially associated with Jaliyasum. They are also offered to Yuyuboi and are burnt at her shrine to avert smallpox. A broom of feathers is sometimes used to sweep a village in order to drive away disease. Shamans often use a peacock's feather to brush a patient's body in order to extract some material substance which has been sent into it by a sorcerer.

[1] Ramamurti says that a man who has transformed himself into a tiger can be restored by being given green ginger to eat.—*Manual*, p. 246.

[2] Hutton suggests that since the Saora arrow 'appears to be degenerate from the Gond form, it is possible that the bow and arrow have replaced a spear as the typical Saora weapon'. But so long ago as 1837 Russell found that the 'only weapons' used by Saoras were arrows, bill-hooks and axes.—Hutton, *Census of India*, 1931, vol. I, pt iiiB, p. 4; G. E. Russell, 'Report' in *Selections from Records of Madras Government*, No. XXIV, vol. I, p. 75.

Fire. The fires in the domestic hearths are kept burning throughout the year. The old Saora custom is to rekindle them when they fire their swiddens. A priest or shaman goes to his swidden, followed by the people, and makes fire there with a drill. When it is well alight, those present kindle torches with it and carry them to their own clearings and fire them. Later the head of each household takes another torch home and kindles new fire in his own hearth.

FIG. 17 Saora guns

But in the more Hinduized villages the Saoras follow the example of such places as Gumma, Serango or Nuagada. Here the Oriyas, on the full moon day of Phag (February-March), build a great fire to commemorate the burning of Kama by Siva, and the Saoras in neighbouring villages take fire from this great bonfire home to their hearths and they cook upon it any new crops that may have recently matured.

Five days after a child is born sacrifice is offered to Alungsungboi, the goddess of the inner chamber, on the hearth, and after this the mother can cook again.

Till recently fire was made by drill and saw, but now many Saoras have learnt the use of matches. There is no special ritual and no rule governing the kindling or the use of fire for cooking sacrificial feasts, but often a smoking coil of rope or straw is taken from the house concerned to wherever the sacrificial meal is to be prepared.

Guns. The Saoras are very fond of noise. It is a protection against unseen enemies. It makes them feel important. It rouses memories of a deep emotional tone.

Of course, it must be the right noise. The Saoras think that the most effective demon-scarer is the clash of brass and the roar of gunpowder. Gongs are beaten and guns fired mainly at funerary rites, but guns are sometimes let off at Harvest Festivals 'to interest the dead in the crops'. At a funeral, and at the Guar, Karja, and Sikunda rites, guns are fired continuously. The aim is no doubt partly to give the dead a sort of salute and to emphasize the dignity of those who have survived him; partly to publish the fact of a death or that ceremonies for the dead are in progress; and partly to scare away hostile gods and ghosts who might interfere. I have been told that the gunfire at the Guar was to warn the ancestors to clear the path to the Under World, for a new resident was on his way.

The Saora gun is a crude enough instrument. One type is little more than a hollow tube six to eight inches long (Fig. 17) which is loaded with powder and set off for purely ceremonial purposes. There is also a matchlock of more substantial size which too is useless for anything but ritual, and a crude muzzle-loader called *jamikibalan* which can kill a bird at short range. Well-to-do Saoras sometimes have shot-guns, but they are not really very interested in guns except for religious use.

FIG. 18 A shaman's dagger

The roar of the explosions down the narrow valleys and the quick impatient clang of the gongs as a party walks with nervous rapid steps across the mountains to fetch someone's bones stirs the hearts of the hearers and contributes not a little to the general emotional atmosphere of Saora religion.

Knives and swords. The shamans have special knives with decorative brass handles for use in taking the omens. I have also seen them use the double-pronged dagger (Fig. 18) called *katar* by the Kanarese. In many houses there are old swords, which are brought out for dances, and may sometimes be used to kill animals in sacrifice. Swords are often painted in the ikons, where they are a symbol of importance, and gods and tutelaries nearly always have a number of retainers armed with swords or guns.

Lamps. Lamps play an important part in Saora ceremonies of divination. The shaman holds a lamp in his left hand when he summons the spirits to come upon him; he puts a lamp in the winnowing-fan or by the bow when he is divining; he holds leaves or the blade of a knife in the flame of his lamp as he takes name after name in his search for the cause of a disease. Lamps are placed in the shrines of ancestors and before ikons.

In the Pottasingi area, a shamanin is not regarded as 'confirmed' in her dedication until she has received the gift of a lamp from an older woman who has initiated her. The lamp must be given before her marriage and by a shamanin of the same type and of the same family group. The famous shamanin Jigri of Boramsingi instructed all three of her brother's daughters, Arari, Amiya and Rogi, in their work, and she gave Amiya and Rogi their lamps and made them fully qualified Guarkumbois. But Arari, although she was married to her tutelary, took a human husband before she received her lamp, with the result that now she cannot be given one; she can perform minor rituals and assist other shamanins, but the spirits do not come upon her.

Lamps are of varied kinds and shapes. Little upright lamps, placed in the shrines, are called *adur-mallin*, 'festival-lamps'; the *tedung-mallin* are undistinguished but convenient lamps used in divination (*tendungan*); the most elaborate are the *karja-mallin* used in the Karja rites and for the initiation of the shamanins. These, considering the very crude methods of Saora pottery, are rather impressive. In form the lamp consists of a bowl, six inches in diameter, which rests on a small pot with a little spout. On the rim of the bowl are images of a horse and an elephant, and the inevitable peacock. On one lamp, in my collection, there is the image of a man being led by a rope; this is said to represent a sick man being led away by Ratusum.

Pots. To the Indian tribesman the earthen pot is the symbol of fertility and increase. To see a full pot on a woman's head is the most favourable of omens; a decorated pot, inverted on a pole, is sufficient to bar thievish ghosts from a tobacco patch. To the poetically-minded the pot recalls evenings by the well or river and girls splashing in the stream as they draw the cool water. The more materialistic remember splendid feasts of pork or beef cooked in pots ranged in long rows above the cooking-trenches, or the pots hanging from a thousand sago palms to catch the wine. It is in such pots that the housewife distils her spirits, stores her grain, preserves the gruel, parches rice: as in prehistoric days the pot is the cupboard of the home. No wonder that the ikons show so frequently the Potter of the Under World and his wife staggering along under great loads of pots.

The pot, so important in social and domestic life, has been adopted by the Saoras as an essential element of their religious culture. There are pots hung from the roof, pots in the shrine, pots on the veranda, pots used as sacred lamps, pots used for the transportation of the soul, pots caressed in divination, pots tested, pots as omens, pots that call tigers, pots to feed the dead, pots smashed in misery and despair.

The Saoras buy their pots in the low-country bazaars or from itinerant Dom merchants. There are also Saora potters known as Kumbits, who live in small groups scattered about the country. They generally live together in their own quarter of a village and do not intermarry with other Saoras, though they do not seem to be regarded as socially inferior. They make pots, bowls, lamps, and occasionally small images from a rough clay which they prepare by means of a wooden hoop. They use a wheel balanced on a stake about three feet high. After shaping the pots, they beat out any irregularities with a wooden block, and finally fire them by heaping straw and wood above them in a shallow pit.

There are few rituals connected with pottery. Once a year a shaman sacrifices a fowl on the wheel for the dead who may otherwise interfere with the work, making the potter ill and his pots flawed. Uyungsum is said to cause the pots to break while they are being fired, and the potters offer him wine from time to time. Although potters figure often in the ikons, I was unable to find any paintings which had been made specially for the encouragement of the industry.

The Kumbit Saoras live as ordinary cultivators, and only their special craft distinguishes them from other Saoras; this is definitely a subsidiary one, and brings them a small additional income.

The Saora custom is to buy a new pot; put into it grain, a copper coin, perhaps a bit of ginger; offer it to a god or ancestor in the course of sacrifice; then hang it up from the roof or in a shrine; and from time to time attach to it flowers, leaf-pipes and ears of grain, bunches of mangoes and pods of pulse as the seasons come round.

Such pots are dedicated at most of the important ceremonies to avert disease such as the Ajorapur, the Uyungpur, or the Doripur. They are always dedicated when an ikon is made for whatever purpose and hung up beside it against the wall. Ancestors are frequently honoured in this way, both by pots in the house and in their own shrines. On the occasion of a shaman or shamanin's marriage to a tutelary, a pot is always dedicated, and it is preserved and its contents renewed throughout a lifetime. A Buyya-priest, and often an Idaimaran or Idaiboi, may have a similar pot, in this case for the ancestors.

Pots containing a little grain or pulse are often prepared at the time of taking out the seed from the store-bins for sowing before the rains; one pot is kept in the house, and others are placed under the roofs of the village shrines. A gourd is sometimes used instead of a pot at this time: every kind of seed may be put in a gourd and

FIG. 19 Symbols of the Sun-god painted on earthen pots

it is hung up in front of the 'fertility-ikon'. For the Saoras say that 'we were born from a gourd, and if we put our seed into one, it will be doubly fertile'.

Very small pots for various gods may be hung from little wooden pillars on a veranda.

When a pot is dedicated to Uyungsum, a symbol of the Sun may be painted on its surface (Fig. 19). At the ceremonies for Ajorasum and other snake-deities, a snake is painted or the rough model of a snake is made with rice-flour upon a pot. Some of the sacrificial food is cooked in it and it is then taken home and hung from the roof.

When a child is sick it is a common practice for the parents to promise the sacrifice of a buffalo or a goat after a few years provided the child's health improves in the meantime. As a guarantee of this a pot is filled with rice and the mouth is carefully closed with the large leaves of the creeper *Bauhinia vahlii.* It is hung up and if it remains undamaged it is a sign that the child will be well; it is considered very unlucky if a rat should nibble through the covering leaves. The pot is sometimes tested by being placed upside down on the ground; the child's mother is made to get on it and 'dance' upon it. If it remains unbroken it means that all will be well.

It is in fact very dangerous to break a dedicated pot. Saoras sometimes offer a special sacrifice to prevent mountain rats (one of the few creatures of whom the gods are afraid) from stealing the grain in the pot, for the gods get very angry if they do. A man who broke a pot dedicated to Mammosum fell very ill with sores in his mouth and it cost him expensive offerings to recover. Another man, when a pot for Uyungsum broke in his house, did nothing about it and also fell ill with a bad head and many sores. Once, when a sexual taboo was broken in a priest's house, one of the pots burst with the noise of a gun being fired; on another occasion a pot fell from the roof on to the head of an offender and killed him.

Pots are used in divination. A shamanin plays with a pot, tossing it in the air, catching it and tossing it up again and again, whispering into it, when in trance. A shaman, anxious to discover which god has incited a man-eating tiger to attack his people, roars realistically into the mouth of a pot and calls on the god to reveal himself.

A pot may be smashed as a last gesture of despair and indignation if the child for whose safety it was dedicated dies.

Rings and bangles. At funerary rites there is often a lot of business with rings. In some villages the rings of the deceased are distributed to the officiants; in other places it is considered dangerous to do this, for the shade may return and demand to see its property. In this case new rings are purchased and given as little tokens. At any ceremony where a sacrifice is not actually offered, but is given conditionally, a ring and bangle may be placed on a child's hand and will only be taken off when full payment is made.

Spittle. The magic power of spittle is illustrated in the myths. In the days when birds did not lay eggs or have chicks, Kittung spat on the ground and told the birds to peck up his spittle, after which they began to lay.[1] In another story, to create a tamarind seed, Kittung rubbed some dirt from his body, made it into a ball, covered it with spittle in his mouth, and then planted it.[2] A shaman spits in his hands and rubs them over his face; he blows spittle into the ears and over the body of a patient. When they see a whirlwind approaching, the Saoras, who believe that this is a ghost back from Assam, spit to drive it away.

Swings and thorns. Throughout tribal India spirit-possession has to be authenticated. The idea seems to be that the human frame, when powerfully reinforced by a visitant from the other world, should be able to resist any assault upon it. The Gond Gunia, once possessed by his deity, proves to the world the genuineness of his experience by thrusting a pointed spike through his cheek or arm. The Muria Siraha in a similar condition flogs himself with an iron scourge and suffers no damage. The Gadabas and Bondos swing to and fro on swings of thorns; others fling themselves to the ground, beat themselves with great stones, and fill their mouths with fire.

I have not seen a great deal of this among the Saoras, but it does exist. At Maneba there was a swing with a seat of thorns upon which the shaman when possessed by Lurnisum seated himself. If the shaman could sit and swing on this uneasy seat, it meant that the place would be safe from smallpox. At Talasingi the shaman danced with a dagger which he thrust constantly into his body, sitting on its point, stabbing himself with it, not always, I thought, as vigorously as he might have done. But thorns and dagger alike fulfilled their purpose; they proved that the man was out of his own wits, truly possessed by a god who was satisfied with what he had been offered.

Thorns are used in Name-giving rites and a thorny branch of *bel* wood is used in the divination ceremony after a funeral. In each case the thorns are put afterwards over the door of the house. At a Name-giving ceremony a baby is made to sit on a circlet of thorns for a moment, and omens are taken from the way the bent thorns rise into position after the child is removed.

Thorns are important for keeping spirits in their place. If anyone is buried, and it is considered desirable to keep the shade under

[1] See *TMO*, p. 309. [2] ibid., p. 155.

control (as when the death is from smallpox) a layer of thorns is put in the grave. Thorns may be placed across a path to prevent Mardisum from entering a village.

The Winnowing-fan. All over India the fan is regarded as sacred. The Saoras use it to protect the grain on a threshing-floor, and it is in constant use by the shamans in ceremonies of divination. To rub rice in a fan is perhaps the most usual method of inducing trance.

X. *The Use of Leaves*

No one who attends a Saora celebration can fail to be impressed by the amount of time devoted to making things with leaves. A minor functionary called the Olabamaran (*olān* is a leaf) has the duty of seeing that these are in proper supply, but the main burden of making the necessary cups, plates, pipes and bundles falls on the shaman and his assistants. Sometimes, as at the Sikunda rite which I attended at Barasingi in 1951, the number of cups required runs into hundreds—so great was the number of ghostly visitors expected from the Under World.

The rules governing the use of these leaves are not very strict, and they vary from place to place, but—as I shall show immediately—certain kinds of leaf are normally used for certain kinds of ceremony.

Only in a few cases do the Saoras connect gods with trees in any permanent relationship. On the other hand, gods and ancestors visiting the earth often rest in or under trees, and the shades before their translation to the Under World can often find nowhere else to live. A common formula used by the shamans when summoning spirits to attend a sacrifice is: 'All you who are living in the forest, come! You who are in the mango, in the banyan, in the tamarind, in the ebony, in the jackfruit tree...' and so on, taking the name of every tree they can think of. The idea seems to be that since the spirits may be wandering anywhere, it is advisable to cover every possible place where they may be found.

The Saoras are not remarkable for any particular respect for trees, though it is taboo to cut the mango, mahua, tamarind and a few other fruit-bearing species. This taboo took its origin from the tears of Kittung, who is a great lover of trees, as the following story from Guli shows.

After the first earth had sunk beneath the waters and the new earth was made, Kittung planted the forest with fruit-bearing trees.

These were the only trees he made. At that time there were few people and no grain; everybody lived on fruit. But when the population increased and men made fields and hill-clearings and sowed them with grain, they needed firewood to cook with and they cut down the fruit trees and burnt the wood. In this way the forest was destroyed.

When Kittung saw this he was very sad, for he loved his trees and had pity on them, and he went to find seed to make new ones. But he could not find any and sat down on a rock and wept. Then the tutelary of Kittung's father[1] came out of the ground and asked him what the matter was. Kittung told her and she gave him seed saying, 'Every tree will bear fruit, but men will be able to eat the fruit only of those which were first made. They will not be able to eat the fruit of these new trees.' Kittung sowed the seed, and when the forest had grown up again, he said to men, 'Do not cut fruit trees till they are dry and useless. Cut the new trees I have given for your firewood and your houses.'

I will now give a few notes on the Saoras' traditions about the more common trees and the way they use their wood and leaves in ceremonial.

Aegle marmelos, Corr. (*kulpatneban*). The *bel* tree. The trifoliate leaves are used in divination: the shaman holds them one by one above a flame, taking names until one of the leaves burns in a certain way. A branch of the leaves is placed by the central pillar of a house at the ceremonies during a funeral. The thorns are used by the shamans at Name-giving ceremonies, and are placed above a door to keep away intrusive spirits.

Artocarpus integrifolia, Linn. (*padasaneban*). In sacrifices in the Sogeda area, the large ovoid fruit is sometimes used as a substitute for a goat: bits of wood are used for the head and legs. It is taboo to cut the tree for, though it is not connected with any god, the fruit —the jackfruit—is very popular.

Bassia latifolia, Roxb. (*abāneban*). A tree of the greatest importance since it provides food, oil and ardent spirits: it is taboo to cut it. In some villages, the tree is said to be the home of Kinchesum. The leaves are used at the Sikunda ceremony.

A story of the origin of this tree describes how once, when Kittung's wife was bringing water from a stream, a little red earth from the bottom of the pot got into her hair. Kittung suspected that some young man had been flirting with her, and he took the earth and planted it in front of his house. 'If it is true that it was not a young

[1] I have been unable to get any explanation of this mysterious reference.

man who put this in your hair,' he said, 'let a tree grow from it.' He went to sleep and during the night an *abāneban* tree grew up. When the wife saw it she was delighted. 'Look,' she said, 'this proves that I was telling you the truth.' And whenever afterwards she saw the tree she reminded Kittung that she had been right. Kittung, by a rather far-fetched pun on *boban* (head) gave the tree the name *abān*, since it had come from the earth on his wife's head.

Bauhinia vahlii, W. et A. The great leaves of this creeper are often used for plates at sacrificial feasts. Its origin is associated with Ramma, who once made a bird-trap with the entrails of a goat. Kittung turned the trap into a vine, and when Ramma protested, told him, 'If you roast the seeds and eat the kernels, you won't want meat, and the leaves will serve for your sacrifices. Its rope will be very useful, even better than a meal of meat.'[1]

Bombax malabaricum, D. C. (*kukuineb*). The cotton tree. In some places Jaliyasum is rather vaguely associated with this tree, and in others it is said to be one of the favourite haunts of the Buttamboi, the female ghost who approaches young men in dreams and robs them of their virility. In a cholera epidemic the wood is used to make the little chariot in which Mardisum is escorted from the village. The leaves are not used ceremonially.

Butea frondosa, Roxb. (*kondrumdaneban*). The flame of the forest. There is no taboo on cutting this tree. The flowers are offered to the ancestors at the Karja ceremony.

Diospyros melanoxylon, Roxb. (*tarelneban* or *kariseneban*). The Ebony Tree. One tradition gives the tree a very ancient origin. When Kittung and his wife emerged from the gourd in which they had escaped the great flood, they made a fire from its broken fragments, and from the charred wood came the ebony tree. Another tale says that the tree grew from the grave of a girl who had been bitten by a snake.[2] There is no taboo on cutting the tree and the leaves are not used in rituals. But a stake of the wood is used in the Lambapur ceremony to impale the head of a sacrificial pig. In some villages a pole of ebony is used to protect a garden of tobacco or chillies, in the belief that if a sorcerer tries to injure the crop his eyes will be attracted by the pole, and 'as this wood is black so the whole garden will appear black (and thus invisible) to him, and he will not be able to do anything'.

[1] *TMO*, p. 124. [2] *TMO*, pp. 126f.

Eugenia jambolana, Lam. (*kurgadneban*). The black plum. A branch of this tree is used to sprinkle medicated water over a herd to drive away every kind of cattle-disease.

Ficus bengalensis, Linn. (*tabarneban*). The banyan. One of the few really sacred trees. It is the *sadru*-shrine of the gods. It is taboo to cut it; should anyone do so in ignorance, he must sacrifice a goat to the gods and Kittungs living there. Cups are made of the leaves at the Guar and Karja ceremonies. At Talasingi the Saoras make offerings to the banyan at the Harvest Festivals, for 'it is our mother', and they tell a story of two fatherless children, whose mother left them under a banyan tree and went away. They would have died, but the milk of the tree dripped into their mouths and kept them alive.

Ficus religiosa, Linn. (*onjerneban*). The pipal. There is a remarkable story about the origin of this fig tree, which is sacred throughout India.

> Before the creation of the world, Kittung and his sister used to live in a gourd. When the new world was made and the gourd broke open, brother and sister came out and made their home on Kurabeli Hill. There were no trees on the earth at that time, and the two had to sleep in the open under the sky. One night while they were asleep, a mountain squirrel bit off four of the fingers of Kittung's left hand. Only the third finger remained. Kittung woke with the pain and cried; his sister also woke and cried.
>
> When the hot weather came, the girl said, 'How can I live in this heat when there is no shade?' Kittung cut off his maimed left hand, and put it on a stone. It soon grew into a tree, and gave shade beneath which Kittung's sister sheltered. This was the *onjerneban*, which has one finger in the middle of its leaves and grows on rocks in the forest.

The leaves are used in sacrifice to Ratusum, who will not accept offerings in any other kind of cup.

Holarrhena antidysenterica, Wall. (*keredneban*). Offerings are made on leaves of this tree, which exude a milky sap when cut, if a palm tree dries prematurely and fails to give its sap.

Mangifera indica, Linn. (*udāneban*). The mango tree may not be cut, though the branches may be. There are special festivals for the kernels of the fruit and for the ripe fruit, and then the shrines are decorated with the leaves. Kittung is said to have created the tree from the thigh-bone of a goat, which had been offered to him in sacrifice and had been left behind accidentally by the worshippers.[1] A concoction of the tender leaves is said to be good for headaches

[1] *TMO*, p. 138.

and a poultice may be made of the shredded bark. In some places, the mango is associated with Kinchesum, a god to whom human sacrifice was formerly offered. When suicides hang themselves from a tree, it is nearly always from a mango.

Melia azadirachta, Linn. (*puineban*). The bitter leaves of this *lim* tree are used in the feast at the Limma rite after someone's death.

Musa sapientum (*kintaneban*). The broad leaves of the plantain, when available, are used in many sacrificial feasts. The leaves, fruit and roots are offered to Kittungsum and Mardisum, but bunches of the fruit may be given to any tutelary or ancestor in substitute for something more expensive. It is said that the first plantain was raised by Bimma, but Ramma was jealous of it, and cursed it to bear only one bunch of fruit and then die.[1]

Phyllanthus emblica, Linn. It is taboo to use the wood of this tree for a funeral pyre. Its branches are used to make the little platforms on which stones are piled and crabs offered at the Lambapur.

Pongamia glabra, Vent. (*karanjāneban*). This is the wood most commonly used on funeral pyres, but Fawcett is wrong in saying that it is the only wood that can be used.

Pterocarpus marsupium, Roxb. (*ameneban*). In parts of the Gumma area it is taboo to cut this tree, but elsewhere the wood is used for making doors. In some places it is regarded as a favourite tree of Gadejangboi. A small branch may be used in the treatment of dysentery, for this is a bleeding tree: the blood-red gum-resin resembles blood. For the same reason, it is dangerous for a woman to cut the tree, for since its branches menstruate she too may suffer from excessive menstruation.

Semecarpus anacardium, Linn. (*araineban*). The leaves are used in the Tonaipur ceremonies; they are considered especially efficacious against sorcery. They are also used in the Gungupur for the protection of cattle, perhaps for this reason. A suitable offering to the tree may be made for anyone suffering from sore eyes. The fruit is sometimes used as ammunition by shamans when they shoot at their patients during the Doripur and similar ceremonies. The leaves are used at the pig sacrifice after someone has been killed by a tiger. There is a tradition that the original dress of the Saoras was in these leaves.

Shorea robusta, Gaertn. (*sargiyaneban*). The images and birds on a shrine should normally be made of this wood. The leaves can be used in any sacrifice where special leaves are not required.

[1] *TMO*, p. 144.

Tamarindus indica, Linn. (*tittineban*). The tamarind was first planted by Ramma with the idea of rivalling Bimma's plantain. In those days the tamarind had great leaves. But Bimma sent his parrots to tear the leaves to shreds and ever since they have been small. The fruit is sometimes offered in sacrifice.

Trewia nudiflora, Linn. Amulets are sometimes made of bits of the bark of this tree and used as a protection against Danunkisum.

XI. *Musical Instruments*

THE essential purpose of Saora music is religious. It is true that men sometimes beat their drums at night to keep animals from the swiddens and support their own spirits, that boys play the flute while grazing cattle, that someone may play a fiddle at an impromptu dance or while children are sitting round a fire at night. But for the proper performance of the various instruments a ceremonial occasion is required.

This is emphasized by the myths about the origin of music. One story comes from Sogeda.

In the old days there were no drums or flutes. Galdu lived in Karbisahi with his two wives and three sons. He died in another village and after his death, when his widows and sons examined the ashes, they could not find a single bone. That night the shade of Galdu came to his younger widow and said, 'If you want to bring me home, send word to the neighbouring villages. When I hear the sound of flutes and drums and trumpets, I will give my bones and you can bring them home.' The woman said, 'But we have no such things. Show us how to make them, and we will certainly bring you home with honour.' So Galdu explained in the dream, 'Make *kadingan* and *tuduman* drums and flutes in such and such a way, and come with them to fetch me.' The woman got up that very night and found a potter to make part of the *tuduman* and she made the other things with her own hands. In the morning she called the people from all the places round and they took the drums and flutes and danced. Now when they reached the burning-ground and looked at the ashes, they soon found bones and brought them home and buried them near by. In this way instruments of music came to the world.

Another story, from Samgainta, points the same moral.

At the beginning men had no instruments of music. When anyone died or was married, there was no means of sending the news to other villages. Kittung wondered how he could remedy this. 'I'll make music so that all men may know when there is a funeral or a wedding, and this will also cheer them.' Kittung made a *dollun* drum and covered it with buffalo-hide. With clay he made a *dagadān* drum and covered it with cowhide. He made a gong with a brass dish. When everything was ready he called Ramma and told him to take the instruments and whenever he sacrificed or when someone died or got married, he should dance, drink and make a noise. Ramma took the things and when he next sacrificed he called the Saoras of four or five villages and gave them wine and made the boys and girls dance with the drums and flutes. The gods were pleased and this good custom spread to every village.[1]

The Saora band consists of three or four drums of various types—the large hemispherical *dollun*, the *tuduman* which is a simple tom-tom, the kettle drum called *dagadān*, and perhaps the *kadingan* hide-gong. Rising above the rhythm of the drums are heard the long wailing notes of the brass horns, which are about three feet long and gently curved. There is always a brass gong, vigorously beaten with a wooden stick,

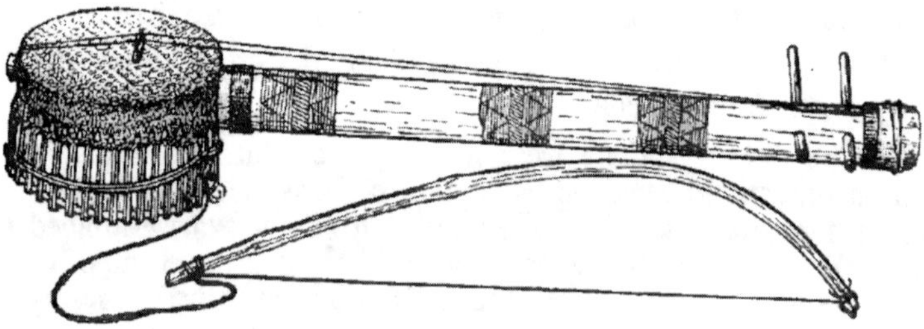

FIG. 20 The *gogerājan*
These vary from 2 to 3 feet in length

cymbals also of brass, possibly a stridulator, and a bundle of reeds which are beaten by hand with a clattering din.

This band performs on all routine occasions, at funerals and when a party goes to fetch the bones or shade of someone who has died in another village, at the Harvest Festivals, at weddings and at the Guar and Karja rites.

For dances the band uses the same instruments, but there is more attention given to the rasps and reed-bundles, and a small fiddle called *gogerājan* is very popular. This *gogerājan* (Fig. 20) consists of a bamboo stem about a foot long, to which is attached a sounding box of half a coconut covered with lizard skin; it has two strings and a bridge and is played with a bamboo bow strung with sago palm fibre.

[1] There is a brief account of Saora musical instruments in *Census of India*, 1931, vol. I, pt. iiiB, p. 203, and a somewhat fuller discussion by G. V. Sitapati in *Bulletin du Musée d'Ethnographie du Trocadero* (Paris, 1933), No. 5.

Ancestors often demand that it shall be played in their honour, and it has also various secular uses: it is 'a love-fiddle, a love-in-girl-arousing' instrument. A youth plays it at night to please a new wife. When everybody is sleeping out in the fields, boys play it to attract girls.

Another stringed instrument, resembling a guitar, is the *memerājan*, or 'breasts-instrument' (Fig. 21). A bamboo neck has four to six frets attached to it with beeswax. Two wire strings, spread apart, are passed over these; the first gives the melody, the second is a drone. Below there are two small gourds, cut out at the bottom, and secured

FIG. 21 The *memerājan*
These vary from 2 to 3 feet in length

to the bamboo neck by their closed ends. The *memerājan* is held with the open ends of the gourds towards the body; they are pressed against it or released to regulate the volume of sound. The wires are plucked by the right hand while the left fingers the stops.

The most important ritual instrument is the *kurānrājan* (Fig. 22), 'at whose music the dead and the gods come and dance before the shaman'. It is made of a bamboo about two feet long, with a headpiece carved in the form of a peacock's head. There are two fibre strings and a large gourd is attached by its back to the bamboo neck. The open outer end of this resonator is pressed against the shaman's body while he sings fingering the strings to keep the time and key.

The *kurānrājan* must be made by a shaman himself, fasting, outside the village, preferably on a hillside. When it is ready he offers his tutelary rice and wine and says, 'Wherever I go with this, may every spirit and sorcerer fly at the sound. But when you hear its music draw near.' The rhythmic drone of the strings often assists a shaman to pass into trance.

Bunches of little brass bells are worn by shamans when they dance ceremonially at festival or sacrifice, and sometimes strings of a large

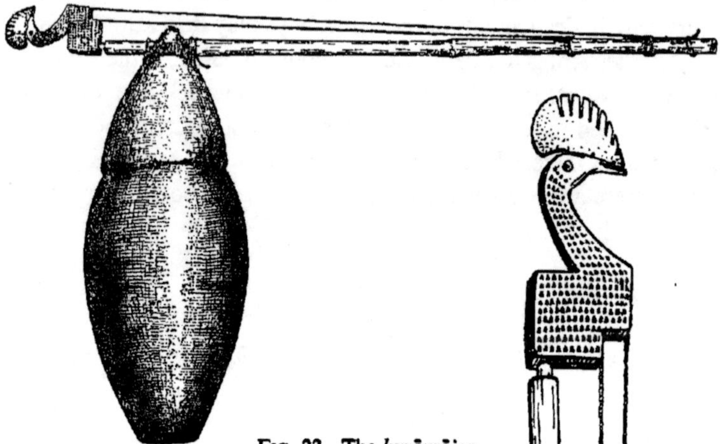

FIG. 22 The *kurānrājan*
These vary from 2 to 3 feet in length

bean or seed are attached to the ankles. The bells may also be worn by laymen at dances, but only if they are fasting; if they are not, they may fall ill.

The *doddurājan* (Fig. 23) is a rasp or stridulator, made of a piece of bamboo down the middle of which has been made a slit which is rugged with small grooves on either side. These are scraped with a stick; the upper part of the slit may be covered with one hand to improve the resonance. Sometimes a buffalo's horn is similarly serrated.

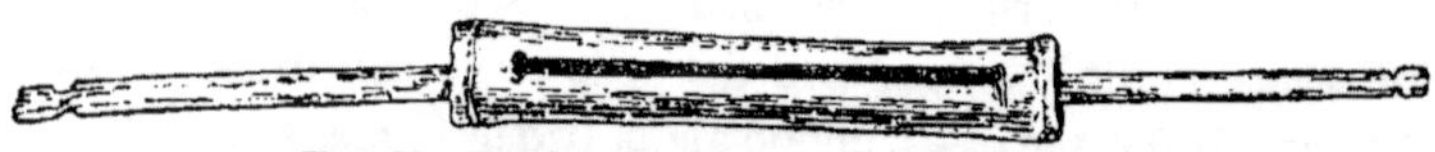

FIG. 23 Bamboo musical rasp or stridulator
2′ long

A special kind of rasp called *ragobdrājan* is used at marriages in the Sogeda area. In this case the serrated bamboo is fitted to the stem of a gourd drinking-dipper, and it is decorated with peacock's feathers. The members of the bridegroom's party go playing on it to the bride's house, where the youth fills the gourd with wine and hands it to his father-in-law. The older man drinks, refills the gourd and hands it back saying, 'Today I give you my daughter. If I change, let this gourd, this bamboo and the peacock-feathers witness against me.'

For the gourd symbolizes a newly-born baby; the bamboo is used at funeral rites; the peacock stands for the Karja ceremony and the shrines—and the three things thus combine to make a powerful oath. The number of slits on the rasp is made to correspond with the number of pots of wine which the bridegroom presents to his father-in-law.

Flutes are popular. The Saoras use one with five stops, another with seven.

Gongs are important as demon-scarers. The Saoras beat them continually after someone's death and until the body is cremated. They use them whenever the band plays during the Guar and Karja rites, and beat them all along the road when they go to escort a dead man's bones home from another village. Sometimes the bones are actually brought home in a gong.

There are various rules governing the use of these instruments. Buffalo horns may be sounded at the time of weeding in the fields and swiddens—'when the crop hears the noise it grows well'—but they should not be blown at threshing-time or harvest, 'or much grain will be blown away'. They may be sounded when the rains fall and when a hunting party sets out for the forest. There is a belief that when deer hear the noise they are attracted and come out of hiding.

Gongs, cymbals and earthen drums should not be played at weddings, perhaps on account of their association with funerals. The proper instruments for weddings are the fiddles—the *gogerājan* and *memerājan*—and the rasps.

The *kurānrājan* should not be played at sacrifices for Ratusum, Rugaboi, Tangorbasum, Mardisum, Madusum and Dorisum, for 'these gods are very bad and do not appreciate music'.

Offerings of rice and wine are sometimes made to instruments at the greater festivals, and at the Guar and Karja rites a little wine is dropped on the drums 'so that they may sound well'.

XII. *The Ritual Purpose of the Dance*

THE NATURE of the Saora dance is suggested by the legends of its origin. One story from Gunduruba describes how a wealthy Saora went to betroth his son and all went well until the bride's father declared that he would only give his daughter if she was escorted dancing to her new home. Nobody knew what a dance was, and the Saora went to Kittung to find out. Kittung taught him to dance, and 'on the wedding day they went dancing for the girl and brought her dancing; all day long they drank and danced'. Another story, from Barasingi, relates the dance to the great funerary rite of the Karja.

Kittung is in the sky. He had a daughter, but she died. He buried her and after three years prepared to celebrate her Karja rites. Her ghost said, 'Father, have a great dance for me, call all the neighbours, buy buffaloes and have a splendid feast.' Kittung arranged it, and he himself danced like a peacock and the guests imitated him. It was in this way that dancing began.

The dance, in fact, did not come into being as a form of recreation; it was not invented only for pleasure; from the very beginning it was serious business. And still today it is not indulged in for mere fun; even its form and shape depend on the function it fulfils in Saora society. Like the classic Bondo and Kond dances it is a serious piece of ritual conduct. It is curiously reminiscent of the ceremonial performances of the Ahir cowherds of central India.[1] Like them, the Saora dances are more of a procession than a dance.

For normally, as in the myth of origin, the Saoras dance to escort someone or something. They dance with a bride to her new home. They process round and round a village at the Harvest Festivals. They dance home with the bones of a woman who has died abroad. They escort a buffalo to a sacrifice and afterwards dance in its blood. They dance to fetch a menhir and escort the water-carrier to the well at a Guar rite. The donor of a buffalo at this rite dances ceremonially through the village. Indeed whenever the Saoras visit another village on a ceremonial occasion they dance through its streets. And so it has come about that the Saora dance has taken on the shape of the village street—a long rectangle. The Saoras rarely dance in a round: in many of the hill villages they could not even if they wanted to: there would be no room. The character and geography of the dance has determined its shape.

The dance itself is of the simplest character, well-adapted to its peripatetic purpose. There is no form or rhythm, there are no ordered steps, there are no rules. Men and women prance about in a confused jumble. They whirl their bodies round, jog up and down, swing their arms to and fro and in the air, jump, hop and stamp; now they move forward with little shuffling steps, now they run; but all the time the rectangle moves on. There is no singing, but everyone carries something

[1] The dancing of the Saoras of Mahendragiri, which the geologist Ball witnessed in 1870, reminded him of the Rajmahal Paharias rather than of either Santals or Kols.—Ball, *Jungle Life*, p. 268.

—a stick, a sword, a bunch of peacock-feathers, a pole with wooden monkeys or lizards, an umbrella—and waves it in the air. The band mingles with the dancers, blowing trumpets, clashing cymbals, beating the drums and gongs, and boys whistle piercingly with one knuckle in the mouth. From time to time they all raise their arms and weapons in the air and give a great shout.

The religious and ritual character of the dance is emphasized by the incidents that occur naturally during its course. A shamanin may be possessed by an ancestor and will career wildly about, wearing his turban and waving his sword. A shaman will dress in the clothes of his spirit-wife and dance like a woman. A priest possessed by Karnosum and shrouded in a sheet may lead the dancers from shrine to shrine at a Harvest Festival. Shamans and shamanins, once possessed, torment themselves with clonic convulsions; they roll on the ground, tear at their hair, sway to and fro in complete abandon, dance on their knees.

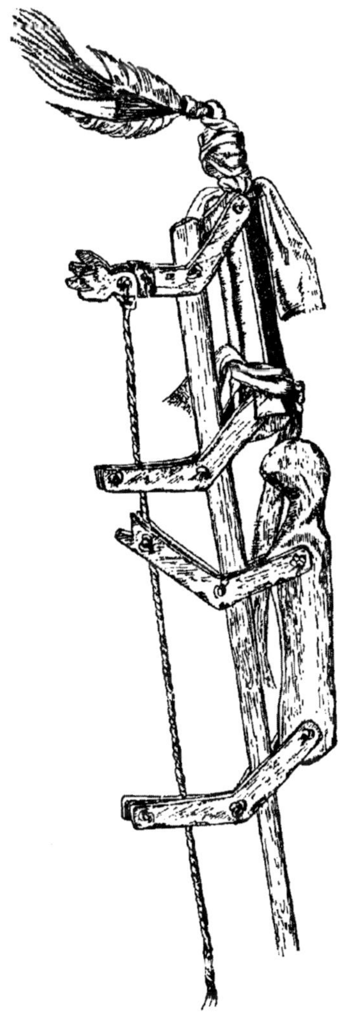

FIG. 24 Toy representing lizards climbing a pole, carried by dancers

In addition to the regular Saora dance, there are special dances for certain occasions. At the Guar the Idaimarans and Idaibois bring out the things of the dead—a man's axe, plough, clothes, box, umbrella; a woman's basket, skirt, ornaments, pots—and dance with them on their heads. In this case, only three or four people dance and the scene of their performance is the street immediately outside the house and the open space before the family menhirs. When performed for the ghosts of suicides and murderers who have been hanged, the dance has special features which are described in chapter XVI.

The shamans often dance by themselves during the ceremonies they conduct. At the sacrifice of a goat or pig which has been dedicated for the good of the crops, a shaman shoots arrows into the decapitated head; as he does so he dances rather slowly, hopping to and fro, gyrating on one leg, running forward in a sort of charge to release his missile. The shaman also dances at the Doripur and similar rites while he shoots balls of magic medicine at his patient. I have often seen shamanins perform quaint little symbolic dances indoors before an altar; possessed by a jovial spirit, they rise to their feet, shuffle their feet and jerk their bodies, waving their arms.

At weddings there is a dance of a more organized type, and this is so unlike the characteristic Saora dances that it is possible that it has been introduced from outside. This dance is called the Gogeraitongan. The girls and boys dance round two or three fiddlers playing their *gogerājans*. They sometimes move in a circle, sometimes in two rows with the fiddlers between them. Now they move to and fro with a skip and a hop, jumping up and down with both feet, kicking out with their feet, sometimes raising their arms in the air. At this dance, but not usually at any other, the girls sing.

Saoras are not good dancers; they do not practise enough; they are too busy for it; my impression is that they are not greatly attached to it. The impromptu character of most of the dancing is very typical; it has to be done, but there is no time to do it properly. Much of it is done under the compulsion of spirit-possession.

Sachs has distinguished between dances that are in harmony with the body, typical of peoples attached to the dance, and dances which are out of harmony with the body, typical of peoples who are indifferent to it. Opposed to the meaning and nature of the body is the 'convulsive dance', which is characterized by a 'state of forceful flexion and relaxation of the muscles which may lead to a throwing about of the body in wild paroxysms. The will has completely or to a certain extent lost control over the parts of the body; consciousness may likewise completely disappear. This condition is therefore not an activity, but a suffering.'

This pathogenic, convulsive dance is a characteristic of shaman cultures. 'It makes its appearance where priestly dignity and magic power are in the hands of the witch-doctor or the medicine man, where as a result of a peculiar racial tendency or of a cultural influence, religious experience and its cult formation rest solely on the rule of hypnosis.' It would not be possible to describe all Saora dancing in these terms, but Sachs points out that a dance 'which has developed in the first place, involuntarily and forcibly out of frenzy and extreme neuropathic disturbance, may continue to live on as an art form among peoples of lesser or of hidden ecstatic tendencies; in such cases control over certain groups of muscles develops generally from the clonic convulsion'.[1] This may have happened among the Saoras. The first dancers were the shamans, and their dances were, as they still often are, convulsive and ecstatic. But when the laity also began to dance a mixed form of art came into being, and control and convulsion combined to produce the Saora dance as we know it today.

[1] Curt Sachs, *World History of the Dance* (New York, 1937), pp. 17ff.

Chapter Seven

THE CAUSE AND CURE OF DISEASE

I

A GREAT deal of Saora theology and ritual derives from the struggle to be fit. There is nothing 'world-denying' about Saora religion; rather it stresses on all occasions the enormous importance of the body. There is little Saora asceticism: the occasional ritual fasts impose the lightest of burdens on those who observe them; the few celibate shamanins lead an exceptionally complete life in many ways; the idea of the body as a coffin, a fetter, a cage is as alien to the Saoras as it is to the most completely world-affirming, world-embracing thinker of the modern age. The body is all they have; it is the vehicle and instrument of all sensation—the delicious apopteia of intoxication, the release of sexual rapture, the delight of a good meal.

Health is the primary need and all else turns upon it. Yet it is an ironic fact that the Saora country, where there is so much to excite and charm the senses and the fields give food and the palm trees wine in abundance, is far from friendly to physical well-being. Since there has been no attempt in Koraput and no serious attempt in Ganjam to keep a record of vital statistics, it is not possible to speak with certainty. But the visitor to the Saoras soon gains the impression that they are a rather unhealthy and certainly a comparatively short-lived people. 'Old men are scarce,' said Fawcett long ago. 'The youthfulness of the people strikes one at once.' And although the Saoras are strong, muscular and wiry, very active and hard-working, he considered that 'they were decidedly physically inferior to the Konds',[1] and I think that most observers would agree with him.

The great scourge of the Saora country is malaria. 'Men were very happy,' says a folk-tale plaintively, 'before fever came into the world.' Of the forty-four species of anopheline mosquito to be found

[1] Fawcett, p. 215. J. D. Beglar, who visited Ganjam in 1875, also considered that the Saoras were 'much inferior to the Konds in strength and general physique. They were both short and thin.'—Cunningham, *Manual*, p. 121. Ball compares the Saoras with the Paharias of the Rajmahal Hills. 'They have not the manly bearing and good physique of the latter.'—*Jungle Life*, p. 267.

in India, no fewer than twenty-three have been discovered in the Koraput District,[1] and the large areas flooded for rice-cultivation provide them with ideal breeding-grounds. Where there are two crops a year involving perennial irrigation, there is continuous malaria transmission. These breeding-grounds are often close to the villages —Sogeda is surrounded by them, Tumulu rises from the midst of them, they are all around Arbun and Abbasingi—and it is hard to see what can be done to check infection. On the other hand, yaws, the scourge of Koyas and Marias to the south, does not seem to occur. Cholera is rare. Venereal disease is almost unknown in the hills, and there is no Saora word for it—where it does exist it is called Sanniboi, a name borrowed from the plains where it is all too tragically common among the 'reformed' or sophisticated Saoras.

Leprosy is prevalent in the Gunupur taluka, where a survey in 1940 showed an incidence of two per cent.[2] Skin-diseases of all kinds are increasing with an increased use of clothes which are seldom washed. Diseases of the eyes are very common among children. Smallpox is frequent everywhere and the general hostility to the vaccinator makes it hard to control. Saoras are very unwilling to go to hospital for any cause.

The Saoras generally name diseases after the god who is supposed to cause them. Thus cholera is known as Mardisum, smallpox as Rugaboi or Lurnisum, epilepsy as Kannisum, a cough as Kukusum. It is significant that there is no special god associated with fever, which in Saora is *asum*, or headache, which is *asuboban*: if there were, his cult would surpass all others.

A number of myths reveal in a clear and vivid manner the Saora theory of the origin of disease, which is—briefly—that the gods and ancestors have to make a living somehow and the only way they can do so is by forcing human beings to support them. I will give some of these stories in full.

The first, about the origin of fever, from Kerubai, attributes this disease to the ancestors who shiver with ague in the Under World. The ghost enters the body of his victim 'like wind' and imparts to it his own sensations of misery.

In the days before fever came to the world, people were very happy. When the time came for them to die, they passed away peacefully in their sleep.

[1] Bell, p. 94.
[2] L. N. Sahu, *The Hill Tribes of Jeypore* (Cuttack, 1942), p. 165.

There was a Saora named Tikara; he had one son. The boy grew up and married and he too had sons, three of them. After Tikara's death, his son performed the Guar rites. Five years afterwards Tikara's ghost came and said he had nothing to eat or drink. He went to Kittung and said, 'For five years I have had no food. Where are my children and grandchildren? I can't find them anywhere.' Kittung said, 'Go to your son and give him fever, and he will be frightened and give you all you want.' The ghost entered his son's body like wind and filled it with fever and pain. The son called a shaman and the ghost declared through him, 'I want a buffalo to eat, and fowls and a pig. If you don't give them to me, I will never leave my son alone.' This was the first fever to come to the world.

In a Dantara story also, it is Kittung who encourages the dead to give men fever and permits Mardisum to afflict them with cholera.

Cholera was the last disease to be created. Before it there was no Mardisum and there were no ghosts. Then Mardisum and the ghosts were born and they lived together. But they found the greatest difficulty in obtaining food and drink and one day they went to Kittung and complained. Kittung said, 'Go to Barlung village, for there are many Saoras there. Let the ghosts give them fever and Mardisum make them purge and vomit. When they begin to die the shaman will call for you. That will be your chance; then you can ask for anything you want.' The ghosts and Mardisum went immediately to Barlung, and there they gave the people fever and cholera and killed twelve of them. Then they told the shaman that unless they had goats and fowls for their food they would kill everyone in the village.

The origin of Kannisum, the god of epilepsy, is traced directly to Kittung.

One day Kittung went to bathe and rubbed some dirt off his body and put it on a stone. Kannisum was born from it and burnt like fire. Kittung was frightened and put his head down and sat still. Kannisum said to Kittung, 'I have been born from your body; tell me what to do and where to live.' Kittung said, 'Go to Kindabul village and find the Chief's eldest son. Go into his head and make him fall down. When he is out of his senses make him throw his hands and feet about as if he was a fowl. When this happens they will call the shaman and he will see that you get food. Then you can leave the boy alone.'

In a Tumulu story, the gods were born in the Under World and made people ill, not for any particular reason, but because it was their nature to do so.

There was a Saora named Dubla living in the Under World. He had four sons; he found them wives and married them, and then he died. The boys covered his body with lotus leaves and carried it to the burning-ground, where they burnt it on a pyre of green wood. From his ashes all the gods were born. They attacked Dubla's sons and made one cough, and another itch, and gave watery motions to a third and smallpox to a fourth. But the eldest son was a shaman and when he discovered what was the matter he made the proper sacrifices and sent the gods to this world. Since then the gods have lived here with the Saoras and have tormented them.

In most of these stories Kittung is represented as sending the gods on their destructive missions for, as we have seen, although he is often a kindly and benevolent deity, his character is ambiguous. According to a story from Potta, Kittung and his sister put disease in the world, almost wantonly, at the very beginning of things.

When the earth was submerged beneath the waters, Kittung and his sister took refuge in a gourd. When they reached land, they broke the gourd open and came out. They made insects to devour trees, put flies in the water and created diseases to affect everything and everyone.

These stories are instructive as showing how Saora thought traces evil as well as good to the same source. The same Kittung who teaches a shaman his benevolent profession instructs the gods of disease to harass and destroy mankind. The gods give disease, partly because that is their nature and partly because they want food, shelter and attention. In the Tumulu story the gods appear almost as if they were germs or bacilli, bound to do damage whether they want to or not, dangerous as a raging fire or a polluted well. A glance at the gods of the Saora pantheon in chapter III will show the very large number who give disease to man; in many cases the only thing a Saora can say about a god is to name the disease he gives. Indeed, if you mention the word 'god' to a Saora, his first, and often his only, reaction will be 'disease'.

In some cases a god is associated with a particular disease, as Kannisum is associated with epilepsy and Gajjisum with itch. But other diseases may be due to many different gods, or to the dead, or to sorcery. And conversely the same god can afflict his victims with several diseases: Uyungsum, for example, may give fever, leprosy or headache. Were this not so, the task of diagnosis would be very simple.

II. *Disease caused by the Gods*

Disease may be caused by the gods, by the dead and by sorcerers. Let us examine these in turn and see what are the motives that excite them.

The first motive, as we have already noticed, is that there is no motive. Many of the gods are sheer malice—there is nothing good in them at all. If the Saoras allowed us to classify them separately, I would call them furies or demons. But the Saoras use the same word *sonum* to describe these creatures of wrath and the comparatively just and benevolent Kittung and Sun-god. The wrath of the gods is wanton and unpredictable; it flares out and destroys the innocent and simple, the most orthodox observer of taboos, the most attentive worshipper. The irrational character of these attacks is specially evident in very serious and incurable cases of paralysis, lameness and insanity.

For example, at Alangda in 1950 I saw a young cripple named Sunanto who, when about five years old, had been attacked by Ettang-Jambosum for no reason whatever. The child was playing in the road; the god passed by and, according to the shaman, wanted to tie him up in a bundle and put him on his back; he made him into a bundle, distorting the poor little body just as if it had been tied up, and the child would have died, but for the sacrifice of a cow. Another cripple, at Kerubai, named Indro was met by Dorisum when he was out grazing cattle as a little boy. A great wind blew, and the terrified child ran home with high fever. From that day onwards Dorisum began to drink the blood of his right leg. The shaman sacrificed a buffalo, but it had no effect, and then Dorisum began to drink the blood of Indro's whole body. When I saw him he had been lame for fifteen years.

Sometimes the shaman decides that no cure is possible. At Barasingi a baby was born dumb, lame and with ears like a goat's. 'She couldn't even cry when she was born.' Darammaboi came upon the shaman and said, 'I have made her like this. There is nothing to be done. You cannot cure her.' This was a merciful economy, for otherwise the family would have gone on offering sacrifice for years; as it is, they explained, 'The child has not cost us so much as a fowl, for since she cannot be cured, what is the use of spending money on sacrifice?'

Delirium and madness is regarded with special apprehension, for it means that a sick man has not only been attacked, but possessed, by a god. In some places delirium is attributed to the malevolent Kond deity, Kinchesum. Fainting may be due to Mannesum's removing a man's soul from his body to take it on a visit to the Under World; there is always the danger that it may stay there.

Madness is due to an androgynous god called Bayyisum, whose attacks generally seem to be entirely unmotivated. If Bayyisum attacks a man in his female form, or a woman in his male form, there is no hope of recovery. When Bayyisum comes, the victim laughs and cries, curses his friends and relatives, eats refuse, attacks people and wanders about in the fields and woods.

In 1948 in Talasingi, two girls—Sombari and Trudeboi—were possessed by this deity. Sombari was quietly husking rice in her house, when suddenly she struck her head with the pestle and began to scream. She went to draw water, but as she brought the pot into her house it broke of its own accord, the water poured over her and she ran screaming down the street. She bit those who tried to soothe her, and when they tied her up she bit her own hands. She used to throw off her clothes and wander about naked. This continued for two years and then, in spite of many sacrifices, the girl died. Trudeboi had much the same experience, and the sacrifices were equally useless.

The Saoras do not like these mysterious unmotived attacks, which make them feel that there is no order or logic in the world. Wherever possible, the shamans attribute a reason for an illness and search unweariedly till they find one. The stories already quoted give one of the most common of these reasons: the gods are hungry and need food and shelter; men will not give them what they want unless they have to; the gods therefore put pressure on men by making them ill and keeping them ill until they get the food-sacrifice they want. There are many examples of this throughout the book, and I will only give one here. In April 1948 at Arbun a shaman called Jiggu was, as he believed, visited by Karnosum. 'The god tied his elephant and horse in the street outside and came into my house. He began to drum on a pot hanging from the roof and made a noise like *bhulbār-bhulbār*. He said, "I have come from afar, but I have nothing to eat; I am very tired, but I have nowhere to rest." I at once fell ill with high fever and vomiting. The shaman told me to make an ikon for Karnosum, and give him a fowl to eat. I did so and soon got well again.'

The gods are believed to be very sensitive to all kinds of neglect or disobedience. They react immediately to any breach of an established taboo. They are fussy about their rights and always ready to be insulted. They express their displeasure by ruining a crop, sending a tiger to attack the cattle, but above all by making the offender ill. Sickness is the routine punishment for every mistake and crime in relation to the gods.

There is a vague idea that the greater gods such as Uyungsum and Darammasum punish men for 'sin', giving leprosy for incest or blindness for false swearing, and the shamans and shamanins are immediately punished by their tutelaries for any breach of the moral code such as adultery. But the great majority of such 'moral' sicknesses are due to faults against ritual exactitude or punctuality and spiritual good manners.

The wrath of the gods breaks out emphatically if there is any unauthorized invasion of their territory. Meriahsum had to be placated when the Saoras moved north in the Kond mountains. Labosum made the people of Gundripadar ill when they invaded his hills for axe-cultivation without first making the usual sacrifice. Hargu took wild spinach from Gungusum's hill and the offended god attacked him with fever. There are a score of similar examples elsewhere in this book.

Most of these troubles could have been avoided, one feels, if the people had taken a little thought. Everybody knows that it is dangerous to enter a new area without sacrifice and to insult a god by taking his herbs and fruits without permission. But there are other cases where offence is given unwittingly and no one can guard against it. A revealing prayer was made by a shamanin at Tumulu on 7 January 1951; she was treating a boy who had been ill for five days with severe headaches and fever. This is what she said:

> You are great Rajas. You were out wandering along the road and this boy met you. You wanted him to sit with you, you asked him for tobacco, but he took no notice of you—how could he? For he could not see you, he could not hear you—and by accident he trod on you and went his way. That must be the reason why you are so angry.
>
> You are always hungry for wine and flesh and rice, and we give it to you willingly. If you are so easily offended, how are we to live? It is a matter of shame that great people like you should attack little people like us for so small a thing.
>
> You must have kicked the boy, or slapped him to give him such pains in head and body. We salute you, we touch your feet, we eat your excreta, but we beg you to let him alone. We will give you a feast at the very place on the road where he unwittingly offended you. Let him alone and we will give you anything you want.

III. *Disease caused by the Dead*

THE motives that prompt the dead to afflict mankind are more varied and interesting. But the reason, both for god and ghost, is the same. There is only one way by which a shade or ancestor can make his

23. Saronti, the eunuch of Sogeda, divining with his bow

24. Sarpoli, on the occasion of her marriage to a tutelary at Sogeda

25. The leper shamanin, Idan of Boramsingi

26. Jigri, the famous shamanin and Chief of Boramsingi, with Amiya who succeeded her after her death

27. A shamanin dances in trance with her sword at Thodrangu

28. Musicians at Gundruba

presence felt, and that is by being unpleasant. This does not mean a change for the worse in the dead man's character; it is rather a reflection on the character of the living. It simply means that there is no other technique possible for getting what one wants. For, as a Saora at Regidi told me, 'The dead have become strangers, and no Saora ever did anything for a stranger unless he had to'. Even as it is, the nightmares which the dead give to the living are generally forgotten directly the day breaks, and if they came in sweet and pleasant dreams no one would think about them at all. The dead, I have been told again and again, do not want to trouble the living; they are driven to it by necessity, sometimes even by affection. If the ghost of a husband makes his widow sick unto death, it does not mean that he has become cruel and evil in the other world, but that he loves his wife so much that he desires to have her with him.

The Saora view of the dead, then, is not that they are wicked or cruel; they are rather pathetic, for they have to act out of character to get anything they want..

All the same, wicked or not, the dead are a very great nuisance. They are a constant drain on the health and pockets of the living. And what is worse, an ancestor is no less tiresome than a shade. When I began my inquiries I had the idea that the proper celebration of the Guar and Karja rites was enough to lay the ghost and save his descendants from further trouble. But that is not so. A shade, in fact, is in some ways an even greater nuisance when he becomes an ancestor. The shades are in the main only concerned about food, drink and clothing and to persuade the living to observe the Guar on their behalf. But the ancestors have many other reasons for visiting the earth; some wish to perpetuate their names in new-born children; some seek for company; one may need a buffalo to plough his fields in the Under World, another may need food for a tutelary, a third may be angry at a failure to repair a shrine erected in his honour.

There is no definite time-limit to an ancestor's importunities. Suicides, the murdered and those who have fallen from trees are said to be troublesome for many years. The ghost of a man murdered at Pandrung appeared eight years after his death and gave fever to a young man who had nothing to do with him at all. Those ghosts who become merged in such gods as Dorisum or Kinnasum continue indefinitely but not, I think, for long as separate entities. A dead shaman who becomes a tutelary has a very long lease of activity on earth, although he does not appear as an ancestor but as a god. Generally, the ancestors appear so long as their memory is fresh and so long as they are remembered and invoked at sacrificial feasts. But there is no certainty that a ghost will not reappear until he has died again in the Under World and has been cremated there with due ceremony.

The machinery by which the dead, equally with the gods, make their wishes known, and by which they emphasize them when they are ignored, is ill-health. They may sometimes damage the crops and send wild animals to attack the herds, but their chief weapon is the sickness they give to human beings. How they do this I have never been able to discover. There is a vague idea that a ghost can possess his victim and communicate to him something of his own misery; the typical ghost-diseases are fever and rheumatism. Fever with its fits of ague reminds the living that the dead are naked and cold unless they clothe them. Rheumatism gives a hint of the misery and pain that the ghost suffers unless his heirs are sufficiently attentive.

What are the chief reasons which drive the dead to trouble the living with sickness?

The period between a man's death and the performance of his Guar is often one of much ill-health for the survivors. The shade plagues them with nightmares and fevers; it fills the house with ill-omened cries and tappings; it makes the wine tasteless and the gruel stink. But every Saora tries to postpone the trouble and expense of the feast as long as he can; he ignores the warning dreams; he puts off the importunate shade with little gifts of rice and wine; and only when someone falls really ill does he get busy with his duty to the dead.

The motives of the ancestors are more complex and elaborate. A common cause of sickness for young children and their parents is the desire of a dead ancestor to perpetuate his name, and in some way reincarnate part of himself, in one of his descendants. To ensure this, he usually gives a dream to the father of a newly-born child, and when this is ignored—and it is almost routine for it to be ignored—he makes the child or its parents ill. At Maneba a grandmother's ghost gave a child fever in order to force the parents to perpetuate her name. At Pandrung a man died, leaving three sons and two daughters. They all married and had children. Then the father came in a dream to one of them and said that every one of his grandchildren, both boys and girls, should be called by his name. The dreamer forgot all about it, and the whole family went down with fever. There was another dream and this time the shaman insisted on the strange command being obeyed, and everyone recovered.

In 1940, the father of the Chief of Talasingi died. Soon afterwards the Chief himself had a little son. The grandfather's ghost came in a dream and said, 'Now my grandson is born, call him by my name and dedicate a goat for him. Then he will grow up happily and have no kind of trouble.' The Chief ignored the dream and soon the baby was seriously ill. The shaman was called in and reminded the Chief of his dream, and he then gave his child the name demanded and dedicated a goat. This goat became famous. It was said that no tiger could possibly eat it; even if a tiger killed it, it would be unable to digest the flesh. Once one of the Bissoyi's agents took away the goat by force for his master's pleasure; but as he went along to Gumma he suddenly got high fever and hurriedly returned the goat to Talasingi, where he found the child also ill because the sacred animal had been taken away.

Sometimes the ancestors, who are, of course, always rather conservative, indicate their disapproval by making their descendants ill. This commonly happens in any case of irregular marriage. A Saora once brought a wife from Dokripanga to Ladiguda. Presently her grandfather's ghost, who seems to have disapproved of the union, came to Dokripanga, and gave a number of people fever. They had to erect a wooden pillar and sacrifice to it before they got well. At Maneba a Jati Saora broke the rules by marrying a Kindal girl. Her dead parents were angry at this and gave her a lot of fever until the husband built a shrine in their honour. When he did that she got perfectly well again.

The life of the ancestors in the Under World is by no means comfortable, but it is settled. The wine is bitter, food is scarce, the climate is abominable, but at least one is part of a society and one has fields, a house and some sort of domestic life. The shade is anxious to join this deformed and frustrated company for just this one reason: he has no home, he does not belong anywhere.

But the very fact of the more settled life of the ancestors leads to complications. An old man who dies leaving a widow and children behind finds himself very lonely in the Under World, and not only lonely but helpless—there is no one to cook for him, no one to bring water. It is thus very common for an ancestor to come back to earth in search of company; he makes a widow or a daughter ill and die so that he can have her help about the house—it is the mark of an expert shaman that he can persuade such a ghost to go away content with some lesser offering.

Out of many possible examples, I will give that of Lingu, an Idaimaran of Pattili, who lost most of his family and nearly died himself from this cause.

When I was about fifty years old, the ghost of my paternal grandfather came to me and said, 'You are getting on now; what is the point of your going on living? Come and look after me and we'll be able to drink together and enjoy ourselves.' I gave him a goat instead and he left me alone. Then my father's ghost came and made one of my daughters desperately ill, for he said, 'Your mother and I are old and feeble and there is no one here to get us water.' He refused every substitute and the girl died. Then my brother's ghost came and took away one of my sons, a boy whom he had always loved and who had sat beside him when he was dying. His own son, his only one, had been taken by Ajorasum and of course could not be with him in the Under World. So my brother took my son instead. Then came the ghost of my father-in-law and tried to take the only son left to me; he said, 'The others have had their share: what about me?' My wife has just died too, taken from me by her brother's ghost. He wanted me as well, for he pointed out that the whole family, or most of it, was now together in the Under World, and what was the use of my staying on earth. I sacrificed a pig, a goat and two fowls, but he refused them all, and now I don't know what is going to happen.

Lingu died about a year after this, and I was told that it was his paternal grandfather who after all got him in the end.

Closely connected with the desire to have one's family around one is the feeling of jealousy at seeing a widow marrying again. In this case a ghost often makes the woman or her new husband ill. I discuss this, for it is a complicated matter, in a special section. More rarely a ghost shows himself jealous at the sight of a dearly-loved child giving its affections to someone else. On 13 December 1944 there was a pig-sacrifice at Bungding for a sick child. This was a little girl whose father was devoted to her: he always had her in his lap, fondling and playing with her. But after his death, one of the neighbours took to her—for she was a great charmer—and used to play with her and hold her on his lap. Presently she fell ill, and when the shaman came her father's ghost came upon him and said, 'I have been several times to see how my little daughter is. She has forgotten me; she sits in the lap of another man and plays with him as if I had never existed. Now sacrifice to me or I'll take her away to play with me in my house in the Under World.'

The dead are very sensitive to neglect, and they get plenty of it. They respond, just as the gods respond, by making the careless and forgetful ill. An ancestor, for example, may persuade his heirs to build a shrine for him; after a time the roof is blown off, or a storm damages the plinth; he comes in a dream asking that it be repaired; no notice is taken and the ghost makes the culprit ill. Similarly, forgetfulness in offering sacrifice, failure to mention a name in an invocation, failure to renew a dedicated pot or an ikon can all lead to various kinds of sickness.

The dead greatly object to their descendants going to the Tea Gardens. Away in Assam, many Saoras forget to perform the proper rites. An interesting example of this is provided by the experience of Jonia, an Idaimaran of Potta, who went to Assam for three years.

When we came back, the family ghosts attacked us, making our legs so weak and thin that we could only hobble along with the help of sticks. For they said, 'Why did you leave us and go to that distant country? We have been starving all this time; we have had no one to look after us.' I sacrificed a buffalo and a pig, but for a long time I was weak in the legs. My eldest son also went with his wife to Assam. My father's ghost came to me in a dream and said, 'Call them back; they are neglecting us, and if they continue to do so, they will both die there.'

A remarkable thing about the Saoras in relation to the other world is their habit of forgetting things. It is easy enough to forget a dream, it is less easy to understand why the Saoras so frequently forget the promises they make at feasts and sacrifices. A good example of what may happen under these circumstances comes from Karanjusingi, where an old man called Punjari died in the house of his son Lerju in the winter of 1936. At the time of his death Punjari owned a number of valuable ornaments and some palm trees. After the funeral, his shade came to demand his ornaments and Lerju promised to keep them for him, but he forgot all about his promise and sold them. Lerju also promised to make special offerings to the palms before tapping them for wine; this too he forgot to do. Punjari's shade, therefore, made Lerju's wife and son very ill; they lay in extremity for over a month. Lerju even then could not be induced to take the matter seriously, though his behaviour was the occasion of much discussion in the village, until at long last he sent for a shaman and on 19 December 1944 offered a buffalo in sacrifice for his father.

Many other examples of such forgetfulness will be found in these pages. It is specially irritating to the dead when it is combined with pride and arrogance. In January 1947, one Lagai of Pattili developed a splitting headache and an earache so severe that he felt as if one side of his head was being knocked off.

My paternal grandfather had died a long time ago and I had forgotten all about him. Then one day he came in a dream saying, 'I am dying of thirst and hunger; give me something to eat.' But I turned over and slept on my left side. By morning I had forgotten all about it, but I began to get this pain. It was because the ghost was angry at my turning proudly on my left side; he declared that he would take everything in the house.

However, when Lagai offered him a fowl he accepted it. Sacrifice was made in the usual way and Lagai recovered.

It will be observed that many of these incidents arise ultimately from an ancestor's desire for food or some other benefit. Often the ancestor desires this for himself; sometimes he wants it for other people. In one pathetic case, a shamanin's ghost made children ill as the only way of getting food for her old tutelary who was starving in the Under World. In another case, the ancestors had no buffalo with which to plough their subterranean fields, and they made an old woman ill so that as a result of the subsequent sacrifice they would get the animal they required.

It is said that when the ancestors get a craving for a meal of buffalo flesh, they send maggots into a wound, which is regarded by all Indian tribesmen as a very great disaster.[1] They may also send fever in order to extract a gift of clothing, as the following example shows.

In the last week of January 1945, Sukki the wife of Rajmo was taking her little son Mali from her home at Kerubai to visit relatives at Potta. On the way they had to cross a stream where, ten years before, there had been a drowning tragedy. A man called Jora had gone with his daughter from Rajintalu to Sogeda for a sacrifice; both had got very drunk and on the way home they slipped in the mud of the stream and both were drowned. Although both Guar and Karja ceremonies had been performed, their ghosts continued to haunt the stream, and as Sukki and Mali were crossing, they caught hold of the boy and gave him fever.

I was present in Rajmo's house when the shaman made this diagnosis. He passed into trance and the two ghosts came together and said,

[1] Cf. my *The Baiga* (London, 1939), pp. 198f.

'We are father and daughter. We went home drunk one night and fell into the stream and were drowned.[1] We had no clothes, for they were carried away by the torrent and now we live naked. We saw this woman and her child and we attacked them to get their clothes. Give us something to wear and we will let them alone.'

This was an unexpected demand, and Rajmo replied, 'But I haven't got any spare clothes.' The ghosts were not to be put off. 'No,' they said, 'we must have clothes; we don't want anything else, only clothes.' Rajmo then said, 'I have no cloth for a man, but there is a girl's cloth here', and he placed a girl's new cloth on the altar. The shaman picked it up, examined it minutely, smelt it and tied it round his waist in token that the ghosts had accepted it. Then the ghost of Jora said, 'So there's no cloth for me; well, never mind, give me a goat instead.' Rajmo said, 'I haven't got a goat, but I can give you a pig.' The ghost replied, 'That will do. Give it to us and we will go away and take our diseases with us.'

IV. *Disease caused by Sorcery*

THE FEAR of black magic plays a comparatively unimportant part in Saora life; the real enemies of human health and prosperity are the gods and the dead; witches and sorcerers exist, it is true, and precautions are taken against them, but they do not have the dreaded significance that they have in ordinary village society.

Sitapati, however, says that the Saora 'dreads the sorcerer more than the spirit' and he refers to 'a secret class of sorcerers whose main business is to injure their enemies or the enemies of their employers and who are, therefore, much dreaded and looked upon with suspicion and contempt'.[2] Ramamurti's Dictionary also gives a rather large number of words for witchcraft and the evil eye:

assolā	to cast an evil eye
giggim-mad	the evil eye

[1] There is a curious parallel, from which no conclusions should be drawn, in the *Katha Sarit Sagara* (vi. 36). A King of the Savaras named Mayavatu goes to bathe in the Narmada river and three water-spirits seize him. He is saved by Mrigankadatta who goes into the water after him with a drawn sword.

[2] Sitapati, 'The Soras', *J.A.H.R.S.*, vol. XIV, p. 11. When Russell and Hira Lal (vol. IV, p. 507) say that 'the Savars are considered to be great sorcerers' and quote the sayings—'The man bewitched by a Saora and the bullock tied up by a Rawat (grazier) cannot escape' and 'Verily the Saora is a cup of poison' they are not speaking of our Hill Saoras. *Sabara-mantras* have long been famous: they are, as distinct from *jadu-mantras*, addressed only to the deified ghosts of those who have met with violent deaths.

isangā	to ruin by witchcraft
kanidan	sorcery
molān	evil eye
poru-	to exercise an evil influence by the evil eye
solāmad-	to look at with an evil eye
tanayan, tanai	sorcery
ural madan	the evil eye.

But of these, *isangā* really means envy, or mischief in general; *tanai* or *tonai*, which is the word most commonly used for sorcery, is not Saora but Oriya; *assolā* actually means to curse; *molān* is an evil spirit and is usually found as an echo-word to *solān*, as in *solān-molān*, evil spirits. These spirits, like most spirits, can be employed by witches, but the word does not mean the evil eye.

Ramamurti and Sitapati were inclined, I think, to read into Saora religion a good deal that was not there; moreover some of their material was gathered from sophisticated and Hinduized Saoras. There can be little doubt that they have exaggerated the importance of black magic in Saora life.[1]

But, of course, every Saora believes that witches and sorcerers exist and I have met individuals, such as the Chief of Sogeda and Jigri, the late Chief of Boramsingi, who were obsessed with the fear of black magic. They were, after all, important people, with many enemies.

Stories of the origin of sorcery are not widely known, but I recorded one at Ladde.

Jammasum fell from above in the form of a weeping child. An old woman found him and took him home as her own. When he grew up, the boy said, 'Mother, go to the Chief and get me two bullocks, and I will plough your field.' But when the mother went to the Chief, he said, 'I have no bullocks.' The boy said, 'Never mind.' He made magic against the Chief and his cattle died.

Then the boy said, 'Mother, go to the priest and get me grain.' But when the mother went to the priest, he said, 'I have no grain.' The boy said, 'Never mind.' He made magic against the priest and his harvest failed.

After that the boy went to another village and said to the Chief, 'Give me work.' The Chief replied, 'I have too many servants already.' The boy said, 'Give me a little food and let me sleep here.' That night two of the Chief's servants died and others fell ill. The

[1] In this opinion I have the support of Fawcett, who says that although the practice of sorcery is 'not unknown' to the Hill Saoras, they are 'not given to dabbling in magic'.—Fawcett, p. 270.

shaman discovered the reason and told the Chief, and he decided to kill the boy. The boy said, 'Kill me if you must. But don't burn my body. Put it in a cowdung pit and after a week come and look at it.'

The Chief killed the boy and buried his body in a cowdung pit. After a week he went with many others to look at it. They found that the bones of the fingers had turned into rings, the hands had turned into rings, the arms had turned into bracelets, and the bones of the chest had turned into necklaces. One man took the rings, another took the bracelets, a third took the necklaces. Each became a sorcerer. They were the first sorcerers and this is how sorcery came into the world.

It is worthy of notice that in this tale it is Jammasum, the god of death, himself (as his name suggests) a recent immigrant into the Saora pantheon, who by his death and the transformation of parts of his body gives sorcery to the world. Another story, from Taraba, describes a sort of college of witches.

Kanjam Saora and his wife grew old. They had seven virgin daughters. One day these girls went to an old Saora witch, named Kabri, to learn sorcery from her. They stayed with her for seven years, and when they had learnt everything from her, they returned to their parents' house. The people of their village got frightened and had one of their women taught sorcery also. One day, the seven sisters, followed by this woman, went to the forest to get wood. When it was cut and ready tied into bundles, a Raja came by hunting.

The eldest sister was very beautiful and the Raja caught her and enjoyed her. But as he was going away, the other girls struck him with their magic and he fell from his horse and died. The sisters took out his brains and liver and started for home. On the way was a river and they halted on the bank, discussing how they might cook and eat the Raja's flesh. They had wood and there was water, but they had no hearth. So the eldest sister took out her vulva and put it on the ground. The others put wood in it and lit a fire, and they cooked the brains and liver that they had taken from the Raja's body. In this way these women learnt how to make a hearth, and when they got home they made one of baked earth in the same pattern. It was in the shape of a vulva, and at the centre was a small tip like the tip of a clitoris. The woman who followed them told the neighbours what she had seen, and they drove the girls away. It was they who spread the knowledge of sorcery through the world.

This ominous story, with its sexual and cannibalistic[1] motifs, suggests the detestation in which the witch is held. Ladde, a village high in the hills overlooking the Vamsadhara valley, is one of the

[1] Compare the stories in *MMI*, pp. 443ff.

rare places notorious for sorcery, and few people care to visit it. Even the police are afraid of going there, and when, some years ago, there was a murder in the village, they called all the inhabitants down to the Station House at Pottasingi, to avoid having to make investigations on the spot. The people of Ladde are rather proud of their atrocious reputation and there is in fact a slightly sinister atmosphere about the place; old crones quaver their incantations at midnight and the shamans have a peculiarly startling whistle and gestures which are all their own.

I have only once actually met a Saora who would admit, even in his cups, that he was a sorcerer. He was an elderly Idaimaran of Borai, who has since died, but whose name I need not disclose. He spoke with pride of his achievements, and declared that in Assam he had enchanted five men, all of whom had died. In his own area, he had killed one of his enemies by sending Mardisum to him with a sharp attack of dysentery. A man and his wife quarrelled with him and he sent Jammasum to them and made them ill. 'No one could cure them,' he added with some complacency, 'so they had to send for me and pay me to make them well.' 'It is when I lose my temper with people,' he went on, 'that I send my magic to them. And when the gods come to trouble me, I have the power to pass them on to others, who fall ill instead of me. They are always trying to turn me out of this village, but they are too afraid of me to do anything much.'

The sorcerers are supposed to do their work either directly, by sending objects into a victim's body, or indirectly by sending gods to do their work for them. The Borai sorcerer sent Mardisum and Jammasum to attack his enemies. A Sogeda sorcerer sent Madusum against the husband of Bejonto the shamanin, gave him leprosy and ultimately drove him to suicide. But the two gods most commonly employed are Tonaisum and Pangunasum, both obvious newcomers to Saora theology. Tonaisum, who is a typical familiar, the Bir of Hindu India, comes in a dream in the form of a pig and drinks an enemy's blood.

Pangunasum is a sort of tutelary. If a man wishes to become a sorcerer, he sacrifices (it is said) a black fowl to Pangunasum and fasts for two whole days. Then the god appears to him in a dream in the form of a small green chilli—'for magic is hot and strong as a chilli'. The next day he comes again, this time as a pig. The third night Pangunasum assumes human form and takes the sorcerer's soul out of his body and shows him the forest and the hills, and where the magic herbs grow, and teaches him how to enchant people and use the medicines of sorcery.

> Now when such a man desires to enchant someone, his big soul talks to his little soul, and the little soul agrees that the big soul should go to call Pangunasum. When the big soul has found its helper, they go together to their victim and he dreams of pigs and chillies and soon falls ill.

A sorcerer may also send Pangunasum to spoil a hunt: the familiar has to be bought off by the sacrifice of a fowl.

A sorcerer can also work directly, without the need of an intermediary or agent. If he can find some of the hair-clippings, or spittle, or nail-parings of a child he can use them to its harm. He can send magic with a hen's egg, or with bones stolen from a pyre, or with rice and chillies. He can put a charm on a path or into someone's wine. A Kerubai sorcerer once sent magic with rice, chillies and little pebbles to the Chief of Sogeda, who had caused great offence by forcing a Kerubai girl to marry his son. The shaman brought two of these pebbles out of the Chief's chest and two chillies from his throat.

Sorcerers are supposed to take a malicious pleasure in interrupting and spoiling the effect of sacrifices, and most ceremonies begin with invocations designed to keep away their evil influence. Sometimes the shaman invites the familiars, together with the dangerous ghosts of the murdered and suicides, to come and accept a drink of wine and then go away. A typical invocation is:

> Let no sorcery approach our house or village. Let no one in . . . [here the shaman takes the names of all the surrounding villages, never omitting Ladde] work evil against us. Let every sorcerer—young man or old, maiden or crone—forget what we are doing today. If they try to put their magic in our wine, our rice, our drinking-water, stop them. Let no one approach who works evil by grubs, by chillies or by rice. If any such come near, let them not enter the house. We will give them wine and rice outside.

Occasionally Saoras who have learnt magic from the Konds—and the Konds, as practitioners of human sacrifice, are regarded as the supreme experts in the black art—may turn themselves into monkeys, cats, tigers, bears, rats, snakes and even insects. When clouds suddenly cover the sky on a fine day, it may mean that such a man has just turned himself into a tiger. But it is very dangerous to do this, and it is said that these sorcerers are quickly seized by Madusum, that is to say, they become lepers. It is safer, and so more usual, for a sorcerer to send an animal to damage his enemy's crops or herds.

The lethal character of a sorcerer's hostility, which may employ more than one method at the same time, may be seen in an account given by Jigri, the famous woman Chief of Boramsingi.

My father was Chief of our village, and when he died my brother succeeded him. But Ganno, the Chief of Kittim, killed him by magic, for he hated him: Ganno had murdered a man in Boramsingi, and my brother reported him to the police. Ganno got three years, and when he returned home, he sent Tonaisum to attack my three brothers. For this he used three eggs. He came by night along a path which he knew my brothers often used, and made three circles of ash and turmeric and put an egg in each; before them he offered rice and wine. Fortunately my two younger brothers when they went out the following day used a different path. But my eldest brother, the Chief, went early before dawn to get palm wine and took the path which led to the enchanted spot. When he came there, he heard a word uttered —*sar sar sar sar*—and he ran home in fright. He brought a torch and returned to see what it was, and when he saw the circles on the path, and the eggs, he realized his peril. He went home and sacrificed a pig, but it was no use; the very next day he fell ill with terrible pains in the head and chest, and the day after that he died.

After the funeral was over, my second brother quarrelled with Ganno and accused him of sorcery. Ganno was very angry, and a month later he went to my second brother's palm tree and did mischief with chillies, putting bits of them into the wine. Directly my brother drank from the pot, he had violent pains in his stomach and ran home, doubled up and crying for help. We put a hundred silver rupees on his chest as a promise that we would spend this on sacrifices if he recovered. But it was no use. We took him to the hospital at Gunupur, but that was not any use either. We brought him home and the next day he died.

A year later, we had reason to fear that Ganno was again plotting something, but before that happened, my father's ghost came to my youngest brother and said, 'You alone are left. He is going to kill you also. So come with me and escape him.' As a result this brother fell ill and died, and since there was no one left, I became Chief of Boramsingi.

As a motive for homicide, sorcery is much less important in Saora than in Maria society,[1] but occasional cases come before the Courts.

[1] Cf. my *Maria Murder and Suicide* (Bombay, 1950), pp. 61ff., but see *Bondo Highlander* (Bombay, 1950), p. 234.

In August 1942, three Saoras killed another Saora called Jadu at Bodaguda in the Pottasingi area. This man was widely suspected of being a sorcerer, for wherever he went people and cattle sickened and sometimes died. On the afternoon of 14 August, the three men —Kakia, Gopanna and Suku—were distilling liquor in the bed of a stream, and were all rather drunk. Jadu approached them, and Gopanna accused him of being a sorcerer and struck him in the face. Jadu knocked his assailant down, knelt on him and tried to throttle him. Kakia, who was expert at killing buffaloes for sacrifice, struck Jadu with the blunt side of his axe on the back of his neck 'just as if he had been a buffalo', and Jadu fell down and died soon afterwards. The three men buried the body in the bed of the stream and agreed to tell everyone that Jadu had gone away to Rangoon. But the crime was discovered, and Kakia was sentenced to three years' imprisonment under Section 304 I.P.C. and the others to a year and nine months each under Section 201.

A rather similar, but more brutal, crime occurred the following year, on 2 January 1943, at Orai. A Saora called Tasu had a bad reputation as a sorcerer. Among his neighbours was one Gopal, whose father, sister, daughter and son died in rather quick succession. Gopal came to the conclusion that Tasu was the cause. One day, therefore, while Tasu was walking down the village street, Gopal—well primed with palm wine—came up behind him and knocked him unconscious with two heavy blows from his axe. Tasu's wife ran to the rescue, but Gopal beat her off with his axe. Then Gopal's own mother, an old woman of over seventy, came and upbraided him, but he struck her violently on the left shoulder-joint, cutting right through the humerus. Then he continued to beat the unconscious Tasu as he lay on the road until he died. The post-mortem discovered nine serious wounds on the neck, shoulders and face; the larynx, oesophagus, both carotid arteries, and both jugular veins were completely severed, and the spinal cord was cut clean through the body of the second cervical vertebra. Such was the very violent revenge that the fear of magic could excite. There was possibly also the unconscious motive that by thoroughly disabling the corpse of his enemy, Gopal would be safe from the resentment of the shade, who would be too crippled to attack him.

One of the common effects of sorcery is the intrusion into a victim's body of some small alien object—a chilli, a bit of bone, a grub, pig's bristles, legs of a crab, even a hairy caterpillar. A shamanin at Boramsingi, engaged in treating a girl for rheumatism, asked her tutelary, 'What has the enemy sent into this girl's body? Is it a chameleon's bone? Is it a lizard's bone? Is it an insect's bone?'

The cure for this condition is by 'medicine' and by manual activity which extracts the foreign substance. On 7 June 1948 I watched a patient being treated at Gailunga. The shaman began by a lengthy diagnosis with his *kurānrājan*, playing on it and chanting.

> Where are you from, magic? Did Labosum send you? Or was it Kittung? Or did the ancestors or tutelaries send you, magic? Was it someone in Kamalasingi, or Thalulaguda, or Sogeda, or Gunduruba, or Ladde? Who was the enemy and why did he send this evil thing? Did this man sitting here eat his enemy's grain? Did he steal his mangoes? Did he take his tamarind? Did he steal his pigs, his cattle, his fowls? Did he rob his fields? Did he abuse or beat him? If not, why did he send this evil upon him? Now we give you grain and husked grain, wine and a fowl. Uyungsum be witness, Labosum be witness that we are giving you these things. Let this man alone.

The patient had a severe pain in the left side, but the shaman declared that anything sent into the body by magic does not stay still, it moves about. He gave the sick man some medicine, of which he refused to disclose the nature, to eat and put a little in the form of paste on the left side above the liver. He then took a peacock's feather and began to brush his patient's body. At such a time, it was said, the tutelary possesses a shaman's hand and it moves of its own accord. The shaman lit a lamp 'for the eyes of the tutelaries find it hard to see by the light of this world'. Then as he brushed all over the man's body, he cried over and over again, 'Whatever thing it is —be it a worm, a bone, rice, chilli—come out!' At the end of the ceremony, which lasted over two hours, the shaman declared that whatever had intruded into his patient's body had been brushed away by his feather.

On another occasion, on 30 December 1947 at Boramsingi, a sorcerer bewitched a man called Kullusing and gave him a belly-ache and a cough, so bad that when he coughed 'he thought his belly would burst open'. Many shamans tried to cure him without success. Then he called a woman from Kanjasingi called Agan who had the reputation of being specially expert in this kind of thing. She gave Kullusing *tonairegaman*, 'sorcery-medicine', to eat and applied some of it externally to his stomach. Then she got a potsherd, put fire in it, and stroked Kullusing's throat until suddenly a hairy caterpillar came out, and she dropped it at once into the fire. She stroked the throat again and some of the caterpillar's hairs came out, and she burnt them also. Then she put some more 'medicine' on the stomach and sucked at it, and produced a fowl's claw. She sucked again and spat out some black blood. After this, and the sacrifice of a pig and a cock, Kullusing felt much better.

At Dantara in 1948 the Chief Sonia was attacked by a sorcerer who sent a caterpillar, flying with Ringesum, the Wind-god, into his body. At Kittim, Surburu quarrelled with another Saora over a field and the latter put magic in his palm wine with a crab's leg and pig's bristles. When Surburu drank it he fell ill with dysentery. Again the shamanin treated him and removed the pig's bristles from his belly and the crab's legs from his back.

Often these things cannot be seen when the shaman removes them, but the Saoras say that they 'know they are real because they can smell them when they are burnt'.

At Jirri, on 20 May 1948, a little girl had worms which had been sent into her by a witch who disliked her mother. The shaman removed them by means of an arrow tied up with a mango leaf in the shape of a pipe. He heated it and applied it to the child's chest and drew out a worm, which the child herself burnt.

The presence of these objects in the body may also be due to Kinnasum, the tiger-god, though it is probable that he usually only attacks human beings when incited to do so by a sorcerer. I witnessed a dramatic treatment for this at Guli on 30 December 1945. Twenty years previously a man called Adiya had been eaten by a tiger and in due course had become Kinnasum. One evening, when Roko, a Saora of Guli, was coming home, an enemy sent the god to attack him; he heard a noise 'as if someone was walking on dry leaves', and when he reached home he got high fever and felt 'as if an animal was clawing and biting him all over'. A shamanin sacrificed crabs and rice in front of an ant-hill on the path, and Roko recovered. But the shamanin declared that it was essential to proceed to more advanced treatment; whatever grub or insect had entered Roko's body as a result of his encounter with Kinnasum must be extracted and burnt. For, as she pointed out, if such a creature escapes alive, it will call a tiger to devour its former host.

Two days later, therefore, on 1 January 1946, the shamanin made her patient sit by the central pillar of his house and offered rice and wine to Kinnasum and the dead. Then she brushed Roko all over with a peacock feather, holding a potsherd in her left hand and brushing into it. Presently two small white grubs fell into it. I saw them myself.

Roko took the grubs to the hearth and burnt them. 'They are the tiger-grubs,' explained the shamanin. 'Had they grown and developed wings, they might have flown away to the hills, turned into tigers and come back to eat him.'

Then Roko's younger brother lit a lamp and ground up some *Shorea robusta* resin. He held the lamp close to Roko's body and threw a pinch of the resin powder at him through the flame of the lamp. It flared up like a firework. He did this over and over again, all over Roko's body, while the shamanin brushed at it vigorously with her feather. This was intended to remove any of the tiger's hairs which might be sticking to the skin; if they remained, the grubs might grow again. Finally, the shamanin blew in both Roko's ears to remove anything else that might be remaining.

At Abbasingi I was told that when Kinnasum's hair and blood enter a man's body, the hair pricks like thorns and the blood makes a man feel as if he has had a heavy flogging.

Another ceremony of this type, which I witnessed at Boraisingi on 19 May 1948, was associated with Jammasum, and there was a curious history behind it. The patient was a boy of about ten years, a pathetic little creature named Pungru, with shocking sores on his ears and cheeks; he had one eye closed and acute pains in the joints. The story was that when he was still in the womb, his mother fell ill. For in the third month, when the foetus was still forming, Jammasum—incited by a jealous sorceress—gave it, along with the human bones, the bones of a pig and a fowl. Jammasum has three wives—Gundpilurboi, Surarami, and Surajangi—and they mixed up the bones and gave the unborn child too many. A shaman was called and made this highly expert diagnosis; he managed to extract the fowl's bones, and the mother recovered and Pungru was born.

But the pig's bones remained in him for ten years.

The ceremony of extraction was done at night and in the house. The shaman, a famous old man called Gamru, prepared the usual materials of sacrifice, and offered wine to Jammasum, calling on him and all the gods.

O mighty Jammasum, Jaganthsuru, Jaganthbena, Karikasuru, Karikabena,[1] it is you who cause women to conceive, it is you who put the bones in the womb. O Jammasum, you give leprosy, you make men blind, you make men deaf, you make the belly swell, you make the eyes red and sore, you cause legs to break, you make the blood to flow. O Jammasum, I call you. Come, sit and eat; sit down here; I have a new pot for you. Sit on it and accept what we offer you. Bring out the bones you put into this child and make him well. Come without fail. I give you wine. You are a blood-drinker: I give you blood. O bone-giving and bone-removing Jammasum, come and save this boy. Tell Gundpilurboi and Surarami and Surajangi not to make such a mistake again.

Then the shaman poured rice into a winnowing-fan and made the sick boy sit by him. He waved a pinch of rice over his head, across his back and shoulders, over his knees and feet, always right to left, and then waved the fan up and down in front of him. He put it down and everyone crowded round eagerly to see if any bones had passed into the rice. After a lot of scrambling they found three tiny scraps of bone, which the shaman declared to be pig's bones, and Pungru took them to the hearth and burnt them at once.

Then the shaman sacrificed a pig in the usual way and offered the blood to Jammasum, and when everything was finished the people feasted. Pungru got much worse after this, but his parents absolutely refused to take him to the Serango Hospital, which was only five miles away. I heard that he died not long afterwards.

In most of the above cases, it will be noticed, the sacrifices are directed towards whatever god has been induced to cause trouble by the sorcerer. The gifts win the god over and he lets his victim go.

But when it is not evident which spirit has been involved, or whether in fact any spirit has been involved, the rite called Tonaipur is observed. For this a special shaman is needed, who knows the secret medicines which are to be used. The Tonaipur is not unlike most ordinary sacrifices; there is a sacrificial feast to which all the benevolent and protective spirits are invited; but the most important element is the application, generally externally, of the secret 'medicine', the *tonairegaman*.

[1] These are all names of Jammasum.

To conclude, Saora belief in sorcery is rather vague and confused. Everyone believes that there are sorcerers, but no one has ever seen one at work, very few have had direct experience of their malice. No one has ever proved a sorcerer's guilt, though the accusation of sorcery is sometimes made very lightly and is not always taken seriously. In practice, action is rarely taken against a sorcerer. On the other hand, special invocations are commonly used to avert the interference of sorcerers during a sacrifice, and there is a regular and elaborate technique of treatment for those who have been afflicted by them.

We should observe the absence of some of the most characteristic features of classical sorcery. The custom, widely diffused over the world and remarkably persistent through the ages, of making an image of an enemy and then destroying or injuring it, seems to be unknown. Equally unknown is the kidnapping of souls. The Saoras have no pointing apparatus or ghost-shooter. Their sorcerers do not single out the liver for attack. They do not buffet their enemies with sudden winds or destroy their houses with inextinguishable fire. They do not fly through the air, they do not assemble in Sabbaths. In fact, I suspect that the Saoras do not really class sorcery among their own rites and customs at all; it is something that belongs to their neighbours the Konds, the dreaded practitioners of human sacrifice, and it is generally only those Saoras who have been corrupted by external influence and example who have turned to the black art.

V. *The Treatment of Disease: Diagnosis*

THE magico-religious treatment of disease is naturally dependent on a correct diagnosis. Since, as the Saoras say, 'there can be no disease without a spirit', and since the spirits vary greatly in the type of sacrifice they require, the task of diagnosis is one of the most important of the shaman's duties.

The simplest and most common method of diagnosis[1] is for the shaman to summon his tutelary and persuade her to find out the truth. Often he starts a regular spirit-hunt in the other world, calling on all the gods and ghosts by name to go and find who was responsible for a sickness and to bring him to reveal his demands. The usual

[1] The Saora word for the divination ceremonies is *ted-ted-puran*, or *tetepuran*, which refers particularly to divination by the bow, but is extended to cover all types of diagnosis.

procedure is for the tutelary either to tell her shaman who was responsible or for her to arrange that the god or ghost should himself come upon the shaman—who is, of course, all the time in a state of trance—and speak to him directly. This often leads to a great deal of argument: the spirit demands a buffalo—the patient offers a goat; the spirit demands a goat—the patient offers a fowl. The spirit usually complains about the quality of the wine he is offered, and at most seances other spirits come upon the shaman with many totally irrelevant demands. But the upshot of the whole business usually is that the shaman is able to tell his patient who has attacked him, and why, and what ought to be done about it.

There are a number of examples elsewhere of how the shamans behave on these occasions, but I will give here a typical invocation, which shows very clearly the kind of questions that are asked, from my report of the proceedings of a diagnostic seance held at Taburda on 18 January 1951. A shaman was trying to discover why a youth called Rupo was suffering from what was obviously remittent malaria. He called first on the tutelaries, then on the ancestors, and then on the gods.

O tutelaries, was it you who sent your messengers for this boy? He has returned from Assam after several years; perhaps you think he has a lot of gold and silver, cloth and tea to give you. Come and tell us whether you have done this.

O ancestors! You who were killed by Uyungsum, by Labosum, by Ratusum, you who hanged yourselves, you who were murdered, you who were hanged because you murdered, you who fell to death from trees, come all of you. For you we have sold our own heads, for you we have run into debt. Go and search for whoever has made this boy ill and bring him here.

O gods! O Mannesum, O Uyungsum, O Labosum, O Kittungsum, O Barongsum, O Galbesum, O Ratusum, O Dorisum, O Ajorasum! We touch your feet, we eat your excreta, you are father and mother to us, we worship you. Come all of you, find out who it was that made this boy ill. Bring him here and when we have satisfied him, drive him away. Open your eyes and see, open your ears and hear. As a monkey I salute you.

Was it you who made this boy ill? Perhaps he was going over the hillside or distant clearing and did not notice you. Perhaps you asked him for tobacco and he did not hear you. Were you angry with him? Did you send a ghost or other messenger to trouble him?

Come, all of you, sit in a row and eat the feast we give you. You have books of gold, books of silver. Bring them with you, and read in them the name of whoever attacked this boy.

Sometimes these inquiries are made with the help of a winnowing-fan half full of rice, which the shaman rubs round and round with his right hand. This 'helps to persuade the gods', as a shaman once told me, and it seems to induce by its rhythmic and slightly hypnotic motion a state of trance which is the basic condition for all a shaman's commerce with the unseen world.

But this may not be sufficient. In that case the shaman resorts to various tests. Perhaps the most popular of these is the *bel*-leaf[1] test. The shaman lights a lamp and places it in a fan half filled with rice. Someone brings him a branch of *bel* leaves. He takes these one by one, and in each he puts an unbroken grain of rice. He holds the leaf in the flame of the lamp and recites names. In this, as in all similar ceremonies, the shaman proceeds as in a guessing-game, gradually narrowing the field of possibility. He begins, for example, by taking the names of gods, ancestors and sorcerers. If a sorcerer is indicated, he then takes the names of all possible villages. When the village is found, he takes the names of individuals.

In the *bel*-leaf test, the answer is given by the grain of rice turning black and sticking to the leaf or by the way the leaf curls in the heat.

A similar test is conducted with the help of a knife. The shaman takes one of the ceremonial knives, with an ornate brass handle, such as is often used in rituals, and passes it through a flame, judging the answers by the way the blade is blackened.

If a shaman wants to know what part of a patient's body has been attacked by a sorcerer, he takes a lamp and passes it over him. When the flame burns up brightly or if the skin shines unnaturally, it indicates the affected part.

A bow is used to track down thieves and sorcerers. The shaman holds an ordinary bamboo bow by the string in his left hand, and throws grains of rice at it with his right, taking suspected names as he does so. When the bow swings violently to and fro, it is regarded as having pointed out the culprit. Sometimes the shaman puts a few grains of rice on the belly of the bow. In this case the process is reversed; it is when the bow does not shake and the grains are not knocked off that it gives its answer.

The *kurānrājan* (see p. 212) is used both in divination and to induce trance. The shaman plays it, strumming rhythmically on the wires, and chanting softly, until he passes into a state of dissociation.

[1] *Aegle marmelos*, Corr.

VI. *The Treatment of Disease: Sacrifice*

We have seen that one of the chief motives which drive the spirits to attack human beings is hunger. Food-sacrifice, therefore, is the first and essential cure for most diseases. Even where a man has fallen ill because he has offended the dignity of a god, or broken a taboo, or has injured an ancestor's vanity by neglect, food-sacrifice is still of great importance for, as a Saora once pointed out to me, the quickest way to soften an enemy is to feed him well.

Every Saora sacrifice includes a number of ingredients that are fundamental, although there are many incidental techniques which vary according to the god who is to be honoured and the inspiration of the shaman. But, in order to avoid too much repetition, I will give an outline of a standard sacrifice, let us say, for example, the sacrifice of a pig for the recovery of a man from fever. Such a sacrifice will proceed, generally speaking, on the following lines.

1. *Preliminaries.* These include the building of an altar (see pp. 176ff.), invocations to the spirits, and the offering of uncooked grain and wine.

2. *Manual treatment.* The shaman makes the patient sit beside him in front of the altar. He takes between the thumb and first finger of his right hand either a pinch of dedicated rice or a tuft of hair from the back of the neck of the sacrificial animal. Then he passes his hand again and again over his patient's head, across the back, down each arm, down each leg. If he is treating a baby, he makes his passes also over the mother's head and breasts. There is not really any rule about the order and direction of these passes; they generally start, naturally enough, at the head and work towards the extremities; they are often, but not always, clockwise in their direction.

The shaman then throws the rice or hair away—he may indeed go through the motions of throwing something away with a twitch of his fingers after each set of passes. Then he blows in his patient's ears, and sucks, bites and kisses his body all over. As he does this, he again pretends to remove something from the body and puts it in his loin-cloth. He cleans his teeth with a bit of ginger and blows again in his patient's ears.

Sometimes, the shaman sweeps his patient's body with a broom; in certain emergencies he strokes it with a feather. He often applies a pinch of dedicated rice to the patient's forehead, knees and back, and he may wave the various offerings of the sacrifice—such as a basket of grain, a gourd of wine and the sacrificial animal itself—round his head.

This treatment, especially when it is applied to children, is done in a very homely and kindly way. A shamanin, for example, does her best not to frighten the child; when she blows in his ears, she laughs, fondles him, pats him on the head and generally behaves as an amiable doctor might when he has to give an injection to a nervous patient.

3. *Dedication of the sacrificial animal.* The pig is brought in and the shaman does three things to it. He plucks off a little hair from the back of the neck and passes it over the patient's body. He picks the pig up and waves it round his head. Having thus established a connexion between patient and offering, the shaman feeds the pig. This is an essential part of the rite. When the animal accepts its food and wine the shaman knows that the spirit has accepted the animal. Often the shaman puts the grain and wine in the patient's own hand and makes him feed the animal himself.

4. *The procession.* In some cases, the entire sacrifice is concluded inside the house. The fowl or pig is killed inside, a goat or buffalo is killed in front of the veranda. But more often there is now a procession out of the village; it may be along any path, and in any direction. All the materials of the sacrifice must be carried out and the women of the house take cooking-pots, wood and water. When they have reached a suitable spot, the shaman makes a little altar, and arranges the materials of sacrifice before it. He prepares leaf-cups and plates, he may trace a rough design on the ground.

5. *The sacrifice.* The animal is now killed. This is never done by the shaman, but there is no other rule; it may be done by 'anyone who knows how'. There are no special duties allocated to relatives at any sacrifice, not even at the Guar. Directly the animal is dead, it is decapitated, and someone carries the head to the altar and lets drops of the blood fall on the things offered there; often one or more leaf-cups are filled with blood, and the head itself is placed on or by the altar.

6. *The feast.* The proceedings now become thoroughly domestic, for they are to do with food. The animal's body is taken some distance from the altar; the blood is drained into a special pot, and the body is cut up. Women have already prepared hearths, and fires are burning under pots of rice or millet. They now cook the meat. Generally the special food for the spirits, and the shaman, is cooked in a new pot on a separate hearth near the altar. When everything is ready, the

shaman offers leaf-cups of cooked meat and rice at the altar, and when this has been done they all sit down and feast.

7. *Ikons and pots.* In connexion with a sacrifice there is nearly always some other activity enjoined on the worshippers. The dedication of a pot (see pp. 200f.) is important. Sometimes an ikon must be drawn; I discuss this in another chapter. Occasionally a shrine must be built. There may be a special dance demanded by the spirit, or a ritual hunt, or perhaps a little cart or bundles of wood or some image is taken out of the village on the scapegoat principle.

8. *Trance.* It is not necessary that a shaman should go into a state of dissociation, for all discussions and bargaining with the spirits should have been done previously, at the time of diagnosis. Indeed many shamans who are not capable of trance could yet fulfil almost the whole of the above programme. But it often happens, either during the preliminary invocations indoors or outside by the altar during the long interval while the feast is being prepared, that the shaman falls into trance and he may then be visited by any god or ancestral ghost.

9. *Application of 'medicines'.* In the course of some sacrifices the shaman applies 'medicine' to his patient. This is often in the form of a paste which he smears on the forehead or over the body; it is usually done after the killing of the animal and before the feast.

10. *Prayers.* There are no standard Saora prayers, no formulas or fixed invocations. The shamans open their rituals with very long lists of names, which vary considerably from place to place. Then there are the prophylactic prayers intended to keep away sorcerers and their familiars. Other prayers follow a general pattern, but they seem to depend largely on the inspiration of the moment; though there are, of course, clichés that recur continually. I will give a few examples of the kind of prayers that are offered in the course of sacrifice.

At Boramsingi on 24 December 1950 a Raudakumboi offered pig-sacrifice for the young Chief Iswar, who was suffering from fever. When the pig's head was placed on the altar, she said,

> We have given you rice and blood. Come and accept it. Do not hide from us and afterwards return to trouble us, saying that we gave you nothing. You who have no settled homes, you who wander everywhere, find those who attacked this boy and bring them so that they can feast on what we give them. O Rajas, O fathers, O Great Ones, you live on every side, we cannot see you, we cannot tell when you will attack us. Yet though we cannot see you, we are driven mad when you come near. We know nothing and you know everything, yet we

give you all you demand. You gave us birth, you injure us, you protect us. As we give presents to important people to win their favour, so we give presents to you. You were very hot with anger, now cool down, and show your favour by accepting our gifts.

The Jammapur was celebrated at Sogeda on 12 April 1946 for an old woman with rheumatism. At the very beginning, before the shaman gave the woman manual treatment or sacrificed his fowl, he made the following invocation.

Jammasum, Uyungsum, Darammasum, you made our hands, our feet, our bones, our bodies. When you attacked this old woman, did you take the form of men or did you come as spirits? What mistake have we made that you should trouble her? How did you get into her house? Did you enter by the door? Did you break through the roof? Or did you meet her as she was walking along the path under the hill? But at all events you came to her somehow or other, and now we are to give you honour. Care for all the children in our village.

When you come, we cannot see you, yet we suffer in hands and feet and bones. You come with such angry power that if you catch a tree it will wither, if you catch an animal it will waste away. How then can a human being escape? Do not be so angry.

If we suffer from purging, it is through you. If there is evil in the water, it is from you. If there is evil in the food, it is from you. You give birth to men and women, birth to us all. We call you: come and accept our sacrifice.

Then when the shaman offered a fowl, making the bird eat rice from the old woman's hands, he cried,

When you attack us, you give pain to hands and feet, bones and body. Now make this woman well. We give you a fowl. You live in the sky; you witness everything, good and ill alike. Be pleased with our offering and go away.

On 12 May 1948 the rite of Tangorbasumpur was offered at Tumulu for a boy named Surato who was suffering from high fever. The shaman sat before the boy and put marks of rice on his forehead and chest and said,

Come all ye spirits. We fall at your feet, we fold our hands, we beg you to come. Come and remove whatever evil is in this boy. Remove it from his body with your tongues, with your teeth, with your nails. Tell us what has happened. Was it that as he was going through the forest you caught him? If so, we fold our hands and beg you to heal him. If you are going to attack us at any moment, whether we are working, sitting about, standing, laughing, talking or eating, what are we going to do?

Perhaps as you were squatting on the path, he walked over you, perhaps he trod on you. If so, we fold our hands and beg you to forgive and heal him. Perhaps he kicked you on the head, perhaps he knocked against your body, perhaps he trod on your feet. If so, we fold our hands and beg you to forgive him and accept what we spread before you.

Come to us and take our offerings. If you are asleep, get up quickly and wash your faces and hands. Get up and come quickly. You who live in the Under World, burrow up from below. Come quickly, like rats making their holes from there to here.

VII. *The Treatment of Disease : Persuasion*

OFTEN it is not sufficient to offer food-sacrifice; the shaman has to use all his wits to persuade the spirit to accept it. This is specially the case when the spirit does not want food, but has made someone ill for another reason, as for example when an ancestor makes one of his descendants sick with a view to obtaining his company in the Under World after he has died. The ancestor does not want food or wine: he wants company; and a shaman has to fight hard for the life of his patient if he is to persuade the ghost to accept a substitute.

I will give two examples of this. My first comes from Potta, where on 7 January 1947, the son of one Bhoinu, a boy called Tungre, fell very ill and was expected to die, since his grandfather, Bhoinu's father Indrasen, had come to take him with him to the Under World. The shaman was called and when he had gone into trance, the ghost of Indrasen came upon him, and the following argument[1] ensued.

Ghost: I am your father Indrasen. Your old mother is with me, but I am lame and blind; I cannot work, I don't even get proper food and drink. You know I was always a heavy drinker, but the wine here is terrible, even when one can get it. But if I have my grandson with me, he will look after me and we will be all right.

Bhoinu (putting some wine into a gourd): Come, father, drink this; it will do you good.

Ghost: Aha, I know your little tricks. You want to send me away, but I'm not going. I want something more than wine. Throw the stuff away.

[1] I must emphasize that this dialogue is in no way fictitious; it was recorded word for word on the spot and, except that it omits some repetitions, represents exactly what was said.

Bhoinu (bringing a goat, and touching the feet of the shaman, who of course represented Indrasen): Take this goat, but let the child alone. We never forget you here and we will always see that you get something to eat.

Ghost (laughing): Well, after all, perhaps... Anyway, let's have a taste of your wine.

Bhoinu (giving him some wine): Take this, father, and be content.

Ghost (tasting it and spitting it out): *Chi chi!* Do you call this wine? It's nothing but water. I told you to give me *wine*. Get me something better.

Bhoinu handed the shaman a gourd of wine from another pot.

Ghost: Ah, this is better. (Laughing) Well, I suppose I'll have to accept your goat. Kill it for me and I'll be back when it is ready.

Many other ghosts followed, all claiming that they had tried to persuade Indrasen not to harm the child, and begging for some wine as a reward. When they had all gone, the shaman offered cooked meat and rice to Indrasen's ghost. I was told that the child recovered.

My other example concerns a family's struggle to save the life of a widow, called by her husband to join him in the Under World.

Bambu, the father of Parsing, died at Kerubai in 1935. Parsing arranged the Guar and Karja rites, offering buffaloes for the dead man on no fewer than four occasions. Bambu's widow Jakti lived with Parsing. All went well for many years, but suddenly at the end of January 1945, Jakti went down with high fever and acute pains all over her body. The shaman declared that the reason was that Bambu wanted his widow to die so that she could be with him. On 31 January a ceremony was performed in Parsing's house at Kerubai in the hope of persuading Bambu to change his mind.

After the usual preliminaries, the shaman went into trance and presently Bambu's ghost came upon him. It spoke in a thin weary voice saying, 'Where is my wife? Bring her to me. I want to take her away with me, for here I have no one to cook for me and she will at least give me rice and pulse and vegetables.' The voice rose a little. 'I won't let her stay on earth; I must have her with me.'

At this Parsing spoke heatedly for many minutes. 'You are dead now,' he said to the ghost, 'and you have become an ancestor. What's the matter with you? We have done the Guar and Karja for you, and hung up a pot in your honour in this very house. Our old mother lives with us; she teaches the children how to do things, and looks after the place. What can we do without her? If you take her away, and don't let her stay with us, we may as well all die. Why not leave her alone, and instead of her we'll give you a good present. Make her well and don't let any other god or ancestor bother her. But don't go tricking us by promising to let her alone and then secretly telling some other ancestor to come and fetch her for you. We won't be stingy; whatever you want you shall have.'

Ghost: Well, suppose I let her be, what am I going to get out of it? At present I don't even get enough to eat. I've come all this way to see you, yet you send me away with only one little cup of wine. But don't talk any more to me. I'm going and your mother will have to follow me in a day or two.

Parsing: Very well, father, if you won't talk to us, you won't, but then who are we to talk to? I am your son; if you don't care for my sorrow, who will? Let the old woman alone for three or four years and then you can have her. Meanwhile, I've already told you I will give you anything you want instead.

Ghost : Well, to begin with, I'm thirsty.

Parsing handed the shaman a gourd of palm wine.

Ghost: *Thu!* There's no taste in this; you're just giving me water.

Parsing then went into the inner room and fetched some wine of better quality, for the usual custom is to offer inferior wine first in the hope that it will be accepted. He gave it to the shaman, who tasted it and chuckled.

Ghost: Aha! That's better. I remember often drinking stuff like this. I used to have it every day, and in the hot days there were always three or four pots of wine in my house and how the Chief and I enjoyed ourselves! Well now, tell me, shall I take my old woman or no?

Parsing: No, father, no. If you do, we will die.

Ghost: Then give me a she-goat.

Parsing brought a cock and handed it to the shaman.

Ghost: I'm not going to accept a little thing like that. I'd better have the old woman after all.

Parsing then brought a pig and held it in front of the shaman, who shook his head vigorously.

Ghost: No, that's no good. I'll have the old woman.

So at last Parsing brought a goat, and then the shaman laughed, and the ghost addressed his widow who was lying near by.

Ghost: Ha! You can stay on earth after all. This goat will do for me. Now I am going.

Widow: Why have you given me such a lot of trouble? You were good to me when you were alive. Here is your family and your property. We are looking after it for you. Now don't trouble any of us any more. Go away and stay in your proper place.

Ghost: Yes, I'll go now. But see that you all look after your mother properly, see to my property and work hard in my fields. If you do, I'll see to it that you have no kind of trouble. But don't blame me if she is attacked by any other god.

Parsing: Naturally we won't blame you for what some other god does. We will give them whatever they demand, just as we give you whatever you demand, provided you really don't bother us in any way. But you must see that our fields bear good crops and that our children grow up well and strong.

Ghost: I won't give you any trouble. After all you are my own family.

Then Bambu's ghost went away and the shaman rubbed his body all over and had a drink of wine. Then another ghost, Simo, Bambu's brother's son, came upon him, and said, 'Our father came to fetch your mother, but I told him that it was very wrong of him to take her away from you all so soon, and I managed to stop him. Don't be afraid, mother. I'll see that father doesn't do any more mischief and you'll get quite all right again.'

Then Simo went away and the ghost of Lindo, Simo's younger brother, came and said, 'I have followed my father and brother; I am tired; do give me something to drink. Whatever happens, don't be afraid. Don't worry about the dead. Your father and brothers are living perfectly happily in the Under World. In fact we are very comfortable there, even though the wine is bad. Don't worry about anything.'

In this case too, the old woman recovered. It often happens, however, that these persuasions and arguments do not succeed, and the patient dies. But this is not regarded as a bad death. The soul goes to join his family and those taken away by their own relations are regarded as being the happiest of the dead.

VIII. *The Treatment of Disease : Magic*

At most of the sacrifices designed to cure the sick, there are elements which can be generally described as magical, and I will now describe them.

There is a wide variety of cures which consist essentially in charming a mischievous god into an object, or an animal, and then removing it.

For this purpose the Saoras often make little dolls or toy animals. In treating someone attacked by Kinnasum, the tiger-god, the shaman makes a model of a tiger with bits of wood tied round with cloth. He keeps an all-night vigil inside the house, and in the morning, after sacrificing a buffalo on the threshold, he offers a little of the flesh, some blood and rice to the toy tiger, and then goes by himself out of the village and throws it away by an ant-hill.

Makrisum (a monkey-god) is believed to attack babies, making them thin as little monkeys, and their faces dry and wizened, with red spots. To cure this condition the shaman makes a toy monkey out of beeswax and passes it over the sick child seven times. Then he takes it out of the village to a *Shorea robusta* tree and sacrifices before it.

Edangsum is the god of the funeral pyre. He attacks little children, making their bodies burning hot as the flames of a pyre and their faces white as the ashes of a corpse. The shaman makes a doll of flour and water to represent the child and a little cot with sticks and thread. After waving the doll round the child's head, he puts it in the cot and carries it out of the village. He builds a little pyre of the same wood and on the same plan as a real one, and puts the doll on the pyre and burns it. As he does so he pretends to wail for the dead. Then he digs a hole and buries the ashes, and concludes by sacrificing a fowl.

Thurston describes how the Saoras 'frequently attend the markets or fairs held in the plains at the foot of the ghats to purchase salt and other luxuries. If a Saora is taken ill at the market or on his return thence, he attributes the illness to a spirit of the market called Biradisum. The bulls, which carry the goods of the Hindu merchants to the market, are supposed to convey this spirit. In propitiating it, the Saora makes an image of a bull in straw and, taking it out of the village, leaves it on the footpath after a pig has been sacrificed to it.'[1]

Little carts are sometimes made. They are loaded with offerings, the spirit is persuaded to sit in them, and they are dragged out of the village. This is one of the ways of dealing with an epidemic of smallpox.

[1] Thurston, vol. VI, p. 342.

There are a number of ceremonies connected with the bloodsucker lizard. Here the god to be satisfied is Tuttumsum who gives babies rickets; he makes their heads and bellies swell and reduces their legs and arms to little sticks by coming into a house and drinking the mother's milk and the baby's blood. The shaman catches a lizard and ties it by a string round its stomach to a branch of dry wood, and keeps it in the house all night. Before going to sleep he offers it boiled rice, boiled gram and palm wine. As he makes each offering, he says, 'O Tuttumsum, will you take rice, will you take wine?' and if the lizard opens its mouth it is taken as a sign that the god will. In the morning the shaman takes the child out of the house and waves rice round its head and body saying,

> For a long time you have taken your share of milk and blood. Today we bid you farewell.
>
> After this let the child grow fat again.

Then he removes the lizard from its branch and says,

> You have drunk this child's blood. You have made it thin and ugly as yourself. Now take your own likeness back. Let there be more blood, more flesh, more fat in the child's body. From today give us no more trouble.

The shaman ties the lizard to the branch again, and offers it wine. He takes some wine himself and gives a few drops to the child. Then he carries the lizard and its branch, together with everything used in the sacrifice, away to the fields or woods, and looses the lizard from its branch but still with the string attached to its body. If the lizard runs away, all will be well. But it is most important that it should not be injured or killed, for there is a risk that whatever happens to it will also happen to the child.

In some places, the shaman plants the branch in the ground, and after passing the lizard round the child's head three times, he puts it on the branch. If it climbs of its own accord, the child is expected to recover.

For Kinnalosum, there is a picturesque ceremony with crabs. This god lives in a stream, and if anyone drinks the water where he is, he may slip down his throat and give him a belly-ache. The cure is to catch a couple of crabs and harness them to a little wooden plough, which the shaman takes down to the stream and drives along as if he was ploughing. He lets one of his 'bullocks' go, and kills and cooks the other. He puts a little of the cooked crab and rice on the patient's head, chest and belly.

If a man gets a splitting headache, and the cause is diagnosed as Tangsirbasum, the shaman takes the patient to the *tangsir* tree, and makes him sit beneath it. He ties a scrap of cloth round his head, throws rice at the tree, removes the cloth and ties it to a branch. He sacrifices a fowl, puts a little of the blood on his patient's head, buries the fowl's head at the foot of the tree, and they go away, saying, 'You gave this man a headache. Now leave him; from today you and I are friends.'

Sometimes a little 'house' is made for a god and this is carried out of a village, in the hope that the god will go with it.

On 8 December 1944 I assisted at a sacrifice at Munisingi on behalf of a child who had been attacked by Kachhinosum with fever. The shaman made a 'house' of three storeys with plantain stalks, and put a little rice in each. He made the mother and the child sit in front of it and waved a handful of rice round them three times. Then he carried the house out of the village to a little glade in the forest near the path where the god had attacked the child, put it down and sacrificed a fowl before it. He put the feathers in the house, and the party cooked and ate the fowl on the spot.

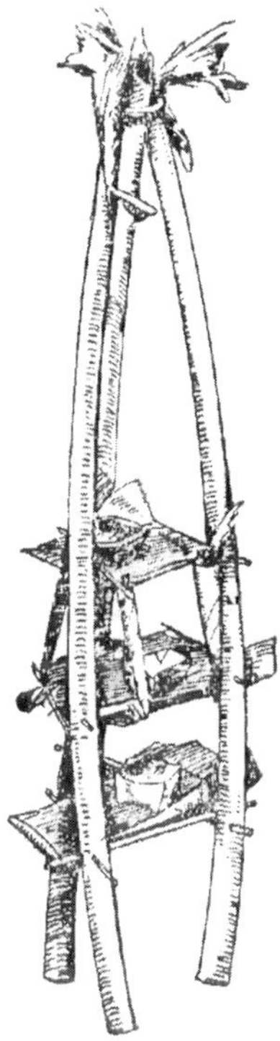

FIG. 25 'God-house' into which a spirit is charmed and then taken out of a village

A few days later, at Bungding, I witnessed a sacrifice based on a similar motif. A little boy nine years old was suffering from sore eyes caused by Lankasum. It is generally said that if anyone has the misfortune to meet this god while going to get wood or water, his eyes will become sore and red. Two years previously Lankasum had met this child when he was going with his mother through the forest and had given him sore eyes; the father sacrificed first a goat, then a pig, with a pot dedicated to the god, and the boy recovered. But in November 1944 the boy's eyes got bad again and the shamanin discovered that Lankasum was angry because the pot which had been hung up for him two years before had been a plain and not a decorated one. As Lankasum is the Sun-god, pots for him are usually adorned with crude symbols of the sun.

The shamanin—it was the beautiful and efficient Sondan—assured the father that if he would prepare a decorated pot and sacrifice a fowl all would be well, and on the early morning of 12 December, therefore, she removed the old pot and threw away its contents. She filled it with fresh rice, decorated it with patterns of rice-flour, and hung it up again. Immediately underneath it she placed a little mat made of strips of date-palm woven crisscross and covered it with leaves. Above this she put a little model plough (for it is on a plough that Lankasum is usually removed from a village at any time of epidemic). She then followed the usual sacrifice programme, and then took the boy and his father down to a stream, to a spot where some great rocks had formed natural caves. There was a ledge some eight feet above the ground on to which she climbed and on the wall of the cave she made a rough drawing (with rice-flour and charcoal) of a circle half divided by a straight line. This was 'to shut the god up'. The straight line represented the god and the circle was his prison. 'There's no door for him to get out,' said Sondan. In this way the god, who had been charmed out of the house in his plough, was imprisoned in the jungle and everyone believed that he would not return. And in fact, I was told, the boy did get very much better.

Other sacrifices which include some sort of dramatic make-believe are offered, for example, to Pungpungdasum. This god makes a man's belly swell with dropsy, and to cure it the shaman fills a new pot with water, ties the mouth with a leaf, and takes it to a running stream. There he sacrifices a fowl or a pig before it, and then smashes the pot with a stone, thus allowing the water to escape. 'For Pungpungdasum fills a man's belly with water and it cannot get out,' but when this is done it can.

On 16 May 1948 the baby boy of a man called Birsinga was suffering from dysentery at Sogeda. It was Gabaldatungboi, said the shaman, who had entered the baby's stomach and cut it inside with her knife, thus causing blood to flow in the stools. The shaman brought a piece of *Pterocarpus marsupium* wood, which exudes a blood-red resin, and tied it up with grass; he made two little wooden 'knives' of the same material. He touched the baby's stomach with the wood, took it outside, sacrificed a pig before it and stuck the pig's head on the

29. A typical Saora village (Thodrangu), built up a hillside

30. Shaman examines rice for bones extracted from a patient's body

31. Tikano, the naked shaman of Potta

32. Shaman dances in trance, wearing dress of his tutelary wife

33. The shaman Kintara of Hatibodi

34. A shaman enjoys a drink during a pause in the proceedings

35 & 36. Scenes at Mango First Fruits Festival at Sogeda

35

36

point. He explained that as blood comes from the wood but he had tied it up with grass to prevent it being seen, so it would be with the baby's stomach. No more blood would be seen.

A barren woman was treated at Gailunga on 6 June 1948. It was assumed that her barrenness was due to Jammasum, and the shaman accordingly sacrificed to him. He tied a pot to the main beam of the house and made the woman lie down beneath it. He put rice on her belly and sacrificed a pig in front of her. He explained that the pot was hung above her 'so that her belly should soon be round as a pot'; when it was, the pot would be removed, and another pig would be sacrificed.

I have only come across one example of the practice, fairly common in other parts of India, of frightening a spirit out of a sick person's body. This was in a treatment for severe pains in the nose, supposed to have been caused by Tangolbobsum. It was at Sogeda in March 1946, and the shaman made two leaf-pipes of mango leaves and put one in each of the nostrils of his patient. Then he drove them up into the nostril with two sharp blows. Blood poured out, and 'the god ran away in fright'.

IX. *The Treatment of Disease: Medicine*

LOGICALLY, since all diseases and even such accidental ills as cuts and burns are regarded as the work of spirits, to be treated by spiritual means, the Saoras should have no use for medicines and other natural methods of cure. In actual practice, however, they do bind up wounds, accept aspirin for their headaches, and occasionally—very occasionally—visit a hospital. For fever in the hot weather they give a concoction of red ants; to assist lactation they give raw papaya. When a would-be suicide was rescued just in time, they revived her with three raw eggs. They know the use of chiretta (*Justicia paniculata*) for worms and other intestinal troubles.

The Saoras have a word *regaman*, which means 'medicine' or 'antidote', and there is a special kind of shaman who is called the Regamaran, the medicine-man. *Regaman* (usually used in its contracted form, *ren*) can be used to describe an ointment or a pill obtained from a dispensary, and it is tempting to suppose that when the Saoras use the word of their own remedies they imply that these are actually medical in their effect. Sitapati indeed considers that the Saoras have a considerable pharmacopoeia at their disposal, and states that he knows of 'successful medical practitioners using some of the Saora drugs with satisfactory results'.[1]

I am very doubtful whether this is so, at least among the Hill Saoras. It is true that they have a number of remedies, such as the application of heat and bandaging, and know a number of healing herbs, but these are always used in connexion with sacrifice, and most of the 'medicines' which are applied externally cannot have any possible direct effect on the patient's body. But before considering this subject further I will quote the life-story of a famous Regamaran which throws a very clear light on the Saoras' attitude to their medicines. I will give Ikam's story in full, for although it contains material not relevant to our immediate purpose, it is perhaps the best, as it is certainly the fullest, account of a shaman's experiences that we have.

Ikam, who is both Regamaran and Raudakumbmaran, medicine-man and shaman, was born in Kamalasingi about fifty years ago. He is a small, energetic, charming person, and of great repute, for there are only a few qualified medicine-men and his services are required not only for the treatment of ordinary disease, but also for the protection of villages where there has been a case of suicide or murder or where someone has been killed by a tiger. The son of Jimbidi, who was himself a shaman though not a medicine-man, Ikam was the eldest of six children, of whom three were boys and three girls. This is his story.

My father's tutelary was called Sundri and he had four children by her, two boys—India and Behera—and two girls—Goi and Ajari. India has married a shamanin at Gunduruba; Goi is the wife of Karana, the shaman of Jirango; and Behera and Ajari are not yet married.

When I was about sixteen, Sundri came to my father with a young tutelary girl called Tinrai and said to him, 'Find me a husband for this girl.' My father thought, 'I have a son. If he marries this girl, he too will be a shaman and will continue my work.' After this, whenever my father offered sacrifice he used to make me sit beside him, though I used to beg him not to force me to this work, of which I was much afraid.

Then one day Tinrai came to me in a dream and said, 'Your father promised to marry you to me; that is why he has been teaching you all these things. Now I have come for the wedding.' I said, 'But I don't want to marry you,' and jumped out of bed.

My father was now very old, so old that he could only hobble about on a stick, and his father's ghost came to take him away. But when a goat was sacrificed he let him alone. Then Dorisum tried to

[1] Sitapati, 'The Soras', *J.A.H.R.S.*, vol. XIV, p. 16.

take him, but Sundri said, 'He is mine and when the time comes I shall take him. In the meantime no one else is to touch him.' Then again my father fell ill and sent for another shaman to treat him, but Sundri came upon him and said, 'The old man is now very old and sick. If he stays longer in the world, there will be no end to the gods and ghosts who will come for him. It is better that he should go with me now.' So she took him and he died. Since he was taken by his tutelary, he joined the other tutelaries in the Under World, and now he himself has become a tutelary.

Four months after this, my mother was taken away by Ratusum, and she herself became Ratusum, and in that form came soon afterwards and took away my eldest sister Jaggi, for she said, 'I am old, and there is no one to bring me water and give me food.' We tried to persuade her by sacrificing a pig to her at night, but it was no use. Then Kukkusum took my second sister Joman, and Rugaboi took the youngest. But my brothers are alive, and both are married and have children.

One night, while my father was living, I had a dream of many spirits dancing and shouting. I was frightened and ran down the street dancing and shouting too. My father offered sacrifice and cured me. But he said, 'It was a tutelary. You will have to become a shaman.' I replied, 'Give them anything you like, but don't make me a shaman.' So my father offered a hen to the tutelary to let me go. But when the hen was offered rice, it refused to eat. All the same my father had it killed.

The next night the young tutelary girl Tinrai came with her whole family on horses and elephants. She left the party to dance on Borong Hill, and she herself with her mother Sindrai, wearing white clothes and with her hair hanging down, came to me. She did not speak a word, but tied my hands and feet, picked me up and took me to Borong Hill. I said, 'What have I done to make you tie me up like this?' Tinrai said, 'I desire to marry you. I will make you a medicine-man and teach you every kind of medicine. But if you refuse I shall take you, tied up as you are, to the Under World.'

Tinrai left me alone on the slope of the hill. A tiger came by. I screamed with fear and tried to climb a tree. Tinrai and her mother stood a little distance away roaring with laughter. Then I sat on a rock and presently the ogre Kambutung came out of a cave and growled at me. In my terror I fell off the rock and Tinrai picked me up. She said, 'You see the dangers that threaten you because you refuse me. Now tell me, will you marry me or not?' By now I was so frightened that I was ready to do anything and I said I would. I awoke and wandered through the village crying loudly.

My father was very disturbed about this, but before he could do anything about it he died. I was very busy then for several months seeing to the affairs of the family and preparing for the Guar. But soon after the Guar had been concluded, Sundri came with Tinrai and said, 'Son,[1] your father promised to marry you to this girl. I am an old woman now and will not marry again. I will live with my daughter-in-law, and whenever you are in any difficulty I too will come and help you.' When she said that, I agreed.

The next morning when I woke up I remembered what had happened and I made arrangements for the wedding. The following Monday I fasted and made an ikon for my tutelary as I remembered my father had done, and dedicated a new pot. I sacrificed two fowls and offered a man's cloth and a woman's cloth. There was another shaman with me. Sundri's father came upon this shaman and said to me, 'I have come to give you my daughter.' Then Tinrai's brother came and said, 'I have come to give you my sister. Look after her well. If you get into trouble over anything, send for me.'

My sister-in-law came and said the same thing. Then my mother-in-law came and said, 'Look, my daughter loves you. That is why she is marrying you. Care for her well. Give her food and clothing. Do whatever she tells you; never try to do anything on your own.' Finally my own Tinrai came, not on the other but on me myself and cried, 'I am pleased with you. Because of my pleasure in you I have married you. If there is ever any trouble I will help you. Prepare a pot for me. Give me cloth and bangles.' So I put rice in a new pot and hung it up, and gave a white cock for Tinrai's relatives, and a cloth for my brother-in-law. They were all pleased and went home happily.

After this I married a wife in this world. One day I beat her and Tinrai came and said, 'I am your god-wife and this other has to live with you. She does all your house-work and gives you good food. I do no work for you and come and go as I please. Yet you do not trouble me; do not trouble her either.'

From Tinrai I have one daughter. She is now four years old and her name is Sitrai. When she was born her mother brought her to me, and put her beside me and lay down herself on the other side of me. When little Sitrai groped for my breasts and didn't find any she began to cry. I jumped up and looked everywhere, but there was nothing. Sometimes Tinrai visits me every night, sometimes not for eight or fifteen days. Whenever I offer sacrifice or go to help the sick, I call her and she comes with old Sundri to help her.

Gradually more and more people came to me and I was kept very busy. Then one day I began the work of a medicine-man. I had been called to Mannemgolu to perform the Doripur ceremony. Soon after I got home, I began to have sharp pains in the stomach. I called another shaman and he had a pig sacrificed for me, but it was no use. That night, Tinrai came and said, 'So long as I am with you, do not run about consulting shamans and wasting your money. I myself will tell you what to do. It was the people of Tammegorjang, an evil village, who did magic against you.' Then in my dream she showed me a certain

[1] Ikam counted as the son of his father's tutelary, and his tutelary wife was thus her daughter-in-law.

hill and a sago palm growing there. 'There is the medicine you need against sorcery,' she said. 'Take it; you will find it bitter; but if you drink it, you will recover.'

Next morning I went to the hill, and there was the tree just as I had seen it in my dream. I offered wine and rice at its foot, and dug in the ground. I found the root of which Tinrai had told me and took it home. I pounded some of it up and mixed it with water and drank it. It was indeed very bitter, so bitter that I vomited. But that was a good thing, for I brought up two little worms which had been sent into my body by the Tammegorjang magicians. After this I gave the *tonairegaman* [sorcery-medicine] to many people.

Another medicine I learnt was the *kinnaregaman* [tiger-medicine]. A man called Tinpa of my own village was caught and killed by a tiger. We were all very frightened and the women did not dare to go out for wood or leaves. We sent for a shaman from Abada who was supposed to know what to do, but he was no use. That night my tutelary came to me in a dream and showed me a great rock on the Barong Hill, and an *abba* tree growing beside it. She told me to get the medicine which I would find at the root of the tree and give it to the people.

So next morning I bathed and went fasting to the rock with four other men. I made them sit down some distance away so that they should not see what I was doing. I offered rice and wine to the tree and then dug up the root. As I dug it up a thrill of fear went through the men who were with me, as if a tiger was approaching, and they shouted and fired their guns. I took the medicine home, and after we had burned the bones of the dead man, I gave some of the root to everybody, and there was no more fear or danger.

Pararegaman is the medicine to be used after a murder or if someone hangs himself. A boy called Mursui, the only son of his parents, hanged himself in his house while the family was out in the hills. We never knew why he did it. That very night I had dreamt that the boy had hanged himself. I was very frightened and did not go to the village for two days, but slept outside in my forest-hut. Then my tutelary came in a dream and showed me a place on the Laso Hill above Gailunga, where a *sargiya* tree was growing. There was a rock beneath it and on the rock something that looked like an onion, which was the medicine we needed. I went to the rock and sacrificed and brought the medicine home. The people were on the point of sending to Rajintalu for a shaman who was said to know what to do, but I told them that I had the medicine and could attend to the matter myself. I sacrificed a pig and mixed the medicine in water and gave it to the people to drink. It was very strong, they behaved like drunken men after taking it, and many of them vomited.

In the same way I learnt the *ajoraregaman* and the *doriregaman* to be used at the Ajorapur and the Doripur, and that is why I can perform these sacrifices as well as the others.

I have given the *tonairegaman* to many people. There was a man in Gunduruba who was a very evil sorcerer. He died and turned into a *tonaikulba* [sorcerer-shade]. In this form he attacked Agari, the wife of Jamno, in Gailunga. They sent for me and I found her suffering from very bad pains in her legs and body. I sacrificed and brushed her with a feather, and when she had taken the medicine I brought two hairy caterpillars and some blood from her chest.

In Sogeda, a man brought some powerful magic with him from Assam. He called a Mannesum and sent him with it against one Bopna. When I went there I found poor Bopna with such severe pains in the back that he could not sit up. After I had given the medicine I brought two fishbones out of his body, and after that he was all right.

Benu and Siap, two men of Mannemgolu, quarrelled over a field and Siap put magic in Benu's wine. When Benu drank it, he fell ill and his body swelled up alarmingly. From his belly I brought out two date-palm grubs and a small bit of pig's bone.

When I am called to administer the sorcery-medicine, I never go that very day. I wait, because for one thing I have to get the medicine fresh and for another I must have the right kind of dream. Some years ago the Chief of Rajintalu was attacked by a sorcerer and four men came to call me. I said I would come the following day. I went to find the medicine, but it took me a long time, for there was none in the usual place. That night I had a dream. I dreamt that as I was going to Rajintalu, I met a bear. That was all right, for I frightened it away. A little later I met a tiger, and I frightened that away too. But as I was approaching the village, while I was crossing a field, Kambutung came out of a stream and attacked me. I jumped into the water and shouted myself awake. After this dream I decided that it was taboo [*ersi*] for me to go to Rajintalu and the Chief had to get someone else who was no good at all.

I have learnt everything from dreams, but when I am in trance I have no idea of what I am doing or saying, and afterwards I do not remember anything.

I am usually called about twice a month to give the sorcery-medicine and perhaps twice in the year to give the *pararegaman*.

Now what is significant about this account is that of the five medicines mentioned two have nothing whatever to do with the pharmacopoeia: one protected people from tigers, the other was an antidote to the spread of violent crime. The other three can only be used in association with a sacrifice; the *ajoraregaman* and *doriregaman* are applied externally to drive away hostile spirits, and the *tonairegaman* has a magical rather than a medical effect.

This is the case too with other medicines. The *abdimmaddāregaman*, which is translated 'soporific' in Ramamurti's Dictionary, is not some tribal Luminol; it is a kind of charm by which thieves can put the members of a household to sleep so that they can then enter the building and rob it with impunity. The *kutamregaman* is a medicine made out of the root of the *kutam* tree; it is used to restore a crop damaged by Labosum.

The administration of medicine is thus magical in character, designed to reinforce the effect of sacrifice and prayer.

The Saoras have a number of minor remedies, which vary enormously from place to place, concocted from roots and leaves, often with turmeric added to them. They may be plasters, such as the poultice of *putla* (*memri*) leaves for a headache, or of the tusk of a wild boar powdered and mixed with castor oil for a swollen cheek. They may be potions of various kinds. For a pain in the chest, *hirwa* pulse is boiled for a long time, and the water is strained off and given to the patient. The sap from various roots and barks is given for dysentery or to stop vomiting. Myrabolams are pounded up and given in water for a cough. For toothache the teeth are rubbed with a twig of *Ailanthus excelsa*. For earache a plug of gourd leaves is heated and inserted in the ear. To cure the habit of bed-wetting, the parents burn the hoof of a cow and make the child sniff it. In 1948, there was a woman with an infection of the breast; her husband heated an umbrella rib and pierced the breast to let out the pus; to keep the wound drained he put a plug of cord in the hole.

But none of these remedies are efficacious, and may indeed be positively dangerous (since such an arrogant display of confidence in one's own powers may well offend a god), unless they accompany the proper sacrifices.

Amulets are made, especially by Saoras who have been to Assam or have come under Hindu influence elsewhere. The word used for them—*dongarān*—is an Oriya one. At the time of an eclipse, a 'medicine' made of little bits of *mogaireng* wood is tied round the neck of a pregnant woman, who may otherwise have a fit of vomiting or a miscarriage. Amulets are often tied round the necks of children at the Ajorapur, and rings or bracelets are often worn in token of promises made to the ancestors. The flesh of a small black mountain rat called *sambiri-kumbulan*[1] is very efficacious against the attacks of spirits; bits

[1] These rats live in holes among rocks, and no gods can live there, for 'gods are afraid of rats'. If one of them comes to a house where someone is lying ill, the god causing the trouble runs away. If such a rat is killed and its body kept in the house, it serves as a powerful protection against every kind of spirit.

of it may be tied round the neck of anyone in danger. Herbs may be mixed and put in a small case made of five different metals and tied to the wrist to ward off black magic. A necklace of bits of the bark of the *Trewia nudiflora* tree is believed to protect a nursing mother from the attacks of Danunkisum.

It is said that if the cord of an amulet breaks of its own accord, it is a sign that it has done its work and may be thrown away. But it is dangerous to break an amulet deliberately.

Sitapati describes a form of treatment for epilepsy, which combines all the different methods of cure. The shaman performed the Kannipur with the sacrifice of a buffalo. He made a string of the beads of the *Canavalia ensiformis*, and after chanting over it the necessary incantations tied it round the neck of his patient. He prepared a medicine from the following formula: seed and root of *Canavalia ensiformis*; root of *Tinospera cordifolia*; bark of *Dalbergia latifolia*; bark of *Cipadessa fruticosa*; root of an unidentified plant called *samapuri*; mustard. He reduced these to powder and the patient had to take two doses a day before meals for a fortnight. During this period he had to avoid the flesh of the peafowl, wild hog and hare. At the end of the fortnight there was a further ceremony.[1]

Treatment for snakebite also combines several elements. The shaman makes a plaster of the roots of certain trees, and applies it to the wound. He makes a potion of the roots of two other trees and makes the patient drink it. But the really important part of the treatment is when the shaman extracts the poison with his peacock feather; he strokes the affected limb towards the extremities and cries on all the snakes by name—'Luanajadan, Bangrubingjadan, Tuneljadan, Bongbongjadan, Luijarjadan, Garpajadan'—whereupon 'blood, white as milk' comes out and with it possibly the snake's fangs.

Another kind of *regaman* is 'man-medicine' or 'woman-medicine', the charms used by frustrated or jealous lovers. Their use was first taught to the world by a shaman.

A great shaman called Kursu lived on Rameli Hill. On the same hill lived Bhainsu with his beautiful unmarried daughter Machho. Her breasts were wood-apples, her slender body was a cow's tail, the bun of her hair a nest of bulbuls. Kursu's wife died, and after that he grew

[1] Sitapati, *J.A.H.R.S.*, vol. XIV, p. 8. Sitapati says that he recorded this 'in a village on the outskirts of the Agency border'. The medical prescription sounds like a parody of something from a dispensary; particularly the instruction 'to be taken twice a day before meals' does not sound genuine Saora.

to love the girl very much and often begged her to come to him. But her mind was not for the old man. After he had tried to win her for a long time, Kursu said to himself, 'Here am I, a great shaman, and yet I cannot do anything about this girl.' He thought and thought, and then on a Wednesday he took a lime, a black chicken, a coconut and a gourd of wine and went naked and at midnight to the shrine of Umahansingisum[1] on Muski Hill. He offered the chicken and coconut at the shrine and sprinkled it with wine, and thus persuaded the goddess to take up her abode in the lime. He said, 'O Umahansingisum, when Machho eats this lime, bring her to my house.' He took the lime to a lime tree growing near the village and climbed into the branches. When Machho came by with her pot on the way to the stream to fetch water, he dropped the lime at her feet. She picked it up and ate it. At once love came to her, and all that day she was restless and at midnight went to the old man's house. Kursu was very happy after that and taught his woman-medicine to many people.

Love-charms are not, however, used very often. A youth relies chiefly on the magic of his own charms, the beauty of his well-proportioned body, his gay manner, his wit, his smile, the feathers in his hair. But it sometimes happens that one is less well-favoured than others, or that his lover has her attention diverted elsewhere, and he then goes to a medicine-man or to the Gontora Saoras (who make ornaments and are said to be expert at this) to purchase the necessary medicine. Before doing so, he must sacrifice a fowl to the dead. The youth puts the medicine, which is a compound of certain herbs, into a cheroot and gives it to the girl, or he flicks it at her with his thumb, or he may be able to persuade some woman relative to slip it into the girl's hair.

But before giving it to a girl, one should first try it on a dog. 'Find one which never comes to you, and rub it on its back. Then if it follows you about, you will know that the medicine is good.'

Like the Baigas, the Saoras consider that the charm must be removed once love is firmly established. If the affair has ended in marriage, the husband should wait until his wife has gone to wash her clothes after menstruation, and should then send her away somewhere, and in her absence turn the stone on which she was sitting upside down. It is important that she should never know either that the medicine was applied or that it was removed.

Women sometimes make medicine for men. The man-hungry woman exists among the Saoras, as elsewhere, and such women sometimes force their way into a man's house and insist on living with him.

[1] *Uma* in Saora means 'to be pregnant' or 'to give birth'.

'Medicine' may also be used in the form of material charms to keep disease away from a house or a village. A piece of bear's skin, for example, is regarded as valuable for preventing the gods or ancestors of another village from entering one's house. A broken bit of an old ploughshare may be set up on a veranda to save the family from getting backache when they go to the fields. But the most striking of these charms are the stuffed monkeys.

Anti-sorcery medicine may be put in a stuffed monkey to protect a tobacco-patch, but the most common use of this charm is to keep cholera and smallpox away from a village.

The Saoras have what is almost a 'joking relationship' with monkeys. An important branch of the tribe is known as Arsi, the 'monkey' Saoras. Shamans delight in drawing monkeys in their ikons. There are two monkey gods, Arsibasum and Makrisum. The Saoras eat monkeys, but do not usually offer them in sacrifice. They have many folk-tales about them, but curiously they do not seem to have any traditions about Hanuman. A tale from Sogeda explains how the use of the monkey as a charm originated.

Men were born first, then monkeys. Kittung's sister had a son and wherever Kittung went he took the boy with him. One day Kittung said to Sima Rani, 'I want a wife for my nephew.' She said that she would do what she could. After some time, Kittung sent the boy alone to her saying, 'Go and see if she is there or not. If she is, I'll come to her.'

The boy found Sima Rani, dressed like a Saora girl, lying asleep. He tried to have intercourse with her as she slept. But she awoke and caught him and went running with him to Kittung crying, 'Look what a rascal your nephew is.'

Kittung was furious at this. He cut off the boy's hair-lock; he blackened his face and made his body rough and hairy. Finally he tied a rope round his neck and hung him from a tree. In this way the boy turned into a monkey and began to chatter *bangad-bangad.* Kittung said to him, 'The Saoras will eat you whenever they get a chance, and even the smallest bit of iron will kill you. Because you have been made in this way, the Saoras will hang your bodies up in their villages to scare away gods and ghosts.'

Monkey-charms are usually, but not always, made when there is a cholera or smallpox scare. Men go out at night and if possible get four monkeys, one for each corner of a village. They skin them, stuff the skin with straw and stitch it up, put a bow and arrow in its hand and a pipe in its mouth. Then they tie them to long poles and set them up, offering a little of the flesh at the foot to Yuyuboi or Mardisum. If they cannot get four monkeys, they stuff one and set it facing the quarter whence they apprehend danger. They believe that when Yuyuboi sees it, she will run away for fear that it will jump on her.

At Mannemgolu in 1946 there were four such monkeys, at Thodrangu one; in 1950 there was one hanging from a tamarind tree on the outskirts of Dungdunga. At Arangulu in 1944, in front of the house of one Apno there was a tall bamboo pole to the top of which was attached the stuffed monkey, a feather in its hair, a pipe in its mouth, a sword over one shoulder, a bow and arrow in its paws. Before the Rogonadur of that year, Apno's wife had gone down with a sharp attack of fever, and when Apno called a shaman the ghost of Kirsaru, Apno's father, came upon him and said, 'Before you celebrate the festival, catch and kill a monkey; tie it to a pole, and on the day you eat the pulse, make it dance through the village with feathers in its hair. Then hoist it on a pole in front of your house. If you do that, your house and the whole village will be safe from Mardisum and Yuyuboi and the attacks of other gods.'

Apno told the other villagers what the shaman had said, and they went out to get a monkey, confident that Kirsaru's ghost would lead them to one. They went first to Apno's own clearing on the hillside, and there they found many monkeys stealing the pulse. A boy killed one of them with a stone and sat on its head. The people skinned it, roasted the flesh then and there and ate it with palm wine in the name of the dead. Then they brought the skin home, stuffed and decorated it, and on the day of the festival danced with it through the village, finally setting it up outside Apno's house. Apno's wife recovered.

X. *The Treatment of Disease: the Doripur*

In this section and the next, I propose to describe two famous Saora rites, the Doripur and the Ajorapur, which are distinguished by special techniques of great interest.

Dorisum is both the god of cattle-graziers and a congeries of all the dead carried away by him. The buffalo-sacrifice in his honour is usually conducted by a special class of priests and in the first instance is for members of a single family. It is, however, permissible to invite guests, and to sell, even to Doms, any of the sacrificial meat that is not consumed on the spot.

On 30 December 1950, I was present at a Doripur ceremony at Potta conducted by the shaman Kondera for an old woman called

Iran who was suffering from rheumatism. Although Kondera was a general practitioner, a Raudakumbmaran, he included, rather exceptionally, the Doripur among his other duties.

The proceedings began in the morning at about 9.15 outside Iran's house. A buffalo was tethered to a pillar of the veranda and near it in the street the shaman spread his impedimenta on the ground. On a winnowing-fan he placed three baskets of rice and grain, a ring, a small bow and arrow, a white ball of medicinal clay, a bundle of medicinal herbs, and three kinds of 'bullets'—some were of rice-flour, some of green wood, and some were the nuts of *Semecarpus anacardium*. By the fan was a large leaf-hat, of the kind used by graziers in hot weather, and an old basket full of leaves with two slats of wood on it: these were for Dorisum's servant.

The shaman Kondera began by singeing the buffalo's tail with the flame from his sacred lamp. He put a ring, some grains of rice and the ashes of the burnt tail into a leaf and folded it up. Then he made old Iran sit before him and passed the leaf over her head and body, while he recited a long litany of the names of the gods and dead.

> Today we give you a feast. Go all of you and find Dorisum and bring him here. You are the Great Ones, you can bring him if you wish to. Come, you who live in the Under World, come you who live in the sky, come flying, come running, come dancing to make this woman well.

Then he put on the grazier's hat, picked up the bow and arrow and began to dance. The bow was so constructed that it would propel anything fixed to the tip of the arrow, but the arrow would not itself be fired. Kondera picked up the 'bullets' one by one on the tip of his arrow, heated them in the flame of the lamp, and shot them first to the four quarters of the world, then at the buffalo and finally at his patient. As he danced he called again on the dead and the gods saying,

> It is Dorisum who has sent this grub into this woman's body. It is for him that we give this buffalo. I shoot with my arrow to drive the grub from her body and send the evil far away.

When he had expended all his ammunition, the shaman sat down and began to beat a drum, slowly at first and then more rapidly.

> Come quickly and accept our offering. Uyungsum, Rugaboi, Dorisum, you give disease to the cattle, to the pigs, to the goats, to the fowls, to men and women. Gather together here and agree to

make this woman well. Ildasum, Mannesum, come and we will give you whatever you desire. Wherever you may be, in trees, in streams, in rocks, in caves, on mountains, come. We give you rice and blood. Come and drive away this sickness.

Then the shaman led a procession out of the village to a pleasant open space among palm trees; near by a clump of trees gave abundant shade. He set out his impedimenta on the path; some distance away under the trees a number of women assembled with cooking-pots and prepared hearths for cooking the feast; others busied themselves with stitching leaf-cups. Under another tree, men gathered to kill the buffalo. The man who killed it, as usual with a sharp blow on the back of the neck, which he followed up by piercing the throat with a sharp stick to let out the blood, had ashes thrown all over him. This, it was believed, would ensure that there would be a lot of fat on the meat.

The shaman took a cup of the blood, let some drops fall on each of his offerings and threw a little to each of the four quarters, saying,

Now there are flowers [i.e., blood] for you. Come and take them away. We give you whatever you desire. Come with your cooking-pots and take away your sacrifice.

Then he sat down and took up his drum and beat it as before, first slowly and then more rapidly.

Dorisum wandering in the forest, Dorisum in the stones, Dorisum in the trees, Dorisum of the mountains, come all of you. Dorisum in the moon, Dorisum in the sun, Dorisum in the Under World, Dorisum in the sky, Dorisum on this earth, come and accept our offerings.

If one of you has been prevented from coming by magic, if I have forgotten anyone, go and fetch him. Stop the sorcery of the mischief-workers. Come all of you and lighten the burden of the sick one, lighten the burden of her arms, her legs, her body.

Kondera then offered palm wine, pouring it over and round the altar. Iran's daughter sat down beside him and began to prepare the 'medicine', pounding up herbs, roots and clay into a sticky mixture. Kondera beat the drum again, calling on his tutelary to come and help him.

Suddenly—it was now just after 11.0—he fell flat on his back, and it took the combined efforts of three women to straighten his rigid body and unclench his fingers. His tutelary had come. He began to talk, not in Saora but in Kui, like a tiresome old woman, chuckling, hawking, and now and then clapping his hands together. Then clenching and unclenching his fists he shouted very fast and angrily. His tutelary was declaring that she had had to come a long way and was tired, and could not understand why she had been called at all. 'I have gone to so much trouble,' she said, 'and you only give me palm wine; why is there no liquor? I shall go and tell Gorusum and Dorisum and ask them to come here.'

Then Kondera was visited by a succession of ancestors; one demanded cloth and Kondera laid a cloth on the altar. Another asked for tobacco and an axe, and these were put in Kondera's hand. Finally Dorisum himself came, and Kondera put on the big hat, took the amputated tail of the dead buffalo in his hand and pranced about in front of the altar, as if he was driving cattle.

Dorisum then said, 'Yes, it is true that it was I who was troubling the old woman. We were short of a buffalo for ploughing our fields, so I had to attack her in order to get one. Now you have given me what I wanted, I will cause no more trouble, and she will soon get well.' The shaman laughed heartily, drank a lot of wine, and made a number of very dirty jokes which delighted everyone.

Then came Dorisum's wife and the shaman put a bundle of cloth and a basket of rice on his head to show that she had accepted these things. Dorisum's servant came and was given his stick to hold.

Then Kondera called his patient, 'kissed' and sucked her body to remove the grub that was lurking in it, put some mud on her head 'to clean it', smeared her whole body with 'medicine', and examined her hair for 'magic lice'. When he had finished, he was like someone waking from a heavy sleep; he yawned, stretched his arms and legs, spat on his hands and wiped his face and eyes. Then he joined the rest of the company at the cooking-place, and presently offered cooked rice and meat, and after that they all sat down and feasted.

The custom of applying 'medicine' by shooting a patient with pellets from a bow is fairly common among the Saoras. Fawcett noticed it in a ceremony addressed to the sun deity who had given a boy fever. He describes the bow used as 'about two feet long, *through* which was fixed an arrow with a large head, so that it could be pulled only to a certain extent: the arrow was fastened to the string so that it could not be detached from the bow'. The shaman 'stuck a small wax ball on the point of this arrow head, and dancing went on with his chant. Looking up at the sun he took aim with the bow and fired the wax ball at it. He then fired balls of wax and afterwards some other small balls which the Oriyas present said were "medicine" of some kind, at the boy. First ball hit the boy on the head, next on his stomach, and then on each leg; as each ball struck him he cried.' Finally the shaman went to a buffalo which was to be sacrificed and fired a ball at its head.[1]

At Kankaraguda, in 1946, I found the same treatment associated with Kannisum (epilepsy). The shaman dammed up a little stream and made his epileptic patient lie down in the bed below and a sacrificial buffalo stand in the water above. He himself stood by with seven arrows. Then, after invoking Kannisum, he touched his patient with an arrow and shot it as hard as he could at the buffalo. It bounced off its hide and fell into the water, whereupon the shaman picked it up and fired it towards the east. He fired off his six remaining arrows, to each of the four quarters and in the air. One of the bystanders was holding a leaf-packet of 'medicine'; the shaman wrested this forcibly from his hand and mixed it in the water above the dam. Then he broke the dam and let the water flow down over the sick man.

At a rite on 12 May 1948, at Boramsingi, the same method was used as a warning to the dead, who had attacked a young girl with sores and fever. On this occasion the fruit of the *Semecarpus anacardium* was used. I was told that the shamanin who shot the fruit at the child was possessed by Uyungsum, and the implication was that the Sun-god himself was doing it and that it was an order to the dead not to trouble the child again; if they did they would be punished by being burnt with marking-nut juice.

XI. *The Treatment of Disease: the Ajorapur*

THE Ajorapur is the central, the classic, sacrifice for the protection of young children. It will be convenient, therefore, before describing the rite itself, to consider the dangers that threaten the unborn and the newly-born, and the means taken by the shamans to avert them.

For in dealing with babies, it is vitally important that there should be no mistakes. There are remedies for barrenness—an ikon for Gadejangboi, and a mixture of roots given to the mother in her gruel

[1] Fawcett, pp. 264f.

—but it is essential that when the mother conceives, the proper sacrifice of a goat should be made to Gadejangboi, or there may be a miscarriage.

Fortunately there are few taboos at menstruation or pregnancy, and the chance of error here is therefore small. But Danunkisum and the jealous Uralbasum are always on the watch for an excuse to cause miscarriage. If a woman suffers one such disaster, then when she conceives again, the shaman sacrifices a goat for Danunkisum and makes the mother eat a little date-palm root. He ties a bit of the same root round her neck as an amulet.

If interference from Uralbasum is anticipated, the shaman ties a dedicated pot under the eaves of the house, putting an arrow with it. If all goes well, then about a month after the birth of the child, he takes down the pot and the mother cooks a little rice in it. The shaman offers Uralbasum a fowl, and performs the customary rites which include the sprinkling of water on mother and child. If this is not done, it is said, the mother may get very thin and the child may die. Pudoisum is another god who may be invoked in the same way.

After the birth of a baby, other precautions may be taken. At the naming ceremony, thorns are put above the door of a house to discourage ghosts who might come to trouble the child. When a child is a week old there is a hair-cutting ceremony. This may be done for different gods: at Tondrangu I saw it done for Uyungboi and Ajorasum, at Gunduruba for Uralbasum. The shaman cuts a lock of the hair, and puts it with his knife on the altar, before which he offers a pig. He dedicates a pot and then mixes the hair with a little cow-dung and smears it on the wall. 'We do not throw it away, for if anyone were to piss on it, the baby would get sores on its head.' Or if a dog were to walk on it, or sniff at it, the baby's head would be covered with lice; in Ladde, I was told that a tiger might attack the father, for the dog is a symbol of the tiger. Sometimes, however, hair-clippings are hidden in the cracks of stone walls, for then it is said that the child will be strong as a stone. Sometimes a girl's hair is thrown away into the branches of a date-palm, and then her hair is expected to grow luxuriantly. The date-palm branches are also a strong protection against ghosts; the body of a child whose hair or nail-clippings are thrown among them, will be 'covered with thorny spikes against every kind of spirit'.

When the first teeth drop out, a child's father throws them on the roof of his house for Uyungsum, saying, 'Take my milk-teeth and give me good ones soon'. Or they may be buried under the mortar where the paddy is husked to ensure that the next teeth will be as 'strong as a pestle and able to chew bones'.

If a child has a big soft umbilical stump, the theory is that Ringeboi the Wind has got into it. The father should poke it gently three or four times with a stick he has brought back with him from the fields. Then the mother should go for water, with two pots, one on top of the other, and a gourd on top of both. With the handle of the gourd she too should poke at the stump. This is said to expel Ringeboi and the stump should become small.

We have already seen how children are subject to illnesses caused by ancestors who wish to have their names perpetuated. Children are also affected by certain gods who seem to specialize, as it were, in children's diseases, and by supernatural snakes and lizards who steal the mother's milk.

Among these gods are Danunkisum, who not only causes miscarriage but gives diarrhoea; Uralbasum, who gives children fever and makes them refuse their mother's milk; Gadejangboi, who catches and destroys young children when they are playing; Uyungboi, who gives them boils; Arangsum, who makes them cry. These are the most commonly troublesome, but any other god may attack a child if he feels inclined.

Remedies follow the usual lines. If a baby has diarrhoea, the mother should bring water from a stream in a new pot and put it in the house for Danunkisum, leaving it there till the motions stop 'even if they do not stop for two months'. When the baby is well again, the shaman should sacrifice a fowl before the pot, and the mother should take it a long way off and throw the water away.

I have mentioned Uralbasum. This is a god who gathers into herself all the misery, jealousy and frustration of the scores of mothers whose children die and who die themselves of sorrow. Such mothers become Uralbasum, a god who is naturally dangerous to happy and healthy babies who excite her envy. There is an *uralba* tree and sacrifice should be made at its foot.

Gadejangboi often sits down to rest among the picturesque rocks and gendarmes that litter the Saora Hills. If any small child comes to play near by, she may attack him. The shaman must then go to the rock and make an ikon upon it and sacrifice.

To console a child who cries continually, the Saoras put a broken pot upside down on the roof of a house, and sacrifice a fowl to Arengsum.

There are various ways of promoting lactation. The shaman may make an offering to any tree whose leaves exude a milky sap in the name of Gadejangboi, and make a medicine of the root which he then gives to the mother to drink. Or he may sacrifice a fowl to Uyungboi at sunrise, mixing a little of the blood with water and sprinkling the mother's body with it. A rather drastic method has been tried from time to time: nearly fifty years ago at Tollana, the mother of Lango, who grew up to become shaman of the village, was treated for inadequate lactation: a cock was killed above her breasts and the blood allowed to pour out over them.

But of all the forces imagined as hostile to the life and health of young children, the most dangerous are the unseen snakes. Ever since the day that Aghasura, king of primeval snakes, attempted to destroy the divine boy Krishna, such snakes have been common in Indian myth and ritual, and ideas about them are widely spread among the tribesmen.

Snakes which can destroy human beings merely by looking at them are as old as the *Secretum Secretorum*, and an ancient Sanskrit name for a snake is *drigvisa* or *drishtivia*, poisonous of aspect. There is a story that Alexander came across a valley on the Indo-Persian frontier which was guarded by deadly serpents whose very glance was fatal. He erected mirrors in which they might stare themselves to death.[1] From Matin Zamindari in Madhya Pradesh, I have recorded a legend of a water-snake 'the colour of ground turmeric', whose glance gives cholera and death within a few days. In Mandla District there is a tradition of a great snake five and twenty cubits long and bright red in colour, whose poison is so powerful that it can blast trees and grass.[2] Forsyth tells the story of the 'loathly worm', slimy and horrid as a great caterpillar, with a scarlet head, whose look was death, that used to haunt the forests of Uprora.[3] Sinclair says that there is a belief in west and central India that the slow-worm or amphisbaena changes its head to its tail and back every year and that its bite causes leprosy. In Poona District it is said that if a buffalo sees a certain

[1] Penzer, *Ocean*, vol. II, p. 299. [2] See *MMI*, pp. 163ff.
[3] J. Forsyth, *The Highlands of Central India* (London, 1871), p. 418.

water-snake with yellow netlike markings, it dies.[1] And in Ganjam District itself, shortly before the time of Fawcett, Goodrich recorded an account of a great snake which was believed to be an incarnation of Bagh Devi and was expected to turn into a tiger.[2]

The Saoras know of many similar snakes: Luurjadan, which places its tail in a baby's mouth and sucks the mother's breast instead; Gondisajadan, striped like a squirrel, which bites you on the forehead; Kadujadan, which has the power of moving backwards and forwards; the fabulous Kudubudan, which guards the gate of the Under World; Angkoilajadan; the great Ajorasum, which looks like a bit of wood with bees flying in and out of its mouth; Jayodensum, which has a red crest and lives on the banks of streams; the horned Rimpayiguri and its wife Pandaigudi and their children, Sunkaro and Sunkari.

These snakes are very dangerous. They may be sent by sorcerers to attack their enemies; they may come to rob children of their milk, a drink of which they are inordinately fond; some of them, all too easily insulted, take a swift revenge.

So great is the menace of these snakes that in some villages sacrifice is offered as a routine measure to one or other of them for all children who live to be a few months old. In other places, however, the sacrifice is done only when necessity arises.

The sacrifice, which seems to be generally known as Ajorapur, even when other snakes are propitiated at it, is an expensive one, for it involves the offering of a buffalo: this is because Ajorasum has horns like a buffalo's. Usually this rite can only be performed by specialists. The first shaman to perform it was named Kurutameru-Arangtameru; he had the body of a man and the skin of a bear. Today there is a class of celebrants who are not qualified to act in other matters—they have no tutelaries and thus cannot perform the more elaborate rites—but who do know the mythology connected with snakes and the ritual for the Ajorapur. It is interesting to note that this is one of the few ceremonies at which the myth on which it is based is recited by the shaman.

I have attended several of these ceremonies, for they are all too frequent in the Saora country, and I will now describe one which

[1] W. F. Sinclair, 'Notes on Natural History: Snakes', *Indian Antiquary*, vol. II (1873), pp. 171f.

[2] H. St A. Goodrich, 'Superstition in Ganjam', *Indian Antiquary*, vol. III, p. 267.

occurred at Sogeda on 29 November 1950 on account of two babies living in the house of a man called Gano. One was Gano's own child, the other was the son of Gano's father by a younger wife. Each was about six months old, thin and ailing, and the shaman declared that it was because a snake was drinking the mothers' milk and so preventing them from getting proper nourishment. The celebrant came from Dungdunga; he was not a full shaman, he had no tutelary, but he was a specialist in this particular rite, and because such specialists are rare he was in demand over a wide area. Since he was incapable of trance, the preliminary inquiries and discussions with gods and ancestors were conducted by another shaman the previous night.

The ceremony itself began just after nine o'clock in the morning, inside the house. The shaman made the customary altar and placed on it a new pot on which he had drawn with rice-flour the figures of two snakes. He sat before it and holding a gourd of palm wine in his left hand began to chant.

> Gondisajad, Luurjad, Kadujad, Anagajad, Kudubud, Ajorajad, snakes of the hills, snakes of the rocks, snakes of the streams, snakes of the bamboo clumps, come to us today. You have horns, you have ears, you have eyes, you have fangs, you have everything you want, come to us with all that makes you mighty. Rimpaigudi and Pandaigudi, come with your children Sunkaro and Sunkari.

The sacrificial buffalo was tethered outside. Gano's younger brother pulled a little hair from the back of its head and gave it to the shaman. The two mothers with their babies came and sat by the altar and the shaman, holding the hair in his hand, made passes over the children's heads as he continued his incantation.

> Gondisajad, Luurjad, Kadujad, Anagajad, Kudubud, Ajorajad, snakes of every hill and village, you are great, you are merciful; we call upon you. Whether you live above or below, there is nothing you do not see. You live in trees, you live in the pot of gruel; it is for you to make these children well. Snakes of Boramsingi, snakes of Sogeda, snakes of Pattili, snakes of Rajintalu, snakes of Potta, come and help us. It is you who steal the mothers' milk, it is you who have made these children thin as leaves, thin as young bamboos. Show your love for us by letting them alone. You are great, leave them alone, and we will remember you. From time to time we will give you goats or pigs or even buffaloes. We ourselves have nothing but the roots and herbs of the hills, yet we never fail to give you sacrifice.

Then Gano's brother took two bits of oily rag from the sacred lamp burning before the altar and tied them to the buffalo's horns, and as the shaman came out of the house with his patients he set fire to them, and the shaman cried, 'Come, Rimpaigudi, come Pandaigudi, we are going to the sacrifice; come with us.'

The party formed itself into a little procession, shaman, the mothers, father, brother, a few members of the family group; carrying with them the materials of sacrifice, the fan, the baskets, cooking-pots, water-pots, they went across the fields to the pretty little stream that winds down the Sogeda valley. Just outside the village the shaman halted, put a stone in the middle of the path, drew a circle round it and covered it with a date-palm leaf, calling on Rimpaigudi and Pandaigudi and their children: 'The gods of the house have sent us here. We shall return home, but you must not follow us past this stone.' He then threw water from a gourd over the legs of the two mothers.

Arrived at the stream, at a place consecrated by long tradition to such rites, the shaman made the usual altar with the fan, baskets and leaves, adding to it a bit of the buffalo's tethering-rope. More women gathered and they busied themselves making hearths and lighting fires. There were present altogether fifteen men and six women and many children. One of the men killed the buffalo with a sharp blow on exactly the right spot and the men all assisted in the task of skinning and cutting it up. This took a long time, for exact divisions had to be made, and a certain amount of meat set apart for sale—this is one of the sacrifices at which meat can be sold, a thing forbidden at the Guar, for example. The women cooked rice and made leaf-cups. The shaman puffed contentedly at his pipe. One of the mothers cooked special rice for the sacrifice in the *ajora-dang*, the decorated pot, on a hearth beside the altar. At last someone brought the buffalo's head and tail to the shaman, who put them on the altar, and let a few drops of blood fall on all the offerings. He then sat down to recite the story of Ajorasum.

In the days of Ramma-Bimma there was a family of seven brothers and a sister living together in one house. All except the girl (who was the eldest of them all) and the youngest brother, were married. One day the girl took the little boy to catch fish. They did not get anything, and decided to bring home herbs and leaves and wood instead. They came to a little stream and while the girl went to pick leaves, the boy sat by on the bank searching for crabs.

On the bank of that stream lived an old python; it was Ajorasum; there were many honey-bees flying in and out of its mouth. The boy thought the snake was a bit of wood, and tried to cut it open with his axe so that he could get the honey. But a stream of blood poured out and he ran frightened to his sister and told her what had happened. She said, 'Let us go and look.' When they came to the stream, the python raised its head and looked at them and they ran for their lives. But the snake followed them and soon caught them up. It said to the girl, 'I am going to devour this boy.' The girl said, 'Do not eat him. I will give you my anklets and bangles instead.' 'No,' said the python, 'I am going to devour him.' 'Then take my hair-pin,' said the girl. 'No,' said the python, 'I am going to devour him.' 'Then take my cloth', said the girl. 'No,' said the python, 'I am going to devour him.' 'Is there nothing I can give you?' asked the girl. 'Yes,' said the python at last. 'Let me marry you, and then I will spare the boy.' 'Very well,' said the girl. But the boy protested, 'No, you mustn't marry a python. Let it devour me, but do not let it bring shame on all of us.' But the girl insisted and they went home, followed by the snake.

When the six brothers saw the great snake approaching the house, they came out with their axes to kill it. But the girl said, 'This is my husband. Kill him if you will, but you will have to kill me first.' So they let it be and the python lived in the house.

Now this was a rich family. They were Chiefs and well thought of by the neighbours. The brothers said to each other, 'The people will laugh at us if they hear that our sister is married to a snake. Somehow or other we must get rid of it.' So one day they said to the snake, 'Brother-in-law, let us go for palm wine today.' When they came to the tree, they said, 'Brother-in-law, climb the tree and bring down the pot.' The snake replied, 'I can climb, it is true, but how shall I use the knife and how am I to carry the pot?' The brothers said, 'Hold the knife in your mouth and tie the pot to your head by a string through your mouth.'

So the snake climbed the tree, cut the branch with the knife and took the pot on its head. Then he called down, 'O brothers-in-law, how shall I come down?' They answered, 'Put your head down and your tail up.' But as the snake came down the tree, the brothers cut it into little pieces and hung them in the branches of the palm.

When they returned home their sister welcomed them and sat down to drink with them. Presently she said, 'But where is your brother-in-law?' 'O he drank rather a lot by the tree and he is sleeping it off out in the jungle. Drink a little more and then you can take him his supper.' But the girl said, 'I will take him his supper first and I will drink afterwards.' When she came to the tree she saw her husband's body hanging in pieces from the branches, and she beat her head and wept loudly. But the snake said to her, 'Don't cry or mourn for me. I have no pain. Put my body together and I will return to life. Then go to my house and live there; all will be well for you but you will see me no more.' The girl did as her husband bade her. She put the bits of his body together and it became alive. It went at once to a stream and disappeared.

The girl went home and lived there alone. After a time the eldest brother's wife bore him a son. But Ajorasum came to the house and bit the child and it died. The snake brought the child's soul and hid it in a box in his wife's house. Then the second brother's wife had a son, and then the third brother's wife; they all had sons and Ajorasum came and killed each of them. He took the souls of the babies and hid them in his box.

One day the eldest brother's wife went to see her sister-in-law; she stayed the night and the next morning the girl asked her to sweep the house while she fetched water. But she warned her not to touch the box where the snake kept its things. But the woman opened the box and the souls of the six children cried, 'Mother, mother!' She heard the voices but could see nothing. She went home quickly and told her husband and the brothers about the strange voices. They called the shaman and Ajorasum came upon him and said, 'I will never forgive you. I shall destroy every child you have.' But when they protested he said, 'Well, if you will sacrifice to me every time a woman has her first child, I will leave your children alone'. They promised to do so, and ever since we have sacrificed a buffalo for a first-born child and fed the snake on crabs.[1]

By the time this recital was ended, it was midday. Someone brought a handful of meat to be cooked in the special pot, and a leg of the

[1] There are several variants of this story. The most interesting of them is one which explains, not why the Saoras worship Ajorasum, but why they cremate and do not bury their dead (see p. 341). This version follows the above tale up to the snake's death, but then departs from it. The girl dies of sorrow and the brothers bury her and the snake in separate graves, but the girl's body comes out of the grave however deeply they dig it until at last they cremate it and have no more trouble.

In an Arangulu variant, it is the sister who asks her brother to cut the log of wood, and the python accordingly attempts to devour both of them. The girl not only offers, she throws away her ornaments and cloth, until she stands naked before the snake, and it proposes to kill her unless she agrees to marry it.

A Potta version says that the seven brothers were the first Kittungs and their sister was named Pandai. The little brother who went with her to the stream was Maddia Kittung. Pandai went along the bank of a stream picking herbs until 'she noticed a bit of wood with a head like the calf of a buffalo. From the nose many bees were flying in and out. She was frightened and screamed loudly. Maddia heard her and was about to hit the head with his axe, when the snake raised its head to strike him. Maddia begged forgiveness. "It was not my fault, but my sister's. Kill her if you will, but let me go." The snake had two horns like a buffalo's and when Maddia spoke as he did, it picked up Pandai on its horns and took her to the salt-country by the sea and married her.' After a time, Pandai wanted to see her family, and the snake took her, riding on its back, to her old home. There the brothers killed the snake, and when the girl made it alive again, they ran away to the sea. All their wives were pregnant, but the snake made them miscarry. In this version the snake's name is Sarapunda-Tikapunda.

buffalo for the shaman; he placed it beside the altar. Then he squatted on his haunches before it and with a gourd of palm wine in his hand began to chant.

> Snakes of water, snakes of trees, snakes of hills, snakes of streams, whoever and wherever you be, you are great; you have become related to us, you have come to us. Whether you live far away or near at hand, we cannot see you, but you care for us as a father cares for his children. Today we give you wine, we give you blood; come and take it. You live under stones, you live in trees, you may not wish to come. But do come and accept our offerings. We give you rice and meat and cooked blood. After today come no longer to our homes; do not enter our houses. We give you whatever we have, blood and wine, meat and rice. What more can we give? You are as father and mother, you are as Kittung to us. Come with all your relatives, eat your fill and go away for ever.
>
> Gadejangboi brought us into being and you came to see us. Now you have seen us, go away. As a child calls his father, so do we call you. Eat your feast, then leave us and our village. From the days of our ancestors we have worshipped you. Now trouble us no more. There is no grudge in our hearts, we give you willingly everything you ask of us. But now go away.

The shaman then prepared some 'medicine', pounding up a few roots with a little wild ginger and water. He offered the cooked rice and meat, putting tiny scraps in individual cups for the different spirits, and then called the two mothers and gave them wine to drink. He applied the medicine in a round blob on the head of each child crying, 'You have given us these children; now see that they keep well. You are the great snakes; leave them alone.' He then rubbed their bodies with the medicine and also the breasts and backs of the mothers. Then once more he squatted before the altar and chanted,

> Uyungsum, Ajorasum, Mannesum, Ildasum, we have offered meat cooked and raw, we have offered rice and blood; gather and eat, then leave us. Do not trouble us on the way as we go to and fro. We have not made our offerings with one hand, but with both hands; we salute you with both hands. You who have ever lived in Sogeda, in Pattili, in Kerubai, in Potta, in Gunduruba, divide the feast and eat. Sometimes you live above the ground, sometimes in holes beneath it. Some of you have horns, some of you are crested like the cock. Come all of you. Sometimes you climb the mango tree, the banyan, the tamarind, the sago palm, the ebony, the cotton tree; sometimes you burrow beneath the earth; sometimes you hide among the herbs, the rice, the pulses, the millet, the oil-seed crop. Come all of you, eat your feast and go away.

Finally the shaman gave the two mothers a little gruel. They took it in their mouths, but immediately spat it out. Someone brought a little fish 'to ward off sorcery'; the shaman gave it to them, and this too they spat out.

After this, everyone devoted himself to the business of food, the shaman finished off his pot of wine, and about four o'clock the company dispersed.

Other Ajorapur ceremonies which I have witnessed followed the Sogeda model in general outline. At Arangulu in 1946, however, there was some attention paid to a rite with crabs. All the women present went to catch crabs which were roasted and offered to Ajorasum. Two years earlier at Munisingi I attended a rite where the god named was the red-crested Jayodensum. This included a test with a new pot: the mother with the baby in her arms was made to stand in a pot and do a sort of dance; the pot did not break and this was taken as a sign that the sacrifice would be acceptable. On both these occasions the story recited and the general ritual were substantially the same.

On 20 April 1946, however, at Sogeda I assisted at a rite which showed some points of contrast. This was a Kambunjorapur—the sacrifice of a pig (*kambunan*) to Ajorasum. The wife of one Igano had recently given birth to a baby boy. She was a weak feeble creature, with no milk in her breasts, and the child was failing for lack of nourishment. A shaman declared that the cause of the trouble was the snake Rimpaigudi. This snake's tail has a tip like a woman's nipple. 'It used to come at night,' said the shaman, 'and when the baby went to the breast it curled round his body and tickled him until he cried. When he did that the snake put the end of its tail into his mouth, and itself drank the mother's milk, with the result that the child grew very weak.'

A pig-sacrifice has never, of course, the atmosphere of a buffalo-sacrifice; it is a smaller affair altogether. But the main ritual was the same except that the shaman made a little model of a snake with rice-flour and water on a pot, and later offered it on the altar. The story he recited on this occasion was entirely different. It ran as follows:

Rangu Saora and his wife made their clearing on the side of Paheri Hill. When their first son was born, the tiger and the bear heard his crying and came to eat him. Rangu tried to drive them away, but they took no notice of him and went into the house. The mother picked up the child's placenta and cord and threw them at the bear and tiger. The cord turned into a snake which bit them in the eyes and made them blind. As they stumbled helplessly away, Rangu took a stick and drove them far into the forest. For twenty-one days the snake stayed by the child and guarded him and every day the mother divided her milk between the snake and her child. At last she sent the snake to live in a hole under the ground. But it still came every night, and while the mother was sleeping robbed her of her milk and the child grew very thin. This is the Ajorajadan that still robs many women of their milk.

At the end of the ceremony, the little image of the snake was left down by the stream to ensure that Rimpaigudi did not return to the house.

XII. *The Protection of Widows*

WHERE the seen and the unseen worlds are so closely linked, and the spirits of the dead have so much to say about the affairs of the living, it is evident that a peculiar situation may easily arise when a widow marries again. Her former husband in the Under World may come and call her away if at any time he feels particularly lonely or disapproves of her conduct on earth. It is necessary, therefore, that proper arrangements should be made to avoid exciting a dead husband's jealousy. Thurston quotes some interesting remarks by Ramamurti.

Whoever marries a widow, whether it is her husband's younger brother or someone of her own choice, must perform a religious ceremony during which a pig is sacrificed. The flesh, with some liquor, is offered to the ghost of the widow's deceased husband, and prayers are addressed by the priests to propitiate the ghost, so that it may not torment the woman and her second husband. 'O man,' says the priest, addressing the deceased by name, 'here is an animal sacrificed to you, and with this all connexion between this woman and you ceases. She has taken with her no property belonging to you or your children. So do not torment her within the house or outside the house, in the jungle or on the hill, when she is asleep or when she wakes. Do not send sickness on her children. Her second husband has done no harm to you. She chose him for her husband, and he consented. O man, be appeased. O unseen ones, O ancestors, be you witnesses.' The animal sacrificed on this occasion is called *long danda* ('inside fine'), or fine paid to the spirit of a dead person inside the earth. The animal offered up when a man marries a divorced woman is called *bayar danda* ('outside fine') or fine paid as compensation to a man living outside the earth. The moment that a divorcee marries another man, her former husband pounces upon him, shoots his buffalo or pig dead with an arrow, and takes it to his village, where its flesh is served up at a feast. The priest invokes the unseen spirits, that they may not be angry with the man who has married the woman, as he has paid the penalty prescribed by the elders according to the immemorial custom of the Saoras.[1]

There is, in fact, a whole range of illnesses which may be called 'widow-sickness', caused either by a dead husband wishing to have his living wife with him in the Under World, or because she has failed to attend to him properly with gifts of food and wine, or because he is jealous of a new attachment or a second marriage. It is said that if anyone tries to make love to a widow, the first point she raises is the danger of her dead husband's jealousy.

For example, Bejonto, a shamanin of Sogeda, recalled what happened at the death of her husband. He was an epileptic who had married not only Bejonto herself, but also her younger sister, whom he had persuaded to leave her husband. Later he developed leprosy, the result—it was believed—of the outraged cuckold who sent Madusum to attack him.

My husband's body was rotten with wounds. We used up everything we had in our efforts to save him, but it was no use. As he grew worse, he used to say, 'You are alive: I am dying. You are not making proper sacrifices, and I know why—you want to marry other men after I am dead. Who will look after my ghost once you have gone to other men? It is no use my living, yet it is even worse to die.' But one day when we two wives had gone to the hills to sow seed in our clearing, he hanged himself in the house. The police came and I had to give them ten rupees and a goat—otherwise they said they would accuse us of murder. Since then we have both lived alone. Many men have wanted to marry us, but we have been too afraid of our husband's ghost, and we have always refused.

Another story comes from Potta. In 1930 a young Saora named Tinipo died in this village, leaving a widow, pretty and childless. A year later she married a man called Porid, and they lived happily together for six months when suddenly Tinipo's ghost came to Porid in a dream and said, 'How dare you marry my wife? I am going to take you away.' Porid fell very ill, and in spite of the sacrifice of a buffalo, died soon afterwards. But the girl was still young, and she went to Boramsingi and married yet again. This time the ghosts of

[1] Thurston, vol. VI, pp. 321f.

both her dead husbands attacked her and she was very ill. Shortly afterwards her new husband fell ill too. But this time they sacrificed two buffaloes and after a time they recovered and had no more trouble.

The motive for these attacks is not only sexual jealousy; it is also economic. The ghost seems to fear, and probably quite rightly, that once his widow is preoccupied with another man, she will forget him and will fail to make the proper offerings for his maintenance. For example, when a widow at Busabo remarried, the ghost of the first husband made the second husband ill, and declared through the mouth of the shaman, 'Before you married I was getting all I wanted, but now who will give me food and liquor? There is no one to look after *me* now; the only thing for me to do is to take you with me, and then you'll have to look after me.' He said to the new husband, 'What business have you to be lying with my wife? Who is going to cook for me and feed me now?' The couple hastily arranged for the sacrifice of a buffalo, and it is said that the ghost returned satisfied to his place.

In order to save her child, Burendi, an Idaiboi of Potta, had to swear never to remarry. 'After my husband's death,' she recalled, 'his ghost came to me and said, "I know the ways of women; you are going to marry again, and then who will look after our child? I am going to take him away and look after him myself." And he made the child very ill. It was only when I swore that I would never remarry that the ghost let him alone. Since then a number of men have come to my house, asking me to marry them, but every time the ghost made my son ill, and I was reminded of my promise, and refused.'

The ghost of a dead wife can be just as troublesome. She may be even more lonely than a man would be in the twilight existence of the Under World. Panchai, an Idaimaran of Gunduruba, told me how 'One night my wife's ghost caught hold of me and said, "Come and live with me, for I am lonely here. I cannot get a drop of liquor, for there is no one to climb these tall trees. I cannot go on living alone." I gave her a goat and plenty to drink and she went away. Some time afterwards I wanted to marry again, but her ghost made such a fuss and made me so unwell that I gave it up.'

The ceremony for the pacification of the living and the dead is known as the Gadding-bong-pur. I had the good fortune to witness this at Sogeda on 25 May 1948. In this case it was the ghost of a dead wife who was jealous of her husband's remarriage to another girl.

Jani's first wife, Gatni, had died a year previously, and after a discreet interval a very pretty girl called Dayam came of her own accord to live in his house.[1] Very soon, however, the ghost of Gatni made her ill and when a shamanin was called declared, 'What are you doing in the house I made? I was there first, and you have entered it of your own accord, and have never given me a thing.'

Accordingly on 25 May, Jani instituted the ceremony of friendship (*gadding*) through the gift of a buffalo (*bongan*) to bring his two wives, the living and the dead, together. A shamanin put two baskets of rice and a pot of wine before the main pillar of the house, and opened the proceedings in the usual way. Presently Gatni's ghost came upon her and said to her husband, 'Why did you bring this woman into my house? I had a little sister; she was the girl you should have married. She would have looked after me properly.' Jani replied, 'But that was the very girl I wanted to marry. I went to her father's house for her. But the old man made such a fuss that we quarrelled. Then this girl came. She works well; you ought to be pleased with her.' The ghost replied, 'Very well. Now where's my cloth?' Jani gave it to the shamanin who, in her character of Gatni handed it to Dayam and said, 'Now you have become my *gadding*-friend we will have no more quarrels and you shall live happily in my house. But what about my bracelets?' Jani produced the bracelets, and the shamanin gave these also to Dayam, and Gatni's ghost said, 'From today your soul and mine will be one.'

Then Gatni's ghost came with great power upon the shamanin and she rushed out of the house and seized the dedicated buffalo and dragged it down the street and out into a field, while all the people pushed and belaboured it until they were tired. They gave it wine to drink and brought it back to the house.

After this two Idaimarans, dressed up to represent the two wives and carrying bows and arrows, staged a symbolic quarrel. They danced about, shot arrows at each other, knocked each other down, and the bystanders threw ashes over them. At the end of what was a first-class knockabout slapstick performance, they sat down

[1] Such a woman is known in Middle India as Paithu, and among the Saoras as Daritamboi, one who herself 'opens the door of the house'.

together for a drink, embraced and fondled each other, thus dramatically signifying that the dispute between the two wives was at an end.

XIII. *The Menace of Smallpox*

THERE is no disease more feared in India than smallpox, so mysterious in its incidence, so fatal in its effect, having the dreadful power, in Macaulay's vivid words, of 'tormenting with constant fears all whom it has not yet stricken, leaving on those whose lives it has spared the hideous traces of its power, turning the babe into a changeling at which the mother shudders, and making the eyes and cheeks of a betrothed maiden objects of horror to the lover'. There is probably less smallpox now than there was once, but many villagers, and nearly all the tribesmen, try to avoid the vaccinator, bribing him to leave them alone: the Saoras go so far as to offer sacrifices after his visit to undo the evil effects of his attentions. As a result disastrous epidemics sweep the country from time to time; to deal with them a special technique has been evolved by the shamans.

The smallpox goddess is known, in various parts of the Saora country, as Rugaboi, Yuyuboi, Lurnisum-Lurniboi, but the old Saora names are being gradually displaced by the Hindu word Thakurani. The name Rugaboi is associated with *rogon*, the red gram which is supposed to resemble the smallpox pustule. Yuyuboi, who is said to give the most virulent type of smallpox, may derive her name from the Saora verb *yu* which in its transitive form means 'to shake', and intransitively means 'to tremble' or 'shiver': another verb *yuyu*- means 'to droop'. I have recorded two stories of the origin of Rugaboi's malice towards mankind; both reveal her as a goddess dominated by ill-temper and revenge.

The first story, from Gailung, emphasizes Rugaboi's connexion with the red gram.

When the gods were born, each went to his own place and did his own business. Tupru Saora lived on Tamchaya Hill. He made a clearing and sowed red pulse. Under one of the shrubs Rugaboi was born; when Tupru went to see his crop he found her like a young girl and took her home. She worked for him, brought him water, cleaned the house. One day Tupru took his pulse and beans to the bazaar. The other villagers went on ahead, but Rugaboi lagged behind and on the way a Dom and a Saora caught hold of her and stole the pulse she was carrying. She was very angry and changed her appearance and took the form of a goddess. The Dom and Saora dropped their baskets and ran for their lives. Rugaboi went to Kittung and told him what had happened and he said, 'You can have your revenge by giving them swellings like pulse and beans on their bodies. They will sacrifice to you and you will get all the food you want.' Rugaboi went back and entered into the bodies of the Dom and the Saora and gave them smallpox. They called the shaman and he made a little chariot, put every kind of grain into it, took it out of the village and sacrificed a pig before it. Rugaboi was satisfied, and the pestilence ceased.

Another story, forgetful of the many myths that make the Sun and Moon man and wife, describes Uyungboi the Sun, Angaiboi the Moon, and Rugaboi as three sisters.

Rugaboi was the eldest and she was very beautiful. Her body was tender as fresh leaves, her breasts were bael fruit, the bun of her hair was a bulbul's nest. One day Ramma-Bimma called the sisters to divide the world between them. Uyungboi and Angaiboi went, but Rugaboi stayed behind. Ramma-Bimma, therefore, gave the night to the Moon and the day to the Sun, and each went to her own place. This made Rugaboi very angry. 'I am the eldest,' she cried, 'and the most beautiful, yet I get nothing.' And she went to Ramma-Bimma, intending to devour him. Now Ramma-Bimma was bringing out of his bins the twelve kinds of seed to give to men, and when Rugaboi came to attack him, he threw the seed at her. Wherever a seed hit her a sore broke out and soon she was hideous with pustules swelling like seeds all over her body. She abused Ramma-Bimma, but all he did was to hand her a mirror. When she saw how ugly she was, she went into the sky and devoured half the body of the Moon. When Ramma-Bimma saw this, he said, 'I will give you all humanity to eat, but leave the Moon alone.' So Rugaboi left the Moon and now she attacks men instead, when she remembers how unjustly she has been treated.

I have found here and there the belief that smallpox is caused by the menstruation of the goddess; it is when she is in her period that she rages through the villages bringing death to the people.

In some places the smallpox deity is called Lurnisum. This god is androgynous in character, and his symbol is an upright stone not unlike a lingam. It is curious that this decidedly male symbol should be used for a disease-deity who is almost everywhere regarded as female. Sometimes there are two of these stones, one for Lurnisum and the other for his wife Lurniboi. Little shrines are made for Lurnisum, always of stone with thatched roofs, and sacrifice is offered in them. To the north, similar shrines are made for Thakurani, but usually of wood.

There are a number of special techniques for dealing with an outbreak of smallpox. At Maneba in 1943 the shaman made a little cart, loaded it with bundles of wood, and dragged it out of the village and along the road to the shrine of Lurnisum. There was a seat of thorns there, and while the others sacrificed a buffalo, the shaman sat on this and prophesied.

At Bungding, where in the same year there was a shocking epidemic that devastated entire streets in the village, 'sweeping the people into a heap', as one of the survivors put it, the attack was associated with the dead as well as with Lurniboi. It is said that not a single child survived, for the goddess was furious because the people only gave her a fowl instead of the usual buffalo. After they had buried most of the victims, the ancestors came upon the shaman and said, 'You have given us nothing, not even the fowl you gave to Kurniboi. We are dying of hunger. Now let every woman bring us rice and a head-load of wood, and every man a fowl and a shoulder-load of wood.' They hurried to obey; the women made tiny bundles of sticks (six to eight inches long) like those they normally carry on their heads, and the men made similar loads—little poles a foot long with bundles of twigs tied at either end. They took them outside the village, made one enormous leaf-plate and piled their rice upon it, sacrificed over fifty fowls (but did not scatter the blood in the usual manner over the rice) and cooked the flesh and offered it, not to the smallpox goddess, but to the dead. I visited the village shortly afterwards and the Saoras there were like people suffering from shock; they moved about slowly, spoke in hushed voices, and there were no children playing in the streets.

FIG. 26 'Cart' with small bundles of wood attached, to remove Yuyuboi (smallpox goddess) from a village
About 2' high

At Sogeda, I was told, at a similar epidemic the shaman made a

37. Shamans offer a fowl at Bungding before a specially-constructed bamboo shrine which has been carried out of the village

38. Image of Ajorasum

AJORAPUR CEREMONY AT SOGEDA (38 to 41)

39. Lighting the buffalo's horns

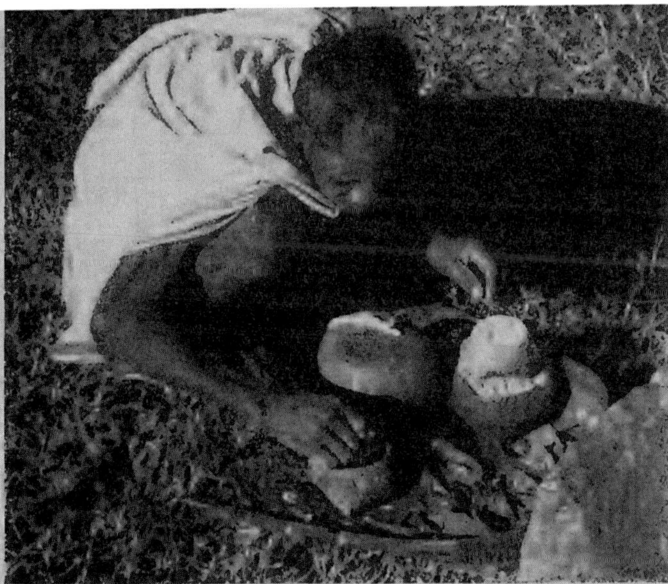

40. Shaman offering rice

41. Shaman feeding pig before sacrifice

42 & 43. Scenes at ceremony described on pp. 268f.

43

trident of bamboo in honour of Rugaboi, tied scraps of coloured cloth to it, put it in a basket and went round the village collecting rice and the usual bundles of wood from every house. Then the shaman went round searching for Rugaboi, for she hides in pots or baskets. He found her in a pot, picked it up and ran as hard as he could towards the village boundary. The householder had to give chase, but before he could catch him up the shaman fell to the ground in trance, the goddess having come out of the pot into his body. The people at once brought offerings of rice and wine which they gave the goddess at the very spot where the shaman was lying. They also sacrificed a pig.

When I visited Kankaraguda village in December 1945, the people told me of an epidemic they had had some years before. The day before the first case of smallpox, both the Chief and the priest dreamt that the village had been burnt down. Then many people fell ill, and the shamans were baffled, for not until twelve children and three adults had died did Thakurani come upon one of them and state her demands. She said,

> All the world gives me food and lodging. I live in every tree and every home and every kind of seed. Your ancestors refused to give me anything, and so now I have come to take my food by force. If you build a house for me, and give me my food, I will give you no more trouble.

The shamans agreed to do this, and they took Thakurani out of the village in a small wooden cart to a mango tree. Beneath this they erected a phallic-shaped stone and put a vermilion mark on it (in recognition of the fact that Thakurani is a Hindu; they would not do this for a Saora god). Later they built a stone house round the stone and sacrificed a sheep.

In Boramsingi and some of the neighbouring villages, there was a special functionary called the Kamanda,[1] who was a specialist in the worship of Yuyuboi or Thakurani. At the killing of the peacock at the Karja ceremony (see p. 381), after the dance with the stuffed body of the bird, the Kamanda takes it to Yuyuboi's shrine and removes the feathers and burns them: the goddess is said to be pleased with the offering 'because it is so pretty'. If there is danger of an epidemic, the Kamanda leads the hunt for a peacock, which is done ceremonially just as at the Karja. If the bird is caught alive, as it should be, the

[1] This custom is not confined to the Saoras. In many villages in Orissa, there is a special male or female shaman known as the Kalasi, who is engaged at outbreaks of cholera and smallpox and interprets the will of Thakurani.

Kamanda feeds it with rice and then kills it. He ties it to a pole and sacrifices a fowl before it. Then he carries it round the village at the head of a dance-procession, and repeats this every night until Yuyuboi is satisfied, whereon he burns the feathers at her shrine. It is dangerous not to burn the feathers, for if a sorcerer in some other village gets hold of them he can send the disease back again.

When anyone dies of smallpox, he becomes, of course, a Rugaboi-Idaisum, an ancestor who is a servant or even part of Rugaboi. At Burda, on 19 December 1946, I attended a ceremony to cure a child who had been attacked by such a ghost. Three years earlier, a six-year-old boy called Sonia had died of smallpox. Then his mother had another baby called Somra. After Sonia's Guar ceremony had been performed, he came in the form of Rugaboi to see his baby brother and gave him, not smallpox, but a severe attack of malaria as a warning. Through the shaman, the young ghost demanded food sacrifice and promised to go away if he got it; but if he did not, he threatened to give smallpox to the child. The shaman made the usual offerings of rice and wine in the house and said,

> Eat Rugaboi, eat happily and go away. You are the mother of the world. You came of your own accord to see your little brother, and we are glad you came, but now let the child alone and go away. For, look, he is only a little baby. We willingly give you a feast. If you do not accept it and go away offended, we shall all die. Yuyungsum, Darammasum, Lankasum, Labosum, be witness that we have given you food. Go! We bid you be gone and leave this child alone.

Then the shaman, with the mother and child, went into the forest to a mango tree traditionally associated with Rugaboi and there offered a fowl. Before they returned, the shaman sprinkled water over all those present, and placed a potsherd with some little offerings on the path to prevent the goddess following them home.

It is possible that from these incidents and traditions we can define three stages in the Saora attitude to smallpox. At first it is attributed to the dead, who are the chief (and perhaps in the earliest Saora thought, the only) agents of disease. Then the responsibility is shifted to a Saora deity Lurnisum, but the prevailing Hindu belief is too strong for this function to be left in male hands and he is therefore given a wife Lurniboi (the phallic symbols for this god suggest that the wife is a later accretion), who also becomes known by names such as Rugaboi and Yuyuboi which suggest the physical manifestations of the disease. Finally, perhaps as a result of the visits of the vaccinator, smallpox is attributed to a Hindu goddess, Thakurani.

XIV. *The Diseases of Animals*

THE THRIFTY and industrious Saoras set great store by their domestic animals and are very good to them. They keep cattle and buffaloes, goats, pigs and fowls, often a dog or two, sometimes a cat. The cowsheds are usually built into the row of houses along a street, and are substantial buildings of the same type as the living houses, with mud floors and wooden doors. Pigsties are sometimes erected separately, more often are built into the veranda of a house. Fowls live with the family indoors. There is no special class of graziers and the task of guarding the cattle during the day is generally left to small boys; one may often see some diminutive urchin driving a whole herd with the help of a stick and much picturesque abuse.

Bulls are not used for ploughing, and only in very exceptional circumstances in sacrifice. Cows and bullocks, as well as cow-buffaloes and castrated buffaloes, are used for ploughing, but never (so far as I know) as beasts of burden. The Saoras have a taboo on milk and its products, and cattle and goats are never milked. Goats, pigs and fowls are generally dedicated or at least preserved for some religious purpose, and the Saoras dislike selling them. They do not like depleting their herds of horned cattle for the purpose of sacrifice, and usually buy a buffalo or bullock from the local Doms when one is needed.

Animals, like human beings, are subject to the attacks of spirits, and their diseases are always regarded as having a supernatural cause. It was Kittung himself, for example, who sent disease to fowls.

At the beginning of things, although other creatures fell sick and died, fowls were free of disease; they were always strong and well, and only died if men killed them. As a result they increased greatly in numbers. Kittung thought, 'All other creatures die of disease, but these cocks and hens never get anything the matter with them.' So he made two kinds of diseases; he scraped some dirt off his tongue and mixed it and the diseases with paddy chaff and scattered it in the streets of the villages. The fowls ran to peck it up and at once fell ill.

The gods who most commonly affect cattle are Gorusum, associated with the Gour graziers; Ringeboi the wind, who gives a windy colic; Rugaboi, who gives rinderpest; Kannisum (god of epilepsy), who gives the staggers. Kinnasum and Senaisum are said to make the throats of cattle swell and cause them to salivate excessively. Uyungsum makes them very thin.

Goats are attacked by Sakurasum, who gives them sores in the mouth which stops them eating. Ringeboi makes their throats and bellies swell. Jammasum affects pigs with loss of appetite and makes them pant heavily. Mardisum troubles fowls, giving them, as might be expected, a sort of cholera, turning their droppings white and causing their feathers to fall out.

The dead also distress domestic animals. If an ancestor in the Under World has insufficient cattle to plough his fields, or if he has to perform the Guar ceremony for one of the dead who has died again there, he may cause the death of a buffalo on earth so that he can take it below. If the Guar ceremony is delayed, a shade may remind the living of their duties by attacking the herds.

Sorcerers may also send disease, or more commonly wild animals, to attack cattle and other animals. In fact, animals are subject to all the risks that attend human life.

They are also subject to much the same treatment. The cattle-shed may be protected by a small pot dedicated to Gorusum, hung from the roof by a cord made of the tail-hairs of a cow, together with a leaf-hat, cords from a carrying-pole, a grazier's stick and a cow-bell. Many sheds have a piece of a hornet's nest hanging in front of the door. Itis considered very lucky if hornets make their nests in such a shed, for they will sting and drive away any alien ghost or other spirit who tries to enter it.

Gorusum is worshipped in a little leaf-hut erected beside one of the paths leading out of a village; Ringeboi is given a fowl; Galbesum receives a pig in her shrine and rice inside the cattle-shed. When there is an outbreak of rinderpest, the shaman takes the cattle outside the village, sprinkles water and rice over them, and sacrifices a goat to Rugaboi. For the staggers, the shaman first gives the cattle a herbal medicine; if this is ineffective, he sacrifices a pig outside by the path. For Kinnasum, he offers dried fish and an egg before an ant-hill.

For foot and mouth disease, the Saoras tie their cattle up in some place where there is plenty of muddy water, the idea being that no insects can infect the sores when the cattle are standing in mud. The shaman throws rice and water over them. Then he finds the foot of a previously sacrificed buffalo, takes it out of the village and, using it as a sort of altar, sacrifices a pig and a fowl upon it. None of the flesh of animals sacrificed for cattle may be brought back into the village.

Nearly all such sacrifices are made outside the village. The shaman sometimes uses the branch of the *Eugenia jambolana* tree to sprinkle the water.

The shaman often applies 'medicines' after offering sacrifice. He gives a sick goat the fruit of the *sakura* tree, rubbing it on a stone, and applying the pulp to the sores. Then he sacrifices a goat to Sakurasum who is believed to have caused the trouble. He gives a pig the pounded root of a deciduous shrub to eat. For a fowl attacked by Mardisum, he gets the bark and leaves of the *Azadirachta indica*, presses out the juice and forces it down the creature's throat. If a hen's eggs prove sterile, the householder breaks them, strings the shells on a bit of broomstick and puts them in the thatch in front of his house. This is supposed to please Uralbasum, who will see that the next setting is fertile.

I will now briefly describe three of the ceremonies for cattle at which I have assisted.

On 21 November 1950 the cattle of Sunmaro Karji of Kerubai were sick. The shaman declared that Kinnasum (the tiger-god) had given them eye-trouble so that they would be unable to see their way about in the forest and tigers would be able to catch them easily. The curing ritual was simple. The shaman took a little basket of rice into the cattle-shed and waved it over every animal that stood there. Then he went out of the village towards the west and when he had found a suitable spot, he placed an old ploughshare in the ground as an altar and sacrificed a fowl before it.

On 14 May 1948 at Tumulu there was a ceremony to protect the cattle of a Christian Saora named Moti who had recently bought three bullocks at Serango and brought them home. Moti was very unwilling for me to be present, for he feared that I would object to his participation in this 'heathen' rite, but I managed to convince him that I was not interested in that aspect of it.

The ceremony was due to the fact that Gorusum, who used to look after the bullocks at Serango, had followed them to their new home. Moreover, since Serango was a mission station, it was believed—even by the Christian Saoras—that it held many witches and sorcerers within its boundaries. The Tumulu shamans therefore had advised Moti to make the customary offerings to Gorusum and Tonaisum.

On the afternoon of the 14th of May, accordingly, Moti put his cattle in their shed and the shaman made an offering of palm wine on the threshold. Then he went inside and threw some rice over the bullocks and waved a pig that it was proposed to sacrifice three times round them. He took the rope with which they had been tethered at Serango and the pig and a fowl for some considerable distance along the path that leads from Tumulu towards Serango. There was then a long pause, for the actual sacrifice had to be made after dark. At about 9 o'clock in the evening the shaman offered the rope to Gorusum, saying, 'Accept this and use it as you will,' and poured some wine upon it. He fed the pig with rice, had the head cut off, and made offerings of the blood. His assistants took the body of the pig and removed the bones, which they crushed and cooked with the blood into a soup. They feasted and at midnight returned home, being careful not to look behind them.

On 22 November 1950, the Gungupur was held at Kerubai; although this ceremony is usually performed in August, the special circumstances of that year caused it to be held later. Its aim is normally to 'drive away weariness and pain at the end of the ploughing', but it can drive away pain and weariness at any time.

A pig was hung up by its feet outside the Chief's cattle-shed. An Idaimaran of the Chief's family group made a cup of the leaves of the *araineban* (*Semecarpus anacardium*) tree and filled it with water. Into this he put a few bristles from the back of the pig's neck and a little rice. The cattle were standing at one end of the street and the Idaimaran went to them and sprinkled water on them with a bundle of leafy branches. After this the people herded the cattle into their shed and shut the door. Two men took the pig and slung it by its feet on a long pole. They stood outside the door, holding the pig before it. The Idaimaran went inside and drove the cattle out one by one. As they came out the men holding the pig banged it vigorously against them. This was intended to drive out any ghost or god who might be possessing the animals.

When this was done and the shed cleared, the Idaimaran set up a little altar inside the shed before a plough and a yoke, putting *araineban* branches before it, with small baskets of rice and grain, and many leaf-cups for the ancestors and gods. Another Idaimaran joined him and the two men offered palm wine and called on the dead, first of the Chief's own house, then of his family, then of the village, then of neighbouring villages, inviting them to come and share the feast, to see that the cattle kept well and that the harvest was so good that even the richest Chiefs of other villages would come to them for loans. The pig was then killed and its head placed before the plough. The flesh and rice were cooked and members of the Chief's family sat down to share the feast. As they ate, one of the Idaimarans sprinkled them with water. When they had finished they tore up the plates on which they had eaten and scattered them about the shed, so that the cattle might stand or lie upon them; this, it was believed, would drive all their pains away.

The Saoras are somewhat uncertain about what happens to animals when they die.

The Under World is certainly full of animals. Tutelaries ride on elephants and horses; they keep tigers and monkeys as pets; the bear and the porcupine have priestly functions. Every ikon that portrays scenes of the Under World is crowded with animal studies.

When animals are sacrificed for the dead they 'go below'; that is why the dead want them. And they seem to go down alive after their death here. A buffalo sacrificed on earth is used by an ancestor for ploughing his fields; or it may be sacrificed again in the Under World for the Guar ceremony of one of the dead who has died again there; an old man at Boramsingi had a favourite cow slaughtered by his pyre so that it could keep him company after death. Most commonly, of course, a sacrificial animal is used by the dead for food, but it is not clear from the way the Saoras talk whether they consider the dead share the feast with the living on earth, or whether a goat or pig 'goes down' and is killed again there to feed, for example, the many ancestors who could not come to the earthly festival. In one ceremony I attended, the tutelary was supposed to be trying to drag away a buffalo to the Under World so that he could enjoy all the meat himself, and those present had to struggle hard with the shaman in order to ensure that they got their share.

There is a further complication. No one can enter the Under World unless the Guar ceremony has been performed. When a pet dog dies, two men sling it on a pole, carry it out and bury it. 'For long ago,' as I was told at Sogeda, 'the dog was our brother—it was a man. It has a shade, but we don't know where it goes. It cannot go to the Under World, for there is no Guar for dogs. That is why we bury them; otherwise we would have to do the Guar for them.' The Saoras also bury cats, wrapping the bodies in cloth, 'for long ago the cat was a woman'. They put rice into the graves of both dogs and cats to feed the shade after death.

It appears, therefore, that the many animals in the Under World are not the ghosts of animals who died here. But animals can be sent down, under certain conditions, for the use of the dead and the tutelaries. As to what happens to the shades of those who die otherwise, there is no certain answer.

XV. *Accidents*

THE IMPORTANT things about accidents, of course, is that they are hardly ever accidental. It is true that an ordinary cut may be regarded as an ordinary cut, but if the wound festers, it shows that a god has been offended: if a man cuts himself with his axe while chopping down a tree, he may have insulted a god living in the branches; if he injures himself while cutting up firewood, he may have annoyed a god who had chosen that bundle of sticks to rest on. It is pus that proclaims the divine hand, while maggots in a wound suggest that the ancestors are craving for a meal of buffalo flesh.

The most common accident is to fall from a tree. Half-drunken men swarm up the tall palm trunks and all too often slip and crash to their death. This is caused by a push from Uyungsum, and when it happens, the shade goes 'above' where the Sun-god ties it up and keeps it without food or water in his house. At the time of the Guar, which naturally should be performed in this case as soon as possible, the shaman sends the ancestors to look for it; they go into the sky, steal into Uyungsum's house and release the unhappy shade.

If anyone injures himself by a stumble or fall while walking, it is attributed to Labosum who must have been offended in some way. For example, Lilamo of Boramsingi went during the Karja ceremony one year to visit someone in the neighbouring village Kittim. As he came home, very drunk, that night, he met Labosum and accidentally kicked him. Labosum caught hold of Lilamo's foot and pulled it from under him, knocking him over and injuring his knee. Lilamo lay unconscious till morning, when his friends found him and carried him home. Labosum came upon a shamanin and said, 'I was out for a stroll and he kicked me, so I knocked him down. He will not recover.' But he did, after a pig had been sacrificed.

Burns are due to Uyungsum, if they occur by day, to the shades if they occur at night. Kannisum also may knock his own epileptics into the fire, but he does not attack other people. The shades are blind (it will be remembered that their eyes are in the back of the neck) and they come stumbling into a house, knock against people, sometimes push them into the fire. At Boramsingi once, Turdang was sleeping by the fire when the shade of his dead brother came bumbling about and stepped into the fire, scattering the embers over Turdang's clothes, which caught fire and burnt his hand. This was strictly speaking a double accident, but the shamanin insisted that it happened because Turdang would not give the thirsty shade enough to drink.

In the same village, the son of one Talsi was sleeping by a fire, when the ghost of Talsi's elder brother knocked a piece of burning wood against his chest. He declared through the shamanin that he was dying of hunger and had come to take away both father and son to work for him in the Under World.

If anyone is killed by lightning, the shaman must inquire from the ancestors whether the corpse can be cremated in the usual place or not. It is said that lightning usually only strikes some great 'sinner', but sometimes it falls by mistake on the innocent. The ancestors do not like having these sinners in their company, and try to avoid it by having their corpses cremated in some unusual place, whence they are able to send the shade to Gadejangboi who returns it to earth as a firefly. But if the ancestors do not object, the body is burnt in the usual manner. Everything to do with lightning is dangerous: if it strikes a tree, the wood should not be used or even touched; if it strikes a house, it should be abandoned; if it kills an animal the flesh should not be eaten.

Injuries caused by animals are regarded as due to the prompting of a spirit or sorcerer. To be killed by a bear is the work of Saluasum, driven to it by the ghost of some murdered man anxious to take revenge on the living. But if one is only injured by a bear, it is due to Labosum who takes a bear's form and wounds and frightens but does not kill, since his purpose is not revenge, but to extort a food-sacrifice.

There is a story—I do not know how seriously it is taken—that the scorpion is an unwanted and unmarried girl who has been sent back to earth to take her revenge.[1] If it bites anyone, no sacrifice is offered, but the scorpion is killed and its entrails are applied to the wound.

The shades of people who die in unusual ways are always troublesome. The shade of a man killed by falling from a tree makes his victim unconscious as if he too had fallen. The shade of someone who has died of burns causes pain in the very place where his own wounds were. The shade of a drowned man causes liquid to flow from the mouth and nose.

[1] See *MMI*, p. 160.

Chapter Eight

THE RITES OF FERTILITY

I. *The Mythological Background*

THERE is no Earth Mother in the Saora pantheon. How extraordinary this is can only be appreciated when we reflect on the enormous influence of this conception over the whole of eastern India, and particularly among the Saoras' nearest neighbours, the Konds. There are, however, a number of gods of no very great eminence associated with the earth. Chief of these are Labosum[1]—*labon* is Saora for earth, soil or country—who is god of the fields, Lambusum or Barusum who presides over the hill-clearings, and Jammolsum who is the god of seed.

Labosum is sometimes called a Kittung, but he does not appear, at least by name, in more than a few myths: in one he comforts a weeping girl, who is trying to sweep a courtyard with her hands, by pushing a broom up from below.[2] In another we are told that it was when he belched that the wind came to blow the chaff away from the threshing-floor.[3] But apart from these two amiable but rather undistinguished interventions in human affairs, Labosum does not appear, either at the creation of the earth, or at the institution of agriculture, or at the discovery of grain.

Nor is Labosum specially or exclusively worshipped for the good fortunes of the harvest. He is remembered constantly in invocations, but he is treated just like any other god, and is generally noticed because he has given someone fever or other sickness. Offerings are made to him in the fields, but they are made at the same time to other gods and to the dead. On the rare occasion of an earthquake, the Saoras offer him a goat, for they believe 'he is angry at not getting enough to eat'. After this no work is done for three days, and the crops are expected to be excellent, 'for the old earth has become new and will bear well'.

[1] Labosum, like many other Saora gods, is sometimes regarded as feminine; but Laboboi or Labosumboi actually means no more than 'Mrs Labosum': the feminine form of the word refers to Labosum's wife.

[2] *TMO*, p. 594. [3] *TMO*, p. 79.

The other gods associated with the earth and its harvests are Lambusum and Barusum and the very large number of local hill-gods. The Saoras sacrifice to them when they cut the trees in their clearings, when they sow the seed and at a significant ceremony when the pulse breaks out in red and yellow flowers. Jammolsum, who lives in the gourd where dedicated seed is put, is worshipped at the important Jammalpur or Surendapur before the sowing at the main cultivating season at the start of the rains.

To the Saora every part of the agricultural process is a religious act; his field is a temple, his hill-clearing a shrine. All that he has and does can be traced back to the mythological past of his tribe. It was Kittung who made the first field and sowed the first seed. It was Kittung who prepared the first threshing-floor—it was twenty-four miles long and twenty-four miles broad. It was Kittung who then taught men how to cultivate.

In the old days there was no grain anywhere. The whole world lived on fruit and roots. But when the people increased in number, there were not enough roots to go round. Kittung came to two brothers, Satiya and Nambo, who lived on the Manjul Hill, and said to them, 'There are not enough roots for all these people. If you will bring grain to birth, all will be well.' The brothers replied, 'But where are we to find grain? We have no seed.' Kittung took them to the Mandarjan Hill, and showed them how to use the digging-stick. He found a flower of the wild fig and in it was every kind of grain. The brothers sowed the grain and learnt which kind of seed was which.

This story was recorded at Bungding; another with a similar motif comes from Baijalo. This too tells how men originally lived on roots, but an ever-increasing population made this more and more difficult. The Saoras went to Kittung for help and he sent his messengers to find grain. They discovered that two rich Saoras had stored some in their house, but they refused to share it with the rest of the world. Kittung sent his officers to arrest the hoarders, and only then did they surrender with great reluctance seven handfuls of grain. 'Kittung had a field made and sowed the grain. When it was ready, he reaped, threshed and winnowed it, then stored it in his house. He called the whole world and distributed it.'

Curious and highly characteristic myths describe how weeds and insects came into the world to damage the crops. These too came from a divine source, for the gods feared that if men grew too rich they would grow proud and neglect them.

At first there were no fields. But when men increased in numbers, they cleared the ground and made ploughs. They used seven kinds of grain and the crops grew well; there were no weeds and no disease attacked the growing plants. Whatever was sown bore splendidly and the people grew rich. There were no poor in the world at that time. Each single grain was so big that it served for a man's meal.

When Ramma and Bimma saw this they sent to Kittung and said, 'If everybody is rich who will be afraid of us?' Kittung said, 'It is all because of their fine crops.' Ramma and Bimma said, 'What shall we do about it?' Kittung said, 'You must make grass and weeds grow in the fields and then men will have to waste half their time removing it.' 'But how can we get grass and weeds?' 'Find the foetus of a six or seven months' woman who has aborted and, stripping yourselves naked, bury it at midnight in a field.'

Ramma and Bimma did as Kittung advised with the result that grass and weeds sprang up everywhere, and 'since then men have no longer been rich'.

It was Jammolsum who created the weevils that damage the grain once it has been stored in the bins.

In the old days people kept their grain for twelve or twenty years in their bins and it never went bad or was eaten by insects. One year, just before the rains, Jammolsum called the Saoras and distributed seed-grain to them. They took it home, and Jammolsum put what was left back in his bin. He clapped his hands over it to remove the dust, and when the dust fell it turned into weevils.

The weevils abused Jammolsum saying, 'Why have you created us? What have we got to live on?' Jammolsum said, 'Live in the grain-bin and eat the grain. When you are reborn after you die I will put you inside the grain and you can eat it from within.'

II. *The Dead and the Harvest*

There is no doubt that all the inhabitants of the unseen world are greatly interested in human agriculture. Those gods who regard themselves as the real owners of fields or hills expect to receive some kind of rent in the form of sacrifice. The other gods and the tutelaries are interested, for unless the harvests are good they cannot expect to receive much in the way of tribute. After all, their prosperity depends on man's prosperity. It is, of course, a rather delicate business, for if man becomes too prosperous he grows proud and careless of his sacred duties; if he becomes too poor he is helpless before them, and the gods do not like a bankrupt.

But the dead have a unique and special interest in the fields and clearings, the threshing-floors and grain-bins of the living. These are the fields across which they themselves drove the unwilling buffaloes, from which they tore the choking weeds, through which they ranged, triumphantly cutting the golden grain. They were their fields once, in a sense they are their fields still, and they demand and expect a share of what comes from them. One would suppose that on this theory, which is undoubtedly the Saora theory, the dead would automatically see to it that the harvests were always good and the threshing-floors inviolate, for it is in their own interest that it should be so. But the dead are like old people everywhere; they are exact, meticulous, severe; if things are not done right, they do not in the least mind penalizing themselves in order to teach their graceless heirs a lesson. And so they drive the living to their will by two strong reins; in one hand they hold the menace of disease and death, in the other the threat of disaster to the crops.

When ghosts come upon the shaman they commonly inquire about their fields and seed, their cattle and ploughs, and how their unworthy descendants are maintaining them. Conversely it is usually from the ancestors, rather than from such earth-gods as Labosum, that the living inquire about the future of their crops. At the Sogeda Mango Festival the dead declared that the harvest that year, with the exception of the red gram, would be good. At the Boramsingi Karja, the ancestors said, 'You have done well and we shall be happy and content. The crops in your fields and clearings will be good.' From time to time ikons are drawn to satisfy ghosts who come in dreams to announce that if they are pleased they will ensure a good harvest in the coming year.

If we accept the view that mythology is a tribe's theology in concrete yet poetic form, the stories about the part played by the dead in creation are relevant. According to one tradition, it was the dead who remade the world after the deluge, preserved mankind and grain for it, and taught the Saoras the principles of axe-cultivation.[1] In another story, it was the dead who taught the Saoras how to love and thus ensured human fertility.[2] A number of transformation stories describe how an ebony tree grows from the body of a dead girl; how the bamboo comes from a foetus; how tobacco springs from a girl's bones unconsumed on the pyre; how flowers grow from the ornaments of a

[1] *MMI*, p. 43. [2] ibid., p. 289.

dead maiden. It is a dead man's bones which turn into salt, a dead man's hair which becomes grass.[1]

Such stories suggest that it would not be impossible for the Saora mind to conceive of the dead as in some way entering into the soil or the growing plants and acting as a kind of fertilizer; for if the dead can become salt and grass, why cannot they become rice and pulse?

But I think there can be no doubt that the general Saora view of the effect of the dead on the harvest is that it is a negative one. If the dead are satisfied, they will not interfere with the normally beneficent purposes of nature, and they will protect the harvest from its other enemies. Just as there are no health-giving, but only disease-giving, gods, and the most man can do to keep in good health is to persuade the disease-givers to let him alone, so in relation to the crops, gods and dead alike are thought of as fertility-destroying but not as fertility-promoting. We come back to the fundamental zenophobic mentality of the Saoras: 'Let us alone and we will be all right.' Man as he was first created had no diseases; the first fields had no weeds, the first grain was not attacked by rust or weevils. Let nature take her course; if he is left alone, man will be fit and strong; if they are not attacked, the fields will bear fruit abundantly.

Writing after a very brief visit to the Saora country, Hutton (with whom I disagree only with the greatest reluctance) says, 'The Guar ceremony coincides approximately with that of sowing and seems never to be performed after the rice is transplanted and I infer from this that the Guar ceremony marks the transition of the soul into the crop which along with the previous dead it probably helps to fertilize'.[2] And he speaks again of 'the single annual festival' at which 'the dead of all the year are commemorated'. 'The souls of these dead are in some way associated with the ensuing crops, and offerings of the first-fruits of the next harvest are made at the stones put up the previous year.'[3] With regard to the Guar Hutton was given inaccurate, or at the best, partial information. It is observed as a 'single annual festival' only in some villages near Serango. The 'time of sowing' is, as everywhere in India, the months of June and July; transplantation is done in August: this period is strictly taboo for the performance of Guar ceremonies. A subsidiary rice crop, the so-called 'mango rice', is raised by some Saoras in some villages, and the seed for this is sown in

[1] *TMO*, pp. 28, 108. [2] J. H. Hutton, *Census of India*, 1931, vol. I, pt iiiB, p. 4.
[3] J. H. Hutton, *Caste in India* (Cambridge, 1946), p. 23.

January before the main Guar season, and the transplanting of the seedlings occurs in the middle of the season and not at the end. But in any case this is a very minor crop; no ceremonies are associated with it—there is no dedication of the seed, or sacrifice at the harvest; and the Guar is not in any way related to it. For this important ceremony can be performed at any time in the open season—'there is no *ersi* time for Guar except in the rains'—and I have known it as early as October and as late as 2 May, when the ceremony was performed for Dipanam Gamang of Gudara on that date in 1947. The main season is February to March, and this time is chosen simply because it is the time of the greatest freedom, when the bins are full of grain, the weather is pleasant and the sago palms give abundant wine.

The Karja is held in the months of February to April; it is 'against custom' to perform it at other times. But this too is not related to any agricultural operations; it comes after the sowing of the mango rice, before the sowing of the main crop; the time is obviously chosen because it is the season of leisure and abundance.

The Guar and Karja rites for the dead certainly assist the crops, for once they have been performed the irritated and resentful shades and ghosts no longer interfere with them. But I very much doubt if any Saora would think of them as entering the soil as fertilizers. All the same, whatever the machinery by which they effect their purpose, there can be no doubt that the dead have a very considerable influence on the crops, and it will be instructive to examine some of the rites which aim at persuading them to use their influence for good, or at the least not to use it for evil.

The erection of menhirs at the Guar, the drawing of ikons in the house and the building of shrines for the dead appear to be parallel activities, aimed at pleasing and flattering the dead, providing them with temporary resting-places and so inducing them to leave the crops alone. In the northern area wooden pillars are often set up for this purpose.

Outside Mandidi village in 1945 there were two carved wooden pillars. One was for Lurup, a former Dhol-behera of the place, and the other for his wife, Mangri. Lurup's memorial was one of the strange 'claw-fingered' pillars, of which the top bends over and projects into a sort of hand with three fingers, characteristic of the area. Lurup died in 1930 and his Guar and Karja ceremonies were regularly performed. Two years later, however, a tiger killed one of the villagers and it was decided to shift the entire settlement to another site, to Kurada. The people lived there for seven years and were reasonably prosperous. Then the crops failed and a tiger killed no fewer than four people. When the shaman was consulted, the ghost of Lurup came upon him and said, 'You deserted me, like the cowards you are, leaving me in the forest alone; you will all be devoured and you will never again get a good harvest until you return to the place where you left me.'

FIG. 27 Wooden pillar at Mandidi
4′ high

The people therefore shifted their village from Kurada back to Mandidi, and sacrificed a buffalo in Lurup's honour. That year his widow Mangri died. The next year there was sufficient rain, but the harvest was poor. Lurup's ghost came again and declared, 'Now my wife is also dead, for I needed her with me in the Under World. Make wooden pillars for us and sacrifice a buffalo for us every year if you want good crops.' The villagers did so, and at once the harvests improved and 'they did not hear so much as the growl of a tiger'.

At Satara too there was a similar pillar outside the village. The story here was that at one time four brothers, sons of the same parents, lived in the village, of whom one was Chief and another a shaman. These four men, Kamru, Jalbang, Mangala, and Pichla, were actually the founders of the village. But they died, one by one in order of their ages, the last of them seven or eight years before I visited the place in 1945. Three years after Pichla's death there was a complete drought. The following year too there was no rain and when the people sowed their seed in their clearings they feared that the harvest would fail again. They called the shaman and the ghosts, it was said, thronged about him, all four brothers 'jostling one another in their eagerness to speak first'. Their instructions were clear: 'Erect a wooden pillar for us and sacrifice a buffalo; then there will be rain and an abundant harvest.' The villagers hastened to do this, and within three hours of the sacrifice down came the rain in torrents. There was a bumper crop, for the dead no longer interfered with its fertility, and to make sure that this happy state of affairs should continue, the people of Satara offer a buffalo before the brothers' pillar every third year.

Among the ceremonies which specifically invite the dead to protect the crops is the Lajap, performed in the fields at the harvesting of the main rice crop, and the Buriyanadur, the festival of small millet, when people grind a little millet into flour, mix it with water and make drawings on the walls of their houses in honour of the ancestors.

The Saoras occasionally sow cotton in their gardens and clearings. To ensure that it grows well, the shaman finds the foot of a buffalo which has previously been sacrificed and grinds some of the bone into flour. He mixes this with rice-flour, makes it into flat cakes, bakes them and offers them to the dead before another old foot used as an altar. After this, it is said, the dead will do nothing to damage the plants.

At Barasingi, in 1948, I witnessed the sacrifice of a goat which had been dedicated to the dead for the benefit of the harvest.

It sometimes happens, I was told, that when an otherwise prosperous farmer gets a run of bad luck in his fields, which the shaman declares to be due to his ancestors' jealousy or indignation, he may dedicate a goat or a pig to the latest of his immediate relations who has died. He does this either in November before reaping or in May-June before sowing. The shaman is summoned and performs the usual preliminaries with rice and wine before an ikon specially drawn for the ancestor to be honoured. Someone brings in the goat and the shaman washes its face, puts turmeric on its forehead, and covers its back with cloths belonging to the dead. He feeds it on rice, and then takes it below the eaves in front of the house, and removes the testes from the scrotum, putting some black soot from the roof into the cavity. If the ghost demands it, he also cuts a little bit of each ear. If a pig is being dedicated, he cuts off a bit of the tail, but he does not do this for a goat. Then he calls the goat or pig by the name of the dead man, and lifts it up as high as the eaves, so that the crops will grow as tall. He promises that it will be sacrificed in three, five or six years if the harvests improve.

The animal is then set free and is treated with great consideration. It must grow fat, for then the harvests will grow fat too. Should the goat butt anyone, it means the ghost is angry and the shaman is called to find out why. The house-people call the goat—and even the pig—by the dead man's name.

Sako Buyya of Barasingi dedicated a pig for his paternal uncle Didiyang and a goat for his father Balima at the same time in 1946. He told me how strange it was to hear the animals about the house being addressed by these familiar names.

On 18 April 1948, Sako invited seven celebrants—two shamans, three Idaimarans and two Idaibois, all of his own family group—for the sacrifice of the goat. They began that evening and sat through the night invoking and conversing with the tutelaries and the dead. In the morning one of the shamans sat on the threshold of the house and had the goat laid on the ground before him. He put a pestle across its body, and the others brought Sako's youngest son, a child of six, who was of course the grandson of the Balima for whom the sacrifice was being offered, to represent the ghost. The shaman dressed the child up in the dead man's turban and feathers and made him sit before him on the other side of the goat. Then he invoked the dead and as he chanted he tapped the goat's body with the pestle. The little boy placed his hand on the pestle and tapped with it too, as a sign that the ghost was pleased. Then the goat was removed and killed, its head being broken with a stone. The shaman put the head before the threshold, stuck an arrow in the ground behind it and tied a thread from the notch of the arrow to a small stone in front of the head. Then he took a bow and a handful of arrows and danced before the head, shooting at it till all his arrows were exhausted.

The ghost of a man killed by a tiger, who in due course turns into Kinnasum, may do a lot of damage to the crops and may carry off the cattle on which so many agricultural operations depend. When a bad harvest is pronounced by the shaman to be due to this, the people promise that if the next year's crop is good they will sacrifice a buffalo and perform the rite called Kinnapur. In token of this they tie up some rice in a little leaf-bundle and hang it up inside the house.

On 25 April 1948 I witnessed this ceremony at Barasingi. The proceedings began in the evening and continued all night and until the late afternoon of the following day. They followed the usual course of such sacrifices, except that when the buffalo was killed the blood was not let out as usual, but retained in the carcass until it was cut up. The shamanin at one point dressed in a red turban with a plume of feathers to represent Kuntikidan, the Lame Tiger, son of Sidibiradi or Sitaboi. She fell forward onto an altar of millet and made the rough marks of tigers' paws with her hands. She then told the story of Sidibiradi's marriage with a tiger, by whom she had seven cubs. Her brothers killed all but one, and that one was lame in one leg, the famous Kuntikidan.[1]

The shamanin was continually in trance, and was 'visited' by a large number of ancestors beside the one who was killed by a tiger; they all promised to see that the crops were good in future.

The dead interfere in a curious and interesting way with the fertility of the sago palms, a thing which naturally causes the Saoras very great concern. Sometimes an ancestor, tired of the bitter wine of the Under World, is exasperated at the sight of his unworthy heirs enjoying themselves at the tree which once was his, and dries up its flow of sap to spite them. Or he may bring a group of friends and drink the wine himself. Sometimes, when an ancestor dies in the Under World, and the other ghosts perform the Guar rite for him, they find they cannot get enough wine for all their guests, and they come to rob the trees here. Occasionally the sap fails on account of Alatuisum (or Dinglatuisum), who is the falling star, the collective name for the ghosts of suicides. Sometimes the trees may be robbed by the ghost of the son of Uyungsum.

If the Saoras find the tip of the spadix of the tree black and sticky like gum, they diagnose the trouble as due to Alatuisum, and take immediate steps to remedy it. I saw the little rite at Tumulu on 8 January 1951. The shaman made a tiny 'umbrella' with a potsherd decorated with stars (see Plate 57) and tied round it small bundles of wine, rice and fish. He offered this, with dried fish and wine, at the foot of the tree, and then climbed up and set a new pot to catch the sap; he said that he expected it to be full by evening.

Fish and crabs, being associated with flowing water, are used in all ceremonies for the palms. The shaman may also smash an egg against the trunk, afterwards attaching the shell to any convenient branch; or he may offer a fowl to Kittung 'so that as the clouds gather and give rain, the palm will give plenty of sap'.

I have already mentioned the belief that the palms may be robbed by the ghost of Uyungsum's son. This goes back to the widely distributed story[2] of the trick played on the Sun by his wife the Moon, which is known to the Saoras in a number of different versions as an explanation of the eclipse. In one version, the Moon has two

[1] For other stories about tiger-gods, see *TMO*, pp. 416f.
[2] See *MMI*, pp. 55 and 74.

sons, the Sun only one. Owing to the heat of the Sun's son, men, animals and the world are scorched and there is danger that everything will be destroyed. To prevent this happening, the Moon hides her own sons in a box and eats a fruit which stains her lips red with the juice. She goes to the Sun and says, 'I have eaten my sons; they were very sweet to the taste.' The Sun then eats his own son. When he discovers the trick played on him by the Moon he is very angry and swears that the ghost of his son will always pursue the Moon and will catch her from time to time.

Another version describes the quarrel as between Gadejangboi Kittung and the great snake Lujadan. Gadejangboi says, 'I am the greatest of all, for I created the whole world.' But Lujadan says, 'No, I am greater, for I can go down to the Under World, devour all the gods and swallow the Sun and Moon.' Gadejangboi loses her temper and picks up an iron rod and heats it. Just as the snake is lifting its head to swallow the Sun and Moon, she strikes it and the flash of the red-hot iron as it breaks the snake's head is the lightning. As it dies, Lujadan says, 'I die, but my ghost shall continue and when it grows hungry it will devour the Sun or the Moon; when it gets thirsty it will go to earth and take wine from the palms.'

When Uyungsum's son's ghost or Lujadan's ghost robs the palms, the Saoras meet the emergency with a special rite called the Guarsal. The theory is that since the trees are being robbed by a restless and unhappy ghost, a Guar ceremony should be offered to content it. Since the full ceremony would be too expensive, however, a fish is used instead of a buffalo and only a little menhir is erected.

I witnessed this ceremony on 16 December 1950 at Boramsingi. A shaman, the owner of the diseased tree and his immediate household, and some of the village elders went to the tree with the usual apparatus of sacrifice. They prepared a hearth, and placed on it a large pot containing rice, turmeric, fish and chillies. In a separate pot they put some dried buffalo meat preserved from another sacrifice. Someone brought a few living fishes in a small tin and the shaman caught one of them and slipped a fine cord through its mouth. As they poured the water over the rice in the pot, the shaman squatted before the hearth and chanted,

From today let no sorcerer, no murderer, no ghost or ancestor approach our tree. Let no medicine-man who might put his medicine on it approach our tree. From today let our wine-pot overflow as the boiling rice in this pot overflows. When we come here tomorrow, let us find our pot full and wine dripping to the ground. Let all be well, let our tree be well.

A boy climbed the tree, examined the empty pot and dry spadix and beat the trunk with his axe to drive away any of the dead who might be there. The shaman made a little altar at the foot and offered wine in leaves of the *Holarrhena antidysenterica*, which when broken exude a milky sap. Presently one of the spectators dragged the fish towards the tree, treating it just as if it was a buffalo, urging it along with a stick; he was followed by another man with an axe. Now the shaman squatted before the altar and called on many gods and ghosts by name:

Today we call you, gods who go along the path, gods who make pits in the middle of the paths, gods who put thorns in paths: come all of you. We call you, ghosts of the Under World, ghosts of the sky, ghost who devours the Sun and Moon, ghost of the snake, ghost who falls as a star from the sky: come all of you. Today we give you rice and wine to eat. Today we give you a buffalo. Accept our offerings and let the sap of this tree flow well.

Then the fish-buffalo was placed before the altar, and the man with the axe raised it high in the air and struck at the fish with great violence, cutting it in half. The others present jumped to their feet and danced round, shouting and whistling. Two men tied a bit of the fish to a pole, put it over their shoulders and went staggering along (as if they were carrying a great load of meat) and put it in the rice-pot. Then the shaman resumed his chant:

Today we have given you a buffalo. You have had the head, the blood. From today have pity, let the sap flow freely. Yours is our body, our soul, all that we have. If you will accept our sacrifice, we give it freely and happily. You teach us wisdom and whatever you ask we will give. If you say, 'This is our tree, our sap', even then we will beg you for it. After today, let all our pots overflow with wine.

Then, led by the shaman, the whole party went down one of the paths leading out of the village and at a convenient spot set up a small stone beside it. The shaman cleaned the ground, rubbed turmeric and water on the stone, set out the usual leaf-cups, rice-baskets, wine-pot and a new cloth for the dead beside it. Then he squatted before it and chanted:

Come Uyungsum, come Angaiboi, come all you stars, Sun, Moon and stars, come. Come spirits and ghosts of the Under World, come spirits of trees and hills, come and hearken. Gods of the path, gods of streams, gods of the fields, gods who live in aeroplanes, come and persuade the ghosts not to rob our trees.

You magic-workers who pass by, you who see us doing Guar, may you forget your evil charms. May your trees dry instead of ours. Let not the passers-by say, 'It is a shame for those people that their tree dried up; they have not done their duty to the dead.' Let them forget what we are doing, let them not speak of it. If they do speak, let no one take any notice.

O ghosts, ghost who devours the Sun and Moon, ghost of the snake, ghosts of those who fell from trees, ghosts of men killed by tigers, ghosts of those bitten by snakes in the forest, do not be jealous of us, thinking that we get more to drink than you did. O dead, do not trouble us with your jealousy because our pots overflow with wine.

The owner of the tree, sitting by, began to weep, crying on the dead members of his family by name:

O father, O mother, O brothers, why did the ghost rob my tree? Where shall I go? Where shall I get anything to drink if even the ghosts rob me? But now I have planted a stone, I have given you a cloth. Let all be well after today.

The ceremony ended with a very jolly impromptu dance, with much shouting, laughter and waving of arms to suggest the state of intoxication that the new sap would induce, and when the company had eaten their food they returned to the village.

I attended an entirely different rite at Tumulu on 12 May 1948. Here there was a rather special date palm belonging to a man called Gopi. Round it he had planted a hedge of tall cacti which made a pleasant little enclosure inside which people could sit round on stone seats to drink the tree's gift of exhilarating wine. This date palm had been planted long before by Gopi's father, Sitno, and after Sitno's death the tree passed to his son. There was a good flow at first, but after a time it dried up, and the shaman declared that Sitno's ghost was drinking the sap with the help of a swarm of butterflies. The sacrifice to persuade Sitno's ghost to leave the tree alone was simple enough. It was held at night, for in this village it was said that Uyungsum, the Sun, must not witness ceremonies for palm trees. The shaman collected a number of crabs, killed and cooked them and then boiled some rice in the water in which the crabs had been cooked.

He prepared a dish of pulse with turmeric and offered a little of the cooked food to the tree. He then took some of it along a path leading out of the village to tempt the ghost away.

The following morning, Gopi lit a fire at the foot of the tree to drive away the butterflies which were still hovering in the branches.

The description of these ceremonies will sufficiently illustrate how closely the Saoras associate the fertility of their crops and trees, the regularity of the rainfall, and even human conception itself, with the ancestors and shades.

But they seem to think always in terms of personal relations; they have long forgotten, or have re-interpreted, any belief in 'soul-matter' which, on leaving the body, might pass into the soil and fertilize it. In general too the help given by the dead is negative in character; if they are pleased, they let the crops alone, and protect them against alien invaders of family property.

At the same time, the application of sacrificial blood to seed, the use of water on the cremation-ground, and the tradition that in former times the Saoras used to get pieces of human flesh from the Konds to plant in their fields, may indicate that a faith in soul-matter did once exist. Hutton has pointed out that the conception of the desirability of releasing soul-matter to fertilize the earth has often been interpreted later as the placation or propitiation of an earth deity, but that 'this must be regarded as a sophisticated justification of a practice the true meaning of which has become obscure or been forgotten',[1] and this may well be true in the Saora context.

III. *The Methods of Saora Cultivation*

A BRIEF account of Saora methods of cultivation will help to clarify the means by which the crops are protected by ritual acts. The Saoras have three kinds of cultivation—on their terraces, in the swiddens on the hill-sides and in the little gardens near their houses.

The carefully-fenced gardens are greatly treasured, for here is grown tobacco, maize, pumpkins, cucumbers and sometimes ginger; they are carefully manured with refuse from the house. Manure is also regularly collected in great heaps and spread on the terraced fields.

These terraces are works of no small engineering skill. Built right up the beds of mountain streams, rising for many hundreds of feet

[1] Hutton, *Caste*, p. 212.

from the depths of the valleys to the hill-tops, they occupy every inch of ground available; sometimes only a few feet broad, they creep round the hillsides. The drop from terrace to terrace may be as deep as fifteen feet, yet so carefully are the stone facings built up and so flat are the platforms that no soil is carried over by the water that trickles from level to level down to the plains below. Ingenious methods of irrigation have been devised to control the flooding of the fields.

The classic area of Saora terracing is in the highlands above Pottasingi on one side and Serango on the other. As one goes north into Peddakimidi and Pinnakimidi, the terracing becomes casual and rather slack; it is not supported by stone walls and the people are obviously more interested in their swiddens. Rice is the main crop

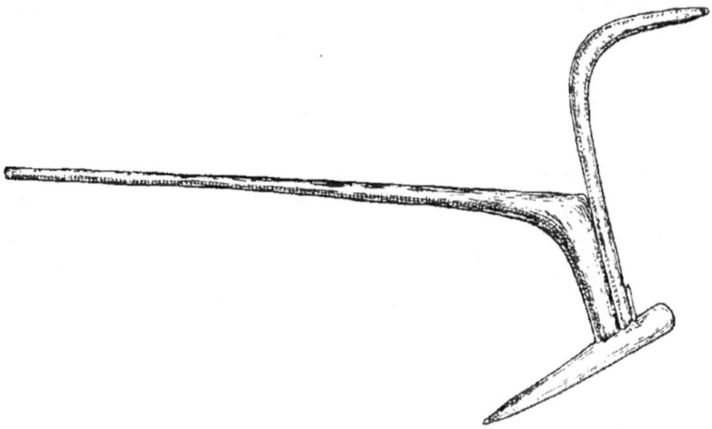

FIG. 28 Saora plough

sown on the terraces and the plough is used even on the narrowest of them. At the end of the season, the threshing-floors are often made on the terraces themselves. Sometimes even villages are built on old terraces and the streets rise one above the other.

The third type of Saora cultivation is shifting-, or as I prefer to call it, axe-cultivation. This is not so important to the Saora as *bewar* is to the Baiga or *penda* to the Maria. The Saoras have no taboo on the use of cattle and the plough, and they use their axes, not for their main crop of rice, but for the lesser harvests of pulses, millets and maize. Except in Peddakimidi, they do not grow beans in their clearings and so do not girdle trees or kill them by heaping combustible matter round them before firing so that the dead trunks may serve as bean-stalks. Nor do they plough over their clearings in Bhuiya fashion.

In the densely populated Parlakimidi and Koraput hills, however, the rotation is now far too short. The Saoras use their swiddens for two and sometimes even for three years, but return after a rest of only five or six years, whereas fifteen is the very minimum required. It is said that the Saoras prefer the tops of the hills to the lower slopes, a steep rather than a gentle gradient, and for some reason they like cultivating in the neighbourhood of rocks. The swiddens are very widely scattered, for the Saoras do not make their villages the centre of their cultivation. A swidden may be miles from a man's home, and during the season when crops have to be guarded, many Saoras spend all the time on the hillsides, living in temporary field-huts, and the villages are almost deserted.

The Saoras, unlike the Baigas, are rather inarticulate about their axe-cultivation; my impression is that it has become an economic rather than a cultural activity. They cling to it partly because of the excellent crops it gives, and partly because they believe it is the one thing of which the Doms and Oriyas will be unable to rob them. Beyond a tradition, common to many tribes, that the Supreme Being taught them how to do it, there is little evidence of any specifically religious attachment to the practice.

The Saoras do not grow wheat, and their main interest and source of profit is the rice crop, although since there is no Harvest Festival for it, it may be a comparatively modern innovation in Saora life. Many, but by no means all, Saoras raise two crops in the year, the main sowing in June, and a subsidiary sowing, the so-called 'mango rice' in January. The first is reaped in November and the second in June just before the rains. The second crop gives just enough to carry the people through the difficult period of the rains, while the main crops are ripening.

Both men and women plough the terraces and the great irrigated fields in the valleys. Sometimes they prepare small nurseries, and when the seedlings are big enough they pull them up and plant them out in little bundles some six inches apart. Sometimes they moisten the seeds and sow them broadcast. Elaborate irrigation canals enable them to control the quantity of water standing in the fields. The boundaries of the fields and walls of the canals are regarded as sacred, and it is a serious matter (though not actually taboo) for anyone to break them down. Once the seedlings are established, the task of weeding begins; the embankments have to be repaired and cleaned; and as the harvests ripen, the fields have to be guarded against the attacks of wild animals and birds. In early November the crop is usually ready for reaping. The Saoras sacrifice a fowl, cut a few sheaves and take them home, and then gradually reap the entire harvest.

Work in the forest-clearings is spiritually more dangerous than in the fields, for hill-gods are notoriously touchy about their rights and may easily be insulted. There are therefore more ceremonies attached to the swiddens. These clearings are regarded like fields, as private property (though the Saoras have actually no right to them at all), and they are bought and sold. If a man does not need all his holding, he shares it with someone and takes a share of the produce. When new swiddens are to be made, the elders agree on how the area is to be divided; it is always done by strips running up and down a hill, never across it. A man gets a right over a particular strip; when he wants to return after shifting elsewhere, he must return to that strip and no other. If a widow is left without sons to support her, the whole village co-operates to clear and cultivate the strips which she inherits.

Before any clearings are made a shaman performs the Kurrualpur, a small ceremony which involves the offering of a pig or a fowl to Labosum and the gods of the hillside 'so that the trees will not fall on anyone and the axes will not slip'. The first tree in a swidden should be cut by a lusty unmarried youth 'who will not tire easily; for if he wearies in cutting the tree, the crops too will grow weary'.

Men naturally carry the heavy burden of cutting the larger trees and creepers, but women and even children assist in clearing the undergrowth. In late April and May when the felled material has dried, firing begins. It is not preceded by any ceremony, and any fire may be used. The ashes are not distributed over the swidden, and charred stumps of trees are left as they are for the following year.

Shortly before the rains, but always after the seed has been consecrated by the Jammolpur ceremony, the Saoras proceed to sow. They usually sow pulses and beans first, dibbling holes for them and dropping the two seeds together. For red gram, they say, is a woman and the bean is a man; the man gets ready first, and the woman, jealous, tries to catch him up. After this the Saoras often sow castor seeds, and when these have sprouted, they sow all the other seeds mixed together, small and large millets, mountain rice, and anything else they have, scattering them broadcast and then working the soil over them with their hoes.

Weeding is a heavy business in the fertile clearings and the task of guarding the ripening crops from monkeys and birds demands constant watchfulness. Many Saoras make a second home in the swidden. The little huts they build are woodland versions of the houses in the villages, constructed on the same plan and roughly furnished. They are often placed in the most picturesque surroundings, on the top of a rock, in a tree, on the edge of a mountain with a wonderful view of hill and forest below. After dark the hillsides are dotted with the fires of the watchers and the throb of drums and the sweet music of the flute is heard.

In September the first crops are ready. The Saoras cut *Panicum miliare* and other small millets with a knife, removing only the ears, which they take home and thresh indoors with their feet. In November other crops are ready. The people reap the ears of *Eleusine corocana* with knives and pile them up on little platforms. In December falls the great Harvest Festival of the red gram; when this is over the Saoras reap the gram by pulling the pods off the shrubs into baskets. They dry them and thresh them with sticks. About the same time, they cut the stalks of *Zea mays* at the bottom and when they have brought them down they remove the cobs.

Every two or three years the Saoras sow turmeric in part of a swidden. They sometimes put down plantains and roots in a third year. They also sow the oilseed *Guizotia abyssinica* and its yellow flowers illuminate the hillsides in their season.

For the Saoras cultivation is something more than just a means of getting food to eat. It is a whole way of life. It is arduous, but it is happy. It unites an entire family in a single task. The keen mountain air, the glory of the scenery, the open spaces of the sky are compensations for the anxiety, the weariness and the danger of the task.

IV. *The Consecration of Seed*

A VERY important event in the Saoras' agricultural year is the ceremonial 'taking out of the seed' from the store-bins for sowing shortly before the rains. The chief elements of this ceremony are the drawing of a special ikon featuring fertility symbols (see Figs. 34-7), sacrifice and the recital of a long story which gives the mythological origin and background of the rite.

I attended the Jammolpur, as it is called, at Tumulu on 13 May 1950.

The ikon was made on the wall of the house near the ground and under the loft on which stood massive grain-bins. The shaman and a lay assistant made an altar with the dedicated pot, which had been hanging above the ikon, and a basket of rice-seed, to which all the members of the family had contributed. This rite may be performed in all the houses of a village, but more commonly is done in the home of the wealthiest and most important of a family on behalf of all its members. The shaman placed a pot of liquor on the altar and before and round it little baskets containing samples of all the kinds of seed which were to be sown. He set out leaves and leaf-cups in rows for the dead and other spirits.

The two officiants sat before the altar and called on the spirits to attend and share the feast. Then the shaman, holding a pot of liquor in his right hand, recited the first part of the story of Jemra Kittung and Sidibiradi.

Long ago there were an old man and woman who had nine sons and one daughter. The daughter's name was Sidibiradi and she was the youngest of the family and very beautiful. The old man was rich with many cattle and fields and a store of gold and silver. One day he called his nine sons and said, 'I have decided to divide my wealth while I am still alive, for if I leave you to divide it after my death you will quarrel.' When the nine boys heard this, they went and told their mother. She said, 'It is good that you boys should divide the property, but what will Sidibiradi get?' They said, 'Father said nothing about her.' The mother said, 'Go back and ask him.' They went to him and he said, 'She will get nothing at present, but when somebody comes to take her away and we drink his liquor, I will give whatever pleases me. For this is our ancient custom.' When the boys repeated this to their mother, she replied, 'What your father says is right.'

A few days after this, Jemra Kittung came with a pot of wine to betroth the girl. He sat down on the veranda of the house and when the old people and the nine sons and the nine sons' wives had assembled, he said, 'I hear that a flower has blossomed in your garden, and the scent has come to our nostrils even far away, for it is very sweet.' The old man said, 'Who knows if the flower is willing to be plucked?' Then Jemra said, 'No, I do not want flowers. I have burnt my hand and I want a spoon to eat with.' The old man replied, 'Is this a sahib's house that we should eat with spoons?' Then Jemra spoke plainly and said, 'I have brought betrothal-wine; will you drink it or not?' The old man said, 'What is the use of asking us? Ask Sidibiradi, and if she is agreeable, then we will drink it.' The mother went in and asked the girl who was hiding under the loft and she said, 'Yes, drink the wine.' So they all sat round together with some of the neighbours, and the Chief came in, and they drank the wine. After that Jemra Kittung went home.

The next time that Jemra Kittung was due to visit the house with a pot of wine, he covered himself with soot and white clay so that he looked like a leper, and he put on tattered clothes. So he came and sat down on the veranda. The nine brothers and their wives asked him, 'Who are you?' He replied, 'I have been betrothed to your sister. Now I am here to marry her.' They were frightened at this, and called Sidibiradi, and when she saw the dirty beggar on the veranda she was indignant and said to him, 'My betrothed is rich and handsome. He is nothing like you.' But Jemra Kittung said, 'No, I am your betrothed.' But the girl cried, '*Thu thu chi chi!* Get out of my house,' and she herself pulled him to his feet and pushed him out.

When Jemra got home he went to his mother, all covered with clay and soot as he was, and said, 'I went to fetch my wife, but she said "*Thu thu chi chi!*" and drove me away.' His mother said, 'You must be mad. Have a good wash and make yourself look nice, and then go and get her.'

So after a few days Jemra Kittung dressed himself smartly but this time he took only a very small pot of wine to his betrothed's house. The nine brothers and their wives greeted him and he said, 'I have come to fetch my bride.' The old man and woman said, 'Where is your wine?' Jemra said, 'Here it is,' and showed them the little pot. They were annoyed and exclaimed, 'What nonsense is this? The wine in such a little pot will not even moisten our lips.' Jemra replied, 'Call everyone in the village and to each give at least one drop. I am a poor man and I could not get any more.' The parents whispered to each other, 'We have agreed to give this man our daughter and we cannot now refuse.' So the father sent out for a large quantity of wine at his own cost and invited the neighbours to the wedding.

When they had all assembled, Jemra Kittung put his little pot in the middle and invited them to drink. But however often they dipped the gourd into the pot it was never emptied and for three days the people drank their fill. When they saw this, they realized that a god was among them.

It was now time for the girl to go with her husband to his house and the mother said, 'What shall we give our daughter to take with her?' The boys replied, 'The pulse is growing in the clearings, the rice is growing in the fields; we have nothing in our store to give.' So they sent the poor girl away with nothing.

But the following day, when the brothers went to their fields and clearings, they found that their entire crop was destroyed.

At this point the shaman broke off his narrative. His assistant handed him a fowl and he made it eat a few grains of every kind of seed on the altar, washed its feet and cut its throat over a pot. He let a few drops of blood fall on the altar, on the different seeds and on the threshold of the house. A woman took the fowl away to cook it.

Then the shaman, again taking the gourd of wine in his hand, began to chant, addressing Jammolsum and Sidibiradi.

At the Mango Festival we sowed our seed in our clearings. Perhaps you suspected that we would give you nothing, that we had forgotten you. But we did not forget. As our ancestors worshipped Ramma-Bimma in the old days, so do we worship you today. If we have forgotten any of your relatives, if we have not put leaf-cups for them, do not be angry and spoil the harvest for a little mistake. We greet you; we offer you every kind of seed.

You are blood-drinkers, so we offer you blood. Perhaps you have been looking up at our bins in the loft, intending to destroy them, but we beg you to leave them alone. One year, it is true, we did not give you sacrifice, and you destroyed our crops, you carried away our seed, you killed our cattle, you ruined our fields. But this year we are giving you everything you can possibly want. Let the seeds for field and clearing be fertile.

The shaman scattered wine over the altar and the seeds, and continued for some time to call on the spirits, being careful to recite the names of every ancestor he could remember. Then he continued his account of Jemra Kittung.

In due time Sidibiradi bore a son. After a month she said to her husband, 'I have not seen my parents and brothers for a long time. Let us go to their house. Perhaps now at last they will give me a present.' Jemra agreed and they both dirtied themselves and dressed in filthy rags so as to look like beggars. Sidibiradi tied the baby to her back in a sling and they went to her mother's house.

Now all the seed belonging to the family was stored in large bins in the youngest brother's house. When Sidibiradi arrived, it was to this house that she went and sat down to rest on the veranda. No one was there. All the members of the family were out working in their clearings. When the brothers returned, each went to his own house. The youngest brother, as he approached, saw a beggar woman sitting on his veranda and asked her who she was and why she had come. She did not say anything, but she changed her appearance, and he saw that it was his sister. He said, 'There are nine of us brothers; why do you choose my veranda to sit on? You must go to your eldest brother for your food.'

By now the whole family had gathered round, and the eldest brother took his sister and her husband to his house for dinner. The next day the second brother entertained them, and so on day by day, brother after brother, until it was the youngest brother's turn. When the visitors sat down in his house and he put their food before them, they did not eat it, but looked up to the loft where the seed was stored. The youngest brother said, 'Sister, why do you not eat? What are you looking at?' Sidibiradi said, 'I have already filled my belly and need no more. I am now remembering how I used to work here when I was a little girl. That is why I am looking up at the store.'

The next day the brothers said to each other, 'Our sister and her husband are eating our food. They ought to do a little work for us in the fields. We men will work in the rice-fields and the women will go to the clearings.' They brought every kind of seed out of the store and said to Sidibiradi, 'Take the seed and put the rice in the fields and pulses and millets in the clearings.' They told Jemra to drive the cattle out into the fields.

Sidibiradi said to her brothers, 'But what are you going to do? You must come and work as well.' The brothers said, 'We will drink a little and smoke a little, and then we will follow you. Our wives will cook the midday meal and will bring it to us. But you two go ahead.' Sidibiradi said, 'No, no, we must all go together.' But they took no notice of her.

So Sidibiradi and her husband went out and when they came to the fields, Jemra Kittung tied the cattle to the ploughs and turned them into clay. Sidibiradi caught grubs and fish and insects and sowed them in the field. They carried the seed to their own house.

Meanwhile the nine brothers sat at home drinking until they were drunk, and only then did they go to the fields. Everything looked dark, and they saw that their ploughs and cattle had turned into clay. When they touched them, the cattle fell to pieces. They sat down and wept.

As they were weeping, their wives arrived with the midday meal. They thought that their drunken husbands were singing and said, 'What are you singing like that for?' The brothers were annoyed and said, 'We are weeping and you ask why we are singing! Look what has happened to our ploughs and cattle.' The wives replied, 'What will be, will be. Go home and get some more seed and at least we will sow it in our clearings.' But when they reached home, they found that there was no seed left in their bins.

They went and told their mother and she said, 'Go to a shaman and seek his help.' The brothers went to find a shaman and on the way they saw a man ploughing in his field and asked him, 'Friend, have you seen anywhere the house of a shaman?' The man replied,

'I am a peasant who ploughs and sows. What should I know of shamans?' The brothers cursed him saying, 'Well, grubs will destroy your crop and as you work you will hurt your feet with thorns and stones, and unless you go to a shaman, nothing will go well with you.'

A little further on they saw a woman weeding in her field and asked her, 'Mother, have you seen anywhere the house of a shaman?' The woman replied, 'I am a woman weeding in her field. What should I know of shamans?' The brothers cursed her saying, 'Well, weeds will choke your field and weevils will destroy your crop, and unless you go to a shaman, nothing will go well with you.'

They went on their way and presently they met a Dom selling tobacco and asked him, 'Friend, have you seen anywhere the house of a shaman?' The Dom replied, 'I am a merchant selling tobacco. What should I know of shamans?' The brothers said, 'At least give us a little tobacco.' But he refused. The brothers cursed him saying, 'Go your way and try to sell your tobacco. No one will buy it and your belly will never be filled.' Ever since the Doms have taken their revenge on the Saoras by cheating them in every bargain.

The brothers continued on their search and next they met an old woman spinning yarn and asked her, 'Mother, have you seen anywhere the house of a shaman?' She said, 'I am an old woman spinning yarn. What should I know of shamans?' The brothers cursed her saying, 'Well, you will spin for a month yet you will not have enough yarn to cover your privates.'

They went on their way and passed a girl engaged in husking grain and asked her, 'Girl, have you seen anywhere the house of a shaman?' The girl replied, 'I am a girl husking grain. What should I know of shamans?' The brothers cursed her saying, 'Well, may you fall asleep over your work, and while you sleep, may the pigs and fowls devour your grain.'

By now the brothers had reached the forest and here they met a porcupine. It greeted them saying, 'O sister's sons, where are you going?' They answered, 'O father-in-law, we are in great trouble and we are searching for a shaman to help us.' 'But I myself am a shaman,' replied the porcupine. With this it took them to its house and they found it furnished with silver and gold chairs and tables. Uyungsum was sitting there with the tutelaries, proud as landlords. The porcupine did not give the brothers chairs, but let them sit on the floor. Then it said to its wife, 'Prepare my bath, for I am going to do Tetepur.'

The porcupine had its bath and then put rice in a winnowing-fan and tested it. It passed into trance and Jemra Kittung and Sidibiradi came upon it and Jemra Kittung said, 'I came to fetch my bride and you drove me away.' Sidibiradi said, 'You gave me no presents at my wedding; that is why I have now taken everything you have.' The brothers wept when they heard this and asked what they should do. The porcupine said, 'Make an ikon on the wall of your house,

44. Saora youth loads his gun at a Lajap ceremony

45. Men dancing on the hillside at Talasingi

each of you, and sacrifice a goat and a pig before it and you will recover all that you have lost.'

The nine brothers returned home, and did what the porcupine had said and at once everything that they had lost was restored to them.

This cautionary tale not only underlines the importance of the shaman, but emphasizes the danger of being stingy in relation to the gods. 'This is why,' concluded the shaman, 'we do the Jammolpur every year, for unless Jammolsum, the god of seed, protects us, Jemra Kittung and Sidibiradi may rob us also.'

By the time the story was finished, the food was ready and the shaman offered cooked rice and meat in each of the leaf-cups before the altar. The family feasted, and then a little of the consecrated seed was distributed to each member to mix with the seed he was going to sow. New seed was placed in the pot hanging before the ikon. The women dipped their fingers in rice-water and made many little dabs, of no special pattern, on the doors and walls.

Meanwhile in a neighbouring house a secret ceremony was being performed for Tundrublutsum, a very touchy god. It is taboo for anyone except the actual householder and the shaman to be present, and when I tried to enter, the door was politely but firmly shut in my face. For if anyone, I was told, drinks any of this god's wine he gets very angry and may do irreparable damage. He can make the fields 'barren as a childless woman' if he is displeased. His pot is hung apart from the others and no ikon is made for him, but otherwise his ceremony closely resembles the usual Jammolpur; samples of seed are offered and blood is sprinkled over them.

The Jammolpur is sometimes performed for Surenda Kittung, who is Jemra's son. It is then called Surendapur, and a different story, which I have not heard, is recited.

V. *The Protection of the Plants*

FROM the time of the Jammolpur, when they carry out the consecrated seed to their fields and clearings, the Saoras watch over them with loving, anxious care. For there is now a long struggle with their unseen enemies, and all the time the plants are growing they perform minor rituals to protect them and stimulate their fertility.

There is, for example, a little rite called Purred, when a fowl is offered to Labosum and Barusum to keep the green parrots away from the ripening ears. At the time of weeding, in the northern area, a buffalo is sacrificed to 'the red star', if the plants show signs of failing. This is the Sukrapur, for which several villages combine. The buffalo's blood is mixed with rice and each householder puts a little in his fields, on his grain-bins and on the roof of his house.

To protect the rice from weevils, there is a rite called Jatrapur in honour of Labosum. Should the paddy stalks turn yellow, the Saoras pull up a handful of them, draw an ikon for Labosum, and tie the stalks in front of it. The shaman plays his *kurānrājan* and sacrifices a fowl. This is called the Orendapur; it is only done when necessary; it is not an annual sacrifice. Later, an offering may be made to Uyungsum, the Sun, if the ears of rice begin to dry, 'for Uyungsum drinks the milk of the tender white grain and exhausts it'.

Fawcett speaks of a sacrifice offered to Sattirasum in the paddy fields round Kehalakot. A stick of ebony 'about five or six feet long, is stuck in the ground, and the upper end is sharpened to a point; on the upper point is impaled a live young pig or a live fowl, and over it an inverted earthen pot daubed over with white rings. The sacrificed pig or fowl is left there and never eaten'.[1] I have heard of this sacrifice, which is called Sattirapur, being offered in the hill clearings; the pig's blood is caught and mixed with rice and then scattered over the growing plants.

I have never witnessed the impaling of a live animal, but a rather similar sacrifice is the Lambapur, which is offered for the success of the red gram crop; this involves the killing of a pig and the impaling of its decapitated head on an ebony pole. At the Lambapur a small platform is made of the branches of the *Phyllanthus emblica* tree; this is laden with small stones until it sags—the idea is, of course, that the platforms on which the grain-bins are supported should also sag under the burden of a splendid crop. Crabs are offered on this platform so that the pods of pulse will be long as a crab's legs.[2]

I was present at a Lambapur celebration on 3 December 1950, at Ladde. This ceremony is performed not only to protect the ripening pulse harvest, but also on behalf of the whole village or of a

[1] Fawcett, pp. 259f. Whitehead notes that 'the impaling of live pigs is practised in the Telugu country'.—Madras Museum Bulletins, vol. III, p. 136; H. Whitehead, *The Village Gods of South India* (Calcutta, 1916), pp. 57f.

[2] The Uraons put live crabs into a fire, and as they crackle in the heat and their legs stiffen, they exclaim, 'May the pulses burst from their pods as the crabs burst in the fire, and may the pods resemble their stiffened legs'.—S. C. Roy, *Oraon Religion and Customs* (Ranchi, 1928), p. 211.

particular family inside it to stop the dead, gods, or sorcerer's familiars damaging the crops or home. A pig is offered on behalf of the whole community, and after that each family repeats the rite with crabs in its own clearing. At Ladde the Lambapur was always celebrated on a path leading out of the village to the north, because this is the direction of the Kond country, the traditional home of evil magic.

After the usual preliminaries in the priest's house, the priest, a shaman and representatives of every household went in procession along the path. The priest set up, in the middle of the path, a pointed pole of ebony which was ringed at seven equal intervals down its length. He put leaves and cups before it and offered rice and wine, calling on all the spirits of the surrounding villages and hills.

> O gods and ghosts! O Tonaisum of Ollenga, Boramsingi, Singjangring, and Kittim! Come all of you, for we are giving you a special feast today. Do not say afterwards that we did not invite you. Do not trouble us or visit our village. Eat your feast and then go dancing away. You go flying, flying to see the whole countryside; you know everything; we salute you. Eat happily and go away. Then we your children too will be happy.

Then the priest tied a folded leaf to the pole. Someone killed the pig by smashing it on the ground; he cut off the head and fixed it on the pointed spike. Both leaf and head were signs to the sky-gods Uyungsum and Ramma-Bimma. They skinned, cut up and cooked the pig, with plenty of rice, and offered five leaf-cups of cooked food; in two of these there was only rice, in three there was meat and rice. The vegetarian offerings were for the female spirits who, like Saora women, do not eat pork. The priest chanted,

> Your feast is ready; come and take it and go away. Like a monkey I salute you. As a monkey jumps from branch to branch in search of fruit, so I have sought you spirits in every tree and branch and leaf. See that the harvest of our gram is good. See that no evil magic enters our village. Let the pods of gram be fat as the legs of crabs. Come all of you and eat.

From time to time, and at the end of the proceedings, the priest put one of his knuckles in his mouth and made a loud piercing whistle to drive away the workers of black magic.

In addition to these formal ceremonies, the fields are sometimes —but not often—protected by material charms. The inverted pot, marked with various patterns, placed over a pole, is an obvious borrowing from popular Hinduism. In the tobacco-patches, serrated poles, over which rings have been slipped, are erected to keep away thieves; it is believed that if a thief approaches such a pole he will fall ill. If the pole is of ebony he will go blind for the time being: everything will appear black as the wood itself. At Bodo Okhra I saw poles with bunches of leaf-pipes attached—these were mute appeals to the Sun to witness, and in one field there was a mirror, the 'eye' of which, I was told, would detect the presence of a human or unseen thief.[1]

A straw monkey (not a stuffed monkey, but a doll made of cloth and straw) may be put among the tobacco plants to keep away thieves and rats. At Burda, a shaman put 'sorcery-medicine' in such a monkey and set it up before dawn in the name of Uyungsum. He explained that if anyone were to steal his tobacco, he would get a cough and find it difficult to breathe when he tried to smoke it.

FIG. 29 Straw monkey for protection of tobacco-patch

The pubic hairs may be used to protect a forest-clearing. If, for example, a Saora cuts down a big tree, he may pull out one of his hairs as it is falling and place it on the stump saying, 'Go, eat my hairs!' This will drive away any god who may have been living on the tree and who, angry at the loss of his home, may do mischief to the crops.

VI. *The Harvest Festivals*

A FINAL discipline controls the farmer eager to enjoy the fruits of his toil. It is strictly taboo for anyone to eat part of a crop until ceremonies have been performed by the elders on behalf of the whole village. The enjoyment of the harvest must never degenerate into a merely individual triumph over nature; the gift of Mother Earth is a corporate thing, given to everyone, and all must accept it together and even, to some extent, share alike.

The Harvest Festivals further acknowledge in a most emphatic way the gods as the real landlords of the fields and clearings, to

[1] It is possible, however, that the real apotropaic effect of such mirror-magic is based on its flashing and dazzling effects. See W. L. Hildburgh, 'Indeterminability and Confusion as Apotropaic Elements', *Folk-Lore*, vol. XL (1944), p. 148.

whom tribute must be paid. They admit the sovereignty of the gods over men, who must not venture to eat first and thus turn the new food into 'leavings'.

Not all crops have these festivals. Those which have been introduced in comparatively modern times, such as the finer varieties of rice, several kinds of gram (horse, black and Bengal), most vegetables and, curiously enough, tobacco have no festivals and no taboos on their use, though it is considered wise to make a token offering to the gods and ancestors before eating any new thing.

But the festivals for the other crops come to nearly a dozen and, distributed as they are throughout the year, provide the people with pleasant holidays.

Most of the festivals follow the same lines. The priest or a leading shaman or shamanin celebrates the rites privately in his own house and then in his field or clearing. Then each household observes the festival at home and in the field, and finally the entire village has a communal celebration with dances, sacrifice and a great feast. It is on these occasions that the *sadru*-shrines are mostly used. Sacrifice is made for the whole village in one or other of the popular shrines and often in one for Tangorbasum outside. Then each family sacrifices in the private shrines that have been erected for their ancestors. For on these occasions the dead come to share the happiness of the living and must on no account be neglected.

Once a festival is over, the taboo on the use of the crop concerned is lifted, and the people go to reap and eat at will. But there are no fixed dates for the festivals, and the feasts shift according to the weather and the inspirations of the shamans, and the times vary greatly from village to village. When, as often happens, a feast is delayed, the people are allowed to reap the crop, but they must not eat any of it.

The visitor who attends one of these festivals may find it difficult to follow the programme of events, for it is continually interrupted by proceedings irrelevant to their main purpose. A father may choose this moment for the dedication of his daughter as a shamanin; sick people may decide to consult the already excited shamans for diagnosis of their maladies; the ancestors are always breaking in, and their coming affords a convenient opportunity to consult them about domestic and other matters. The idea seems to be that since in any case there is a considerable assembly of beings from the Under

World at these festivals, it is as well to take advantage of their presence.

The Harvest Festivals are a delight and comfort to the hard-working anxious farmer. Everyone is pleased and at his best. Girls put on clean clothes and stick flowers in their hair; boys wind gay-coloured turbans round their heads and decorate them with plumes of feathers. The shrines look pretty with their decorations of leaves and bunches of fresh pulse or mangoes. It is pleasant to have a change of diet—fresh roasted pulse, new roots and sweet potatoes, the long-desired mango.

And many deeply-rooted religious needs are satisfied. The gods are honoured and flattered by being given the first fruits of their land. The dead are remembered at every shrine. Disease is often removed from the village by some kind of scapegoat. Prayers for the future are offered and the people hope that they have been heard. The beloved tribal community is bound together once more by its attachment to a common task in which living and dead, human and divine, all have a share.

I will now describe the festivals one by one, taking them for convenience in alphabetical order.

ABBANADUR

In April or early May, the *Bassia latifolia* trees are covered with fresh copper-red leaves and the flowers begin to open. Soon the long, cream-coloured corollas begin to fall and are eagerly sought after by men and animals. But before they can be eaten or distilled into spirit, the Abbanadur must be observed. In some villages, the custom is for the priest or shaman to rise before dawn and go alone to collect the corollas. When he comes to one of the trees, he throws stones at it until a few drops of the milky sap flow from a damaged branch. It is believed that this will cause the tree to flower more abundantly. The shaman collects as much as he can carry home; he dries the corollas for two days in the sun and then puts them in a pot with a little fruit from the marking-nut tree. After five or six days he takes the pot to a home distillery in the bed of a stream and, after offering a fowl to the dead, he distils it. When the spirit is ready he takes it to the tree at which he threw his stones and offers an egg and some rice, with a few drops of the spirit, before it, and drinks some of it himself. After this everyone is free to distil and drink. In villages where there is a cult of Jakersum, the sacrifice is made specially for him.

The *Bassia latifolia* varies greatly in the abundance of its flowers, but one or two good crops may be expected every three years. Sometimes the flowers are destroyed by hail before they have matured. The tree is liable to attacks from the *loranthus* parasite. This variability gives rise to the belief that the tree is specially sensitive to interference from the unseen world, and especially from the dead, who are jealous of their descendants getting the good liquor of which they themselves are deprived. If some of the corollas rot and begin to stink, the shaman should offer a black fowl to the ancestors in order to save the rest of the crop.

BURIYANADUR

This festival is held in August for the *Panicum italicum* and other small millets. It follows the usual lines, except that in some villages every householder makes a small ikon for the dead with flour made from the new grain.

ENLUDANADUR

This festival, held towards the end of the rains for the new cucumbers (*Cucumis sativus*), does not seem to be observed by the Koraput Saoras.

GANUGAYANADUR

This is essentially for the sweet potato, *Dioscorea alata*, but it is usually extended to cover all kinds of wild roots. It is observed in July and the villagers bring the potatoes and roots to the house of the priest or shaman, with rice, in little baskets. The shaman's wife cooks them and the shaman offers the cooked food to the gods and the dead and, after eating some himself, announces that henceforward everyone is free to dig for roots or potatoes as he will.

KONDEMANADUR

This is the festival of the coarse *kondem* rice (called *kondemmulu* in Telugu), which is supposed to be preferred by the gods, for it is an older crop than the finer rice which is now often cultivated on the terraced fields. It falls about the end of September, and the offerings are made specially to Labosum. The small pots dedicated to this god are taken down and, if damaged in any way, are renewed; a little of the new rice is put into them, and they are hung up again with a few ears attached.

KUROJANADUR

The festival for the small bulrush millet, *Holcus spicatus*, which occurs in October.

OSANADUR

The festival for the important millet, *Eleusine corocana*, which is held in October.

PUJJINGADUR

Although the Saoras call this an *aduran*, it is not really a Harvest Festival. It is a small rite performed in July or August at the time of heavy weeding of the fields. Everyone makes an offering to the gods and the dead in his own field, with the intention of keeping weeds, rust or weevils from spoiling the maturing crop.

ROGONADUR

This is one of the major Saora festivals, for the harvesting of the red gram, *Cajanus indicus*, which falls in December or January according to the weather. I have witnessed this on a number of occasions,[1] and I will describe the preliminary rites, as I watched them at Boramsingi, in some detail, for the incantations are instructive for an understanding of Saora theology.

The custom at this festival is for the priest or shaman to observe it privately in his own house, and for the rest of the villagers to follow his example a week, or even a month, later. After the priest has concluded his own rites, he and his immediate household may eat the pulse, but no one else may do so until the general celebration has been observed.

At Boramsingi on 17 December 1950, the shamanin Aganti performed the preliminary rites in her own house. It was a little after five o'clock in the evening. She made an altar with two baskets of rice, bunches of the fresh gram, a large pumpkin and a pot of palm wine, with the usual leaves and cups. She squatted before the altar and began to chant:

> You who live in the clearings now overgrown with trees, you who live in pits, you who live above, you who live in water, you who live in water where there are fish, you who live in the fish, you who live in bones, you who live in the bones of men, you who live in the stones of the walls between fields, you who live in the trees of the forest, you made us and gave us birth; come all of you to take your offerings.

[1] At Tarcbil, 18 to 20 December 1944; at Uoma, 2 January 1945; at Boramsingi, 17 December 1950; at Regidi, 1 January 1951.

For you we sowed the seed, and now that the plants have grown and borne fruit we offer them first to you. We have not yet cooked the pulse; we shall cook first of all for you and feed you first. You watched over the harvest and so we give first to you. All these things are yours; we give them to you first. Do not say afterwards that we gave you nothing. Be pleased with our sacrifice.

Therefore you dead, mothers, fathers, brothers, sisters, I call on all of you. Come for your gifts, then go away dancing and singing with happiness. You are great, you are kings. We cook pulse with rice-flour to please you. O great ones, O kings, come.

Then Aganti offered a bunch of green pulse on the altar with rice and wine. Other women were busy cooking rice and roasting the pulse, and when it was ready Aganti offered it and cried,

Spirits of the house, spirits of the stones, spirits of the pots, Uyungsum, Jammasum, Labosum, spirits coming to sit on these leaves of sacrifice, spirits resting by the hearth, spirits sitting on the roof, spirits on the loft, come willingly and go willingly. Let us live happily.

O grandfathers, O grandmothers! Come from the Under World, come from below, come from above, come just as men of this world might come. Spirits sitting on the trees, spirits sitting on stones, spirits in caves and streams, come. This pulse is for you, come and take it.

Then Aganti, assisted by another shamanin, while a third sat by to learn, changed her posture, sitting now with legs extended and hands on her knees, and called on her tutelary.

Come! However many gods may be crowding the paths, push your way through and come. If there are great rivers in the way, make bridges over them and come. If there is a stream, throw a log of wood across it and come. Spirits of the Paruasing Mountain, come. Gonjlikumboi, Taraikumboi,[1] you also come.

Then the shamanins clenched their hands, began to tremble all over, leant forward and were still. There was a pause of complete silence, then somebody straightened their arms and unclenched their fingers. The women cleaned their teeth with bits of wild ginger, and then leant forward again, breathed heavily and Aganti suddenly cried 'Ram Ram!'[2] in a high-pitched unnatural voice. She laughed, gesticulated and beat her head and breast. The tutelary had come. As usual he had nothing but complaints. Speaking through Aganti he declared, 'You told me there was rice and pulse to eat, but I don't

[1] Famous shamanins who have become tutelaries.
[2] A Hindu greeting which she would never use in ordinary life.

see so much as a bunch of your pubic hairs.' Everybody began to talk at once till the chatter sounded like the noise and bustle of a bazaar. They protested that they had provided a sumptuous feast, and the tutelary spoke again. 'Very well. I am great. I am a king. If you give me plenty, I will look after you. Bring your pulse and let me look at it.'

Aganti picked up the bunches of fresh pulse and waved them above her head. She jerked her knees up and down as a sign that the tutelary was dancing with pleasure at the sight of the new harvest. She picked up the pumpkin and waved that about. She beat her breast and stomach and the tutelary exclaimed, 'This pumpkin is as small as a new-born baby. Am I a Dom that you should give me so little? You called me, and I have come, expecting a feast, but you give me absolutely nothing. I have a large family in the Under World; how am I to feed them?' Then Aganti rose to her feet and danced with an axe in her hand. The tutelary called on all the other spirits to come and eat with him. 'Don't say later on that I ate everything myself like a thief.' Then Aganti cut the pumpkin in half with her axe, putting half on the altar and cutting the other half into small pieces. Suddenly she threw these pieces out of the door into the street, 'for the spirits that have crowded like dogs outside the house', as she put it. She again picked up the bunches of pulse and shook them.

Aganti, still representing her tutelary, now drank some wine, but the tutelary shouted, 'This water is bad,' and she beat with her hands on the ground. She put a new cloth on her head, and the tutelary said, 'Why hasn't this cloth been sent to the washerman?' She dressed Hindu-fashion in the cloth and danced crying '*Jaisu dungsu dungsu!*' in imitation of a drum-rhythm.

Then the tutelary said, 'You must give offerings to Koraitu Kittung who made the herbs, for he is greatest of all.'

Finally he said, 'Now I am going. Many other spirits will come. Feed them all. Do not eat everything yourselves as if you were a lot of thieves.'

After this spirit after spirit came upon Aganti, all demanding food and plenty of it, generally complaining of its quality. The long arguments continued until at nine o'clock the last of the visitants departed, and Aganti, now more than a little drunk with the wine she had taken on their behalf, turned to the business of changing the contents of the sacred pot, to which she attached a bunch of the red gram. Then at last she and her family ate a hearty meal of rice and the new pulse.

On the day of the general festival, a band of drummers goes round the village visiting each shrine in turn; the dancing is continued for at least four days. Early in the morning, the people go to their hill-clearings to gather bundles of the pulse and collect gourds of palm wine. Women repair and wash the shrines with red earth and water. The priest or a leading shaman, after making the usual offerings in his own house, goes round the village shrines, tying bunches of pulse to the roofs and pillars, and offering rice and wine. Each householder offers pulse to the ancestral dead in his own house. In the afternoon, there is often a rite for the protection of the cattle. They are fed on the leaves and stalks of the pulse; if there is a shrine for Dorisum, the priest sacrifices a fowl before it, and scatters the feathers over the cattle, and throws rice at them. In the evening the people devote themselves to food; the women cook large meals of rice, the new red gram, often the *Phaseolus radiatus* pulse as well, and any beans that may be ready. Well-to-do people often offer a fowl to the ancestors. Nearly everyone gets a little drunk.

After the festival is finished, there may be a final rite two or three days later, when the ceremonial dancing has come to an end, 'to bid farewell to the gods' and drive them away. On this day a small party of drummers, with boys beating gongs and cymbals, goes right round the forest-clearings collecting a little pulse from each. I watched this done at Regidi on 1 January 1951. When the party returned they went with the priest and a shaman along a little path to a shrine on the hillside some distance out of the village. This shrine was dedicated to Gusada Kittung, and near it in the midst of a dense thicket were two roughly carved poles, one of which had an inverted pot above it; these represented two local hill-gods called Ormara and Sarpalla Kittung. There was a flat altar stone in front of them.

The shaman put two baskets of rice inside the shrine and decorated it elaborately with bunches of pulse. At the same time, the others roasted pulse over a small fire and the boys beat on their drums and gongs. The shaman squatted before the shrine and offered wine saying,

O Babu, Babu, it is your festival today. We give you the new pulse. Come and take it. We give it to you raw, we give it to you roasted. We call you, come and hear what we have to say.

He scattered rice round the shrine and then went to the pillars, pushing his way with some difficulty through the bushes, and offered rice and wine there also and said,

> Ormara Kittung, Sarpalla Kittung, come and hear. We give you pulse. We give it even though you allowed it to be eaten by grubs and monkeys and tigers. Sojuljiraji, Damdajiraji, Babu, Babu, we give you pulse; come and take it. Bring with you all the subjects of your kingdom, and all the members of your family so that no one can say that we did not give you all that you required.

Then the shaman offered pods of roast gram here and in the shrine, and then we all sat down and ate some of it ourselves. When everything was done, the Saoras returned home silently, for fear that the gods to whom they had now bidden farewell would follow them.

TANKUNADUR

This is a festival for the stones of the mango. The Saoras, like many other tribesmen, remove the stones from the unripe mangoes and preserve them by drying them in the sun and sprinkling them with salt. Before they do this, they make offerings to the gods and ancestors. The festival is a minor one and irregularly distributed.

UDANADUR

The festival of the ripe mangoes, however, is one of great importance and is everywhere elaborately observed. There are more breaches of taboo in connexion with this than with any other festival, for the temptation to pick a luscious mango from a tree is very great. I have twice been present at this festival, at Sogeda on 15 April 1946 and at Abbasingi on 1 May 1948; the course of events was largely the same in either place.

For four days before the festival there was dancing at night, and during the day the people were busy distilling spirit, cleaning and repairing their houses and the shrines, washing and mending their clothes; men brought loads of big new red pots from the plains; women fetched firewood and leaves. On the morning of the festival every house was freshly cowdunged; men went to taste the freshly-distilled spirit; girls who had been up half the night husking grain for the feast bathed and washed their hair. The shamans started the day by drawing ikons wherever these were required.

I will describe what I saw at Sogeda. At about 9 o'clock in the morning, a shaman accompanied by a band playing trumpets, drums and gongs, went along a path out of the village to the shrine of Tangorbasum and repaired it. Representatives of every household came with small baskets of rice, and the shaman put these on the shrine together with freshly picked mangoes, and pots of wine and spirit. He decorated the shrine with mango flowers and leaves (at Abbasingi they tied a white cloth all round it); then he perched a cock on his shoulder and made a formal offering of two mangoes. He fed the cock on rice, wine and spirit. He filled his own mouth with spirit, spat it onto his hands and rubbed his face with them; 'This is the oil of the gods,' he exclaimed. Then he said, 'Today we celebrate the Mango Festival. We have come to you, O Tangorbasum, first of all; you eat first and we will follow.' He cut up a green mango into slices and ate them on behalf of the god. He said, 'From today let our children, our cattle, our goats and pigs and fowls be untroubled!'

Then the shaman distributed pieces of mango to all those present. Someone killed the cock and the shaman let its blood drip on the shrine. There were no women present and the men cut up the fowl, cooked the rice and they feasted on the spot. Before they left the shaman offered cooked rice and meat at the shrine.

The next feature of the festival was a procession from shrine to shrine. The band preceded the shaman down the street, and a crowd of dancers and onlookers followed him. At the shrine of the ghost of one Ritanu Gamangan, his family had tied the dead man's turban round the pillars and had placed inside it his cloth, his sword, umbrella and ornaments. The shaman decorated the shrine with bunches of mangoes, and made a formal offering of two mangoes, liquor, wine and rice. The ghost came upon him and said to his widow, 'I have come to share your feast of mangoes; eat them and give me my portion.' The widow replied, 'See then that our crops are good.' She brought seeds of every kind out of her house and put them in the shrine and said, 'Tell us which of these will be good and which will be bad.' The ghost replied, 'Every harvest, except the red gram, will be good.' There was a long discussion and finally someone sacrificed a cock for the ghost, decapitating it with a single blow of his sword.

This, or something like it, was repeated again and again. During the proceedings the shamanin Sinaki was possessed by her tutelary and several sick people came to her for treatment. There were long arguments with the dead; some of the shades demanded that their Guar rites should not be delayed; ancestors insisted that their names should be given to grandchildren; a ghost came to summon his widow to the Under World and had to be bought off with the promise of a goat. Feasting and dancing continued late into the night.

The next morning there was a special sacrifice at the shrine of Uyungsum, and the shaman swept his own house and the street outside with a broom of peacock-feathers to drive away disease. In the late afternoon, after a day of feasting and dancing, a shaman brought a sheep and adorned it with garlands. He put turmeric on its forehead and led it round the village; as he went he threw water coloured with turmeric over the roof of every house he passed, calling to the gods, 'Come out; we are bidding you farewell. We are going to take you out of the village.'

Each householder brought a little bundle of sticks and a packet of every kind of seed mixed together. Led by the shaman and the sheep, the procession left the village towards the setting sun, and when they had gone some distance they all very quickly opened their packets and threw the seed on the ground. Then they offered their bundles of sticks, someone killed the sheep with the sharp edge of his axe, and the shaman sprinkled the blood over the seed and the sticks and then threw the head along the path away from the village. The people removed the sheep's liver and cooked it separately, and the shaman offered it to the gods where the rice lay on the ground; the rest of the meat was cooked with rice some distance away. After the feast was over the people returned to the village, glad that a tiresome and rather dangerous taboo had been lifted and that now they and their children could eat mangoes to their hearts' content.

VII. *Rites of the Threshing-floor*

AFTER the Harvest Festivals, the point of tension shifts from the fields to the threshing-floors, for here the sheaves and the grain lie exposed to every hostile influence. If they are not guarded, Jammolsum and Dobasum, to say nothing of the hungry and jealous dead, may carry part of it away. On the other hand, if the proper precautions are taken the grain may actually increase in quantity.

After the sheaves have been stacked by the threshing-floor, a pig or a fowl may be offered to the dead. I saw this done at the rice-harvest, on 8 December 1944, at Munisingi.

The shaman made his altar on top of the stack of sheaves; he turned a basket upside down and poured rice-flour over it, covered it with leaves and poured more rice-flour over them, and made offerings of rice and wine.

Then the shaman and his assistant—his own son whom he was training—went to the field, where they cleared and cowdunged a patch of ground. On this the shaman traced a large square with rice-flour and then, rather as if he were laying out cards, he put nine leaves face-upwards in rows of three and on either side four leaves face-downwards. He put a little rice on each leaf.

He also made a large number of little leaf-pipes, in each of which he put some rice.

The shaman's son had in the meantime returned to the threshing-floor, where he climbed on to the stack and cut the left ear of a hen and allowed the blood to drip over the offerings on the altar. He came down and carried the bleeding bird round the stack three times. He put the hen on the ground and took a bowl containing rice-flour and water in his hands. He carried this also round the stack three times, spilling the contents of the bowl as he went so as to make a double circle of blood and of flour-water right round the stack. Now, explained the shaman, 'no god or ghost will be able to steal the grain; in fact more grain will be attracted to the floor from outside'.

The boy took the hen to his father in the field, and the older man cut its right ear and let the blood fall on the offerings before him. Then the boy cut off the hen's head and plucked out the feathers, sticking them into the mouths of the leaf-pipes. 'The hen's ears were cut for women, its throat for men.' The shaman called on all the gods, especially Sitaboi and Manneboi, and the dead, and offered them wine. The shaman's wife and daughter cooked the fowl and a pot of rice, and the family ate everything there on the threshing-floor before returning home.

The threshing is done by cattle who are driven round in a line, roped together, but not tied to a pole in the middle of the floor. The work is often finished off by men and women who beat the broken stalks with long poles. For threshing millet this is the usual method. The Saoras winnow by shaking the grain from fans on to a long mound—which may be from twelve to fifteen feet long—right across the floor. Two men then make long vigorous strokes of their fans to blow away any chaff that may remain. When the mound is about two feet high, the winnowers carefully smooth it over and treat it almost as if it were an altar. The owner of the grain puts a winnowing-fan face down at either end, and then with ashes or grains of husked rice traces a rough pattern at either end and across the mound at intervals of about a foot; in the middle he puts a small basket of rice with an egg in it. At Maneba I saw a pole erected in the middle of the mound and from it were hung the tethering ropes of the cattle which had threshed the grain. At Pattili, a beak of the Indian Hornbill, and at Abada an axe with a polished brass head, was put beside the little rice-basket. Finally, the baskets in which the grain will be carried home are placed irregularly round one end of the mound.

These precautions have the effect of enclosing the grain within a sort of protective shell; even the irregular placing of the baskets has a purpose—it prevents ghosts or gods from 'creeping through and going with the grain into the store-bins'.

Then the householder sits down at one end of the mound and at the other sits his eldest unmarried daughter or sister with her legs stretched out over the grain as far as they will go. As much grain as her legs can cover will be hers to buy ornaments with as a reward for her help in gathering the harvest. But this is not allowed to a married woman. Other men and women sit round her.

The householder takes a few grains of rice and puts them under the soles of his feet. He picks up the winnowing-fan from the end of the mound and throws a handful of grain into the nearest basket. He shovels grain into the fan, empties it into the basket, takes a handful of grain out of the basket and returns it to the fan, and continues to do this until the basket is full. He works slowly down the mound, filling one basket after another until he reaches the end, whereupon the men and women who have been waiting pick up the baskets all together and go in procession to the house; the little rice-basket with its egg goes in the last of the baskets. Sometimes the egg is placed for a moment on the grain in every load.

When all the grain has been removed, the householder buries an egg in the middle of the floor, offers fish and crabs with cooked rice to Kittungsum, Jammolsum and the ancestors, and the workers have a feast.

It is not always done exactly like this: sometimes the grain is heaped in a large pile; there are differences of detail—one man puts grains of rice on his fan, not under his feet; another throws rice left and right before starting; but the main outline of the procedure has been the same wherever I have witnessed it.

The general atmosphere of the threshing-floor, once it has been suitably protected, is one of merriment and recreation. Sometimes little sheds are built nearby so that people can sleep on the spot to guard it. Children love to tumble in the straw, and they play every sort of riotous game: boys attack girls, pull their hair, grab at their breasts, snatch the cheroots from their mouths—I have seen girls stripped naked and rolled on the floor amidst screams of laughter. Once at Tumulu, when the people were threshing millet with long poles, they sang and three of the men put their poles across their arms and danced about, pretending to play the poles as if they were fiddles, and chanting obscene little songs which gave pleasure to all. But at the time of removing the grain to the house, everyone is very solemn; there is no laughter and little conversation.

VIII. *Control of the Rains*

IN Saora legend rain is caused by the tears of a girl who is unhappily married to a sky-god.[1] Bimma (Bhimsen), widely regarded in tribal India as the rain-giver, does not seem to have this function among the Saoras; there is instead a rain-goddess, Ganurboi, to whom sacrifices are sometimes made for the increase or lessening of the rainfall. The mountain Jumtangbur gives rain to its immediate neighbourhood if the proper sacrifice of a cow is made every year. But this custom is falling into disuse, and many Saoras refuse to sacrifice cows and employ Doms to do it for them. On the other side of the valley, on the slopes of Deogiri, Hindus and Saoras together make offerings of milk, ghee, country sugar and coconuts to persuade the hill to give them rain.

The dead may intervene to stop rain from falling, and the technique of bringing rain is thus to satisfy the dead who then in some way which is never explained allow the rain to fall. At Satara and Mandidi villages the dead prevented the rain until they had been honoured with appropriate wooden pillars (see pp. 304f.).

Another method of getting rain is to dig a small pit somewhere in the village, put a frog in it, cover the mouth of the pit with a plank of sago-palm wood, erect sticks on either side and join them with a bit of cord. The shaman pulls the cord taut and taps it; the sound is

[1] *TMO*, p. 72-3.

supposed to resemble the croaking of the frog, and the frog in the pit replies, 'O Mother Rain, come! They have shut me up in jail. I will only get out when you come.'

Or the shaman may go to a *Bassia latifolia* tree and sacrifice a pig at its foot. He makes a new bow and arrow, and an unmarried youth fires the arrow at the tree. The shaman ties a thread seven times round the trunk and the rain falls.

If the rains are too heavy, a man naked but for a small loin-cloth takes an old plough and sets it up with the share in the ground. He beats it with a stone until it stands firmly, and then he throws ashes over it. He goes into his house crying, 'I am hot and thirsty; give me something to drink.' The shaman gives him salt and water. After this the rain is expected to fall more moderately.

At Dokripanga I was told of an ingenious method of stealing water from another village. If a spring dries up for lack of rain, a shaman goes at night with two or three friends to the spring of a neighbouring village and sleeps beside it. Labosum comes to him in a dream and promises water if he will make the necessary sacrifices. The shaman gets up, has a pig killed on the spot, takes a cocoon and puts a few drops of water from the spring into it and hurries back to his own village. Here he throws the stolen water into the dry spring and sacrifices a fowl. As a result it is believed that the water of the other spring will be transferred to this.

There does not seem to be any way of stopping a hail-storm. Hail is regarded as the tears of the Sun; 'his little tears are the little stones, his big tears are the big stones'. At the right time, hail is regarded as very lucky. If there is a storm before sowing, the Saoras expect that the growth of weeds in the fields and of shrubs in the clearings will be light. Hail also foretells a good crop of red gram.

Chapter Nine

THE RITES FOR THE DEAD

I

ALTHOUGH the Saoras have a clear enough idea of how disease came into the world, they do not seem to have any comparable theory of mortality. At Munisingi I recorded a story about the origin of death, but it had obvious Hindu elements: the leeches drank the water of immortality, which was intended for men, and they then began to die. It may be that the Saoras, unlike other tribesmen, regard death as a natural thing which does not need explaining. It is, after all, the logical conclusion of their theory of disease; it is the means by which the Under World is populated; it is the first step to apotheosis.

For the Saora, death is an embarrassment; it is an expense; every death in a family adds a new danger from the other world. But it is not a separation; it is not an end. Life goes on. The shades and ancestors are always at hand; there is not a festival or ceremony which they do not attend; they are there, affectionate and aggressive by turns, interested in what is going on, always ready to talk, all too often ready to interfere.

How far this close and continued communion with the dead robs death of some of its sorrow it is hard to say. This is not a thing that can be measured, and the question is complicated by the custom that forces the bereaved to make a formal display of grief. But I have witnessed scenes of such genuine sorrow as that described later in this chapter, when his parents mourned the death of their little son at Tumulu. At Kankaraguda too, on the death of the old man Jagantha on 27 December 1947, there seemed to me a very genuine note in the plaint of his daughter-in-law who led the mourning:

O father, father, you were a royal man like Mahaprabhu himself. How could you leave us like this? What shall we do now? Who is to care for us now? When you were here, we cut our clearings, we did our work and you looked after us. For us you brought roots and herbs from the forest, and we lived and ate. Now who will do this for us? When you were here, you brought us cloth, rings, necklaces, bracelets, oil. But now, O father, who will bring these things for us? Now you have joined the gods, who will go to borrow pigs and fowls from the merchants for sacrifice when we fall ill? O father, father, when will you take my soul with you? Who will watch our joys and sorrows now? O father, you have left us, you have left us.

In 1940 a man named Indimo, of Jarasingi, lost his wife in child-birth, though the baby survived. His grief was so intense that when the body was taken to the pyre and the wood was lit, he put the child beside the mother's corpse, crying, 'The child will have no milk or food, for how am I to get it?' The bystanders rescued the child, but not before he had received a few small burns. He was taken to hospital, but after four days tetanus developed and he died. Indimo was sentenced to six months' imprisonment, the Court holding that he had been more or less out of his mind with grief.

Are the Saoras afraid of death? They should be, for all their teaching declares that the shade is in for a bad time, at least until the Guar is performed, and that may not be for several years. Even then life in the Under World, if the reports of dreamers and shamans are to be believed, does not seem very attractive. Here again is something that cannot be measured. Those Saoras whom I have seen at the point of death have been patient and resigned.

The funerary rites of the Saoras are complicated and important, for on their proper performance depends the condition of the dead, and thus the welfare of the living. There is some difference of custom, particularly in the Serango Mutta, but the main ceremonies may be summarized as follows:

First day	Preparation of the corpse and cremation.
Second day	Stripping of the pyre and burial of the bones and ashes. This may be preceded, or sometimes followed on the third day, by a ceremony of sacrifice and divination and a feast, the Limma.
Later (at any time from a few months to several years)	The Guar ceremony, which includes a buffalo sacrifice and the erection of a menhir. In a few villages this and the Karja are combined.
Afterwards	The Sikunda, an elaborate but economical version of the Karja, which is celebrated between the Guar and the Karja, or even before either of them, when the people cannot afford the expense of the greater ceremonies.

Every second or third year	The Karja ceremony for all who have died since the preceding Karja.
Finally	The Lajap, a minor rite which has special reference to the crops.

II. *The Funeral*

EXCEPT in cases of smallpox and cholera, the Saoras nowadays cremate their dead, but there is a tradition that this was not the ancient custom.[1] At one time, it is said, they used simply to throw the bodies away and leave them to be eaten by wild beasts. Later, they buried the dead standing upright with the heads protruding above ground: people used to remove the skulls and use them as hearths for cooking. The change from burial to cremation is explained by a long story which resembles the myth recited at the Ajorapur (see pp. 277f.). A girl is forced to marry a great snake and takes it to her home. Her brothers are very angry and kill it. When the girl hears of it she dies of sorrow.

The brothers buried her beneath a sago palm. They buried the snake in another grave near by. But that evening, when they went for their wine, they found the girl's body had come out of the grave and was standing under the tree. They dug another grave, a deeper one, and buried her again, but when they returned the following evening, they found the body had again come out of the grave and was standing beneath the tree. They dug yet another grave, deeper still, but the third day they again found that the body had come out of the ground and was standing beneath the tree.

They were terrified, for they thought that the girl's shade would certainly destroy them. But that night Kittung came to the eldest brother in a dream and said, 'Burn the corpse and it will not return.' They did so and had no more trouble. Ever since the Saoras have burnt and not buried their dead.

After death the corpse is laid on its back across the mortar in the central room of the house, and is covered with a cloth. A funeral is strictly an affair of the deceased's own family, and none of the other villagers—even though they may have been close friends or relatives by marriage—attend or give any assistance. Young men let off guns and beat gongs and drums to announce the tragedy and summon the mourners. The family Idaibois busy themselves fetching water

[1] J. D. Beglar, who visited Ganjam in 1875, says that the Saoras buried their dead. Cunningham adds that the Malwa Saoras of Vizagapatam did so also.—Cunningham, p. 121. But only twelve years later Fawcett found cremation the rule everywhere.

and preparing turmeric, and a number of men hasten to the forest for wood to make the pyre.

The cremation-grounds are near, and sometimes in, a village, and there is a separate ground, as there is a separate group of menhirs, for each family. The pyre is always made of green wood. Fawcett says that 'the only wood used is that of the mango and of the *Pongamia glabra*',[1] but this is not so; any wood can be used, though *Pongamia glabra* is preferred. In some places there is a taboo on the use of *Phyllanthus emblica*, for as the leaves and fruit of this tree fall readily, it is supposed that its use may cause many people to fall and die. The pyre is a substantial affair, and it is sometimes said that it should be built of seven layers of wood for a man, of eight for a woman. 'For a man has seven ribs and a woman eight.'

Meanwhile women carry the corpse out of the house and lay it on a plank of wood in the street outside. They remove most of the ornaments, bathe the body and comb the hair. Other women sit round weeping, and the young men maintain a ceaseless cacophony of gongs, drums and trumpets.

When all is ready, the corpse is carried to the pyre. This is done in several different ways. I think that the old custom was for women to carry it, and they still often do so, but nowadays in some villages women only carry a female corpse, and in some only the corpses of children. I was told that if a suckling child dies its mother[2] takes it out, for 'a mother feels very sad at the death of such a child, but if she herself carries it her memory of it soon goes. If others carry it, she will always sorrow.'

Sometimes the corpse is carried by hands and feet; sometimes a man may take it on his back, the head being tied in position face upwards by a cloth that covers both living and dead. Sometimes, it is said, the hands and feet of a corpse are tied together and it is slung on a pole.[3] Where Dom influence is strong, a rude ladder is made to serve as a bier.

Before the corpse is taken away, the relatives pile every bit of the deceased's cloth upon it: not a scrap should be left in the house.

[1] Fawcett, p. 249. [2] On 19 December 1947, at Boramsingi, when a one-year-old boy died, it was the father's sister who bathed him and carried him in her arms to the pyre.

[3] Rice, *Occasional Essays*, p. 108. I have never seen this done by the Saoras, but it is not uncommon among the Bondos. Rice says, 'Many of my readers may have seen, and seen with indignation, a pig slung on a pole in a similar way'.

Fawcett says that in his day everything was taken out and burnt. 'Everything a man has, his bows and arrows, his *tangi*, his dagger, his necklaces, his cloths, his reaping-hook for cutting paddy, his axe, some paddy and rice, etc. are burnt with his body. I have been told in Kolakotta that all a man's money too is burned, but it is doubtful that it really ever is, a little may be.'[1] The reason which the Saoras gave Fawcett for this was that if they did not burn a man's property, his shade would come to demand it, and that would be a nuisance. But personally I have found that the shades who appear at the divi-

FIG. 30 Men placing a corpse on a pyre

nation ceremonies after a funeral are very indignant if all their property is not available for their inspection.

The body is taken to the pyre and laid upon it with the head in any convenient direction, most commonly perhaps to the west. The Siggamaran, who is here the most important figure, covers it with some dry wood and additional green logs. It is the custom for the mourners to contribute a little grain towards the expenses of the funeral, and this is piled on the ground at the head of the pyre; if

[1] Fawcett, p. 249. At a Sogeda funeral in 1948, four brass pots were placed on the pyre, but they were removed before it was fired.

a rich man dies and there is a lot of rice, it is laid out in a long mound beside it. Then while the people wail, and the drummers beat their drums, the Siggamaran lights the pyre. Since the wood is green, the body takes a long time to burn, and the Siggamaran may have to spend hours feeding the fire. If the wood is specially obstinate in burning, the Siggamaran exclaims, 'If you loved your children and your property so much, what did you want to die for? Give up your love for the world and go.' He picks up a twig, breaks it and spits on it, and throws it on the pyre crying, 'Go!' It is said that when this is done the corpse at once turns to ashes.

The following day, the mourners visit the pyre. The Idaibois pull it to pieces and take each of the unburnt logs (and generally there are a good many) and wash them. The Siggamaran examines the ashes for any signs that may reveal the cause of death. Then he digs up the ashes of the last person to die, and buries the new ashes and most of the bones in the same pit. If the deceased came originally from another village, he separates a few of the bones and buries them separately in a little pot. Grass and logs are then laid over the pit, and sometimes a little hut is built above it.

In some places, if the dead man had a sword or a gun, it may be buried near by. The Siggamaran may also take the dead man's bow and shoot all his arrows in different directions, finally breaking the bow and throwing it away.

If the death occurs at the right season, the male members of the family may go for a hunt in the dead man's name. Before starting, they throw some rice towards the Sun saying, 'Show us whether he was a bad man or a good'. If the hunt is successful, it means that the dead man was good; if not, that he was bad. But I doubt if this is often done, or in any case taken very seriously as a means of obtaining a moral verdict on a man's life.

During or at the end of these ceremonies, the shamans busy themselves with attempting to divine the cause of death. An altar is made in the house where the death occurred, a branch of *Aegle marmelos* leaves is set up on it, and one or more shamans or shamanins of the special type qualified to deal with funerary matters sit before it and pass into trance, whereupon the shade returns and tells them what really happened to him. There is often a long, and sometimes acrimonious, discussion about the disposal of his property.

In the evening, a fowl is sacrificed at the cremation ground and this is cooked with rice and the bitter leaves of the *Melia azadirachta*;[1] each of the mourners takes a cup of this food to his own home and offers it to the ancestors there. It is said that these leaves are eaten 'because of the bitterness of separation'. This little feast is sometimes called the Limma.

III. *The Soul-house*

FAWCETT refers to a miniature hut that is built over the place where the ashes and bones of a dead man are buried, and Hutton describes how he saw in a village which was probably Munisingi—the time of his visit was March 1931—a thatched hut, which, he says, 'is used to accommodate a rough wooden figure (the one I saw was purely conventional but clearly female and a question elucidated the fact that the last person to die had been a woman) which serves to accommodate the soul until the Guar ceremony'.[2] Fawcett gives a detailed account of a hut which had been erected after the Limma rite; he does not say where it was, but it must have been in the neighbourhood of Kehalakot, only a few miles from Munisingi.

I once saw a gaily ornamented hut, evidently quite new, near a burning place, and inquired as to its *raison d'être*. The ornamentation was ridiculous. Rude figures of birds and red rags were tied to five bamboos which were sticking up in the air about eight feet above the hut—one at each corner and one in the centre; and the bamboos were split and notched for ornament. The hut was about four and a half feet square on a platform three feet high, no walls, but only four pillars, one at each corner, and inside a loft just as in a Saora's hut. A very communicative Saora said he built the hut for his brother, who died a month before, after he had performed the Limma, and had buried the bones in the raised platform, in the centre of the hut. He readily went inside and showed what he kept inside for the use of his dead brother's shade. On the lofts were baskets of grain, a bottle of oil for his body, a brush to sweep the hut; in fact everything the shade wanted, as if he were still a Saora. Generally, where it is the custom to have a hut for the shade, such hut is furnished with food, tobacco and liquor; the shade is still a Saora, though a spiritual one.[3]

Fawcett says that only two miles away, in another village, the people did not make such huts, and still today the custom is restricted

[1] This custom may have been borrowed for, under the name of *pithapona*, it obtains among the Oriya inhabitants of the plains.—Thurston, vol. VI, p. 326.

[2] Hutton, *Census*, 1931, vol. I, pt. iiiB, p. 4. [3] Fawcett, p. 254.

—so far as I know—to the area where it was noticed many years ago. Except far to the north, the only place where I have seen these huts is Barasingi, between Munisingi and Kehalakot in the Gumma Mutta. In January 1951 there were three huts on one of the Barasingi burning-grounds, built and furnished exactly as Fawcett saw them over seventy years before. In the same village, two years earlier, there was an elaborate hut, six feet square, with a roof ten feet high, solid walls and a roughly carved door. Rising from it were nine bamboo poles eight to ten feet tall: each had a little perch for a pair of wooden birds (Fig. 31) which were attached to them by wooden pins and decorated with red and white strips of cloth. Inside was a loft, with pots and baskets. On the ground floor, a wooden gun leant against the wall; there was a hearth, and a layer of straw covered the pit where bones and ashes had been buried. The hut had been built by one Addia for his brother Mano who died in March 1948.

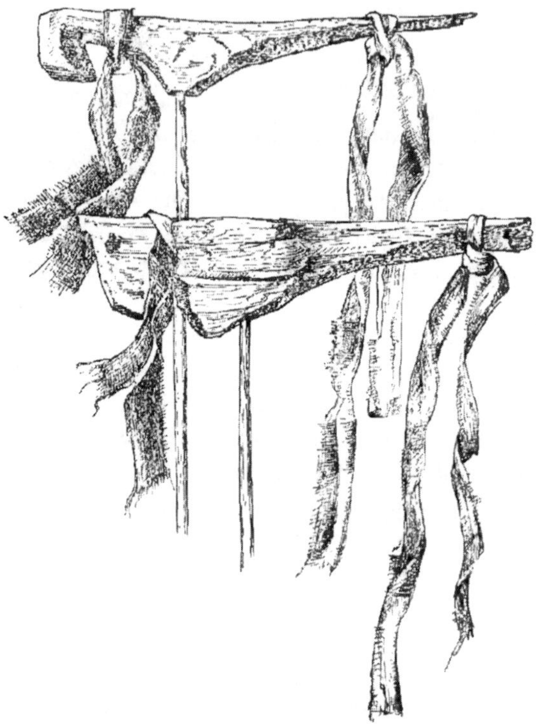

FIG. 31 Wooden birds on a soul-house at Barasingi

In the northern area I saw a regular *sadru*-shrine on one of the burning-grounds at Sinkulipadar. It was draped with a white cloth, and had been put up for Surano Jani, a rich old priest whose ghost could not be ignored (Fig. 32). In Jamudia, long bamboo poles decorated with flags (Fig. 33) were erected above the ash-pits and small circular fences were made round them.

In all the other villages I have visited the only accommodation provided for the shade has been a sort of symbolic hut—a few logs laid above the ash-pit with an upper covering of straw.

Saora thought on this, as on many other matters, is inconsistent. The universal complaint of shades who possess the shamans is that they have nowhere to live and are forced to shiver in the dubious shelter of trees and rocks. When the shamans summon them to attend a ceremony, they speak of the shades as living in trees and streams and on the mountainside. Moreover soul-houses are built at other times to persuade the dead to visit a village. Thus at Barasingi, at the Sikunda rite in 1951, elaborate miniature huts were erected on each of the burning-grounds, though no one had been cremated there for months and the priest stood before them and cried,

FIG. 32 Shrine wrapped in cloth near a burning-ground at Sinkulipadar
About 10′ *high*

> O ancestral dead, today we call on you. Where are the newly-dead? Fetch them from the trees, the rocks, the pits where they are living. We have made houses for you. Come and sit in them and accept our offerings.

This certainly does not sound as if the shades had been accommodated in the grave-houses since their death. Probably the building of the huts is intended rather to flatter the shades with a show of consideration than to provide them with adequate housing.

Another kind of house made for the dead is the regular *sadru*-shrine which is built for important people in front of their houses. Here too the ghost is not imagined as living in the shrine; it is rather a place where he can rest when he is invited to attend a festival; it is a monument which tickles his vanity and keeps him quiet.

IV. *A Funeral at Tumulu*

THE course of events, and the emotions which they inspire, can best be understood if I narrate some actual incidents.

On 26 December 1944, in the house of Manisuh and his wife Salke at Tumulu, towards evening, their beautiful little son Passigo died. He was about five years old, 'big enough to graze the cattle', and he died after only thirty-six hours' illness. Sickness and mortality left no mark upon him and the perfect little body with its bright ornaments looked fresh and lovely even in death.

FIG. 33 Flags erected above a hut for the dead, on a burning-ground at Jamudia

There was a younger boy, and the children had been ill before. A year before the shaman had dedicated a pot to Dorisum for their health, with the promise of a buffalo if they kept well. So now when Passigo fell ill, his father hastened to sacrifice—but he was a mean drunken man and, breaking his promise of a buffalo, offered Dorisum nothing but a fowl. The god came upon the shaman and declared that 'a fowl is not enough', to which Manisuh replied, 'A fowl is all you will get'. It was generally believed in the village that this was the real cause of the child's death, which indeed occurred on the very afternoon of the sacrifice.

Directly the mother was sure that the boy was dead, she laid the body across the mortar and covered it with a cloth. Crying loudly she took down the pot dedicated to Dorisum and smashed it to pieces before the house. Her husband was out in the forest and she abandoned herself to a frenzy of grief. I found her throwing herself about the house, now rolling on the ground, now clasping the child's body and burying her face in the cloth that covered it, now sitting to wail loudly. Presently an old woman joined her, and then the father with tears pouring down his face came in and he too threw himself upon the child. Their dog ran anxiously round and round the body, and licked the tears from the faces of the mourners.

Directly the news spread, all the men of Manisuh's family went to build the pyre. The cremation ground was very near, immediately behind the house, and within an hour they had a substantial pile of large green logs. At the four corners they dug holes in the ground, put a little rice and a copper coin into each, and set up poles to support the pyre.

Meanwhile the mourners in the house continued their desperate cries which began in rhythm like a song and ended in a hoarse shout of despair or a loud shout of 'Raja'. Manisuh's old mother abused Salke. 'We told you to sacrifice a buffalo and a pot of wine, but you refused and only gave a fowl. What are you crying for? Do you want to roast and eat the boy? If you were afraid of giving even a little wine, how will you ever get another son like this?'

Then the father talked to his dead child. 'When I went to drink wine you used to say, "I'm coming too" and we would go out together. O my father, who will go with me now? To save you I sacrificed a fowl, but I was wrong; it was not enough. You told me, "I am going to die of this fever; I won't be staying in this world." You said that and you were right. To save your life I offered sacrifice and, thinking you would be well, I went to my work. And now in my absence you have gone away without a word of farewell. O Raja, where have you gone?'

The mother's memories were naturally the most tender and intimate. 'O my father,' she cried, 'where have you gone? Where shall I stay now? How am I to live? You used to say, "One day I will go to Assam; I will get a lot of money. I will buy fields, bullocks, buffaloes; I will become a great merchant." That was how you talked to the other boys. But where have you gone now, my Raja? You used to wander through the village, driving home the goats and cattle, and you would shout, "These are my cattle". Now who will bring them home? You used to say, "I am going out to graze the cattle; give me my food quickly". Now who will take the herd to graze? At first I had no baby and your father quarrelled with me and said, "You have no children. I married you for nothing. I will drive you out and get another wife." Yet in the end I bore him two sons, but O my Raja we had no means of knowing whether your life would be for joy or sorrow. Now you have left me, to what strange land have you gone? You used to say to the other boys, "When I'm grown up I am going to make a lot of money. I will get good food for my father and mother. I will be the richest man in the village." But your talk was only for your death. O Raja, when shall I see your mouth and ears again? Why were you ever born? Had I remained barren it would have been well. You have left behind your little brother and he too is ill.'

Manisuh had three brothers living in the same street, and the daughter of the eldest of them, a very capable girl called Durpano, who was an Idaiboi, collected rice from each of them, put it in a large basket and placed it by the dead child's head. As she was doing this, the mother suddenly jumped up and with great fury hurled a fine brass pot out of the door. 'We have no further need of wealth,' she said.

Durpano, on whom the larger burden of the work now fell, brought pots of hot water and some turmeric. Manisuh's elder sister pounded the turmeric on a rock outside the house. Durpano pulled a broad beam of wood into a suitable place in the street and washed it with hot water. Then another Idaiboi, an eighteen-year-old girl named Sirindi, daughter of Manisuh's second brother, carried Passigo's body from the house.

A quite appalling scene followed. Sirindi laid the little body on the wood and removed the cloth that covered it. The old women, seeing the beautiful child, lost all control. They fell on the body, struggled to possess it, passed it from hand to hand. The limbs were beginning to stiffen: one bent the legs, another the arms, a third smeared turmeric on the chest, a fourth tipped a pot of hot water over it. Then the mother rushed screaming from the house, seized the child's body from the others, hugged it, kissed it, clasped it to her in a passionate gesture of possession. I well remember the horror of the scene, for the child seemed to come alive as he was tossed to and fro by the frantic women.

At last the ritual bath was over, and 'water ran down the street' as tradition demanded. Sirindi wrapped the body in the same cloth and picked it up. Darpano fetched fire from the hearth on which the boy's last meal had been prepared; then she stood with her back to the door and pulled some grass from the roof. The entire party escorted Sirindi as she carried the body to the pyre. There she laid it on the wood, head to the west, and removed the cloth. Darpano put the grass and fire on the ground near by. Manisuh's sister brought two baskets of grain and put them at the head of the pyre.

Now the Siggamaran took charge. He covered the body with a few pieces of dry wood and piled on more logs until it was enclosed in a sort of oven of green wood. Then he lit the kindling grass with the fire from the house; he had to do this by waving it to and fro till it ignited; he was not supposed to blow on it. Then he went clockwise round the pyre setting light to the wood. The wood caught slowly and reluctantly for, as the watchers said, 'Had the dead one been old, it would have blazed up quickly, but this was a child and he still loved the world'.

When the body was laid on the pyre, the mother had climbed up and thrown herself upon it, kissing it passionately. Now when the wood was lit, she tried to throw herself into the fire. Her husband had to drag her away, and at last she fell into some bushes and crouched there screaming. All night her wild cries reminded the village of her loss. As the moon brightened, drummers and trumpeters, and a crowd of men, gathered by the pyre; from time to time a woman would creep up to it, wail loudly, and go away.

The Siggamaran was kept busy for hours. The wood burnt slowly and needed nursing and feeding. At last when he was sure that the body had been consumed, he spread some dry grass round the pyre and set fire to it. About midnight everyone went to bed.

Next morning, not very early, about nine o'clock, the Idaibois took pots of hot water to the cremation-ground; someone from each household in the family brought a pot. The Siggamaran came to examine the ashes, but there were no signs, so no one could say what the cause of death was. The Siggamaran and the girls pulled the logs apart—there were over thirty left, many only slightly burnt—washed them and threw them aside. The Siggamaran gathered the ashes into a mound, carefully removing any bits of grass or wood. He dug a small pit to the west of the pyre; as he dug he threw out the old ashes of other children—and older people—long since dead. Then he offered rice, a broken egg-shell, and a bunch of *dub* grass in each of the four corners of the pit. He removed a ring from his finger, bent a branch of *Pongamia glabra* into a hoop, slipped the ring onto it and then used it to draw the ashes into the pit, and the girls poured water and cleaned the place till all the ashes were buried. The Siggamaran raked in the old ashes and earth into the pit, trod it down with his feet, and placed two green logs over it. On these again he spread freshly-cut thatching grass and three more logs to hold it in place. 'For the soul is naked now,' he said, 'and it will need shade.'

The band of drummers and trumpeters played throughout the ceremony. The child's parents were not present, and the only note of grief was struck by Manisuh's old mother who wailed intermittently. The rest of the party were cheerful.

On the third day, 28 December, a shaman, the Siggamaran and the two Idaibois assembled in Manisuh's house. The shaman put rice, leaves and cups of wine before the mortar where the corpse had lain. He took the names of all the ancestors he could remember (the others echoing him) and cried,

> Who took this child away? Where is he now? Gather together all of you, search for him, and look after him. Care for him well, as we did on earth, for we can look after him no longer. We do not accuse you, we do not say it was you who took the child away. But we do leave him in your hands.

Then they went to the cremation ground. The shaman and Siggamaran lifted up the logs and grass from above the pit, and laid out a row of leaves each with a small offering of rice upon it. The two men and the two girls stood in line at the foot of where the pyre had been; each held a little rice and chanted, calling on the dead by name,

> We do not know whether this child has gone above or below, or who took him away. We only know you are there, in the Under World. Gather together, all of you, and find the child, and for your food we give you rice.

They blew on the rice and threw it on the ground. Then the Siggamaran returned the grass and logs to their place.

After this the party moved away a little into the surrounding trees and sacrificed a fowl. The Idaibois took it away to cook. Each household of the family contributed rice. The shaman put a few drops of the fowl's blood in a leaf-cup, and mixed blood and rice for the ancestors. The band played and the Siggamaran went round looking at the sun and sprinkling everyone with water to drive away any ghosts who might be inclined to molest them. Then they returned to the house, and the parents of the dead child, who had fasted till now, at last sat down to eat.

In the evening, Manisuh cooked rice in a new pot and himself put cups of rice and water near the ash-pit. This was for the dead who would come that night, bringing the child's shade with them. And in fact, the Tumulu people said, that night a great host of the dead came talking and calling to one another, and in the midst of the din could be heard the faint gasping cry of the dead child. Manisuh and his wife were so afraid of this visitation that they locked up their house and went to sleep somewhere else, no one knew where. The dead went round the village searching for them, and many people that night saw their loved ones in dream and their sleep was disturbed.

A FUNERAL AT BORAMSINGI

THE death of Passigo was a tragedy, and his funeral was marked by the most moving manifestations of grief. Simanto, an Arsi Saora of Boramsingi, who died in the early morning of 25 December 1947, was an old man whose passing evoked only formal expressions of regret.

I saw Simanto the night before he died. He was a very poor and lonely man, for he had survived all his children and his brothers. There was only a decrepit old woman, his younger brother's wife, to look after him.

Boramsingi is divided into nine family groups, of which seven are Jati, one Kindal and one Arsi. The Arsi group is very small: there are only four households; and because of this, and because Simanto was old and friendless, members of the other groups—contrary to the usual custom—collaborated in the funeral arrangements.

By nine o'clock in the morning, the preliminaries had been completed, and eight women carried the corpse on an old cot to a very beautiful spot above the village, where the pyre had been made on a little hill, on the Arsi burning-ground. There two Idaibois climbed on the pyre (they were maidens: had they been married they could not have done this) and made a rough bed of old rags. The body was hoisted up and laid upon it, the head towards the east. The Idaibois removed Simanto's ornaments, such as they were, even his little nose-ring, stripped off his old clothes and covered him with a red cloth. As the Siggamaran lighted the pyre, he saluted the Sun crying, 'When he was alive we used to sit and drink with him; now we burn him but let no blame attach to us'. Guns were fired and boys beat their gongs and drums. The women stood by watching, the men retired to a little distance, and slowly the wood blazed up and the body was consumed. When the pyre was burnt out, the mourners removed the big logs and gathered the ashes into a pile.

On the following morning, a shamanin (a Guarkumboi) went with the two Idaibois to the dead man's house, and proceeded to take the omens with *Aegle marmelos* leaves. After some time, one of them responded to the name of Labosum. Then the shamanin passed into trance and there was a long conversation between her tutelary and Simanto's only surviving relative, the old woman Induri. Induri wept loudly and said, 'You have taken away my husband and my son, and now even this old man. If you wanted food-sacrifice, why didn't you say so?' The tutelary (speaking, of course, through the mouth of the shamanin) replied, 'It's nothing to do with me; it was Labosum. Why don't you ask him? Perhaps there was some sorcerer who coveted the old man's field and sent Labosum to take him away.' Induri wept louder than ever. 'Send for Labosum,' she cried, 'and I'll ask him.' The tutelary went away to search for Labosum and presently the god came on the shamanin. Induri said, 'You have taken everything I have; now who will give you pigs or fowls? If you had once asked for something, I would have given it to you.' Labosum replied, 'I didn't want the old man, but Deko sent for me and asked me to remove him, for he wanted to plough his field. He promised me food-sacrifice, and so I took the old man away.'

Deko was sitting near by, a rather sinister old man with a fiddle in his hands; he strummed nervously on it as he heard this monstrous accusation.

Then Labosum went away, and the ghost of Induri's son came on one of the Idaibois and Simanto's shade came on the shamanin. There followed a lively conversation between the two spirits and Induri. When Simanto possessed the shamanin, she covered her head with a bit of his cloth and put his axe on her shoulder. She drank some water, holding the gourd with both hands as if she were very old, trembling as he had done in his last illness. Induri embraced the shamanin and said, 'You have left me all alone. Who will look after your cattle? Who will plough your field? Who will reap your crops? Who will use your hoe? Now your sitting-place is empty.' Simanto's shade replied, 'I've gone now. What do these things matter? Very soon I'll come and take you with me.' And the ghost of Induri's son said, 'I'm glad the old man is dead. When I was alive and ill once with a splitting headache, he drove me out to work. He was a nasty old person and never gave me anything but curses. It is very good that Labosum has taken him.'

But Induri his mother cried, 'O my prince, my princely son, my young son, you have all left me. Now who will look after me? Who will care for the cattle? Who will plough the fields? Why did you leave me, son of my king?'

Simanto's shade said, 'Now I've gone, I've gone. But give me the cow I used to plough with. I love it and I want it with me.'

At this the Siggamaran went out of the room and took the cow up to the pyre. There he killed it with one of the logs of unburnt wood from the pyre, and left the carcass lying there.

Meanwhile, in the house, Simanto's shade departed, and several other ghosts and gods came upon the shamanin and they all accused Deko of sorcery. Finally the ghost of Induri's own husband came and begged her to join him in the Under World. 'Here you are living like a dog,' he said. 'You work all day and you might be a dog for all the food they give you. Far better come away with me.'

It was now midday, and the Siggamaran took the whole party to the cremation ground. He put seven leaves on either side of the pile of ashes and made little offerings of *dub* grass and rice upon them. On one side of the pile he put a hoe, on the other an iron axe-head. He offered rice to the Sun, throwing it to east and west. Then he stepped over the ashes, placing his feet on the magic iron on either side, and one of the assistants made a hoop of bamboo through which he crept: by this means he freed himself from the menace of Simanto's shade.

The two Idaibois also were careful to put their feet on the leaves and bits of iron as they proceeded to wash the ashes. To do this they held large bunches of *Pongamia glabra* leaves and poured the water through them. They did this, they said, for several reasons: the leaves checked the flow of water so that it did not scatter the ashes; by letting the water seep down slowly there was a chance that it might isolate a bone or a bit of wood that would reveal the cause of death; and it was believed that the leaves were cooling and soothed the scorched body of the dead.[1]

[1] It is possible that we have here an example of 'the connexion between the souls of the dead and the fertilization of the ground' which is reflected in their 'very frequent association with water'. Hutton gives several examples of tribal practices of this kind which are expected to bring rain.—Hutton, *Caste*, p. 209.

Then the Siggamaran removed the two pieces of iron and two bits of charred wood and gave them to one of the Idaibois; she wrapped them in a bit of cloth and put them aside. The Siggamaran dug a hole and then, bending a bit of bamboo into a hoop, slipped a ring onto it, and with his back to the pile of ashes and his legs apart pulled the ashes between his legs into the pit. He washed the bamboo hoop, removed the ring, broke the hoop and threw the pieces to the north and south. Then he took another bit of bamboo and repeated the process, but this time he threw the broken pieces east and west. The Idaibois poured water everywhere and gradually swept and cleaned the place until every scrap of ash was in the pit.

Then in the middle of the ashes, the Siggamaran made a small hole, and into this he put the bones and charred wood which had been put aside by the Idaiboi. He covered this with a potsherd, plastered it over with wet mud, put some cooked rice on it and covered everything with a pot placed upside down. Then he put two large logs on either side, covered them with grass and leaves, and put more logs on top.

Then the Siggamaran and the Idaibois bathed and anointed themselves with turmeric oil. The people carried the carcass of the cow into the village, cut it up and distributed the meat throughout the village.

Nothing ever was done about the accusation against Deko; the neighbours were perhaps a little wary of him afterwards; but Simanto had no relatives to carry on a feud and the matter was soon forgotten.

A DIVINATION RITE AT TAREBIL

I WILL give another example of the divination ceremonies which are held during or immediately after a funeral, for they throw a vivid light on the Saora's conception of death and what comes after it.

On 16 December 1944 an old widow named Sinari died at Tarebil. She was cremated the same day and on the 17th her bones and ashes were buried. On the 18th a shaman and the Siggamaran (a hideous leper) visited her house to divine the cause of death.

The two celebrants made a pile of rice over the mortar, and held a knife wrapped in a piece of cloth point downwards over it. Each held the knife with his right hand and had a little rice in his left. As they began to chant, they threw some of the rice towards the door as an invitation to the gods and ancestors to be present.

Presently the shaman passed into a state of trance, and his tutelary came upon him. 'Why have you called me?' she asked. 'To discover why Sinari died. Was it a god, was it Uyungsum, or Labosum, or Dorisum, or Galbesum?' 'It was none of these. It was her own husband who took her away.' So saying, the tutelary 'went down again'.

Then Sinari's own shade came, and now the shaman, when she was supposed to be talking through him, spoke in a thin and weary voice, uncanny to hear: you felt as if the shade was really speaking. 'Here there is no one to give me water,' she said, 'and I am very thirsty.' The Siggamaran held a gourd to the shaman's lips and made him drink. There were two widows sitting by and they said, 'Tell us: who took you away?' Sinari answered, 'It was my husband who took me away, I don't know why, for now he won't have me with him. He ties a gourd to a stick, puts the food in it and feeds me at a distance.' 'Then why did you go to join a man like that?' 'He is my husband. What else could I do?' 'Yes, we understand,' said the widows. 'You thought that if you went to join him you'd be better off than you were here and would get plenty to eat and good water.'

Then Sinari said, 'Bring my ornaments, my necklaces, bracelets and cloth, for I am naked here.'

Sinari's sister produced one bracelet which had been rescued from the pyre and handed it to the shaman, but he threw it away angrily crying '*Chi*' and scattered the rice over the floor. 'Bring all my things at once,' he said.

Sinari's sister then brought out a bundle tied up in a red cloth; in it were Sinari's necklaces, nose-rings, bracelets and cloth. The shaman picked up two of the bracelets and said—he was, of course, all the time representing Sinari's shade—'But where are the other two? Where are my ear-springs? Bring them quickly, for I cannot stay here very long.' Sinari's sister said, 'But this is all we have.'

Sinari, however, insisted and her sister had to collect all the ornaments in the house. The shaman chose a few of them and tied them in the bundle with the rest. He put the bundle on his head and said, 'Good, now I have my things, I shall go away.' He shivered, clenched and opened his hands and declared that the shade had left him.

There was a little pause, while everybody had some palm wine. Then the shaman again went into trance and this time Sinari's husband, Surju, came upon him. 'Was it really you who took the old woman out of the world?' asked one of the widows. 'Nobody took her. She was my wife and I wanted her with me. I am not the sort of person who runs off with other people's wives. None of you in this house ever did anything for her, so she naturally came to me.'

'But why,' asked the widow again, 'don't you treat her properly now that you have got her? Why do you give her food at a distance?'

'If you will do the Guar for her, give a buffalo for her, plant a stone, she can live with me as she did on earth. At present the poor creature stands shivering out in the road where the cattle go to and fro. I don't like it and she is very wretched. But I can't do anything until you give a buffalo.' Then the husband went away and the shaman had another brief respite.

But after a few minutes, Kurosi, Surju's elder brother came and said, 'I want a drink.' The Siggamaran handed the shaman a gourd of wine and he drank it eagerly on Kurosi's behalf. The ghost asked for more, but the Siggamaran said, 'The trees give us nothing nowadays; how can we give you more?' Kurosi said, 'When I was alive there were always great pots of wine; how is it you have so little now?' The Siggamaran said, 'The trees have dried up; we made offerings to you, but you did nothing about it.' All the same he gave the shaman a little more wine and then Kurosi's ghost departed.

Little more was done. The shaman and his assistants continued to chant and drink wine until they were all hopelessly intoxicated, whereupon the proceedings terminated of their own accord.

But they had given some comfort to the shade, and had established that the death was due to the husband's intervention and that the Guar ceremonies should be performed as soon as possible.

V. *The Guar*

THE Guar is a ceremony of the utmost importance; it is the central rite round which the entire elaborate fabric of Saora sacrifice is built. It is the means by which the shade is admitted to the company of the ancestral dead and given the freedom of the Under World. It is usually performed for individuals (and it must be performed for all individuals who have been cremated) at any time from a few weeks to several years after death. But in some villages, particularly those in the neighbourhood of Serango, it is combined with the Karja and celebrated for all who have died within a certain period.

The word Guar is derived from the verb *gu-*, meaning 'to plant' or 'to sow seed', and *ar*, a contraction of *arangan*, 'a stone'; this suggests that the planting of a stone or menhir is the primary feature of the rite. To this is now added the sacrifice of buffaloes and the exchange of ceremonial gifts. Although the most popular time for the Guar is February, after the harvest has been gathered and there is little to do and plenty to eat, it may be celebrated at any time in the open season, and I have records of its occurrence as early as October and as late as May. It does not coincide with any agricultural operation, such as the sowing or transplanting of rice.

The Guar is established in the mythology and a number of stories are told to explain its origin and importance. The following tale comes from Dungdunga.

Long ago a brother and a sister lived together. The brother had a wife and children, but the girl was unmarried. While she was still young she died, and her brother burnt the body and buried the bones. But he did not plant a stone for her, for that was not the custom. The girl became a shade, and whenever her brother went to his clearing at night to guard it, she used to wander round in the forest weeping and calling to him, 'O brother, you have so much, fields and house and children, but what use is it? I am your sister and I wander here, naked and hungry, yet you do nothing for me.' After she had talked like this for several nights, the brother said to himself, 'My sister is dead; how is it that she can talk as if she was alive?' and the following night he called her to come near and asked her, 'What can I do to help you?' She said, 'Plant a stone and kill a buffalo for me.' He did so, and the ghost complained no more.

Another story, from Boramsingi, stresses the belief, common among India's tribesmen, that the soul becomes an outcaste by contact with the stain of death.

In the days before the Guar began, the shades of dead men had to live separate in the Under World, just as Doms and Ghasis are not touched by the Hindus. Their bodies were black as charred wood, and their hair was wild and dirty and shaggy, for they had no oil or water. They were always hungry, for no one would give them food.

So the shades were always coming back to earth to visit the homes of their relatives and to eat their cattle and goats. One day when a shaman was in trance, many shades came upon him and said, 'We are the Doms, the untouchables, of the Under World. Our bodies are black as charred wood; our hair is wild and shaggy. We have no food, no oil, no water. That is why we have come here to eat your goats and cattle. But if you plant stones for us, and pour water and oil and turmeric on them, and kill a buffalo for each of us, we will be able to mix with the other spirits and there will be no need for us to take your cattle.'

That is why the stones at a Guar are washed with water—so that the dead can get a bath in the Under World—and oil and turmeric are used so that they can anoint themselves and do their hair. For whatever is given at the Guar goes straight down to the Under World.

Yet another story, from Pattili, explains why the sacrifice of a buffalo is necessary as well as the erection of a menhir.

An old couple had three sons and a daughter. They were of a Chief's family, and rich. The brothers were married, but the girl was still a virgin, and before she could be married, she died. They burnt her body, and buried the bones, and planted a stone for her. But they did not sacrifice a buffalo, for that was not the custom.

The girl's shade went to the Under World, but the spirits there drove her away. She came back to earth, but Labosum drove her away. She went to the hills, but Mannesum drove her away. 'If you would stay,' they all said, 'you must give us something.' 'But I have nothing,' said the poor naked shade. 'What can I give you?' And she wandered from place to place weeping bitterly.

Then her father had a dream and the girl said to him, 'I have nowhere to live, for I have nothing to offer to the gods.' Next morning the father called the shaman and told him the girl's story. The shaman called Kittung to come and tell them what to do. Kittung came and said, 'When you plant a stone for the dead, you must at the same time sacrifice a buffalo. If you do that, they will be able to enter the Under World and stay there.'

The theory is that the shade is hungry, cold and naked—and untouchable—until the Guar is performed, and that it reveals its dissatisfaction by making members of its family ill or by killing their cattle until they do their duty. The shades, in fact, are a great nuisance at this time. Sometimes they come in the form of owls hooting mournfully round the house. A man taken by Labosum comes riding on a pig, for the pig is the horse of Labosum. Anyone taken by Galbesum comes flying on a peacock. A man struck by magic returns as a buffalo and comes grunting round the house.

Some shamans are adept at recognizing the shades by the noise they make. The shade of a young girl clinks her bangles and makes a *chat-chit* sound as if she were husking grain. An old woman's shade comes with the tapping of her stick. A drowned man makes a noise *chubur-chubur* in the water-pots and sometimes splashes out the water.

The shade of a young boy whistles, the shade of an old man grunts and pants. It is specially dangerous when a shade comes crying *Tirrai-tirrai titte titte titte!* for this is how the Saoras call their buffaloes and it means that some of the herd will die.

When the shades visit a house, they often have an unpleasant effect on the food and liquor. If the shade touches the liquor he weakens it, and if he is the shade of someone who has died by Kinnasum (the tiger god) or Madusum (leprosy), he makes it stink. A shade may turn cooked rice, palm wine or gruel bitter and white as ashes. If the shade of a suicide, of one who fell from a tree, of a murdered man or of one who was hanged for murder touches the food, it turns the colour of blood and gives a hateful smell.

These visitations are intensified if a family delays the performance of the Guar. Children fall ill, the cattle die, the house is full of ghostly noises, the whole family gets nervous and upset.

Sitapati mentions a tradition that there are shades who have been forgotten altogether, and these hover eternally round the villages trying to catch hold of children and swallow them.[1]

The Guar does not put an end to the demands and importunities of the dead, and an ancestor can be just as troublesome as a shade. But until the Guar is done, there is not even a beginning of appeasement of the dead.

Each family has its own menhirs, just as it has its own burning-ground. It is essential therefore, that the Guar should be celebrated in the deceased's own village so that a new menhir can be added to the old ones. In the case of a man, this rarely causes trouble, for the Saoras do not often migrate to other villages. If a man dies outside his own village while on a visit somewhere, his body is brought home; if this is impossible, it is buried and not burnt. If a man migrates to another village and settles there, he can—provided that someone in the relationship of mother's brother, father's sister, or their sons is living there—be admitted to a sort of honorary membership of their family. He can then attend their ceremonies, but he does not cease to be a member of his original group—he cannot, for example, marry anyone within it—and when he dies his Guar must be performed in both places. But this is said to be an unusual event.

Nearly every woman, however, has two homes—her birthplace, where her parents and brothers live, and her husband's home.

[1] Sitapati, 'The Soras', *J.A.H.R.S.*, vol. XIII, p. 128.

A woman does not change her family as a result of marriage, and parents can even demand a dead woman's body from her husband so that they can cremate it in her original village. But this usually only occurs when a man is very poor or on bad terms with his parents-in-law, and the usual custom is for the body to be cremated in the husband's village and a Guar ceremony to be performed there at the husband's expense. Some of the bones are brought to the parents' village and are buried there, and another Guar ceremony is performed at the expense of the parents or brothers.

In the case of a man, the expense of the Guar falls on whoever inherits the property. If the only surviving direct relative is a small boy or girl, someone in the family performs the Guar and adopts the child and takes charge of the property. The cost of the Guar remains as a debt and when the child grows up and takes charge of his property, he will repay it.

A cremation must be, but a burial cannot be, followed by a Guar. If for any reason a man is buried, and his relatives later wish to do the Guar for him, they dig at the foot of the grave and find the bones of the dead man's feet. They take these home and cremate them on the burning-ground, and bury the ashes. After this they can perform the Guar.

Except where a Saora dies in Assam or in jail, when the matter is treated as a special case, the normal rule is that the Guar cannot be performed without some part of the cremated body, and the shade, of the deceased. Where someone dies abroad, then, some of the bones and the shade must be brought home.

In anticipation of this, when the Siggamaran buries the bones and ashes, he separates two or three bits of bone and puts them in a small pot; he covers it carefully and buries it near the main ash-pit.

At any convenient time after death, but generally after the first Guar ceremony and before the second, the deceased's relations come from the original village with drums and trumpets to fetch the bones.[1] They sacrifice a fowl, dig up the buried pot, and an Idaiboi wraps it in a red cloth and carries it home. When they get back they rebury the bones in the burning-ground, men and women dance, and they drink far into the night.

[1] I have seen a score of such processions in various places. At certain seasons of the year, they may be observed almost every day, and the valleys are sonorous with the echoes of gunfire and the clanging of the gongs. The ceremony is called Pangjangan.

Some time afterwards the party makes a second visit, this time to fetch home the soul or shade. Now the ritual is a little more elaborate. I can best illustrate it by narrating the course of an actual rite at which I assisted.

At some time in 1940 a man called Salbong migrated from Thalulaguda to Boramsingi and built a house there. A few years later his mother Ubub followed him, but after only a few months in the new village died at the beginning of December 1944. Her son had her cremated in Boramsingi and celebrated the Guar within a month. Then the Thalulaguda people came and removed her bones to their own village and buried them there. On 5 February 1945, members of Salbong's family in Thalulaguda came to take home the shade, in readiness for the Guar ceremony which they were proposing to perform a few days later.

The proceedings were brief—they only lasted some twenty minutes—but they were significant. Although the setting was Boramsingi, only the Thalulaguda people took part, though the Boramsingi folk were interested spectators. A shamanin sat by the mortar in Salbong's house and called on Ubub's shade.

> Come, for you were born among us. You were married there and your children were born there. Here you have done nothing but die, and now your brother's son has come to take you home. Come dancing; we shall take you dancing.

Then the Siggamaran, holding a small bowl of water, climbed up onto the roof, while other members of the party danced before the house, and others let off guns and some wept loudly. From below the shamanin pushed a stick up through the roof above the mortar and immediately below placed an earthen pot on a heap of rice. The Siggamaran poured water over the tip of the stick and it ran down it and fell into the pot below. As it fell it wavered and this was taken to mean that it was alive and that the shade had entered the pot with the water. An Idaiboi immediately tied the pot up in a red cloth and placed it on her head.[1] Then the party formed into a long file, led by the Idaiboi, and they returned over the hills with much beating of drums and gongs.

Arrived at Thalulaguda, the Idaiboi poured the 'soul-water' over the place where they had buried the bones and threw some palm wine

[1] At Kerubai, where I witnessed this rite in 1950, the water was allowed to fall into a bamboo basket, and the Idaiboi wrapped it in a white cloth and took it away tucked under her right armpit.

on the roof of the house where the dead woman had spent most of her life.

The Guar ceremonies are often delayed, sometimes for several years, for they are expensive and the economic exchanges involved are complicated. There are always many guests to feed, and the providing of sufficient rice, wine and meat is not an easy matter.

The problem of rice, however, is solved by the fact that everyone brings his own. Before the ceremony begins there is a long procession of people—members of the family and others who have been invited to attend—coming with carefully measured quantities which they put into the common stock. The arrangements about buffaloes are more elaborate. One buffalo is always provided by the host; this is the essential sacrificial animal offered for the dead. But one buffalo is rarely sufficient for all the guests, or for the prestige both of living and dead, and there is an arrangement whereby friends and relations may assist by ritually determined gifts.

A buffalo contributed by a mother's brother (or members of his family) or a father's sister's son (or members of his family) is called the Sarebongan. This buffalo, after the head has been removed for ceremonial purposes, is cut exactly in half; half is given for the Guar and the other half is taken home by the donor. The half given for the Guar is eaten at the Guar feast and the donor and his family get their share. In the end, therefore, the donor recovers a little more than half of what he gave.

A buffalo given by a specially close friend of the host or of his father, or by someone who stands in the relationship of father-in-law to one of his children, is called Panangsibongan. It too is carefully divided. The host receives three legs and the head; the donor keeps one hind leg and all the rest of the meat, including the liver. But after the feast is over (in which the donor and his family share) and the donor has gone home, the host sends him one of the legs, together with a basket of rice and a pot of wine. Again the donor gets rather the best of the transaction. This gift is indeed made for 'pleasure, not duty' and it is always repaid, when the donor has to celebrate a Guar in his own house.

The host's own buffalo is divided like this: the head and one leg is put on the menhir and goes to the Siggamaran. Two of the other legs are cut up and distributed as presents to the guests. One leg the host keeps for himself. The rest of the flesh and the liver is used for the immediate feast and for the sacrifice.

The sacrificial meat and rice are distributed among the various officiants: the Idaimaran gets a portion of rice and bits of flesh offered on the menhir; the shaman or shamanin gets the basket of rice used for divination and about two measures of meat. Each Idaiboi is given a stick with bits of meat strung on it.

Each family, as I have said, has its own group of menhirs. These are erected inside or outside the village, usually under a tree—it may be any tree—and are always huddled very close together. They may measure anything from one to eight feet in height and can be very narrow or as broad as four feet. There is no rule that an important man should have a large stone and a poor man a small one, but in practicc there is a natural tendency to bring a big stone for an elaborate and expensive celebration. For babies little stones are often 'planted'.

At Sinkulipadar—but I have not seen this elsewhere—where there was a great cathedral of over three hundred menhirs, many very tall, there was a shrine for a famous Chief, Bopna.

Occasionally wooden pillars—this happens more particularly in the northern, Kond-influenced hills—are erected as well as menhirs at the Guar. At Ladiguda I saw five of these pillars and the Saoras there said that before sowing their seed they took it to these pillars and sacrificed before them to promote the fertility of the harvest.

In other places, wooden pillars are sometimes erected instead of menhirs if a man is very poor, and then only a fowl is sacrificed instead of the usual buffalo.

If the dead man had many sago palms, and was a heavy drinker, he may appear to his heir in a dream and ask him to plant palms near the menhirs. When such trees begin to give sap, it must always be first offered to the dead.

What is the motive for the erection of these monuments? I have heard Saoras use expressions which suggest that they regard the menhirs as houses for the dead. In an article on similar stones put up by the Bhils and other tribes of Central India, Koppers suggests that the outstanding motive is to provide a permanent resting-place for the spirits of the dead. 'Menhirs and menhirlike monuments, that is to say "resting-places" raised above the ground, merit special attention, calling to mind, as they do to anyone familiar with India, the widespread belief that the evil-minded spirits of the dead desire high resting-places.

These *bhuts*, or troublesome spirits, are not supposed to feel comfortable on the ground. It is not without reason that older writers already tried to establish a connexion between this belief and the fact that all Indians desire to lie flat on the ground in the hour of death. There is also the further question in how far all these things may be related to the cult of Mother Earth which is so widespread in India.'[1]

On the other hand, the whole point of the erection of a menhir is to admit the ghost to the Under World, and shamans and other dreamers tell many stories of the houses which the dead occupy there. Indeed the very method of placing these menhirs so close together, so that a group of them look like a crowd of figures huddled close together for warmth and comfort, suggests that the function of the stone is to bring the new ghost into close association with the other ancestors rather than to provide him with an earthly home. It is of loneliness and social isolation that the shades most frequently complain, and the erection of the menhir saves them from this. A shrine, a menhir, or an ikon may be a temporary resting-place on earth (and it is true that in every case this lodgement is raised above the ground), but the ghost's permanent home is in the Under World.

A GUAR CEREMONY AT THODRANGU

ON 14 December 1944, three menhirs were erected at Thodrangu for the members of the family of an important Saora named Doniya. The first was for his father Makla, the second for Makla's sister Jalebap, and the third for Doniya's youngest son, Somra.

Jalebap was a widow and she died at Kamalasingi in March 1944, and was cremated there. Nine months later, her relatives went across the mountains from Thodrangu to fetch her bones and her shade. When they reached Kamalasingi, they went to the burning-ground and offered wine to the gourd in which the bones had been buried saying, 'Come and join your own family group. We have come to take you home.'

An Idaiboi from Thodrangu removed the bones from the gourd and put them in a brass gong which she held under her left arm and covered with a bright new red bazaar cloth. Then the party escorted her, going in file, beating gongs and drums, back to Thodrangu. They took the bones straight to the burning-ground and there the

[1] W. Koppers, 'Monuments to the Dead of the Bhils', *Annali Lateranensi*, vol. VI (1942), p. 200. Compare W. Crooke, *The Popular Religion and Folk-Lore of Northern India* (Westminster, 1896), vol. I, p. 237.

Siggamaran threw rice and wine over them and buried them, placing a stone above them with no further ceremony. Two days later the party went again to Kamalasingi and brought back the woman's shade.

This was on the 13th: on the 14th a group of men belonging to Doniya's family group went to get the menhir stones. They brought three stones, each wrapped in a red cloth, with no further rites than a certain amount of drumming and beating of gongs, to where the family menhirs stood, to one side of a terraced field on the slope of a hill which commanded a magnificent view of hills and valleys down to the Vamsadhara river. They laid the new stones on the ground in front of the old menhirs and a shamanin placed a number of *Pongamia glabra* leaves before them and on each leaf little baskets of rice and brass rings. The men lifted the stones on to the leaves, and then covered them with date-palm branches which they weighed down with smaller stones. This was a test; if by the following morning the rice was in place, all would be well with the ceremony. The date-palm branches were 'to keep the stones warm and guard them from sorcery'.

The next morning, 15 December, early, everybody in the village brought rice to Doniya's house: members of the family brought three measures each, others brought three-quarters of a measure. In every basket was a small brass ring. The rice was heaped up over the mortar in the main room of Doniya's house.

The shamanin and the Idaibois now arranged for the provision of fire and water. They made cups of the leaves of *Bauhinia vahlii*, filled them with the fine chaff of rice and set fire to it. This fire must be allowed to smoulder throughout the day and everything must be lighted from it: on no account must it be allowed to go out. The shamanin then took two new earthen pots, slipped a ring over the blade of a long sacrificial knife and traced lines across the pots and sprinkled them with liquor in the name of the dead. Then two Idaibois took new pots and one of them covered herself with a red cloth. The shaman and the Siggamaran with a number of drummers escorted the girls down to the well. The Siggamaran took leaf-cups of rice in his hands, the shaman carried a red cloth on a pole over his shoulder. At the well the shaman offered rice and wine to the water and the girls filled their pots. One of them powdered a little turmeric and they rubbed each other with it. The shaman washed the girls' left arms with turmeric, rice and water and then playfully smacked their bottoms.

Then the party escorted the Idaibois to the menhirs and the Siggamaran, prepared a hearth and the girls set their pots upon it.

The two women carried the pots to the terraced field in one corner of which stood the menhirs. A slit trench for use as a hearth on which the guests' food would be cooked had already been dug and one of the pots was placed on this. In the middle of the field was a small menhir about two feet high to mark the place where the food for the family group would be cooked. A shaman removed the stone and dug a trench, set a large green log across it, and balanced the other pot —the one which had been covered with the red cloth—against it. The Idaiboi lit a fire with the smouldering chaff which she had brought from the house. All this time, old women were wailing and drums were being beaten in the village.

The shamanin went to the new menhirs and removed the date-palm branches which covered them. She lifted up the stones to see if the rice below was undisturbed. All was well, and she slipped three rings on to her knife and traced lines across the stones as a sort of dedication. 'May no god or ghost come to trouble us!' she exclaimed. Then the Siggamaran moved the stones to one side and with an ordinary digging-stick dug three holes in the ground in front of the existing menhirs and set the new stones in place. The tallest was for Makla and the smallest for young Somra; all three stones were put very close together, leaning against the others.

Then the shaman put a number of baskets, big and small, by the hearths and dropped a ring into each. He filled the central cooking-pot with rice and the shamanin stirred it. A rather ubiquitous woman, of a type which religious ritual seems to produce in every land, Dubli, who was Makla's brother's daughter, now took a considerable share in the proceedings. She busied herself with the cooking and presently took a handful of powdered turmeric and smeared it on the menhirs, wailing loudly, then sat down beside them weeping and gazing out over the mountains.

In front of the stones the Siggamaran built a little booth about two feet high of *Pongamia glabra* leaves and branches. He spread more leaves above and below it, and put a pinch of rice on every leaf. He rolled up the red cloth, put it in the booth, piling rice and putting a ring upon it.

Now came the moment for the slaughter of the buffaloes. There were five of them. Two were provided by Doniya himself, and one by

Jumbong Makla's brother's son, for the dead. One was brought by visitors from Gailunga and one from Kinteda. The story of the Gailunga buffalo was this. Tokla's father's sister, Kujji, was Makla's widow; she had come to Thodrangu from Gailunga. Makla had thus been Tokla's father-in-law. When Tokla's father had died seven years previously, Makla took a buffalo with gifts of rice and wine for the Guar. Now Tokla was returning the gifts. A party of about twenty people from Gailunga escorted their buffalo dancing in procession round the village with drumming and trumpeting.

The buffalo from Kinteda was brought because Makla had been a special covenanted friend of a man called Katela of that village; their forest-clearings had marched together and on their hill had been many sago palms. While working in their clearings the two men had become close friends, and had even agreed to share the wine from their trees. When Katela's father died, Makla presented a buffalo for his Guar, and now Katela was returning it.

The two buffaloes donated by Doniya were led to the door of his house and offered rice and water. When they accepted it it was taken as a sign that the dead were pleased. A woman's cloth was laid over the back of one of them for Jalebap.

Then all five buffaloes were taken to a field a little above the menhirs and tethered there. One of the Kinteda men who was regarded as expert slaughtered them with blows from the back of his axe. He killed three of the animals instantly, but he had to strike the other two several times. This was not considered a good omen and the bystanders shouted and threw dust and dung at the man and smeared his back with it. At the same time a boy killed a fowl by dashing it on the ground. The others proceeded to skin and cut up the carcasses. This took an hour and a half and attracted far more attention than any other part of the proceedings. The skins were very carefully removed and spread in the sun to dry; they would be returned in due course to the Doms from whom the animals had been purchased.

The shaman and Siggamaran offered two of the heads, two legs, and bits of liver and chopped meat at the booth in front of the menhirs. The shamanin took up her position at the booth and began to chant, calling on the dead to be present and to accept the offerings. It was now midday and she stayed there for five hours till nearly sunset.

The rest of the company spent the time dancing, drinking and distributing and cooking the flesh of the buffaloes. There was much amiable gossip and not a little flirting among the younger people. The Gailunga visitors retired to a camp of their own at one side of the village; the Kinteda people made another camp elsewhere. On the paths between these camps and Thodrangu village offerings of blood and rice were made to prevent any traffic of dissatisfied gods or ancestors.

The distribution of the buffalo meat was followed by everyone with absorbed attention. There were carefully adjusted exchanges between hosts and visitors. The head and one leg of the Gailunga buffalo and the head and one leg of the Kinteda buffalo were taken to Doniya's house and put before his door. The rest of the flesh of these two animals was taken to the Gailunga and Kinteda camps. Then Doniya went with drums and trumpets to the two camps and presented each with one leg of his own buffaloes and a share of the rice, gruel and wine that had been contributed. Doniya returned to his house, and then the Gailunga and Kinteda people each sent him two more legs. The visitors ate as much as they could in their respective camps, chopped up what was left and took it home.

The rest of the afternoon and all the evening was spent feasting, drinking and dancing.

The shaman and shamanin spent a lot of time before the new menhirs, arranging leaves in rows and making offerings of rice and blood to the dead. They placed the buffaloes' heads on the menhirs. The shamanin made a small image about five inches long, of rice-flour and water, to represent Makla. She held it in her left hand and fanned it with a banyan leaf saying,

> You died when we least expected it. Now you are mingled with the gods, and you will sit on the banyan, the mango, the tamarind, the jackfruit tree. Today we offer you sacrifice. Help us; do not trouble us.

She covered the little figure with powdered turmeric, laid a banyan leaf upon it, and put it by the newly-erected menhirs.

A GUAR CEREMONY AT THALULAGUDA

At the Guar, as at all Saora ceremonies, the main course of the ritual is constantly disturbed by shamans and shamanins who fall into trance and are visited by the gods and ancestors who, it is supposed, are attracted by the smell of wine and meat. In particular, shades for whom the Guar has not yet been celebrated gather round and are clamorous with their claims for attention. At Thodrangu, inside the house and near the menhirs, shamans were engaged all day in this commerce with the other world. In the following account of a Guar ceremony at Thalulaguda, I shall emphasize this aspect of the proceedings.

On 7 February 1945, three menhirs were erected at Thalulaguda. One was for the old woman Ubub, of whom we have heard earlier in this chapter; another for a little girl Kuntari, not a close relation, but of the same family group; and the third for another little girl, Kachmi, who had died five years before. Ubub's brother, Madhu, gave a buffalo for his sister and for the two children fowls were considered sufficient.

The proceedings followed the same course as those already recounted and need not be repeated. But they were enlivened with a remarkable dance which symbolized the work of axe-cultivation. After Ubub's stone had been erected, five old women danced round the menhirs. One carried a hoe, one a digging-stick, one a sickle, a fourth a pot, the fifth a cloth. As they danced one pretended to dig up the ground, another swept it with her cloth, another pretended to cut shrubs with her sickle. The pot, which was actually full of wine, stood for the pot of gruel which a woman takes to her husband in the clearing. The sickle symbolized the cutting of grass and shrubs for burning. The hoe and digging-stick suggested the work preparatory to the sowing of the seed. The woman who swept the ground did so in honour of the ghosts who live in the forest and always hover about the growing crops.

The Guar, like all Saora ceremonies, lasted a long time: it began at midday and continued well into the night. By sunset the whole village had gathered round the menhirs, and the shamanin sat in the midst calling on the dead to come and indicate their pleasure. They were slow in approaching, but when they did come they had a lot to say.

The shamanin began by saying,

> We went all the way to Boramsingi to fetch you home, and we carried you through Kittim, Rajintalu, Pattili, Tollana, Ragaisingi and Arradalu. Come all you ancestors of those places and bring our ancestors with you. Come quickly, for we have been waiting a long while.

Then she took the names of all the ancestors and shades of her own village, very many of them, all she could remember. But she forgot the name of an old woman who had been devoured by a tiger and for whom a menhir had been erected in a place apart. Suddenly, as she was chanting, a hawk swooped down and carried off a bit of meat from the offerings laid on the new menhir. This caused a great sensation and the crowd was genuinely perturbed. Matters were not improved when, the shamanin now having passed into a state of trance, her tutelary came upon her and rebuked her sternly.

> I am very angry with you. Here you are, all of you, sitting round and you allowed Kinnasum [the tiger-god] to come in the form of a hawk and carry away the flesh offered to the dead. Why did you allow such a thing to happen? There will be a great disaster as a result of this. One of you, at least one, will be eaten by a tiger. You will have to make special sacrifices, or the village will be destroyed. If you don't believe me, well, I am going away now, and you can ask the other gods whether what I have told you is correct or not.

The shamanin called on the ancestors and one of them came and said that what the tutelary had said was undeniably correct, and there was a great clamour of people crying that they would make whatever sacrifices were necessary.

Now the ghosts were beginning to throng round the menhirs, and the shamanin was continually being possessed by one or another of them, jerked about and made to tremble and quiver with the force of their possession. First an old priest, long deceased, came and said,

> Those of you who have spent some money on this sacrifice will be all right. I have only come to see if you my descendants are doing your work properly and are continuing the customs of our tribe. Now I am going away, for the old Chief wants to talk to you.

He left the shamanin, who instantly relaxed, but then began to scratch her armpits as a sign that another ghost was in her. This time it was a former Chief, dead five years past. His daughter cried from the crowd, 'Father, I have brought your cloth: please accept it.' But he replied through the mouth of the shamanin, 'I don't want my cloth. I've not come here for that. I have only come to see what you are doing for my sister.' The shamanin gave him a drink of wine—by the simple process of swallowing it herself—and he said, 'I have never tasted such bad liquor in my life. I'm off; I'm not going to stay where I am insulted.' The shamanin cried in alarm, 'But at least tell us whether we are doing our work properly or not.' But the angry ghost said, 'Don't talk to me. I'm going away. But I'll send my brother and you can ask him anything you want.'

Then the ghost of the Chief's brother came and said, 'You did well in doing the Guar for my sister. We will let her join our company and we will take her below with us. She won't have to sit cold and hungry by the roadside where she has had to wait so long.'

He went away, and the brother of one Kaya, who had died five years before and whose widow had only survived him by two years, came upon the shamanin. He called for Kaya and said, 'I died and I took my wife away after two years, for she was seducing the young men. Now the wanton has to live with me and she can get men no longer.'

Then another of Kaya's brothers came. He had died four years before and they had not yet erected a menhir for him. He said, 'I have been dead four years and I am still wandering by the roadside. You have not sent me to the company of my father and brothers; you don't even give me anything to eat.' Kaya, considerably embarrassed by all this, said, 'I am a poor man; what can I do? I have been to the money-lenders and the Doms, but they wouldn't give me anything. What am I to do?' The shade replied, 'I know all about that. I too have lived in the world and I know how hard it is. But don't blame me if things go wrong with you.'

Now came a man called Rabjang. He had died five or six years previously. He had had a great friend called Boya who was still alive. Rabjang's ghost called for Boya who came and sat down by the menhirs. The shamanin began to chuckle for she was now representing Rabjang and said, 'Well, my friend, when I was still unmarried and we were all young, what fun I used to have. What a lot of other people's wives I used to have!' A wave of apprehension passed over the whole company. The ghost went on, 'Don't you remember? Surely you can't have forgotten. When I was a young man what fun I had.' The shamanin with more chuckles made some singularly obscene gestures. Boya tried to stop her, for after all one never knows what a ghost will say next, and exclaimed, 'How can you talk like this with all these young girls sitting round? Why do you say such things?' The ghost replied, 'What does it matter? I am only a poor ghost. I can see you but you can't see me. I'll say anything I like; you can't embarrass me. What have I got to be ashamed of? Tell me, who are you having nowadays?' There was another tremor and a good deal of fidgeting all through the company, especially in the female and younger part of it. But the ghost did not wait for an answer. 'When I was a young man, there wasn't a girl I didn't make lie down'—and he began to mention them by name, one after another, in spite of screams of protest from the audience—'and when I did anything I did it so vigorously that it went right through their bodies and into the ground below. Well, that's all I've got to say. I'm going now.'

There was a general sigh of relief, especially when this most embarrassing visitant from the other world was replaced by the ghost of a former Siggamaran's mother, who seemed to be entirely concerned with economics. 'When I was ill', she declared, 'you people did not spend enough on me and so I died.' The Siggamaran was also dead, and his ghost came on another shamanin and spoke through her; there was thus an argument between the two ghosts. The Siggamaran was indignant: 'But there was no end to my expenses,' he protested. 'You forget how many fowls and pigs I sacrificed. But you had to die, and there was nothing I could do.' 'Well, at any rate, give me my cloth,' said the old woman. Her daughter fetched it from the house and gave it to the shamanin who laid it on her shoulders and then the ghost 'went below'.

Then came the ghost of Ubub, the old woman for whom the Guar was being performed. The women who were sitting round said,

> We have called you to tell you to go and join your father and mother. Don't now give any trouble to the people in your husband's house, for otherwise everyone will laugh at us and say that we did not do the Guar properly.

Ubub said, 'I have come of my own accord and all the dead are pleased with me. But to keep enemy ghosts away, carry the buffalo's excrement out of the village.' Some of the younger men got up and did this immediately. Then Ubub's ghost said again,

> When I was ill, my son did nothing for me, and that meant that I had to die. Now you have sent me to join my parents in the Under World. When you were bringing my shade, I saw a Sahib by the roadside and he took my photo. He seems to have come here also, following me about wherever I go. That is very flattering to me. I am very pleased. I never had my photo taken when I was alive, but I have had my shade taken after I was dead. Does the Sahib approve of what is being done? Now give me my clothes and ornaments.

The relatives brought out the old woman's clothes and ornaments, and the shamanin put bangles on her own wrists and a pin in her hair, and laid the cloths over her shoulders. Satisfied, Ubub went away.

Then came a ghost who had died of smallpox. He said, 'Lurnisum took me away. Now let men bring loads of wood every Tuesday and let women bring loads of leaves and offer them to me. Otherwise you will soon see how many of your people will die. I have come to warn you.'

Now the Siggamaran began to distribute rice to the people. Suddenly the shamanin's tutelary came upon her and spoke very angrily. 'Here are these ghosts coming and going, and the sacrifice is not yet complete. What are you distributing the rice for? You have made a great mistake and you will have to pay for it.' But the shamanin said, 'No, this is only what was left over. Your share is there, over by the fire.' Hearing this, the tutelary was consoled, and presently departed.

Finally, the whole assembly got up and led by the drummers and trumpeters went round the village, visiting every shrine in turn. But on the way, the shamanin fell into trance again; this time it was Rugaboi who possessed her, and a very hostile and irritated Rugaboi it was. 'Last year, when the red gram was green, you didn't sacrifice to me. So now I am going to sow seed among you.' The people replied, 'O mother, we made a mistake; we admit it; forgive us, but do not punish us.' Rugaboi said, 'Very well then. Bring loads of wood for me, and I will forgive you. Put the wood on the path and if any other gods try to get into your village that way, I'll ask them where they are going and I'll send them back.' At that the people promised to make a special sacrifice on the following Thursday. 'No,' said Rugaboi. 'It must be Tuesday, or I'll sow seed among you.' At last after much discussion they agreed and Rugaboi went away.

That ended the proceedings. It was now close on eleven o'clock and everyone was tired. Within a few minutes the village was quiet and not a soul was to be seen.

VI. *The Sikunda Ceremony*

THE Saoras are a thrifty people and although they spend a great deal of money on their religion, they are always glad of an excuse to spend less. The normal course of events, as we have already seen, after a death, is first the Limma feast, then the Guar, then the Karja and finally the Lajap. But in some places the Limma and the Guar are combined in the interests of economy; in other places the Guar and the Karja are combined; and in a few villages of the Gumma Mutta there is an elaborate, but comparatively inexpensive, ceremony called the Sikunda, which supercedes the Limma and enables the Guar or Karja to be postponed.

The Saoras of these villages do not have any feast at a funeral. They perform the Guar, not for individuals, but for all who have died in a village within a certain period. If they cannot afford the buffaloes for the Guar, they postpone this by a celebration of the Sikunda; if, on the other hand, they can afford a Guar, they perform it, and use the Sikunda as an excuse for postponing the Karja.

The Sikunda, then, is a rite which is performed at irregular intervals, when a number of people have died in the various families of which a village is composed. It does not admit the shades to the Under World—only the Guar can do that—but it does give them consolation and encouragement.

I was present during the Sikunda ceremonies at Barasingi on the 25th and 26th of January 1951. Since the last celebration two years before there had been deaths in five houses representing two families, and sacrifice was offered in each of these houses as well as at the two burning-grounds.

The proceedings began at sunset of the 25th, when a party of men and women went to the burning-grounds with pots of rice and pulse and water. While old women wept, the men made hearths, left the pots on them and returned home. Then the Buyya-priest went from house to house inviting the dead to attend the ceremony. He offered rice and wine on *Bassia latifolia* leaves and said,

> O ancestors, O grandfathers and grandmothers, O shades, come dancing, come to share our feast. If you are eating your food by the wayside, get up and come quickly. If you are eating a fowl, if you are eating a pig, if you are eating a buffalo, if you are drinking liquor, if you are drinking wine, leave it; get up and come quickly. Bring with you those who live in trees, in streams, on the hillside. Today we desire to please you. Come dancing, come happily. Come and sit with us and share our feast.

The following morning, at about nine o'clock, men and women went to build ghost houses on the burning-grounds. They built them very carefully, with little lofts inside, with doors, hearths and cooking-pots. Women cowdunged the floors and planted turmeric round the doors. In each house they put an old fan with a supply of rice, pulse and water. When the houses were ready, the priest came and sacrificed at each house in turn, members of the two families attending only to their own house. He put leaf-plates, one for each of the dead, in two rows on the roofs, and scattered rice all round. He called on the dead, saying,

O ancestors, grandfathers and grandmothers, we call on you. Where are the shades of the newly-dead? Are they in the trees of the forest, among the rocks, in streams, in pits? Seek for them and bring them with you. We have made a house for you. Come and sit in it and share our feast. If any of the dead are in jail, or are engaged as servants of others, or have gone on business somewhere, bring them here. If any of the dead are babies, too young to come, feed them with milk, bathe them, put oil and turmeric on them and bring them with you. Today we give you a feast; come dancing, come happily, to share it.

Then the priest poured wine over the house and round it, and for each of the dead he gave a ring, which he afterwards collected as his perquisite. Old women wept, young men fired off guns, a group of boys banged discordantly on their drums. When the rite was finished for both houses, the people removed all the leaves and cups that had been used and hid them carefully under stones.

Then everyone went back again to the village, and there was now sacrifice in each of the five houses. A great deal of time was spent in measuring and dividing the rice that had been contributed for the feast. In the main house, the priest's own house, all the materials of sacrifice were collected. There were plantains, pumpkins, two new pots, a dozen pots of wine, a winnowing-fan, a sword, a spoon, a brass knife, a bunch of peacock-feathers, pots of water, a bundle of tobacco.

At about midday, the whole company, carrying these things, went up the hill above the village to a picturesque spot below a mango tree where there was a great stone, in front of which was a traditional place of sacrifice. The old hearth was there and the old ashes were cleared out; the ground was cowdunged; and presently the priest set out over two hundred little cups, one each for everybody who had died within living memory. Women started cooking. The priest and a shaman offered rice and wine and called on the dead as usual. Then an Idaimaran took a sword in his hand and led the Idaibois down to the stream to fetch water.

Then under another mango tree near by—it was now just on three o'clock—the shaman cleared a space, scattered turmeric powder over it, placed the sword tip downwards in the ground, and sat down before it. Then five women, representing the five people who had died, came with rice tied in their clothes, and circled round the shaman three times. They put the rice on the ground, piling it up round the sword. Someone brought a winnowing-fan and they filled this too with rice. On top of the rice they put millet, and on top of the millet more rice. On top of everything, they put peacock-feathers, a lamp and a knife.

Then the priest with a shaman, a shamanin and two Idaibois, sat in a row before this altar, and the five women sat in a row behind them. The shaman proceeded to test the omens in order to discover the reason why the five people of their village had died. He had already done this before, and the reasons were perfectly well known, but the thing had apparently to be checked once more. The shaman smeared his knife with oil and held it in the flame of the lamp. As he did so, he took name after name of gods, ghosts and sorcerers. If the knife blackened in a certain way at any particular name, it was understood that the name of the spirit responsible had been revealed. This took a very long time, and it was not until the sun was going down that nine chickens were sacrificed and the people had their feast.

Till late that night, and all through the night, guns were fired, and all next day there was cooking, feasting and drinking in honour of the dead.

VII. *The Karja Ceremony*

THE last major ceremony for the dead is the Karja, though even this may not satisfy them and additional sacrifices may have to be made for years afterwards. The Karja is held every two, sometimes every three, years, in February or March after the harvest has been gathered in and plenty of food and wine is to be had. It takes a long time, is very expensive and demands therefore a season of comparative leisure. Every Saora who dies is commemorated at three successive Karja ceremonies which means that all the dead of the previous six years are honoured at any one Karja.

As Fawcett observed long ago, in some places the Guar and Karja rites are combined. But this is not common, except in the villages round Serango, and the normal practice is for the Guar to be performed first for individuals and then, since, in Fawcett's words, this 'does not *quite* satisfy the *kulba*, there is the great biennial feast to the dead'.[1] In Fawcett's day the drinking and dancing lasted for twelve days; the shamans ate only after sunset; guns were continually fired and the people 'gave themselves up to sensuality'.

The main feature of the Karja is the slaughter of buffaloes. In the following account of the Boramsingi Karja of 1945, twenty-one buffaloes were killed, but Fawcett says that at Kehalakot in 1886 there was a slaughter of at least a thousand.

Fawcett also describes the burning of houses. 'Every house,' he says, 'in which there has been a death within the last two years is on this occasion burnt.' But Fawcett did not himself see this done, and does not seem to have been able to get any actual evidence of the practice. If this was ever done, it is no longer, so far as I can discover, done today.

I attended the Karja ceremonies held at Boramsingi in February 1945, being present throughout the three critical days, the Saturday, Sunday and Monday, 3rd, 4th and 5th. Boramsingi is a large and important village, in very beautiful surroundings, and at that time was distinguished by the fact that the Chief was a woman, a very remarkable woman, Jigri Gamangan. Jigri with her assistants[2] Amiya and Arari—all three women were Guarkumboi shamanins—conducted the greater part of the ceremonies, which were conducted in the house of one Tikamu on behalf of his father's brother Biroila (who had died four months previously) and eighteen others who had died during the period covered by the last two Karjas, a total of six years.

Unlike the Guar, the Karja is performed for an entire village, all the family groups co-operating, though each group has its separate sacrifices in addition to the main ones and its separate food arrangements. Tikamu belonged to the Gamangan family-group and was a prominent citizen of the place and hence his house was chosen for the main rituals.

On Friday 26 January, people came from every house where there had been a death, bringing to Tikamu a small basket of husked rice, a ring and a gourd of wine. These offerings were placed in a row in the main room of the house and the three shamanins sat before them and began the invocations of the dead, calling them by name, and suggesting at interminable length the different places where they might be hiding. When the dead came and asked, 'Why have you called us?'

[1] Fawcett, p. 252. [2] The assistants were not fully 'qualified' and Arari had not yet fallen from grace. See p. 146.

Jigri replied, 'We are going to do your Karja. If you are agreeable, we will be very happy.' She offered the dead a drink of wine and then performed a rite which was to be repeated again and again during the coming days. This was the exhibition of their property to the dead. All the clothes and ornaments of the nineteen dead persons were collected in Tikamu's house, and there were also axes, sickles, baskets and other odds and ends which had been set aside for this purpose after the funerals. The dead are very touchy about these possessions, for they suspect, not unnaturally, that the living want to divert them to their own use. Again and again, therefore, every individual piece of cloth, every bangle, each umbrella had to be brought out, examined and its presence verified—a process that took well over an hour each time.

After this had been done, the three shamanins, possessed by the dead, danced inside the house. Then they sat down again and collected the rings that the mourners had brought. They tied eight of them on a string to give to the potter who would bring a special lamp for use during the ceremony. The remaining rings and the rice were distributed among the people who were to be the chief actors in the Karja—the shamanins themselves, the Siggamaran, several Idaibois, and the Debdingmarans, the drummers who attend the sacrifice and accompany the dancing.

It is the custom in this and other villages situated at not too great a distance from the Kapu Saora settlements, for the Kapu or Kindal Saoras to bring whatever bamboo baskets or mats are required for the Karja and for them to be repaid, not with money, but with ceremonial gifts. On the 27th of January, therefore, each household again brought baskets of rice, rings and gourds of wine to be given to the Kindal Saoras. This evening the dancing began.

For the next five days the villagers were engaged in their preparations for the feast. Buffaloes had to be bought, invitations issued, rice prepared. On Friday, 2 February, a potter came from Alangda with the Karja-lamp: it was a finely decorated pot with a wide mouth on which the actual lamp, a bowl with little figures, rested. He was paid fifteen measures of rice, a rupee in cash and eight rings. He did not bring the little human clay figures that are sometimes used, for Jigri considered his charges—a bullock for two figures each six inches high—exorbitant and refused to order them. Later in the day came some Kindal Saoras with nineteen baskets and a special mat. They were given the same presents as the potter, but with the addition of nineteen gourds of palm wine. The shamanin sprinkled wine on the baskets and distributed them among the various households.

That Friday evening, the Siggamaran, who had been fasting all day, cut a bamboo and brought it to Tikamu's house. He climbed the roof, made a hole in the thatch and let the pole down through it until it stood on the ground in the main room of the house. This was the 'heavenly ladder' which was in evidence throughout the rite. The shamanins spread the new mat before it, and the people came again with baskets of rice, rings and pots of wine, and set them by the ladder.

Tikamu provided a fine crowing cock and the shamanins made it perch on a projecting branch of the ladder some four feet from the ground. The cock had to sit here during every ceremony, and when it crowed from time to time it was taken as a sign that the dead were pleased.

The shamanins kept an all-night vigil. They sat with their legs stretched out before them, clutching a knife in their hands, calling on the dead. When they came, Jigri would pour a little wine on her toes, then drink for the dead, and give some to her assistants. Then they would get up and dance. Five times during the night did they exhibit the clothes and ornaments to their ghostly visitors.

On the Saturday morning, the shamanins, the Siggamaran, and all the Idaimarans and Idaibois (since Boramsingi has nine family groups, each with two or more Idaimarans and Idaibois, there were many of these) and the drummers had to fast until midday. During the morning a dance went in procession round and round the village 'to call the dead from every house'. Then a party of men went out to catch a peacock. The rule is that the bird must be caught, and not killed or damaged in any way. About midday the men returned with a fine peacock and they were met by the drummers and escorted to Tikamu's house. There the man who caught it offered the bird some wine to drink and it was supposed that it would then die of its own accord 'thus proving the power of the dead'. But things did not work out quite so happily and the bird was actually killed in a very cruel way. The belly was slit open while it was still alive; the entrails and flesh were removed and taken out of the village and cooked: a little of the cooked flesh was sent to every house. Then the body was stuffed with straw and stitched up and tied to a pole. With great enthusiasm an Idaimaran took it round the village, escorted by a crowd of wildly gyrating dancers.

The man who caught the peacock was rewarded with a leg of one of the sacrificial buffaloes, six measures of rice and a whole pot of liquor.

At about two o'clock the shamanins sat again before the sacred ladder and lamp, with the solemn cock perched above them, and discussed with the dead whether the Karja was being properly performed. The people again brought rice, rings and palm wine, and the dead yet again demanded an exhibition of their property.

Outside the village, on the road leading to Rajintalu, an Idaimaran made special offerings to the god Manduasum (god of the path) who is a vegetarian and might be offended 'by all the throwing about of blood' that was to come.

Then the shamanin Amiya went with an Idaimaran and the drummers to find a bloodsucker lizard. They went like a hunting party, axes over the shoulder, gourds of wine in the left hand, bows and arrows in the right; someone carried a blazing torch. They found a bloodsucker without much trouble, and the Idaimaran killed it with an arrow. Two other men tied the little creature to the arrow and carried it back on their shoulders 'as if it was a deer'. They took it to the ladder and placed it before it. The shamanin buried twelve kinds of seed at the foot of the ladder. The Idaimaran cut the bloodsucker's throat with a knife and Tikamu's wife took it away and cooked it, cutting the body into small pieces. She mixed these in a pot of wine. Then the Idaimaran offered the mess to the ladder and then took it round the village. Wherever he saw anyone drunk, he said, 'Open your mouth' and when his victim, hoping for a refreshing drink, obeyed, he popped a bit of the flesh inside.

Until the bloodsucker is killed, the Karja cannot proceed, 'for the bloodsucker is the sambhar of the ancestors and they are very pleased when we give them one'.

Later in the afternoon, the head of each of the households where there had been a death offered rice and wine in front of the ikons in his own house and called on the family dead in whose honour the Karja was being held. At sunset each prepared the buffalo to be sacrificed during the night, tying it up in front of his own house and covering it with a new cloth, a man's or woman's as the case might be.

Two other buffaloes were brought as gifts: one came from Karjasingi to Sudbudu's house, a present from his sister's son, and the other came from Alangda to the Dol-behera from his sister's husband. Later a special 'cart' was made: it was an old basket and filled with the dung from the intestines of the dead buffaloes and sprinkled with blood; and it was dragged out of the village to free the place of any alien spirits who might have invaded the place, riding on the buffaloes from outside.

It was a pathetic sight to see the twenty-one buffaloes, dressed in their finery, waiting patiently for the dawn that would mean their death.

Shortly after sunset the Siggamaran went to the spring and offered palm wine before it. He cleaned the spring, scooping out the mud, and put date-palm leaves above it to keep the cattle away and as a sign that no one should fetch water there. At nine o'clock in the evening, a large party of dancers, from Boramsingi itself, and from Karjasingi and Alangda, went to the spring with much waving of torches and beating of drums, escorting representatives of the various households concerned in the Karja. Each of these carried a new bamboo basket full of rice, covered with leaves. The shamanin Jigri removed the leaves from the baskets and offered a little rice on all sides of the spring. Then she stood with her two assistants in front of the spring, each having one foot on a ploughshare, and they chanted together for a long time. As they sang they threw rice over the water. The dancers on the bank above marched up and down with a thunder of drums and a loud noise of gongs and trumpets. Then each of the mourners went to Jigri in turn and she, filling a small pot with spring water, washed their left arms and legs. Finally she poured water over the baskets of rice and the mourners took them home and fed the sacrificial buffaloes with rice and a little pulse. They cooked the rest of the rice in special new pots and kept it for the morrow.

During the night the buffaloes were killed. There was no ceremony about it and it was done whenever the head of a household felt inclined. Only one buffalo was kept for a special ceremonial killing, the one tethered in front of Tikamu's house, by which the Siggamaran slept on guard.

All night the shamanins kept vigil with the dead. At midnight, when I went to the house, they were drunk with sleep, falling over as they sat, forgetting what they had to do; it was the second night that they had had no sleep and all day they had been busy, their one support the wine which they drank steadily for forty-eight hours.

I found the little room crammed with people. On the pole, now decorated with new cloths, sat the solemn patient cock. Below burnt the lamp on its decorated pot. All round were laid out the materials of sacrifice. Above on the loft sat the drummers. The three weary shamanins sat gripping the sacred knife; they were heavy with sleep, yet they still urged their limbs to dance when the dead came upon them. From time to time an Idaimaran would try to climb up the heavenly ladder. 'For the dead who have gone to Kittung,' I was told, 'come upon us and force us to climb upwards towards the abode of Kittung in the sky.'

Jigri asked the dead, 'Is our work good or bad?' and they replied, 'It is good, and that is why the cock has sat on its perch for two whole days to show that your work is true.' 'What shall we do with all this old cloth?' 'Give it to anyone you please.' At this everyone woke up and there was a lot of discussion about the proper distribution of these perquisites. Then the dead gave a blessing to the mourners.

> You have done well and now we shall be happy and content. The crops in your fields and hill clearings will be good: you will get enough to eat and your children will keep well. We will help you whenever you are in trouble.

All night the procession of ghosts filed through the little room. Each had his special demands and had to be appeased with promises and flattery. At three in the morning the people from the other houses, where the buffaloes had been killed, came with the specially washed rice which each had cooked at home.

Then suddenly the cock crowed and they roused the sleeping Siggamaran. Dawn was on the way, and the cock crowed again. The Siggamaran got up and killed the last buffalo with a single blow of his axe. He also killed two fowls contributed by very poor families who could not afford anything more. Then he climbed on to the roof and pulled up the bamboo pole and threw it away.

During the morning the whole of Boramsingi was given up to the smell of meat. There was meat everywhere: slices of meat were drying in the sun, pots of meat were boiling on the fire, strips of meat were being carried on poles by enthusiastic children for distribution; there were quarrels about meat, jokes about meat, sacrifices of meat, gifts

46. Preparing for a feast at Sogeda

47. A potter at work on his wheel

48. Ikon No. 34

of meat for friends, portions of meat for creditors—and in front of every house the head and stomach lay by the door 'so that the spirits would know what had been done'.

In the evening about eleven o'clock there was a final ceremony in front of Tikamu's house. Sixteen of the buffalo heads, each with the stomach balanced on top of it, were placed in a row before the veranda and thirty-five new pots, each covered with a basket, were ranged along the street. A great crowd of people assembled. In the middle, out in the street, on the sacred mat, sat the indefatigable Jigri and her assistants: in front of her was the head of Tikamu's buffalo and the sacred lamp. She held an axe and a bamboo stick in her hand and tapped the head with these as she sang to the dead a long chant of which the burden was, 'Are you pleased with us or no?' She told those of the dead who had been honoured in three Karjas that their business was finally completed; she promised the others that they would be remembered again.

This was the real conclusion of the Karja. But there was still a good deal of distribution of rice and meat to be attended to. The following morning the heads and stomachs of the sacrificed buffaloes were removed from the front of Tikamu's house. The Siggamaran, the Idaimaran and Tikamu shared equally the rice that was left on the altar. The head and stomach of Tikamu's own buffalo, together with the cloth from its back and all the pots and baskets used during the Karja, were given to the three shamanins, Jigri getting the larger share. Each householder distributed the flesh of his own buffalo: he made shares according to the number of houses in his family group —if there were ten houses he made eleven shares, giving nine to the neighbours and keeping two for himself. Large handfuls of chopped meat went to near relatives and relatives-in-law.

Special arrangements were made about the two buffaloes that were brought from outside. Sahibo, who brought the buffalo from Karjasingi for his mother's brother Sudbudu, gave the head and stomach and the two forelegs to Sudbudu, and took the rest of the flesh to the camp made for the Karjasingi visitors outside the village. He also gave Sudbudu three measures of rice and a pot of wine. Sudbudu sent nine measures of rice, a larger pot of wine and a leg of his own buffalo to Sahibo for the entertainment of the visitors in his camp. The same conventions were observed for the buffalo from Alangda. At a later Karja at Karjasingi and Alangda, the Boramsingi people would return the gifts.

Everyone in the village, not only the mourners, everyone who contributed wine, got a little meat during the distribution, and all that day and night the feast continued.

VIII. *The Lajap Ceremony*

AFTER the Guar and Karja have been completed, there is another, though minor, ceremony to be performed. This is the Lajap, which is celebrated when the rains are over, at the time of the big rice harvest, to show that the work of the dead is now finished and to persuade them to give good crops in future.

For this rite each family makes its own arrangements, and the sacrifice is offered partly in the house and partly in a field, always the same field, belonging to a leading member of the group in which any death has occurred during the preceding two years, or whatever period has passed since the last Lajap.

I attended the Lajap rites at Alangda on 23 November 1950. There were three families in this village and in each of them someone had died. Three separate ceremonies were therefore conducted simultaneously. I attended the proceedings in the house of one Sumanto, in honour of his dead father, Dasmo. Sumanto paid for a cock, a new fan, baskets, pots and a sickle; the other members of the family brought their own rice and wine for the feast. The actual rite was conducted by the Idaimarans and Idaibois; no shaman or priest was present. The Idaimarans collected the dead man's possessions, his loin-cloth, his bow and arrows, his axe and a pot, and put them with the new baskets and other things as a sort of altar inside the house. They sat before this, one of them holding the other's wrist, and called on the dead to come and share the feast.

Then they took everything out into the field. There they made a small clearing amidst the growing and nearly ripened rice, and made an altar with baskets, the dead man's possessions and a winnowing-fan, and laid out rows of leaves of *Bauhinia vahlii* before it, offering a little rice and wine on each leaf.

Then the Idaibois fetched water in new pots and cooked the rice. One of the Idaimarans fed a cock with rice and liquor, stunned it by striking it against the ground, cut off the head and let the blood fall over the leaves and into a pot. Guns were fired. An Idaimaran offered cooked rice and meat to the dead. Then everybody feasted.

Sumanto explained that the new things he had bought were a token that the work for the dead was now complete: there was a new sickle to ensure a good harvest, a new fan to winnow the grain which would be abundant, new baskets to carry home the splendid crop that must follow. He stressed the fact that only members of one family could eat together at this time and share the food consecrated to the dead. 'Only those of the same *idai-birinda*, ancestor-group, can share it.'

Since no shaman was present, there was no possibility of communicating with the dead, with the result that this ceremony was remarkably straightforward and expeditious, free from the endless irrelevancies of trance.

IX. *The Anamanpur Ceremonies*

IMPORTANT rites for the dead, at which only those shamans specially dedicated for the purpose—the Guarkumbmarans or Guarkumbois—can officiate, are those in which ancestors are honoured and given some kind of further life on earth by the naming of children after them.

Saoras normally get their names from the day of the week on which they were born—Addian or Addin (Sunday), Mangadan or Mangadi (Tuesday), Budan or Budi (Wednesday) and so on. In addition to this, as they get older, they often collect nicknames. A boy may be called Tala because he has a head like a stone, Melad because he squints, Jelumu if he has a big nose, Kabunglud if he has big ears. A boy at Boramsingi was called Jumbong, because while he was still in the womb Kinnasum attacked his mother and a buffalo was sacrificed for him; hence Jumbong, eater of buffaloes. Usually a man takes the title of his family group after his proper name; thus, Jumbong Gamangan, Sukku Buyyan.

But other children are called after their ancestors. Sometimes after he has been named in the ordinary way, a child may refuse its milk and cry a great deal, and when the shaman is called he may discover that the reason is that one of the ancestors wishes the child to bear his name. As we have seen in chapter II this constitutes a sort of nominal reincarnation: the ancestor gets a new lease of life through the existence of his name on earth. When this happens a ceremony, with the sacrifice of a goat or buffalo, may be performed immediately, or the name may be given and a ring or bangle put on the child as a token with a promise of a regular ceremony after four years when he can walk.

I will now give some account of two of several Anamanpur ceremonies which I have witnessed, for they form an important part of the Saora tendance of the dead: the first was for a baby who was named after her maternal grandmother; the second was for a child named after a paternal grandfather who after death became a tutelary.

THE MANEBA CEREMONY

MAKLE, a young Saora of Maneba, was so troubled by the Doms of Serango, that he went away to Assam to earn some money to buy them off, leaving behind his pregnant wife who took refuge in her brother's house.

After the child was born—it was a girl—her maternal grandmother's ghost began to torment her with constant fever. A shaman was consulted and the ghost came upon him and said, 'Give the child my name, Pissari, and she will have no more trouble. For then I will be in her, and if any god or ancestor comes to attack her I will drive him away.'

On 22 December 1944, therefore, a ceremony was held at Maneba to give the child the new name and to cure her sickness. Her mother's brother made an ikon on the wall of the main room of his house. The shaman built an altar of rice and other offerings above the mortar. He made many cups of leaves and a circlet of thorns.[1] The mother's brother took the child in his lap and sat down opposite the shaman on the other side of the altar. The shaman made the usual offerings of rice and wine on the altar and in front of the ikon and made a mark of rice on the baby's forehead in the name of the dead, and called upon them saying,

> Kittung has given us this child. She is a bamboo pin, she is a leaf; come and make her fat and strong.

The mother took the child in her arms, and the shaman picked up a hen and washed its feet in water. He proceeded to a lengthy invocation of the ancestors.

> O grandfathers, grandmothers, sisters, mothers, father's sisters, we beg you all to come. When you do come, we will wash your feet and anoint them with turmeric and oil, and most lovingly make you

[1] The leaves and thorns of *Aegle marmelos*, Corr., the *bel* tree, are invariably and exclusively used during the Anamanpur ceremonies.

sit amongst us. You say that you live among the menhirs, but in fact you go abroad to visit every land. You traverse the great mountains, the rocks, the thorny places, you go down to the Under World. Yet you return to live where the stones are placed. We do not know where you are now. Come quickly and tell us. If we had no child to worry about, do you think we would call you? Whether you are short or tall, ugly or beautiful, even if you have lame feet and broken arms, in whatever form you come, you are our ancestral dead, and we shall honour you as kings. As is a Raja's body, so is your body; as a Raja dresses so do you dress; as a Raja rides on an elephant or horse, so do you. We do today all that Kittung taught us in the old days. Come, you are great, we honour you.

The shaman then put a tiny cup of rice and a bit of ginger in the baby's hand, and made the hen peck at it; the child was naturally frightened and there was an extraordinary din, the child screaming, the hen squawking and the shaman chanting invocations to the ancestors. Then the shaman took the bit of ginger in his mouth, chewed it up, spat it into the baby's ears, sprinkled her with water and cried 'Pissari, Pissari!' and everyone present echoed him.

Then the mother's brother killed the hen and the shaman sprinkled the blood over the rice and other offerings. Then he placed the circlet of thorns on the altar of rice, covered it with a cloth and made little Pissari sit on it. Afterwards he carefully examined the thorns: if those which had been bent down by the weight of a child's body rise again into their usual position it is considered a good omen. It was so today and everyone was pleased. The shaman took the baby in his lap and they all leant forward to pet and fondle her, for it is considered very lucky to take a baby in one's lap or even to touch one at this time: wounds heal and old diseases are healed. As they did this, the shaman took up his chant again:

O grandfathers, O fathers, come and see this child. Put your hands on her body. Today is a day for happiness. Come and feel her body with your hands. Her body is tiny as a tamarind leaf, thin as an *aonra* leaf. Come and look at her. Make her fat and strong. Today is a great and lucky day, and on it show your love for the child.

The shaman gave a little wine to the mother and she put a few drops in the baby's mouth. She handed the child to the shaman and he held her to his breast and called on the grandmother to come and see the child in whom her name would now be living. She came and declared herself pleased with what had been done and promised that her young namesake would grow up strong and well.

The actual rite was now finished, but members of the household and a few visitors spent the rest of the day drinking and singing; in the evening they had a feast.

THE SINGJANGRING CEREMONY

THIS second Anamanpur occurred on 26 December 1950, and was performed for the four-year-old son of a Saora named Shanku. Shanku's paternal grandfather, Saitino, had been a well-known shaman, and after his death and the due performance of all the funerary rites, he became a tutelary in the Under World, where he was given the new name of Ribano.

When Shanku's baby was born, tutelary Ribano came upon the shaman who was inquiring what name it should be given and said, 'Give this child my names, both of them, Saitino and Ribano.' The parents replied 'We will certainly give the child your names, but', they added, being of a canny and economical turn of mind, 'let him walk first. If he grows strong and well, we will name him after you.' 'Very well,' replied the tutelary. 'Make an ikon, dedicate a pot, and sacrifice something in my name. When the time comes, name the child and have a fiddle-dance.'

Four years passed and the child grew into a strong and healthy little boy. On 26 December, therefore, there was an imposing gathering to fulfil the old promise. There were five officiants, two Raudakumbois, two Guarkumbois, and an Idaimaran: the chief shamanin, Jigri, having recently died, an old woman called Aganti came over from Boramsingi for the occasion.

Underneath the ikon which had been made for Ribano, Aganti made an altar of rice and put fourteen leaves upon it, seven for the tutelaries, seven for the ancestors; on each leaf she put a leaf-cup. On the left she placed a basket of rice, a pot of wine and a new white cloth. She began the ceremony by putting a few grains of rice and some drops of wine into each of the cups before her and by chanting an invocation against sorcerers.

Today we are to name a child. Let no sorcery approach our house or village. Let no one in Kittim, Singjangring, Boramsingi or Ladde work evil against us. Let every sorcerer—young man or old, maiden or crone—forget that we are naming a child today. If they try to put their magic in our wine, our rice, our drinking-water, stop them. O tutelaries, O ye departed, Kittungsum, Uyungsum, Mannesum, you are great kings, there is nothing you do not know. We give you rice and wine. O Tongarbasum, Manduasum, Borongsum, let no one approach who works evil by grubs, by chillies or by rice. We give you rice and wine. O tutelaries, if any who died of snake-bite, or hanged themselves, or were murdered, or were devoured by tigers, or fell from trees—if any such come near, let them not enter the house. We will give them wine and rice outside.

Then the Idaimaran put some wine in two cups, took them outside and whistled loudly. He returned and the shamanins offered rice and wine at the main pillar of the house, calling on all the dead by name.

Come all of you and see. We are giving this child his name. Let him live happily. Do not trouble him. Come and drink your wine; we invite you in all honour.

Then two of the shamanins (the Raudakumbois) and the Idaimaran went outside and stood in line before the door, which was then shut. There was a bundle of thorny *Aegle marmelos* branches; they picked its leaves and put them in their hair. One shamanin held the bundle and each of the three put an axe over the shoulder. They now represented the tutelaries and spoke in that character.

We have come in love, O brothers, we have come willingly. We have brought a bundle of thorns. We will give you no trouble. We have come to make you happy. We have come from far carrying our thorns, all the way from the Under World, travelling through every land, keeping back the witches that would follow by placing thorns on the path behind us. O brothers, O fathers, we will not trouble you. We will accept our wine and food with pleasure.

Then from inside the child's parents answered, and a long conversation followed.

Parents: Whence have you come and why?

Tutelaries: We have come from the Under World to give you happiness.

Parents: From which hills and forests have you come? It is true that we called you and we are very glad that you have come.

Tutelaries: We were in the Haldibagor [a hill-clearing in the Under World, where only turmeric is grown], but when you called us, long though the road was, we came at once.

Parents: Have we made any mistakes? Have we ever forgotten to honour you? You are those who give joy and sorrow.

Tutelaries: You have done no wrong. You called us and we came. But why do you keep us standing outside the door ? Open it and let us in.

Parents: You live on the hills and in the forest. It is you who drive men to hang themselves, you make men murder one another, you cause them to fall from trees, it is you who carry men away. But we do not blame you, we speak no word against you. We are glad you have come. Speak the truth to us and we will let you in.

Tutelaries: There was a great hill on the way and we are weary. Many started with us, but some returned home and others lagged behind. We had to cross many streams and hills, and pass by many villages, to bring you these thorns. Why do you keep us waiting outside? It was we who gave you this child; why are you hiding him from us?

Parents: How many children and old people, how many girls and boys, have you taken away? Yet we never stopped you; we will let you in.

Tutelaries: Do, for we are tired of standing here outside. We are the Great Ones, we give and we take away, we give birth and death, we know all things, we are the kings of the Under World.

Parents: Yes indeed, we know you are kings, you are Brahmins, you are Kshattriyas. Come in, we welcome you.

At this the three 'tutelaries' standing outside put their left feet together on the threshold. One of the bystanders handed them a gourd of water and they washed their feet and rubbed turmeric on them, and then washed their left hands and arms. Then they cried, 'Why is the door still shut? In our house the dead are as many as the leaves on a tamarind tree. We have left them and come to you. Do not be afraid; we have come to help you.'

Then they pushed at the door with their axes and when it swung open they went inside and placed the bundle of thorns and their axes on the altar of rice before the ikon. They sat down and the mother bathed the child and rubbed turmeric and oil on his body.

Now all five officiants sat round the altar and called again on the dead. So as not to forget anyone, they took the names by the days of the week on which they had died, saying, 'All ye who died on Monday, come and aid us. All ye who died on Tuesday, come, all ye who died on Wednesday, come. . .'

Now the two Raudakumbois prepared for the coming of the tutelaries. They stretched out their legs towards the altar, and Aganti took the little boy on her lap, tied the new cloth round his head as a turban, stuck some cock-feathers in it, and made him sit on the bundle of thorns. Then she and the other Raudakumboi went into trance, and when their legs had been straightened and their hands unclenched, Aganti cried, '*Daring-daring!* Saitino and Ribano have come!' She put the child by her and the two women patted his back, and addressed him for a long time, as if he had actually become Saitino-Ribano.

Daring-daring! We call you son, but in fact you are our father. You are great; you have lived in the Under World; now you have come here. We take you in our laps and fondle you to make you happy. When you were in the Under World, you wandered like a wild pig in the jungle, like a tiger on the hills, like a bear in the thick grass. You are great; you are Brahmins; you are Hindus; yet you have come here to us. You were living in water as fish do, on trees as birds do, and we could not see you. Yet we never say that because you are beings without blood or bones you cannot speak, that because you have no hair you cannot teach us.

Now that you are born here, you must eat the flesh and blood of the excreta-eating pig. Did you get permission to come from your relatives in the Under World? How did you manage to leave the dead there, thick as leaves on the tamarind? But however you did it, you are born here now, and that is why we make you sit on thorns and call upon your name. Now you will have to use the plough, you will have to clear the forest, you must climb the sago palm, you will have to fetch wood, you will have to graze the cattle, you will have to chat with anyone who passes by, you must eat what others eat, and live just like the rest of us. You have come from the Under World and it may be that your relatives there will have something to say about all this. You had great happiness in the Under World; how is it that you have come to taste sorrow here?

In the old days you were a famous shaman. In the Under World you soon became a tutelary. But now you are one of us. As you were a shaman before, so you will be a shaman again. All the things you once had, the houses, the fields, the garden, cattle, money, they are here: nothing has been lost. Do not let your relatives come and say, 'This is our man; we are going to take him back again.' As you came willingly, so live here happily.

The shamanins then put the child down, and called on the gods and tutelaries again, and many of them came, full of complaints and demanding better treatment. Aganti's own tutelary said,

In the Under World the sky is always overcast. Now you have called me, what do you propose to give me? You have made me very angry. As a grazier gathers his cattle, so have we herded the dead together for you. We are too important to be called to earth for trivial things.

Then the tutelary Ribano (who at the same time was Saitino) came full of complaints.

We told you that when you gave this child our names, there must be a fiddle-dance. We see no sign of it. And we asked for a new cloth; where is it? You have given us our milk (that is palm wine) in a small pot; we want a big pot of it. What are we to say to our relatives in the Under World? There is not enough to give them one drop each.

There was a long discussion at this, everyone talking at once and explaining that times were hard and that they were giving all they could. In the end the tutelary declared himself satisfied, and the shamanins cleaned their teeth with ginger and washed their faces with spittle. Aganti again took the child in her lap crying, '*Daring-daring!* Live happily. Do every kind of work. Never forget that you come from the Under World.' She dressed him in new clothes and tied his turban, putting a tuft of white feathers in it.

Then tutelary Ribano said, 'Where is my horse?'

A goat was brought in and the shamanins washed its feet and rubbed turmeric on them; they put some rice in the child's hand and made the goat eat from it; then they cleaned the child's teeth also with ginger.

Then tutelary Ribano called to Shanku and said, 'Now I am your child. But I told you to give me a coloured turban. Why have you given me a white one?'

The father promised to give a fowl at the next Festival of Pulses and this seemed to satisfy the tutelary. He took hold of the goat and said, 'Very good' and sang,

> You did not give me a coloured turban.
> You only gave me a tiny pot of milk.
> What a little horse you have given me!
> I have no profit by becoming your son.

Shanku replied, 'We didn't ask you to come here; you came of your own accord. Take what you have got and be content.'

Then Shanku put a new cloth on the goat's back, made the little boy sit on it, and led him round the village, while the people danced and the boys beat their drums and one man went before them with a fiddle.

At last the boy was taken down from his 'horse' and the two shamanins who represented the tutelaries caught hold of the goat and dragged it out of the village. The others caught hold of them and pulled them back, and there was a regular struggle which only ended when Shanku gave the shamanins some wine. Then they let the goat return. The meaning of this was that the tutelaries wanted to take the goat as it was to the Under World and eat it all there. But the villagers naturally wanted their share and so they dragged it back.

The shamanins went back to the house, and tutelary Ribano said to Shanku, 'We are very pleased with this. We came of our own accord and we shall live here happily.'

Then someone killed the goat on the threshold, stunning it with a stone and then making a hole in the throat. The Idaimaran offered some of the blood on the altar. They cooked the meat and when it was ready the shamanins offered cooked rice and flesh on the altar, first giving a little to the child. They put the thorns over the door and then they all sat down and feasted.

For her work on this occasion Aganti received twenty measures of rice, a pot of wine, the new cloth, and the head and a leg of the goat. She was escorted home to Boramsingi, a mile away, by a party of boys and girls who danced and sang round her. She placed her gifts under the ikon of her tutelary and gave the boys and girls the pot of wine to drink.

X. *Special Precautions*

THE unusual is always risky. Against the sudden, the dramatic, the extravagant it is essential to take precautions. And so, when people die out of the routine, all sorts of special rites and taboos are observed to protect those who are still alive. I consider elsewhere what is done when someone is murdered or dies by his own hand. I will now describe the precautions observed for those who die of smallpox, who die abroad, and who are killed by tigers and bears.[1]

The bodies of those who die of smallpox are not immediately cremated. They are first buried, with a rather furtive little ceremony,

[1] 'The chief objects of reverence amongst the Savaras, and all the other aboriginal races, are the deified ghosts, or spirits of persons who have died a violent death, either accidentally or in battle.'—Cunningham, p. 138.

attended only by members of the actual household. No cloth or turmeric is put on the body. The grave is shallow, only waist deep, and the corpse is laid on its side, a man's on the left, a woman's on the right, and the feet pointing to the north. The proceedings are directed by a Siggamaran, who is the first to throw earth upon the body. After about a foot of earth has been filled in, the grave is firmly packed with stones. Then comes another layer of earth, then a layer of thorns, and then more earth and stones. This is to prevent any hyena or other wild animal digging up the body; should this happen the shade would become a *kinna-kulba*, a 'tiger-shade' and cause endless trouble.

But the Saoras do not like to leave the body in the ground. Unless they cremate it, they cannot have a Guar ceremony for the dead man, and that means that his shade cannot find entrance to the company of the dead in the Under World. On the other hand, there seems to be some idea that, since the ghost will in any case join Rugaboi, goddess of smallpox, there will be no harm in delaying this for a time by not pressing on with either cremation or Guar. As long as the shade is in the grave, well packed down with thorns and stones, it will have to stay there, and that saves a lot of bother for everyone.

But after about a month, or when the epidemic has ceased, a shaman calls on the ancestors and inquires if they are willing to have this dangerous ghost among them. 'If we burn the body,' he asks, 'will he return to torment us?' If the dead reply that they will accept him, then the people of most villages, even of those who have officially adopted the taboo on beef, sacrifice a bullock. They dig up the corpse, take it to the burning-ground and cremate it. Later they perform the Guar, erecting the menhir at a little distance from the rest.

It is said that if there is a great epidemic, with many dead, they do not do this, but leave the bodies in the ground.

In some places, those who die of cholera, epilepsy and leprosy are given a double burial in the same way.

I have been told that when a pregnant woman dies, the Saoras cut open the belly down the middle after the corpse has been laid on the pyre, for they fear that otherwise the belly may swell up and burst, throwing the foetus to the ground.

It is a bad thing to die abroad. The shade finds itself in unfamiliar country; the funeral may not be conducted properly—logs of green wood may be unobtainable, there may be no Siggamaran or Idaimaran, the proper offerings may not be made. Saoras do not, in fact, often die outside their own homes, for they rarely migrate, seldom go to hospital, and do not often get hanged in jail. But they do go in fairly large numbers to Assam, and some of them die there.

When this happens the other Saoras in the colony do their best; sometimes they even send little pieces of bone all the way back to Orissa. But the shade has a difficult time finding its way home. If it can meet Ringesum the Wind, they come together with 'a rushing sound like the noise made by a motor car'. When the shade reaches its village, it proclaims its presence by blowing the grass off the roof of its house, and by making ill anyone it catches in its blast. A whirlwind is, in fact, usually regarded as a shade returning from Assam.

If the Guar is delayed, the shade visits the house of its relatives and makes a noise like a railway train or a car to frighten them into doing their duty. Special ikons are often made, featuring aeroplanes, cars and trains (see pp. 440ff.) to satisfy them, and to please the other dead, who strongly disapprove of people leaving their villages. They are by no means ready to admit these errant shades immediately, and sometimes even after the Guar put thorns on the path to the Under World to prevent them coming. 'Why did you go away?' they are supposed to say. 'In your absence there was no one to feed us. Why should we accept those who neglect their duties?'

Strangers and orphans are usually buried. This is a measure of economy, not because it is cheaper to bury than to burn, but because burial eliminates the necessity for a whole series of costly ceremonies. Everyone who is cremated must have his Guar, Karja and Lajap. But if he is buried, he cannot have any of them.

It is a serious matter to be eaten by a tiger. It is tiresome for the shade and dangerous for the living. The shade goes to the Under World in the form of a tiger, and the tutelaries and ancestors go out to hunt it. When they succeed in killing it, they cremate the carcass with castor wood, and perform a Guar ceremony, and the shade becomes an ancestor. He then comes in a dream to his relations and points out that since he has now been accepted in the Under World, there is no reason why they should not perform the proper ceremonies for him on earth.

The ghost becomes Kinnasum, the tiger-god, and it is in the form of a tiger that he usually visits the earth. He is very dangerous, especially in the early stage before he has been hunted down and killed by the other dead, and often enters into and inspires the same tiger who killed him to kill other people too.

Similarly a man killed by a bear turns into Saluasum, but he acts as the shaman of the Under World. Saluasum can be employed, as it were, by the ghosts of murdered men to attack the living in revenge for their tragic fate.

The sequence of events is something like this. First of all, the Saoras search for the body, and when they have found it, and it has been inspected by the Chief and village elders, they cremate it on the spot. A medicine-man is summoned if there is one within reach, otherwise an ordinary shaman does what he can. In some places the people take everything the dead man possessed, even gold ornaments, to the place, and these become the property of the shaman, who holds them on behalf of the ghost: it is too dangerous for anyone else to have them. There must be no dancing, no firing of guns, no blowing of trumpets as at an ordinary death. As they go to and fro the mourners must be silent. When the funeral is over they bathe and wash their clothes, and the medicine-man sprinkles 'medicine' over them. He may also throw medicine over all the houses in the village.

While the pyre is burning, the medicine-man or shaman attempts to divine the reason of the tragedy. Wild animals never act on their own. They are in themselves neutral; they only become dangerous when inspired and directed by some other power. It is therefore important to discover who it was, and there is a special technique of divination for this.

The shaman holds an earthen pot to his mouth and roars into it; the pot acts as a resonator, and the resulting noise is satisfyingly tigerish; he calls on the tiger to say who sent it. He takes the name of a god, and roars. If there is any answering noise from the forest, it is assumed that this was the god responsible. If there is no reply, the shaman takes another name, and roars again. He goes on with the names of many gods, then of the dead, especially any others who have been killed by tigers, then of any possible sorcerers. If this method fails, the shaman turns to the lamp and the knife, and he calls on the tiger, saying,

> Are you a real tiger, or were you specially made for this deed? Were you actually born a tiger? Are you a man changed into the form of a tiger? O Ramma-Bimma, Kittung, Kinnasum, you gods who gave us birth, come and tell us the truth.

The following day the villagers perform the first Guar rite, which has the effect of sending the shade below in its tiger form to be hunted by the ancestors. For this, the mourners assemble in the village, and someone ties a pig by its feet to a rope. He then pierces its throat with a sharp stick and dragging it bleeding behind him leads the way into the forest towards the scene of the tragedy. The mourners follow along the trail of blood, until they come to an ant-hill as near as possible to where the death occurred. In some places, however, it is regarded as dangerous to do this, for the trail of blood may lead the tiger back to the village. Instead they drag the pig along, kicking it and trampling on it, and finally beat it to death before the ant-hill.

Ant-hills are always connected with Kinnasum and tigers, and when the party find one that is suitable, the shaman stands with his back to the hill and bumps it with his backside as he calls on Kinnasum to come and partake of the feast which is being prepared for him. It is a good feast, for in addition to the pig, a buffalo is also sacrificed, and the whole of the meat must be eaten on the spot. Nothing may be brought back to the village. A small menhir is erected by the ant-hill, and this completes the first 'little' Guar.

Later, when the relatives have been convinced as a result of dreams and divination that the tiger-shade has become an ancestor, they perform the full Guar in the usual place.

For example, a woman named Damni, of Potta village was killed by a tiger in 1943. The villagers performed the little Guar in the forest at the place where she had been killed, and her shade went as a tiger to the Under World. It was not, however, for several months that the ancestors managed to hunt her down and kill her. But then she became an ancestor and began to give her surviving brother attacks of fever until he celebrated the full Guar ceremony for her in 1946.

There are many small variations of practice. In the third week of January 1945, a tiger killed one Bariko, a Saora of Gunduruba, dragging him from his field platform in the swidden where he was sleeping beside his little niece. The child ran home with the news, and in the morning the people went to look for the body, but all they could find was the head, with part of the hands and feet. They burnt these relics on the spot, took their 'medicine' and the following day performed the pig ceremony and the 'little' Guar. On this occasion, they mixed pig's blood with palm wine and scattered it all over the place 'to drive back the tiger in the name of the dead'.

A few days later Bariko's widow had a pig sacrificed in her house, and a shaman went out to drive a nail into a tree at the village boundary 'to close it' and prevent the shade returning. On this day everyone in the village had to pass one by one through Bariko's house; the shaman stood at the front door with a broom in his hand and brushed each individual as he passed through, crying repeatedly, 'Go away! We have given you a pig. We have driven nails into a tree. We have done our duty. There is no need for you to trouble us any more. Go away and leave us alone.'

The strict rule of quarantine where a tiger-tragedy has occurred is illustrated by what happened at Latur where the wife of one Karu was killed on 19 December 1944. None of the villagers were allowed to leave the place and no one was permitted to go in. The woman's relatives were not allowed to come from her home-village for the funeral. The police came to investigate and they, of course, were privileged, but the Saoras who carried their baggage had to buy a small pig from Karu's house, and sacrifice it by the path before they could enter the village. Had they not done so, they would have been in great danger of being killed themselves.

In this village the shaman protected the village differently. Early in the morning, he sacrificed a pig, and while it was still dark led a party of mourners right round the boundary, dropping grains of rice as he went along. He found a *Pterocarpus marsupium* tree, and went round it three times. Then withdrawing from it about eight feet, he took a bow and shot an arrow with all his strength into the trunk. It is necessary that the arrow should penetrate so deeply that no tiger can pull it out. Should the shaman miss or the arrow break, it is a very bad omen, and a pig or even a buffalo must be sacrificed at once. But if the arrow hits the tree squarely, it is believed that if the tiger approaches the village again, it will become blind when it reaches the charmed boundary.

Chapter Ten

THE ART OF THE IKON

I

AN IMPORTANT and characteristic feature of Saora religion is the custom of making drawings on the walls of houses in honour of the dead, to avert disease, to promote fertility and on the occasion of certain festivals.

These drawings, which are called *ittalan*,[1] a word I translate as ikon, may be made by 'anyone who knows how'; he need not be a priest, but the artist who becomes adept achieves a sort of dedicated position and is known as the Ittalmaran, 'wall-writing-man' or, in fact, artist. Many of the shamans also combine this art with their regular professional duties.

The routine procedure, which is almost standardized, is for the shaman to recommend the painting of an ikon as one of the means of satisfying a god or ancestor who has brought trouble on a home. The making of the ikon may be the pivotal point of a ceremony, or may be auxiliary to its main business, but it is always associated with some sort of sacrifice. As the regular festivals come round, the renewal of the old paintings, especially those for improving the fertility of the crops, is accepted as a normal religious obligation.

When an ikon is to be made, the householder may either paint it himself, following the inspiration of his dreams, or he may send for a shaman or Ittalmaran and tell him what has to be done. In this case the artist comes to the house and spends a night there before beginning work. In the evening the householder places a small basket of rice and a pot of palm wine on the ground before the wall on which the picture is to be made. If necessary his wife washes the wall with fresh red earth and water to provide a good background. The artist offers the rice and wine to the god or ancestor concerned and says, 'I am an ignorant fellow; I know nothing; but I have been told to

[1] Probably derived from the Saora root *id-* which means 'to write' and *tālan*, a contracted form of *kitālan*, a wall—*ittalan* thus meaning 'the writing on the wall'. Ramamurti gives the word as *jotālan*. In some villages the drawings are called *sedatal*, and the person who draws them is the Sedatalmaran. *Seda-* is a verb meaning to select, and Sedasum is a tutelary who selects a shaman.

make you a house. If I make any mistakes, do not punish me, for it will not be my fault.'

The reference to the 'house' is significant. The ikons are the one-dimensional homes of the spirits. 'A spirit', I was once told, 'sits in his picture as a fly settles on a wall.' The same idea is emphasized in a story which I recorded at Kinteda.

Before ikons were made the ancestors used to give people a great deal of trouble. One day an ancestor came to Bojai the shaman in a dream and said, 'I have nowhere to live; I want to stay with you.' The shaman said that there was nowhere for a ghost to stay in his house. The ancestor was angry and made him very ill with fever. Bojai sent for another shaman and when the ghost came upon him, he said, 'Sacrifice a goat and make me a house on your wall.' The poor shaman, who had no idea what to do, tried to build a house with bamboo against the wall, but the ghost came and laughed at him. At last Bojai went to Kittung and asked him what to do. Kittung mixed rice-flour with water and showed him how to paint a house on the wall and furnish it. In this way the custom of making ikons began, and as a result the spirits were pleased and did not trouble people quite so much.

Another story, from Sogeda, gives a highly charged magical significance to the ikons, though I doubt if the ordinary Saora of today regards them in quite this way.

After the world was made, Kittung built a house for himself. On the wall he made drawings of a man and woman with white earth. At that time, all creatures, except men and women, had been made; Kittung wanted to make them, but he had no notion of how to do it. He went to Uyungsum and asked what he should do. Uyungsum said, 'Cover your drawings of the man and woman with leaves. After seven days cut your little finger and let the blood fall on the drawings, two drops on the man, three on the woman.'

Kittung covered his drawings with leaves and let his blood fall on them, as Uyungsum had said. Nine days later from the woman's picture came a girl: she at once began to cry. Next day a boy came out of the man's picture. Kittung looked after them, and when they grew up, he asked Uyungsum to marry them to one another. From them came all mankind.

The artist sleeps on the floor beside the dedicated rice and expects to have a dream telling him exactly what to do. Sometimes, however, the householder or a shaman has the dream instead, and then the artist works under his guidance. But invariably, I think, the ikons are directed by dreams.

In the morning the artist gets up and has a wash, but he must not eat—though he may drink palm wine—until he has finished. He again makes offerings of rice and wine before the wall, and then settles down to work.

He uses a twig slightly splayed at the end, and his canvas is, of course, the red-washed wall of the house. For paint he has rice-flour and water mixed in a small bowl, or sometimes ashes and water, a mixture which looks a dirty grey at first but dries a sharp white. Occasionally he gives emphasis to his figures with a little lamp-black or red ochre. Unlike other tribesmen who make their pictures in red or black on a white background, the Saoras nearly always paint in white on a red background.

Most of the ikons are built up round the idea of a 'house'—a square, circle or rectangle, which is filled in and surrounded with the figures of men and animals. The artist makes the outline of the house first, for this determines the approximate size of the picture, and then proceeds to decorate and fill it in. He draws the frame with multiple straight lines, with lines elaborately enhanced or with rows of dots or stars. But he always follows the same technique, whether he is making a house, a human figure or an animal. He first makes the outline and then fills it in. In drawing a human figure, for example, he first makes an outline of the whole body with two opposed isosceles triangles which meet at the tips. He adds the arms, then the legs, then the head, and finally fills in the two triangles to make a solid body with a sharply accentuated waist.

For an elephant, the artist first makes the outline of a rough rectangle, adds the legs, tail, head and trunk in that order, whites in the body and finally draws the rider. He makes a horse with two triangles similar to those for the human figure, but turned on their side. He then adds legs, head and rider, taking great care to suggest the hair by fine strokes along the neck and tail. Similarly in making a bear, after he has filled in the body, he draws hair all round it. Equal attention is paid to a peacock's tail, a deer's horns or a porcupine's quills.

When the artist has finished the preliminary draft of the picture, he sends for a shaman who at once proceeds to complicate the course of true art with fussy religious inspirations. He offers rice and wine before the ikon, and calls on the spirit for whom it has been made to come and inspect it. He falls into trance, takes his sacred lamp in his hand, and inspects the drawing by its light; he criticizes it and suggests improvements. 'You have not given me a comb,' he may say, or 'There are not enough chaprassis sitting at my gate' or 'When I was alive I once sat on a bicycle; why haven't you put it in?' This is one of the ways whereby the pictures get so overcrowded; the spirits do not seem to like blank spaces; every inch of wall must be filled with symbols of honour; their greed abhors a vacuum. I once watched the symmetry of an admirably balanced picture being destroyed by this kind of supernatural interference.

I attended the dedication of an ikon at Abbasingi on 5 May 1948, when Gurpanu, a shaman, made a new painting for his tutelary. On a mud platform in front of the picture, he put two pots of rice, a small mirror, the bowl of rice-flour used by the artist, many little leaf-cups for the tutelary and her relatives, and on either side bunches of green plantains. He offered rice and wine while an assistant rang a bell, and called on the gods and ancestors and particularly on his own tutelary.

> I have made a house for you. Here are your elephants and horses. Come riding on them. Here is your tiger and your bear. Here are your birds. Come and see what a fine house I have made for you. Tutelaries of the sky, come and see the house. Tutelaries of the hills, come and see the house. All is ready. Come and feast with us and examine your new house. Bring your clerk and your chaprassis. We are watching the road for you. Come quickly, for here is your house and door. Your elephants and horses are ready. Come quickly.

The shaman passed into trance and his tutelary came upon him. There was a long argument about the quality of the entertainment provided and it was only after the shaman had offered rice, plantains and wine and had promised a fowl at the next Harvest Festival that the tutelary condescended to examine his new house. The shaman lit a lamp and looked it over carefully. The tutelary said, 'Yes, that's all right. But where's my lizard? I always have one as a pet in my house. I must have my lizard.'

The shaman hastily promised to add a lizard to the picture, and the tutelary at last declared himself satisfied and went away. The shaman concluded the ceremony by dedicating a new pot into which he put some rice and a copper coin; he hung it up with a branch of plantains above the ikon.

Once it has been accepted and dedicated, after sacrifice has been offered and a pot or gourd hung up above it, the ikon is regarded as a little temple within the house. Offerings are made before it on every ceremonial occasion, and bunches of fruit or ears of grain are hung round its pot at the Harvest Festivals. In certain cases the ikon is repainted every year, often with variations, so that in some houses there is a sort of palimpsest effect, old designs showing dimly behind the bright outlines of the latest drawing.

The ikons are so important, as an element in the cure of disease, for the fertility of the crops, in the marriage of a shaman with his tutelary, and for the light they throw on Saora theology, that it will be necessary to consider them in detail. I propose to examine, and illustrate, fifty of these pictures under various headings according to the purpose for which they were made.

II

1. IKONS DESIGNED TO PROMOTE OR PRESERVE THE FERTILITY OF THE CROPS

Ikons are painted at the Jammolpur, the ceremonial removal of the seed from store for sowing, when a sacrifice is offered to guard it and improve its fertility. Such ikons often depict agricultural operations such as ploughing or hoeing and include fertility symbols. They may, for example, show a man ploughing, a pregnant woman, a woman carrying seed, a potter laden with pots, gods seated on an elephant. These are friendly and auspicious symbols, and each kind of seed is offered before them with a prayer that the gods and ancestors will be favourable.

Such ikons are made as a matter of routine every year, and others are painted for the Harvest Festivals and retouched annually. Other ikons for the protection of the crops are made in emergency, and may then be of a rather different pattern.

The fertility ikons are made either for Labosum, the earth-god, or for the ancestors, whose interest in the harvests is thus emphasized.

1. *In the priest's house at Karanjaju. Length*, 34" (*TAMI*, p. 191[1]).

For Labosum. Painted at the Jammolpur, this ikon shows a ploughman with a characteristic (and auspicious) pipe in his mouth, with his son, engaged in ploughing. The cow is followed by its calf. There is a pregnant woman carrying seed on her head. A potter and his wife bring loads of pots to cook the bumper crop which is expected. On an

[1] Some of the ikons are illustrated in my *The Tribal Art of Middle India*, and are referred to with the page number and abbreviation *TAMI*.

elephant sit Jemra Kittung and Sidibiradi (see pp. 316ff.), who are specially placated at this time. This ikon, with its fertility symbols, may be taken as a sort of standard picture, for in various forms it is reproduced all over the Saora country.

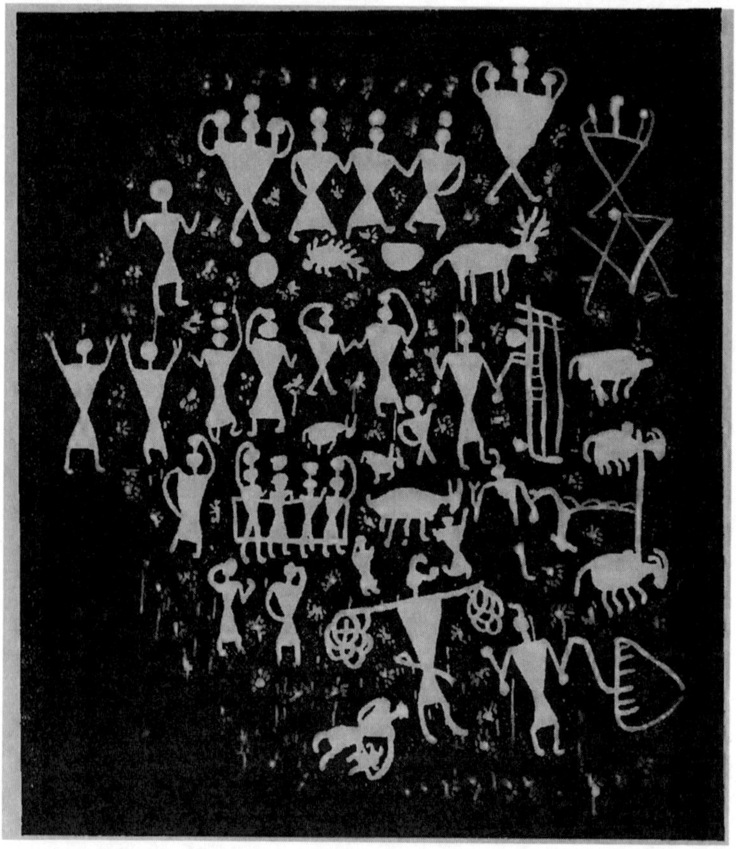

FIG. 34

2. *In the house of Saronti, the eunuch, at Sogeda. Height*, 23" (Fig. 34).

This ikon, also made for Labosum at the Jammolpur, though it lacks the simple dignity of the preceding picture, displays a scene of great exuberance. While the ploughmen and men with harrows continue with their work, a party of merry-makers dance round them, some waving their arms in the air, some carrying pots on their heads, some holding them on their shoulders. A few people carry two pots to suggest that the harvest will be twice as good as usual. The sun and moon look down as witnesses. Birds, deer and a porcupine are painted in the belief that if they are honoured here, they will not go into the fields and damage the growing plants.

FIG. 35

3. *In the Chief's house at Gunduruba. Height*, 28" (Fig. 35).

This ikon was painted at the Jammolpur for the ancestors by an Idaimaran, priest of the dead, as this was considered to be specially his concern. The main building is the palace of the ancestors. Monkeys frolic on the roof and attendants and guards surround the building as they do the bungalow of any very important person on earth. Below to the left is a house for three tutelaries and beside it is their armoury. The tutelaries themselves are seated on an elephant, carrying umbrellas in their hands; their clerk rides on a horse before them.

This picture illustrates the Saora doctrine of the second death; there are three dead men here, and it was explained to me that the two groups, one on each side of the house in which two men are shown carrying a third (rather incongruously drawn as sitting upright with an umbrella), are in fact bearers taking corpses to the pyre. A potter carries a load of pots for the funeral ceremony.

There is nothing here about agriculture, but it was supposed that the ancestors would be so flattered by the ikon that they would do their best to help. Speaking of this picture the Chief said, 'So long as this is on the wall, there will be no fear of thieves. The ikon is the watchman of the home.'

4. *In the priest's house at Pandiguda. Height*, 46" (*TAMI*, p. 191).

Another Jammolpur ikon for Labosum. It shows one man ploughing, another with his hoe, a row of women going to weed, potters with their pots. At the bottom Labosum sits on his elephant. Sun and moon witness to the bargain that if the picture is made there will be a good harvest.

5. *In Singraju's house at Arangulu. Height* 32" (Fig. 36).

Singraju painted the usual ikon for Labosum at the Jammolpur. He sacrificed a fowl before it, dedicated his seed, and planned to go the following day, a Friday, to sow it. That night, however, he dreamt that as he was carrying his seed to his clearing a tiger tried to kill him. He fled and, as he was running away, he saw his mother and father—both long dead—and they drove the tiger away. The next morning he sent for a shaman and the father's ghost came upon him and said, 'Don't take your seed to the clearing today, for your picture is all wrong. Rub it out and make a new one and take out your seed next Monday. Unless you do this, your harvest will be a failure.'

Singraju was now in a quandary, for he had no idea what kind of picture was required. But that night he had a dream, and his father showed him just what he had to do. On the Sunday, therefore, he fasted and painted the new ikon. He sacrificed another fowl, and on the following morning sowed the first seed of the year and in due time reaped a fine harvest.

The picture shows, within an unusually elaborate border of stars, the forest-clearing, in the middle of which is a house for Singraju's parents. One man is ploughing, and another breaking up the soil with a harrow. There are two women with hoes on their heads and three with sickles. Another woman is bringing food for the workers, with pots of rice and gruel on her head. Singraju is drawn consulting the shaman, who is playing his *kurānrājan*. There is a very old snake which is trying to swallow the sun: this motif is included to avert any possible danger from eclipses.

FIG. 36

6. *In the Chief's house at Mannemgolu. Height*, 18" (Fig. 37).

The Chief's younger brother Dampo died in 1942, and his Guar and Karja ceremonies were duly performed. Two years went by and the family was not once troubled by the ghost. But in 1944, at the time of the Osanadur, the Harvest Festival of the millet *Eleusine corocana*, Dampo's ghost came to his brother in a dream and showed him a pattern on the wall. 'Make a painting for me like that,' he said. 'Then your millet crop will always be very good.' The Chief at once drew the picture and Dampo's ghost came in another dream and said that he was very pleased and that he would personally see to it that the millet crop was good. This ikon is in the same simple style as No. 1, and shows the usual agricultural operations in progress.

FIG. 37

II. IKONS DEDICATED TO GODS TO AVERT DISEASE

In some, but by no means in all, of the sacrifices offered to the gods in an attempt to avert disease, the shaman prescribes the painting of an ikon. Such pictures usually aim at flattering the god by showing what a splendid palace he has and how many servants and pets, and what important people come to call on him. But occasionally, as in the case of some of the ikons for Uyungsum, the picture may be very simple, consisting of nothing more than a rude symbol of the god.

I have noticed that comparatively few of the gods in the Saora pantheon are honoured in this way. Although I have seen a great many ikons, in all parts of the Saora country, I have never seen them made for any of the smallpox deities, or for Dorisum, Ajorasum, Ramma-Bimma, Tuttumsum, Kannisum or Kinnasum, among the more important gods, or for a great many of the less distinguished ones.

This does not mean that such ikons are never made, but it does suggest that they are uncommon.

Gods of local cult, Kittungs and hill-gods of the neighbourhood seem to be honoured more frequently with ikons than the great popular gods, for whom the more expensive sacrifices are made.

7. *In Karika's house at Arbun. Length,* 62" (Fig. 38).

Addia and Karika were two brothers who for some years lived together with their father, but after the old man's death set up separate establishments. Addia had made an ikon for Gadalsum, Karnosum and Madisingsum in his house, and when Karika built his new home

FIG. 38

they came to him in a dream and said, 'We have already got a house with your brother, but we want to live with you also.' Karika forgot about his dream, and this made the gods angry; one night when he was coming home drunk in the dark, Karnosum gave him a vigorous push in the back and knocked him down. Then Gadalsum and Madisingsum beat him as he lay on the ground, and he reached home a very sick man. He summoned a shaman and the three gods declared through him that, 'This man's father used to worship us, and so did his brother. So long as he lived with them he joined in the worship, but now he has separated from them, he neglects us. If he wishes to recover he must honour us in his house also.' Karika, therefore, begged the shaman to paint an ikon without delay, and one evening after dark a goat was sacrificed before it, and the gods were apparently satisfied, for Karika recovered.

The ikon shows the houses of the three gods. Each is crowded with servants, and one has a party of dancers with feathers in their hair. The gods, with their clerks, are riding on elephants and horses. A man carries a bundle of grass for Gadalsum, and potters bring pots for a feast.

8. *In Addia's house at Arbun. Length,* 22" (Fig. 39).

This rather poor ikon is for Gadalsum, the god of grass-cutters. Addia's father, Poraila, once went to Gunupur and on the way met Gadalsum and the god followed him home. On his return Poraila fell ill and Gadalsum told the shaman who came to treat him, 'I was

FIG. 39

looking after my grass, and since I was all alone and hungry I followed this man home. I want a house and some food.' The shaman therefore painted this ikon and offered a fowl.

The picture shows Gadalsum's houses, in each of which the sun stands as witness. The human figures represent grass-cutters; Gadalsum himself stands on the left with a bundle of grass, protected by two snakes which will bite anyone who comes to cut grass before the proper time.

9. *In Budda's house at Dantara. Length,* 43" (Fig. 40).

At the time of the Harvest Festival of red gram, the Saoras celebrate the Gadalpur, at which sacrifice is made to Gadalsum. It is strictly taboo to cut grass before this. The custom is for the priest to cut the grass first, and when he has finished for the villagers to follow his example.

Long ago there was a very famous priest who broke this taboo. Retribution came upon him swiftly. As he returned home with his load of grass, a tiger (sent by the offended god) came out of the forest and stood in his way. The tiger was invisible and the priest advanced confidently towards it, and the tiger said to itself, 'This is such an

FIG. 40

important person that he is afraid of nothing; how can I eat him?' But Barusum, who with Gadalsum watched over the affairs of the hillside, said, 'How do you mean he is important? I am much more important than he is, and yet he carries away my grass and gives me nothing for it.' In a temper he went up behind the priest and knocked him down. The tiger, relieved of its doubts, sprang on the unfortunate man and devoured him. Back in the village, the priest's relations watched the road for him and when he did not come by nightfall sent for a shaman. Barusum came upon him and described what had happened. Then the unhappy shade of the priest himself came and said that he would become Gadalsum (not Kinnasum, as is usually the case when a man is eaten by a tiger) and warned the people never to cut grass before the Gadalpur. The shaman sacrificed a goat and drew this ikon for Gadalsum and Barusum; it appears to be a traditional subject which has been redrawn many times.

In the picture we see the priest with his load of grass, his 'long-tailed' loin-cloth hanging from his waist. A substantial tiger prepares to spring upon him. The houses are for Gadalsum and Barusum; the people in them are grass-cutters. The priest's tutelary sits in an easy chair, Gadalsum and Barusum ride on their elephants, and other gods and tutelaries ride and stand about. There are three little birds, which usually give warning when a snake or a tiger is in the neighbourhood, and it is said that these birds tried to warn the priest, but he was so conceited that he took no notice of them.

10. *In Sonia's house at Talasingi. Height,* 44" (Fig. 41).

The ancestors of Karbu, a Saora of Munisingi, a village in the valley below Talasingi, used to live in the Kond country to the north. After migrating to his new home, Karbu kept up the worship of Kondasum to protect himself from the malice of any Kond sorcerer who might send his magic after him. Some years afterwards Karbu's daughter, a young woman named Lobari, went to Assam and while she was there married Sonia. A year later Sonia and Lobari returned and settled in Talasingi. One day they went down the hill to Karbu's house to attend a sacrifice offered to Kondasum. When Lobari came home she fell ill. When the shaman came to make his diagnosis, Kondasum came upon him and said, 'You came to my feast and I have come home with you. You were drunk and danced wantonly, but I too was dancing and saw everything that you did. Now I am going to live in your house, you in one room and I in the other.'

Sonia had an ikon painted at once, but Kondasum said, 'That is all very well, but I am a drinker of human blood.' The Saoras replied 'We are not Konds; it is not our custom to kill human beings.' They gave the thirsty god pig's blood to drink instead, and he declared himself satisfied.

The ikon shows the two-roomed house which Kondasum demanded; in one the people are dancing at his feast, in the other are his armed retainers.

11. *In the Chief's house at Kattumeru. Height*, 62" (*TAMI*, p. 203).

In 1943 the wife of the Chief of Kattumeru fell ill, so ill that she was practically insane. The shaman diagnosed the case as the result of the hostility of Jaliyasum. 'Make an ikon in his name,' he said, 'and

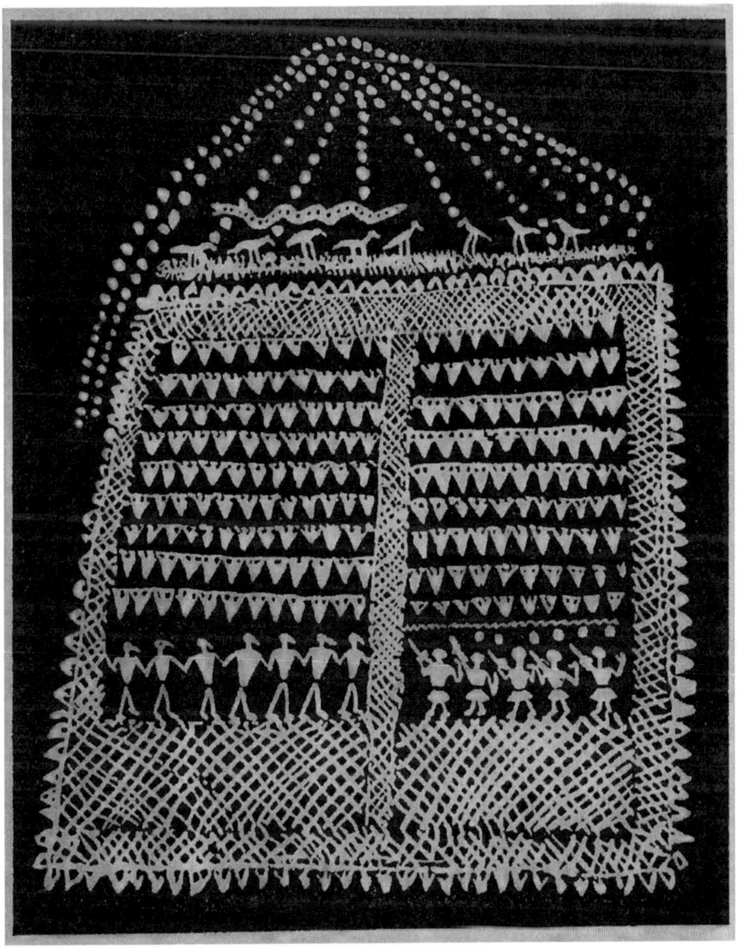

FIG. 41

sacrifice a fowl, and she will be all right.' That night the Chief dreamt that he was to make a picture representing the marriage of the gods.

The picture, therefore, shows us Jaliyasum's own marriage. In the centre is the palace; people are dancing in it, led by the god himself; on a tree outside, monkeys too are dancing for joy. Approaching the building are Jaliyasum's mother, sister and daughters dancing in a row. There is a comb, obviously inserted as an afterthought, for Jaliyasum's mother. Sun, moon and stars shine down on the scene. Sahibosum comes to the wedding on an elephant. The potter of the gods brings pots for rice-beer. The local landlord comes on a mare followed by its foal; he brings two she-goats for the feast. Two men bring in a sambhar killed by the god's servants. The Range Officer also attends and sits with his family on chairs. An unwanted guest is caught by Jaliyasum's dog—a tiger—and another dog attacks a lizard while a man shoots at it with his bow and arrow.

The obvious intention of all this is to show what an important person Jaliyasum is, how many servants he has, what powerful friends he can command, what an expensive wedding he can afford. And in fact, since the Chief's wife recovered, the neighbours believed that Jaliyasum was sufficiently flattered by this attention.

12. *In the house of Sondan the shamanin at Bungding. Length,* 24" (Fig. 42).

This ikon was drawn for Karnosum, and it was redrawn every year at the Harvest Festival for the red gram. At any time when Karnosum made people ill sacrifices were made before it. In the street

FIG. 42

before the house there was formerly a small shrine where Karnosum's horse and elephant could be stabled when he visited the village.

The picture shows men carrying Karnosum and his relatives in a litter. He has a potter with him, for this god is regarded as a Hindu

49. Ikon No. 40

50

50 to 53. Scenes at the Doripur at Potta

51

52

53

54. Head of Raudasum on the top of a shrine at Bhubani

55. Sahibosum images at Parisal

and he cooks every meal in a new pot. There are two knives, one to cut up Karnosum's meat and the other to cut his hair.

13. *In the house of Sartino at Angda. Length,* 58" (*TAMI*, p. 212).

Sartino fell ill, and the shaman advised the painting of an ikon with three 'houses', one for Karnosum (who had caused the sickness), one for Jammolsum (so that fertility-sacrifices could be made before it) and a third for Sardasum.

We see in this not very distinguished picture the three 'houses' filled to capacity with relations of the three gods—it is one of the embarrassments of godhead to have as many relatives as there are leaves on the tamarind. Below there is a procession, led by Sardasum's clerk on a horse and followed by the servants of the other gods on elephants and horses. Potters and their wives bring up the rear, for (as we have just seen) Karnosum needs a great many pots since he uses a new one at every meal.

14. *In the Chief's house at Bodo Okhra. Length,* 19" (Fig. 43).

I include this ikon as a contrast to the elaborate and delicate work done by some of the Saora artists. At the Festival of red gram, the Chief of Bodo Okhra got very drunk and lay down to sleep it off

FIG. 43

in his clearing in the forest. All the other villagers brought branches of fresh pulse for the festival, but there was no sign of the Chief.

After some time his wife went to fetch him and brought him home. But when he neared his house, he got high fever and collapsed on the veranda. There was a shrine in front of the house at which a shaman was sacrificing at the time. He went into trance and Karnosum came upon him and said, 'You have got fever because you neglected the festival. But if you make an ikon and sacrifice a fowl you will recover.' The Chief himself painted the ikon on the wall of the veranda just where he was resting. It had, I was told, no special meaning: 'It was his own work; the work of a drunken man, a man with fever.' That is what it looks like.

15. *In Kutano's house at Dantara. Height*, 26" (Fig. 44).

One day Kutano fell very ill with fever, and the shaman prescribed the sacrifice of a fowl to Tangorbasum. But this was a mistake, for Kutano got no better and after a day or two a god whom the local Saoras called Orissa-Manjorsum, the god of Puri, came upon the shaman and said, 'I have not come with the desire to cause you trouble. I want to be friends with you. As a usual thing, Rajas, great landlords and rich peasants come to me but as a special sign of my favour I have come to you. Now make a house for me and sacrifice a goat so that the people may know that I am the greatest of all the gods.'

The significant thing about this ikon is the representation of Orissa-Manjorsum as two men with a woman in the middle, shown seated on an elephant at the bottom of the picture, an obvious echo of Jagannatha.

16. *In the Chief's house at Barasingi. Height*, 38" (Fig. 45).

In 1945 the Chief's son Sukta went to Gumma for a festival for Gosai Mahaprabhusum. He returned home the same night and four days later developed high fever with acute pain in all his bones. Gosai Mahaprabhu came upon the shaman and said, 'This boy came to my festival. I saw him and wanted to go with him, but he returned home without asking my permission. Had he asked me I would have come and looked after him. But he took no notice of me and now I am going to take him away.'

The people begged Gosai to have mercy and at last she agreed to release the boy provided a temple was built in her honour and she was given a goat in sacrifice. The ikon is the temple that was made. Inside there is growing a tulsi plant and on the top is the peacock watchman of the Saora shrines.

This ikon is interesting as showing how the Saoras believe that even the Hindu gods can attack them and behave for the time being exactly like the Saora gods.

Fig. 44

17. *In Buab's house at Barasingi. Height*, 40" (Fig. 46).

Buab had a daughter, a beautiful dark girl named Legamiboi. One day Kittung Mahaprabhu attacked her with fever and made her temporarily dumb. When the god came on the shaman he declared, 'I am going to take this girl away; I shall not allow her to live here. For I have no maidservant in my house and she will do very well to look after my kitchen and garden.' But when the shaman promised to sacrifice a goat and make Kittung an ikon, he relented, and soon after the painting was completed, the girl recovered.

The ikon shows the usual overcrowded establishment of a Saora deity. The house, with its peacock watchman on the roof, stands in

FIG. 45

the middle of a compound. There is a tree with monkeys clambering over it, deer, a pet tiger, a shaman divining with his fan, two rows of retainers. Two chaprassis carry the shades of the newly dead in a litter. At the bottom is Mahaprabhu himself on an elephant, followed by servants armed with guns and two clerks on horseback. Sun, moon and stars look down from above.

FIG. 46

18. *In the house of a shaman at Liabo. Height,* 22" (Fig. 47).

A Kittung was passing by Liabo and got tired. He gave the Chief's son fever as a sign that he wanted to stay in his house. The shaman advised the painting of a 'house' in which the Kittung could stay and this ikon is the result. It illustrates the crude and simple style of the painting in this area.

We see Kittung's house and Kittung himself sitting on his horse. A servant brings his bicycle and his wife comes with a comb in her hand. Another servant has a snake which has coiled round his leg— this is probably a half-forgotten eclipse motif: the snake is swallowing Uyungsum the Sun in human form. In a kitchen to the left are three Brahmins who are engaged to cook Kittung's food.

FIG. 47

19. *In Hargu's house at Arangulu. Height*, 24" (*TAMI*, p. 199).

One day Hargu went to Boramsingi and got very drunk. He staggered home across the hills and the next day felt extremely ill. The shaman told him that 'Benasum came with you from Jopsir Hill and it is he who has made you ill. If you are not careful, he will give you a lot of trouble.' He called on Benasum and the god came upon him and said, 'Hargu was very drunk, rolling along the path, when he met me. I was hungry, but he was rude to me and would not even give me a scrap of tobacco. So I followed him home. Now if he gives me somewhere to live and plenty to eat, I'll let him alone.' That night Hargu dreamt of the sort of picture he must make, and the next day he made an ikon showing the Jopsir Hill—the wavy lines, he explained, represented his tracks as he walked across it.

20. *In a deserted house at Angda. Height*, 36" (*TAMI*, p. 127).

This ikon is for Sahibosum. 'Long ago', said the Saoras of Angda, 'our ancestors warned us that the sahibs would come and give us a great deal of trouble. But they said that if we made ikons for Sahibosum and his wife, things would not be so bad.'

The ikon shows a row of men, who represent Sahibosum and his friends. Below Mehamsahibosum or Sahibosumboi stands in a row with her friends. The crisscross lines in the middle represent a cot for Sahibosum to sit on.

21. *In Bopna's house at Sogeda. Height*, 12" (Fig. 48).

This and the following pictures illustrate the very simple ikons that are sometimes made. In Bopna's house, there were two such ikons, almost identical in size and pattern, on the same wall. One of these was for Tutiyumsum, who is the god of a mother's nipple. This god made Bopna's wife, who was nursing her baby, ill with a swollen breast and painful nipple. The other was for Uraljungsum, who had attacked Bopna's son-in-law, Suddo, with toothache so acute that his face swelled up and he sweated with the pain. Suddo's own wife, the shamanin Sinaki, diagnosed the trouble and declared that unless a suitable ikon was made and sacrifice offered her husband might get an attack of epilepsy.

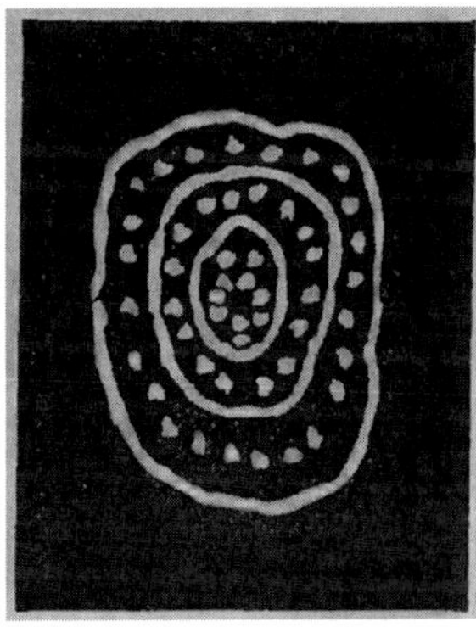

FIG. 48

22. *In the house of Jigri, the shamanin, at Boramsingi. Width*, 27" (*TAMI*, p. 209).

This is a conventional symbol for Uyungboi or Uyungsum, the Sun, and may be drawn for the relief of anyone suffering from fever caused by the god.

23. *In Japno's house at Kerubai. Height*, 14" (Fig. 49).

This is another conventional symbol for Uyungsum. In this case it was made on behalf of Japno's two-year-old son who had been afflicted with diarrhoea by him.

24. *In Sida's house at Barasingi. Length,* 17" (Fig. 50).

It often happens that, after a large central ikon has been painted on the wall of a house, some other god or ancestor may demand attention. In such cases a single figure may be added near the main ikon, or perhaps an elephant or a tree or a little shrine. In this ikon at Barasingi a row of dancers was added for Karnosum above an older ikon previously made for the ancestors.

FIG. 49

One night as Sida was returning home from a neighbouring hamlet he fell ill with fever. The reason was that he had met Karnosum and his relatives going to a dance and had offended them unwittingly. The ikon shows Karnosum and his relatives wearing tufts of feathers for their dance.

III. IKONS MADE TO ASSIST CHILDBIRTH

There are various means of accelerating delivery and one of them, though it is not very common, is the painting of an ikon. Such pictures always contain a pregnancy or delivery motif, and are generally made

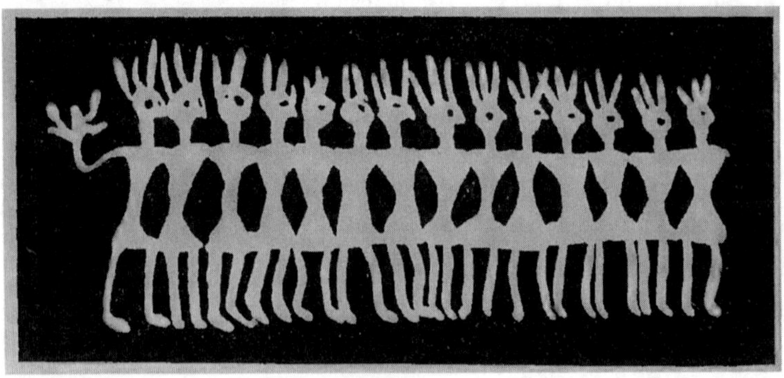

FIG. 50

in the name of Gadejangboi or one of the deities who are notorious for interfering at this time.

25. *In the house of Redga, Barasingi. Height,* 27" (Fig. 51).

Redga's wife Sukiboi had a great deal of trouble at her first confinement and the shaman recommended sacrifice and an ikon for Darammaboi and Gadejangboi.

The ikon is not very clear, but it was explained to me that the group in the lower right hand corner includes Sukiboi herself and that Gadejangboi is holding her. Darammaboi has her hand on the

FIG. 51

mother's belly, ready to remove the child from the womb. Darammaboi's daughters have come with pots of water to bathe mother and child after delivery.

26. *In the house of a shaman at Thodrangu. Height*, 21" (Fig. 52). This ikon, which was painted for Gadejangboi when the shaman's own wife was faced with a difficult delivery, shows the pregnant woman with her attendants, and Gadejangboi herself with pots of water for the bath.

IV. IKONS WHICH REPRESENT SHRINES AND HILLS

Most of the ikons are built up around some central figure which represents a house, shrine or hill, for (as we have seen) the ikon is the 'house' of the spirits. I found many pictures of this kind in the beautiful hill-village Arangulu; they were simple and effective, and in a style which I had not seen elsewhere. Shrine-ikons are often made when spirits demand some sort of place to rest on their visits to a village; they are much more economical than actual shrines. Hill-ikons may be painted if one has inadvertently offended a hill-god by cutting a clearing on his hill or by picking herbs or leaves without his permission.

27. *In Singraju's house at Arangulu. Height,* 24" (*TAMI,* p. 196).

Long ago Singraju's father made a shrine for Karnosum. After his death, the shrine fell into disrepair and Singraju forgot all about it. But one night towards the end of 1943, his father's ghost visited him in a dream and said, 'I made this shrine for Karnosum and offered

FIG. 52

sacrifices there while I was alive. Repair it at once and make an ikon for him inside the house.' Singraju repaired the shrine, but considered that in demanding an ikon as well the ghost was asking too much. But shortly afterwards Singraju's wife fell ill, and when the shaman was consulted he declared that the trouble was due to this misguided attempt at economy. That night Singraju had another dream: Karnosum came to him, insisted on an ikon and himself designed it, tracing the outline on the ground with a stick. The next day Singraju had the drawing made and his wife recovered. The picture shows Karnosum's shrine, with the characteristic peacock watchman on the top.

28. *In Singraju's house at Arangulu. Height*, 23" (Fig. 53).

Just before the Harvest Festival of the red gram Singraju had a dream about his ancestors. They said to him, 'Make a shrine for

FIG. 53

us where we can rest when we come to feast with you, and we will see that your next harvest is the best you have ever had.'

29. *In Hargu's house at Arangulu. Height*, 20" (*TAMI*, p. 197).

One of Singraju's neighbours, an elderly and rather drunken Saora called Hargu, had a regular picture gallery in his house, which might be taken as illustrating the influence of the hangover on tribal art. For whenever Hargu returned home from a drinking-bout, he woke up the next morning convinced that some singularly unpleasant god was persecuting him and had an ikon made to put things right. We have had one example of this in No. 19; three others represent various hills on which the drunken Hargu got into trouble, his own interpretation being that he was accosted and followed home by the gods living there. A hill-god's house is, of course, a hill, and these pictures give an interesting idea of the Saora's symbolization of a hill-house. This ikon was made for the god Barongsum—*barongan* is an old Saora word for a mountain; it shows the hill with the god standing below.

30. *In Hargu's house at Arangulu. Height,* 27" (*TAMI*, p. 198).

After another orgy Hargu made an ikon for Kurtisum of Deogiri, the great mountain of the Saoras, and in a dream he promised to keep all other gods away. Hargu, who was an Ittalmaran, drew these pictures and those in Singraju's house, himself; in this ikon he portrayed Kurtisum standing on the summit of the hill with his umbrella and his son to one side with a tuft of feathers in his hair.

31. *In Hargu's house at Arangulu.*

One day in 1943 Hargu went to the forest on a hill called Ladiolenga to get some wild spinach. Directly he got home he went down with a sharp attack of fever and vomiting. The shaman declared that Gunjusum a local god living on the hill had been annoyed at the theft of the spinach from his home and had followed Hargu back to the village. 'There will be no end to the trouble I am going to give this fellow,' declared the god. The alarmed Hargu immediately made an ikon of the hill with Ganjusum standing below it, sacrificed a pig and in due course recovered.

32. *In the shaman's house at Gundripadar. Height,* 42" (Fig. 54).

The people of this village go to make their clearings on a hill, not far from their homes, called Surjibudi. When they first went there many of them fell ill, for Labosum was angry at being disturbed. At about the same time Uyungboi gave a number of people fever, and a composite and rather elaborate ikon was made to satisfy both gods.

In the upper right hand corner of the ikon there is a design of concentric circles and above it a shrine out of which grows a banyan tree. This is the house of Uyungsum the Sun. In the centre is Surjubudi Hill and Labosum and his wife riding on an elephant. All round are the various animals and birds which live on the hill. To the top at the left, the ghost of Uyungsum's son (see p. 307) riding on a dog is about to swallow the sun.

While the artist was painting this picture, Tangorbasum came upon the shaman and insisted that he should have a share in it. So in the lower left hand corner we find Tangorbasum's house—this god's shrine was actually on a path leading to the hill—and there are monkeys climbing over it, and a potter with his load of pots stands near by.

The man on the bicycle is a Forest Guard who has come to see what was going on. At this time there was a good deal of friction between the Saoras and the Forest Department, which was trying to stop axe-cultivation, and the Guard was included in the ikon in the hope that he would henceforth leave them alone.

FIG. 54

33. *In the Chief's house at Liabo. Height* 22″ (Fig. 55).

This is another ikon for Labosum who was offended because the people of this village cut clearings on his hill without permission. It gives a rough outline of the hill with Labosum's house inside it, and various poorly drawn figures including a gigantic lizard.

V. IKONS MADE IN HONOUR OF TUTELARIES

Ikons are always painted at the time of a marriage between a shaman and his tutelary, or a shamanin and hers; they may also be made at any other time when a tutelary feels that he or his relations are not receiving sufficient attention.

These ikons are generally rather elaborate, for many of them tell in picture form the story of a tutelary's relationship with the shaman and this is often complicated.

34. *In the house of Sundaro the shaman at Ladde. Height,* 55" (See pl. 48).

Sundaro's father, Lungut, was also a shaman and was very anxious that his son should continue in the same profession. When Lungut died, his tutelary Arjuni came with her son Malinga and made Sundaro ill. A shaman was summoned and Arjuni declared through him that, 'Your father was a shaman, but now he is dead we get nothing to

FIG. 55

eat and no attention. There is a nice girl called Daruli here in the Under World. Marry her and you will be able to work as a shaman and feed us all.' Sundaro replied, 'I don't want to be a shaman, I can't be a shaman. But I'll give you food, certainly. Here is a fowl; take it and go away.' But Arjuni was not satisfied with this and Sundaro got worse.

The shaman was called again and this time Lungut's ghost came and said, 'I showed you what to do when I was alive; I'll teach you all over again now I am dead. Do what I tell you to do and you will get well. But if you disobey I will take you away with me.'

Sundaro again protested and sacrificed a goat. But on that same night he had a dream that Arjuni, Malinga, Daruli and his father's ghost came to him and carried him away to a very dense forest. There were mountains on every side, a stream in the midst, and on either bank banyan trees heavy with honeycombs which snakes and a tiger were eating. Lungut's ghost went to kill the tiger with his axe, leaving his son alone, whereupon another tiger seized him and carried him away. Sundaro screamed and awoke sweating with fright.

This is considered a singularly ominous dream, and so Sundaro sent for the shaman again at once, and now the shaman's own tutelary came on him and said to Sundaro, 'You will have to do the work of a shaman. There is no way out. Make an ikon for all four spirits who took you away and sacrifice to them; if you don't, a tiger will certainly eat you.'

So at last Sundaro gave in and arranged for the Ittalmaran to paint the ikon, and he celebrated his marriage with Daruli and became a shaman.

The ikon is a large and detailed one, and is said to be based on Sundaro's dream. At the bottom a procession of tutelaries approach the house which stands above. In the litter are Arjuni, Malinga, Daruli and Daruli's sister. The tiger that attacked Sundaro can be seen at the top right hand corner and a little below it is the shaman in trance.

35. *In Lebo's house at Singjangring. Height*, 47" (Fig. 56).

Lebo's younger sister Impuri was being trained by her father's sister to be a shamanin. But the old woman died, and nothing more was done about it. But presently the girl fell ill and her father's sister, who herself had become a tutelary, came upon the shaman and said, 'Here in the Under World I have a son. I am going to take Impuri away and marry her to him. For I am old now and no one takes any notice of me or gives me anything to eat or drink.' Lebo protested, 'But you are too great for that. We all regard you with the greatest honour. Don't take this girl away. We will give you a feast instead.' But the tutelary replied, 'No, I don't want your fowls. I want an ikon. Make it in my name and the name of my son and Impuri. Then the girl will get well. When you have made it we will come and sit in our house, as a fly sits on the wall.'

Accordingly Lebo himself painted the ikon at the next Mango Festival, and Impuri was married to her tutelary and began her labours as a shamanin.

36. *In Dalimo's house at Kerubai. Height*, 57" (Fig. 57).

When Dalimo first became a shaman, there was a certain tutelary in the Under World, who earned his living as a potter. It was this

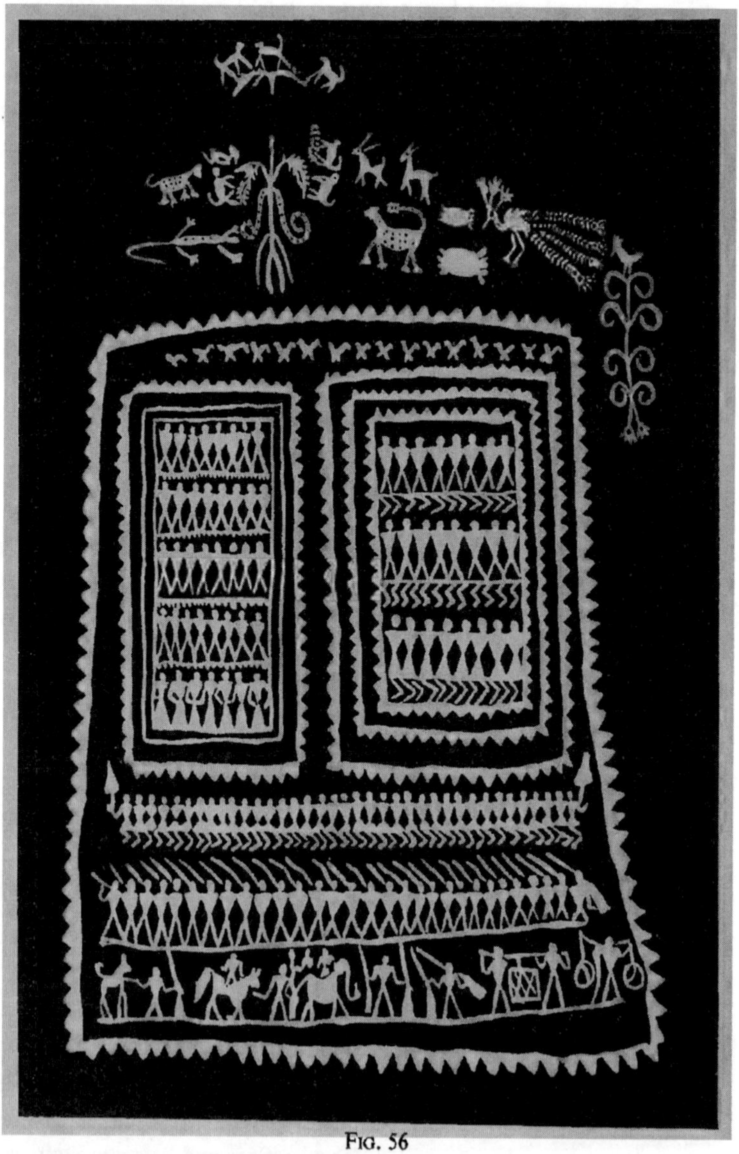

FIG. 56

tutelary's wife whom Dalimo married when he began his work as a shaman. But some time later another woman in the Under World,

who had the duty of clearing away the cowdung from the cattle-sheds belonging to the wealthier tutelaries, began to make a nuisance of herself and frequently visited Dalimo in dreams, begging him to marry

FIG. 57

her instead. At last he promised to do so; he killed a goat for her and dedicated a pot in her honour, hanging it up beside the pot previously dedicated to his first wife.

The unfortunate Dalimo now began to suffer—in his strange other-world of trance and dream—all those embarrassments which are the lot of men who are a little weak in dealing with women. If he went to diagnose the cause of a neighbour's fever, his first tutelary, who should have been at his side to guide him, refused to come. If she did come, she would make herself so unpleasant that Dalimo would run out of the house like a madman. His practice naturally began to suffer. When he should have been listening to the words of the gods, all he could hear were the wrangling voices of jealous and possessive women. He consulted one of his colleagues who told him, 'You first married one tutelary and then another, so naturally the first is angry. You must make these two wives friends.' Accordingly Dalimo made two ikons, but the tutelaries were not satisfied. At last he painted one large picture of the palace in the Under World where the two of them lived together. They were pleased at this, and Dalimo at last got some relief.

FIG. 58

This fantastic story is entirely normal in the Saora setting, and the elaborate detail of the picture is almost as real as life in the everyday world. It contains two points of special interest. At the bottom the two wives are shown engaged in grinding grain together—a domestic touch which is rather uncommon—and at the top, immediately below the sun and moon, the shaman is shown in congress with one of his wives while the other lies asleep beside them.

37. *In the house of Dalimo at Kerubai. Height, about* 12" (Fig.58).

To satisfy the tutelary still further Dalimo added a number of miscellaneous images at the side of the main drawing described above. The most important of these is a painting of Dalimo himself engaged in sexual congress with his tutelary,[1] while a servant armed with a gun keeps watch near by.

[1] The interpretation given at p. 207 of *The Tribal Art of Middle India* is incorrect.

38. *In the house of Durpan at Potta. Height*, 39" (*TAMI*, p. 208).

One night, Durpan, a shaman of Potta village, was visited by his tutelary in a dream. 'You have married me,' she said. 'I am your woman and you are my man. But what about my relatives? Make them a house on your wall and then none of the gods will be able to trouble you or your children.' That night she showed him what sort of picture he was to make, and the next day he fasted and painted it.

The picture shows Durpan's tutelary and her relatives, and with them Sumantisum, a local hill-god. The people of the Under World can, it is said, intermarry with the spirits living on the Sumanti Hill, and the ikon shows such a marriage in progress; at the bottom men are carrying a litter and are followed by a marriage-party on horseback. There is an elephant also which has been brought down from the hill with the bride's treasure tied to its back. On each side of the picture is a banyan tree with honeycombs hanging from the branches, and there are monkeys coming to steal the honey and squirrels climbing. There are peacocks, always associated with the Saora dead, and a bear which acts as a priest in the Under World. To show the importance of the tutelary's family, there are sahibs among the guests; they sit on chairs outside the house, one smokes, another reads a book. Servants bring flowers; snakes and birds are the family pets.

39. *In Gamru's house at Boramsingi. Height*, 42" (*TAMI*, p. 211).

This beautifully designed ikon tells a vivid story of the Under World. Gamru, who drew the picture, was a shaman and his paternal grandfather, Somra, was of the same profession. Somra had a daughter from his tutelary; the girl was named Daruni and she had a romantic history. When Somra died and his ghost was admitted to the Under World, he took Daruni to live with him. One night he came to Gamru in a dream and said, 'We have no one to feed us here and this girl Daruni badly needs the right kind of husband. You must marry her. Many tutelaries have come for her, but she won't have any of them.' And Somra took Gamru's soul out of his body and took it to the Under World and showed it everything. When Gamru awoke he made this ikon to protect himself against any possible dangers that might arise from his adventure, and also in honour of Daruni whom he now married.

The ikon is said to be an exact reproduction of Gamru's dream. In the centre is the great shrine in which the tutelaries have their home; on the roof is a peacock and a snake on guard. To the right is a banyan tree with a shrine built in the branches, and monkeys stealing honey. On the roof of the shrine a cock is covering a hen, and another cock comes to contest their union. This may symbolize the rivalry between Gamru and the tutelaries for Daruni's affections. Inside the shrine Daruni herself is shown hiding from the tutelaries who have come to betroth her with gifts of wine; two of them are searching for her at the foot of the tree. Some of her own servants, however, shoot at them with their guns. At the bottom of the picture are two porcupines, who are the shamans of the Under World; they are being consulted by two of the visitors who want to know whether or no Daruni will be agreeable to their proposals. Nearby, Somra himself divines with his fan. Next to him, in the centre of the picture, is a horse on which one of the tutelaries is riding, and above are still more suitors for the elusive but obviously attractive young woman. On an elephant are the two spirit-children who are born to Gamru and Daruni after their marriage. Strict chronological accuracy was evidently not considered necessary in an ikon designed to flatter Daruni by showing how attractive she was before marriage and how fertile after it.

In this picture too the shaman and his tutelary are portrayed in sexual intercourse: the couple are so intimately united that they have only one body between them. When two bodies melt into each other in this way, I was told, conception inevitably follows.

40. *In the house of Pajino the shaman at Jirrl. Height*, 62" (See pl. 49).

This exceedingly detailed and elaborate ikon was made on the occasion of Pajino's wedding with his tutelary, and represents the jubilation in the Under World when it occurred.

41. *In the shaman's house at Abbasingi. Height*, 33" (Fig. 59).

When Pidgu became a shaman he married a tutelary who was herself already married to a husband in the Under World. When she came to Pidgu's house, therefore, her spirit-husband came in search of her, playing a fiddle to reveal his presence. When he discovered what had happened, all he said was, 'Make an ikon for both of us, but give me separate food.'

In this picture, which stylistically resembles closely the ikons of Dantara, only a few miles distant, we are shown Pidgu's tutelary and her spirit-husband sitting above the sun; their clerks stand on each side. Below them are the pigeons and a mongoose which are the pets in their house in the Under World. Underneath the main design are two of the tutelary's children riding on an elephant, and what were explained as a plantain tree, millet plants and flowers. On the right is the spirit-husband searching for his wife with his fiddle. Still further to the right is a two-headed figure which represents Pidgu and his tutelary united as a single person.

FIG. 59

VI. IKONS MADE IN HONOUR OF THE DEAD

Although the ancestors are continually complaining about the miserable life they lead in the Under World, the ikons made in their honour invariably portray them as successful and important, with large comfortable houses, rooms full of wives and servants, visited by significant and wealthy friends. They ride about on horses and elephants, bicycles, cars and even private aeroplanes. But none of this, the Saoras will tell you, is really true; it is just flattery, designed to humour the dead who in fact are miserable enough, and largely dependent on the attention of the living for the most meagre comforts.

42. *In Jamburu's house at Mannemgolu. Height*, 50" (*TAMI*, p. 202).

At the time of the Jammolpur ceremony in 1944, the ghost of Jamburu who had died five years before began to pester his widow for attention. He gave her fever; made sinister noises at night among the water-pots; visited her in dreams. One night he showed her a house—'That's the kind of house I live in; make me one like that on your wall.' Then he showed her men riding on elephants and horses—'That's how the other ancestors come to visit me.' He showed her his potter and his pet lizard, and concluded, 'Draw all these things before you take your seed from the store; otherwise your crop will be ruined.' Early next morning the widow hurried to the shaman and found that they each had had exactly the same dream. The Ittalmaran drew the picture under their direction; its central feature is a substantial two-storeyed house, with three rooms crowded with the dead Jamburu's wives and other dependants.

43. *In Saitino's house at Kamalasingi. Length,* 32" (*TAMI,* p. 200). Saitino's father was old and ailing and one night his father's ghost appeared in a dream and announced his intention of taking the old man to the Under World to keep him company. Saitino protested, but to no purpose, and the following day his father died and he performed the customary rites. But a year later he himself fell very ill, and now his own father's ghost came and declared that he was not satisfied with a mere Guar ceremony and that he must have an ikon in his honour as well. 'Draw a man on a horse,' he said, 'and make a cowbell for my cattle here in the Under World. Give me a bit of a honeycomb to eat, with a bee sitting on a branch, and a woman bringing me a bowl of gruel. Do it like this,' he continued, tracing the pattern on the ground, 'and you will recover.' Next morning, Saitino himself painted the picture, and the ghost visited him again and professed himself very pleased. Perhaps the crudity of this ikon is due to the fact that when he made it, Saitino was a very sick man.

FIG. 60

44. *In Raviwaria's house at Guli. Height,* 23″ (Fig. 60).

The brother of Raviwaria's father, Gangai, died in 1941, but Raviwaria did not do anything about it, beyond the usual Guar ceremonies. Accordingly, one day five years afterwards, Gangai's ghost attacked him, and Raviwaria lay unconscious just as, it was said, Gangai had lain unconscious for days before he died. The shaman was called, and Gangai's ghost came upon him and said, 'In the Under World I have a fine house and I have brought all my relations to live with me in it.' Then he gave the shaman a dream showing him how the ikon was to be made.

The picture, which is drawn with a simplicity characteristic of this area, shows Gangai's house in the Under World. In the upper storey are four figures representing Gangai himself and Raviwaria's own father, brother and paternal grandfather, all long dead. On the horses below are three friends who have come to visit them. At the very bottom of the picture, Gangai's servants are dancing in his honour.

45. *In Sardar's house at Guli. Length,* 18″ (Fig. 61).

Sardar died at about the same time as the Gangai mentioned in the preceding section. The two ghosts became close friends in the

FIG. 61

Under World. When Raviwaria made an ikon for Gangai, Sardar got jealous and demanded a house for himself. Raviwaria, therefore, drew this picture in his neighbour's house.

46. *In the house of the Chief at Taburda. Length,* 27" (Fig. 62).

This simple ikon was painted to please the ghost of the Chief's father who made his son ill during a dance at the Mango Festival,

FIG. 62

when no special offerings had been made for him. The ghost is shown riding on an elephant, and the people are dancing below.

VII. IKONS MADE FOR THOSE WHO HAVE BEEN ABROAD

The influence of civilization is seen in the ikons made for people who have been to Assam, and have either died there or died after their return. Motor-cars, trains and aeroplanes[1] are necessary for the transport of shades and ghosts and are usually featured in the pictures.

[1] The Saoras are naturally fascinated by aeroplanes; some of them experienced air-raids in Assam during the war; others saw the wreckage of a plane forced down in the Ganjam hills during a typhoon. The general idea is that an aeroplane is the vehicle of the gods, like the wind-horse or wind-elephant on which tutelaries visit the earth, and ikons show that shades and ancestors can also travel in them. At Talasingi I attended a rite for the cure of the village children who were down with fever because a plane had passed overhead. In the hills round Ladde a new weed had sprung up in 1948, which two years later was threatening to choke the young trees; the Saoras declared that the seeds had been dropped by Japanese planes during the war.

47. *In the house of Tissano the shaman at Tumulu. Height,* 52″ (*TAMI*, p. 195).

Tissano took his wife to the Tea Gardens in Assam. He had bad luck from the start, got very little money, his wife sickened and died, and he himself fell desperately ill. A shaman there told him that his troubles were due to Karnosum and his own tutelary, who felt herself neglected. An ikon was made on the wall of his hut in the Tea Gardens and he recovered sufficiently to return to Tumulu.

But after a year at home, Tissano again fell ill, and now the local shaman declared that Karnosum and the tutelary were very annoyed that Tissano had left them behind sitting like flies on the wall of his hut in Assam. 'We had to get two aeroplanes,' they said, 'and flew after him, but now we are here there is nowhere for us to stay.' Tissano at once painted an ikon for them, and this is said to resemble exactly the ikon he made in Assam, except for the aeroplanes which the gods had chartered. It shows the tutelary on an elephant, his clerk on a horse and his servants standing in a row. At the bottom of the picture Karnosum also appears with his servants. There are two banyan trees with monkeys after the honeycombs that hang from the branches. When the picture was ready the two spirits came to inspect it and complained that it did not include the aeroplanes which they had taken with such great trouble and expense. These were quickly added and all was well.

48. *In the house of Laboi at Tumulu. Length,* 65″ (*TAMI*, p. 213).

Laboi was a shamanin who went to Assam. She fell ill there and an Ittalmaran made an ikon for her. On her return she again fell ill, and the same Ittalmaran, who had come home at the same time, repeated the ikon on the wall of her Tumulu house, adding to it the car and train in which the tutelary who had caused the trouble had come from Assam. The two tents on either side of the train were used by the tutelary for his camp during the long journey. The train itself will be immediately recognized by anyone who has ever travelled in the 'Little Ease' of the Parlakimidi Light Railway.

49. *In the house of Lakkia at Angda. Length,* 6″ (*TAMI*, p. 214).

The three sons of Lakkia died and their ghosts went to Assam to make their fortune. This they did so successfully that they were able to buy a car for three thousand rupees. They drove back from Assam to the Saora hills, only to find themselves forgotten in their own home. They made their father ill, but when he made an ikon showing their car they allowed him to recover.

50. *In Ganjano's house at Kerubai. Height*, 64" (Fig. 63).

Ganjano is a shaman and this ikon reflects the usual history of struggle and resistance before he surrendered himself to his profession and agreed to marry his tutelary. Ganjano's father's sister was a shamanin who died in the Tea Gardens. After her death her tutelary Ura came from Assam and declared that he had a daughter, Irpani, whom he must marry. Ganjano did nothing about it, and presently he dreamt that a great crowd of people came to him in a train and the girl Irpani

FIG. 63

tried to pull him out of the house. He cried, 'No, no, no!' and clung to a pillar. There was the roaring of the train in his ears and he awoke. That day he was so ill that he could not lift his head for pain. He decided to accept the situation, but did not know how to make the necessary ikon; it was to be very big, but that was all he knew. Then Irpani came in a dream and showed him.

The main feature of the ikon is Irpani's house, in the midst of which she is sitting with her fan and many patients who are waiting to consult her. The train is shown at the bottom.

III

The ikons are made for use rather than for display. They are for the eyes of spirits, not of men. Often they are painted in the darkest corner of a house, or may be hidden behind gourds and pots. In fact, it is desirable that human beings should not look at them, for there is always the danger that a careless word or an unguarded giggle may offend the spirits. In the painting itself, symmetry and balance are less important than the inclusion of everything likely to please the spirit for whom it is made: a comb, a lizard, a cycle may be added without any consideration of its effect on the general scheme. The gods are not interested in beauty; they want flattery.

Yet the Saora artists often put their very best work into their ikons, and sometimes it is astonishing what good results they achieve. An expert does seem able to build up a large picture—without any preliminary sketch—so that the details fall into place, and its architecture is reasonably designed.

The ikons vary in style, but they show a remarkable general similarity throughout the area. The variations are often due to a greater or less degree of elaboration. The largeness and extravagance of the people in the fertile Sogeda valley is reflected in the great size and complicated detail of their pictures; the economy and simplicity of such small hamlets as Guli and Arangulu, set deep in the hills, expresses itself in little paintings with a single motif. But we cannot really generalize from this: one of the most elaborate of the ikons comes from remote and elevated Ladde, and in Sogeda itself I have seen paintings of an extreme simplicity. The subject of the ikon may affect its style; on the whole the ikons made for tutelaries are the most elaborate, for they often have to recall the story of the shaman's relations with his spirit-partner and must include flattering references to the tutelary's family, often numerous as the leaves on a tamarind. Similarly, 'modern' features such as motor-cars, railway trains, aeroplanes and bicycles are not likely to appear in an ikon for a rural-minded hill-god. But they do often occur in ikons made for the ghosts of those who have died abroad.

The drawings are conventional, but on the whole realistic. There is rarely an attempt at symbolization; I have not, for example, noticed any representation of a thing by its parts, such as a bird by its wings. A porcupine looks like a porcupine, a peacock like a peacock, and often the Saora artist takes a lot of trouble with the quills and the peacock's tail.

But houses and mountains are shown symbolically in geometric patterns of great variety. Dancing too is suggested rather than portrayed with any sense of movement. Figures are painted in a row; feathers are put in their hair; they may be given drums or trumpets; sometimes their arms are raised above their heads.

It is curious that, although in wood carvings of the human figure the Saoras exaggerate or distort the sexual organs, they never draw them in the ikons, where there is hardly any sex differentiation at all. A woman may be recognized by a pot on her head or a bulge at the side if she is pregnant, but otherwise the only way to distinguish male and female figures is by their occupation. Sexual intercourse may be suggested by the drawing of a body with four arms and legs and two heads; the union of a shaman and tutelary by a single body with two heads.

The word *ittalan* suggests writing rather than painting, and it might be argued that the ikons belong to literature rather than to art. In one sense they are graphic messages to the spirits; they tell a story, they recite a prayer of praise and flattery. In another sense, however, they might be classed as architecture—for they aim at giving the spirits earthly 'houses' in which they can reside.

The Saoras have no art that is not inspired and directed by religion. Their wood-carving is always of the figures of the gods, or of peacocks to adorn their shrines and musical instruments. They have no secular art of decoration. They are unusually deficient in the art of bodily adornment; they can, it is true, dress up, but only for festal and sacred occasions. In the ikons illustrated in this chapter, we see in an unusually vivid manner how cult and myth can move a people to some sort of artistic expression. Here is the record of their dreams, their eschatological hopes and fears, the dramatization of their theological beliefs.

Chapter Eleven

THE COST OF RELIGION

I

RELIGION is a heavy item in the Saoras' budget. It is impossible to say in what proportion it stands to the total expenditure, for there are no reliable figures, but no one who has attended the elaborate and costly ceremonies of the tribe can doubt that it is high. 'We are all made poor by the exactions of the Bissoyi overlords and of the gods,' said a Saora of Gumma, and the shamans repeat again and again in their prayers such not altogether hypocritical phrases as 'We have been stripped naked by your demands' or 'For you the best meat and wine—for us the thinnest gruel and roots'. And from time to time men and women are driven to actual suicide, not only by the distress of a long illness but by the impoverishment caused by the sacrifices through which they have sought a cure.

Religion is the most fruitful cause of Saora indebtedness. The people do not like to deplete their own herds if they can help it, they can no longer steal from the people of the plains, and when a shaman says that the sacrifice of a buffalo is necessary they usually go to the local Doms to buy one. There is rarely sufficient cash to pay for it, and the Saora has to promise to pay in kind, at the cheapest rate, at the time of the next harvest with the usual interest added. And since the matter is urgent and he is in a hurry, and perhaps in great distress and anxiety, the Dom has little difficulty in driving a hard bargain to his own great profit.

Of course, a lot depends on the type of shaman you consult. There are expensive shamans and shamans who are not so expensive. The poorest people often have to be content with a mere taker of omens, a man or woman who has no tutelary, whose information can only be a guess, who is not in real touch with the other world. Such shamans usually recommend cheap and simple sacrifices, even though they may not be effective, and their own perquisites are modest. But a famous and important shaman often has big ideas; he prescribes the offering of buffaloes, goats, the painting of ikons, the building of shrines. I do not mean that he deliberately exploits his patients; it is simply that he lives in a world of higher and more expensive standards; he is used to things done well; and being what he is he dare not make the gods inferior offerings.

It is interesting to find hypochondriacs among the Saoras, generally rich men who do not mind how much they spend on their religion so long as they can keep themselves interesting to themselves and their friends. The rich and powerful Chief of Sogeda, for example, likes to live in an atmosphere in which he believes himself constantly threatened by supernatural dangers. There is nearly always someone ill in his large household and one or more shamans are almost continually employed there. He himself, in constant fear of magical attack from his many human enemies, watches jealously over his splendid body and at the least sign of sickness sends for a shaman. He frequently also arranges for prophylactic rituals to protect his family and crops. He has an obsession—and it costs him a great deal of money.

The young Chief, Iswaro, of Boramsingi, showed every sign of being turned into a similar kind of neurotic when I was staying with him in 1950. He had three shamanins in the family, and two of them —an aunt and an elder sister—lived in his house. They used to fuss over him absurdly: he had a slight headache—it was Uyungsum, they must sacrifice a fowl; a stuffed-up nose—they must offer a goat; a touch of fever and they must give a pig.

In addition to the actual cost in money and kind, the ceremonies are a heavy drain on the Saoras' time. Before a sacrifice, say, of a buffalo, at least two men must spend a whole day buying the animal; others must fetch firewood and get sufficient wine. The women must collect the large number of leaves required for cups and plates; they must husk rice, fetch water, prepare turmeric. On the day itself, at any important ceremony, the donor, the officiant and his assistants, and at least one household (often most of the members of a whole family), will be kept away from work all day. And at most rites many visitors are present. At Sogeda, at the end of November 1950, at one of the busiest times of the year when everybody was working hard to get in the harvest, no fewer than fourteen lusty young men took a whole day off for an Ajorapur, and two days later nineteen assisted at a similar rite—and this was in addition to women and children of whom there were over a score on each occasion. The number of working-hours diverted to sacrifice is considerable.

Yet on the credit side, it must be admitted that religion is in some ways a stimulus and support to Saora economy. The remarkable industry of the tribe is not unconnected with the need of grain and money for its ceremonial. If a Saora has to perform a Guar rite, it is essential that he has a good harvest, and he exerts all his energies to see that he does. Religion gives him that extra spur to effort which so many Indian farmers, who are content to make a bare subsistence, lack.

Religion also comforts and strengthens the Saora in his economic struggle. He gains confidence and goes to his fields with greater energy when he knows that they are protected by supernatural sanctions; he does better work on the threshing-floor once he is sure that his unseen enemies will not steal the grain he winnows. Agriculture ceases to be a dreary chore; it is a great adventure of faith and effort; from the moment the seed is taken from the store to the day the sheaves are cut and the first-fruits offered to the spirits, it is surrounded by an aura of poetry and legend.

And finally, most of the material and effort devoted to religion does not go out of the tribe; it is consumed at home. It is true that there is often loss in bargaining and through debt, but what a wonderful source of real good heavy meals religion is! The constant feasting not only binds society together by association and a common purpose, but it ensures that the people are well fed. If it were not for the large quantity of meat enjoyed by the Saoras at their ceremonies I doubt if they would have the stamina and the impetus to work as they do. It may be said that their religion makes them drink too much, and certainly if they took spirits this would be harmful to them. But what they drink is palm wine and this is rich in food values.

II

Let us first consider the circumstances of those who earn, if not their whole income, at least a substantial part of it as professional religious functionaries. The number of these varies, for it depends on how many families compose a village: each group must have at least one Idaimaran and one Idaiboi to assist in the funerary ceremonies. There is no such rule about the shamans, of whom there may be many in a small village and few in a large one, but generally—since the profession of shaman is one which is not undertaken lightly—the supply of these does not exceed the demand. In villages where there is a Buyya-priest, there is always one official Buyya and he often has a son or nephew in training.

I will give a few examples which will illustrate the proportion of men and women dedicated to religion in relation to the rest of the population.

BORAMSINGI VILLAGE

Number of		Number of	
hamlets	4	shamans	7
families	9	priests	1
households	80	Idaimarans	16
		Siggamarans	2
		Total	26

In this village, 8 of the 9 families had an Idaimaran and Idaiboi apiece; one group, a very small one, was entitled to borrow them for their funerals. The two Siggamarans could work for any group. All seven shamans were women and, of these, six were Raudakumbois and one was a Guarkumboi. The Guarkumboi had a young niece in training.

TUMULU VILLAGE

Number of		Number of	
families	5	shamans	3
households	74	priests	1
		Idaimarans	28
		Siggamarans	5
		Total	37

This village is remarkable for the small number of its shamans (only two) and shamanins (a Raudakumboi, only one) for 74 households, and for the large number of officiants associated with funerals. Each family group had at least three Idaimarans and two Idaibois and one Siggamaran. Although elsewhere the Siggamarans are permitted to officiate for any family beside their own, here they were restricted to their own groups.

LADDE VILLAGE

Number of		Number of	
families	4	shamans	3
households	25	priests	1
		Idaimarans	16
		Siggamarans	3
		Total	23

56. Clay images of ancestors, made by Saora potters, used at the Karja ceremony

57. Offerings for the improvement of a sago palm near Tumulu

58. A shamanin at Taraba divines with the help of an earthen pot

Each family had two Idaimarans and two Idaibois; the three Siggamarans were normally restricted to their own groups, but could work outside them in an emergency and for the group which had none. One of the shamans was a woman, a Raudakumboi. The priest officiated for the whole village.

These examples are fairly representative. Each family group has at least one, and generally two Idaimarans and Idaibois. There are two or more Siggamarans who may generally assist at the funerals of the whole village. The shamans, of course, may officiate anywhere in their own villages and outside. In Kerubai, with some thirty houses, there were three shamans and one shamanin; in the larger Rajintalu, there were two shamanins and one shaman; in the very large Sogeda, there were four shamans (three of whom were Ajorapur or Doripur specialists) and two shamanins—one Raudakumboi and one Guarkumboi; in the very small Singjangring there was no shaman, but a Raudakumboi and a Guarkumboi.

The Idaimarans and Siggamarans are, of course, much less expensive for the community to maintain; they are in less demand, being restricted to rites connected with the dead; they are not capable of trance—always a costly business in its results; and the perquisites allowed them are comparatively moderate.

On the whole, in view of the strong attachment of the Saoras to their religion, the number of priests and shamans is not excessive.

The funerary assistants are, of course, drawn from every class of Saora society; they have to be, since each family must have them. They come too from rich or poor homes within the groups; it is by no means uncommon for the son or daughter of the wealthiest Chief or priest to follow this profession, at least for a time. The shamans too may be drawn from any group; the fourth wife of the important Chief of Sogeda was a shamanin, and so was Jigri herself, the Chief of Boramsingi, with her considerable property and large concerns. On the other hand, some shamans come from very poor homes, and one of the shamans at Tumulu and a shamanin at Boramsingi were both Arsi Saoras in largely Jati villages. I do not think that economic considerations ever impel, as they do not restrain, a Saora in the choice of a religious profession.

But can a shaman make a decent living? In answering this question, we must remember first that the shamans and shamanins live for a large part of their time the ordinary lives of Indian peasants. A shaman has his property, his fields and his herds, he may engage in trade, he may work for Government. A shamanin is generally married, she performs the ordinary duties of the home; she works in the family fields and clearings, plies the spinning-wheel, takes her produce to market and earns her living like any other woman.

But on the other hand, a shaman or shamanin, especially a popular one, has to spend a great deal of time away from the ordinary business of life, and this is one reason why young people are so reluctant to obey the dreams that summon them to a dedicated life: the constant interference in the work of the fields or house does involve an economic loss; after an exacting ceremony a shaman may be too exhausted or too fuddled with wine to do any work that day; and his attention too is diverted—the dream world in which he lives is not the best setting for agricultural success.

Yet the profession of shaman is not unprofitable. He receives, in kind, a small but useful income which compensates for the considerable loss of time and energy involved in his work, and this income—it must be remembered—is additional to the regular annual profit which comes to him from his fields and clearings, his herds and palm trees.

As in other professions, there is a very wide diversity in the shaman's receipts. A shaman who is qualified to act over the whole range of ceremonial, is known to be favoured by the spirits, and has a practice extending over a number of villages, will naturally have a larger income than one who can, for example, officiate only at the Ajorapur, or who has no tutelary and thus cannot enter into trance, or who is restricted by custom or competition to his own village.

An important aspect of a shaman's life is the fact that for much of his time he lives free of cost. Since every Saora ceremonial ends with a feast, and since it is essential that the shaman should share it, he gets a very large number of free meals. Some shamans get at least one such meal every day, some get even more. And these meals are good square meals—plenty of rice, vegetables, perhaps crabs and fish, and nearly always a generous share of meat. And of course as much palm wine or liquor as one can hold. It is not easy to estimate the value of such a meal in cash. In a town it might well cost two or three rupees; on Saora standards it is probably worth about a rupee.

I will now examine the actual incomes of some shamans and shamanins, and try to assess what they really come to. The Saoras share to the full a common human frailty, a reluctance to reveal the truth about their incomes, but I found that though a shaman was very unwilling to say what he received from agriculture, he was much more forthcoming about his ritual profits. For, in the first place, these are known to everybody; they are on a more or less fixed scale; and they are not taxed. In the second place, the shamans felt that they grew in dignity as they counted up their takings. I do not think, however, that they exaggerated: there were too many friends and neighbours present during my inquiries, and every figure was publicly checked.

Ikam

Ikam, the medicine-man of Kamalasingi, is an adept and famous practitioner, and since he is the only medicine-man in his part of the country, he is summoned to villages over a wide area. The following is his own estimate of his income for the year 1950.

There are first a number of ceremonies, for which it is taboo for a shaman or medicine-man to receive payment. On these occasions he shares in the feast, but he cannot take anything away with him. Ikam said that during 1950 he performed the following ceremonies:

Parapur	Twice
Ratupur	4 times a month
Lambapur	10 times in the year
Kurrualpur	10 times in the year
Jammolpur	6 times in the year

The last three ceremonies are for the dedication of seed, for the protection of the hill-clearings before sowing and for the profit of the pulse harvest. Ikam goes each year to ten different places for these and, at each, feasts with the people, but can take nothing away. At other rites there are definite perquisites, and I give their approximate value at 1950 prices in the Saora country.

Ikam said that he celebrated the Tonaipur and Doripur on an average twice a month, and the Uyungpur, for the Sun-god, three times a month. He was even more in demand for the Ratupur, which he estimated at four times a month. Obviously these figures are approximate, but they may not be so far out, for they are the sacrifices which are most generally offered. Ikam, therefore, on his own estimate, received in 1950[1] a total of Rs 24 in cash and Rs 254–2–0 in kind.

[1] In 1950, in this part of the Saora hills, rice was selling at Rs 2 a measure, a fowl cost from Rs 2 to Rs 4, and buffaloes were from Rs 25 to Rs 35 without the skin.

IKAM[1]

Ceremony	No. of times cele-brated	Approximate value of goods received on each occasion				
		Meat	Grain	Wine	Miscel-laneous	Total for the year
General rites						Rs as ps
Tonaipur	Twice a month	Rs 2	Re 1	4 as	Cash, Re 1	102 0 0
Doripur	Twice a month	Rs 2	12 as	4 as	—	72 0 0
Uyungpur	Thrice a month	—	4 as	4 as	Pot, 2 as	22 8 0
Ajorapur	4	Rs 3	4 as	4 as	Pot, 2 as	14 8 0
Gungupur	6	Re 1	12 as	2 as	—	11 4 0
Festivals						
Rogonadur	1	—	Rs 3	Rs 3	Pulse, 8 as	6 8 0
Udanadur	1	—	Rs 3	Rs 3	—	6 0 0
Kondemadur	1	—	Rs 3	Rs 3	Pumpkins, 2 as	6 2 0
Funerary rites						
Guar	2	Rs 2	Re 1	8 as	Ring, 1 as	7 2 0
Lajap	10	—	4 as	4 as	Sickle, 2 as	6 4 0
Anamanpur	1	8 as	8 as	4 as	Cloth, Rs 2	3 4 0
Karja	1	Rs 4	Rs 4	8 as	Cloth, Rs 12 Ring, 2 as	20 10 0
					Total	Rs 278 2 0

But in addition to this he had no fewer than 187 good meals, which I have suggested were probably worth a rupee a time. We may, therefore, to be on the safe side, estimate Ikam's annual income as a medicine-man at about Rs 450.

There was no death from tiger during the year, but even if there had been it would hardly have affected the total; for at this and the Parapur which is celebrated in cases of suicide and murder, the shaman may not accept anything but his food.

The expert and vivacious Guarkumboi, Amiya of Singjangring, also did very well in 1950. She had seven villages in her circuit, and there were many calls upon her in spite of the fact that she was confined to ceremonies connected with the dead.

[1]In these tables I have not included the rites for which the shaman receives no perquisites.

AMIYA

Ceremony	No. of times cele-brated	Approximate value of goods received on each occasion				
		Meat	Grain	Wine	Miscel-laneous	Total for the year
						Rs as ps
Guar	8	Rs 3	Rs 2	8 as	—	44 0 0
Karja	7	Rs 3	Rs 10	Rs 2	Cloth, Rs 6	147 0 0
Lajap	4	Rs 2	Rs 5	Re 1	Fan, sickle, baskets, Rs 6	56 0 0
Idaipur	6	8 as	Rs 5	8 as	—	36 0 0
					Total	Rs 283 0 0

In addition to this total of Rs 283, Amiya attended at least two funerals or name-giving ceremonies a month, and a large number of other festivals and ceremonies at which she did not take a leading part but at which—since there is no occasion into which the dead do not intrude—she was often asked for assistance. On all these occasions she got her food and drink; she considered that it would not be an exaggeration to say that she got at least two and often three meals a week in this way. If, therefore, we add Rs 100 to Rs 120 as the value of the food she received, we may say that Amiya's income from her professional sources alone came to about Rs 400. But Amiya also had taken over the management of the late Chief's affairs on behalf of her nephew who was still a young boy, and she was on tribal standards a prosperous woman at the end of 1950.[1]

On the other hand, another shamanin, a Raudakumboi named Dyan, also of Boramsingi village, put her income at not more than Rs 5 a month. She officiated at about six ceremonies in the month and was poorly paid. And a shaman at Sogeda estimated that he treated some ten patients a month and did not get more than six annas a time in rice and liquor. But he did not include the meat he received. Probably the estimate of a shaman at Tumulu is closer to the average. He said that in a good year he performed the Doripur twice a month at least and received about Rs 6 worth of goods each time; he did the

[1] The official National Income Committee estimated the per capita income for 1948-9 as Rs 255, but Dr V. K. R. V. Rao has pointed out that this sum was actually about Rs 5 less in purchasing power than the Rs 65 which was estimated as the per capita income for 1931-2.

Uyungpur three times a month and got ten annas, and four ordinary sacrifices a month which were worth to him eight annas a time. This comes to Rs 190–8, of which the greater part comes from the Doripur, always a profitable rite for the shaman. To this we must add the income from funerals, Guar and Karja ceremonies as they occur, feasts at the Harvest Festivals, and at least 130 free meals in the course of the year, so that the total income comes to between Rs 300 and Rs 350. This is, I think, the sort of income that most of the reasonably adept shamans and shamanins can expect.

An expert, however, may get much more. But not many are as successful as Indano, the shaman of Tammegorjang. He was a man who had seen the world; he had been to Calcutta and Assam; he talked a little Oriya; and was a very intelligent and rather tricky person. In his own and surrounding villages, there was rather a dearth of shamans and shamanins in 1950, and since he himself was qualified to perform every kind of sacrifice except those reserved for the medicine-men, he was kept very busy. He told me that he sometimes performed as many as three ceremonies in a day, a fact which was confirmed by my own observation.

This makes the impressive, if rather approximate, total of Rs 554–4. It is approximate because Indano was unable to give the exact number of times he celebrated, say, the Idaipur in the year; he could not possibly remember all the occasions, but he insisted, and the other villagers supported him, that it was once a week and often twice: he thought six times a month would be a fair estimate and I accepted this. Similarly, he declared that he was in constant demand for ceremonies addressed to Labosum and that these came to at least five a month. And so for the Doripur, Uyungpur and Tonaipur, which occurred not less than once a week or once a fortnight.

In addition to this, Indano said that he had celebrated the Ratupur about a dozen times, the Lambapur once, the Jammolpur once, and the Kurrualpur once. On these occasions, as we have seen, it is taboo for the shaman to accept anything but his food and drink. In this area the same taboo applies to the Lajap, which Indano celebrated 7 times in 1950. He thus officiated on his own estimate 284 times during the year, and so to his income of Rs 554–4, we must add Rs 284 for his food and drink, making a total of Rs 838–4. In a year when the Karja is celebrated, or when the mortality is higher and there are more funerals and Guar rites, his income may well approach a thousand rupees.

INDANO

Ceremony	No. of times celebrated	Approximate value of goods received on each occasion				
		Meat	Grain	Wine	Miscellaneous	Total for the year
General rites						Rs as ps
Gungupur	8	—	6 as	4 as	—	5 0 0
Doripur	Thrice a month	Rs 2	Re 1	4 as		117 0 0
Uyungpur	Thrice a month	—	6 as	4 as	Pot, 2 as	27 0 0
Tonaipur	Twice a month	Rs 2	Re 1	8 as	Cash, Rs 5	204 0 0
Labopur	At least five times a month	—	8 as	4 as		45 0 0
Ajorapur	Once a month	Rs 2-4	8 as	4 as		36 0 0
Festivals						
Rogonadur	1	—	Rs 3	Re 1	Pulse, 6 as	4 6 0
Udanadur	1	—	Rs 3	Re 1		4 0 0
Kondemadur	1	—	Rs 3	12 as		3 12 0
Funerary rites						
Guar	6	Rs 2	Re 1	4 as	Ring, 1 as	19 14 0
Anamanpur	5	8 as	4 as	8 as	Cloth, Rs 2	16 4 0
Idaipur	At least six times a month	8 as	6 as	2 as		72 0 0
					Total	Rs 554 4 0

This is a considerable sum for an Indian tribesman, when it is remembered that it was a supplementary income, in addition to the earnings of agriculture, but I do not think it is exaggerated, and Indano certainly gave the impression of being comparatively well-to-do.

III

Let us now approach the problem from the other side, from that of the layman who has to spend the money. I will give four examples of 'religious budgets', which will give some indication at least of the way the money is spent. Each of the households examined was of fair substance, midway between poverty and affluence. The period in each case was for December 1949 to November 1950, and the expenditure was incurred in both cash and kind.

NILAM DOLBEHERA OF BORAMSINGI

Month	Sacrifice	Expenditure				Total
		Animal offerings	Grain	Wine	Miscel-laneous	
						Rs as ps
1949 Dec.	Uyungpur	Fowl, Rs 3	8 as	4 as	—	3 12 0
	Ratupur	Pig, Rs 5	8 as	4 as		5 12 0
	Idaipur	Goat, Rs 15	Re 1	Re 1		17 0 0
1950 Feb.	Karja	Buffalo, Rs 32 Fowl, Rs 3	Rs 3	Rs 6	Pots, 12 as Cloth, Rs 5	49 12 0
March	Kurrualpur	Fowl, Rs 3	Re 1	Re 1		5 0 0
April	Udanadur	Fowl, Rs 3	Re 1	Re 1		5 0 0
	Jammolpur	Pig, Rs 6	Rs 2	Rs 4		12 0 0
June	Idaipur	Buffalo, Rs 30	Rs 8	Rs 4		42 0 0
August	Ganugayan-adur	Fowl, Rs 3	8 as	Rs 2		5 8 0
September	Gungupur	Pig, Rs 10	Rs 3	Rs 3		16 0 0
	Lambapur	Pig, Rs 4	Re 1	Re 1		6 0 0
October	Guar	Buffalo, Rs 32	Rs 3	Rs 5	Pots, 6 as	40 6 0
	Doripur	Buffalo, Rs 30	Rs 4	Rs 2		36 0 0
November	Doripur (repeated)	Buffalo, Rs 30	Rs 4	Rs 2		36 0 0
	Lajap	Fowl, Rs 3	Rs 3	Re 1	Pots, baskets, fan, sickle, Rs 1–14	8 14 0
					Total	Rs 289 0 0

This was in a year in which no member of Nilam's family died.

GAIMA OF RAJINTALU

Month	Sacrifice	Expenditure			Total
		Animal offerings	Grain	Wine	
					Rs as ps
1950 March	Kurrualpur	Pig, Rs 6	Re 1	Rs 2	9 0 0
May	Doripur (for his sick son)	Buffalo, Rs 25	Rs 3	Rs 3	31 0 0
November	Kittungpur (for a sick baby)	Fowl, Rs 2	Re 1	Re 1	4 0 0
				Total	Rs 44 0 0

In addition to this, Gaima made small contributions of grain and wine at each of the village festivals, at the funerals of members of his family group and at the Guar and Karja ceremonies to which he was invited, but with which he had no personal concern. He said that the total value of all such donations was about Rs 5. His total expenditure on sacrifices and festivals during the year thus came to only Rs 49. He was, of course, fortunate in having no Guar or Karja ceremonies of his own to pay for, and in the fact that his own health and that of his family was good throughout the year.

JIVANO OF SOGEDA

Month	Sacrifice	Expenditure				
		Animal offerings	Grain	Wine	Miscellaneous	Total
						Rs as ps
1949 Dec.	Doripur (for a sick son)	Buffalo, Rs 20	Rs 2	Rs 2		24 0 0
1950 Feb.	Idaipur (for his sick wife)	Fowl, Rs 3	Re 1	8 as		4 8 0
March	Karja (for his father)	Buffalo, Rs 24 Cock, 4	Rs 2	Rs 2	Cloth, Rs 4	36 0 0
April	Udanadur	—	8 as	6 as		0 14 0
May	Jammolpur	Fowl, Rs 3	8 as	12 as	Cash, 8 as	4 12 0
	Ratupur (for sick son)	Pig, Rs 5	Re 1	8 as		6 8 0
July	Idaipur (for himself)	Goat, Rs 10	Re 1	Re 1	—	12 0 0
August	Gungupur	Pig, Rs 6	Re 1	Re 1	Cash, 12 as	8 12 0
	Pijjinganadur	—	8 as	4 as	Cash, 4 as	1 0 0
Sept.	Kondemanadur	—	8 as	8 as	Cash, 6 as	1 6 0
Nov.	Lajap (for his father)	Fowl, Rs 4	Re 1	Re 1	Rs 1–6	7 6 0
					Total	Rs 107 2 0

Jivano too said that he contributed small quantities of grain and wine to the funerals and ceremonies of other people, which amounted in all to five or six rupees; we may, therefore, put down his expenditure for the year at Rs 112.

Finally I will give an account of Jomsiya, the Dolbehera of Sogeda, a man important in the social and political life of the village, but of only moderate wealth.

JOMSIYA OF SOGEDA

Month	Sacrifice	Expenditure				
		Animal offerings	Grain	Wine	Miscellaneous	Total
1949						Rs as ps
Dec.	Lajap	Buffalo, Rs 30	Rs 2	Rs 2	Rs 3–8	37 8 0
	Idaipur (for his daughter)	She-goat, Rs 20	Rs 2	Re 1	Cash, 6 as	23 6 0
	Uyungpur	Cock, Rs 3	8 as	4 as	Cash, 6 as	4 2 0
1950						
Jan.	Rogonadur	Fowl, Rs 3	8 as	8 as	Cash, 4 as	4 4 0
March	Karja (for his father)	Buffalo, Rs 32 Cock, Rs 4	Rs 2	Rs 2	—	40 0 0
April	Udanadur	Fowl, Rs 3	4 as	4 as	Cash, 6 as	3 14 0
May	Jammolpur	Fowl, Rs 3	4 as	8 as	Cash, 4 as	4 0 0
June	Ratupur (for his wife)	Pig, Rs 6	12 as	8 as	—	7 4 0
August	Gungupur	Pig, Rs 5	4 as	4 as	Cash, Re 1	6 8 0
Sept.	Lambapur	Pig, Rs 4	12 as	12 as	—	5 8 0
					Total	Rs 136 6 0

If we again add a few rupees for miscellaneous expenses, we reach a figure of Rs 140 for the year. Jomsiya too had no Guar ceremony and no funeral to pay for during the year, or his expenditure would have approached Rs 200.

It will be noticed that by far the heaviest expenditure is for the dead. Nilam spent on this, for his

	Rs	as	ps
Idaipur, to appease an ancestor who had made him ill	17	0	0
Karja, for his dead father	49	12	0
Idaipur, for his widowed mother whom his father's ghost wished to take away	42	0	0
Guar, for his dead elder brother	40	6	0
Lajap	8	14	0

— a total of Rs 158–2–0 or over half the total year's expenditure on sacrifices.

And Jomsiya spent an even higher proportion on three rites:

	Rs	as	ps
Lajap	37	8	0
Karja	40	0	0
Idaipur	23	6	0

— or Rs 100–14–0 out of a total of Rs 140.

Expenditure on wine and liquor is relatively low, and in fact—where so many people have to share what is available—there is little drunkenness at the great ceremonies. It is the shamans and shamanins, and the Chiefs and other village officials, constantly treated by their friends, who generally end the day in a sort of stupor.

Sometimes the even course of the budget may be upset by some extravagantly expensive illness. Thus the wife of Mangu Buyya of Ondrunguda in 1947 had a difficult delivery, and before the child was born Mangu had spent Rs 6 on a pig for Labosum, Rs 10 on a goat for Gadejangboi, Rs 2 on a fowl for Kittung and Rs 32 on a buffalo for the ghost of his paternal grandfather—a total and unexpected expense of Rs 50.

Chapter Twelve

PRAYER AND TRANCE

I. *Prayer*

'THERE is no part of the religious service of mankind,' says Farnell, 'that so clearly reveals the various views of the divine nature held by the different races at the different stages of their development, or reflects so vividly the material and psychologic history of man, as the formulas of prayer.'[1] To this we may add Deissmann's words: 'One might write a history of religion by writing a history of prayer.'[2]

A study of Saora prayer is thus of the first importance, for in it we not only have clearly and authoritatively displayed the deepest Saora beliefs about the spiritual world, but we may also trace an anticipation, however dim, of the splendid creations of prayer which religious genius in its loftiest experience has achieved. In Saora, as in all the prayers of preliterate peoples, we study prayer in its simplest and purest form. 'In the popular religions of highly developed civilized peoples prayer lives with native energy and simplicity, but it is strongly repressed by ritual prayer and the fixed forms of exorcism and the magic spell . . . The literary fixation of ritual prayers and hymns brings about a restriction of free prayer which is not possible to the same extent among non-literary peoples.'[3]

Even though they move within certain well-defined limits, Saora prayers are largely the free expression of immediate need and individual character. There are no fixed forms; it is impossible to write down a definitive text of Saora prayers. There are, however, a large number of conventional phrases, epithets, stock forms of praise and intercession that are always being repeated. Such clichés occur even in the ordinary conversation of simple people, who cannot always be

[1] L. R. Farnell, *The Evolution of Religion* (London, 1905).

[2] Quoted by F. Heiler, *Prayer*. English translation by S. McComb (New York, 1932), p. xvi.

[3] ibid., pp. 1f. Unhappily the English translation of Heiler's great work omits the documentation of quotations, of which there were over 2,000 in the original version. Some of the prayers put onto the lips of primitive man seem unduly romanticized, and without knowing the sources from which they have been taken one hesitates to accept them as evidence. But that apart, the breadth, wisdom and spirituality of Heiler's work is beyond praise.

creating fresh expressions, and find relief in falling back on the familiar and the defined. But in Saora prayer these clichés are continually being mixed and sorted, rearranged and revitalized. But they never organize themselves into a formula: every Saora prayer is a new adventure in which fresh inspiration mingles with established phrase.

Saora prayer is in the main social, expressed sometimes by the head of a household, more often by a priest or shaman. But individual prayer, in which a man gives spontaneous expression to a personal need, is not unknown. After a dangerous dream, an individual may make a small sacrifice for himself and pray for his own safety; a shaman may sometimes be seen sitting alone before an ikon invoking a spirit whom he fears he has offended. But prayer without sacrifice is not regarded as very effective, and in personal need the Saoras tend to perform little ritual acts or gestures, with brief invocations. Whenever the shaman Kintara went on a journey, he offered wine at the pot dedicated to his tutelary, and asked for her help. Others take a pinch of rice from the pot in the village shrine and pray for protection. A shamanin does not only ask her tutelary to keep hostile spirits away; at the same time she puts a bit of ginger in her mouth. The little offerings of drops of wine or grains of rice which many Saoras make before drinking or eating are in effect prayers, and are often accompanied by the muttering of a few names and some such phrase as 'I drink; come and share what I have'.

But the ordinary man prays little; when he does he is inarticulate and brief. For all his greater needs he goes to the shaman. For it is of little value to pray unless one is capable of direct communication with the unseen world, and unless one has a tutelary to help. And so Saora prayer is largely, though not exclusively, conducted through the gifted individuals who are married to supernatural beings.

It is significant that the shamans and shamanins are not restricted to the service of their own families or even their own villages, but can go anywhere to sacrifice and intercede for their fellows. They pray, of course, for individual homes and families; they specially pray for their village community as a whole; but their prayer has been socialized to include the entire tribe within its scope. They may even pray for outsiders who come to them for professional assistance. A shamanin once offered fervent prayers as well as sacrifice for me when I was suffering from fever and invited her aid.

Prayer may be offered by an individual shaman or by two, three or even seven together. At a burning-ground at Tumulu two men and two women stood together in a row and chanted their invocations; at the Boramsingi Karja, three shamanins sat together holding hands and praying in unison night and day. At the Barasingi Sikunda, there were seven officiants who held each other and prayed in chorus. When a spirit possesses a shaman, a whole crowd of people may speak to him at once—this is a kind of congregational prayer since it is addressed, in however homely a fashion, to a spirit. Often, however, the congregation takes little notice of what is going on. At a festival or funerary rite, especially when a buffalo is sacrificed, and the problem of dividing and cooking the meat fills every mind, the shaman is usually left to pray before the altar alone or with one or two assistants. The rest of the company chatter, joke, and busy themselves with food without taking the slightest notice of what is going on between their representative and the unseen world.

Let us now consider some of the elements of Saora prayer, always bearing in mind that this is our classification and not that of the Saoras.

The Invocation

Every Saora prayer begins with an invocation, which may continue for as long as fifteen or twenty minutes. Its aim is to drive away the unwanted, to summon the desired, the appropriate spirits. It often begins with an invocation to foreign ancestors, the familiars of sorcerers, the ghosts of those who have been hanged or have hanged themselves, the ghosts of the murdered, of those killed by tigers, of those who fell from trees, all the spirits, in fact, whose baleful influence might interrupt and spoil the even course of prayer and sacrifice. They are invited to come, accept some wine and rice, and go away.

The invocation then proceeds to enumerate a great number of ancestors, tutelaries and gods. Certain names, which are often included, have in the course of time lost all meaning and no one can now say to whom they refer. The list includes such names and echo-names as Manninji, Sunninji, Jalbanji, Bulkanji, Radobanji, Raganji, and many more. Then the shaman calls on his own tutelary, the ancestors of the family concerned, the gods to which the rite is addressed. He may summon a vast company from the Under World to go and find a particular spirit. It is not expected that all those whose names are taken will attend the rite, but they expect to be remembered, and their help is often needed to ensure that the spirits who ought to be present will really come. For if prayer is to be effective, the spirit to whom it is offered must be present.

And here it should be said that prayer may be offered equally to the gods, the tutelaries and the ancestors. In broad outline the prayers are much the same to whomsoever they are addressed, but naturally prayer to the great, more aloof deities of the sky is more respectful; prayer to dangerous gods like Ratusum is more cautious and more obsequious; the prayer of a shaman to his tutelary wife is intimate, even casual and witty; the prayer of a widow to her dead husband's ghost may be plaintive and reminiscent.

Praise

After the invocation, the shaman often proceeds immediately to praise. There are many stock forms of greeting: 'We salute you with both hands' or, 'Like a monkey I salute you,' or, 'We salute you; we touch your feet, we eat your excreta.' In dealing with the gods, one must apply flattery with a trowel, and the shaman says everything that he can to please. 'As is a Raja's body, so is your body; as a Raja dresses, so do you dress; as a Raja rides on an elephant or horse, so do you ride. You are great; we honour you.' 'You are the Great Ones; you are kings, you are Brahmins, you are Kshattriyas.' At the Ajorapur the shaman flatters the supernatural snakes: 'You have horns, you have ears, you have eyes, you have fangs, you have everything you want. Come to us with all that makes you mighty.'[1]

It is essential that the giving and accepting of a sacrifice should be enveloped in an atmosphere of praise, that there should be the utmost good-humour and pleasantness on both sides. Man must make his offering ungrudgingly; the spirits must come willingly to accept it. This theme recurs continually. 'We give willingly; we bear no grudge.' 'Come dancing, come happily. Come and sit with us and share our feast.' And even to Rugaboi, the dread smallpox goddess, the shaman can say, 'Eat, Rugaboi, eat happily and go away. You are the mother of the world. You have come of your own accord; we are glad you came.'[2]

Praise creates the atmosphere for a friendly correspondence between the human and the divine.

[1] See p. 276. [2] See p. 290.

Petition

Saora prayer is generally excited by urgent and concrete necessity. Someone is ill, a child is to be named as a protection against danger, the rains have failed, there is a threat of sorcery. The Saora does indeed pray for health, for good crops, for riches. But most of his prayers aim more at preventing calamity than at obtaining a positive benefit. Indeed, as we have seen elsewhere, the basis of the Saora attitude to life is summed up in the saying, 'If only we are left alone, whether it be by gods or men, all will be well'. This spiritual zenophobia means that the most characteristic Saora petition to the spirits is 'Leave us alone and go away'.

I have never heard a Saora pray for virtue, for purification of heart so that he can commune better with the divine, for deliverance from temptation. After all, the gods do not reveal themselves so much to the pure of heart as to the open of hand.

Intercession

Altruistic sympathy is an attractive trait in the Saora character; it is indeed from this fine quality that the shamans draw their influence and power. Intercessory prayer, which is the verbal expression of sympathy, is the most important, as it is the most common, element in Saora prayer. The shaman is always praying for other people; many examples will be found in these pages. A shaman at Tumulu addresses Tangorbasum: 'Come and remove whatever evil is in this boy. Remove it from his body with your tongues, with your teeth, with your nails. We fold our hands and beg you to heal him.'[1] At a Jammapur the shaman prays, 'Care for all the children in the village'. At a Tuttumsumpur, the shaman exclaims, 'Let there be more blood, more flesh and fat in this child's body'. At the Potta Doripur, the shaman cried to the gods, 'Gather together here and agree to make this woman well... Come all of you and lighten the burden of the sick one, lighten the burden of her arms, her legs, her body.'[2]

Saora prayer does not depend on the belief that the gods can be compelled to give a favourable reply. There are no spells which produce an inevitable result, no magic rite which is bound to work; the shaman cannot by his ascetic power bend the spirits to his will. Saora intercession proceeds on the assumption that there is something in the nature of the spirits on which man can build with faith and hope.

[1] See p. 248. [2] See pp. 268f.

It is the mark of greatness to love. In the twenty years I have spent in tribal India, this rather surprising fact has come home to me: these people who are so generally supposed to respect power and show, to interpret greatness in terms of wealth and influence, do in fact admire above all things love, tenderness, sympathy, forgiveness; to them there is no greatness higher than disinterested love.

The Saoras obviously do not attribute this quality to all their gods or all the time to any of them. But the idea is there in their minds, and it is the basis for their intercessions.

THANKSGIVING

Heiler rightly points out that the absence of a word meaning 'to thank' in many tribal languages and even in the rich verbal treasury of the *Rigveda*, does not necessarily mean that the element of thanksgiving is absent from the tribal religions. 'Whenever one acknowledges to the Giver that one has received from him some special favour, that is thanksgiving.'[1] Thanksgiving, it is true, is sometimes flavoured by an ingenuous eudemonistic desire to ensure future benefits by acknowledging those already received. It is also true that where great stress is laid on sacrifice, there is less emphasis on thanksgiving, for the natural tendency is for man to feel that he has done his share and that it is only proper for god to do his. Indeed some Saora prayers give the impression that the shaman feels that it is the god who should be thankful to him rather than he who should be thankful to the god.

But in a simple way there is certainly something that can be called thanksgiving in Saora religion. The Saoras, for example, usually offer a little 'grace' in the form of a drop or two of wine before drinking themselves, and who shall say that there is not sometimes in their minds a sense of gratitude to the spirits who have provided or at least have not stolen the precious fluid? The element of thanksgiving cannot be excluded from the Harvest Festivals, even though the main emphasis is on paying due honour to the divine landlords and ensuring good crops in future. And in such phrases as these: 'You gave us birth. You injure us. You protect us', or 'We cannot see you, but you appear to us as a father appears to his children', or 'You are as father and mother, you are as Kittung to us', there is an acknowledgement of protection and care which amounts to gratitude.

[1] Heiler, *Prayer*, p. 38.

This may also be seen in a typical Harvest Thanksgiving prayer at the Rogonadur. 'For you we sowed the seed, and now that the plants have grown and borne fruit, we offer them first to you. You watched over the harvest, and so we give first to you. All these things are yours; we give them to you first.'[1]

Sacrifice and Vows

'As we give presents to important people to win their favour' said a shaman at Boramsingi, addressing the gods, 'so we give presents to you.' It is impossible at this date to say whether prayer or sacrifice came first in the history of Saora religion, but it is probably true that today there is no prayer without some kind of offering, however small it may be, even if it is only a few drops of wine, a few grains of rice. As we see in another chapter, the Saora pictures the spirits, if not exactly like himself, at least like the officials, overlords and merchants whose favour he has to win from time to time. Sacrifice has been called embodied prayer, and it may be that in the Saora mind the offering is more important than the arguments, the pleadings, the rich outpouring of words which accompany it.

'Wherever sacrifice in support of prayer predominates', says Heiler, 'the level of religion is inevitably lowered. The feeling of absolute dependence upon God which animates the worshipper is weakened by the thought of a service rendered to God, which obliges God to do a service in return; it is completely crowded out by the belief that the gods live on man's offerings and are, therefore, dependent on man. Thus in the sacrificial transaction, it frequently appears that the worshipper, instead of being in subordination to God, is on an equality with Him, or even superior to Him.'[2] The level of Saora religion has undoubtedly been lowered by this association of prayer with sacrifice, as witness the very undignified arguments that occur at almost every ceremony about the quality of the offerings, and the greed that is attributed to the gods. But I do not think that the Saoras have thought things out so far as to consider that the gods and ancestors are sufficiently dependent on them as to put them in a commanding position. So deeply implanted in them is the fear of pride, so strong is their belief in their powerlessness before the unseen world, that although they may argue with the spirits, may sometimes abuse and reproach

[1] See p. 329. [2] Heiler, op. cit., p. 25.

them, the general atmosphere is one of entire subordination: 'We are at your feet, we eat your excrement.'

But this does not exclude the note of pleading and reproach from their prayers. Addressing Tangorbasum, a shamanin said, 'If you are so easily offended, how are we to live? It is a matter of shame that great people like you should attack little people like us.'[1] And again, 'If you are going to attack us at any moment, whether we are working, sitting about, standing, laughing, talking or eating, what are we going to do?'[2] And there is a constant fear that the gods may trick their worshippers. 'Do not deceive us,' cries the shaman. 'Do not eat the feast and then say we gave you nothing.' And, 'Do not eat and promise to leave us alone and then secretly send another spirit to trouble us.'

At many ceremonies, the shaman calls on the great gods of sky and earth, Uyungsum, Darammasum, Lankasum and Labosum to bear witness that prayer and sacrifice has been duly offered.

This suspicion that the gods may not fulfil their side of the bargain, which has grown up naturally enough from bitter experience of a thousand wasted sacrifices and unanswered prayers, has given rise to the custom of the conditional sacrifice. Especially for little children, the Saoras often make a token gift and promise that, if all goes well, they will present the residue after a period of years.

SELF-JUSTIFICATION

Other notable elements in Saora prayer are connected with the very varied means of persuasion that the shaman employs to win the spirits over to his side. He flatters them, appeals to their power, and even to their love, reminds them of the years of service he has given, stresses the social and family bonds that hold them. He threatens and accuses, protests and rages. He appeals to their sympathy, and their self-interest. He excuses himself, begs for forgiveness, but above all continually attempts to justify himself.

The Saoras invariably remind the spirits of the trouble they have taken to arrange a sacrifice and tell them in great detail exactly how much everything has cost. 'We went to a distant land for thorns,' said the shamanins at a Name-giving rite, mendaciously, since in fact they only went just outside the village. 'We suffered much in gathering them. We have taken such great trouble.' At the Ajorapur the

[1] See p. 227. [2] See p. 248.

shaman protested, 'We ourselves have nothing but the roots and herbs of the hills, yet we never fail to give you sacrifice.' It is curious that the shamans generally depart very far from the truth in these protestations and the spirits often reply that they know better. On one occasion at Boramsingi, for example, when the villagers were proclaiming their poverty and their great self-sacrifice in offering a rather small pig, the ghost of shrewd old Jigri, the former Chief, replied, 'I've been watching you ever since I died. You may trick others, but you can't trick me. You can't see me, but I can see you. I know just how well off you really are.'[1]

The Saoras are also anxious to justify themselves as ritually correct. 'Have we made any mistakes?' they ask anxiously. 'Have we ever forgotten to honour you?'

And they also stress the fact that in spite of all the spirits may do against their interests, they bear no grudge and harbour no resentment. In a significant passage, a shaman says, 'It is you who drive men to hang themselves, you make men murder one another, you cause them to fall from trees, it is you who carry men away. But we do not blame you, we speak no word against you.' 'We give you pulse,' said the priest at a Rogonadur ceremony, 'even though you allowed it to be eaten by grubs and monkeys and tigers.'[2]

But though man thus forgives the gods, he is never tempted to abuse his position; the servant forgives his master, the criminal his judges; but there is no real reversal of their roles.

Conclusion

Man may forgive the gods, but he also seeks forgiveness from them. With the plea for pardon goes naturally confession of guilt or mistake. At the Jammolpur at Tumulu, a shaman said, 'One year we did not give you sacrifice and you destroyed our crops, you carried away our seed, you killed our cattle, you ruined our fields. But this year we are giving you everything you can possibly want.' And again, 'If we have forgotten anything, do not be angry and spoil the harvest for a little mistake.'[3] At a ceremony for Tangorbasum, for the relief of a sick boy, the shaman enumerated all the possible ways in which he might have offended and said, 'If he did this, or this, or this, we fold our hands and beg you to forgive him and accept what we spread before you.'[4]

[1] See p. 475. [2] See p. 332. [3] See p. 318. [4] See p. 249.

The Saoras also appeal to the pity and sympathy of the spirits. 'Look, he is only a little baby.' 'It is a child thin as a bamboo.'

The important thing to notice about Saora prayer is that it is real prayer. Even though it is to some extent modified by the bargaining implicit in the idea of sacrifice, it is not magic. There is no coercion about it. It is a real commerce between men and 'personal' spirits, who are imagined as being very like human beings, open to the same sort of persuasion, reasonable creatures to whose pity and understanding an appeal can be made with some hope of success.

'The idea of the kinship of man with God,' says Farnell, 'belongs to the alphabet of true prayer.' Men and the spirits are one family; after all men have the actual blood of the ancestral ghosts in their veins; the shamans are linked by marriage to their tutelaries; many of the gods are themselves halfway to being ancestors as a result of taking so many of the dead into themselves. And so Saora prayer is a social phenomenon; there is a real interchange, a genuine intercourse, between men and the spirits on the plane of men's actual social and economic relations with one another. Prayer is the 'reflex of human social relations'.[1]

The forms of Saora prayer are those which Heiler summarizes as characteristic of all prayer. They are 'as manifold as the forms of human speech; appeal and address, greeting and benediction, complaint and petition, praise and thanks, invitation, allurement, persuasion, threatening, insult, accusation and apology—all these modes of speech reappear in prayer. As man's speech is not only utterance, communication, but also aims at a real influence, a prevailing upon, a change of another's point of view, so prayer especially is of use in moving the god to grant help or to fulfil man's desire.'[2]

II. *Trance*

THE trance[3] occurs, or may occur, as a feature of any ceremony at which the spirits are invited to be present, provided there is a shaman qualified to accommodate them.

But if the ceremony is being conducted by an ordinary priest, or by an Idaimaran, or by a shaman not fully qualified, then it proceeds

[1] Heiler, *Prayer*, p. 58. [2] ibid., p. 58.

[3] A trance may either be a cataleptic or hypnotic condition marked by the suspension of consciousness, or a state of mental abstraction from external things, absorption, exaltation, ecstasy (*O.E.D.*). In the Saora trance the shaman is abstracted from external things but not wholly unconscious of them.

to its conclusion more expeditiously, but without the excitement and interest that a shaman in trance invariably provides. Shamans may also fall into trance on occasions at which they are performing no official function; I have often seen shamanins fall to the ground in a state of spirit-possession at entirely secular dances or during the processions of a Harvest Festival. On more than one occasion I have been somewhat embarrassed by a shamanin going into trance as a result of listening to my gramophone.

Once a shaman passes into a state of dissociation anything may happen. The belief is that he is possessed by a spirit, or more usually, a succession of spirits who speak and act through him. He is supposed to be completely under their control and to have no knowledge of what he is saying and doing. Yet although there is no programme, and there is endless diversity in detail, there is a remarkable general similarity throughout the whole Saora country in the way the shamans talk and behave at these times.

There is generally great confusion and, as I say, anything may happen. There may be revelations and discussions about matters entirely unrelated to the sacrifice or festival at which the trance occurs. The dead are always breaking in, for—it is said—'at the least sign of love the dead approach'. A ghost may take the opportunity to give instructions about the disposal of his property or to demand a quite different sacrifice later on; a god may give warning of an epidemic or threaten ruin to the crops. The regular course of the proceedings may also be interrupted by visitors who drop in for a consultation. For once it is known that a shaman is in trance, it is economical to consult him, for it is supposed that now the door to the other world is open, the spirits are there thronging to get through, and it is a good time to consult them about one's personal affairs, however irrelevant they may be to the matter in hand.

There is a fairly definite routine of entering on an officially-induced trance (as distinct from those which occur spontaneously), and there are several ways of preparing for it. It is generally preceded by a period of invocation when the shaman[1] squats on his heels before the altar or ikon, makes offerings of rice and wine, and calls on the spirits to attend. When he feels that 'they are on the way', he changes his posture, sitting upright on the ground with his legs stretched out straight in front of him. He takes a fan of rice in his left hand and

[1] All this will apply equally to a shamanin.

lights a little lamp which he waves above the rice and places by the altar. Then he begins to rub his right hand round and round in the rice, calling as he does so on his tutelary to come upon him. He continues doing this for as long as perhaps five minutes, and his voice grows fainter until suddenly he gives a start, his whole body stiffens, his arms extend straight before him and both his hands clench themselves tightly over his fan. His attendants at once catch hold of his arms and legs and bend them and unclench his fingers; this sometimes involves a regular struggle to break down the rigor which the trance induces.

Then there is a pause. The shaman sits with head bent, legs straight forward, his arms stretched along them. And then all at once he begins to speak in a high-pitched unfamiliar voice, sometimes using a few Kui or Oriya words; this is the voice of the spirit who has come upon him.

After this there is no programme, no routine. The shaman *becomes* whatever spirit has possessed him for the time being, and within an hour he may play a dozen different parts. He appears to be entirely out of his own control. He weeps, laughs, jokes, curses. Now he is a woman and pretends to give suck to a child; he puts anything given him on his head as a woman does. Now he is an old man, wears a big hat and hobbles round driving imaginary herds before him with a stick. Now he is a tutelary's horse and demands water and drinks it with great noisy gulps. A bawdy ghost comes upon him, and he demands a woman, catches hold of one, and makes a token attempt at intercourse. As an old man he coughs and spits; as an old woman he sheds tears, pats his shrunken breasts and combs his hair. When the ghost of old Jigri came one day at Boramsingi, the shamanin tottered about on a stick complaining of her sore foot just as Jigri used to do in life.

Although a shaman engaged in sacrifice or incantation may be left severely alone, there is always a crowd when he goes into trance. For here is pathos and humour, bargaining and gossip; a good shaman provides first-class entertainment. And there is nearly always a hot discussion, the congregation remonstrating, pleading, arguing; the spirit complaining, abusing, threatening at first, then gradually softening in the face of promise and persuasion.

Normally a shaman's own tutelary comes upon him first, and after that a succession of gods and ghosts. The sign that one is going and another coming is that the shaman's voice falters and dies away; his body jerks convulsively and his hands slide down his legs to his feet; sometimes he scratches his armpits. There is a pause and then he begins to speak in a different voice.

When everything is over, the shaman relaxes; he spits into his hands, rubs them together, rubs them over his face, yawns, stretches himself; he is like someone waking up.

Although the most common way of inducing trance is by the aid of rice in a winnowing-fan, there are several other methods.

A new earthen pot, which will later be dedicated to a spirit, may be used to induce a sort of auto-hypnotism. The wife of Somra, at Taraba, who was a well-known shamanin, affected the use of the pot in preference to any other method. I once watched her in trance for two whole hours as she talked with her tutelary and his relatives. After hanging up two coloured cloths for her daughters in the Under World, she dedicated a pot to the tutelary and began to speak into it, holding it close to her mouth, first to one cheek and then to the other. She threw it up and down, catching it in both hands and all the time calling on her tutelary husband to come to her. For a time he did not come and she wept. Her attendants sat behind her ready to catch her when he did come. Suddenly she stiffened and fell back into their arms. The tutelary refused wine and demanded a little rice-beer; the shamanin had to mix some rice-flour with water and drink it. Then one by one all her relatives in the Under World came upon her and she talked to them in turn, singing into the pot which she held caressingly to her mouth. Sometimes she held the pot with one hand and rubbed rice in a fan with the other. When all was over she hung the pot up before an ikon.

The *kurānrājan* and the hide-gong are also used to induce the proper rhythmic atmosphere for trance. The shaman accompanies his invocations on the fiddle, and soon the quiet rhythmic music accomplishes the desired result. The steady beating of a hide-gong serves the same purpose, and so may a dance. The shamans are very sensitive to any kind of rhythmic music or movement.

I can best give some idea of what happens in trance by describing an actual case, one of scores which I have attended. On 22 December 1950, Iswaro the young Chief of Boramsingi, and nephew of old Jigri, fell ill, and an old shamanin, by name Sahadri, was summoned to discover why. The actual period of trance lasted from 2.30 to 3.45 in the afternoon.

Sahadri sat with two Idaibois to assist her before a small altar consisting of a basket of rice and a pot of wine, beneath an ikon for her tutelary. Her patient, Iswaro, sat just behind her. She began in a squatting posture and, taking a pinch of rice between her thumb and forefinger, passed it over the boy's back as she chanted, calling on the ancestors:

> Was it one of you who threw a bit of wood at him or sent a worm into his belly or hit him on the head with a stone? Why has he got this pain? Come and make him well. I call you with rice. Whether you be Rajas, whether you be servants, come all of you. Come Jigri, come Jigri's mother, call the other ancestors. Do not come by a roundabout way, come by the straight road. Do not rest in caves or under trees or on the banks of streams, but come straight here.

She threw away the rice and, turning to the ikon, offered wine before it. Then she stretched out her legs and took a fan in her lap. One of the Idaibois handed her a small basket of rice. Sahadri lighted her sacred lamp and waved it round and round above the basket; she examined it carefully, smelt it, took out some of the rice and peered at it, passed her hand through the flame of the lamp and then threw a few grains towards the ikon. She poured the rest of the rice into her fan, and began to rub her right hand round and round in it, calling on her tutelary as she did so.

> There is a good road. Come quickly and help me discover what is wrong here. Whether it is a big matter or a small matter, it is for you to see to it. Is this boy's pain due to sorcery? Is it the work of a god? Is it a god of this world or of the Under World? Is it Uyungsum? Is it the god who lives in aeroplanes? Gogoji Rajaji, take this matter into your ears and attend to it. Goiyaraji Kararaji [famous old shamans who had become tutelaries], come and help. Whether it be tough or tender, soft or hard, come to us and help. Look in your books and come. Do not trip or stumble on the way; do not stub your toes against stones in the path. You who live with Kittung, come. If there is a rock in the way, break it open; if there is a tree in the way, knock it down; if you are in an aeroplane, descend.

The shamanin continued in this strain for about fifteen minutes, calling on every god, ancestor and tutelary she could remember, and then gradually her voice began to die away; she herself seemed to grow weaker; you could almost see her passing out of normal consciousness. She spoke slowly, then more slowly, until she was silent but for little gasps and cries. She gave a sudden start, her body tensed and stiffened, her hands gripped the sides of her fan.

The Idaibois at once caught her arms and legs, and after a little struggle relaxed them; it was harder to force open the clenched hands. There was then a pause of about a minute of complete silence, and for once there was not so much as a whisper among the onlookers. Then Sahadri jerked her body sharply and picked up some rice, smelt it, threw it up in the air and began to rub the rice in her fan. Suddenly she gave a loud scream, which indicated that her tutelary had come. Through her he cried, 'What are you bothering me for? What is it you want now?' The Idaibois and the others in the room at once began to explain, all speaking at once with a tremendous chatter. 'Tell us,' they said, 'was it a god of the forest or a god of the path?' 'Why,' asked the tutelary, 'had the boy been somewhere?' 'Yes, he'd been to Jampapur.' 'Then I'll go and find the god who did it and bring him here. But it might have been a plot of your enemies in Boramsingi and Kittim. Personally, that's what I think it was, but I'll go and find out.'

The shamanin jerked forward, her hands slid down her legs, and she remained silent with bent head for a couple of minutes. This was supposed to allow the tutelary time for his inquiries. Another violent jerk announced his return. The shamanin put her lamp beside her and began to rub her rice again. Once more everybody began to shout questions. The tutelary refused to answer till he had a drink. The shamanin took a long draught of wine, but the tutelary (speaking through her own lips) abused her. 'This is water. Get me some proper wine, and in a tumbler. There is a sahib here. That shows that this is an important occasion; I must be treated right.' There was another pause while someone went off to my camp to get a tumbler. When it came, it was filled with wine and the shamanin took a long drink. 'That's better,' said the tutelary. 'Now tell me again, what is it you want?' More screaming voices answered him.

'There was a banyan tree', said the tutelary at last, 'on the path to Jampapur, and the tutelaries of Singjangring and Jampapur had put their pots of gruel in its shade while they had a chat with some ancestors from Ladde who were returning home after a sacrificial feast. The boy kicked one of the pots over as he went by. You must give a pig in compensation at once.'

After another drink, the shamanin gave another jerk as a sign that her tutelary had departed. She was then visited by a procession of ancestors. One of them, Iswaro's paternal uncle, admitted that he had been there under the banyan tree, but disclaimed any share in the incident. Then the ghost of the shamanin's own dead husband came and discussed family matters with her sister who was sitting near by. Rather late, for owing to the sore on her foot she could only hobble along, the ghost of Iswaro's formidable aunt Jigri arrived. She demanded to see the pig proposed for sacrifice. She now showed that she had taken with her to the Under World those sound financial gifts which had made her so prosperous in life. The shamanin (in her character as Jigri) took the pig in her lap and carefully examined it. 'It is not very fat,' she complained. 'You paid far too much for it. Couldn't you get some of the money back? In any case, it's too small. When we have important visitors in the village, we ought to do better than this. Why don't you sacrifice a buffalo?' The spectators explained volubly, stressing their poverty, their debts, the failure of the crops that year, the endless demands upon them. Jigri laughed derisively. 'I've been watching you ever since I died. You may trick others, but you can't trick me. You can't see me, but I can see you. I know just how well off you really are.'

Then an old man with an obvious hangover, who was not even related to Iswaro, came in and insisted on the shamanin inquiring into the cause of his bad head. Sahadri passed her hands over his body, removed something from it and placed it in the fold of her cloth, then pulled at his fingers and toes. The ghost of a man who had been murdered some years previously came upon her, saying that he was now Uyungsum and that the old toper must give him a buffalo. This was rather more than he had bargained for, and he hastily put some rice in the shamanin's hands and clasped them in his, saying, 'Look, you and I are old friends; we used to go drinking together; you wouldn't want to bother an old friend.' But the ghost swore with an oath that unless he had a buffalo he would take his old friend away.

This interesting discussion was interrupted by the return of Jigri's ghost; she was not satisfied about certain matters concerning the disposal of her extensive property, and in particular insisted that her niece Arari, who had let her down by marrying before her dedication as a Guarkumboi had been completed, should not be given the keys of any of the store-rooms.

The proceedings continued with a score of irrelevancies. Young Iswaro was completely forgotten. Sometimes the talk was homely and good-natured; the spirits laughed and made the people laugh with them. But sometimes they discussed the scandals of this and the other world, and a ghost would be angry and abusive.

At last, when it was approaching four o'clock, the shamanin's tutelary returned and showed an interest in the patient of the day. He made the shamanin blow violently in his nose and ears, feel his ribs, blow on his stomach, stroke his legs and thighs, squeeze his arms. Then he said, 'He's going to be all right. Sacrifice that pig at once, and there will be no more trouble. Give me something to drink and I'll be off.'

The shamanin took a long drink out of the tutelary's special tumbler, jerked violently to show that the spirit had gone, and then relaxed completely as a sign that she was coming out of her trance. She spat on her hands and rubbed them over her face, yawned and sat up. Then without any pause she turned to me with a beaming smile and asked for some medicine for itch!

What are the shaman's own sensations while he is in trance? Some say that they feel intoxicated, as they well may in view of the amount they drink on behalf of their spirit-guests. One shaman compared the trance to his first experience of sexual intercourse: 'Everything went black before my eyes.' Another also compared it to a first intercourse, but more poetically: 'It was as if the sky and the earth were made one.' A shamanin at Baijalo rubbed her eyes on coming out of trance because, she said, 'Owing to the god everything was dark'. Yet another said, 'My throat is parched and I feel very thirsty. I feel like someone lost on a lonely road.'

All shamans agree that they know of what goes on during the trance, the details of the conversations, which spirits came to them, how they themselves behaved. But some of them say that their inner experiences of a sort of dream world vary according to the kind of spirit that possesses them. The dead, for example, are far more exhausting than other spirits. A shaman at Tumulu described his experience like this:

> When a god comes on me, everything is dark: people look very small and of many colours; sometimes I see a bazaar, a river, hills and many animals—horses, elephants and monkeys. When everything is over, two lovely young girls come to me and catch me by the hand and cry, 'Come with us to our world'. I resist them and it is the act of pushing them away that wakes me up.

Another shaman, Samiya of Sogeda, had similar experiences of the Under World while he was in trance.

When a tutelary comes upon me, I see a great white house and a broad straight road with elephants, horses and soldiers, just as they might be here, but all very small. There is an office with clerks writing at tables, and the police bring in people naked with their hands tied behind them. I see a banyan with many monkeys and gods sitting in talk below. When the tutelary is on the point of going away, two pretty girls catch me by one hand and two other girls catch me by the other and they say, 'Come, come!' I wrench my hands free, and the tutelary departs.

It is bright when a tutelary is with me, but when the ancestors come everything is dark. I do not know where I am or what I am doing. I see nothing but mountains and a winding road. There are houses in rows, very small, and their doors are as small as windows. Many tigers prowl round the villages. The women are dressed like Saora women and their babies are usually crying for food. There are great rocks and people sitting on them; they are silent as if they were thinking about something. When the ancestors depart, I feel as if I am falling into a pit, and after they have gone I am completely exhausted.

This seems to be the general opinion, for Sondan the shamanin also said that 'When a god comes, everything looks beautiful to me, and when he leaves me I do not feel at all tired. But when an ancestor comes, everything is dark and when he goes my body is worn out and aches in every bone.'

These experiences compare, of course, with the dreams of the Under World which every shaman has and the general picture compares with those of the ikon paintings. But the sense of exhaustion, and the motif of the pretty girls who would keep the shaman for ever in the world of dream are peculiar to the trance-state.

But whether the shamans know what they are talking about or not, they do in effect give a dramatic exhibition of what the spirits are supposed to be like. The records of these trance-sessions, therefore, throw much light on Saora theology, on the relations of living and dead, of human and divine, and above all on the character of the gods.

The picture that emerges is a curious one. On the one hand, we discern traces of kindliness and amiability, even of love, a willingness to help, a concern for human welfare. On the other, there is greed, temper, selfishness and an extraordinary lack of dignity.

In the first place, the spirits are revealed as very touchy about the order of precedence. At one ceremony I attended, the shaman's tutelary was indignant because some of the ancestors had been called before her. At another, Uyungsum complained that the ancestors were always arriving first and getting the best food.

Then again, the spirits continually complain about the quality of their entertainment. A ghost, speaking through a shamanin at a Name-giving rite, smelt the wine he was offered and said, 'What kind of liquor is this? Did you put your hand into your thing and bring it from there?'

It is not perhaps unreasonable, on the Saora theory, to suppose that the dead will make a good deal of fuss about their food. For everyone knows that the unhappy shades live on the frontiers of starvation, and even the ancestors are often hungry in the Under World. But the tutelaries are pictured as doing themselves very well; they have large houses, many servants, are constantly giving parties, and some of them maintain private zoos. Yet a tutelary visiting a shamanin will be as exacting in his demands for food and drink as any ghost. And the gods are as bad, though they have many sources of income.

Indeed a large part of the communion between the spirits and their votaries is taken up by tedious arguments about food.

The unseen visitor invariably finds the wine insipid, the food inadequate, his worshippers lacking in respect.

But when the session continues for some time, and as the shaman grows more and more mellow with the offerings of wine which he has to consume, his representation of the spirits mellows also. Soon they begin to joke, often obscenely; they show a keen ear for gossip; they themselves let out scandals at which no one living has yet dared to hint; they swear friendship. At a ceremony at Barasingi, a ghost demanded a woman, 'a Dom woman' he insisted, amid roars of laughter. On the same occasion a shamanin threw her arms round the necks of two men at once and banged her head against theirs in token of a spirit's friendship. At Ladde the ghost of a man named Sobha possessed his widow in a dream. The woman fell ill, and when the shaman came to assist her, Sobha's ghost came laughing upon him and said, 'Oho, what a fine time I had with her! She was going to leave my children and marry someone else. So I had her and made her ill. Now draw an ikon showing what I did.' And the shaman had to paint what is called a *tutun-ittalan*, a 'copulation ikon', showing Sobha with his widow.

If the behaviour of the spirits during a trance is familiar and undignified, the conduct of the human worshippers is often equally familiar, casual and even frivolous. Death itself becomes a matter for jest. At the Potta Doripur, an old woman joked with a ghost who possessed the shaman. The ghost said, 'I have left my fields and the reaping of my harvest to come here. Everything is in a muddle. Let me go quickly.' The old woman protested, and the ghost said, 'Then why not come with me [die] and help me reap my crop?' 'Not me,' said the old woman, chuckling as at an enormous jest. 'I've plenty to do here.'

People are not afraid of abusing the spirits. At a Name-giving ceremony, they said to an ancestor, 'You are always coming here to get things to eat, but you don't really help us at all, and our children always die.' And at another similar ceremony, a sick child's mother cried, 'You gods and ghosts only think about eating goats and pigs and fowls. All you want is liquor. But when it comes to helping us, you do nothing at all.' At a Rogonadur celebration, the shamanin scattered scraps of food on the threshold 'for the spirits that are crowding like dogs outside the house'. And at a Doripur ceremony for a sick boy, his father who had had heavy expenses in the attempt to cure him, cried, 'You are always lying to us, promising that if we give you this or that, you will be content. But you always come back for more. I cannot see gods and ghosts, but if I could, I would kick you all.'

But the atmosphere at most ordinary ceremonies is informal and relaxed. I remember that once at Abbasingi, when a shaman fell into trance, his attendants shouted with laughter as they bent his stiffened arms and legs. At Barasingi in January 1951, everyone was very jolly at the Sikunda ceremony. The priest who should have performed this important rite did not bother to turn up at all, and his place was taken at the last moment by an elderly shaman who was completely blind. The congregation found this tremendously amusing, shouted encouragement after every mistake, offered him contradictory advice, and ragged him unmercifully. Later, there was a procession to the burning-ground to dig up the bones of a woman from another village. As these pathetic relics were exhumed, there were roars of laughter from the crowd, and boys and girls chased each other in and out of the throng.

Long before, at a buffalo sacrifice for an ancestor at Karanjasingi on 19 December 1944, I had been impressed by the frivolous behaviour of most of the participants in the rite. The donor of sacrifice, one Leju, was a very casual young man with an indifferent notion of his filial duties, which he had long postponed. But the others present seemed equally indifferent to any danger from the potentially dangerous spirit. Women joked and giggled; bathed their babies and put them to the breast under the very shadow of the ghost. Two little boys led off the dedicated buffalo to its doom with derisive cat-calls; as they went they played at killing it by beating it on the back of the neck with their little sticks. The actual sacrifice was performed by irreverent youths with loud sniggers of amusement; they made dirty jokes about the executioner because he did not kill the unfortunate victim with a single blow.

When I myself arrived, the ghost declared through the mouth of the shaman that he was afraid to remain. 'A very important person has arrived,' he said. 'How can I show myself?' The people laughed at this and said, 'What are you afraid of? You're only a poor old invisible creature; he can't see you, nobody can, so how can he get hold of you to beat you or take you to the German war? It's we who ought to be afraid, not a bodiless thing like you.' I thought this was rather well put, and so apparently did the ghost, for he made no further objections to my presence.

There are times, however, when everyone is very serious. At the funerary rites after an ill-omened death, there is fear and silence. At the first moment of a trance, when the shaman awaits a spirit to possess him, there is complete quiet. At ceremonies for the dangerous Ratusum or for the smallpox goddesses, there is no laughter, and no irreverence.

An interesting book might be written on the influence of alcohol on the development of tribal theology.

The shaman does his work on an empty stomach, and from his first invocations he begins to take sips of the wine he offers to the spirits. After he has passed into trance, he drinks constantly, perhaps for several hours, as spirit after spirit demands refreshment. For since the spirit occupies the shaman's body, and since after all wine is a material thing, this body is the only channel through which the wine can reach its divine recipient. Sometimes the programme continues long into the night, occasionally even till dawn, and it is little wonder that the shaman, without food or sleep, and alternately stimulated and depressed by the quantities of alcohol he has consumed, should experience functional disturbances of his organs of sense.

The effects of this gradually maturing intoxication is to be seen both in the attitude of the shaman himself, and later in his dramatization of the conduct of the spirits who are supposed to possess him. The shaman approaches his task of divination, sacrifice and trance rather timidly, as becomes one who is about to address beings of incalculable temper in an enterprise where mistakes are easy and quickly punished. But as he proceeds with his invocations, as he drives away now a sorcerer's familiar, now a suicide's ghost, now a tiger-shade, and as he takes sip after sip of the heart-warming fluid in his gourd, his manner changes. Self-criticism and self-restraint fall from him. He is no longer timid. His fears of the unseen are one with the anxieties of yesterday. He no longer bothers his head about ritual mistakes. He is on top of the world, even of the Under World. Where previously he grovelled, declaring his willingness to eat the excreta and drink the urine of the gods, he now commands and threatens. He now feels that he is a great shaman.

By the time a shaman is ready to pass into trance, he is generally slightly intoxicated already, and once he has passed out, or rather once a spirit has passed in, his alcoholic exuberance is regarded as characteristic not of him but of the spirit who has possessed him.

For once a shaman is in trance, he is of course no longer himself. Up to this point, he was the representative of society and spoke for the people; now he is the representative of the society of spirits and speaks for them. He can no longer say a word for himself. The shaman in trance is no more the mouthpiece of the congregation; the congregation becomes the mouthpiece of the shaman.

A great deal of research has been done on the effect of alcohol on human beings. Partridge gave four university students (they were teetotallers) six doses of alcohol, each of 100 grams of 16 per cent, at intervals of from half an hour to an hour. Shortly after the first dose, he noticed in each of his subjects an increased feeling of self-confidence, 'which gradually deepened into recklessness and bravado'. At a later stage, the students began to lose their self-control and 'to throw off all restraint'. In each case there was a period when they were very humorous. And they revealed a strong sense of superiority towards the world.[1]

Scott describes the effects of intoxication as follows. 'It results,' he says, 'in an apparent intellectual stimulation. The person becomes

[1] G. E. Partridge, *Studies in the Psychology of Intemperance* (New York, 1912).

more lively, his ideas flow more freely, and his conversation is less restrained, so that he may indulge in vulgarisms which would be repugnant to him under normal conditions. He laughs readily and immoderately. He sees the world through a rosy mist, and loses the caution which might prevent him from making mistakes. In most cases, there is a general excitement which may give place later to argumentativeness or to outbursts of easily provoked rage.'[1]

All this might well be a description of a shaman's dramatic representation of a spirit. At first the spirit is full of bravado; he demands food and drink in a loud voice; he is full of complaints. Later, he mellows a little, begins to laugh, gets up and dances round the room, makes dirty jokes. He is very superior, the god on a visit to poor mortals. Then suddenly he loses his temper and the most appalling threats and the filthiest abuse flow from the shaman's mouth. As time goes on, incoordination of the shaman's muscles becomes evident, and now when the spirit tries to make him dance he tumbles over to the delight of all.

When everything is done, the shaman often quietly passes out and spends the rest of the day asleep. When he wakes up, he usually remembers nothing of what has happened; this alcoholic amnesia probably accounts for the fact that most shamans cannot remember anything that they did in trance.

The very entertaining antics of the shamans and shamanins are obviously due to that disappearance of self-criticism and the dulling of inhibitions that is always characteristic of intoxication.

Seligman has emphasized the predominance of the extravert disposition among what he calls 'savages' and its reinforcement by social forces. He notes 'the relative ease and frequency with which many of them enter into states of dissociation', and raises the interesting consideration 'how far this quality of facile dissociation is due to causes intrinsic to the organism, causes which might be called neuronic, and how far it is to be attributed to extrinsic, that is social, conditions'. Saora social life obviously favours the adept in dissociation; it treats him with the greatest honour and respect ; but I agree with Seligman that the main causes of dissociation are intrinsic—the phenomenon is too deep and widespread to be caused by merely social factors. I think it is also obvious that among the Saoras 'the

[1] G. M. Scott, 'Alcoholism and Criminal Behaviour', in *Mental Abnormality and Crime* (London, 1949), p. 166.

Unconscious passes into the Conscious more readily than among the white races'. Seligman found that among European neurotics there was, broadly, a greater tendency to exteriorization and dramatization. This tendency is equally strong among the Saoras.

'The little I have been able to learn', says Seligman, 'of dramatization among our own psychotics and psychoneurotics has impressed me with the comfort and sense of security which dramatization brings with it. If it be permissible to predicate this effect for savage peoples it would explain the quality of earnestness they commonly bring to their ceremonies, as well as the prolonged duration and their delight in such long drawn out and complicatedly dramatized rites as the Australian *intichiuma* ceremonies.'[1]

The 'savages' whom Seligman had in mind were obviously very much more 'primitive' than the Saoras, but his words are entirely applicable to them. The 'comfort and sense of security' which the shamans and the people gain after the dramatizations of a trance-seance is very striking.

It is impossible to watch one of the greater Saora shamans or shamanins in trance without being impressed by their extraordinary quality. For his work a shaman must not only have a good grasp of theological principles, but a considerable knowledge of local geography, history and economics; he must be acquainted with the circumstances and genealogies of every family in his circuit; and he must also be well aware of village gossip. In the state of dissociation, all his varied knowledge and experience comes to the fore and is expressed in a dramatic performance which often has a genuinely healing effect.

[1] C. G. Seligman, 'The Unconscious in Relation to Anthropology', *The British Journal of Psychology*, vol. XVIII (1928), pp. 374ff.

Chapter Thirteen

THE NATURE OF SAORA SACRIFICE

MANY and varied are the theories about the origin and types of sacrifice and this is no place for an academic discussion of them. The basic motif of Saora sacrifice arises simply and logically from Saora anthropomorphism. The circumambient unseen world is imagined to be generally similar to this; its population is driven by the same fundamental desires as ours—the need for food, drink, social and sexual companionship, the clinging to prestige, the urge to possess property and exert power. The spirits are wealthier, they have a superior social position, in some ways they are very much like the petty officials and landlords of the neighbourhood—they are out for what they can get, and they will do nothing without a bribe. The spirits being what they are, everything in Saora sacrificial practice is logical and natural.

But this is not the whole story. The spirits are something more than irritable and greedy bureaucrats; as we shall see, they are sometimes pictured as having altogether grander and deeper qualities. And Saora sacrifice too is something more than a mere ritual gift; prayer, thanksgiving and communion are allied to it; sometimes magic reinforces it. I propose, therefore, to discuss Saora sacrifice under a number of different headings. It will, of course, be understood that the Saoras themselves do not analyse or classify their rites in this or any other way, but for our own understanding of them, it will be convenient to do so.

Sacrifice and Magic. Loisy defined sacrifice as the combination of a magic rite and a ritual gift;[1] in this, Tylor's view of sacrifice as pre-eminently a gift to a supernatural being is modified by Frazer's theory of sympathetic and contagious magic. Here, as usual, we are in trouble over words. 'Magic' has been used so widely and in such a variety of senses that this book might well have been called *The Magic of the Hill Saoras* or *Saora Magic*: from one point of view, 'the range of magic', as Hutton Webster rightly says, 'is almost as wide as the

[1] A. Loisy, *Essai Historique sur le Sacrifice* (Paris, 1920), pp. 10f.

life of man'.[1] But in this book I use the word to cover only those activities, especially those associated with the use of inanimate objects, which work automatically, without the intervention of a supernatural being. Despite all the discussions and controversies, I doubt if we have ever really progressed beyond Frazer's division of magic into Homeopathic and Contagious, both depending on the Law of Sympathy, the first based on the principle that like produces like, or that an effect resembles its cause; the second, that things which have once been in contact with each other continue to act on each other at a distance after the physical contact has been severed.[2]

But so absorbed are the Saoras in their belief that all life and all events are controlled by personal unseen beings, and so weak is their belief (if indeed it exists at all) in the occult power residing in material things, that magic in the sense that I have defined it does not play a very important part in their lives. The thing that is real to them is the gift, the prayer, the discussion, the bargain with the spirits.

But there is something that we can only call magic used as an auxiliary to the ritual gifts and bargains of their sacrifices; there does not seem to be any very special reason for it, and the Saoras themselves treat it rather lightly, almost as a spiritual joke. For example, when they go out hunting, they send a shaman ahead into the forest. He puts his bow and arrows across the path and hides among the trees. They then play a sort of hide-and-seek; if the others find him quickly they are pleased, for they know that this dramatic rehearsal will make the real hunt speedily successful. If they do not find him within a reasonable time, they make an altar of their own bows and arrows, summon the shaman to appear, and get him to sacrifice a fowl to the local god to come and help them.

At the Lambapur, where the essential thing is the sacrifice of a pig to Lambasum, a sacrifice which by itself is supposed to achieve everything that is necessary, the Saoras build little platforms in their swiddens, load them heavily with stones and offer crabs, with the intention that the platforms supporting their grain-bins will be similarly loaded and that the pods of pulse will be fat and strong as the legs of crabs.

[1] Hutton Webster, *Magic : A Sociological Study* (London, 1948), p. 55.

[2] 'Although', says Malinowski, 'I started my field work convinced that the theories of religion and magic expounded in *The Golden Bough* are inadequate, I was forced by all my observations in New Guinea to come over to Frazer's position.' —B. Malinowski, *Argonauts of the Western Pacific* (London, 1932), p. 32n.

In chapter VII, I describe a number of dramatic tableaux by which the shamans complete the work of sacrifice. Most of these, however, are concerned with spiritual beings, but there are one or two which appear to be entirely magical. For example, in the course of a sacrifice to cure a child of dysentery, a piece of *Pterocarpus marsupium* wood is wrapped in cloth so that as the red exudate of the wood disappears beneath the cloth, the red blood of the child will cease to stain its motions. At a sacrifice to Pungpungdasum for the cure of dropsy, a pot is carried down to the nearest stream and broken there, so that the water in the patient's belly may likewise flow away. And at a difficult delivery, a pot may be tied to a woman's belly and then removed and broken.

In these cases the act of sympathetic magic is auxiliary to the sacrifice. The sacrifice can be, and often is, performed without the magic, but the magic is never attempted without the sacrifice. The use of 'medicine'—various magic herbs and roots which are made into a paste and applied to a patient's body; the manual acts of stroking with the hand or a feather are never attempted by themselves. They are part of the sacrifice, and it is not always clear why they are necessary, especially when a spirit has declared himself satisfied and agreeable to do what is required of him.

Magic divorced from sacrifice is rare among the Saoras, and where it occurs may be due to external influence. The milk teeth of young children are buried beneath the mortar so that their new teeth will be hard and strong as a pestle. Hair-clippings are thrown into the thorny branches of a date palm to ensure that the body will be covered with thorny spikes as a protection against sorcery. The frog may be used as a rain-bringer, and there is a little rite of burying it in a pit until the rain comes and frees it, which does not seem to involve the intervention of any spirit. But these customs are known to the Saoras' neighbours and may well have come from them.

The same may be said of the charms designed to protect a house or village. A shaman draws rude designs on a path and puts a palm leaf above them to prevent the return of a spirit. Bits of bearskin are treasured as a protection against ghosts; an egg or the beak of the Indian Hornbill is placed on the threshing-floor to prevent spirits stealing the grain; a hornet's nest is hung outside a cattle-shed to keep it free from alien gods.

But on the whole, compared to other communities at a similar stage of development, the Saoras seem to place little trust in magic.

At the time of pregnancy and delivery, there are hardly any of the countless means of sympathetic magic by which the mother is assisted and the future of the child assured. The idea of eating certain animals to absorb their qualities is unknown. It is only very occasionally that one sees a material charm erected to protect a field.

And it is possible, I suggest, that even the few rites to which I have been able to refer may not really be magical at all. They may be rather a sort of code message to the spirits, a picture language which they will be able to understand. 'The spirits are very stupid,' a shaman once remarked to me. Perhaps it is not enough to feed and wine them and get their promises; they may not understand properly or they may forget. A little drama showing in action what is required, a tableau which will stand as a permanent reminder, is perhaps necessary. To put crabs' legs in a field of pulse cannot of itself make the pods grow fat, but it may remind the gods of their duty. Pungpungdasum may possibly not be able to grasp the fact that he is required to cure a case of dropsy until he sees the broken pot and the water running out. To sacrifice a fowl for a woman who cannot feed her child should be sufficient, but how much more powerful and dramatic an appeal is made when the god sees the fowl killed and the hot blood flowing over the mother's breasts.

The Saoras do not believe that the results of sacrifice and magic are inevitable. The spirit cannot be coerced, either by gifts or by supplication or by conjuring tricks. The magical act emphasizes the meaning of the rite of which it forms a part; the magical charm is an embodied sacrificial prayer against an invading spirit. But the smallpox goddess may, and unhappily often does, ignore the stuffed monkey which bars her path; a wandering ghost may attack a shamanin even if her cheeks are stuffed with ginger; an ancestor may be implacable in his resolve to take away the living; a god may be in a wayward or angry mood and refuse to listen to the most flattering prayer and praise. The most that even automatic magic can do is to reduce the risk; it cannot eliminate it.

Let us now turn to a consideration of other types of sacrifice.

Honorific sacrifice. In the ceremonies for the Harvest Festivals, the sacrifice is a simple acknowledgement of overlordship. There is no evidence that the Saoras ever thought in terms of eating a Corn Spirit. The festivals are based on two fundamental ideas—the Saora conception of the ownership of land and a belief in the enormous social importance of who eats first. Whatever Government or the

Maharaja may say, the land really belongs to the gods, and there are many stories of the disasters that befall those who trespass. To clear a swidden without sacrificing to the local hill god inevitably causes trouble.

The Harvest Festivals acknowledge this ownership; they also ensure that the gods partake of a new crop before men do. This brings us to a very important Saora, and even Indian, tradition. If I eat something from a dish of food I turn what is left into 'leavings', and anyone who accepts those leavings admits that he is inferior to me. In one of the myths, we are told that, long ago, 'when the Saoras first took honey from the comb, we used first to taste it and then give it to the Raja, with the result that he ate our leavings. And we boiled turmeric in our pots and when it was dry we sold it. In this way everybody ate our leavings. We first eat the fruit of our fields, and then the rest of the world buys it and gets its food. Thus the Saoras are the first and greatest of all mankind.'

By giving food first to the gods and ancestors, therefore, the Saoras acknowledge their own creatureliness, and the overlordship and importance of the spirits.

There is something more than this; there is a bargain. In return for the emphatic honour they give them, the Saoras expect the spirits to see that the crops grow well and are not damaged by blight or weevil. But the essential point of these sacrifices is the honour that they pay to the true lords of the soil.

Propitiatory sacrifice. The Saoras derive many elements of their theology from the social milieu in which they live. A rapacious moneylender will be more accommodating if he is given a drink and a good meal; an excise inspector will not inquire too closely if he has money in his purse; a constable or forest guard who discovers one of the hundred illegal secrets of every tribal village must naturally be propitiated with an appropriate gift. Those who from pride or a conviction of innocence refuse to pay, will always suffer in the end. Even in the ordinary relations of tribal life, when someone is in a temper, the easiest way of restoring his good humour is to give him a present, even if it is only a leaf of tobacco or a sip of wine.

The spirits make men suffer in order to emphasize their own importance, to extort food and drink, or because they feel they have been insulted or neglected. In many cases, there probably has been guilt of a sort on the part of the Saora who has broken a taboo, failed in his duty to the dead or been careless in his religious observance. To calm the violent anger roused by the breach of a taboo, it is essential that sacrifice should be offered immediately, and in all cases where a sacrifice has been necessitated by the belief that a spirit has been offended the stress is on its propitiatory character, which restores harmony between the living and the dead, the worshipper and his gods.

Substitutionary sacrifice. Sacrifice often takes the form of an animal substitute for the human being who is demanded by the spirits. This has nothing to do with human sacrifice: its aim is not to take human life, but to save it. For example, after certain kinds of nightmare, which are believed to mean that Ratusum is about to cause the dreamer's death, it is essential to offer this god a substitute without delay. Then again, it frequently happens that a ghost comes from the Under World to carry off one of his family to keep him company or serve him. If he is offered a goat or a buffalo, he may be persuaded to accept it instead of taking the human being. An angry deity may declare that he is going to kill many people in a village, yet when the time comes he accepts an animal victim instead.

Sacrifice as an act of hospitality. Sacrifices are often made to spirits in regard to whom there is no danger to be averted, no anger to assuage, no special honour to be given. But just as the duty of hospitality is one of the most important obligations of Saora social life, so the shaman makes offerings to the crowds of spirits who visit him every time he falls into trance. The theory is that these spirits come a very long way; some of them burrow up from below, others make weary journeys over hills and rivers, breaking the rocks and felling the trees that stand in their way. Some come by train, some charter private planes. When they arrive, therefore, it is only proper that they should receive refreshment, and much time at almost every sacrifice is occupied by providing this. And when a shaman summons his tutelary to a divination rite, when spirits come to a Name-giving or a house-warming, they do not come as beings to be propitiated or even honoured, but as friendly visitors to be entertained.

Sacrifice as a contract. An offering may be in the nature of a more or less straightforward *do ut des* contract. This is common in the case of rituals designed to protect little children and in the dedication of animals for the benefit of the crops. There is a preliminary sacrifice, in which the god is given a token instalment, with a promise of payment in full if a child survives in good health for so many years. An animal is dedicated to an ancestor with the promise that it will be sacrificed after two, three or four years if in the meantime the harvests are good. There is nothing magical about these contracts; although a spirit may have accepted his token gift or dedicated animal, there is no certainty that he will fulfil his part of the bargain. He is expected to, for there is a genuine faith in the decency and honour of the spirits, a belief that if they are treated properly they will not be slow to respond. But the Saoras have learnt by long experience that the unseen world is as incalculable as this, and that the most they can do is to invest wisely and hope for the best.

Zenophobic sacrifice. The zenophobic type of sacrifice, based on the desire to be left alone, to be free of strangers, to live one's own life without interference, is very characteristic of the Saoras. The burden of every Saora invitation, to divine as to human visitors, is 'Come by all means, if you must, but please go away as soon as possible'. If you camp in a Saora village, the first question you will be asked (not rudely or offensively, but with perfect simplicity) is, 'When are you going?' And in all the incantations that accompany offerings to the gods, we find repeated over and over again such phrases as, 'Eat, drink, and depart'; 'You have come willingly now go willingly'; 'Leave us alone'.

An image of Sahibosum is erected, and sacrifice is offered to it, outside a village to keep this deity away. When a man returns from jail, or from Assam, or even from a visit to another village, he may be accompanied by alien spirits and sacrifice must be offered to keep them out. At the conclusion of the Harvest Festivals, special rites are performed to speed the departure of the supernatural guests who should not overstay their welcome. Many sacrifices include a procession outside the village, in the course of which all manner of things, little carts, bundles of wood, bamboo 'houses', bloodsuckers, dedicated goats and sheep, are taken out with the belief that the spirits concerned will go with them. The idea in this is not the transference of guilt to an animal or a thing, but that the spirit will ride in its vehicle and make its way to its own place.

Sacrifice for a spirit rather than to a spirit. There are certain rites in which the main emphasis is on the benefit of the dead rather than of the living. The great rites of the Guar and Karja relieve the living of the more aggressive importunities of the dead, but their fundamental purpose is to benefit the shades themselves, to give them a new lease of life and ensure them social standing, accommodation and the necessities of existence in the Under World. Some Saora theologians say that the sacrificed buffaloes go straight down to the Under World and are feasted on there; that the turmeric and oil smeared on the menhirs also goes down and is used by the shades to anoint their bodies and tame their matted locks.

According to the myths, the original purpose of sacrifice was to enable the hungry and neglected gods to make some sort of living. And it is true that a considerable part of what we may call the divine income is derived from the offerings made by men. But with the passing of the years, the spirits—whether they be gods, tutelaries or ancestors—appear to acquire resources of their own; they have their own herds, their own fields, their own palm trees; and it is only when these are insufficient for their needs that they come to demand help from man.

Cathartic sacrifice. The notion of ceremonial impurity exists, but it is very weak, among the Saoras. A shaman or priest should technically bathe before offering sacrifice: the custom is for him to wash his feet and hands first, then to salute Uyungsum, then to bathe his face and body. But there is no insistence upon this; it is not part of the ritual; and it is often omitted.

There are certain lustrations at the funerary rites. The corpse must be washed, and so thoroughly that 'the water will run down the street'. After the cremation is over, the pyre is stripped and each of the great logs that has survived the flames must be carefully washed. Then an Idaiboi washes the very bones and ashes, slowly and carefully pouring water upon them. After they have been buried, she cleans the ground and gives the Siggamaran water to wash himself. In some villages all the mourners bathe before returning home. At the Guar and Karja ceremonies there is a formal washing of the rice that is to be offered to the dead, and the doomed buffaloes are given a sketchy—though ritually adequate—bath before execution. The officiants at the Guar and Karja are also bathed during the ceremonies; the custom is to wash only the left leg and left arm. Shamans representing tutelaries who stand outside a house at the Name-giving ceremony have the left leg and arm washed; this may be an act of hospitality to remove the stains of a long journey from the Under World.

As we have seen, menstruation—the most obvious form of ritual impurity—is not taken very seriously by the Saoras. A shamanin cannot function at a ceremony during her period, but that is not because she is filled with a baleful influence, but because if she did so it would anger her tutelary, who is a Hindu. A shaman can sacrifice when his human wife is in her period, but not when his spirit-wife, his tutelary, is in hers; this again is because she is a Hindu.

What is the real reason for the ceremonies that follow a violent or an evil deed? When someone has been killed by a tiger, or has taken his own life, or has been murdered, sacrifice is offered, everyone concerned must endure a certain ritual discipline, and medicine is administered. When a convict returns from jail, he must offer sacrifice and pay a fine to the community before he is admitted back into the fellowship of the tribe. Is the reason for this that individuals are toxic and contagious in themselves, or is it that what they have done has attracted dangerous spirits to them or excited the hostility of the gods or dead? Are they, as we might put it, actually infected with parasites, or merely bothered by mosquitoes who may bite them and other people?

A study of the actual rites suggests that their main purpose is to banish the dangerous spirits who may attach themselves to anyone who visits an abnormal place or puts himself into an abnormal situation. There is hardly any conscious idea of ritual defilement which will be washed away by the blood of sacrifice; purification, either inward and spiritual, or external and formalistic, is not a Saora way of thinking. But it is possibly slowly penetrating the Saora mind as a result of external influence.

Sacrifice as a sacrament of communion. Sacred meals may be of various kinds. The simplest is when the members of a community devoted to a common cult eat together in fellowship, commemorating perhaps a dead founder in whose honour they meet. Secondly, a god is supposed to preside over the feast, and the common meal implies some kind of communion with him. Thirdly, there is the belief that in the sacred meal the votaries partake of the god; in the rending and eating of a sacrificial victim, especially if the animal is believed to be a form in which the god appears, there is a more than ordinary communion, there is the assimilation of the divine flesh into man's.

Every Saora rite ends with a feast, in which part of the cooked food is set apart for the spirit in whose honour it has been prepared, some for the multitude of other spirits who are always present, and the remainder for the celebrants and the people who are qualified to attend, members of the family, the villagers and their guests. Sometimes, as in the feasts after sacrifice to Ratusum or for an abnormal death, everything must be consumed, not a scrap may remain uneaten or at least unburied, but generally there is no such rule, and after most buffalo sacrifices some of the meat is dried and kept to offer again if the spirit should be tiresome later on.

These feasts are obviously something more than a common meal of votaries congratulating themselves at the conclusion of a rite. There is a definite sense of sharing; the gods and ancestors eat first, by reason of their superior status, and their worshippers eat afterwards, but all the stress is on the fact that they eat together.

But is there anything more than this? When a frenzied worshipper buries his face in the flesh of a newly-killed buffalo and tears off bits of raw meat with his teeth, is there any idea that he is thereby eating the god? Is the drinking of blood, or of wine which is ritually a substitute for it, ever regarded as a means of taking the god, or at least magic power, into oneself?

The Saoras cannot eat their totems, for they have no totems. The sacred animals of the Under World, the porcupine and the bear, are never offered in sacrifices on earth. At the Ajorapur, the image of a snake is made of rice-flour, but it is not eaten; it is thrown away. The only animal which is sacrificed and eaten, and which has some sacred function, is the peacock. This bird is associated with both Jaliyasum and Galbesum—it is said that 'when a man is killed by Galbesum, his soul flies up like a peacock'—and with the dead. It also appears constantly both on the shrines and in ikons as the watchman of the gods. But though semi-sacred, it is not a god.

The same is true of the monkey. There are two monkey-gods, Arsibasum and Makrisum, and monkeys are killed and their skins stuffed and set up as charms to prevent disease entering a village. But the Saoras do not sacrifice monkeys, and though they eat monkey-flesh and in particular eat the flesh of the monkeys whose skins they stuff as charms, they do not seem to regard this as in any way an eating of a god.

Ajorasum, the snake-god, has the horns of a buffalo and must be offered a buffalo. Do the worshippers, when they partake of the buffalo flesh, ever think that they are eating Ajorasum and assimilating his magic qualities?

There is a hint that certain animals are identified with the dead. At the Guar and Karja rites, the dedicated buffaloes are dressed in the clothes of the dead, treated with honour and ceremonially fed. There is a belief that Ratusum sometimes turns a human being into a buffalo, and then has him sacrificed, and of course eaten. When a pig or a goat is dedicated to an ancestor for the protection of the crops, it is called by the ancestor's name and treated with the greatest consideration, until it is killed for the sacrificial feast. The giving of a ghost's name to a living baby is supposed to effect some kind of reincarnation, and it may be that giving an ancestor's name to an animal has the same result. In that case there is a sense in which, at the time of sacrifice, the dead are eaten in animal form.

But the Saoras are inarticulate about this; their beliefs can only be dimly inferred from their practice.

Human sacrifice. It is probable that the Saoras never practised human sacrifice. It forms no part of their tradition, and it does not occur in their mythology. But they know of it as a Kond custom of significance, and it is possible that the Saoras living in the northern areas not far from the Kond villages used to share in the rites.

In 1838 Taylor made an abstract from 'a fragment of loose papers without covers, mark, or numbers' written in Telugu which he found in the Government Library, Madras; this gives an account of the Toki festival among the 'Savaralu, the Conda-Savaralu, and Malijala-Savaralu'. By Conda-Savaralu he appears to mean plains-Saoras and the Malijala or Maliya Savaralu, who lived in 'the proximate neighbourhood of Vizagapatam, Kimedi and Ganjam', seem to be our Hill Saoras. The Toki festival was held annually, forty or fifty villages uniting in the celebration. 'It was done in honour of Jagrata devata, the local numen.' Some friendless man, or woman, of the age of twenty-five or twenty-six years, was seized and put into confinement; he was highly fed and allowed the free use of intoxicating beverages. 'At the time of sacrifice, the victim is taken out in public procession, for eight or nine successive days, proceeding around the village where the sacrifice is to be held. The precise act is held at four o'clock in the morning, or an hour or two before sunrise. The victim is then killed by a weapon, herein named *Gandagodali*, and the blood is used as an offering to the aforesaid idol. Nothing is herein mentioned of eating the flesh of the victim. The person is always kept in a state of intoxication; and is usually insensible at the time of sacrifice. The people imagine that by this sacrifice they increase the fertility of their lands, and render their villages more valuable.'[1]

The evidence of an anonymous and undated paper is not perhaps very trustworthy, and Campbell, our chief authority on the Meriah rites, declares,

> The Saoras do not sacrifice human beings, nor is female infanticide known among them, but some of them participate in the Meriah by procuring flesh from places where the sacrifice occurs, and burying it in their fields. They did not seem to attach much importance to the rite, and at once promised to have nothing more to do with it—refraining from it even as spectators.[2]

Fawcett, writing many years later, refers to this passage, and says, 'I have not heard of the Saoras being concerned in human sacrifices any further than this'.[3] He says again,

> About fifty years ago, though human sacrifice was discovered to be in full swing among the Konds, there was no trace of it to be found amongst their Saora neighbours. The Saoras say that they never practised human sacrifice, and I know of nothing that may be a distinct relic of it. The story about the sun eating up his children may or may not be a real Saora story. All the hill people of the Eastern ghats, the Saoras perhaps excepted, seem to have practised human sacrifice.[4]

Today, in certain villages, the Saoras sacrifice every year to Meriahsum, the god of the Meriah victims; to Kinchesum; and to Kondasum, the 'blood-drinker'. An instructive incident occurred at Talasingi (see p. 414), when Kondasum declared that he was not satisfied with ordinary sacrifice, since he was 'a drinker of human blood'. To this the Saoras replied, 'We are not Konds; it is not our

[1] W. Taylor, *Catalogue Raisonné of Oriental Manuscripts in the Government Museum* (Madras, 1862), vol III, p. 472. The context of Taylor's remarks makes it clear that he is not confusing the Savaralus, or even the Conda Savaralu, with the Konds. 'Toki' was a word used of the Kond Meriah sacrifices, but since it simply means 'child' it might be used of any human sacrifice.

[2] J. Campbell, *A Personal Narrative of Thirteen Years Service amongst the Wild Tribes of Khondistan* (London, 1864), p. 204.

[3] Fawcett, p. 259.

[4] ibid., p. 258. And the official *Madras Administration Manual*, published in 1886, says that 'though this race is considered far more wild and savage than the Dravidian Konds, they have had no share in the Meriah or human sacrifices formerly performed by the latter'.—p. 109.

custom to kill human beings,' and they gave the thirsty god pig's blood instead.

There is a Saora word *andadukka* or *andakeran*, which means someone who kidnaps children for human sacrifice, and even now there are occasional scares when it is reported that such a person is in the neighbourhood.

In one village to the north, at Dariambo, the Saoras admitted that their ancestors used to participate in the Meriah rites.

> In the old days we Saoras used to offer human beings in sacrifice to the Kond gods. When we did so, we always had good crops, and no tigers attacked our cattle. We used to get young boys or girls from other villages. The thief who brought them was called the Andadukkamaran.
>
> After the sacrifice was over, the Andadukkamaran used to take the hair, nails and some of the flesh to his own house. The hair made the millets fertile, the nails made the pulses fertile, and the flesh made the rice fertile. The gods were frightened of the flesh and if we kept a little in the house, they dared not approach. We used to bury the bones or any flesh left over; we did not burn it. Once, from fear of Government, we burnt the bones and the god was angry and sent tigers to us. Now that the sacrifice has been stopped we give the Kond gods a pig instead. An old man in our village had a bit of human flesh which he used to keep tied to his waist, and this saved him from every kind of danger. He lost it in the end, and the gods at once attacked and killed him.

Even as far south as the Gumma area, at Dantara, I was told that the Saoras used to attend the Meriah rites.

> When the Konds sacrificed the Meriahs, we also used to go and get bits of the flesh. If we put them in the swiddens they kept wild animals away and the crops were always good. We had to make friends with the Kond priests to whom we would give a goat or a pig in exchange for a bit of human flesh.

Many Saoras believe, without a scrap of evidence, that the great Chiefs of the Pottasingi valley still offer human sacrifice in the privacy of their homes, and that is the reason why their crops are always so good.

There can be no doubt that the Saoras regarded, and indeed still regard, the Kond practice with respect as a powerful means of protection and fertility. It is possible that a few Saoras in the northern villages, who were under strong Kond influence, themselves once practised the rite; others undoubtedly attended and purchased small portions of human flesh. But the main body of Saoras were always probably, and in the last hundred years certainly, innocent of any actual participation.[1]

[1] Hindu tradition has always, however, associated the Saoras with human sacrifice. B. C. Mazumdar refers to the poet Vakpati, who flourished during the last half of the 7th century A.D. The hero of his poem *Gauda Vaho* describes the Vindhyachal shrine, at which a goddess named Kali Vindhyavasini was offered human sacrifice by leaf-clad Saoras.—Mazumdar, *Aborigines of Central India*, p. 10.

Manning recalls a story from the *Dasa Kumara Charita* about a child who was dropped by his nurse and hid behind a dead cow. A tiger seized the cow, but it was killed by a Saora who rescued the child, intending to sacrifice him to the forest goddess of his tribe.—C. Manning, *Ancient and Medieval India* (London, 1869), vol. II, p. 335.

In the collection of Prakrit tales, *Samaraicca Kaha*, by the Jain writer Haribhadra, which is ascribed by Jacobi to the 9th century, there is an account of the Sabara chief Kalasena who captured Dharana, who was travelling from Dantapura in Orissa, and led him towards the temple of Chandika for sacrifice.—H. Jacobi, *Samaraicca Kaha of Haribhadra* (Calcutta, 1926), pp. lxxvii, 435.

The *Katha Sarit Sagara* (see N. M. Penzer, *The Ocean of Story*, London, 1924–8) refers to Saoras practising human sacrifice on three occasions. The first (vol. I, pp. 115f.) describes how Sridatta fell into the hands of a band of Savaras, and was prepared by them for sacrifice to Chandika. He escaped, however, through the love of Sundari, daughter of the Savara chieftain.

The second story (vol. II, pp. 141f.) is related by Jimutavahana. He was captured by robbers in a forest and led in chains to a temple of Durga, 'terrible with a long waving banner of red silk like the tongue of death eager to devour the lives of animals'. He was presented to the Chief Pulindaka to serve as a victim to the goddess. But the Chief, 'though he was a Saora,' had pity, and was about to sacrifice himself instead, when he was prevented by a heavenly voice.

The third incident (vol. VII, pp. 153ff.) concerns Sundarasena, who was imprisoned by the Savara troops of King Vinhyaketu, who is called successively the King of the Pulindas, the Savaras and the Bhillas. The King sends Sundarasena and other prisoners to the temple of Durga to be sacrificed, but the King recognizes him and falls at his feet, and Sundarasena persuades him to let all the human victims free.

We must, however, remember that the Savaras of the *Katha Sarit Sagara* may be anybody; the name is used as synonymous with Pulinda and Bhilla; moreover, the temples in which the human sacrifice is to be offered sound more like Hindu than tribal shrines, and the goddess is always Durga. It is worthy of note that in five of these six examples, the sacrifice apparently was not consummated.

One modern instance has been recorded. In August 1936 a young Saora named Pita, belonging to Jharani village of Patna State in Orissa, was transported for life on a charge of sacrificing a Mussalman boy before a stone image of the Brahmin goddess Chandi.—C. C. Das Gupta, 'Human Sacrifice and the Sabaras of Orissa', *Man*, vol. XXXVIII (1938), p. 16.

For an interesting account of human sacrifice in classical Hindu times see Rajendralala Mitra. 'On Human Sacrifices in Ancient India,' *J.A.S.B.*, vol. XLV (1876), pt. i. pp. 76–118.

Chapter Fourteen

THE IMPORTANCE OF DREAMS

IN THIS chapter I propose to give a brief account of the importance which Saoras attach to their dreams and to describe some of the type-dreams which they experience. The reader must already have appreciated the fundamental significance of dreams for Saora religion, and it will also be obvious that these are, in the main, of two types. 'The dreams and visions of so-called primitive peoples,' says Lincoln, 'always fall into two distinct classes, the unsought, or spontaneous dreams occurring in sleep, and the sought or induced "culture-pattern" dreams of special tribal significance.'[1] The second kind of dream is, of course, of greater importance for religion, but the unsought, unexpected dream frequently has meaning for the Saoras and compels them to action.

Saora 'official' dreams are of several different kinds. The most important is the visionary experience of the shamans and shamanins, which consists of a sequence of dreams described in detail in chapters IV and V. In the opening dreams a tutelary appears with a proposal of marriage. The proposal is nearly always rejected by the dreamer, and the next dreams in the series are characterized by experiences of flying and falling, of threats of death and sickness, which cause a condition of *angst* which often leads to actual breakdown and extreme neurosis. After some time there is a final dream of surrender, which is followed by immediate action on the part of the dreamer: the girl or youth is dedicated to the profession of shaman, the sense of guilt and anxiety disappears, and the dreams are henceforth as pleasant as they were previously alarming. Now the tutelary comes and lies in rapture with the shaman, spirit children are born of the union, and the tutelary imparts to the shaman a complete course of Saora theology and ritual.

These dreams follow a regular pattern and all over the area they resemble each other even in the smallest detail. They exactly reflect the picture of the Under World and its inhabitants which is to be found in the ikons, the myths and the conversation of Saora theologians.

[1] J. S. Lincoln, *The Dream in Primitive Cultures* (London, 1935), p. 22.

Other religious functionaries are appointed in dreams, but these lack the special features of the shamanic vision: there are no nightmares, no ecstatic union with a tutelary. The Buyya priest's appointment is hereditary, but before he takes up his sacred duties he is confirmed in them by a dream of his dead father who instructs him in all he has to do. Idaimarans and Idaibois are also appointed in dreams, nearly always by the ghosts of father or mother, and the dream is accepted as sufficient authority, subject to certain tests of fitness.

The life of a medicine-man is, even more than that of other shamans, motivated and directed by dreams. Not only does he have the usual dreams that precede his dedication as a shaman, but each medicine is revealed to him separately by his tutelary. The life-story of Ikam (see pp. 258ff.) is particularly instructive. 'I have learnt everything from dreams,' he declared, and he claimed that after his tutelary had shown him the root or herbs required and the place where it could be obtained, he would go the following morning and find everything exactly as he had seen it in his dream. He would not go to treat any patient on the very day that he was summoned; there always had to be a night between the call and his response, and unless he had a favourable dream he would refuse to go.

Stekel quotes Maeder as saying that 'the dream is perhaps the primitive equivalent of a work of art', and Stekel himself adds that 'every dreamer is a poet'.[1] Certainly the painting of the Saora ikons is almost always directed by dreams which are expected by the artist. When a man is called to make an ikon he sleeps for a night on the floor in front of the wall on which he is to paint it and expects to have a dream showing him what he is to do. Many ikons are painted in response to a dream, and sometimes gods or ancestors come and show the dreamer himself what is to be done. In one case a god came and traced the pattern on the ground with his stick; in another an ancestor declared that the painting originally made was wrong and in a second dream showed how it should be done correctly. At Potta the tutelary of the shaman Durpan demanded an ikon in a dream and revealed the actual picture that she desired.

Names are often given in dreams, especially when an ancestor desires that kind of semi-reincarnation that follows the bestowal of his name. Here too the dreams follow the conventional pattern.

[1] W. Stekel, *The Interpretation of Dreams* (New York, 1943), vol. I, p. 74.

In the last two instances, instructions are sometimes given by the spirits in dreams, sometimes through the lips of a shaman whom they inspire. There is no very clear line drawn between the dream and the trance, and indeed some of the visions seen by the shamans in a state of dissociation closely resemble what they see in dreams. But the revelations of trance are naturally more easily remembered, for they are given before witnesses. A trance-vision is a kind of public dream.

Many of the Saora myths may have originated in dreams, and in some of them we find dreams within the myths whereby various elements of Saora culture were revealed. Thus the custom of drumming and sounding trumpets when a party goes for the bones of a dead woman married into another village originated in a dream which is now established in a myth.[1] It was in a dream that Kittung told the Saoras to wear cloth and how to get it,[2] in a dream that he revealed the use of palm wine,[3] and gave the seeds of the sago, date and toddy palms to men. It is not clear why, at a time when Kittung is portrayed as speaking freely to men and mixing with them, he has on occasion to resort to this method of communicating his instructions.

The ghost of Raja Gehil came to a Saora in a dream and revealed the use of salt.[4] The shade of a girl came to her mother in a dream and told her how good mushrooms were to eat.[5] The ghosts of a mother and father imparted by precept and example the method of sexual intercourse to a young dreamer who was ignorant of how to take his wife.[6]

Warnings are frequently given in dreams, but although these are commonly expressed in the plainest manner, without secondary elaboration, displacement or dramatization, the Saoras nearly always ignore or forget them, and it needs a sharp attack of fever or other sickness to recall them to their minds.

But warnings are also given in disguised symbolic form. Dreams of fire are always dangerous, for the dead are cremated and fire suggests death. 'Thakurani burns down a village as smallpox burns the body.' To dream that one is burnt may mean that Mardisum is on the way and that one will die of cholera. To dream that one's cloth is burnt means that a baby will die, for babies are tied with

[1] *TMO*, p. 626. [2] *MMI*, p. 473. [3] *TMO*, pp. 197-8. [4] ibid., p. 28.
[5] ibid., p. 171. [6] *MMI*, p. 289.

cloth round a mother's body. But the fire-dream may also mean quite simply that a house is going to catch fire. The Chief of Gailunga once dreamt that 'the crop in my clearing caught fire. I was running to and fro, trying to put it out. A sago palm was giving a great deal of sap and I slept beneath the tree and the sap dripped all over me. My cloth was burnt; I took it off and stood naked.' After this dream the Chief sacrificed a fowl to Uyungsum (the Sun-god, a source of fire) for fear that his house would actually catch fire.

Dreams of raw meat are always bad; they suggest that someone in the village will die, or that a relative in another village has died and that the news will arrive soon after the dreamer wakes. This is probably associated with the fact that at the great funerary ceremonies of the Guar and Karja, the sight and smell of raw meat is the most obvious physical feature. The motif of the news coming from another village may also be connected with the gifts of meat from other places at these ceremonies.[1]

To dream of a bear means that the family ghosts are hungry and have sent their pet bear to frighten the living into giving them food. Alternatively it may mean that the dreamer really will meet a bear when he next goes through the forest, or that Jaliyasum (who appears in the form of a bear or peacock) should be worshipped.

A dream of a falling tree is a death-warning. If the trees are being felled in a swidden it suggests the coming of an epidemic, the approach of Rugaboi (smallpox) or Mardisum (cholera), when corpses will litter the ground like tree-trunks in a clearing which await the cultivator's torch. If an unfruitful sago palm falls it means a young girl will die, for the sago palm is a maiden. But if a sap-giving tree falls, it is peril for a mother who is nursing her child. Similarly, if an old thick dry *Shorea robusta* falls of its own accord, it portends the death of one of the village elders. If the dreamer himself falls from a tree, it means that someone is going to hang himself.

To dream of a tooth breaking (one of Seligman's universal type-dreams) augurs a bad harvest and the loss of domestic animals.[2]

[1] Seligman has shown how widely distributed is the belief that this dream is 'thoroughly bad, presaging bad luck and misfortune', and he suggests the common association with death ceremonies.—C. G. Seligman, 'The Unconscious in Relation to Anthropology', *Br. J. of Psychology*, vol. XVIII (1928), pp. 378ff.

[2] Compare C. G. Seligman, 'Anthropology and Psychology', *Journal of the Royal Anthropological Institute*, vol. LIV (1924), pp. 37ff. The most common interpretation of the tooth-losing dream is the loss of a close relation or friend; among the Saoras the harvest or a cow might well symbolize either.

To see paddy or chillies in a dream is a warning that a sorcerer is working against one. For the sorcerers send grains of paddy or chillies into the bodies of their enemies. A dream of snake-bite suggests that one should be on the watch for an attack by Ajorasum, the horned snake so dangerous to little children.

The rather straightforward character of many of these dreams suggests, as Lincoln has pointed out, 'that the symbolism among primitives is more directly connected with the symbolized than among ourselves, on account of the low threshold between the conscious and unconscious, and that secondary elaboration is not intensive because repression is only skin deep'.[1]

Most of the dangers adumbrated in these dreams can be averted by a small sacrifice the following morning. The danger arises when the dreamer forgets his dream and does nothing about it. This is in fact what usually happens, and it is only when the calamity occurs that the dream is recalled. Perhaps it is only those warnings which are fulfilled that are remembered.

The dream of flying and falling, which is another of the universal 'type-dreams', is experienced most commonly by the young shamans and shamanins who, on resisting the demands of their tutelaries, are carried by them to great heights or dropped by a thread to the Under World. These kinaesthetic dreams, among which Kimmins includes 'the great variety of falling sensations, gliding, floating on air or water, often accompanied by loss of muscular and speech control',[2] occur widely in primitive cultures, but care must be exercised in their interpretation. Craighill Hardy has rightly stressed the 'need for caution in analyzing dreams of non-European peoples in terms of any symbolism, psychoanalytic or religious, other than that derived from and implicit in the native cultural heritage and the local environment'.[3] Here the dreams of falling, floating and flying—and the dread of falling—are obviously derived from the general tradition of the Under World being situated far below the earth, and approached by a thread or by the horses of the wind.

[1] Lincoln, *The Dream*, p. 99. [2] C. W. Kimmins, *Children's Dreams* (London, 1931), p. 26.

[3] R. S. Craighill Hardy, 'Dreaming in relation to Spirit Kindred and Sickness in Hawaii', *Essays in Anthropology presented to A.L. Kroeber* (California, 1936), p. 127. And compare Paul Radin's opinion on an Ottawa dream in which, he says, the flying motif 'is not simply the well-known dreams-theme, but the last vestige of a mythological motif quite common in Ottawa and Ojibwa folklore'.—Paul Radin, 'Ojibwa and Ottawa Puberty Dreams', ibid., p. 234.

On the other hand, it is perhaps worth noting that Kimmins found that, while children under the age of nine or ten years rarely experienced the kinaesthetic dream, from ten years of age it increased in frequency 'fairly steadily up to the age of seventeen or eighteen ... and that children who had had any type of malady accompanied by high temperature were particularly susceptible to it'.[1] Malaria, with its heats and rigors, is endemic among the Saoras, and the dreams certainly occur with greatest frequency among young people of between fourteen and eighteen.

They are not, however, confined to the young or to shamans. The dream may be a warning of death, which is natural enough when we reflect that the place to which the dreamer is most likely to fly or fall is the abode of the dead. Thus the Chief of Gailunga dreamt: 'I went to the Under World in the form of a monkey, jumping and flying from tree to tree. I grew very small. When I got half way down, I saw the people of the Under World coming out to hunt and I joined them.' This dream was considered so dangerous that the Chief at once sacrificed a buffalo to his ancestors to leave him alone.

Another flying dream, of a shaman at Gudara, was associated with Rugaboi. The goddess came to him and said, 'Come with me.' Then in his dream, 'Rugaboi made me fly like the wind. And as I flew I saw a hill where there were many gods, some had no hands, some were without feet, some had great teeth, some enormous heads. They were all chewing raw meat and blood trickled from their mouths. I tried to fly away, but I knocked my foot against a rock and awoke.'

Another dreamer was taken by his father's ghost, whom he had neglected, down by a spider's thread to the Under World. 'There my dead mother, brothers and other relatives caught me by the hand and made me sit down. They had a great pot of palm wine. They asked me, "Who is looking after your field and clearing? Who is caring for your children now you have come here?" And I realized that they thought that I was dead. But just when I might have been lost for ever, my tutelary came on a wind-horse and put me on it and flew with me back to earth.' Another man dreamt: 'I flew up into the sky and looked down on many men and women working in a swidden. When I came down a cow attacked me.'

All these dreams were regarded as highly ominous. But in one village I was told that a dream of flying like a bird simply meant that

[1] Kimmins, op. cit., p. 27.

before going to bed one had eaten off a plate made of the leaves on which a bird's droppings had fallen.

Straightforward sexual dreams do not seem very common, but young men experience dreams akin to those of the Churel in other parts of India. It is said that when an unmarried girl dies, she asks Kittung where she should live, and he says, 'At night wherever unmarried youths sleep. Go to them in their dreams, sleep with them and make love to them.' Babusum may also take the form of a woman and drain young men of their energy, and there is the curious idea that if a man sees and admires a beautiful tree, this tree may take the form of a woman. The dreamer must go to the tree, cut one of the branches and make it into a plough, whereupon the dreams will cease.

The relations of tutelary and shaman are sexual, but are imagined in a very decorous way. But Pingo, an elderly shaman of Tollana, recalled that thirty years earlier, before he was married to his tutelary, a girl came from the Under World; she was bael-breasted, dressed in a silk cloth, with ornaments of gold, and she lay down beside him as he was sleeping in his swidden. He had a spirit-child from her in the Under World, but since it happened before marriage, his tutelary-wife did not seem to object to the existence of this spirit-bastard.

Finally, there are a number of dreams that can only be classed as nightmares, though it is interesting that, in spite of the Saoras' detestation of the horse, this animal does not actually occur in them. Ernest Jones describes three cardinal features of the true nightmare: an overwhelming dread, a sense of oppression or weight at the chest which alarmingly interferes with respiration, and the conviction of utter powerlessness.[1] Each of these features is present in greater or less degree in the Saora nightmares. Many Saoras are subject to attacks of the *angst* neurosis, that 'combination of fearful apprehension, of panic-stricken terror, of awful anxiety, dread and anguish', which has been related by Freud to the pathological repression of the psycho-sexual system of a man's activities.

Sometimes the nightmare takes the form of a visit from an ogre. Kambutungsum has the head of a man and the body of a bear. Above a mass of hair rises a long hideous face. He approaches growling, mounts the dreamer's body and as he presses him down in utter

[1] E. Jones, *On the Nightmare* (London, 1931, 2nd edition, 1949), p. 20.

helplessness prepares to devour him. The dreamer wakes sweating from head to foot with fear. 'This is a very bad dream,' I have often been told. 'People die of it.' For Kambutungsum is the messenger of Ratusum, from whose attacks there is no recovery. The dreamer should not wait even to call a shaman, but should himself immediately sacrifice anything on which he can lay his hand.

Another ogre is Bobmaisum who has a great head covered with long hair, and a huge pendulous belly supported on thin stick-like legs. He prostrates himself upon the dreamer's body and attempts to drink his blood. That is all he wants; he is a solitary and a blood-drinker, living alone in caves and under rocks. If one dreams of him, one must send for a special shaman, 'the kind of shaman who will sacrifice blood from his own finger', to make offerings in secret: it is taboo for anyone to go near him. At Tammegorjang a man called Sodano had this dream, did nothing about it, and died.

An equally dangerous dream, though not so outwardly horrible, is to see a man wearing a red turban, in a red cloth, with feathers in his hair, dancing in the middle of a road. This is Ratusum again and the danger is that he will turn the dreamer into a buffalo and eat him. And the worst of that unpleasant fate is that the soul will be for ever separated from his own people in the Under World. If the man in red is just standing still, the danger may be averted by prompt sacrifice, but if he dances there is no hope: death is certain.

Such a dream is not a nightmare in the ordinary sense, but in the degree of *angst* it produces it is as terrible as any. So are certain apparently pleasant dreams. There is nothing worse than to dream of an ancestor who sits by one and talks amiably, for he is certainly planning to carry the dreamer away with him to the Under World. And what could ultimately be more horrible than old Idan's dream of the handsome youth who sat by her laughing and tickling her, but leaving in every place touched by his thrilling fingers the hateful marks of leprosy?

Dreams of the dead are very common. They may be pleasant, as we have just seen, and may then be dangerous. They often convey warning or instruction. They are sometimes threatening, as when an angry crowd of ancestors comes to remove a shaman who is interfering in their traffic with the living. They may be descriptive or panoramic, and the dreamer sees the dead unhappy and deformed and his own shy soul among them. But it is said that once an ancestor has died again and has been cremated in the Under World, he is seen no more.

People can give dreams to one another. A love-sick youth can by appropriate charms excite a girl with dreams of his attractions. A wife can give an absent husband dreams and even bang his head against the ground in sleep. A sorcerer can make his victim dream of pigs and paddy, by means of a special technique. The sorcerer's big soul talks to his little soul and the little soul agrees that the big soul should leave the body and go with a familiar to the enemy, to whom they give the ill-omened dreams which soon make him ill.

The Saora theory of dreams is, of course, the very common one that the soul leaves the body in sleep, but here we find soul and familiar apparently entering someone else's body in sleep to cause a dream.

Not all dreams are bad, and some of the most cherished are those of spirit-children in the Under World. Elderly women particularly find consolation in these; an old shamanin declared that they were the only dreams she remembered, for she had no children here, and her husband had been dead for many years.

I have made no attempt to analyse Saora dreams. That is the business of the psycho-analyst into whose mystery the amateur intrudes at his peril. Moreover—and this is a very important point, and one insufficiently appreciated, I think, by students of tribal dreams—where the culture context is so prominent, and where dreams largely follow regular and predetermined patterns, individual associations are of less importance and may not occur at all. The dreamer's explanation is invariably the traditional one; the key to the symbolic code is not individual but is known to all; it is almost impossible to obtain a *personal* reaction.

Individual dreams (the 'little' as opposed to the 'big' dreams of Jung) are not of great importance; they are not easily remembered and are seldom recalled in detail. Nearly all show, in their manifest content, clear traces of tribal culture and belief.

But the great official dreams and visions, which resemble each other—though with some variety within the general pattern—are vividly remembered and are described in great detail, willingly and often with enthusiasm. The Saoras are proud of such dreams, and they recite them as if they were poems, which in fact they very often are.

Chapter Fifteen

THE SAORA ETHIC: TABOO

I

THERE are two words which have an important influence on the conduct of the Saoras—*ersi* which means, roughly, taboo, and *ukka*, a word derived from the Oriya, which means custom.

Ukka is traditional behaviour and conduct, fidelity to tribal rules, the normal, the socially approved. It is good conduct which is directed by tribal opinion, but not supported by supernatural sanctions. To depart from *ukka* may earn you a fine from your offended neighbours, but it does not bring down upon you the wrath of an outraged god. *Ukka* controls the kind of dress you wear, the sort of ornaments you affect, the architecture of your house, your general moral behaviour, the family from which you get your wife.

Ersi, on the other hand, covers a range of behaviour, which is often more trivial yet may be infinitely more dangerous. Thus it is against *ukka* to lie, steal and murder, but it is only *ersi* if you lie in the name of a god, steal the food offered at a sacrifice, and kill a dedicated animal. It is not *ersi* for an ordinary layman to commit adultery with an unrelated woman in another village: that is only a breach of *ukka*. But it is *ersi* for a priest or shaman to commit adultery with anyone, or for anyone to commit it with a forbidden relative. It is not *ersi* to kill your aunt, but it is to kill the lizard that has been set free after the Tuttumpur rite. *Ersi*, in short, relates mainly to man's conduct as seen by the spirits; *ukka* to his conduct as seen by his fellow men.

A breach of *ukka* often leads to punishment: the culprit may be ostracized or fined. But it is not automatic punishment; it can be modified by discussion, argument, excuses, apology; there is some sense in it. But the danger, the awe-inspiring character of a breach of *ersi* is that it leads to automatic retribution which reaches out to the offender from the world of spirits and against which there is no appeal. The punishment can often be averted, the sentence (as it were) can be reduced by the payment of a religious fine in the form of sacrifice, but this is not always possible and it often happens that a man only becomes aware of his offence when he begins to pay its penalty.

There is no little confusion over the use of the word 'taboo'. Freud uses it in one sense; Wundt in another; Frazer in a third. A recent handbook of anthropology defines it as 'a customary restraint or prohibition laid upon certain words, things or actions',[1] which seems to me too wide. On the other hand, Hutton Webster unduly narrows the meaning of the word. Taboos, he says, 'form a specific series of thou-shalt-nots. They are not to be confused (as in popular usage) with social conventions and regulations of a negative sort, conventions and regulations without an obvious utility. They are to be distinguished from restrictions resting on the vague notion of unluckiness which attaches to certain acts or things or times, restrictions found in the lower culture and, under the attenuated form of a survival, lingering among ourselves. More important still, there are innumerable prohibitions, both animistic and non-animistic in character, which must likewise be excluded from the conception of taboo if this is to possess any scientific validity and retain a place in ethnological theory. Taboos are prohibitions which, when violated, produce automatically in the offender a state of ritual disability—"taboo sickness"—only relieved, when relief is possible, by a ceremony of purification.'[2] Yet in practice Hutton Webster finds it impossible to follow his own definition, for his book on taboo is full of examples which are nothing more than animistic or sympathetic prohibitions. Radcliffe-Brown regards a taboo as a ritual prohibition, which he defines as 'a rule of behaviour which is associated with a belief that an infraction will result in an undesirable change in the ritual status of the person who fails to keep to the rule', this change involving the likelihood of some minor or major misfortune for the person concerned.[3]

The Saora idea of *ersi* contains a number of elements, each of which combines to produce a complete picture of taboo. The essence of a breach of *ersi* is the automatic reaction which it produces, and this distinguishes it from other offences against the spirits. For example, if a man fails to celebrate the Guar for a dead father within due time, the shade may make him ill; but it is not *ersi* to fail in this

[1] M. Jacobs and B. J. Stern, *Outline of Anthropology* (Cambridge, 1947), p. 319.
[2] Hutton Webster, *Taboo* (London, 1942), pp. viif.
[3] A. R. Radcliffe-Brown, *Taboo* (Cambridge, 1939), p. 9.

filial duty and the illness is not exactly a punishment—it is rather a reminder, the only way in which the spirit can express his wishes with emphasis. Nor is the illness automatic; one man may fall sick after a week, another after two years, a third—by being careful to make regular offerings to the shade—not at all. But if, during the Guar, the son were to steal some of the food dedicated to the ancestors, he would fall ill at once and automatically, for that would be a definite breach of *ersi*.

In either case, however, the relationship with the other world is a personal one. It is dangerous to profane a shrine, not because it is filled with a mysterious power which will discharge itself upon the offender, but because the spirit to whom the shrine belongs is easily offended by insult or neglect. It is *ersi*, or taboo, for a woman to touch a shaman's fiddle, the *kurānrājan*, not because the inherent sacred property of the thing will be damaged by a female hand, but because the spirits will be annoyed at a breach of manners.

Ersi, in fact, is a particular code of etiquette for dealing with the inhabitants of the other world. Some of its regulations are due to the fact that these citizens are of a higher social standing; some are based on their well-known irritability; some arise from the danger of attracting them towards one's person. It is taboo for a shaman to commit adultery because such an act outrages the feelings of his tutelary who, as a Hindu woman, has a high standard about this sort of thing. Similarly, a shamanin must observe menstrual taboos ignored by other Saora women out of consideration for her spirit-husband.

But there is something more than this. Sympathetic prohibitions, which Frazer describes as a sort of negative magic working in accordance with the laws of similarity and contact,[1] are rare, but they do occur. A woman must not touch a tree which exudes a blood-red gum-resin or she will suffer from menorrhagia. It is taboo to look at the constellation of Cancer; if you do, you will feel as if crabs were tearing at your belly with their claws. It is taboo to throw a baby's hair on the ground, for if anyone urinated on it the child would get sores on his head.

In these taboos the spirits do not seem to be concerned, and the same may be said of a few others, which the modern Saoras are unable to explain. For example, it is *ersi* to hold a gourd-dipper by the bowl;

[1] J. G. Frazer, *The Golden Bough* (abridged edition, London, 1923), p. 19.

if you do, you will get a headache. But to do this does not appear to offend any god, and the origin of the rule may be a commonsense one, that since it is the bowl that is dipped into the pot of wine it should not be soiled by dirty hands. It is taboo to blow a certain kind of horn at harvest time; to do so will cause the grain to be blown away. Nor is it easy to understand why milk is taboo; to eat beef, nowadays in many villages, outrages the feelings of the gods, but to drink milk does not—yet both practices are *ersi*.

A number of taboos are probably due to external influence, and as education spreads among them the Saoras will doubtless adopt many others. The taboo on a pregnant woman going out of doors during an eclipse is common throughout India,[1] and so of course are the menstrual taboos[2] that are an obvious importation into Saora culture. The taboo on beef is recent and is growing with the growth of Hindu influence.[3] To touch a dead dog or cat is also forbidden by many other tribes,[4] and the Gadabas have a similar taboo on the horse.[5] To look back after leaving the scene of an ominous rite,[6] to throw away hair-clippings and nail-parings, to utter the names of the ill-omened dead are taboos so universal that they hardly require comment.

Some prohibitions which are widely distributed throughout the world are known to the Saoras, but are not regarded as taboos. Thus it is dangerous, but it is not *ersi*, to have intercourse with strangers. The images of Sahibosum are set up to protect a village against the strange gods that a visitor may bring with him. After any outsider has camped in a village, all relics of his presence are destroyed, and sacrifices are offered for fear his presence may have been displeasing to the local gods and to banish any of his own gods who may have lingered after his departure.

So too manslayers are dangerous, but they are not taboo. A murderer back from jail may bring alien spirits with him, and immediate

[1] J. Abbott, *The Keys of Power* (London, 1932), p. 268; W. Crooke, *The Popular Religion and Folk-Lore of Northern India* (Westminster, 1896), vol. I, p. 22.

[2] For a full account, see my essay 'Primitive Ideas of Menstruation and the Climacteric' in *Essays in Anthropology presented to S. C. Roy* (1942), pp. 141-7.

[3] A Congress politician who visited Serango had only two things to tell the Saoras: that they should become teetotallers and should give up beef.

[4] Perhaps because the dog is associated with Yama, the god of death. See Crooke, op. cit., vol. II, p. 218. See also Risley, vol. I, p. 79.

[5] Thurston, vol. II, p. 243. The Kols also have this taboo.—W. G. Griffiths, *The Kol Tribe of Central India* (Calcutta, 1946), pp. 35 and 199; and so do the Bharias (Russell and Hiralal, vol. II, p. 250) and the Baigas (see my *The Baiga*, p. 375).

[6] Abbott, op. cit., pp. 52, 116, 325 etc.

action must be taken to drive them away, but such a man in his own person is not taboo. A man in whose body the angry blood is moving (see p. 545) is to be avoided at times of drunken revel and must not be crossed; but that is a rule of commonsense: the man himself is not *ersi*.

On the whole, taboos rest rather lightly upon the Saoras, and it is interesting to notice how many things are not forbidden to them. Many of the ordinary folk-tale taboos—the unique prohibitions, the forbidden tree, relieving souls in hell, letting the sun shine on a girl before a certain age, building a tower to reach to heaven—naturally do not occur in real life, yet some such motifs might well have been expected in the fantasy world of the Saora shamans. The large range of taboos regulating conduct with a supernatural wife in other cultures—not to look at her naked, or in childbirth, not to question her or boast about her or reveal her secrets—do not seem to occur, nor is there any taboo—far from it—on mentioning the origin of a supernatural child.

There are few name-taboos; the names of gods can be used in abuse or jest; the names of tutelaries frequently occur in familiar conversation; and the names of the dead can even be given to goats or pigs who are dedicated to their honour.

There are no totemic taboos, for the Saoras have no totems. There are no lucky or unlucky days. There is no taboo on pointing, though this is found in neighbouring tribes.

Social and family taboos are also unusually weak. There is no taboo on a mother-in-law or any rule of avoidance between a girl and her husband's elder brother. On the other hand, the rules governing marriage and other sexual relations are strict and generally carefully obeyed. The greatest of all *ersi* crimes is 'incest', which covers all relationships between persons of the same blood, descended from a common paternal ancestor.

Most remarkable of all is the absence of sympathetic prohibitions during pregnancy and childbirth, particularly when we remember the numerous and complicated rules that govern the life of a Hindu or other tribal woman at this time. There is nothing in Saora tradition about not tying knots or stopping up holes or sitting on ashes or weaving the strings of a cot or sitting on an ant-hill. But as we see in other aspects of their religion, the conceptions of similarity and sympathy do not have a strong hold on the Saora mind.

Saora social life, then, is not greatly affected by taboos. The most tiresome, as they are the most commonly infringed, are those on eating a new crop, or gathering fruit, or cutting grass before the appropriate festival. Here there is a real interference in the daily life of the people and temptation is sometimes great, as when children see the new mangoes beyond their reach; it may be all the more tiresome when a festival is delayed by a shaman's dream or to suit the convenience of a Chief.

Breach of a taboo usually affects only the individual concerned. There is, however, no guarantee that it will not injure the community, especially when it is in regard to something that is deeply felt by everybody. In one village which had recently adopted the taboo on beef and was feeling rather proud of the fact, many people fell ill when one of their number offended against it. Sometimes a shaman may fall ill if other people eat before a Harvest Festival. But the Saoras do not seem to have any strong idea of ritual disability or uncleanness; their minds revolve rather about the ideas of guilt and propitiation, of offence and appeasement.

When a Saora breaks a taboo, and directly he realizes what he has done, he takes action to put things right. This involves confession, in many cases to a shaman, in all cases to the spirit whom he has offended. Sometimes a man does not realize that he has broken a taboo until he falls ill and begins to wonder why; more often he does realize it, and the realization makes him actually ill. Aldrich has described what may happen in such a case.

> The breaking of a convention, he says, is a very serious thing to the primitive's mind; his ideas of right and wrong are clear-cut and immutable; white is white and black is black with him; there are no delicate shades of grey between them, as with the civilized. He lives under a code of morals . . . To know that he has broken a commandment puts him at once in a state of terror; it splits him psychically; and he naturally flies to the priest to unburden himself of his guilt. With these ideas firmly fixed in his mind, I have no doubt whatever that he really falls physically ill under the weight of a guilty secret, and that he recovers when the burden of sin is removed.[1]

The guilty Saora not only unburdens his conscience; he takes remedial action, he sets in action some form of what Rivers called 'manipulative activity', and soon faith and hope come to him and

[1] C. R. Aldrich, *The Primitive Mind and Modern Civilization* (London, 1931), p. 220.

59. A party fetches a menhir from the hillside above Tumulu

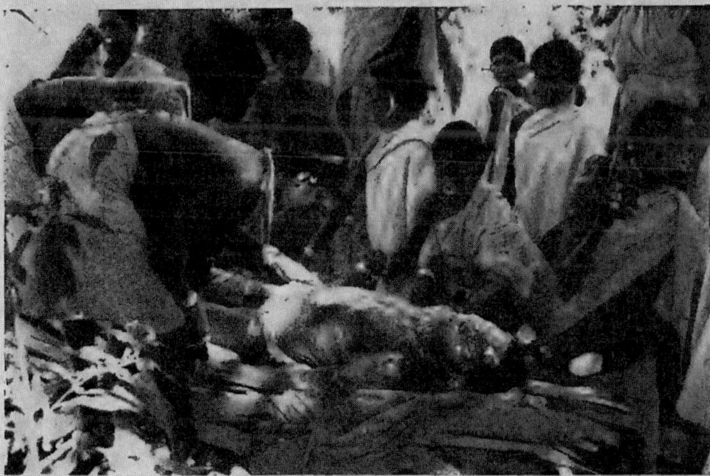

60

60 & 61. Scenes at a funeral at Boramsingi. Note important part played by women

reinforce the courage that has been renewed by the removal of his secret burden. And there can be no doubt about it at all: the majority of Saoras who suffer from taboo-sickness recover directly they confess, propitiate and promise to amend.

I now propose to give some account of the Saora taboos in detail, classifying them according to the clear and convenient method adopted by Stith Thompson in his *Motif-Index of Folk-Literature.*[1] Many of Stith Thompson's motifs could not occur in real life, and he himself says that he has made no attempt to cover taboo in actual practice. Yet it is remarkable how fully his Index does cover the Saora notion of *ersi*; we see here the folk-tale in action before our eyes.

II

C0–C99. Taboos connected with Supernatural Beings

C30 *Taboo: offending supernatural relative*

C31 Taboo: offending supernatural wife

A shaman who has married a supernatural wife in the Under World has to be very careful that his conduct on earth does not offend her. The tutelary wives carefully watch the relations of their human husbands with other women. There are many stories of how shamans who have committed adultery have been punished by their tutelaries with fever or other sickness.[2] One shaman who attempted to seduce his future wife before marriage was warned by his tutelary that he would go blind if he succeeded.[3] The worst thing that can happen to an offending shaman is that his spirit-wife will leave him, for without her aid he cannot divine properly.

C32 Taboo: offending supernatural husband

The shamanins have to be equally careful not to offend their tutelary husbands, who are quick to punish any misconduct. A shamanin at Sogeda who committed adultery with a human lover was ill for months afterwards, and it was only when her tutelary had been satisfied by the sacrifice of a buffalo that she recovered. A tutelary husband may also be offended if his human

[1] Stith Thompson, vol. I, pp. 376ff. Items marked with an asterisk do not occur in the original index. [2] See pp. 133f. [3] See p. 136.

wife breaks the menstruation rules, if she fails to fast at the proper time and if she forgets to give him his regular offerings of food.

C40 *Taboo: offending spirits of water, mountain, etc.*

C41 Taboo: offending water-spirit

It is dangerous, if not *ersi*, for women and children to go alone to springs, especially at midday when the water-spirit Ganorsum comes out of the water and sits on the bank; if he is disturbed he may give the intruder a bad cold. It is taboo to cross a stream where anyone has been drowned.[1]

C42 Taboo: offending mountain-spirit

There is no rule more easily broken than this, for every hill and mountain has its population of deities, who are the real landlords and expect tribute which is often denied them. The most common cause of offence is to make a clearing without offering apology and sacrifice.[2] But it is also possible to offend a god by picking a few herbs without permission,[3] by cutting grass at the wrong time[4] or even by staggering drunkenly across his domain.[5] Many examples will be found in this book.

C50 *Taboo: offending the gods*

C51 Taboo: profaning shrine

At Boraisingi a missionary burnt down a shrine to prove that the Saora gods were powerless. Nothing happened to *her*, but the children of the owner of the shrine fell seriously ill, and he had to build a new one. Ordinarily the shrines are treated rather casually; children climb over them, and people dump things in them. It is only deliberate disrespect that is dangerous. One form of profanation is to allow a shrine to fall down, and this is a common cause of sickness,[6] but I do not think it is *ersi*, for the punishment does not follow automatically.

C51·1·2 Taboo: stealing from altar

A priest once stole honey that had been offered in a shrine and died as a result.[7]

[1] See p. 230. [2] See p. 426. [3] See p. 428. [4] See p. 413. [5] See p. 422. [6] See p. 229. [7] See p. 174.

C51·2 Taboo: stealing from god

Ceremonies in honour of the god Tundrublutsum have to be held in camera, for if anyone other than the actual officiants drink his wine, he regards it as a theft and in a fit of rage will make the fields barren as a childless woman. Young shamans sometimes find the rules of fasting difficult to observe; at a Karja celebration a youthful Idaimaran stole some of the food dedicated to the ancestors. There was an immediate reaction: his throat swelled up and he was in terrible pain, and it was not till long afterwards, when he sacrificed a buffalo, that he really got well again.[1]

C52·2·2 Taboo: cutting sacred trees

The Saoras do not actually regard any trees as sacred, but there is a taboo on cutting fruit trees. The banyan is regarded as the shrine of the gods, and is often drawn in the ikons: it is taboo to cut it.

C54 Taboo: rivalling the gods

Any kind of pride is particularly offensive to the Saoras, whose strongly equalitarian traditions regard humility and docility (among themselves) as the highest of virtues. If a breach of taboo can be interpreted as due, not to drunkenness or forgetfulness, but to pride, so much the worse for the offender. At a Rogonadur ceremony a shaman at Angda once ate the pulse himself and then offered it to Barusum. This was a breach of C231, but it was more—it was regarded as an act of pride, and Barusum declared through another shaman, 'This man is so proud that he thinks even the gods obey him. But it is I who am great, not he, and I should eat first.' The shaman fell very ill in consequence.

C59* Taboo: profaning sacred ceremony

There are many ways in which ceremonies may be profaned. Some may not be performed inside a village, as those for Kannisum, Ratusum and Rugaboi. Some may not be performed by daylight, as those for Ratusum. It is taboo to bring any of the sacrificial meat from certain rites back into the village. It is taboo for any unauthorized person to disturb a ceremony. Once at Sogeda the shaman

[1] See p. 143.

was offering buffalo flesh to Kannisum on behalf of an epileptic named Jugta. As he was doing so, one Lakha came along the path; he was completely drunk and though he belonged to a different family and had no business to be there, he grabbed some of the meat and ate it. Kannisum immediately attacked him and he fell down in a fit. I was told that Jugta recovered but that Lakha died of epilepsy. Again at Potta, a shaman had taken a goat along the road to sacrifice to Rugaboi; the meat had been cut up and was being cooked, when a man called Singo came by very drunk; he snatched up a piece of the meat and took it home. The result of this was that Rugaboi followed him, and first his wife and then four others died of smallpox.

Another way of profaning a ceremony, and thus not only undoing the good it might do but also bringing the participants into danger, is to bring back to the village materials which should be left on the spot. Nothing may be brought home after any rite for someone killed by a tiger. It is taboo to remove the wood that has been used for cooking the feast at a Guar ceremony; the half-burnt logs must be placed on the menhirs. Although in some ceremonies such as the Doripur it is allowable to sell any surplus meat, it is strictly taboo to do this on other occasions.

C63 Taboo: failing to heed message of god

This would not be classed by the Saoras as *ersi*, but it is a very dangerous thing to do, and yet this whole book is a witness to the extraordinary indifference of the Saoras to the divine commands, whether these are given directly in dreams or by the mouth of a shaman.[1] The Saora, almost as a routine measure, forgets what he has to do, or decides that he may as well do it later on, and it is only when he falls really ill that he makes up his mind to obey.

C90 *Other taboos in connexion with sacred beings*

C92·3* Taboo: injuring sacred beings

How far it is actually true, or how far they dramatize their myths in daily life, it is hard to say, but many Saoras

[1] See pp. 139, 229f., 500.

undoubtedly believe that they have injured Ajorasum by mistaking him for a log of wood which they have tried to cut. This always leads to a child falling ill and to an elaborate and expensive sacrifice.[1] It is possible to injure the spirits unwittingly; for since they are all over the place, sitting in the shade of trees or crowding along the paths, one may easily tread on them or kick them by accident—and the offender is immediately seized with fever.[2] It is taboo to injure any animal dedicated to a religious purpose, especially the pigs and goats named after ancestors and promised for sacrifice in due time for a good harvest.[3] It is taboo to kill the lizard used in the Tuttumpur ceremony.[4]

C94·2 Taboo: false and profane swearing of oath

This is a very dangerous thing to do. A Saora of Kinteda who swore to abstain from liquor went blind as a result of breaking his oath. To swear by Darammasum or Uyungsum as witness that one is innocent of something that one in fact has done, may cause blindness or other infirmity.

III

C100–C199 Sex Taboos

C110 *Taboo: sexual intercourse*

In general the Saoras take sex rather seriously. Although premarital irregularities, so long as they are not 'incestuous', are tolerated, even these are not very common, and within the marriage bond fidelity is expected and generally achieved. There is a double standard here; shamans and shamanins are supposed to observe a stricter code than the laity.

C111 Taboo: loss of chastity

Although it is rare for men to live celibate, some of the shamanins, especially the Guarkumbois who attend to funerary rituals, are expected to remain unmarried. If they marry before they have been fully dedicated by the gift of a sacred lamp, they lose much of their power—

[1] See p. 278. [2] See p. 249. [3] See p. 305. [4] See p. 254.

for the gods and tutelaries do not come upon them. Even if they marry after dedication, they may fall ill —as in the case of one unfortunate woman who became a leper[1]—or at the least they lose authority and prestige.[2]

C113 Taboo: sodomy

Homosexuality and bestiality are definitely *ersi* and are expected to bring immediate punishment from the gods or an outraged ancestor. I have never heard of a queer Saora; there are no stories or jokes and no terms of abuse based on sodomy. In one village, only in one, at Ladde in 1950 where there were a number of remarkably good-looking young boys, I noticed a slight tendency to paederasty. The older boys held the younger ones in their arms, fondled them and performed a number of pantomimes in which they graphically imitated the sexual act. But it was always the normal act, and the fact that they did it publicly amid ribald shouts of applause shows that they were entirely innocent of any fear of a taboo.

C114 Taboo: incest

Incest is *ersi.* The Saoras regard as incest connexion with any girl within the family, that is with anyone who is related by blood. There is a general idea that it is against *ukka* to marry someone in your own village, but this is not *ersi* and nowadays when most villages are inhabited by members of several families, the rule is rapidly being forgotten. At Kankaraguda I met a leper who traced the origin of his disease to the fact that when he was a young man he once got very drunk and lay with his father's sister.

C115 Taboo: adultery

Adultery is only *ersi* when it is committed by priests and shamans. For ordinary people, it is simply an offence against *ukka*; if he is discovered, the offender may have to pay a fine, but he does not incur the anger of the gods.

C117 *Nuptial taboos*

C117·1 Taboo: intercourse at hunting season

It is taboo for a priest or a shaman to lie with his wife before a hunt, particularly before the peacock-hunt at

[1] See p. 152. [2] See p. 146.

the Karja or a hunt undertaken because the rains have failed.

C117·2* Taboo: intercourse before ceremony

A shaman or priest must not approach his wife before or during any ceremony in which he is to take part, nor of course may a shamanin approach her husband. This rule also applies to friends or relatives who may be staying in the house. For example, a priest had his daughter and her husband staying with him at the time of the Rogonadur Festival. On the evening before the feast they all got drunk and the daughter and son-in-law lay together underneath one of the ikons. The dedicated pot hanging above them 'broke of its own accord with the noise of a gun', and husband and wife both fell ill. It is worth noting that the priest himself was not affected.

If nuptial intercourse is taboo at these times, any kind of adultery is still more dangerous. At Angda the people still recall the cautionary instance of Badgu, the paternal grandfather of the present priest, who was himself a priest. On the night before the Osanadur, the priest and his wife and a younger brother were sleeping in the same house. The priest was very drunk and fell into a heavy sleep and the younger brother took the opportunity to seduce his wife. As he did so, the string of a dedicated pot hanging above them broke of its own accord and the pot crashed down onto the brother's head, knocking him senseless. The wife developed high fever. The priest awoke and realized what had happened. The younger brother died after three days, and the priest's wife only recovered after a pig had been sacrificed to the offended ancestors. Here again the priest himself was not affected by the profanation of his house.

C117·3* Taboo: intercourse at time of earthquake

Sexual intercourse is strictly taboo for everybody when there is an earthquake. This may be because it is believed that an earthquake is caused when Labosum goes to his wife. Or of course it may be an entirely commonsense rule made because at such a time people ought not to be lying about indoors. Since however no earthquake has shaken the Saora country within living memory this taboo does not impose a very heavy burden on tribal continence.

C140 *Taboos connected with menses*

The imposition of the menstrual taboo varies greatly among the Saoras, according to the degree of external influence to which they have been subject. My own opinion is that originally they had no such taboos at all, but that the influence of the Doms and the outsiders they have met in Assam and elsewhere has led some Saoras to adopt them. In Fawcett's day 'women were not considered unclean during menstruation, and cooked their husband's food as usual'.[1] Where the rules are observed they resemble those in force elsewhere. A menstruating woman must not fetch water, or husk grain or cook. She should not take part in a dance. If she is a shamanin she must not divine or sacrifice and she should not touch a sacred pot. Most shamanins observe the stricter rules, even in places where these are not generally observed, out of respect for their tutelaries who are regarded as Hindus.[2]

C142 Taboo: sexual intercourse during menses

This is everywhere regarded as taboo, even by those who do not observe the other rules. A shaman of Angda, bemused by palm wine at the end of a lengthy sacrifice, went to his wife while she was in her period. She kept saying, '*Ersi, ersi!*' but he took no notice. The next day he fell ill and, in spite of many sacrifices, he died.

C150 *Taboos connected with childbirth*

C152 Taboos during pregnancy

There are exceptionally few restrictions on the pregnant woman, except that during the later months sexual inter-

[1] Fawcett, p. 220.

[2] See also p. 160. Menstrual blood can actually be used for a beneficent purpose. If the people are unsuccessful in a hunt, they dig a trench across a path and put into it their guns, knives, bows and arrows, and carefully cover them with leaves and branches. Then someone persuades a menstruating woman, without telling her why, to go along the path. If she steps over the trench, the Saoras believe that their hunt is bound to be successful. If it is, they give a special share of the meat to the woman as her reward. But it is essential that up to that point she should know nothing about it, for if she does she may suffer later from menorrhagia.

course is forbidden. During an eclipse she should keep indoors. She should not go fishing, for her presence will cause more water to flow in the stream and this will help the fish to escape. A shamanin may continue her work of divination and sacrifice right up to her confinement, though after her child is born it is taboo for her to perform any rite for about three months.

C154* Taboos during the period of lactation

After the birth of a child it is taboo in some villages for either parent to eat fish or meat for ten days; if they do, the umbilical stump will not heal and the lochial fluid will continue to flow. It is taboo for the mother to see her father-in-law or her husband's elder brother for three days.

C180 *Taboo confined to one sex*

C181 Taboo confined to women

There are not many things that women cannot do, but there are some. A woman must not kill an animal for sacrifice, and ought not really to kill any animal at all. She must not dig a grave. She must not collect the bones or bury the ashes after a cremation. She must not fill the baskets with grain on a threshing-floor. She must not climb a sago palm. She must not play, or even touch, a *kurānrājan*, the sacred fiddle of the shamans. A story from Kankaraguda explains the reason for some other taboos. 'In the old days women used to carry loads on poles as men do now; they used to kill animals for sacrifice; they ate pork; and when they went to their husbands they used to be above while the men lay below. But one day two women took a large pig, slung by its feet to a pole, to sacrifice to Labosum in a field. As they went they disagreed about the way they should go, and the woman in front turned round and faced her companion, and they stood for a while, the pole over their shoulders, the pig between them, arguing, and in their excitement pushing and pulling their load to and fro. As they did so, the pig's snout went into the parts of one woman and its tail into the parts of the other, for in those days they were naked. The women threw the pig down and swore that never again would they kill animals in sacrifice, nor would they eat pork, nor would they carry loads on poles, and in future they would lie beneath and not above their husbands.'

IV

C200–C299 Eating and Drinking Taboos

C220 *Taboo: eating certain things*

The Saoras eat almost anything they can get their hands on, but they have a taboo on the flesh of the horse, cat, dog and frog.[1] For some reason, they regard the frog with particular distaste.

C221·1·1 Taboo: eating ox

The taboo on beef is gradually invading the Saora country, though it is still far from universal. Once it has been accepted, however, it is taken very seriously. Some Saoras say that they can sacrifice and eat a cow or bullock if a god demands it specially, but not otherwise. At Boramsingi I saw a cow sacrificed at the request of the shade of a man who had just died and wanted to take this favourite animal with him to the other world. Idaimarans and Idaibois must never touch beef, even if the other members of their household do so.

Long ago in Abbasingi a man decided that he must sacrifice a cow to Yuyuboi, the goddess of smallpox. But since his village had accepted the taboo on beef, he invited some Doms to perform the sacrifice for him. But when the time came, he found himself unable to resist going to share the feast. Immediately, as a result —it was said—of the indignation of Labosum and Barusum, his belly swelled up and he died the following day. The shaman could do nothing to help, for his tutelary and the village ancestors declared, 'The fellow has become a Dom; we won't touch him'. So seriously was the offence regarded that many people in the village fell ill, and they had to sacrifice a goat and a buffalo

[1] The Saoras, says Russell (1837), 'have none of the ordinary prejudices of caste, and eat anything except the dog, domestic cat, beasts of prey, vulture, kite and snake.'—G. E. Russell, *Selections*, vol. II, p. 4.

and promise to abstain from beef for ever before they recovered.

C221·1·3* Taboo: for women to eat pork

I have already given one story to account for the taboo on pork. Another tale, from Sogeda, gives an entertaining picture of the first shamanins. 'At first, women ate every kind of meat, and themselves killed the animals they ate. One day a shamanin went to one house and sacrificed a fowl for Uyungsum; then she went to another house and sacrificed a pig for Kittungsum; then she went to a third house and killed a buffalo for the ancestors. But as she was doing so, she struck the buffalo so hard with her axe that she broke wind loudly and everybody laughed and said, "What a smell! Whatever has she been eating?" A crowd quickly gathered, all laughing and jesting, but the ancestors were affronted and went away. After that the dead decided that women should not eat pork, for the smell of their wind was too strong afterwards.'

At pig-sacrifices, special vegetarian offerings are made for female ancestors and goddesses, for the taboo applies to them as well.

C221·1·4* Taboo: for women to eat certain kinds of fish

It is taboo for women to eat a kind of fish called *laibing-aiyo*; this fish has few bones but a lot of blood, and if a woman takes it she will suffer from menorrhagia. She must also avoid the eel-like *loitra* fish, for this may cause the retention of the placenta when she bears a child.

C221·1·5* Taboo: on eating river-snails

It is *ersi* for Idaimarans and Idaibois, though not for other people, to eat river-snails, possibly on account of the resemblance of their shells to the conches which are traditionally used by the dead.

C221·3 Taboo: eating certain parts of animals

Women and children, 'whose hair has not yet grown', should not eat the head of an animal killed in the chase; if they do, it will affect the success of the next hunt. Idaimarans and Idaibois must not eat the entrails, mouth or tongue of any animal, or the feet of pigs and fowls, though they may eat the feet of other animals.

C230 *Taboo: eating at certain times*

C231 Taboo: eating before a certain time

There is no rule more commonly broken, in spite of the drastic penalties involved, than that which forbids people to eat any part of a crop before its Harvest Festival has been celebrated. One year at Potta, some of the villagers ate mangoes before the Udanadur and the shaman fell ill. He discovered the reason, and had to make a special sacrifice before beginning the Festival. If anyone eats any of the products of the *Bassia latifolia* tree before the Abbanadur, Kinchesum may cause watery swellings, resembling the white oblong corollas, to break out on his body.

It is also taboo for a priest or shaman to break the rule of fasting before he offers sacrifice. This is considered to show pride or at least indifference towards the spirits, who object to taking the 'leavings' of human beings.[1] Here Saora and Hindu sentiment agree. Young Idaimarans often break their fast too soon, especially at the Karja ceremony where the period of abstinence is long and taxing. One Idaimaran who did this died the following day. At Chodangpur, in 1938, the little son of the shaman ate some food before a sacrifice to Kinchesum. Three days later, when the shaman, whose name was Bindang, was out in his clearing, he was killed by a tiger. A shaman at Arbun ate some food before performing the Guar and fell seriously ill, for the ancestors were offended.

C270 *Taboo: drinking certain things*

C271* Taboo: drinking milk

In most places it is against *ukka*, and in some it is actually *ersi* to drink any kind of milk. The reason is obscure. There is a general idea that to milk a cow or she-buffalo will make the calf weak. At Boramsingi I was told that 'Kittung said we might eat any kind of meat, but he never said anything about milk'. Nowadays, the taboo

[1] See p. 488.

on milk is being related to the taboo on beef: it is safest to leave the cow alone.[1]

C300–C399 Looking Taboos

C310 *Taboo: Looking at certain person or thing*

C315·3* Taboo: looking at certain stars

It is dangerous to look at the planet Venus, who is the son of Uyungsum, and a ghost-star, appearing when it will. It is also taboo to look at the Crab, for if you do, you will feel as if the claws of a crab were tearing at your belly.

C331 Taboo: looking back

At most ceremonies where disease has been taken out of a village in a scapegoat or chariot, or at such dangerous rites as those for a man killed by a tiger, or for a suicide or someone who has been murdered, or on those occasions when the gods have been bidden farewell outside a village at the end of a festival, it is taboo for the worshippers to look back as they are going home. If they do so, the spirit may follow them back into the village, and then everything will have to be done all over again.

C400–C499 Speaking Taboos

C401 Taboo: speaking at certain times

It is taboo to speak on the way home from any of the occasions mentioned under C331. It is further taboo to speak or make any kind of noise throughout the rites for someone killed by a tiger. At the Kurrualpur, when the leaves of the young plants of millet are brought home and worship is offered with rice and wine in the dark, it is taboo for anyone but the shaman and his assistants to speak.

C430 *Name taboos*

These are remarkably few. The Saoras have no hesitation about using the names of the gods—they even use some of them in abuse, as when they speak of a Rugaboi or

[1] That this taboo is not due to external influence is suggested by G. E. Russell's observation, made so long ago as 1837, that the Saoras 'draw no milk from any description of animal'.—G. E. Russell, op. cit., vol. II, p. 4.

'poxy' cat and call each other Kinnaboi, Maduboi or Mardisum; or of the tutelaries, about whom they may make dirty little jokes; or of the dead. Nor do they normally use kennings for such ominous animals as tigers and bears. In fact, they do not hesitate to use the words *kinān*, tiger, or *kambud*, bear, as terms of abuse, as for example in *kambudtāngan*—the bear-cow, *kinnaguman*—the tiger-rain, *kinna-raman*—the tiger-cat. The few exceptions are noted in C435 and C437.

C435 Taboo: uttering spouse's name

Like women all over India, Saora women will not use the names of their husbands. Saora men too—although this is not an absolute taboo—do not take their wives' names unless they have to, as for example in official business.

C437* Taboo: uttering the names of the ill-omened dead

The Saoras do not use the name of a suicide or a murdered man or of someone killed by a tiger until ceremonies have been performed to appease his angry and indignant shade.

C500–C549 Taboo: Touching

C510 *Taboo: touching tree*

It is taboo to touch the wood of a tree struck by lightning, for to do so may attract the lightning to one's own house. A woman must not touch the *Pterocarpus marsupium* tree, for the trunk exudes a blood-red gum-resin—it is in fact a menstruating tree—and if a woman touches it she too will menstruate excessively.

C530 *Taboo: touching (miscellaneous)*

C543·1* Taboo: touching horse

It is taboo for a Saora to touch a horse or to tread on its excreta. Even if he hears the word 'horse' he will spit and exclaim '*Chi chi*' in detestation. One reason sometimes advanced to explain this is that horses are the vehicles of the gods, and especially of the Kittungs, and so are not for men, but this hardly seems adequate. The Saoras have no objection to painting horses in their pictographs. It is possible that the horse is a symbol of the civilization of the plains, the vehicle not of the Kittungs but of the Bissoyis, the money-lenders and the tax-gatherers, and is thus disliked.

C543·2* Taboo: touching dead animal.

It is taboo for a Saora to touch a dead dog or cat. If the body is to be thrown away he may lift it up with a pole, but on no account touch it with his hands. But there are special rules governing the disposal of dead pets.[1]

C544* Taboo: touching house at certain time

When sacrifice is offered in a house for Madusum (leprosy), it is taboo to touch or clean any part of the building. Once at Sogeda sacrifice was being offered to Madusum on behalf of one Samna who was in an advanced stage of leprosy. A little boy called Mutku came in and touched the wall, and though the people there cried '*Ersi, ersi!*' and drove him away, he died soon afterwards.

C545* Taboo: touching forbidden food

There are not many foods forbidden, but when they are it is taboo even to touch them. For example, a man called Bamra, of Angda, a village where beef has been made taboo under Hindu influence, went one day to Serango and found some Christian Doms weighing and selling beef. But they were weighing it incorrectly and Bamra, who was a rather officious man, said, 'Let me do it' and did. On his way home, he says, he met a stranger who beat him with his stick until he fell senseless to the ground. A shaman inquired into the case and Kittung came upon him and said, 'It was I who beat him. He has touched beef; he is a Dom. I will never let him alone until his punishment is complete.' They sacrificed a goat, and Bamra recovered, but he still carries on his back marks which he claims were made by Kittung's stick.

Priests must not eat gruel made of *Eleusine corocana* millet and it is taboo for them even to touch a pot of it. Breach of this rule may drive a man mad. Once a priest named Kuringa, of Charguda village, sat down drunk

[1] See p. 295.

to a meal of pork and rice. A pot of the forbidden millet gruel was standing near by, and Kuringa, thinking that it was a pot of water, put out his hand and touched it. Suddenly he put his fingers to his mouth and gave a loud whistle, then jumped up and ran out of the house into the hills. He came finally to Arbun where he behaved like a madman and no one dared to go near him. A shaman diagnosed the trouble and said that Barusum was angry that a worshipper of the gods should have touched a pot of millet. A fowl was sacrificed and Kuringa recovered.

C700–C899 Miscellaneous Taboos

C720 *Taboo: attending toilet needs*

C721·1 Taboo: bathing during certain time

In some places there is a tradition that the gods bathe in the hill streams in the middle of the morning, and it is therefore taboo for human beings to bathe at this time.

C722·2* Taboo: throwing away hair cuttings

It is taboo to throw away the first hair cut from a baby's head, for if anyone urinated on it, the baby would get sores on his head; if a dog sniffed at it, he would get lice or a tiger might attack the father. In fact, it is safest to throw all hair away in a date-palm bush or bury it somewhere.

C750 *Time taboos*

C755 Taboo: doing thing during certain time

It is taboo to blow a certain kind of horn during harvesting or threshing, or much grain will be blown away.

C830 *Unclassified taboos*

C847* Taboo: forbidden to go about alone

Saoras always go about in company. It is so dangerous to go alone, in a world where one may be attacked by the spirits at any moment, that a custom has become a virtual taboo. When the Chief of Sogeda was prosecuted in the Courts at Rayaghada and Jeypore, he took with him a bodyguard of twelve men to the first place and eight to the second, and their travelling expenses were a very heavy item in the budget of his trial. But, he explained, he had no idea what gods might be in these towns and thought that it was well worthwhile giving himself adequate protection.

C848* Taboo: to hold the bowl of a gourd while drinking

It is taboo to hold the bowl of a gourd dipper when drinking palm wine. This is definitely *ersi* and his companions abuse a man who does it. He himself will certainly get a headache.

C849* Taboo: counting above a certain number

It is taboo for a Saora to count above 12. Fawcett describes how a Chief 'in order to count 20 began on the left foot (he was squatting) and counted 5; then with the left hand 5 more; then with the first two fingers of the right hand he made 2 more, i.e., 12 altogether, then with the thumb of the right hand and the other two fingers of the same, and the toes of the right foot he made 8 more. And so it is always; they have names for numerals up to 12 only, and to count 20 always count first 12, and then 8 in the manner described, except that they may begin on either hand or foot... The Chief was a long time telling me how many annas there are in a rupee, and at last said, "12 and 4"... There is a Saora story accounting for their numerals being limited to 12. One day, long ago, some Saoras were measuring grain in a field, and when they had measured 12 measures of some kind, a tiger pounced on them and devoured them, so ever after they dare not have a numeral above 12 for fear of a tiger repeating the performance.'[1] Another reason given is that in the days of Ramma-Bimma, there were 12 Saora brothers and since they were the first Saoras no one should count above their number.[2]

C850* Taboo: building with certain materials.

It is said to be taboo to build with bricks and tiles, for if they were used the spirits would be attracted and would come too often. Tamarind wood must not be used, or tigers would prowl round the house. The use of banyan, pipal and cashew wood is also taboo.[3]

[1] Fawcett, p. 241.

[2] See *TMO*, pp. 416ff., for the text of two stories on this subject.

[3] A. C. M. Munro and G. V. Sitapati, 'The Soras of Parlakimidi', *Census of India*, 1931, vol. I, pt. iii, p. 201.

Chapter Sixteen

THE SAORA ETHIC: THE REGARD FOR HUMAN LIFE

I. *Rebellion*

THE Saoras, who have so strong and obvious a regard for human life when it is a matter of trying to cure the sick, show themselves somewhat indifferent to deeds of violence. The reason for this is partly historical. They have behind them a long heritage of turbulence, a tradition of independence when life in their hills was free and unconstrained, a scorn for the plains people from whom they used to take what they wanted by force, and the example of their Kond neighbours for whom human life was a trifle beside the demands of an exacting religious faith.

Stirling, whose judgements of the people of Orissa are unusually severe, says of the Saoras to the north of Ganjam who were then found chiefly in the jungles of Khurda, from Banpur to Cuttack, and in the woods of Atgarh and Daljora 'which skirt the foot of the hills for some way to the northward of the Mahanadi', that they are in general 'a harmless, peaceable race, but so entirely destitute of all moral sense, that they will as readily and unscrupulously deprive a human being of life, as any wild beast of the woods, at the orders of a Chief, or for the most trifling remuneration. Thus during the insurrection which prevailed in Khurda, they were the agents employed to carry into execution most of the schemes of revenge planned by its instigators, whenever helpless individuals were to be the sacrifice, and the quantity of blood shed by the hands of these ignorant savages without motive or remorse, during the above period of anarchy and disorder, is almost incredible.'[1]

Campbell says of the Saoras whom he met in 1852 that they 'are professed thieves and plunderers, and are the terror of the inhabitants

[1] A. Stirling, 'An Account, Geographical, Statistical and Historical of Orissa Proper, or Cuttack', *Asiatic Researches*, vol. xv (1825), p. 42. One Khurda rebellion occurred in October 1804, and another in 1817, but according to R. D. Banerji it was the Konds, not the Saoras, who took part in them.—*History of Orissa* (Calcutta, 1931), vol. II, p. 286.

of the plains. Even the Konds, so ready to fight among themselves, would rather avoid than seek a quarrel with the Saoras; the latter generally make their attacks under the cover of darkness, a mode of warfare rarely adopted by the others.'[1] And Fawcett says that in war 'the Kond is all straightforwardness; the Saora all subtlety'. He is 'all for ambushes and surprises'.[2] Another early account from an undated Telugu manuscript, published in 1862, says that the Saoras,

> ... cultivate independently and pay tax or tribute to no one... If the zamindar of the neighbourhood troubles them for tribute, they go in a body to his house by night, set it on fire, plunder and kill; and then retreat, with their entire households, into the wilds and fastnesses. They do in like manner with any of the zamindar's subordinates, if troublesome to them. If they are courted and a compact is made with them, they will then abstain from any wrong or disturbance.[3]

There is no doubt that these historical circumstances have left their mark on the Saora country, which is still hard, quick-tempered, swift to revenge, leaning to rough justice. I will consider the expression of this violent temperament under three heads—the *fituri* or rebellion, suicide and murder.

The *fituri* is the inevitable reaction of a proud and independent people to conditions that would be judged intolerable anywhere. The Saora regards the *fituri*, as another man regards his duty to fight for his country, as a just and proper assertion of his rights. He tries pacific means first; he negotiates and writes memorials; but when these fail he takes the law into his own hands. In the past the *fituris* have been directed against the Bissoyis, the Doms, and occasionally against Government itself. To understand them we must briefly review the causes which have excited them.

On the relations between the Saoras and the Bissoyis and other plainsmen, I will allow one of the plainsmen themselves, a resident of Parlakimidi, the late Mr G. V. Ramamurti, to speak.

> The Bissoyis and their retainers are Oriyas or Oriyaized hillmen and speak Oriya. The relations between them and the Saoras are not friendly... This hostile attitude must be due to the oppression of

[1] Campbell, *Wild Tribes of Khondistan*, p. 204.
[2] Fawcett, p. 240.
[3] Taylor, *Catalogue Raisonné of Oriental Manuscripts in the Government Library* (Madras, 1862), vol. III, p. 469.

their Dravidian and Aryan conquerors for ages which has reduced them to their present condition. They are still suspicious of all 'outsiders'; and, though timid, are extremely irritable and, thanks to their habits of drinking, commit at times the most atrocious crimes. In pre-British days the people of the low country suffered much from the ravages of the Hill Saoras who plundered their villages, burnt their houses, and destroyed their crops, in retaliation for the cruelties inflicted on them by the then Rajas of Parlakimidi, who attempted to subdue these barbarous people by the most barbarous methods of that period. In 1822, after the Parlakimidi zamindari was delivered over to the Raja, his peons committed atrocities 'revolting to humanity'; in a plundering expedition five Saoras were apprehended and killed, their heads afterwards severed from their bodies and exposed *in terrorem* on the four sides of Kimedi . . . Even now (1931) we hear of petty revolts of the Saoras and police raids, sometimes led by the highest officials in the district, to enforce obedience to orders and to restore peace; for the Saoras are prone to defy the Government and refuse to obey their orders when they do not like them.[1]

The Bissoyis, as we have seen, are feudal overlords who were appointed in the turbulent days of old to keep the peace and collect taxes. At that time they did valuable work, but they have long outgrown their usefulness; their armies of Paiks and Pessanias have increased out of all proportion; and throughout the Ganjam Agency they have been a heavy burden on the people and one of the chief causes of their impoverishment. A. A. F. Minchin, a Deputy Conservator of Forests, says in an annual report on Ganjam District :

The Saoras are neck over crop in debt to Panos (Doms) and plains sowcars already; and what crop produce they succeed in concealing from either the sowcars or from the dependents of the Bissoyis, the Paiks who come round like raging lions and collect the dues for the Bissoyis (together with whatever they can snatch for themselves) is just sufficient to keep them alive and more or less clad . . .

They [the Saoras] are not numerous and are not successful in defending themselves against the Paiks, the servants of the Bissoyis, who come round with violence and threats and to collect one tribute for the Bissoyis and another for themselves. This results in a very wretched physical condition and timidity and depression.[2]

[1] Ramamurti, *Manual*, p. vi.

[2] Stirling describes the local chiefs (Patros and Bissoyis) 'who claim to represent the regal military class' as 'grossly stupid, barbarous, debauched, tyrannical and slaves of the most grovelling superstition'. He says of the Paiks that they 'combine with the most profound barbarism, and the blindest devotion to the will of their chiefs, a ferocity and unquietness of disposition, which have ever rendered them an important and formidable class of the population of the province'.—*Asiatic Researches*, vol. xv, p. 38.

C. F. MacCartie gives a detailed account of the oppression inflicted by the Bissoyis and their agents in the Parlakimidi Maliahs, in the Muttas of Gumma and Serango. 'The Paiks', he says, 'may be described as the rank and file, and their Sirdars as the titular centurions of a semi-military force whom the Bissoyis employed to overawe the Saoras to curb their irruptions into the low country . . . Though the times are no longer warlike, the establishment survives in enjoyment of the customary *inam* land, the tenure of which is strictly conditioned.'

> The Paiks live at headquarters, but they are allotted to each Saora village in squads proportioned to its size. The village finds the *mamuls* of these men, thatches their houses, and often reaps and transplants their crops; in return for which the Paiks perform such miscellaneous duties as may be required of them, the chief of which may be described as summoning the villagers to work for the Bissoyi or Government on occasion, collecting the Bissoyi's dues and estimating them.
>
> The collections in kind include the income assigned to the establishment of Sirdars and Paiks . . . miscellaneous collections which under the generic appellation of *mamuls*, include very extensive realizations in kind such as chillies, red gram, rice, salt, onions, honey, castor oil and other seeds, fish, pots, goats, fowls, presents of fruit and vegetables. Under this head also will fall the much abused custom of unpaid labour, in accordance with which each village has to furnish a contingent for sowing, weeding, reaping, transplanting, thatching, etc.
>
> It will be easily understood how wide a door is opened by the unrestricted development of this system to unlimited oppression, of the existence of which in parts there is no doubt; however ancient therefore, the custom may be, reforms must be introduced as in the case of *mamuls*.[1]

But although this was written many years ago, and though official after official urged the reform of the system, it was still in full force in 1950. In the Gumma Mutta there has been as shameless exploitation of a tribal people as anywhere in India. The difference in general prosperity between the Saoras of Ganjam and Koraput, where there are no Bissoyis, no army of Paiks to support and where the Dom money-lenders are in considerable awe of the powerful local Chiefs, is startling. And in modern times the *fituris* have all occurred in Ganjam.

The Bissoyis and their Paik servants, then, are one cause of constant irritation; another is the cunning and intelligence of the Dom usurers. Even though in many ways the Doms have made themselves

[1] From Taylor, *Manual*, p. 47.

indispensable to the Saoras, their exactions are most grievous, as I have shown in chapter I.

The disturbances of 1941 may be taken as typical of the Saora *fituri*. The second week of January of that year witnessed a widespread reaction against the unbearable economic pressure, the detested cultural and sexual interference, the inability of Government to remedy the situation. On 10 January a mob of about a thousand Saoras, armed with cudgels and spears and shouting war-cries, descended from the hills on the Pano quarter of Rayaghada. They declared afterwards that since the Doms had robbed them of their possessions, they were going to recover them by force. But the Doms had notice of their coming and gave them a hot reception. Before much damage could be done or a single Dom injured, the great mob had been scattered and two of their number lay dead on the ground.

The following day two more armies of about five hundred Saoras each, drunk and furious, came to retaliate and revenge themselves for the death of their comrades. This time their attack was more successful, even though by now a number of Government officials were assembled on the spot. The Saoras set fire to the Dom settlement, burnt the Pastor's house to the ground, killed three Doms and injured others, and carried off as much of their property as they could. Their aim was, as they said later in Court, 'to kill the Doms and drive them out of the Agency, since Government had refused to do so'.

At about the same time a band of some sixty Saoras attacked the Doms of Ballidi village, broke down their houses and looted their goods and cattle.

A few days later, on 14 January, a mob of two hundred Saoras attacked the Christian Doms settled in Parisal and chased them out of the village. They looted their property and returned home without shedding blood. The reason given was that the Doms were buying their goods forcibly at a very cheap rate and that they were now getting some economic compensation. Again on 18 January, another angry mob attacked the Dom houses at Tabarada. Shortly before this the Saoras had held a meeting and had decided that the Doms must be removed from the Agency. As Government would not act, they decided to take matters into their own hands. The Doms heard of this and sent their women and children away, with as much of their property as they could carry. When the Saoras made their attack, the Doms, who were not of such stout mettle as their brethren in

Rayaghada, fled to the jungle and the Saoras were able to wreck their quarters and loot their property. Among other things they took goats and pigs, which they killed and ate on the spot.

There have been a number of similar *fituris*, not often of very great magnitude, sometimes directed against the Doms, sometimes against the Bissoyis and Patros.

In Koraput District there have been no *fituris* in recent years, but there were two outbreaks in the middle of the last century. 'The first,' says Carmichael, writing only a few years afterwards, 'occurred in July 1864; it was occasioned by the hasty and improper arrest of one of the headmen of Pottasingi by an Inspector of Police. The villagers fell upon the police, murdered several of the party and rescued the headman. The outrage was entirely unpremeditated and originated with the people of Pottasingi alone; but blood once shed, the entire Saora community for a time seemed determined to make common cause against us. In the November following, a combined force of Ganjam and Vizagapatam police marched into the country, destroying Pottasingi, with sundry villages in the neighbourhood, and otherwise punishing the insurgents.'[1] With the help of the Raja of Jeypore, twenty-four of the Saoras were captured, and nine of them were sentenced to transportation and five hanged at Jaltaru. In the following year a body of police who were sent to establish a post at Pottasingi were attacked and forced to retreat down the hills; a large force was then assembled, and after a brief but harassing campaign the post was firmly occupied in January 1866 and still remains today, an entirely unnecessary survival from another age. Three more Saoras were transported for life after this rising. The Saoras remained timid and suspicious for some years afterwards, and as late as 1874 the reports mention it as a notable fact that they were beginning to frequent markets on the plains and that the low-country people no longer feared to trust themselves in the hills.[2]

[1] D. F. Carmichael, *Manual of the District of Vizagapatam* (Madras, 1869) p. 246. Francis, *Vizagapatam District Gazetteer* (Madras, 1867), p. 258, and Bell, *Koraput District Gazetteer* (Cuttack, 1945), p. 35, reproduce this account with some additional details, among them the fact that the Raja of Jeypore was presented with a rifle as a reward for his assistance.

[2] Francis, op. cit., p. 258. It is possible that some of these Saoras were among the hillmen seen by Sir W. W. Hunter when he visited the Puri District Jail. In a letter to his wife, written on 9 February 1870, he says, 'Among the prisoners were 37 hillmen, the relics of 48 sent here in December 1868. Eleven dead already and two more sinking. My blood boils to think of the way we bully these poor tribesmen. Their only offence was obeying their chief's behests.'—F. H. Skrine, *Life of Sir W. W. Hunter* (London, 1901), p. 182.

Against Government, the Saoras have found themselves, at least in recent years, in conflict over the question of shifting cultivation. In Koraput the Forest Department has been content to let well alone, but in parts of Ganjam serious attempts have been made by a succession of officials to save the forests. The first information we have about the condition of the forests in the Parlakimidi Maliahs dates from 1834, when the woods are said to have been so heavy as to be almost impenetrable. But by 1877 the forest round Gumma and Gaiba had almost disappeared. In 1881, C. F. MacCartie reported that 'the once famous forests of the Kimidi Maliahs have disappeared under the combined influence of shifting cultivation and indiscriminate felling for sale', and urged—not the abolition of Saora axe-cultivation—but the 'absolute protection from the axe of the low country speculator for many years'. In 1907 H. T. Reilly, a civilian, and S. Cox, a Forest Officer, made a report on the Parlakimidi area and insisted on the seriousness of the forest situation. They found that denudation of the hills had seriously affected the water supply, and that the pressure of population had already resulted in far too short a rotation in the use of clearings. 'The free stools have lost their vitality and the resultant coppice-growth has become poorer and poorer until in places it has almost ceased to come up at all.' The Reilly-Cox Report advocated the reservation of about 15 per cent of the entire area of 275 square miles.

It was fortunate that a few years later there was appointed to Parlakimidi an exceptionally understanding and tactful Forest Officer, H. G. Welchman, for there was widespread opposition to the plans for reservation. Welchman managed to persuade the Saoras to agree to the reservation of a considerable area, but even he had his troubles. In 1912, there was a scare, perhaps rather an exaggerated one, when the Saoras of the Jirango Mutta decided that they would not allow any further reservation and threatened Welchman with a great show of violence, though it is perhaps doubtful whether they ever intended to do anything in fact. At all events, when Welchman brought out his camera, the whole mob took fright and scattered after firing a few arrows into the air.[1]

[1] In later years Welchman formed the Ganjam Labour Corps of Konds, Saoras and Oriyas. He died of dysentery and appendicitis in 1919, while still in charge of it. He was so popular among the Saoras that some of them adopted his distinctive method of dressing a moustache. The combination of bluster and timidity, which is still typical of the Saora temperament, was noted by Russell in 1837. The Saoras, he says, 'are a contemptible enemy anywhere but in a thick jungle, and even there, their dread of firearms is so great that they seldom ventured near enough for their arrows, which with a bill-hook or axe, are their only weapons, to do any harm.'—G. E. Russell, *Selections*, vol. I, p. 75.

The work of reservation went on steadily if slowly, and the Forest Department now has some splendid forests to show for the patience and care of those early years. From time to time, the Saoras resisted, though seldom violently. It is impossible to give here a full account of such reactions, but a few examples will be of interest. In 1927 the entire male population of Taraba, thirty-eight men in all, invaded the Velladi block at the beginning of February and cleared the forest for cultivation. It was considered that the people had a good case, but in the interests of discipline they were sent to jail for six weeks. When they came out they got their clearings. This was a generous gesture on the part of Government, but it had unfortunate results. The idea spread among the Saoras that once you were punished for cutting a piece of forest, once you paid your fine or went to jail, you automatically established a right over the swidden for which you had suffered. In 1937 many acres in the Raida block were cleared by the Karmatal and Munisingi Saoras. They were imprisoned and returned home firmly convinced that henceforth the forest would belong to them. They cleared it again the following year and again in 1940. In the end the Forest Department adopted the distasteful, and indeed indefensible, policy of uprooting any crops sown in a forbidden area, and the Saoras were no longer punished in any other way.

A few years ago, when the people of Bodo Okhra were preparing to fell part of the Reserve, the priest of that village performed a special sacrifice of buffaloes and pigs to Labosum and the local hill-gods to ensure that the Forest Officer would not interfere. His sacrifices were lamentably ineffective.

These instances will show that the Saoras have not yet lost all the turbulence which once made them so notorious, though today much of it is show and bluster. Yet we must remember that from the moral point of view there is no doubt that in all these cases the Saoras believed they were in the right. If they looted the property of the Doms they were only, they considered, taking back what really belonged to them. If they felled the forest, the forest was theirs and had been so for centuries; it was their life and they were (they believed) entirely justified in resisting any attempts to banish them from its boundaries.

II. *Murder*

THE Saoras are often described as particularly prone to murder. I have not been able to get statistics, but the number of cases in the

Record Room at Koraput did not suggest that, in relation to their large population, Saora homicides were specially numerous.

As among other tribal populations, many Saora murders are committed for the most trivial reasons and suggest a predisposing condition of strain, weariness and hunger. The 1908 murder at Jaltaru occurred during a quarrel about a pig; in 1940 a dispute about a handful of chillies at a village near Gaiba ended in the death of one and the serious injury of another of the disputants. At Rajintal, in 1911, an uncle killed his nephew for allowing some cattle to stray into a neighbour's field. The previous year at Regadiguda two middle-aged Saoras laughed at a third who was rolling home drunk and told him that he was walking like a bear. He resented this and in the ensuing quarrel was killed. A senseless quarrel about the loan of a door led to a murder at Sarsang in 1943.

In only a few cases are Saora murders due to sexual jealousy, partly because in this unusually continent tribe occasions for jealousy do not often arise. But in 1944 two Saoras of Sindisingi, Jumbang and Ajul, were sentenced to life-imprisonment for murdering a man who, while Ajul was away on military service in Burma, seduced his wife. Both men made themselves drunk in order to nerve themselves for their deed, which was carefully premeditated.

There was a curious case at Tiddisingi in 1936, when a Saora named Kuara murdered the ten-year-old son of his cousin Bamuda because the latter refused to get him a wife. Kuara's wife had left him some years previously and he seems to have spent the interval in a very frustrated condition. He was always pestering Bamuda to find him a girl, and one day in November 1936 threatened to kill him or his son if he did not. The following morning, Bamuda went to another village, leaving the little boy on guard over the millet crop. Kuara persuaded the child to go with him to trap rats, and while he was setting the traps he stunned him with a stone and then shot him through the body with an arrow.

In 1937 there was a Saora, Jigu, at Pandrung who had a beautiful daughter, named Jansi. One day one Tamru of Kanjasingi sent men with two pots of wine to betroth the girl to his son. Jigu agreed and accepted the gift. But in the meantime, Jansi fell in love with a youth of Pandrung, Jhoba, and went to live with him. When the Kanjasingi people heard of it, they came in a body to Jhoba to demand a penalty—for in Saora custom it is an offence to divert the affections of a girl, whether she be married or only betrothed. The Chief and other elders gathered to discuss the matter and said to the Kanjasingi party, 'You brought two pots of wine; that is all the expense you had; take two rupees and go.' And Jhoba said, 'That's right; you won't get a pie more than two rupees.' This rather arrogant speech annoyed Tamru's elder brother Yokla, who had been hoping for something more than that and he abused him. 'You've robbed us of our girl, and she's only worth two rupees to you. My pubic hairs won't touch such a wretched sum,' and so on. In his temper Yokla slapped Jhoba and knocked him down. Unhappily, as he fell and put out his hand to save himself, he caught hold of a stone. He grabbed it, and raising himself from the ground struck Yokla a heavy blow on the side of the head, killing him immediately. The Pandrung people scattered in all directions, but the Kanjasingi party—more confident in a clear conscience—carried the corpse to an empty house and sent for the police. Jhoba was sentenced to two years' imprisonment, and when he was released the first thing he did was to find Jansi and marry her.

Economic motives for murder are fairly common. Some of these arise from the almost intolerable oppression of outsiders and have the character of small *fituris*. On 14 February 1945, four Saoras of Jamudal village killed Chowdury, a Dom of Pottasingi. Two years previously one of the Saoras, Kupi, had borrowed two rupees from another Dom named Parit, and on this day Parit came with Chowdury to support him to demand repayment of the two rupees with eight rupees interest. After a long dispute the Saoras took the Doms to a stream to have a drink of the spirit they were distilling there. There was a quarrel, and Chowdury was killed. Three of the Saoras were sentenced to two years' imprisonment under Section 325 of the Indian Penal Code.

In 1936 at Abbasingi, a youth named Turku killed his paternal uncle Mangra. There was a field in dispute between them; Turku said it was his, but one day his uncle took his cattle and ploughed it up. At midday he went to his palm tree for a drink; Turku was hiding by the road and when the older man came by jumped out and stabbed him in the belly. For some reason, Turku only got six months for this, but when he came out, Mangru's son Akla was waiting for him and cut his throat. And then a strange thing happened; before the police could come to arrest him, Akla fell into a fever and died. It is said that it was Turku's indignant shade which killed him.

Quarrels over palm trees often lead to tragedy, for these trees are the most cherished of a Saora's possessions. An uncle killed his nephew in 1936 at Mingili, a nephew killed his uncle in 1939 at Kutini in disputes about the ownership of trees. At Kimunda in 1936 two young Saoras killed their uncle's son who had abused them for tying thorns round the trunk of their palm to prevent him stealing the wine.

At Pattili in 1949 there was a quarrel about a cock. Adu had a very fine bird, but it was killed in a fight by the cock of a neighbour called Dissintaru. Adu was very angry and demanded compensation. Dissintaru offered his own cock instead, but Adu said, 'I want my cock back again.' The Chief was called and he said that Dissintaru should give two cocks and told Adu that was very fair—which it was—and that he should stop making a fuss. But Adu insisted that he wanted his own cock. 'I wouldn't take four cocks if you offered them to me,' he said. 'Tell this fellow to make my cock alive again.' The Chief said that in that case he had better take the matter to a magistrate.

Two days later Dissintaru and his father-in-law Dassiya went for their evening drink as usual and on the way met Adu who was already drunk. Adu tried to kill Dissintaru with a knife, but Dassiya intervened and in the struggle wounded Adu fatally. The police did not come till the following morning, and it is said that during the night Adu's shade reanimated his corpse and it attacked one of the men who was guarding it.

I have not recorded many cases of murder with a magical or religious motive. I discuss elsewhere the few murders that have been caused by the fear of black magic (see pp. 236f.). In 1944 a boy, Budda Buyya of Sindisingi, killed his father (accidentally in the judgement of the Court) during a quarrel about a sacrificial fowl. Budda's sister was ill and the boy brought a fowl to offer in sacrifice. The father thought this was an unnecessary extravagance; he was rather drunk and not only beat the boy but threatened him with a knife. The boy wrestled with him and in the struggle the older man fell down from the veranda where he was standing; he struck his head against a stone and was killed.

The importance of equal sharing at feasts is seen in the 1942 murder at Amaisingi, when Punya stabbed Kudringi for not inviting him to a betrothal feast.

Among the records at Koraput I discovered details of two very old cases in which the general tension and misery caused by a patient's failure to respond to the treatment of a shaman led to murder. The first was tried by my uncle, the late E. B. Elwin, at Vizianagram in 1896. Jogadu, the shaman of a village near Pottasingi, had been treating the son of his neighbour Potila for fever. Potila had supplied one fowl for sacrifice, and on the morning of 28 April 1896 Jogadu demanded another. Potila replied that he had not even got clothes to wear, so how could he get another fowl? 'I have given one already,' he said, 'and all you did was to eat it yourself.' The two men abused each other and seem to have spent the day sulking and drinking. Potila refused to take his morning meal, saying that he would have to go to a money-lender to get the fowl, and that in any case he could not afford to eat with all these shamans about. In the afternoon, Jogadu again asked for the fowl and Potila again said he could not produce one. However, he was sufficiently impressed by the urgency of the matter to set out to visit his money-lender. After going a few hundred yards, however, he turned back and the shaman, thinking that he had changed his mind and was not going to follow his instructions after all, took his bow and shot him in the stomach with an arrow. Potila crawled away, and was carried down to the hospital at Gunupur, where he died two days later. Jogadu was sentenced to death.

The circumstances of this murder are not altogether clear, but I think it is probable that Jogadu, the shaman, already disappointed by his failure to cure his friend's son, was deeply affronted by Potila's insulting suggestion that he had used a sacrificial fowl for his own pleasure, and had not in fact played fair in a professional matter. Shamans are accustomed to obedience, and when Jogadu declared that the gods required another fowl, he expected it to be provided. When he saw Potila apparently change his mind, it was too much for him; the insult, the thought that his prestige would suffer a further blow from the impossibility of concluding the sacrifice properly, irritation at not being obeyed, roused his temper and he killed his troublesome client.

Another case, which fell in 1913 and was tried by F. W. R. Robertson, was that of Panchu, a shaman of Mallapodoro in the Pottasingi area. This man had for some time been trying to cure his wife of a persistent fever by the sacrifice of fowls, but without success, and both husband and wife apparently were in a state of tension and anxiety such as always befalls those whose sacrifices are unsuccessful. On 12 May 1913 Panchu came home tired and worried from the fields and told his wife to hurry up with his food. Her own nerves were on edge and she replied that she would get the meal ready when she felt like it. The stored-up anxiety and resentment (resentment at his wife for not getting better quickly) exploded in the weary Saora's brain and he flew at his wife, struck her several heavy blows on the chest and back and kicked her violently in the stomach, rupturing the peritoneal walls. On the afternoon of the next day the unfortunate woman died. The Court, holding that Panchu had no intention of killing her, sentenced him to five years' imprisonment.

The attitude of Saora society to murder depends on who is murdered and why. There is little, probably no, condemnation of someone who kills a sorcerer or witch, provided it is not done on mere suspicion. Similarly, there is no slur on the man who kills an exacting money-lender, especially if he is a Dom, or the agent of a Bissoyi. But the murder of a fellow Saora, even to avenge one's sexual honour, is emphatically disapproved. It is not *ersi*, but it is wrong, and it is actually *ersi*, taboo, to kill a woman, 'for a woman knows nothing of the world, only of her own house, and it is she who gives us children'. And this disapproval is none the less emphatic because it is commonly believed that a murderer is driven to violence by forces outside himself.

For it is Uyungsum, the Sun, who drives men to murder and suicide. He has two kinds of messenger, the Siarasum and the Dinglatuisum. Dinglatuisum is the falling star and makes men hang themselves with ropes that resemble his long tail. Siarasum is very bad-tempered and obstinate. When Uyungsum sends him to earth, he 'gets a couple of men together, and inflames their tempers, and soon one of them has killed the other'. But this belief does not make murder any more excusable; it merely makes the entire business more dangerous.

Saoras condemn murder because it is 'bad'; it cuts short a life; it brings sorrow and economic loss to the living; above all, it has serious consequences.

There is first the trouble, and the expense, of having to report to the police and attend the trial of the murderer. This means the loss of many working-days to the elders, members of the family and witnesses. For although the witnesses receive what is called 'diet-money' in India, this does not really compensate them for the nervous strain they suffer and for the loss of time, perhaps at a critical moment of the agricultural year. And a village which has been the scene of a murder has the embarrassment and expense of supporting a police party during the investigation, for these official visitors pay little or nothing for what they consume during their stay. At every turn, therefore, a murder or a suicide involves the people in economic loss, and for this reason, if for no other, is regarded as anti-social.

Because of the trouble involved, the Saoras sometimes agree to hush up a murder, provided the murderer is docile and obedient, and is prepared to offer the necessary sacrifices—which operate in practice as a sort of compensation to the village. I have heard of a case where such a fine came to as much as seven buffaloes. This happens specially when a murder is socially approved, as when at Ladde some years ago two very tiresome and turbulent villagers were put out of the way and the entire village agreed to say that they had been killed by a tiger. The police discovered the truth in the end, but only after a great deal of trouble.

Then there is the danger to be apprehended from the ghost of the murdered man. This ghost is imagined as quarrelsome and resentful, not only because it has been taken untimely and suddenly out of life, but because in most cases the corpse is taken away by the police for a post-mortem and is disposed of officially, and certainly not in proper form. This makes it difficult to perform the Guar. If such a shade returns to its own village it may 'enter the bellies' of the people and excite them to hatred and violence against each other. If it goes too soon to join the ancestral dead, it may rouse them also by quarrelling with them or by the story of its wrongs.

The shade of a murdered man may come in the form of a bear or a dog, 'for bears and dogs quarrel when they meet', and this shade is irritable. It may attack people and give them pain in the place where it received its own wounds.

There are, therefore, elaborate ceremonies performed to prevent the approach of such a ghost or the ghost of a suicide. If the body is available, it is cremated away from the usual burning-ground; otherwise the shade may corrupt the other dead and lead to more deaths. The mourners who carry the body to the pyre must endure a special ceremony of protection or their crops may be ruined. The shaman sacrifices a pig to Uyungsum; the pig is beaten to death by the whole company, for the idea is that the shade is in the pig, and the beating will drive it away. Everyone struggles to get in a blow. Then the shaman rubs some of the blood on the mourners' bodies, and prepares a special medicine of the roots and leaves of three shrubs mixed in raw blood. Everyone drinks a little of this; it causes a feeling of intoxication, and they defecate and vomit, which is an additional sign of the shade's departure. Finally the shaman dips an arrow in blood and treats each mourner in turn by tracing a line from the big toe and over the body to the back of the head. The party must return to the village in silence and without looking round.

If the corpse is not available, a shaman leads the villagers along a path in the direction of the place where it was cremated, and performs the pig-ceremony there. Sometimes everybody in the village must take a little of the 'medicine'. The pig ought to be paid for by the murderer's household which should also present a pot of wine on this occasion to the relatives of the murdered man.

The Saoras do not perform the Guar rite for at least two years. This gives the ghost time 'to cool down a little' and to forget its wrongs before going to join the company of the dead. A menhir is erected, but in many places a buffalo is not sacrificed. Instead the shaman takes the members of the family group along the path on which the police took the corpse, and sacrifices a fowl and rice, mixing the blood with the rice. The shaman takes this to the burning-ground and buries the hen's body there and erects a little hut over it. The menhir is 'planted' in the usual place, but only a pig or a fowl is offered before it. There is a special dance: the Idaibois dance with brass pots on their heads and the Idaimarans with whatever kind of weapon was used for the murder. If an axe was used, they hit the pots with their axes crying, 'Come, this is how you were killed'.

In spite of these precautions the shade may return to take his revenge. In the Abbasingi murder of 1936, the resentful shade returned almost at once and killed the murderer. When Dolai of Potta came out of jail after serving a life-sentence for murder, he was attacked by the ghost of the man he killed; his hands and feet swelled, and in spite of many sacrifices, he soon died. On 20 December 1944 I attended a ceremony at Pandrung to appease the ghost of Yokla who, as described above (pp. 538-9), was murdered in this village seven years previously. The curious features of this incident were, first that

62. Shaman sacrifices before building a 'house' above the buried ashes of a corpse at Tumulu

63. Shamans and shamanins chant before a burnt-out pyre at Tumulu

64

64 to 66. Scenes at the Guar ceremony at Thodrangu

65

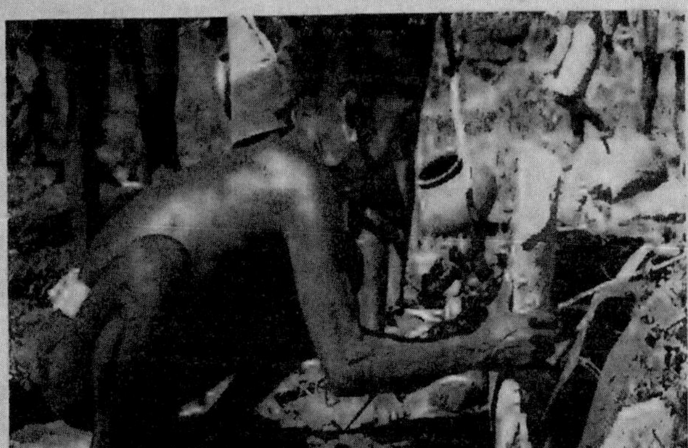
66

THE GUAR CEREMONY

67. Women fetch water, while a shaman stands by with the ghost's cloth

68. Buffaloes about to be sacrificed, dressed in ghost-clothes

the ghost waited such a long time, and secondly when he did come it was to attack a boy who was not related to any of the parties in the original quarrel and give him high fever and a splitting headache in the very place on the side of the head where Yokla himself had received his fatal wound. When the shaman passed into trance, the ghost of Yokla came upon him and said, 'If you give me rice, fish and crabs I'll let the boy alone; otherwise he must die to repay my village for the wrong done it by the people of his village.' The shaman sacrificed fish and crabs, had them cooked with rice, and by evening the afflicted boy was perfectly well again.

Precautions must also be taken against the murderer. If he is hanged in jail, his shade may appear as a rat, 'for rats are caught in a trap as a murderer is'. It is impossible of course for the family to obtain any part of his body, so the usual custom is to go in procession towards the jail with drums and trumpets. The shaman calls on the shade to come and they take it back to the burning-ground, sacrifice and bury a fowl, and make the usual offerings of wine and rice. After this they can celebrate the Guar, which they do in much the same way as for the murderer's victim.

But only a few Saoras are hanged; the majority receive sentences of varying terms. When a murderer returns from jail, special precautions must be taken, for though he is not exactly taboo, he is spiritually in a highly toxic condition.[1] There is first the curious theory of the blood.

When a man kills another, the blood of his victim passes through his axe or stick into his own body. This blood collects round the soul in the middle of his chest. 'It jumps about and keeps the murderer always irritable, and he may kill somebody else.' When a murderer returns from jail, therefore, it is essential that this blood should be removed. A shaman takes the man to a crossroads outside the village, sacrifices a fowl and a pig, and brings out the blood with a peacock's feather, using the same technique as he would to extract a bone or grub sent into the body by a sorcerer.

In 1943, for example, a man called Mursuru insulted a neighbour, Maku, accusing him of stealing his palm wine. 'Your whole family are thieves,' he shouted. 'You drink my wine as if it was my urine.'

[1] Ramamurti's statement that 'the open palm of a murderer bears blood-marks which cannot be washed away or erased' (*Dictionary*, p. 32) sounds like an echo of missionary teaching.

In the course of the quarrel, Maku killed Mursuru with a pestle, but he was acquitted on technical grounds. Since he had not been convicted it was thought unnecessary to remove the blood, and Maku went on for three years with it jumping about inside him and making him more and more irritable. One day he had a row with his younger brother Arsinga, a worthless youth who drank all day and did no work. They came to blows and Arsinga inflicted a deep wound with his axe on Maku's shoulder. This meant that Maku's blood now passed to Arsinga, and, despite his wound, Maku was a happier man thereafter. A shaman was engaged to remove the blood from Arsinga.

At Boramsingi a rather prominent and clever Saora tried some years ago to kill another with a knife; he wounded him seriously, but the man recovered and the matter was not reported to the police. But the blood of the injured man passed along the knife into the other's body. He refused to have it removed, and it made him excitable and irritable. When I visited the village in 1950, I found everybody afraid of him; they kept out of his way when he was in liquor; personally I found him charming one moment, rude and arrogant the next. It was generally expected that sooner or later he would commit an actual murder.

A murderer back from jail threatens the community with other dangers and a ceremony must be performed to eliminate them. The ceremony has a threefold purpose: it aims at driving away any alien spirits who may have accompanied the ex-convict home; it clears him of his association with Doms and other persons of low caste in the prison; and it attempts to prevent a repetition of the offence and the growth of a blood-feud.

Even after imprisonment for a minor offence, Sahibosum or some other god may return with the released prisoner. A number of Saoras at Dariambo were jailed for short terms for breach of the forest rules. While they were in jail there was an outbreak of cholera, and they were terrified that they would bring Mardisum with them back to their village. Accordingly, directly they returned home, the shaman prepared a chariot, decorated it with flowers and plantain leaves, and took it out of the village and sacrificed a goat to Mardisum. Even this was not sufficient and within two days half the village was down with various vomits, coughs and purgings. The rite was repeated, this time with the offering of a pig, and all was well.

The experience of the Chief of Sogeda, who was accused, and acquitted, of compliance in a murder at Gunduruba in 1949, is instructive. The real torment of prison to him was its invisible population. 'I thought I would die there,' he said, 'for it was lousy with gods. People from many different places and tribes were there, each with his crowd of spirits about him. When I myself first went in, my ancestors were angry and abusive, but after a few days my father's ghost came to console me saying, "You have done no wrong. Don't worry; everything will be all right," and after that when the ancestors came they comforted me.' When the Chief was released, he approached his village with circumspection. When he reached the stream at the boundary, he himself killed a fowl, twisting off its neck; he let some drops of blood fall for the ancestors, then threw it backwards over his shoulder and stepped forward over the blood, to stop the jail-gods following him home. He repeated the ceremony with another fowl at the door of his own house. Next day he offered a pig to the ancestors to prevent anyone taking advantage of his depressed condition by working magic against him. Then he gave a goat for the ghost of a dead wife who was angry because he had neglected her while he was in jail. Finally he sacrificed another goat, to protect himself against the malice of his enemies who were deeply chagrined at his acquittal.

The father of my interpreter Somra served a long sentence for homicide. When he returned to Taraba on his release, he was 'treated' with a rite which laid emphasis on rather different things. He sacrificed a pig at the village boundary, and when he reached his home he was made to stand outside. The shaman heated a new ploughshare and put it in front of the door. The old man himself killed a fowl and let the blood fall on his feet, then threw the fowl's body onto the roof: it was taboo for anyone to eat it. He bathed, then stepped on the ploughshare and entered the house. The elders gathered and said to him, 'You made a mistake and you have been in jail for many years. Now you have come back. Are you going to live well hereafter, or are you going to kill someone else? If you do, we shall report you, and this time you will be hanged.' The old man swore by Uyungsum, Labosum and Kittung that he would never repeat his crime. Then the elders said, 'While you were in jail you ate with Ghasis and Doms. We are not going to eat with you, and your ancestors will not eat with you or come near you.' And they refused to use the same gourd-dipper for wine, and would not share his pipe until, a few days later, he sacrificed a buffalo to the ancestors, and distributed the flesh to his fellow villagers. After the feast there was no more trouble; the old man had the blood removed from his body, and lived peacefully thereafter.

Sometimes an attempt is made to make peace between the families of the murderer and the murdered. Where, as is usually the case, the tragedy is an exclusively male affair, the women of the two parties have to be reconciled. The murderer's wife is persuaded to prepare a feast of meat, rice and plenty of wine. The Chief places a ploughshare in front of the house, and the wives of murderer and victim are set down side by side, and induced to drink together. The wife says to the widow something like this: 'My husband killed yours, it is true; but mine is also lost to me; he is in jail and who knows whether I will ever see him again. So we have both suffered, and anyway it is not *our* fault. We didn't do anything. So let us be friends and live in peace together.' They go on drinking for a time and then the murderer's wife feeds the widow and they become friends.

A man, if he wishes and can afford it (though he is not obliged to do so), may give some sort of compensation to the family of the person he killed when he has re-established himself after his release.

III. *Suicide*

THE Saora attitude to suicide is controlled by the belief that in most, if not in all, cases the victim is driven by external influence. As we have seen, Uyungsum has two classes of servants whom he uses to take his messages. The first, the Siarasum, incite men to murder; the second, the Dinglatuisum, drive them to suicide.

Dinglatuisum takes the outward form of a falling star, the tail of which is regarded as the suicide's rope. When Saoras see such a star they cry, '*Thu thu*, go away over there!' and they believe that somewhere in the world a man has hanged himself.

Dinglatuisum, which is a sort of collective noun embracing all those who have died by their own hand, is constantly recruited. A suicide does not go to the Under World, but to the sky; there he joins Uyungsum and becomes one of his messengers, a Dinglatuisum, and goes when required to reproduce his own tragedy in some other person.

The intolerable persecution of other gods may also drive a man to suicide. When sacrifices fail, and the shaman confesses himself impotent, death is the one way out. The only way to escape from god, we might say, is to go to heaven.

There is, therefore, among the Saoras no social condemnation of the suicide. The deed is regarded with pity and understanding. But at the same time it causes considerable alarm. For quite apart from the tiresome and often expensive investigations by the police, it is essential that the funerary rites should be performed without mistake. All violent deaths are dangerous for the living, and those of suicides are specially so. There is the risk that the shade may inspire other people in the neighbourhood to imitate him. There is the fear that he may call a wife or child to go with him to comfort his misery. A suicide's ghost too may be naturally supposed to be angry and resentful, and may spoil the crops or bring sickness to a village.

Special precautions, therefore, must be taken. The corpse is not taken to the usual burning-ground, and when it is cremated, if the dead man hanged himself from a tree the branch he used is cut and placed on the pyre, for others might use it for the same purpose or if anyone climbed on it by mistake he might fall off and be killed. The following day the ashes are collected as usual, but buried somewhere else. Before returning to the village, the shaman—or a medicine-man if one can be found—performs a rite to protect the mourners. He cuts a plantain-stalk, splits it open down one side, kills a pig over it and lets the blood flow down the slit. The mourners put their feet in the blood and return home, silent and without looking back. When they have all gone, the shaman and his assistants bring water and wash the plantain-stalk clean as a sign that there should be no more suicides in their village. When a medicine-man is available he administers to everyone in the place the *pararegam*, or 'medicine', which will protect them against the influence of the unhappy shade.

The Guar is not performed for several years, with the idea that the ghost should not disturb the other dead. When it is performed, it has certain special features. A thread is suspended from the roof above the mortar, so that the shade who used a rope to go into the sky can now descend. The actual rope used in the hanging is carefully preserved, and now it is brought out and the Idaimarans dance with it. After the dance a shaman ties it round a brass pot, lifts it up and suddenly drops it. As he does so, the ghost comes upon him and explains the reason for his death.

Let us now examine a number of actual cases which will illustrate the Saora psychology of suicide. We shall notice that although the Saoras believe that suicide is caused ultimately by divine intervention, there are always subsidiary natural causes. The Sun-god's messengers do not inspire perfectly happy and contented people to kill themselves; they must have something to build on. And the Saoras themselves say that suicide is usually committed by women when they cannot do their work properly or get enough to eat or fall out with their husbands, and by men if they are grievously insulted in a quarrel or are afraid of some incurable disease.

It is by no means easy to get at the facts. The police of the Gunupur and Pottasingi Station Houses have evolved a convenient formula which, in a list of suicides they sent me, accounted for 80 per cent of the cases cited. The formula—'suicide due to intolerable colic pains'—is rather like the 'suicide while of unsound mind' of a British jury, but it springs from a less kindly motive, for generally the police investigators do not trouble themselves very much about discovering the motives of the dead; they content themselves with bullying the living. Throughout tribal India, it is almost routine for the police in a case of suicide to threaten the family with a murder charge as a means of exacting a heavy bribe.

Statistics, even if they were available, would be of little value, for so many things are not reported at all and so many are twisted from the truth. I give here only those incidents which I was able to investigate personally. That too was not easy, for the Saoras do not like to talk about suicide at all, for fear of annoying the ghost, and they have a natural fear that the investigator may be wanting to reopen questions that had long ago been settled.

In every case known to me, the method used was hanging. There are no rivers or lakes which would be suitable for drowning, and few wells; the Saoras do not seem to be very expert at poisons; it is perhaps curious, however, that in an area where so many accidental deaths are reported as due to falls from trees, the method of jumping from the top of a tall palm has not been adopted. Of course, it is not impossible that some of the supposedly accidental deaths are in fact suicides that have been hushed up.

I refer to twenty-four cases of suicide in this chapter. Eleven of these were of women, thirteen of men;[1] ten of them were young people, fourteen elderly; in eleven cases the act was done inside a house, from the main beam of the roof, in thirteen cases it was done outside, from the branch of a tree, often a mango tree.

I will first consider tragedies which were attributed primarily to the intervention of Uyungsum. In 1941 a girl named Adi married a youth of Gudang village and lived with him happily for four months. Then one day when her husband was away, she cooked some buffalo-flesh and rice, set aside part of it for her husband, ate the rest herself, shut the door of the house and hanged herself. The villagers could give no reason; it was, they said, the doing of Uyungsum and they recalled that before her marriage the girl had made two previous attempts at suicide.

Bengbang, an elderly Saora of Kumulusingi, hanged himself in 1947. It was the sequel to a long struggle against the inexorable gods of disease. He went to Assam, and shortly after his return his feet swelled and he got acute pains in the stomach. He gave a pig to Labosum and recovered. Then he began to suffer from headaches; he gave a fowl to Uyungsum, and got better. Then he had fever after fever and grew very thin. The shaman first said this was due to Dorisum, and he sacrificed a buffalo—with no effect. Then the shaman said it was the ancestors, and demanded another buffalo. But Bengbang's resources were exhausted; he was indeed so poor that the neighbours used to bring him food—when they remembered to. On the day the shaman asked for the second buffalo, Bengbang himself cooked a little rice, ate half of it, left half in the pot, and then hanged himself at midday in his house.

The case of Simbero of Rajintalu was similar. He was an epileptic and no one would marry him from fear of Kannisum. When he was about fifteen years old Madusum attacked him with leprosy. He went to Assam for three years and spent a lot of time there in hospital. On his return he sacrificed to Madusum a goat, a pig and a buffalo. He tried to find a wife; no one would go near him. At last he hanged himself in despair one night in 1944.

Tangai, who hanged himself from a mango tree at Kadasi in 1945, was following the example of his father who twenty years before had

[1] The sex-ratio was almost exactly the same among the Bison-horn Marias. See my *Maria Murder and Suicide*, pp. 48ff.

committed suicide 'because Madusum had attacked him and his fingers and toes had rotted away, and no sacrifice had done any good'. Years later, Darammasum, angry that Madusum had treated the father in this way, showed his displeasure by attacking the son. Tangai got what seems to have been tuberculosis, and in spite of many sacrifices of fowls, pigs and goats to Darammasum, grew steadily worse, until in despair he brought his sufferings to an end. The story of Podo, a Saora of Angora, who was an epileptic leper, was the same. In Angda in 1938, a man called Rata hanged himself when he had used up most of his money on sacrifices designed to cure a tumour in his stomach. On that night he ate a hearty meal, drank a pot of wine, took his baby son on his shoulder and did a dance, had intercourse with his wife, and then when everybody was asleep went quietly out of the house to the burning-ground and hanged himself from a mango tree which overhung it.

At Singjangring there were two lepers, father and son, living together in 1945. They offered four successive sacrifices, to Labosum, to Ratusum, to the ancestors, and to the dead, but they only grew worse. The son first, and then the father, committed suicide inside their house.

A pathetic example of a ghost's intervention comes from Kulusingi. Iswaro Dhol-behara was very fond of his wife Lodan, but he was equally fond of liquor. One day in the hot weather he came home very drunk and demanded food. His wife had been out working in the clearings and the meal was not ready. Iswaro abused and beat her, and then lay down on the veranda and went to sleep. Lodan cooked the food, fed her two small children and hanged herself from the roof. Iswaro was inconsolable. He said, 'She was such a good wife and she died for such a small thing—a little beating when I was drunk.' On the day he celebrated her Guar, he got very drunk again and during the ceremonies slipped away from the crowd and hanged himself from a mango tree. 'These two,' I was told, 'loved each other very much. Iswaro hanged himself because his wife's ghost forced him to it. She came for him, and now they will be together in the Under World.'

A number of suicides may be connected with the somatic and psychic disturbances of adolescence. We have seen the strong resistance put up by young girls to an entirely spiritual marriage with a tutelary. Some girls are equally opposed to marriage with human beings. This could only occur in a tribe where marriage is taken seriously. Suicide for this cause is almost unknown, for example, among the Gonds and Pardhans of Madhya Pradesh, whose girls either refuse to go to a husband they do not like or elope with someone else.

In 1936 a girl called Igai hanged herself because her brother insisted on her marrying a man older than herself. In 1946 a family from Baijalo came to betroth a girl called Dolmi at Kulusingi. The girl's brother refused to accept their liquor and they decided to carry her off by force. On the morning they came for her she slipped out of the house and hanged herself from a mango tree. In the hot weather of 1945, a girl ran away from her husband at Baghmeri. He brought her back and shaved her head as a punishment. She hanged herself the following day. In 1948, Lengdu, a Saora of Angda, brought home his bride Gangi, on whose betrothal and marriage he had spent a considerable sum of money. But when he approached her, she lifted her legs and kicked him across the room crying, 'You may be a rich man with fields and cattle, but I don't want them. I hate you, I hate you.' She ran away that night, but Lengda brought her home. This happened three times, for Lengda said, 'I have spent a lot of money on you, and I am not going to let you go.' At last the girl escaped to her own village and hid in her brother's house. The next day, her brother and a friend were up on the roof mending the thatch, when it suddenly began to shake. They climbed down and found Gangi hanging from a beam. They cut her down and gave her three raw eggs and she recovered. But after four days she disappeared, and no one ever saw her again.

A girl at Taburda hanged herself in 1945 because she was afraid of tigers. When her husband took her to his clearing to guard the growing crops, a tiger prowled round the hut, and next morning she ran home in terror after a sleepless night. The husband tried to make her return to work but she hid from him. This went on for days, and at last the husband came with some friends to take her to the clearing by force. But she escaped from them into the forest where she took her own life.

Domestic conflict sometimes ends in suicide. At Ladde, Angari quarrelled with her husband Arjuno. She was in any case not very well, and was not sorry to end her life. At Tiddasingi in 1948 a man called Budda quarrelled with his wife, of whom he was very fond, because she had not given him a child. 'I have no happiness with you,' he said. 'If I had another wife, she'd soon give me a child.' That day the woman hanged herself. But afterwards Budda could not bring himself to marry anyone else, for he always remembered his wife and how well she had looked after him. At last, it is said, his wife's ghost took him away, and a year after her death he was dead too. But this was not through suicide, and the Saora theologians were doubtful whether the couple would be together in the next world. It was possible, they said, but not certain.

In two cases, religious motifs combined with domestic stress. A Saora named Narsing of Dayar was attacked by Kannisum with epilepsy. He sacrificed a goat and a buffalo and this landed him in debt. His wife used to nag him about it. 'Your sacrifices do nothing but get us into debt. You are no better, for all your goats and buffaloes. You do no work and expect me to feed the children.' This depressed the unfortunate man and at last one day he ate a good meal, and then went to his clearing and killed himself there.

At Liabo lived one Mundgu, a drunken quarrelsome fellow. One day when he was drunk he broke down the shrine of Karnosum, and his wife publicly abused him: 'You eat my excrement and drink my urine.' She refused to give him anything to eat that day. The next morning, hungry and miserable after his debauch, apprehensive of the consequences of his affront to the gods, his wife's insulting words ringing in his ears, he hanged himself on a mango tree above the village.

The complications of polygamy may drive a husband or wife to despair. Gangna of Arbun had two wives, the younger being a girl who came of her own accord to his house and at that time with the approval of the older woman. For a time all went well, but soon the inevitable conflicts began. The elder wife insisted that the house belonged to her; the younger threatened to go and claim it through the police. Then the elder wife took to following Gangna about in order to stop any love passages between him and the younger girl; she never left him for a moment. Soon the younger woman was doing the same, and Gangna began to feel literally haunted. He made separate huts for the two women and went to one or the other as he felt inclined. Then the elder began to repulse him: 'I'm only an old woman; what do you want with me? Go away.' The younger too repulsed him. 'The one you really love is that frightful old hag. What do you want with me? Just to eat my excreta, I suppose.' In the end Gangna got so weary of it that he hanged himself.

Tobab of Ladde had two wives. The younger woman, who was named Doiman, had a club foot and was not much use for work in the fields. So normally Tobab used to go out with the elder wife, and Doiman stayed at home. There she had to do everything, get the water, chop the wood, husk the rice, powder the sago, look after her baby, and if anything was not done in time the elder woman used to abuse her. After some months Doiman could stand it no longer. She put her little son to sleep on the floor one morning in the summer of 1947, and hanged herself from the roof above him.

Sorrow and loneliness sometimes drive elderly people to complete disgust with life. Adangu hanged himself at Singjangring in May 1944 after the death of a dearly loved son. Sombari, an old widow of Gailunga, was looked after by her daughter, for the other relatives did not treat her properly. One day the old woman went to another village, and when she returned she found that her daughter and her husband had gone away to Assam. She could not face the future alone, and hanged herself.

I only know of one case where a Saora hanged himself to evade arrest. This was Chaitan, a man of twenty-eight years, who killed himself in his cattle-shed at Kusumguda in June 1943, after he had been caught red-handed in the murder of his wife. It is possible, of course, that it was as much remorse as fear that caused him to do this, for tribal wife-murders are rarely premeditated.

Among the causes of suicide, the economic distress created by the demand for expensive sacrifices, and the despair which follows their failure, are of special significance. We do not, however, find suicide as a ceremonial act, as a way of escape from an unforgivable breach of taboo or tribal law. It is possible that the methods of evasion, by which a Saora can escape the consequences of almost any ritual error by offering an appropriate sacrifice, are responsible for this.

Suicide does not seem to be very common among the Saoras. The few cases discussed above are all that I was able to discover during my inquiries over a very wide area. There must obviously have been other suicides of which I did not hear, and doubtless others which were never reported to the police, but my impression is that in relation to the large population the incidence is not high.

Chapter Seventeen

THE SAORA ETHIC: VALUES AND MOTIVES

I. *The Saora Character*

VERY different judgements on the Saora character have been passed from time to time. Thus, M. W. M. Yeatts who, as Census Commissioner for Madras in 1931, had some contact with the tribe could write:

> One of the most interesting circumstances of the Madras Agency Tracts is the presence in adjoining areas of representative tribes of so widely differing types as the Kond and Saora. They differ in almost every way and provide a vivid illustration of the racial differences which exist in India. Eikstedt found the Konds 'cheerful, mobile, friendly and self-possessed', the Saoras 'reserved, suspicious, refractory and obstinate (*hartnackig*)'. Most will agree with that general differentiation. In general 'Mongolism' and savageness go together, he says, and the most intractable people he came across were those with most apparent Mongol traces. The Kond is open, the Saora closed.[1]

With Eikstedt's judgement, made after he had spent only a few weeks in the Saora country, we may compare the opinion of N. Macmichael who was there for years, and was Agent in Ganjam in 1914-15: 'The more one sees of the Saoras, the more one realizes what thorough gentlemen they are.'

Yet Eikstedt's view has its supporters. H. B. Rowney, for example, in a quaint little book which is only worth quoting because it was written so long ago, says of the Saoras: 'They are fiercer than the Konds and so entirely destitute of moral sense, that they will unhesitatingly commit the greatest crimes for the paltriest advantages. They are not straightforward in any of their dealings; they always take every unfair advantage, even though there is no question that they are quite as courageous as any other tribe.'[2]

[1] *Census of India*, 1931, vol. I, pt. iiiB, p. 200.
[2] H. B. Rowney, *The Wild Tribes of India* (London, 1882), pp. 108f.

A typical outsider's view is that of an official holding a responsible position in Ganjam District in 1943 who, when asked his opinion about the establishment of Co-operative Societies in the Agency, endorsed a file as follows:

> Saoras are not only not civilized, they are very much unlike human beings. They are like wild beasts—not even merely beasts. Many animals, e.g., bees, elephants, etc., live a corporate life. They are far better than Saoras. To think of a co-operative society of Saoras is a big joke and any attempt to introduce it will meet with immediate failure.[1]

Other officials have stressed the 'backwardness' and 'dullness' of the Saora. J. C. Molony says he is 'a matter-of-fact, not very interesting person'.[2] J. S. Wilcock, Agent in Koraput in 1939, wrote in a judgement of a murder case:

> The accused are Saoras, aboriginals in a primitive stage of civilization, little above the level of savages. Their character is evinced by the fact that after committing a ferocious murder for the flimsiest of motives, they made no attempt whatever to conceal the crime or their participation in it... The appearance and demeanour of all except one of the accused is that of children, although it is clear that the youngest of them is not less than twenty-three years old.

R. C. S. Bell, who was also at Koraput, wrote in one judgement, 'The accused is a Saora. His mental development is probably equivalent to that of a normal child of fourteen,' and in another case he speaks of the Saoras as a 'volatile tribe, liable to sudden gusts of passion which are at once regretted'. But Bell considered that Eikstedt's comparison between the Saoras and the Konds was 'perhaps unfair on the Saoras, who are an attractive race when their reserve has been penetrated. But obstinacy and intractability are certainly among their most prominent characteristics and have frequently proved a difficulty to the administrator. The Saoras are probably more intelligent than the Konds and undoubtedly more industrious.'[3]

Eikstedt's opinion is probably due to the rather jaundiced view of Saora life which he must have had as a result of making his headquarters at Gumma, the centre of a Paik and Oriya population, and surrounded by Saoras whose one defence against exploitation has

[1] And long ago, Ghose referred to the Saoras as 'a set of dangerous people... barbarous, who are bad subjects and not trustworthy'.—B. K. Ghose, *History of Puri* (Cuttack, 1848), p. 65.

[2] J. C. Molony, *Census of India*, 1911, vol. XII, p. 6.

[3] Bell, *Gazetteer*, p. 70.

always been a sullen refusal to oblige: from one village Eikstedt and his party had to make a rapid retreat in the face of threatening hostility. The idea that the Saora has a childlike mentality probably arises from the fact that in Court an accused Saora, bewildered and shattered by the sudden tragedy that has fallen upon him, unable often enough to understand the attempts of the official interpreter to make the proceedings intelligible, has no means of communicating his thoughts and naturally appears a fool. The Saora's intractability and obstinacy are due to his resistance against laws and regulations that he knows will ultimately destroy his economy: he resists the forest laws because he knows they will impoverish him, the excise laws because they will rob him of his happiness, and the attempts to educate him because he sees in them an attempt to invade his country by an alien speech and customs.

In assessing the character of a people, it is essential that we should not judge them by their reactions towards ourselves, but by their behaviour towards one another.

From this point of view, is it true that the Saoras are bad citizens of their own community, incapable of co-operation, obstinate and intractable towards the tribal Chiefs? They have their faults, certainly. They are 'volatile'—it is a good word—quick-tempered, and when excited by wine unable to temper their present conduct with the fear of future consequences. They do not have a very high regard for human life and they are apt, as we have seen, to break into mob violence under the stress of economic pressure or social injustice.

Some Saoras are arrogant and conceited; some are embittered and quarrelsome. But such men are strongly condemned by tribal opinion.

Saoras can be cruel. A man murdered in 1921 had his testicles kicked until he died. In the Bungding murder of 1938 five Saoras literally hacked their victim to pieces. It would be hard to find a more sadistic type than Panchu of Gailunga, whose story I tell at p. 169 of this book. Birds and animals are sometimes sacrificed in a very cruel way. Yet the mass of the population is gentle and kindly enough; methods of sacrifice are dictated by ancient custom and generally Saoras are very good to their animals; we cannot condemn a whole people because of an occasional outburst of savagery.

And on the other side, what great virtues the Saoras have! They are an affectionate and sociable people, very fond of each other, loyal and devoted friends, good domestic partners, lovers of children, hospitable to strangers. They are good citizens—on their own standards and in their own way. It is important to emphasize that. They do not take readily to new regulations in the making of which they have had no say. They are not inclined to co-operate in making roads for the convenience of merchants who will come to exploit them or in the building of schools which they believe will do their children harm. They very much object to acting as porters for subordinate officials who do not pay them properly. Many of their supposed 'faults' are in fact the natural reactions of a much-exploited tribe against the outside world, and in other circumstances these very faults would be praised as tokens of manliness and independence. Within their own republic, the Saoras are remarkably co-operative. They frequently combine in labour on the terraces and swiddens. They have a passion for the exact division of food and labour. They obey their Chiefs—even when he was a little boy, as at Boramsingi in 1950, the Chief's orders had the force of law.[1] They combine in many of their religious ceremonies and are always ready to help the poor and needy.

Perhaps the greatest of the Saora virtues is industry. Fawcett considered that the Saoras were superior in activity and industry to the Konds, though 'decidedly physically inferior'. He adds that 'the Saora's endurance in going up and down hill, whether carrying heavy loads or not, is wonderful'.[2] Minchin, a Forest Officer, praises the Saoras for their work in clearance of the forest and the upkeep of lines. 'The Saoras', he says, 'accept this as a duty and the lines are *remarkably* well kept. The cairns are pictures of what a cairn should be. I have never seen such good lines and cairns in any other forest division.' Francis also praises Saora industry.

They are known for the industry with which they cultivate. They terrace the steep hillsides with great revetments of stone, often fifteen feet deep; grow splendid *Sorghum vulgare* twelve or fourteen feet high on the slopes; preserve every pound of fodder by cutting the crops close to the ground and storing the straw on platforms or up trees to save it from damp; and utilize for irrigation every rill in the country. Their well-kept fields, with the numerous *ippa* trees

[1] G. E. Russell, writing in 1837, stresses the 'clannish feelings' of the Saoras. 'During my stay in Kimedy', he says, 'I had more than 200 of them in confinement at different times, yet, of the whole number, only three could be induced to give any useful information or lead our troops against their Chiefs or confederates.' —G. E. Russell, *Selections*, vol. I, p. 75.

[2] Fawcett, p. 216.

scattered about them, have been likened to Italian homesteads surrounded with their dark olives.[1]

The construction of the terraces must have involved enormous labour, and the stone walls round many fields and swiddens must have kept the people busy for years. The work of axe-cultivation is very exacting, and it must be remembered that the Saoras, unlike such tribesmen as the Hill Marias or the Baigas, do not have only one type of cultivation. Directly they have finished with the swiddens, they must get to work on the terraces; directly they have done with the terraces, they must turn to their gardens. I have never seen such hard-working tribesmen. Women are up long before dawn husking grain, and during the harvest season they work by night as well as all day. They are intelligently laborious too; they do not waste effort. No one returns from the woods without a load; a man brings a long bough over his shoulder for firewood; children bring vegetables, leaves, grubs, sticks for the hearth. Women fill in their spare time with spinning and sewing; every scrap of cloth is saved, and sewed together to make at least a baby's garment. If the Saoras have a fault it is that they are perhaps a little too serious, their days are overloaded,[2] they live too hard, and as a result—so Fawcett thought—they do not live long.

The Saoras are in the main a clean people. They bathe whenever they can get at water. This is not always easy, especially high up in the hills where every stream is tapped for irrigating the terraces and a whole village may depend on a single spring. Clothes tend to be dirty and while this does not matter so long as the Saoras retain their tradition of semi-nudity, it does mean that they suffer when they begin to dress. Filthy little blouses and shirts soon lead to every kind of skin-disease. Houses are kept spotlessly clean, but in many villages, though not in all, the streets are filthy.

II. *Saora Ethical Ideas*

It is obviously insufficient to discover what the Saora character is like; it is more important to see what a Saora thinks his character

[1] W. Francis, *Vizagapatam District Gazetteer* (Madras, 1907), p. 257. And G. E Russell noted that the Saoras were 'wonderfully expert' at clearing jungle and removing stumps.—Russell, *Selections*, vol. I, p. 77.

[2] M. W. M. Yeatts says of the Kond: 'He is called lazy and compared to his disadvantage with his industrious Saora neighbour, but there is little doubt which gets more out of life. The Kond has put work in its place and life also. Neither is ever allowed to oppress him.'—*Census of India*, 1931, vol. XIV, pt i, p. 366.

should be like. We have already discussed the two fundamental concepts of *ukka*, custom, and *ersi*, taboo, and in chapter XV have considered the Saora taboos in considerable detail. Most of those taboos governed man's behaviour towards the spirits; in this chapter I shall discuss ideas and principles which come mainly under the head of *ukka*, man's conduct towards his fellows, the tribe and the law of the land.

The Saoras always find it hard to generalize. They can say that so-and-so is a bad man; they do not find it easy to draw a general picture of 'badness'; they are rather inclined to estimate someone by a single trait—he is a thief, he is a quarrelsome fellow, she is a miser—than to make an elaborate analysis of character.

Probably the most universally condemned character is the proud man. To so united and democratic a tribe, to a people who have learnt the need of humility before the incalculable dangers of the unseen world, pride is naturally distasteful; it divides the community, it destroys the good-fellowship of drinking parties beneath the palms, it threatens a sudden dramatic explosion that will bring tragedy to a village.

An insolent man is called *asongbobmaran*, one who relieves himself on someone else's head. An *adaibobmaran* or a *duaiymaran* is a proud man, 'one easily provoked; if someone's cock fights his, he makes a thing of it. If anyone asks him for help, he answers rudely; he refuses to feed the hungry; he is overbearing to his wife; he cannot hold his liquor.' There was such a man at Boramsingi; he was a heavy drinker, a gossip and slanderer: the whole village was afraid of him. Again and again, at a dance, a drinking-party, a sacrifice I saw him flare up over a trifle. He was always pointed out to me as the perfect example of the proud man. 'When he is drunk, he goes into anybody's house, demands food and drink, and lies down to sleep on the spot, caring nothing for the embarrassment he may be causing.' 'His sword wants to eat human flesh; when he is angry he says that even his breath will blow his enemies away.' But in this case, it was not all his fault; he was a victim of the 'murderous blood' that had clotted round his soul (see p. 546) and this drove him to a sort of madness.

There was another proud man of the same type at Kinteda, always drinking, quarrelling with his neighbours, beating his wife. The other villagers refused to drink or even to sit near him at festivals. He was a *rankamaran*, a bad man, a *kinnamaran*, a tiger-man, described at Thodrangu as 'one who quarrels without cause, one who beats other people, a jealous man who cannot bear to see his friends prosper. He does not obey the village elders; he is arrogant in the presence of officials; he pays no heed to anyone'.

The miser, the *ersuamaran*, is also disapproved. 'A miserly mean man who never shares things' is a kind of thief. He likes to drink alone, so that he can have his own, as well as his neighbour's, share. There was a man like this at Sogeda, and the others had learnt not to invite him to go with them to the sago palms or to call him to share in the sacrificial feasts. 'For he always wanted a double portion, and when it was his turn to give he always disappeared.' A mean woman is one 'whose door is shut to beggars and the poor' and who grudges the smallest gift of wine which her husband offers to a friend.

The miser is an obvious misfit in Saora society, which is bound together by mutual hospitality, co-operation, the ritual exchange of gifts, and a very strong tradition of tribal solidarity. In the myths, the noble Raja Gehil cuts bits of flesh off his own body to feed the poor; Galbesum amputates his own leg to make a plough for men; Kittung gives his own fingers to make a tree.[1] 'We give willingly' is a phrase repeated at every sacrifice. The free, generous, almost extravagant bestowal of gifts is a Saora ideal; it is not always achieved; but it is there, and its betrayal is a real slur on tribal fellowship.

A scandal-monger too is a kind of thief, for he steals a man's good name. For this reason, he is said to have been conceived under the shadow of Ratusum, and like the adulterer or 'coitus-thief', goes to Ratusum when he dies. This is not, of course, a theological opinion, for moral defects are not punished in the other world; but it is an expression of ethical judgement—the detested and feared Ratusum, the god of night and darkness, is naturally attracted by the detested gossip. 'The bones of a scandal-monger,' I was told at Tumulu, 'the bones of his elbows and knees are weak; that is why he talks so much, for his soul wanders to and fro. Such a man will be always sickly: Ratusum is on the wait for him.'

Greedy people upset the even course of ceremonial life. At the distribution of meat after a sacrifice, they want more than their

[1] See p. 577.

share; they drink more than they should when they sit with the neighbours round a pot of wine. One is always uneasy in their presence. They may break essential taboos by stealing food from the gods; they may eat before the Harvest Festivals. They are a nuisance and a danger to the community.

The Saoras are exceptionally afraid of jealousy, and they attribute this defect to the spirits as much as to human beings. The dead are often regarded as jealous of the prosperity of the living; the gods do not like to see human beings doing too well. When I offered to photograph the Chief of Sogeda, he refused on the ground that his ancestors would be jealous: they would complain that they had never been photographed, so why should he be? Sorcerers are often excited to their evil devices by the success or pretensions of a neighbour.

This fear of jealousy has an enervating effect on Saora life; it cramps initiative and stifles genius. Everyone should be like everyone else; there must be no individual distinction; no one should stand out. This has a bad effect on art: it is dangerous to make a beautiful thing, for someone may be jealous of you. It is a brake on achievement; for if you make good, an ancestor, a god or a sorcerer may try to do you down.

Theft, or at least theft from a fellow Saora,[1] is strongly condemned. 'A thief is like Ratusum, for when Ratusum attacks a man, not even the shamans can say who is responsible. When a thief dies, the ancestors refuse to have him with them, and sell him to Ratusum.' But theft brings its own punishment. 'A thief is always hungry; wealth does not stay in his house, and his harvests are always poor.'

A man who does not work is a thief, for he takes his share of food without doing his share of labour. A special kind of thief is the *rankaboi*, a daughter-in-law who eats out of the pot or takes food secretly without getting her mother-in-law's permission. But any solitary eater is a thief. A man or woman who cooks food on the quiet and eats it secretly without sharing it with the rest of the household is regarded as having stolen it.

The belief that a truthful man is the pre-eminently virtuous man is common among Indian tribesmen, some of whom speak of *Sat*

[1] In the last century, the Saoras were notorious for their thefts of cattle which they took from non-Saoras to sacrifice at the Guar and Karja rites.—Francis, *Vizagapatam District Gazetteer*, p. 204.

(Truth) as a sort of abstract power dwelling in the tribe so long as it does not turn from its traditional customs and beliefs. The Saoras use the word *daramma* in this sense, and they are generally believed to be truthful among themselves and have a good reputation in the Courts; they certainly praise the truthful man and teach their children not to lie. A deceiver is compared to a fox.

But the common belief that the Saoras never attempt to conceal their crimes is incorrect. Not only are many crimes hushed up by general agreement and never reported to the police, but Saora murderers sometimes attempt to disguise their crime even from their own people. Thus when Dhemma of Sandusahi killed a man in 1936, he put the corpse at the foot of a sago palm and tried to make it look as if it had fallen there. In the Kimunda murder of the same year, the murderers took a goat from their own shed, twisted its neck and killed it, then dug a hole in the wall, and declared that they had done nothing more than kill a thief who had been stealing their property. One of the accused, who actually shot four arrows into the body of his victim, stated in Court that the dead man must have tripped and impaled himself upon them. At Regadiguda, after a murder, the murderers dragged the corpse to a lonely place and buried it, telling the villagers that they had no idea where their enemy had gone. When Saniya of Kutuni killed his uncle in 1939, he and his father dragged the body deep into the jungle and burnt it, afterwards covering the ashes with green branches.

It is true that directly the police began their investigations, the Regadiguda murderers themselves took them to the place, dug up the corpse and made a full confession. The Kutuni murderers did the same. I do not think, however, that we can accept confessions made to the police as evidence of a frank and truthful nature.

Oaths are regarded very seriously. They are usually taken on Darammasum and Uyungsum, for since they live in the sky they are the 'witnesses' of human actions. One method is for a man to take some salt, put it on a piece of dry cowdung, and stand facing the sun. He says, 'O Uyungsum Mahaprabhu, you are in the sky; you rise in the east.' He turns about and says, 'O Darammaboi, you are in the sky; you sink in the west.' He touches the ground and says, 'O Labosum, you are witness that I am telling the truth. If I lie, let me melt as this salt melts in water; let my body be consumed as this cowdung is consumed by fire.'

Another method is to raise the right hand to the sky saying, 'O father, there is Darammasum. There is the sun and moon. There is Kittung. Here is the earth. If I have done wrong or told a lie, may I perish.'

Few Saoras dare to tell a lie after so powerful a challenge to the august witnesses above and below. It is very dangerous to play with this sort of thing.[1]

A Saora of Kinteda, the drunken, quarrelsome man already described, one day repented of his behaviour. He took an egg in his hand and called on Uyungsum and Darammasum as witnesses, and said, 'I swear on this egg that I will drink no wine for three years. If I do, let my eyes break open as I break this egg.' He touched his forehead with the egg, and broke it by throwing it on the ground. But he could not keep his oath. He soon took to drink again and went blind in both eyes.

Yet, I was told, he could have broken his oath with impunity, if he had had the sense to offer a pig to his two 'witnesses'. But he was too proud for that, and his punishment was for pride rather than for false swearing.

A wiser man was Bamra of Angda village who once, when he was suffering all the torments of a severe hangover, swore on a rupee (which he called Lakshmiboi) that he would not drink for a whole year. He kept his word, but directly the year was up, he bought a fowl with the rupee, sacrificed it to Lakshmiboi, and got gloriously drunk.

Like other tribesmen at the same stage of cultural development, the Saoras combine a tradition of some freedom in the pre-nuptial period with considerable strictness of sexual behaviour within the marriage bond. There is no such thing as a Saora dormitory and no attempt to regulate or discipline the relations of boys and girls, but sexual opportunity is to some extent restricted. Although it is not forbidden for a boy to have an affair with a girl of the same village, provided she belongs to a different family group, the fact that most agricultural and ritual activities are organized by these groups does mean in practice that boys and girls of the same group mix together. And sexual opportunity outside one's village is limited to some extent by the conditions of Saora life; there are no dancing expeditions (as among the Bhuiyas and Juangs), no great clan festivals

[1] See also p. 517.

(as among the Marias and Murias) where thousands of young people gather and have a chance to meet; the Saoras do not go very much to bazaars; they do not celebrate the orgiastic festivals of Pus Parab and Chait Parab, nor have they adopted the Hindu erotic festival of Holi. In fact, as Maltby says, the Saoras 'have a better idea of chastity than the Konds, and it is said that some of the women are old maids'.[1]

But of course, boys and girls do meet. They accompany their elders to Guar ceremonies in other villages; they escort bride or bridegroom on the many ceremonial visits of a betrothal and marriage; they go in procession about the country to bring home the bones and the souls of those who have died abroad. Marriages are ordinarily arranged by the parents, but boys and girls fall in love and every now and then elope together. When they do, the elders try to catch them and bring them home. They do not approve, but they take a sensible view of the irregularity. 'When you have fitted an arrow to the bow,' they say, 'how can you take it out?' and unless there is some barrier of taboo the young couple are allowed to marry. A pre-marital pregnancy is not taken very tragically, and is covered up by an immediate marriage, either with the youth responsible or with the official fiancé. The Saora attitude to the love affairs of young people is, in fact, tolerant and kindly; there is certainly no suggestion that there is anything wrong with the act of sex, provided it is not indulged by persons who are forbidden to one another.

In two cases known to me, and I am told that such cases are not infrequent, an irregular conception was attributed to a divine being. At Kankaraguda, when a young unmarried girl was found to be pregnant, she declared that the father was Labosum, and her claim was accepted. In Sogeda a young widow became pregnant two years after her husband's death, and she took a public oath that the only person she had slept with was her dead husband's ghost.

But after marriage the position alters. Marriage is not only, or even primarily, a sexual union. Its character is illustrated by a lecture given by the elders at Maneba just before the formal consummation of a marriage. 'Look,' they said to the bridegroom, 'we have brought this girl for you. The price has been paid in full. Keep her well. Do not quarrel with her. If she falls ill, offer due sacrifice to the

[1] T. J. Maltby, *The Ganjam District Manual* (Madras, 1882), p. 87.

spirits. A husband must look after his wife's affairs and the wife must look after her husband's affairs. The minds of both should agree. When relatives on either side come to your house, feed them well.'

This association for mutual assistance and child-bearing must not be interrupted by the wayward fancies of lust. Adultery in the old days was punished drastically by the murder of one or both of the offenders, and society approved the act. Even today such a homicide is considered theoretically appropriate and occurs, I believe, more frequently than is reported to authority.

The real evil of adultery,[1] to the realistic Saora mind, is that it is a tampering with another person's property. The word for adultery is *jumburtun*, stolen coitus. A loose woman is *junjuriboi*, a thief. A man who carries off another's wife is compared to the snake-god, Ajorasum, who robs babies of their milk. 'When such a man dies, the ancestors sell him to Ajorasum.' To make a success of illicit love, it is said, a man must have the cunning and strength of a tiger; in fact it is those who have been eaten by tigers and have returned to earth as tiger-men who are the great seducers. It is generally considered that it is men who are at fault, but women who menstruate excessively are always in pursuit of men, and there are lecherous women whose minds 'have been made bad by Uyungsum'.

A loose widow is no more approved than a loose wife. At the Thalulaguda Guar ceremony, a ghost came upon the shaman and declared that he had taken his widow to join him in the Under World because after his death she had seduced the young men of the village. Now, added the ghost grimly, 'the wanton has to stay with me and she can get men no longer'. It was obvious that the people approved this rigorist attitude.

Prostitution is unknown among the Hill Saoras. Incest is taboo and is regarded as dangerous as well as reprehensible. Sodomy and bestiality are not even a joke. The Saora attitude to sex is frank and simple. They have few repressions or inhibitions. Their open and natural delight in the beauty of the human form, the absence of futile and tedious taboos, the freedom of their speech, a certain lightness of touch, helps them to approach this beautiful thing without shame or guilt; it enables them to fulfil their lives with happiness.

[1] For some reason, a meteor is called *jundada-tiyan*, adulterous star.

III. *Rewards and Punishments*

It is often said that while the tribal religions have their ethical codes and often attain a high moral ideal of daily conduct, their morality does not derive from religion but exists independently of it, drawing its strength from secular custom and tradition. This is often true, but I do not think that it gives a complete picture of Saora ethics.

It is true, of course, that Saora religion does not aim at making people better, nor are its rewards and punishments awarded for moral character or behaviour. There is no idea that 'the pure of heart shall see God'; there is no such prayer as 'lead us not into temptation'. At the close of a Doripur ceremony members of the congregation return home with full bellies rather than with uplifted hearts. A shaman does not come out of trance ennobled by communion with the divine; he generally passes into a fuddled sleep.

Yet at the same time, it must be admitted that the shamans and shamanins are almost always very good people, by any standards. They are kind and affectionate, hard-working and unselfish, not only because it is 'good' to be so, but because the duties of their profession inspire and demand it. They observe a high standard of sexual morality, and the struggles of some of the unmarried shamanins to preserve their chastity have an entirely religious motive.

No one would write an *Imitation of Kittung* or a *Little Flowers of Ramma-Bimma*, yet there are elements in the character of some of the gods that are certainly worthy of man's imitation. I show elsewhere that Kittung, ambiguous as his character may be, is often generous and amiable, does things for other people, looks after them, tries to make them happy. He is good to animals, giving the dog a tail, the cock its comb, and teaching the tiger how to behave. He is genuinely concerned over the unhappy lot of men and does his best to remedy it. He often appears as the ideal shaman, giving himself to the service of mankind. The other gods are too vaguely imagined to be imitated, but some of them have their noble qualities; Uyungsum and Darammasum stand for justice and truth; they witness to the evil of swearing falsely.

Moreover the general tradition of how men should behave towards the gods emphasizes the way they should behave towards their fellow men. It is dangerous to act with pride before a god; humility is one of the most treasured of the human virtues. It may be fatal to steal from a god; theft is universally condemned in daily life. Disobedience to a spirit's commands brings speedy retribution; obedience, conformity, keeping in step, is one of the essentials that govern human relations within the tribe.

The stress on duty, the importance of working hard and doing one's share, the charm of hospitality, the need to avoid violence and lies, the priority of the community over the individual—these things are not specially enjoined by the religion, but the religion is of such a kind that it forms the natural soil in which they can grow.

Among the forces making for a good life we must, therefore, put the general atmosphere of Saora religion. Another force, even harder to assess, yet of the first importance, is the influence of the reign of law and ordered government. The Saoras have now lived for well over a hundred years under the provisions of the Indian Penal Code, and there can be no doubt that it has gradually, imperceptibly moulded their ideas as well as controlled their actions. Previously, they were unabashed cattle-thieves, plunderers and marauders, and they had no hesitation about their deeds of theft and violence. Today they are restrained from them, not only by the fear of punishment and the existence of superior force, but because they have been subject for a very long time to the quietly persuasive education of the working of the law. Whatever defects there may be in practice, every police investigation, every trial before the Courts, is an education in certain aspects of the moral life, and it has certainly had its effect upon the Saora conscience.

It is true that even today, the Saora ethic reaches its full development only within the borders of the Saora tribe. A Saora still does not think it nearly so bad to murder a Dom as to kill a fellow Saora, or to cheat a merchant, lie to a constable, or insult a forest guard as to do these things to his own people. But, as we saw in the last chapter, certain other factors enter into this: the Saora, still at war with the outside world, often feels that he is simply asserting his rights (as indeed he very often is), and few of his assaults on outsiders are altogether devoid of excuse.

The rule of external law is, of course, strongly reinforced by tribal discipline, and it is this which commands the Saora's most unquestioning loyalty. The problem of discipline, articulated into its three subordinate problems of institutionalism, formalism and rigorism,[1] is of fundamental importance for any ethical system.

[1] K. E. Kirk, *The Vision of God* (London, 1931), p. 10.

Corporate discipline, or institutionalism, in every religion has to face the fact that the majority of people are not greatly interested in spiritual values. This is true even of the Saoras, for though none of them could be called irreligious, and they have not yet produced a heretic, there are a great many who accept their religious duties as a matter of course rather than from any great enthusiasm. How far are such people to conform to the shaman's standard of a 'good' man?

There is no Saora Church—or perhaps we should say the tribe itself is the Church, for our modern division of life into sacred and secular is alien to Saora thought. There is no religious hierarchy, no centralization; if a shaman wishes to perform a ceremony back to front or upside down, there is no synod to which he can be reported—and he can at once disarm criticism by claiming that he is only following the instructions of his tutelary.

The Saoras are not priest-ridden. The Buyya has political influence, not because he is a priest, but because he is an official appointed and recognized by Government. A shaman has no special say in tribal affairs, but of course his opinions are heard with respect; they have influence, but they are not mandatory. The way Saora institutionalism exerts its discipline is by the pressure of tribal opinion expressed in every possible way and all the time. And this opinion is inexorable; it does not ask people to be 'religious' but it does insist that they conform; the rules of *ukka* and *ersi* are absolute, and there is no sympathy for the person who breaks them and suffers supernatural penalties in consequence.

Human penalties are also inflicted for breach of the *ukka*, or customary, traditions. Fines are inflicted on those who make the wrong sort of marriages or infringe tribal custom in other ways. But the anathema, the dread weapon of excommunication, which is wielded with such devastating effect by the elders of other tribes, is hardly used by the Saoras.

It is through formalism that tribal discipline is made easier for the ordinary man. The ethical codification is of external actions, rather than of virtues and dispositions; it is not burdensome, but exact, not heroic but meticulous; and though it is unwritten, and in a way untaught, it is known to every child. It defines the limits within which one should walk, and so long as those limits are observed it is an insurance against ghostly evils. These cautions, prohibitions, rules sometimes lead to a self-conscious scrupulosity, sometimes to an irritating assumption of complacency, but on the whole they help the Saora to live well. Although most of the taboos and cautions are in externals, others have a truly moral basis, as for example those that are based on a recognition of the evil of pride and those that discipline the extravagance of sex.

The danger of Saora, as of all formalism, is that it leads to an excessive timidity—the *eulabeia* which the early Christians found characteristic of rabbinism,[1] an excessive cautiousness which often paralyses action and initiative. It also tends to make what society regards as a good life too easy; it leaves nothing to the individual conscience. A great historian has characterized the 'pagan' of classical antiquity as one who had 'no inward discipline',[2] and though this is not quite true of the Saoras, it is true, I think, that they lack the hardy moral development that comes from the pangs and struggles of conscience and the battle against temptation.

Saora life then is disciplined, but it is not rigorist. The contrast between humanism and asceticism, between a rigorist other-worldliness and a world-embracing code of ethics, has been elegantly discussed by Brémond. And although it is perhaps a little pompous to apply a word like 'humanism' to the simple and inarticulate ideas of an Indian tribe, yet the Saoras are undoubtedly in this great tradition. 'The fundamental doctrine of humanism is simple. It is an accepted axiom that a man feels little interest in that which he holds contemptible. The humanist does not consider humanity contemptible. He wholeheartedly takes the part of human nature; even when he sees it miserable and impotent, he excuses and defends and raises it.' It is 'the toleration of humanity in the tenderest sense of the word'.[3] It is, in India, the poet as against the puritan; the free, uninhibited, happy life of the hillmen as against the morbid restrictions of the ascetics and the prudes. The rigorist ethic of self-denial and ascetic renunciation, the dismal code of condemnation of free happiness, are alien to the Saoras. They have no sadhus, and are not inclined to respect those who visit them—if for no other reason than that they do no work. They do not regard celibacy of any special value. There are occasional instances of ritual nudity and self-torture, but their motive is not ascetic.

[1] Kirk, op. cit., p. 133.
[2] F. M. Powicke, *The Legacy of the Middle Ages* (Oxford, 1926), p. 30.
[3] H. Brémond, *A Literary History of Religious Thought in France* (Eng. trans., London, 1928), vol. I, p. 9.

But it is possible to have a cult-rigorism—as a preparation for the ritual approach to the spirits—which is entirely distinct from a philosophical asceticism. The one is temporary, intended to protect the priest or shaman from danger; the other is fundamental, based on the belief in the inherent evil of the flesh and the joys of the world. Cult-asceticism is practised by the Saoras. There is a general rule that every officiant should perform his duties fasting. This fasting applies only to food; it does not affect the consumption of wine or liquor, which is more nourishing than some kinds of food. If the occasion is solemn or important, sexual abstinence is also enjoined.

Why do the Saoras fast? They have no idea at all that asceticism can influence the gods or the Dead; that is a Hindu notion. They do not appear to think that it does the abstainer any moral good; that is a Christian one. I think there are two reasons. The first is that the Saoras have picked up the idea from their Hindu neighbours, that it is a decent and proper thing to fast before you approach anyone so extraordinary and terrible as a denizen of the other world. But I believe that the real reason is more practical. The Saora has discovered that a diviner can do his work better on an empty stomach. He is more sensitive, more suggestible; the palm wine will work more quickly; it will be easier to fall into that condition of slightly fuddled trance when the voice of the other world will be clearly heard.

Of course, for all practical purposes a Saora 'fast' does not mean very much. The shaman, who has a large dose of palm wine in the early morning and who in any case is not accustomed to eat breakfast can last without much difficulty till midday or even late afternoon and have all the better appetite for the enormous feed awaiting him when the ceremonies are over.

The general climate of religious thought and practice, the existence of an all-powerful, if external, penal code based on the highest contemporary Hindu and Christian ethic, the gently formalist and humane discipline of the tribe all help the Saora to be a *bangsamaran*, a good man, rather than a *rankamaran*, a bad one. How far does the hope of reward, or fear of punishment, here or hereafter, reinforce these influences for good?

The general traditions and conventions of Saora society are, of course, very powerful; I doubt if the fear of punishment by the law is equally strong. Punishment by the gods is a more serious matter. All gods punish any diversion from the formalist path of safety; the breach of a taboo leads to almost immediate, and certainly automatic, retribution. But the greater gods, such as Uyungsum and Darammasum, are said to punish men for 'sin', for which the Saoras use a borrowed Oriya word. By 'sin' is meant, first and foremost incest, then false swearing, and perhaps pride, neglect and breach of any taboo.

Punishments inflicted by these gods are not, however, automatic and are curiously uneven. But this reflects the Saora's own experience of human justice. One murderer is hanged; another gets two years' imprisonment; a third, obviously guilty, is acquitted on legal grounds which no one understands; a fourth conceals his crime and is not even suspected.[1] So too Uyungsum punishes one offender with leprosy, while another gets nothing worse than a bad cold.

I think, however, that the fear of divine punishment is certainly a deterrent in many cases, and this is particularly true of the shamans and shamanins in their struggle to preserve their sexual integrity. The hope of reward, too, is an incentive to a more cautious, if not a better, life. The proper observance of taboo and sacrifice is everywhere expected to be rewarded by health for oneself and one's children, by good crops, and general prosperity.

The Saoras seem to have no idea of ultimate rewards and punishments, which do not, therefore, enter into their ethical scheme at all. It is true that they sometimes say of a bad man that Ratusum will take him, or that the ancestors will sell his soul to Ajorasum. But this seems to be only a manner of speaking, as a modern man who has no belief in the after-life may yet tell somebody to go to hell.

There are distinctions in the fate of the soul after death, but these depend first on the cause of death, and then on the proper performance of the funerary formalities. Indeed a tragic death that in other parts of India may be regarded as a punishment for sin, may be looked upon by the Saoras as entirely fortunate. Thus a man killed by a thunderbolt is regarded as happy in his death, for he will go straight to Jammasum and will have a good time in the other world. It is a good death too to be taken by one's own tutelary, for there is a chance of promotion and apotheosis later on. But for a devoted couple to die of different causes is tragic, for they will be for ever separated in the Under World.

[1] The extraordinary diversity in the severity of the sentences given by judges and magistrates in India is a constant source of perplexity to the tribesmen, and indeed merits the attention of criminologists.

The cause of the death, not the character of the life, determines a man's ultimate fate.

And the cause of death is not, except in certain exceptional circumstances, determined by anything a man does here. Of course, if he commits suicide he will have a different kind of after-life than if he is taken away by an ancestor. But it may not be a worse kind of life, indeed it will probably be better, certainly more varied and exciting, than that of the ordinary dead. If a man breaks an important taboo, and an indignant god kills him for it, the death itself is a punishment, but after death the soul will go to the god responsible and again may have a better after-life than if the offender had died innocently in his bed at the summons of a family ghost.

Again, a man may have been a loving father, a good husband, an excellent citizen; he may have lived a life of extreme formalism, faithfully observing every taboo and ritual rule, yet all his merit will avail him nothing if he is not properly cremated, or if his heirs fail to celebrate the Guar in his interest. The best man in the world will be punished with all the pains of thirst and hunger if the living do not provide food and water for his shade. The greatest villain will grow fat after death if his family can afford to maintain his cult.

Ultimately, a good life is to be lived for its own sake, for it is the way of happiness. A good man 'speaks kindly to everyone, helps those in trouble, is not envious of the success of others, receives rich and poor, neighbours and strangers, alike, tries to compose quarrels, makes a visitor feel at home, is docile and obedient'. He lives this kind of life for its own sake, because it is the only kind of life that agrees with his religion and because it brings peace and welfare to the community, respect and honour to the individual. For, as a Saora once said to me, 'a good man is loved, a bad man is avoided'.

IV. *A Religion of Fear?*

It has been said that fear is the father of religion, and love its late-born daughter, and a study of the Saora gods and their attributes suggests at first that we have here an almost typical example of a faith based on that neurotic dread and apprehension which is most clearly expressed in the German word *Angst*. Consider this vast pantheon of gods, every one a potential enemy of man; consider the jealous and resentful ghosts, the hungry naked shades; consider the dangers that lurk in every stream, by every path, on the quiet hillside;

the frequent and expensive sacrifices; the taboos so easily forgotten; the nightmares. We must consider too the social and political setting in which this religion has developed: the Saoras at war with the world, even today suspicious of strangers, hostile—and naturally hostile—to the outsiders who only visit them to lie and cheat and rob.

For a long time, therefore, I was inclined to see Saora religion in terms of fear; I could find no evidence, in fact there seemed to be no place, for love and gratitude. It was only after a considerable time, largely as a result of recording the texts of incantations and prayers and of a closer acquaintance with individuals, that I began to see that this was not the whole story.

First of all, however, let us admit the very strong element of fear in Saora religion. Before there was such a thing as religion, say the Saoras, there were no gods, no shamans and men lived wealthy and at ease. Fear came with the coming of the gods, for Kittung told them to frighten men by illness into making food-offerings. Gods and ghosts combined, by the hateful machinery of human tragedy, to keep men down, to prevent them growing proud through wealth, or independent as a result of freedom from fear.

In some of their prayers, the shamans acknowledge the angry power of the gods in vivid phrases. 'If we suffer from purging,' says one, 'it is through you. If there is evil in the water, it is from you. If there is evil in the food, it is from you.' And again, 'You come with such angry power that if you catch a tree it will wither; if you catch an animal, it will waste away.' And in an invocation to Jammasum, a shaman cried, 'O mighty Jammasum, it is you who cause women to conceive, it is you who put the bones in the womb. O Jammasum, you give leprosy, you make men blind, you make men deaf, you make the belly swell, you make the eyes red and sore, you cause legs to break, you make the blood to flow.'

Some Saoras develop this dread of the rest of the world and of the other world to a pathological degree. Such rich and prosperous people as the great Chiefs of the Pottasingi area, and especially those of Sogeda and the late Chief of Boramsingi, live in a continual state of *angst*, of anxious dread, not that their enemies will be greedy and rob them of their wealth, but that they will be jealous and rob them of their lives. The fear of sorcery envelops them, their ancestors are the more exacting when they see the wealth of the living, the gods are in ambush along the course of every action that they may plan.

This is the obvious and expected picture. But is there any idea at all among the Saoras of a love which the gods have for man, or that man has for the gods? In spite of the sombre picture of the divine character with which the observer cannot fail to be impressed, there are hints and traces of a nobler conception. We have already noticed the element of compassion in the character of Kittung, the concern he has for men; how he exerts himself to make men comfortable and happy: 'men must be happy', he says.

Even more remarkable are the stories, in which the gods mutilate themselves for the benefit of mankind, from which the element of love cannot be excluded. The first of these concerns Galbesum, in many places regarded as one of the highest, if not the highest, of the gods. Ramma and Bimma grew weary of the digging-sticks with which they scratched the ground in their swiddens, and one day Bimma went to Galbesum and said, 'Digging, digging with our hands we grow weary; show us some other way to break up the earth.' Galbesum had nothing to give, so he cut off his left leg and gave it to Bimma, telling him to use it as a plough. 'Afterwards', he said, 'you can make a wooden plough on the same pattern.' It was in this way that the use of the plough, with its incomparable benefits, came to men—for in this story Bimma and Ramma are regarded as ordinary Saoras living in the world.

Another story describes the self-sacrifice and kindliness of Angaiboi, the Moon. At one time Jammasum was causing much distress among the Saoras, and Angaiboi said to him, 'Why do you worry them so much to get your food? If you want anything, come and tell me. If there is any sacrifice to be made, I will give it for men.' So the next time Jammasum felt hungry, he sent a great snake to demand payment of the debt from Angaiboi; the snake swallowed her—and that is the eclipse.

The extraordinary image of the maimed Kittung is associated with the myth of the origin of fire, and though it is not stated that the god deliberately inflicted mutilation on himself, the wounds were the result of his search for fire to give to man.

One day on the Rawangiri Mountain, Kittung Mahaprabhu broke open a rock and fire came out. The rock burst and a bit of it flew up and hurt Kittung's head on the left side. So fierce was the fire that Kittung's hands and feet also were burnt; the wounds were so

69

69 & 70. Scenes at the Gungupur (69) and Lajap (70) ceremonies

70

71. Group of menhirs outside Parisal village

bad that he remained lame and maimed on Rawangiri. The fire spread and burnt all the jungle and many animals. Men found the burnt carcasses and ate them; they liked the taste and took the fire home to their houses. Formerly they had eaten their meat raw; now they began to cook.

But in their gratitude to the discoverer of fire, they made an image[1] of the maimed Kittung, and worshipped it.

Another story of Kittung's sacrifice dates back to the beginning of the world, before there were any trees. Kittung and his sister used to sleep out in the open and one night a squirrel bit off four of the fingers of Kittung's left hand, leaving only the third finger. In the hot weather the sister wept for the heat, and Kittung cut off his maimed left hand and planted it, whereupon it grew into a fig tree and the girl sheltered in its shade.

The next story does not concern a god, yet the picture it gives of a great and good king of the days before the flood, whose bones were transformed into the vital benefit of salt, throws light on Saora ideas of greatness.

Raja Gehil was a good and generous king who ruled in Manigarh. If anyone wanted meat for dinner and there was none to be had, he would cut a bit off his own body and give it to him.

After his death his bones were mingled with the waters of the great flood, and ultimately turned into salt. A Saora found it, and the king's ghost came to him in a dream and told him how to use it.

I am aware, of course, that these stories of self-mutilation can be interpreted in a very different sense. Yet even if they do point to some obscure nuclear complex or fear of castration latent in the Saora mind, there is no doubt that their obvious and manifest meaning, which is what is really important to the Saoras, is that the gods are capable, out of their sympathy towards mankind, of acts of sacrificial love.

Nothing banishes fear more quickly from the hearts of simple people than the certainty of obtaining justice. The guilty will always tremble, but where there is justice the innocent need not tremble too. And the Saoras believe that the highest gods are just. The Saoras call on the Sun under his various divine names, and on Labosum the earth, to validate their oaths and witness the proper performance of

[1] Illustrated in *TAMI*, p. 119.

sacrifice; they insist that these gods at least will see that they are not deceived by the lesser deities. Indeed, the fact that sacrifice is offered at all suggests that the Saoras suppose that the gods will respond in a fair and equal manner. It takes two to make a bargain and, though the shamans often express the fear that they will be cheated, they do expect in the main to get a square deal.

Saora prayers and incantations contain many expressions which imply a possible response of love. 'Show your love for this child,' urges a shamanin. 'Show your love by letting this child alone.' And at a Name-giving rite, the visiting tutelaries declare, 'We have come in love, we have come willingly,' and again, 'We have come from the Under World to give you happiness.'

And this leads us to a very important point. Not all the gods are on the same side. There are some who are for man against the others. It is especially the duty of the tutelaries, who are sometimes called the Mannesum, the docile kindly spirits, to protect and help mankind. The tutelaries can indeed be tiresome and even dangerous, but at the same time they can be very helpful. The female tutelaries 'love' the shamans they marry; they are 'pleased' with them. The male tutelaries are attracted by the virtue and beauty of human girls; they prefer their suits like any human lover. Once married, they make it their business to guard their human consorts; they drive away hostile spirits; again and again a tutelary tells his shamanin, 'Don't waste your money on unnecessary sacrifices; I will see that all goes well with you.' There was a significant story from Arbun about a shaman called Duga who was actually brought back from death by his tutelary. He died, and as the mourners sat round him weeping he suddenly sat up and asked, 'What are you crying for?' The people were terrified, but he explained that although Tangorbasum had indeed taken away his soul—'he carried me to a place I had never seen and made me sit among great rocks in the midst of thick darkness'—his tutelary had come to find him and had brought him back from the land of death.

It is not uncommon for gods to take individual households under their protection and drive away spirits hostile to them. And there are gods of the home and of the cattle-sheds who, if they are properly propitiated by sacrifice, protect their charges from unauthorized intruders. Just as sorcerers can employ certain gods to harass their enemies, so the shamans can employ other gods to protect their friends. The great advantage of Saora religion is that it enables a man to *do* something about his worries. It personifies them, which in itself makes things easier, and tells him that there is a way of putting things right. And directly anyone takes that way, he gains consolation and support from the sympathy of society. The neighbours, the family, the Chief himself express their sympathy and rally round to banish his anxieties. It is only when a man fails to do his duty by the gods and the dead that society shrugs its shoulders and says that whatever he gets is only what he deserves.

In spite of all the trouble that the shades and ancestors cause those on earth, the Saoras never lose sight of the fact that living and dead are one great family. 'Whether you are short or tall, ugly or beautiful, even if you have lame feet and broken arms, in whatever form you come, you are our ancestral dead and we shall honour you as kings.' They say to the ancestors, 'When you come, we will wash your feet and anoint them with turmeric and oil, and most lovingly make you sit amongst us.' The mourners commit to the care of the ancestors the pathetic shades of the newly dead. At the funeral of an old man, they wept: 'He has left us for you. Now you must care for him. From today he is no longer ours; he has become yours. Guard him well.' At another funeral, the people urged the ancestors: 'Care for the dead as we cared for him on earth. We leave him in your hands.' And once I heard a ghost promise: 'We will care for the child better than if he had been at home.' Another ghost said, 'I will build a shelter round the child.' This suggests a relationship of what can only be called love between the living and the dead.

At the end of a Karja ceremony, the ancestors promised: 'You have done well and now we will be happy and content. The crops in your fields and swiddens will be good; you will get enough to eat and your children will keep well. We will help you whenever you are in trouble.'

'We will help you.' The dead have a concern for the living. 'Who is looking after our fields and clearings? Who is caring for the children?' is their constant inquiry. They long for the company of the living, even though this longing may be an embarrassment. They are jealous, but it is often the jealousy of love. And 'at the first sign of love, the dead approach'.

This evidence, taken cumulatively, certainly suggests that to call Saora theology a doctrine of fear is at the least exaggerated. In fact George Tyrrell thought that the awe and terror of the supernatural which anthropologists ascribed to savages was such that it was surprising that the latter ever went to bed at all.[1]

We must remember, however, that a religion which takes into account the element of fear, recognizing the danger of living and devising some means of dealing with it, is not necessarily bad. Indeed William James goes so far as to say that 'the completest religions seem to be those in which the pessimistic elements are best developed'. Although in its attitude to sin Saora religion may be classed as 'healthy-minded', it is pessimistic in its general recognition of the evil in the world and the dangers to which all men living are exposed. But is this altogether a drawback? Life for the Saoras has many incidents of terror and despair, of anxiety and sorrow, and—as James says again—'the method of averting one's attention from evil, and living simply in the light of good is splendid as long as it will work ... But it breaks down impotently as soon as melancholy comes; and even though one be quite free from melancholy oneself, there is no doubt that healthy-mindedness is inadequate as a philosophical doctrine, because the evil facts which it refuses positively to account for are a genuine portion of reality; and they may, after all, be the best key to life's significance, and possibly the only openers of our eyes to the deepest levels of truth.'[2]

The Saora picture of the unseen world and its population, which is no more than a projection on the gigantic canvas of eternity of a realistic understanding of the world, is a chiaroscuro of light and shade, in which the darkness predominates. That the darkness should be there is natural, inevitable; what is splendid and heartening is that it should be shot through with gleams of light. Because Saora religion faces the facts, accepts life—the life of poor and ignorant people—as it is, it is able to give some sense of security, or at least of hope, in a tragic world.

We must now turn for a moment to an allied, though somewhat different, point, and consider whether the Saoras have any conception of what Otto has called the 'numinous' element in religion. The numinous is that which fills the worshipper with awe and dread before the infinite mystery, the 'wholly other' character of the unseen, instilling in him the 'emotion of a creature abased and

[1] G. Tyrrell, *The Faith of the Millions* (London, 1901), p. 244.
[2] W. James, *The Varieties of Religious Experience* (London, 1902, reprinted 1941), p. 165.

overwhelmed'. Otto has isolated a number of elements in this emotion: there is the *mysterium tremendum*, the *majestas*, the sense of energy and urgency, the recognition of something entirely different from ourselves. 'Its antecedent stage', he says, 'is "daemonic dread" (cf. the horror of Pan) with its queer perversion, a sort of abortive offshoot, the "dread of ghosts". It first begins to stir in the feeling of "something uncanny", "eerie" or "weird". It is this feeling which, emerging in the mind of primeval man, forms the starting-point for the entire religious development in history. "Daemons" and "gods" alike spring from this root, and all the products of "mythological apperception" or "fantasy" are nothing but different modes in which it has been objectified.'[1]

'Though the numinous emotion in its completest development', Otto continues, 'shows a world of difference from the mere "daemonic dread", yet not even at the highest level does it belie its pedigree or kindred. Even when the worship of "daemons" has long since reached the higher level of worship of "gods", these gods still retain as *numina* something of the "ghost" in the impress they make on the feelings of the worshipper, viz., the peculiar quality of the "uncanny" and "aweful", which survives with the quality of exaltedness and sublimity or is symbolized by means of it. And this element, softened though it is, does not disappear even on the highest level of all, where the worship of God is at its purest. Its disappearance would be indeed an essential loss.'[2]

We find it, puzzling and baffling as it may be, in the Wrath of Yahweh, in the *Orge Theou* of the New Testament, in the mysterious *ira deorum* of the classical religions. 'To pass through the Indian Pantheon of gods is to find deities who seem to be made up altogether out of such an *Orge*, and even the higher Indian gods of grace and pardon have frequently, beside their merciful, their "wrath" form.'[3]

There is probably an element of this in Saora religion. The tremendous mystery of earth and heaven, the majesty of the hills and the great powers of nature, the energy and urgency of the lightning flash has impressed itself on their minds no less than the incalculable stroke of accidental or ill-omened death, the sudden onslaught of mortal sickness, the sense of helpless 'creatureliness' before the vast, dimly imagined powers of the unseen world. I well

[1] R. Otto, *The Idea of the Holy*, trs. J. W. Harvey (London, 1950), pp. 14-15.
[2] ibid., p. 17. [3] ibid., p. 18.

remember the 'tremor' which passed over the people at a Guar rite when a hawk swept down upon the sacrifical offerings, when the clouds changed as a warning that a man-tiger was on the way, when the thin piping voice of a dead child was heard in the night. And although the homeliness and familiarity of much Saora practice tends to obscure the fact, I think it is certain that they appreciate—in certain moods—the majesty and mystery of the divine power.

But Otto makes an important point when he shows that directly men begin to rationalize their experiences they weaken their mystery. 'Representations of spirits and similar conceptions are one and all early modes of "rationalizing" a precedent experience, to which they are subsidiary. They are attempts in some way or other, it little matters how, to guess the riddle it propounds, and their effect is at the same time always to weaken and deaden the experience itself. They are the source from which springs, not religion, but the rationalization of religion, which often ends by constructing such a massive structure of theory and such a plausible fabric of interpretation, that the "mystery" is frankly excluded. Both imaginative "myth", when developed into a system, and intellectualist Scholasticism, when worked out to its completion, are methods by which the fundamental fact of religious experience is, as it were, simply rolled out so thin and flat as to be finally eliminated altogether.'[1]

The whole structure of Saora theology and mythology may in fact be regarded as an attempt to make the mystery and horror of the unseen more bearable. The burden of the 'wholly other' was too great for them to bear, and so they produced ghosts who were related to them, deities who had the same desires and passions as themselves. Such ghosts and gods might still be alarming and dangerous, but they were not overwhelming; rationalization, of however simple a sort, had drawn their sting.

The ultimate conclusion, I think, must be that the numinous element in Saora religion is rather weak, for with the creation of another world into which it is possible to marry, about which one has the most detailed geographical, social and economic information, a good deal of the *mysterium tremendum* disappears. There are many epithets one might apply to a spirit mother-in-law, but 'numinous' is hardly one of them. But the conception of the *ira deorum* remains; if the gods are not ministers of 'wrath', they are at least extremely

[1] Otto, op. cit., p. 26-7.

touchy; and some of them in their rage and horror can reduce their victims to a quivering, helpless subservience, an abject prostration before their power.

The Saoras have always been renowned equally for their bravery and for their 'subtlety', and they treat their gods, as they have treated men, with all kinds of 'ambushes and surprises'. In their religion, they have created a realistic picture of life seen *sub specie eternitatis*; they face it, in all its dismal trappings, with courage; but it is not fear of things as they are, but a courageous appreciation of them, which has brought it into being. Their most sublime discovery is that beyond the desolation, the fever and the fret there are values and realities that can only be described in terms of love.

BOOK LIST

BALL, V., *Jungle Life in India* (London, 1880)

BELL, R. C. S., *Koraput District Gazetteer* (Cuttack, 1945)

CAMPBELL, J., *A Personal Narrative of Thirteen Years Service amongst the Wild Tribes of Khondistan* (London, 1864)

CARMICHAEL, D. F., *Manual of the Vizagapatam District* (Madras, 1869)

CUNNINGHAM, A., 'Report of a Tour in the Central Provinces and Lower Gangetic Doab in 1881-2', *Archeological Survey of India*, vol. XVII (Calcutta, 1884)

DALTON, E. T., *Descriptive Ethnology of Bengal* (Calcutta, 1872)

EIKSTEDT, E. VON, 'Die Soras', *Anthrop. Anz.*, vol. IV (1927), pp. 208-19

'Die Soras', *Ethnol. Anz.*, vol. I (1928), pp. 376-82

ELWIN, VERRIER, *Maria Murder and Suicide* (Bombay, 1943)

The Muria and their Ghotul (Bombay, 1947)

Myths of Middle India (Bombay, 1949). Described in the text as *MMI*

The Tribal Art of Middle India (Bombay, 1951). Described in the text as *TAMI*

Tribal Myths of Orissa (Bombay, 1954). Described in the text as *TMO*

'The Saora Priestess', *Bulletin of the Department of Anthropology*, vol. I (Calcutta, 1952)

FAWCETT, F., 'On the Saoras (or Savaras), an aboriginal Hill People of the Eastern Ghats of the Madras Presidency', *Journal of the Anthropological Society of Bombay*, vol. I (Bombay, 1888)

FRANCIS, W., *Vizagapatam District Gazetteer* (Madras, 1867)

GANGULY, M. M., *Orissa and her Remains* (Calcutta, 1912)

HUNTER, W. W., *Orissa* (London & Calcutta, 1872)

HUTTON, J. H., *Census of India*, 1931, vol. I, pt. IIIB (Simla, 1935)

Caste in India (2nd edition, Bombay, 1951)

MALTBY, T. J., *The Ganjam District Manual* (Madras, 1882)

MAZUMDAR, B. C., *The Aborigines of the Highlands of Central India* (Calcutta, 1927)

MUNRO, A. C. M., 'S'Ora (Savara) Folk-Lore', *Man in India*, vol. X (1930)

MUNRO, A. C. M. & SITAPATI, G. V., 'The Soras of the Parlakimidi Agency', *Census of India*, 1931, vol. I, pt. IIIB (Simla, 1935)

RAMAMURTI, G. V., *A Manual of the So:ra (or Savara) Language* (Madras, 1931)
Sora-English Dictionary (Madras, 1938)

RICE, S. P., *Occasional Essays on Native South Indian Life* (London, 1901)

RISLEY, H. H., *The Tribes and Castes of Bengal* (Calcutta, 1891)

RUSSELL, G. E., *Selections from the Records of the Madras Government*, No. XXIV (Madras, 1856)

RUSSELL, R. V. & HIRA LAL, *The Tribes and Castes of the Central Provinces of India* (London, 1916)

SITAPATI, G. V., 'The Soras and their Country', *Journal of the Andhra Historical Research Society*, vols. XII-XIV (1938-43)
'Sora Musical Instruments', *Bulletin du Musée d'Ethnographie du Trocadero* (Paris, 1933), No. 5

STIRLING, A., 'An Account, Geographical, Statistical and Historical of Orissa Proper, or Cuttack', *Asiatic Researches*, vol. XV (1825)

STITH THOMPSON, *Motif-Index of Folk-Literature* (Helsinki, 1932-6)

THURSTON, E., *Castes and Tribes of Southern India* (Madras, 1909)

INDEX OF AUTHORITIES

INDEX OF SUBJECTS